THE AMERICAN ALPINE JOURNAL
2000

Andrej Štremfelj near the summit of Siguang Ri, Tibet. See page 75.
MARKO PREZELJ

COVER: *Steve Sustad in the Arwa Valley, Garhwal Himalaya, India, with the unclimbed northeast face of the Arwa Tower in the background. See page 46.* MICK FOWLER

ABOVE: *Taeko Yamanoi on the first ascent of "Nameless Peak," Pakistan Karakoram. See page 350.*
YASUSHI YAMANOI
RIGHT: *Cecilia Buil on the first ascent of* Yawira Batú, *El Gigante, Chihuahua, Mexico. See page 247.*
CHRIS GILES

ABOVE: *Teatime at Camp VII. Einar Wold on the north face of the Pulpit, Great Trango Tower, Pakistan Karakoram. See page 90.* ROBERT CASPERSEN

LEFT: *David Fasel, Stefan Siegrist and Greg Crouch climbing toward the Helmet on the first winter ascent of Cerro Torre's West Face route, Argentine Patagonia. See page 276.* THOMAS ULRICH

Ten days into it, Joe TerraVecchia tops out on the south face of Mount Foraker, Alaska Range, Alaska.
The French Ridge is in the background. See page 22. STEVE LARSON

THE AMERICAN ALPINE JOURNAL

710 Tenth Street, Suite 140/Golden, Colorado 80401
Telephone: (303) 384 0110 Fax: (303) 384 0111
E-mail: aaj@americanalpineclub.org

ISSN 0065-6925/ISBN 0-930410-87-4

THE AMERICAN ALPINE JOURNAL

VOLUME 42   2000   ISSUE 74

CONTENTS

The American Alpine Journal artists:
Mike Clelland • Sean McCabe
John Svenson • Clay Wadman

THE AMERICAN ALPINE JOURNAL

Christian Beckwith, *Editor*

Advisory Board
John E. (Jed) Williamson, *Managing Editor*; Michael Kennedy, Phil Powers

Editorial & Production Assistants
Michelle Bevier, Paul Horton & David Swift

Associate Editors
Geoff Tabin, M.D., *Mountain Medicine;* Brent Bishop & Chris Naumann, *The Mountain Environment*;
David Stevenson, *Reviews;* Frederick O. Johnson, *Club Activities*;
David Harrah & Angus Thuermer, Jr., *In Memoriam*

Translators
Marina Heusch, *French*; Maxim Rivkin & Henry Pickford, *Russian*; Ana Perčič, *Slovenian*; Emanuele Pellizari,
Italian; Christian Santelices, Christian Oberli & Adam French, *Spanish*; Christiane Leitinger, *German*

Indexer
Jessica Kany

Regional Contacts
Raphael Slawinski, *Canadian Rockies*; Steve Schneider, *Yosemite*; Alan Bartlett, *Sierra Nevada*; Evelio
Echevarría, *South America*; Hernan Jofre, *Chilean Patagonia*; Rolando Garibotti, *Argentine Patagonia*;
Damien Gildea, *Antarctica;* Bill Ruthven, *United Kingdom*; Lindsay Griffin, *United Kingdom*; Bernard
Domenech, *France;* Franci Savenc, *Slovenia*; Vladimir Linek, *Slovakia*; Vladimir Shataev, *C.I.S.*; Vladimir
Kopylov, *C.I.S.*; Harish Kapadia, *India*; Elizabeth Hawley, *Nepal*; Asem Mustafa Awan, *Pakistan;* Sasaki
Kazuyuki, *Japan;* Kim Woo-Sun, *Korea*

With additional thanks to
Jeff Achey, Richard Anderson, Conrad Anker, Valeri Babanov, Fred Barth, Antonio Bohórquez, Jim
Bowes, Roxanna Brock, Ann Carter, Helen Cherullo, John Climaco, Nick Clinch, Jia Condon, Michael
Covington, Liana Darenskaya, *Desnivel* magazine, Cecilie Dunlap, Glenn Dunmire, Charlie Fowler,
Lindsay Griffin, Tsunemichi Ikeda, Renny Jackson, Hans & Nancy Johnstone, Jure Juhasz, Danny Kost,
San Lightner, Jr., *Rock & Ice* magazine, Jim McCarthy, Chris McNamara, Brian McCray, John
Middendorf, Dina Mishev, Jiri Novak, Joy Parker, Andy Parkin, Baker Perry, Gary Pfisterer, Marko
Prezelj, Joe Quinn, Lou Reichardt, Mark Richey, Rick Ridgeway, Darío Rodriguez, Galen Rowell,
Minako Satokuma, David Shlim, Filip Silhan, Eric Simonson, Chrissy Spinuzzi, Carles Valles,
Joe TerraVecchia, Clay Wadman, Bradford Washburn, Mike Wood, Kinichi Yamamori

FRIENDS OF THE
AMERICAN ALPINE JOURNAL

The following provided financial support for Volume 42 of The American Alpine Journal:

Ann Carter
Yvon Chouinard
New York Section of the AAC
Peter McGann, M.D.
Gregory Miller

The H. Adams Carter Endowment Fund
for The American Alpine Journal

THE AMERICAN ALPINE CLUB

OFFICIALS FOR THE YEAR 2000
*Directors ex-officio

Preface

On November 2, Slovenian Tomaž Humar reached the high point of his climb on the south face of Dhaulagiri I. Behind him lay an audacious seven-day ascent on a steep 4000-meter face that was documented on both film and the internet. He was exhausted, and the decision regarding the summit some 170 meters above was easily made: to go on, he said later, would have been to die. He traversed to the northeast ridge, climbed down to 7300 meters where a tent had been left for him by an American team and bivouacked for his eighth night on the mountain. Two days later, with the aid of a helicopter, he was back in Kathmandu.

As evidenced by the other two routes on the face, the south face of Dhaulagiri is both dangerous and hard. In 1981, ethnic Slovenians Cene Berčič, Emil Tratnik and Stane Belak Šrauf made a nine-day alpine-style ascent on the right-hand side of the face, reaching 7950 meters on the southeast ridge before they decided to descend. Leaving their tent, stove and food behind, they continued for six days down the northeast ridge. Hungry, troubled by storm, weakened by dehydration and the simple magnitude of their climb, they barely survived the mountain. A 1986 Polish team's ascent of a line to the left of center encountered friable rock and thin ice that was overcome only with great effort and extensive use of fixed ropes, but this team too was severely challenged by the difficulties and turned back short of the summit. Humar's climb was carried out solo with a paucity of equipment that ruled out retreat. It did not result in the perfect directissima he had envisioned and invoked ratings that have raised eyebrows, but its full import may not be known until a second ascent of the route occurs, and who will be bold enough to undertake that?

If Humar had simply walked away from the mountain at the finish of his climb, his ascent would have opened a window on what is possible at the highest altitudes in a manner not witnessed since Reinhold Messner's 1981 monsoon-season solo of a new route on the north face of Everest. From the object of exploration's greatest adventures, the high peaks of the Himalaya have evolved into quotidian affairs that are increasingly guided, skied, blasted in single-day pushes, climbed in winter, parapented. Now Humar had soloed a tremendous face in a fine effort that gave Himalayan climbing the short, sharp shove it needs to interrupt its myopic focus on routes first climbed in the 1950s. But Humar's climb was also a "production," and in that regard it reflects even more closely the modern state of climbing. Helicopters whisked him into and away from the mountain; radio contact with Base Camp monitored his progress and informed him on route-finding during the climb. Film documentation and an internet broadcast covered the expedition far in advance of the ascent itself and celebrity status awaited Humar upon his return to Slovenia. Taken as a whole, the climb was an event, an ascent marked by originality and verve, spiced with recklessness, captured in the bright lights of media in all its forms. So ends the century. Fittingly, we might add.

Other climbs that shared the media's affection in 1999 did not advance the style we bring to the mountains. Business climbing in general is ill-suited to push physical and mental limitations, encumbered as it is by a need for immediate documentation that precludes speed on technical terrain. The way we tell our stories is changing, spurred on by the internet and its real-time recounting, with results that can be more notable for the press generated than for any climbing done along the way. But how does this affect climbing itself? Few would argue that the increasing prominence of commercialization in modern climbing influences styles, objectives and, ultimately, climbing's evolution, yet it rarely sees candid discussion. Beginning on page 151, we offer three perspectives on the subject in an effort to bring it into the public dialogue.

The above notwithstanding, there is still plenty of climbing being done in the alpine arena, where the cameras remain secondary to the outcome of the climb. Witness Lionel Daudet and Sébastien Foissac on the southeast face of the Burkett Needle, proceeding in autonomy for 40 days in the isolation of Alaska's Coastal Range; Joe TerraVecchia and Steve Larson on their tenacious ascent of the south face of Mt. Foraker; and Doug Chabot and the late Alex Lowe on Mount Huntington, romping up the east face of what Chabot calls "the most beautiful 12,000-foot peak in the world" in a quick three-day ride. Rolando Garibotti, Silvo Karo, Bruno Sourzac and Laurence Monnoyeur continue to push what can be asked of modern climbing on the granite spires of Patagonia, while Jérôme Thiniéres, Stéphane Benoist and Bruno Ravanat made an intriguing foray into the Hindu Raj with their route on the northwest pillar of Chuchubalstering. Minus the hoopla, the scope for wild times in high places is in no way the sole domain of the expeditions with budgets in the tens (or hundreds) of thousands of dollars. And while the question of why we climb is at this point a tired one, it is one of the joys of compiling an overview of climbing in the Greater Ranges to watch the different answers people bring to the question in the form of their personal ascents.

Simultaneously, one of the more difficult parts of publishing an annual volume of climbing is turning down many submissions simply because they are not new climbs. One such climb that you won't read about in this volume was the ascent of the normal route on Nevado Ojos del Salado by Vlastimil Sňída and Jan Cervinka of the Czech Republic. The mountain is of moderate altitude and difficulty and has seen numerous ascents; we declined to publish their note as we do with many accounts simply because it was not significant to modern climbing. Or was it? Sňída is in his late 60s, Cervinka recently celebrated his 70th year, and both have been climbing in the high mountains all their lives. The goal of keeping the Journal's focus on its role as a record of significant climbing often comes at the cost of missing stories such as this that speak volumes about the spirit we can bring to the mountains over time. Though we may not cover it, a great day at the crags, a great week in the mountains, discovering cause for celebration that would sound vain if it ever appeared in an article, continue to be some of the better reasons for doing what climbers do, even if the stories don't show up in these pages.

Approach the contents of this journal, then, with perspective. The climbs recorded here may be very difficult, but they hold nothing that cannot be reached by us all. With friends, watching from our aerie the play of light as it evolves over the course of a day, we discover anew the ancient rhythms of the world—and that is sorely needed. If we look away from the crags and mountains and toward the life we are forging around us, we see what an ignorance of such rhythms can bring. We build the dams and a generation later realize they can cause more harm than good; we exterminate a species from an ecosystem only to find that the ecosystem depended on the species for balance. In climbing, the wildflowers chase the snowline, a cloud forms out of blue sky, the sun loosens a wall's grout, all factors in the problem of our ascent. Here, in change, lies harmony—paradoxical, beautiful, a foil for our cries to harness, domesticate, control. Climbing teaches us to work within the natural context to accomplish our goals. Such lessons are in short supply in our workaday lives, but they are the magic of climbing, a magic central to all of our stories. May you discover a bit of your own on your next adventure.

CHRISTIAN BECKWITH, *Editor*

The South Face of Dhaulagiri

An interview with Tomaž Humar

by Antonella Cicogna, *Italy*
translated by Emanuele Pellizzari, with Christian Beckwith

The south face—or, more accurately, the south-southeast face—of Dhaulagiri I sweeps up over 4000 meters to end at the 8167-meter summit of the seventh highest mountain in the world. It is a broad concavity of a wall, steep and dangerous, pocked by large active seracs and, at over 7000 meters, cut by a 300-meter swath of fractured rock. The eight-kilometer-long southeast ridge defines its rightmost boundary, while on the left, a more complex architecture composed of various pillars and buttresses converges at a broad plateau at ca. 7300 meters. From this plateau, the cleaner lines of the southwest ridge continue to the summit, forming the border of the south face on its left side.

Both the southeast and southwest ridges were first climbed in 1978 in separate expedition-style efforts by Japanese teams. Rising from the South Col, the Southwest Ridge (or South Pillar, as it is known in Japan) was first attempted in the pre-monsoon of 1975 by a team led by Takashi Amemiya. The effort ended low on the route when five men, including two Sherpas and a local porter, were killed by an avalanche as they slept in Camp I. Three years later, Amemiya returned to try the same line. The expedition left Pokhara with a team of 450 porters in late February. Two months after establishing base camp, five members made it to the top on May 10 and 11. One man was killed in the ascent.

In the post-monsoon of the same year, Seiko Tanaka led an 18-member expedition to the southeast ridge. Described by Gaston Rébuffat as "[i]ncredibly long and technically very difficult," the ridge had already rebuffed two strong American efforts to climb it, including one in 1969 that claimed seven lives. Though the summit was reached on October 19 and 20 by six members of Tanaka's team, it came at a high cost: three members were killed in September in an avalanche between camps IV and V, and the climbing leader, Katsuyoshi Kogure, died ferrying loads on October 20 on the same stretch.

The south face proper saw its first ascent in 1981. On October 15, after nearly two weeks of reconnaissance, Yugoslavians Stane Belak Šrauf, Cene Berčič and Emil Tratnik started out from a base camp at 3924 meters. The trio climbed for five days on the right side of the south face before joining the Southeast Ridge route at the rock band at 7185 meters. They continued up the ridge for four more days, reaching their 7950-meter high point near the junction of the Southeast and Northeast ridges (the mountain's normal route, climbed in 1960 by a predominantly Swiss expedition for the first ascent). In increasingly unstable weather and leaving behind their tent, food and stove, they began their descent of the northeast ridge. Four days of open bivouacs in strong storms followed before they reached the base of the mountain. By the time they regained safety in the village of Kali Pani, they had gone six days without food.

The south face of Dhaulagiri, showing left to right: 1: the Southwest Buttress (Coudray et al, 1980); 2: the South Pillar/Southwest Ridge (Amemiya et al, 1978); 3: the Polish South Face (Chrobak et al, 1986); 4: Mobitel Route (showing bivouacs; first bivy is hidden) (Humar, 1999); 5: Yugoslavian South Face (Belak-Berčič-Tratnik, 1981); 6: Southeast Ridge (Tanaka et al, 1978). MICHAEL COVINGTON

In the post-monsoon of 1986, Eugeniusz Chrobak led a predominantly Polish team that established the second line on the south face. The team set up base camp at 3800 meters on September 16. The challenge began with the 1200-meter rock wall on the prominent buttress just left of the center of the face. There, they encountered sustained climbing up to 5.8 on rock "so friable that a bolt hole could be made with a few blows." Next came an ice rib of 60 to 70 degrees with passages up to 85 degrees; 3200 meters of fixed rope was used to this point. The upper part of the buttress involved mixed pitches up to 5.7 before the broad plateau at ca. 7500 meters was reached. Camp V on the plateau was established on October 30 by Maciej Berbeka and Mikolaj Czyzewski. During the night, the wind tore their tent apart. The next morning, Berbeka climbed alone over easy snow to reach the 1978 South Pillar/Southwest Ridge route. Though the way was now open to the summit, bad weather and lack of time forced the team to give up, and they retreated back down their route to base camp.

Soloing in the strict sense of the word means that one is alone at all times above base camp. On June 2, 1981, Japanese Hironobu Kamuro achieved the summit via the normal route. He was accompanied to his first high camp at 5720 meters by two teammates, and his arrival at the end of the spring climbing season allowed him to use fixed ropes and a tent left behind by another team who had just left the mountain. On October 19, 1990, American George Lowe reached the summit, also via the Northeast Ridge route. Nuru Sherpa had accompanied him to 6400 meters, but the day he summited there was no one else above base camp. His descent to his bivy tent at 7280 meters, which he reached three hours after dark, was carried out under difficult conditions with poor visibility and strong winds.

On September 26, 1999, Slovenian Tomaž Humar arrived on the north side of Dhaulagiri by helicopter. The traditional post-monsoon season had not even begun at this point; heavy rains and snowfall had continued through September. Unsettled conditions would linger into early October, followed by more stormy days in the middle of the month brought about by a cyclone in nearby India. Indeed, hampered by the weather, the majority of the post-monsoon Himalayan expeditions would accomplish no noteworthy climbing whatsoever.

Humar's expedition included equipment for a live broadcast of his climb over the internet, a film to be made from base camp and radio communication with base camp to aid in route-finding during his climb. He acclimatized on the normal Northeast Ridge route, climbing to Camp I (5800m) on September 29 and 30 and then to Camp III (7300m) on October 10-12. On October 15, Humar was flown by helicopter to Base Camp at 3800 meters on the south side of the mountain. On October 25—the day after Dawa Sherpa and British climber Ginette Harrison were killed in an avalanche while attempting the normal route on the other side of the mountain—he began his ascent on the south face of Dhaulagiri, leaving BC at 5 p.m. with gear and food for ten days. His plan: with only a 45-meter static 5-mm Kevlar rope, three Friends, four screws and five pitons, he would solo everything, foregoing self-belays. When the climbing was too difficult to achieve with his pack, he would leave it behind, climb up, fix the line, then descend to retrieve the pack.

Climbing throughout the night of the 25th, Humar reached ca. 4600 meters at the base of the huge narrow gully that cuts through the lower part of the south face. In the early hours of October 26, he made various attempts to overcome the gully via an ice line. He continued his efforts for the rest of the day, stopping at 5 p.m. to wait for the return of cooler temperatures. His efforts, which began again at 11 p.m., were also unsuccessful. He stopped to bivouac at 2 a.m.

The next day, at 8 a.m., Humar decided to rock climb the first pillar to the right of the great gully. This he managed to do with a final traverse estimated to be M7. He bivouacked under the second pillar at 4 a.m.

On October 28, Humar left first thing in the afternoon for the second pillar, climbing the rest of the day and into the night on difficult ground up to M7+. He bivouacked at 2 a.m. in a cave to avoid avalanches. The next day, avalanches of ice, rock and snow continued to fall in the central part of the wall. He had hundreds of ridges to cross, one after another, before he could make his fourth bivy. On October 30, he pushed on, traversing over a series of frightening seracs that he dubbed "the Praying Mantis" before putting up his tent inside a huge crevasse at ca. 7100 meters, on the Praying Mantis's head.

The route to this point had followed his vision of a direct line on the south face, but now, on his seventh day, Humar saw the great horizontal rock band above him and realized that it would take two or three days to overcome this formidable barrier. Instead, he traversed to the right some 1000 meters to the southeast ridge, where he bivouacked at ca. 7300 meters. On November 1, he left the tent and the majority of his equipment behind and traversed back out onto the south face. At around 7600 meters, he climbed through mixed ground, drytooling on terrain he estimated to be around M5-M6 before bivying at 7800 meters in his sleeping bag. At 2:33 p.m. the next day, he reached the highest point of his climb at ca. 8000 meters when he exited onto the southeast ridge. From there, he joined the normal Northeast Ridge route for his descent, spending the night in a tent of an American expedition at 7300 meters (Camp III). On November 3, he descended to Camp I at 5700 meters, where other members of the expedition had come to meet him. They then waited for a helicopter, which arrived the next day to bring him to Pokhara.

The following is an interview with Italian journalist Antonella Cicogna, conducted in Humar's home in Kamnik, Slovenia, after the climb. (Certain details were subsequently added to the interview by Humar via e-mail.)

EDITOR

Antonella Cicogna: How do you rank your climb of Dhaulagiri?

Tomaž Humar: The south face has everything. It's the highest face of Nepal, damned overhanging and steep. It's the face par excellence, more than 4000 meters of climbing, the dream of the super-strong [Stane Belak] Šrauf. The idea was also born thanks to him. I chose it for this reason. It's my nirvana. I place it at the top of my present climbs because of [the initial] 1700 meters of rock as well. . . . I don't love climbing solo on rock, because I'm too slow.

How was the start?

Hard. I was afraid. Really, you can't figure this face out until it's above you, until you are in the middle of it. It's immense, 4000 meters of practically liquid ice, of snow, of frighteningly rotten rock. This climb was something unknown, even though I had studied it in all the details. The face was different compared to my photos of 18 years ago. It was too warm; my initial plan was to climb on frozen lines of ice, but conditions were prohibitive. Many plans on paper changed radically when I found myself in action. I tried to forecast different scenarios, particularly over 7000 meters. So I brought with me 45 meters of [5-mm] Kevlar [rope], five pitons, three Friends, four ice screws, some slings, many carabiners. I left BC at 3800 meters a day after the full moon. It was October 25.

Having climbed the first rock pillar, Humar points to his line. His pack is visible just beyond his fingertip. TOMAŽ HUMAR

In your own plans, where did you expect to first bivouac?

My goal was to make my first bivy after ice climbing the great narrow gully that furrows the lower part of the south face. But I was not even at the foot of the gully when three very difficult rock bands presented themselves. Once I got to the base of the gully, the first real problems started.

What was the altitude then?

I was at 4600 meters. But I can't swear about the altitude. I didn't have an altimeter with me and everything is so enormous on a face [like that] that you lose a sense of things. Among the altitudes I remember with some precision is the one of October 31, the sixth bivouac. Because [by then] I had reached the Japanese [Southeast Ridge] route, so I had more precise reference points. And it was also the day when [Janez] Jeglič disappeared on the west face of Nuptse W2 in 1997 when we were together. I prayed for him.

What about once you were at the base of the great gully?

I lost my sense of time. I tried all night to overcome this gully via ice, pausing now and then. Avalanches and lots of water continued to pour down on me, soaking me. By this point it was about 5 a.m. I stopped for three hours and then started again, but the ice line was impractical. At 5 p.m. on October 26 I decided that the only possibility was to wait for night and then go on with the colder temperatures]. I waited until 11 p.m. I started to climb 15, maybe 20 meters on steep ice, but the pillar was not adhered to the rock. It broke loose, it swayed, it felt like climbing on a swing. Water kept pouring down on me with the snow, even in the middle

Looking down at the icy gully from the second bivouac. Tomaž Humar

of the night. I was frozen solid. The only way up was to stay on the right side of the gully and find a route on the rock pillar, but I decided to start again with the light of day and at 2 a.m. I made my first bivouac.

So, on October 27, in the morning, you started rock climbing what you call the "first pillar"?

Yes, it was 8 a.m. on the third day. On the easy parts I climbed with the pack. On the harder leads, I left it at the belay to retrieve later. I used the static Kevlar 5-mm rope only for rappelling. On overhangs I rappelled using one carabiner on the rope. I climbed without rest. Three avalanches hit me, but in the early afternoon I got to a mixed section. From this spot I thought I saw a good ledge. "Here we are! I found the way," I shouted over the radio to Stipe Bozic. So I descended, picked up the pack again and soloed back up, and I still had these enormous black walls to climb. I kept climbing up, and it was almost dark. I had to climb some very thin couloirs, almost rotten, of ice, snow and terrible rock. It was very difficult (M6-) with the heavy pack. But I made it. I was convinced I was out of [the hard parts]. But instead, I found myself facing a very delicate traverse, thin hard ice, 70- to 80-degree aid, and right in the middle of it [there was] a rock formation like a big coconut, a huge coconut, blocking the way. It was dark. It must have been about 7 p.m. I was forced to climb it like a chimpanzee. At a certain point I could go neither forward nor back. There were no cracks. So

I placed a single Friend in between the rock and ice on top of the coconut and hung on it, and [makes a sound] *giiing giiing* started to make a small pendulum in this part which overhangs like a balcony, swinging on the Friend while the protection creaked under my weight. It was crazily exposed, a 20-25 meter traverse. There was nothing to hang on to. One of the most dangerous things I've ever done. I rated it A0, but it doesn't really matter. At the end of this traverse, under a little overhang, I was forced to stop and wait. I waited for hours, from 8 p.m. until 1 a.m. Above was hell: avalanches, falling stones, ice. It was the warmest temperatures of the entire climb. I was hit many times by snow and four times by serac avalanches. At this point, I was sure that I was finished, because I was hanging on ice screws. Then, finally, I managed to get out, and climbed on mixed ground (M7) to the second pillar, where I made my second bivouac. The last avalanches only missed me by about ten minutes.

Was the M7 traverse the hardest part of the climb?

No. The worst came later, on the second pillar on October 28. I started early in the afternoon. It's shorter than the first pillar, but with pitches that were truly extreme for me, up to VII [5.10d] and M7+. In the beginning, the rock was worse than rotten; it was all flakes. I never managed to get any gear worth trusting: when I rappelled to get my pack, I kept one hand on the rope and the other on the rock [in case the anchor gave way].

I knew I had to climb this thing before nightfall. I climbed, rappelled and climbed again without any protection. And where it was overhanging, it was fatiguing as hell to make my gloves slide on the rope. (Twisting a glove around the rope to descend is one of my basic tricks that I use when I climb solo on delicate and loose rock.) I was forced to take my gloves off, and I smashed my hands. They hurt badly.

By now I was in the upper part of the second pillar. I had risked much at this point. My leg hurt as well. I was hit by a big piece of ice at the beginning of the day and the violence was such that I thought I had broken it. At a certain point I couldn't progress any more. I was literally beneath continuous water- and snowfall. I had to climb a terrifying roof. I somehow cleaned it of snow and with a contortionist's moves managed to get through it. I was totally drenched. The water was freezing on me, and it shattered into a thousand pieces with every move I made until it seemed as if I were a robot. At this point my toes were completely gone. Frozen. I was stuck again. I had my pack. Dark had fallen. The next 50 meters took two hours. The face was plastered. Ninety degrees steep. And under ten centimeters of powder snow was rock that felt more like sand. It was all dust. I had no idea how I would get up this part. At this point I was really at the "life border," at the limit between life and death. And after the 50-meter traverse (M7), I came to a snow field. I sat down to rest in a kind of cave, safe from the avalanches that continued to come down a little ways away from me the next morning as well. It was deep dark night; I was at my third bivouac (2 a.m., October 29).

In the most difficult moments, what helped you the most?

God. And a little shoe, that of my son, Tomaž. He's eight. I always keep it with me, clipped with a carabiner on my pack; it brings me luck on the riskiest climbs. And then, all the messages they sent me by radio. All the e-mails that were sent to me via the web site that was broadcasting my climb live in Slovenian and English.

How much e-mail did you receive?

In the most difficult moments the e-mail was huge. My companions in BC read it to me over the radio. I was surprised to receive messages from unknown people. In total, my web site beat the Slovenian records for hits. On November 2, there were more than 1.7 million hits with 50,000 visitors who were following [my climb]. That day I received 550 e-mails.

Back to the climb. How was it from the third to the fourth bivouacs?

On October 29, ice, rock and snow fell continuously down the center of the face. I had a "million" ridges to surmount. Delicate, one after another. And from where I was I could see this huge serac. It was the head of the great Praying Mantis (I gave names to every serac on the wall), with her horrifying open mouth. Her long legs seemed to stretch out to me, as if she wanted to reach me and hit me with the sharpness of a scythe. I climbed onto a ridge crest. I had to traverse the grand couloir and get to the left. I started out three times. Right in the middle, rockfall began from above, bombardments of ice, landslides. Fortunately my position was protected by a little ridge. I watched as everything passed overhead. Jesus. . . . But at the end I arrived at the fourth bivouac. Here, with my pocket knife, I pulled out a tooth that had been tormenting me. Unfortunately I started on healthy teeth, but at the end I broke the painful one. I had a dental granuloma; I sucked it out and then went to sleep. The torment was over.

On October 30 you arrived on the head of the Praying Mantis, and there you put your fifth bivouac.

Yes. I didn't have any particular problems that day. I kept on climbing, crossing frightening seracs. And then, I put up my tent inside a huge crevasse at about 7100 meters. It was the sixth night on the wall.

On October 31 you decided to traverse 1000 meters to get to the Japanese [Southeast] ridge?

It took too many days to get to this point, and now I had very little gas left for the stove. I didn't want to repeat the adventures of Nuptse, and I knew I had to have some [gas] for the descent as well. At least half a canister. Continuing directly was out of the question. The rock band above was overhanging, terrible rock. I understood that the protection I had left (two Friends and four pitons) wouldn't have given me even a minimal amount of security. The only thing to do was the traverse. A countless number of couloirs to cross, like organ pipes, with one rock pitch of V [5.7] . In the photos you don't even see it. . . . Then I climbed more organ pipes and a mixed couloir up to VI+ [5.10a], and arrived at the Japanese Route. And here, on the ridge at ca. 7300 meters, I found a piton and traces of their climb. I bivouacked nearby.

Humar at ca. 7100 meters, five days into the route.
Tomaž Humar

At the exit of the south face, Humar holds up the good luck shoe of his son. TOMAŽ HUMAR

Did you think you'd get to the summit the next day?

The next day I started out, leaving behind the tent and all unnecessary gear. I wanted to summit light; with a big pack, I was scared the wind would blow me away. I climbed on mixed terrain. At 8 o'clock in the morning at 7350 meters I was forced to climb loose rock (5.10a) and an icy crack without gloves. It was very cold. The weather wasn't good—too windy. I was scared some lightning would roast me. And at a certain point, at the edge of the east and south faces, the climb was too rocky and difficult. I couldn't go further. I was halfway between camps VI and VII. I again moved toward the center of the south face. And again, on the very last section, there was an extreme part, a vertical section at 7600 meters, mixed ground. It took all my strength to get through it, dry tooling. (At that altitude, loose rock is not fun.)

Dry tooling at 7600 meters? Maybe you're the only one in the world?

I don't know. I only know that at the end, when I decided to bivouac at about 7800 meters, I was so spent I thought I had gotten edema. It was terribly cold. Obviously I didn't have the tent, only a sleeping bag. Plus my stove did not work anymore, and I was thirsty.

The next day, on November 2 at 2:33 p.m., you exited from the face.

Yes. I popped out on the Southeast Ridge. I found myself on the highest point of my climb at around 8000 meters, and my line on the south face was finished. I had reached my personal nirvana.

And the summit?

The summit would have been the cherry on the cake. And also in the end, the face or summit is not so important. The main goal is coming back home and dreaming on.

Tomaž, what did you expect in the event of success? How was it then?

Personally, I expected to reach my nirvana. But I also knew that this ascent would not have an exclusively personal value. If you climb these kind of faces, there's a responsibility before all of alpinism. That's why Stipe Bosic made a film from BC, we documented the climb on the internet and I took photos.

After your nirvana, what will the next climb be?

I look ahead. There are a lot of faces, the Lhotse traverse, the direct line on the west face of Makalu. . . . The challenges are always there. But it depends on a lot of things, above all on my "third eye." The money doesn't matter, nor the difficulties. Whatever the climb, only when

I feel the mountain welcomes me, then will I go.

After [making the first ascent of] Annapurna, Herzog said, "There are other Annapurnas [in the lives of men.]" I agree with him. There are still other Dhaulagiris [awaiting me in my life].

SUMMARY OF STATISTICS

AREA: Dhaulagiri Himal, Nepal

NEW ROUTE: *The Mobitel Route* (VI 5.10d A0 M7+, ca. 4000m) on the south face of Dhaulagiri (8167m), October 25-November 3, 1999, Tomaž Humar, solo

PERSONNEL: Tomaž Humar, Stipe Bosic, Gorazd Suhadolnik, Andrej Kmet, Lado Ogrin, Tomo Drolec, Vinko Bercic, Josko Bojic and Dr. Anda Perdan

Humar on day 3, approaching the "enormous black walls" between bivies 1 and 2.
TOMAŽ HUMAR

Tomaž Humar was born in 1969. He first came in contact with the mountains in 1987, through the Kamnik Alpine Club. He has devoted himself solely to alpinism since 1992, making more than 1,200 ascents, some 60 of which were new routes, solo. Most of these routes remain unrepeated. Often his most difficult ascents are put up solo. He has soloed the *Reticent Wall* on El Cap, and his Himalayan ascents include a variation to the Japanese route on the southeast face of Ganesh V (with Stane Belak Šrauf), Annapurna I, the *Stane Belak Šrauf Memorial Route* on Ama Dablam (with Vanja Furlan), *Golden Heart* on the northwest face of Bobaye (solo), *Talking About Tsampa* on Loboche East (with Carlos Carsolio and Janez Jeglic), Pumori and the Humar-Jeglič line on Nuptse's west face. He lives in the town of Kamnik, Slovenia, with his wife and two children, to whom he dedicates his extreme ascents.

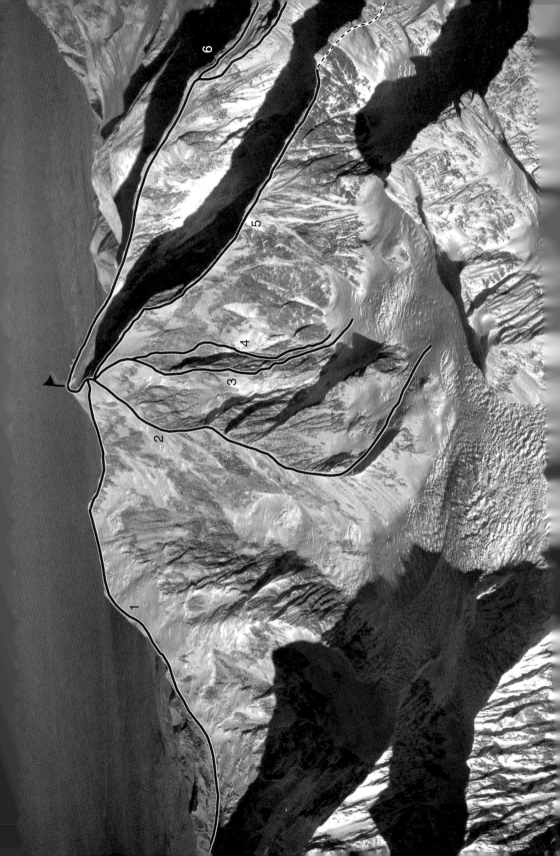

The South Face of Mount Foraker

Trying harder in the Alaska Range

by Steve Larson

July 4th, 1998, and I am spending the weekend with Joe TerraVecchia sport climbing in Rumney, New Hampshire. We are in the parking lot, outside Joe's truck. Joe reaches behind his seat and pulls out a black bag. Before he opens the bag, he looks over his shoulder. The check is quick, but thorough: no one is watching.

Joe produces a photo he took while flying out from the *Moonflower Buttress* of Mount Hunter in 1997. He and Carl Tobin had Paul Roderick, owner of Talkeetna Air Taxi, fly by the *Infinite Spur* on Mount Foraker to check it out. Luckily, it was a perfect day. When Joe got home and saw the photos, though, it wasn't the *Infinite Spur* that caught his eye. Instead, he recognized a line beginning to the right of the *Infinite Spur* that gained the beautiful diamond-shaped wall above.

Joe went to Alaska in the spring of '98 to try the route with Carl. 1998 was an El Niño year, and they never got beyond Anchorage. Now, Carl is becoming a dad, and Joe has asked me to take Carl's place. Joe and I had met on the *Moonflower*, each of us members of separate parties. That was more than a year ago, and I am now looking for a route to provide similar climbing. One look at the line seemed to show that the upper half would be steep enough. Joe did not have to ask me a second time. By the end of the weekend, we had agreed to return together the following spring to the Alaska Range.

Joe and I were fortunate to receive the Mugs Stump Award for an alpine-style attempt on the south face of Mount Foraker. We had Paul Roderick drop us off on the Kahiltna Glacier at the base of the southeast ridge of Mount Foraker, rather than the traditional airstrip on the southeast fork. This not only put us closer to the start of the route, but, with both the southeast ridge and the French Ridge of Foraker just across the glacier and the bulk of Denali looming above the head of the Kahiltna, we had an extraordinary setting to ourselves.

Our proposed route on the south face of Mount Foraker begins with a long gully to the right of the *Infinite Spur* at 8,000 feet and ends with a mantel 7,000 feet higher. The gully, which keeps the climber to the left of any discharge from the hanging glacier above, provides the first 2,000 feet of climbing and ends at the Rock Step, the route's first technical challenge. The Rock Step accesses the Shoulder to the left of the hanging glacier. At the top of the hanging glacier lies a 3,500-foot, diamond-shaped wall. The route follows a line of weakness just right of center, exiting about 400 feet right of the wall's apex at 15,000 feet, where it joins the *Infinite Spur*. The *Infinite Spur* gains the apex of the south face from the left, and our route joins the *Infinite Spur* at that point. It then ascends another 1,800 feet to the broad summit plateau and finally ends on the north summit at 17,400 feet.

The South Face of Mount Foraker, showing 1. Southwest Ridge (LeRoy-Goforth-Liddle-Marvin, 1977). 2. Talkeetna Ridge (Bertulis-Bleser-Williamson-Baer, 1968). 3. Infinite Spur (Kennedy-Lowe, 1977). 4. South Face (Larson-TerraVecchia, 1999). 5. French Ridge (Agresti-Agresti-Bouquier-Créton-Galmiche-Thivierge-Landry, 1976). 6. Southeast Ridge (with 1974 variation on left) (Duenwald-Richardson, 1963). BRADFORD WASHBURN #8049

We left Base Camp on May 23 with 12 days of food and 14 days of fuel for the climb. We knew we would have to cross two ridges to get to the base of the south face but were surprised to find that the second one involved technical pitches. That was the end of the road as far as our sleds were concerned. We pared down and left a cache.

Crossing the second ridge was a difficult day, climbing with enormous packs and eventually getting caught in the sun. We cut through the sheath of our haul rope hauling the first pitch, and trashed the rope in the five pitches it took to get to the top of the ridge. We had decided to bring a 7.6-millimeter rope for a haul rope. We were expecting too much from too little. Tired and frustrated from our day, we went to sleep thinking the route might be over before it had even started.

The next morning we both woke with the same idea. We would return to BC to wait for Paul to fly in another rope. The up-side was that we could retrieve our cache and sleds and bring it all back to BC. At least we would not have to clean up after ourselves once we had returned from the route.

Eventually, Paul arrived with an old rope he found laying around in his office. After nearly a week's delay, we had replaced our rope and covered the approach for the third time, finally getting our first view of the face on May 31.

We moved to within half a mile of the base of the route during a storm and were in position when the weather finally broke. We spent June 3 watching the route to assess activity on the face. We were especially concerned with the effect that direct exposure from the sun might have. The entire day passed without any rock- or icefall, and we started toward the bergschrund once the sun went off the face.

We planned to minimize our exposure by climbing the initial gully at night. While we were on the fan approaching the bergschrund, the gully avalanched. Fortunately, it was just a powder avalanche, but it would have been quite a scene to witness: catching sight of the enormous cloud of powder heading toward us, we each dropped our packs and ran in opposite directions. Tied together, of course.

As I was leading the second pitch, Joe called me back to the belay. He had noticed that our lead rope had two inches of core exposed about 60 feet from my end. We discussed retreating but finally decided we just hadn't tried hard enough yet to cash in our chips. We decided to tape up the sheath and continue to lead on the rope. Our rationale was that leading on the rope would subject it to less abuse than hauling with it.

When the sun finally hit us, we had no choice but to stop. We had been up for more than 24 hours. We each chopped a body-sized ledge and tried to sleep in the sun until the gully went back into the shade. Once things froze up, we got underway again. At the top of the gully, we found four mixed pitches through the Rock Step. Here the granite, which had previously been compact, offering few cracks and virtually none greater than a quarter of an inch in width, now became fractured with clean, sharp cracks. The rock would remain that way through to the top. The Rock Step brought us to the Shoulder, to the left of the hanging glacier. Elevation: 10,440 feet.

The sun played a much larger role than either of us expected. During the first five days, climbing in the sun was out of the question. Nonetheless, on four of those five days we got caught in the sun before we found a suitable bivouac. Not only did the snow turn to bottomless corn, but the heat was oppressive, especially considering that we were dressed for climbing through the night.

We arrived at the Shoulder at the end of our second day and saw the 3,500-foot upper wall for the first time. Perched above the hanging glacier, the wall from this perspective was unrecognizable compared to our route photos. It was our second consecutive long day; we had gotten four or five hours of sleep in between. We were too tired and discouraged to piece together the route, so we just went to sleep.

With four hours of rest, we simul-climbed up the hanging glacier to the bergschrund. I was exhausted and felt as though I was not pulling my weight when Joe suggested that we bivouac in the 'schrund.

"Sure," I said. "If *you* want to."

Above the hanging glacier, the route steepens and begins its transformation into what we had come for. We gained the diamond-shaped wall by way of a corner with a very narrow ribbon of ice up its center. This kept us left of anything funneling down from the snow fields between our route and the French Ridge. We climbed to the base of the Couloir, the obvious weakness through the steepest section of the wall. Elevation: 12,120 feet.

At the base of the Couloir, we tried to find a

Thirty-five pitches up and in the midst of the difficult climbing, Steve Larson wonders whether he can get another 25 pitches out of his rope. JOE TERRAVECCHIA

sheltered spot to bivouac. We were in the sun, and falling ice and rocks were coming uncomfortably close. Out of options, we chopped a ledge but hit rock before it was big enough for the tent. We set the tent up anyway at two-thirds its normal size, crammed into it and tried to sleep with our helmets on. That night it snowed, spindrift collapsed the tent and we had to get suited up and go out into the weather to install the awning that we should have put on when we set the tent up in the first place.

Both Joe and I dislike climbing with big packs. We had agreed that if the route was steep enough, we would haul the packs and enjoy our leads unencumbered. It had worked for me on the *Moonflower.*

Joe TerraVecchia on the second pitch in the Coulior, day 5.
Steve Larson

Thirty pitches into this route, with another 30 to go, the fabric of our packs was failing. Titoune Bouchard, owner of Wild Things, had suggested we bring haul sheaths, but I had opted to save the weight. Both packs had numerous three- to six-inch rips, and the contents threatened to fall out. The problem got exponentially worse each day. Sewing the fabric back together became a daily routine.

The seven pitches up the Couloir provided fantastic climbing. Throughout its length, the Couloir was rarely wider than six to eight feet across. Virtually every pitch had sections to vertical or beyond. Only one pitch allowed for straight-ahead ice climbing; the balance of the climbing was mixed. Joe pulled off a couple of impressive leads here.

When we started the Couloir, we decided to switch our ropes, leading on the haul line that Paul had flown in for us and hauling with the damaged lead rope. As Joe was hauling the second pitch, the sheath blew apart where we had taped it on the first day. It had totally failed, and two feet of core was now exposed. We cut out the damaged section and tied the rope back together. From then on we would have to pass the knot every time we hauled a pitch. This knot would also make retreat a more complicated option.

The weather was deteriorating as well. Snow was beginning to fall and, as a result, spindrift was beginning to slough off the snow field above, funneling down the Couloir. I put on my ski goggles and headed up the next pitch. It was steep, but I figured that because it seemed to be all ice, I could get up it in spite of the spindrift. Even though I could no longer see well enough to place rock gear, I reasoned that, if necessary, I should be able to place an ice screw.

As I climbed the pitch, both the snow and wind increased markedly. In a matter of minutes, the goggles became so fogged I had to remove them. As I neared the end of the pitch, the ice petered out, but the angle had yet to ease. Screws were no longer a choice. My last screw was only halfway in, tied off and well below my feet. Joe says the spindrift was so intense that he was having a hard time breathing through it. At least I had figured one thing

Steve Larson at the belay in the corner system above the Coulior, day 6, pitch 40-something.
Joe TerraVecchia

right: I couldn't see well enough to place any rock gear.

My being was reduced to the next five or six tool placements. I have no idea how long it took, but it took more time than Joe had patience. I rapped off as soon as I got to some ice thick enough to take a screw.

The storm passed during the following day, and we attempted the Couloir that evening for the second time. We ascended our two fixed lines and I re-led my ice pitch. As a sting-in-the-tail, the wind began to pick up again as I neared the top of the pitch. The wind and spindrift continued to intensify as Joe took the next lead, forcing him to stop several times to wait. Fortunately, the wind blew itself out and we were able to carry on.

We were finally high enough to climb during the day, and the sun felt wonderful. The climbing was outstanding as well. We climbed up and right from our bivouac (elevation: 13,230'), and gained a corner system that went for several pitches, allowing us access to a ramp angling up and left. A gully capped with a short wall brought us through a rock band to another snowfield. By the end of the day, the wind started blowing again and we needed to find a place to bivouac. It was a gift to find a snow arête where we could get the tent up without any chopping. Elevation: 14,000 feet.

Our final day on the face was spent in and out of the clouds. Eventually, the storm won out, but not until we were off the face. From its apex, we were able to follow a snow arête upward in blowing snow and white-out conditions. When the arête began to broaden, we decided to bivouac, because we were not certain we could stay on it and we did not want to wander into one of the bowls on either side.

The following day, June 14, the weather cleared by late morning and we started up the remaining 1,800 feet to the summit plateau. We spent several hours on a tedious slope of a single, unrelenting angle, trying to avoid isolated pockets of wind slab. We gained the summit plateau and moved toward the north summit. Eventually, the weather forced us to hole up for a day and a half 500 feet below the summit. By now the difficulties were basically over, but it was frustrating to be caught in another storm, on this side of the summit, with very little food.

Summit day dawned clear and remained that way for the first half of the day. The summit was calm, but high clouds suggested we not linger. After about 20 minutes, we started down. Joe had done the classic Southeast Ridge earlier in his career and knew that he did not want to do it again. We chose the Northeast Ridge to the Sultana Ridge over to Mount Crosson by default and dropped 5,700 feet that afternoon.

Traversing the Sultana Ridge would be a glorious way to spend a clear day, but that was not our lot. Fate provided us with deep snow, poor light and white-out conditions.

The weather improved the following day. As the sky cleared, the temperatures climbed. We now found ourselves in the sun, overdressed and overheating. I was stumbling along toward a spot on the horizon where I planned to shed some layers. Joe was watching me from behind when I disappeared from view. I fell what seemed to be a long way, pulling Joe off his feet and dragging him along the snow. Finally, I stopped in a chimney position, wedged between my pack, my hands and my knees. It took me a minute to decide that I was OK. Fortunately, I had an ice tool in each hand and was able to chimney up and out.

We continued up over the summit of Crosson and began our final descent to the Kahiltna. We had started with 12 days of food, but this was our 16th day. For most of the last week, we had been on half rations. As we descended lower, the snow got worse, and we decided to eat what little food we had left (less than one man's portion for dinner) and wait for it to get colder. Later, when we arrived at a camp at 8,500 feet, we found an abandoned cache being torn

Steve Larson on the summit. JOE TERRAVECCHIA

apart by ravens: bagels and cheese, pita and peanut butter and cookies, cookies, cookies... fat city.

Once we hit the Kahiltna, it was a night of postholing and dead ends. It took several attempts, but eventually we found our way through a maze of crevasses and across the glacier. At 4 a.m., as the east face of Foraker was bathed in the alpenglow of another day, we arrived at the airstrip on the southwest fork of the Kahiltna.

Perhaps doing a big alpine route is all about dealing with a steady diet of problems with nothing more than reason, determination and a bit of duct tape, but that is not how I remember the experience. My journal reminds me of fatigue, mood swings dependent predominately on the prevailing weather, problems with gear and a concern with the lack of food. But my memory is of the climbing, the situation and my partner. So many pitches, for most of which there is no record; lovely answers to a constant stream of questions. All in a remote setting, a spectacular place, a place where our heroes have climbed. And yet, all of this would ring hollow if not for the partnership: that relationship between two individuals, committed and pulling hard for a shared goal, and what they, through the synergy of their mutual desire, can pull off.

SUMMARY OF STATISTICS

AREA: Alaska Range, Alaska

NEW ROUTE: The South Face (Alaska Grade 6, 9,400') of Mount Foraker (17,400'), June 4-20, Steve Larson, Joe TerraVecchia

Steve Larson. JOE TERRAVECCHIA

Steve Larson, 43, a self-employed custom builder and woodworker, began his alpine career in 1976 in the Canadian Rockies. He had led his first 5.9 at his home crag that summer and had done a couple of pitches of aid, so it seemed reasonable to expect to give the North Face of North Twin a go. He settled for the North Face of Athabasca instead and has been learning from his mistakes ever since. He lives in Eaton Center, NH, with his wife, Tricia, and his two children, Brita, 10, and Michael, 8.

The Burkett Needle

The voyage of the celestial tramps

by Lionel Daudet, *France*
translated by Marina Heusch

Beginning the triple portage on the Baird Glacier. LIONEL DAUDET

Unbelievable! He is there, unmoving, having landed just next to us. His wings barely quiver on the cold, white snow. It is one of the first traces of life that we have encountered: a butterfly, red wings flecked with black. Brother Butterfly. Later on, we will see a fly, a spider, a few foolhardy birds, and that will be all. Whatever can he be doing here, so far from everything, at our first bivouac?

And we, what are we doing as well, cut off from the world, isolated in this inhospitable region? To climb a mountain. What a great excuse for Seb and me to find ourselves in the middle of this very wild coastal chain of Southeast Alaska! Just think: 41 days, during which we will have the luxury of savoring every second. But also, 41 days without listening to the radio (or having a radio, for that matter) and 41 days of eating nothing but pasta. And 25 days on the wall!

When we pulled our double pulkas onto these immense white tentacles separating us from the ocean banks where, a few days earlier, a boat had dropped us off, we did not yet realize any of that. And certainly, it was much better that way. . . .

A storm of unparalleled fury, and here is our mangled tent, our pulkas blown away. Welcome to Alaska! A bad night in a snow cave dug out in great haste, and now there is nothing left to do but get back to the portaledge, up there, at the foot of the fantastic Burkett Needle.

From the beginning of the game, the pitches prove difficult. A first dihedral of perfect rock, ideal for warming oneself up and awakening one's senses. A seam of honeycombed black rock shows me the route before it peters out on a short, difficult, overhanging section. Above, as soon as I recover my balance by locking off on small crimps, a smooth slab. . . . On vague smears, I shift from the left, hesitate, climb a bit, downclimb, resolve to put in a bolt.

"Watch me!"

An attentive hand takes out the extra slack. The gaze of the belayer ascends the length of the wall, coming to rest at the front end of the rope. I hesitate to commit completely, so far from the bolt. A fall, now that we have no possibility whatsoever of rescue, is not really an option. We can't afford to smack into anything up here. My mind empties itself, becomes as white as the snow, fills up with a surreal light. Delicate crossing of the feet on questionable little nubbins, my fingers dig into vague relief in the rock and I move on. . . .

The days pass in this way. Time appears to crystallize into a single instant of eternity. We fix pitches higher and higher, without the difficulty letting up, taking everything out of us. Protection is at times delicate to place, low temperatures do not facilitate movement. I toil on the fixed ropes. Behind me, Seb cleans everything. A last pitch on the empty horizon leaves my toes cold. Icy feet too tight in rock shoes—but how could I have climbed otherwise? Insidious, sneaky frostbite sets in.

The summit of the first buttress! A great happiness in the blue sky, a timid sun that does not tarry to cloud over. We celebrate the event with a delicious almond paste. The following snowy arête sends us into ecstasy. We walk between heaven and earth in the middle of a spectacular landscape: these flat glaciers, these gigantic faces, the lofty soaring of the Burkett Needle above our heads and far away, very far away, the Pacific Ocean.

We move the bivouac by hoisting abominable bags up a snow couloir to the breche, grunting like boars with the effort. Backtrack to set up the Tyrolean with the arête: pendulous rappel, climb a rock pinnacle. It's one of the rare moments of touching warm rock, and it is so good.

We, the celestial tramps, pursue our voyage to the summit by moving the portaledge one last time to the middle of the Needle. The "Negresco Bivouac" welcomes us. Indeed, it equals all of the palaces of the world. So much the better, because we will stay here 14 nights!

A blizzard of wind and snow sweeps down upon us, obliging us to retreat into the Negresco Bivouac. The days play out slowly. Reading, writing, eating, talking. Occasionally, more than 48 hours pass without being able to stick our noses outside. When we can go out, it is to remove the snow from the portaledge, which threatens to be buried under heavy snows.

This morning, May 29, we woke up at 4:30 a.m. And for good reason: it is beautiful out. The stove purrs, the snow melts. The usual chicory and chocolate semolina is soon ready. Then we are hard at work. Aid climbing in this section, disquieting from below. Plant the small copperheads, place the micro-nuts, dance, dance in this pendulum that brings you back to a dihedral covered with verglas at the end of a 50-meter pitch.

Sébastien Foissac on the snow arête at the top of the first buttress. LIONEL DAUDET

Sébastien Foissac on the headwall. Lionel Daudet

Alas, the good weather of the morning is but a brief lull, and the storm doubles in strength again. Today will not be the summit day, though the summit is only 50 meters away. The snow pitter-patters, rolls along the icy wall, the blizzard of white breath angered by the two poor tramps. But tomorrow, certainly tomorrow, we will return for the last act.

On this last pitch, I find my greatest struggle. A triumphant icicle imprisons my beard and mustache hairs. My hair transforms itself into a chalky wig. The terrible wind molds me harshly into ice armor. Blinded, I take off my iced-up glasses. The refinements of free climbing no longer apply here. It's all about moving on. Simply moving on!

Fifty meters become 30, then ten. And yet the top has never seemed so far away. Aid in the etriers, which fly away horizontally, Friends and carabiners that I disengage from a layer of ice, blessed cracks that I clear of snow. Struggle! Struggle without end! Not a single moment of respite in this white tornado. And Seb, who belays me, pursues a formidable stationary combat with this blizzard, which attempts to rip warmth and life away from him.

Summit! Unhoped for, unbelievable. . . . And yet I have just emerged here, on this snowy, ill-defined platform. No visibility whatsoever. A great silence inside and out, a long, white, infinite silence. Suddenly, I understand: what surprising luck! At the summit, we are sheltered from the wind, a haven of relative comfort that allows us to refresh ourselves before facing the elements again.

It is past 7 p.m. and nothing is finished. On the contrary. We face a difficult descent to find life back in the portaledge. Seb will take hours, twisting in the evanescent fog, to hammer away at the sheath of ice covering a fixed line. Finally, at two in the morning, we are able to throw ourselves into our bags, the only refuge of warmth in the middle of a landscape now occupied by ice.

Days beyond exhaustion as we return toward the world. Nights of barely four hours' sleep, awakening with swollen eyes, bloated face, slow and uncertain gestures. Ski! Pull this monstrous bag! Come on, another step—one you will not have to repeat! Pause. Today, a couscous

The Burkett Needle, showing 1. South Pillar (Cauthorn-Collum-Foweraker, 1995). 2. Le Voyage des Clochards Celestes *(Daudet-Foissac, 1999).* LIONEL DAUDET

record: 600 grams each. We need that to hold up, to tackle the endless meters of the Baird Glacier.

The sections that we feared pass easily, and we will pull our bags much farther down than expected, thus avoiding tiresome double-load carries. An ugly glacial rain declares itself and chills us to the gut. This evening it is June 3, our 40th day. The celestial tramps finagle a last camp—a tipi—with the avalanche probe, the skis and the portaledge canvas. The water streams down the dirty ice and soaks our things. Too quickly, in spite of the bivy sack, our sleeping bags become saturated. Tomorrow, we will do one last carry on this dangerous spring ice; we will have the pleasure of finding Dieter and his hospitality, Ken who was worried, the inhabitants of Petersburg. We will see green grass.

There is a purity I am intimately acquainted with. I saw it in the gray sky, I breathed it in the flower growing arduously in the middle of the gravel of Thomas Bay, I caught it in Seb's smile full of kindness, I heard it in the emotional voice of Vero, to whom I announced our return. Purity is there, everywhere, for those who wish to receive it.

SUMMARY OF STATISTICS

AREA: Coastal Range, Southeast Alaska

NEW ROUTE: *Le Voyage des Clochards Celestes* (VI 7a+ A3+, ca. 1200m) on the southeast face of the Burkett Needle (ca. 2590m), May 6-31, Lionel Daudet, Sébastien Foissac

Lionel Daudet was born in 1968. He is a mountain guide, but does not work often as such because he has sponsors who support him. He travels widely and enjoys mountaineering with a strict ethic: no radio, no assistance, a traditional approach. In this way, he feels the real dimension of the mountains. He lives in L'Argentière-la-Bessée, France, a small and sunny village in the south of the Alps, with his wife, Véronique.

Lionel Daudet. SÉBASTIEN FOISSAC

The Bear's Tooth

Teaching the new dogs old tricks

by Jim Bridwell

Jim Bridwell on pitch 16, The Useless Emotion. GLENN DUNMIRE

Except for myself and Glenn Dunmire, our team of five were alpine neophytes. The group had been hastily put together at the biannual Outdoor Retailers Show in Salt Lake. Four of us—Glenn, Brian Jonas and Fly'n Brian McCray—met at my house in Palm Desert, California, to pack the many bags for the flight. The fifth member, Terry Christensen of Canada, would meet us in Anchorage. Our objective was the formidable 4,700-foot east face of Peak 10,070', a peak I had previously named the Bear's Tooth.

On the morning of our departure, I awoke to the excruciating lower back pain of a recurring injury. The pinched nerve was debilitating, but we couldn't miss the flight. My wife ordered a wheelchair at the Palm Spring airport and gave me the last of a couple of muscle relaxers. We were off to Alaska.

In Talkeetna, Talkeetna Air Taxi pilot Paul Roderick thought we should fly as soon as possible, so we arrived on the glacier the next day to see the beast. It had become one of my demons; this was my fourth attempt to purge it. For the others, it was their first view. The

The north and east faces of the Bear's Tooth (left) and the Moose's Tooth. The Useless Emotion *on the Bear's Tooth is marked.* ROGER ROBINSON

lower pillar's stunning beauty captures the eye with sweeping elegance, a coy distraction from the upper half of the route. On my third effort, with Mark Wilford, we had climbed a few hundred feet shy of the pillar's top. An inner voice had whispered then, "Above lies the test for success." But Wilford had been struck in the calf by an errant ice missile that ushered in the defeat of our hard-fought battle.

After camp was pitched, Glenn set up the telescope for each to have a look while I described the route to my previous high point with Mark. It was May. Hoping for less snow on the wall, we had come a month later than Mark and I had previously, but the conditions were much the same as before.

The next day, we approached the wall carrying light loads. Though the weather was a little unstable, it looked good enough to get some work done. Glenn took the lead over the bergschrund and up the steeper snow above to the base of the pillar. Being primarily a mountaineer, Glenn's forte was snow and ice. He was not a technical rock whiz, but I knew he was a hard worker and had solid expedition skills. Still, the leaning, ice-choked, mixed corner that loomed above was probably not his cup of tea. Who would step forward?

Fly'n Brian seconded Glenn to join him at a small stance, leaving the rest of us below. Brian's ice experience was limited to following me on two pitches in Lee Vining Canyon on the east side of Yosemite. I turned to go back to camp as the two of them discussed the immediate future. My back was still giving me fits, so I would give it some time to get better and let the others have a chance to gain experience.

Fly'n Brian was half way up the lead by time I reached camp. Brian Jonas joined me shortly to share the box seats at the telescope. Fly'n Brian finished the pitch as the weather took a turn for the worse. Terry followed; he and Brian Jonas would lead the next day. Glenn, who had a barometer on his watch, started a weather log that evening. From my past knowledge of the area, I knew the necessity of climbing in bad weather.

Two climbing days later, we had managed only three more pitches. I'd hoped for better progress, but having led most of the first 12 pitches before, I knew this was a tough climb to cut your alpine teeth on. Terry had only been climbing five years, and Brian Jonas's 5.12 free ability would likely not be of great value on the dubious rock of the Bear's Tooth. Protection was usually poor, far between or just not possible. Big wall aid climbing skills were the ticket, and only Fly'n Brian and I had seats to the game.

Bad weather kept us grounded for a day, but the next afternoon Fly'n Brian and I hauled supplies and set up a hanging tent at our high point. We melted snow and settled in for the night. In the morning, in bad weather, we climbed four more pitches and returned to the tent. Terry and Brian Jonas hauled more food and fuel, and I spent the night with Terry, who had never slept in a hanging tent. The weather was atrocious the following day, so Terry and I rappelled to save food and fuel. Late the next day, four of us hauled food, fuel and another hanging tent to spend the night when the weather turned to shit.

Avalanches of spindrift cascaded over the fragile tents though the black hours. In the morning I peeked out the zipper door to a winter wonderland. Real horror show stuff... an avalanche brought rapid door closure. I brushed the snow off me into the tent bottom and snuggled back in the bag to do the hang.

Around noon, Fly'n Brian could hang no more.

"I'm going up," he declared with purpose in his voice. I spent the night in the tent with a crazy guy, I thought.

"Really," I said. "Have you looked out?"

Brian McCray leading the hook traverse on pitch 10 in full conditions. Moments after this photo was taken, McCray took a large penduluming fall while hooking, ripping other consecutive hook placements and sending a shower of rock chunks down onto Jonas and Dunmire.
GLENN DUNMIRE

An hour later, he was on the ropes. I was impressed. I have never seen anyone climb technical rock in conditions this bad. I remember this being the most technical pitch to my previous high point. A pendulum to loose hooking...lots of it...with little protection, then looking for two rivets on the snow-plastered wall.... This ought to be good, I pondered.

A long time passed after the pendulum, with occasional moments of disgruntled vocabulary. Hooking must have been tough with everything hidden under snow. Then came a crashing rattle of hardware and excited language. Soon after, a repeat performance was heard through the hiss of avalanches. A while later, a great sigh of relief signaled Fly'n Brian's success. When I quizzed him that evening, he confessed, "I wanted to see what it would be like."

The following day, it cleared. Terry and Brian Jonas would try to fix two more pitches while the rest of us went down to get enough supplies to finish the route. That same afternoon, we hauled to the hanging bivy as Brian Jonas finished the second lead. The next morning, Fly'n Brian and I ascended the ropes to our high point. I began leading the rock-chopping pitch, which required chopping holes in the rotten rock to place camming devices. Fly'n Brian used the wooden belay seat as a shield while I worked through crumbly rock. I was literally breaking new ground. He followed, grumbling about the lumps he had received while belaying.

Pitches like these stretches the usefulness of the presently used rating system. We opted to rate this one PDH, which stands for Pretty Darn Hard. Fly'n Brian led the next two pitches before we came down to help set up hanging tents.

A logistical screw-up had tempers flaring. Brian Jonas had descended in the wake of a verbal altercation. The next day, Glenn and I pushed the ropes three pitches higher while tempers cooled. Things had worked to our advantage. Brian Jonas returned the following morning, bringing the last of our fixing ropes, while Glenn and Fly'n Brian took the lead. We were hoping for a snow cave or a tent platform at the top of the pillar, but as the day slipped away, we decided to dig a snow scoop where we were for the bivouac. When the lead team descended, they informed us that we had made the right choice. They had reached the top of the snow, and there was no suitable place above for a cave or a platform.

The weather was still holding well, and the next day we would have a go for the summit. Wake-up call was 4 a.m., and by 5 a.m. Fly'n Brian and I were headed up the ropes. As I jugged, I got my first bewildering view of the upper wall. A series of complex corners breached the wall above for several pitches before going out of sight. After a brief visual sort-out, I decided on the least horrendous and most direct of the group nearest our high point. Glenn was coming up the ropes as I finished the first lead. I yelled down to him to confirm that I was in the left-most of two large corners.

"Yes!"

Fly'n Brian joined me, then quickly started up his first true ice lead. . . ever. He moved up the thin, 80 percent ice-over-rock like a seasoned pro. I led another similar pitch around a huge snow overhang to a steep rock slab. Looking down, I could follow my route. It was marked by red blotches. Apparently, fingerless gloves were not the best choice of hand protection. Fly'n Brian aided up thin cracks and disappeared above an overhang. Brian Jonas joined me at the belay, bringing the last of our climbing ropes. Some clouds were filtering in when Fly'n Brian called down, "Off belay." Despite the unsettled weather, I was full of optimism when I joined him. Looking up, I recognized our location from studying the route through the telescope at camp.

An intuitive chill challenged my usual aggressiveness, and I found myself hesitating, momentarily lost in an internal debate. Above, a thin sheet of ice clung to a shallow depression in the slabby face. To the right it was blank; featureless rock was on the left and at the top of the ice sheet lay unstable sugar-like snow. The only thing hopeful: a thin, straight-in crack. I might be able to reach it from the top of the snow. I fought the internal dialogue and the growing fear, then moved onto the ice. A long nightmare ensued.

The first swing of my blunt ice hammer shattered the ice; the second bounced off the rock beneath. Twenty-five feet up, I drove in a good ice hook piton for protection. Twenty feet higher I tried another, but it didn't happen. Against better judgment, I continued 40 feet more to the snow. Once I left the ice and started climbing the snow, there was no turning back. A fall here was not worth contemplating. It was very rude to discover the crack I was banking on was only a groove and the snow I now stood upon was a foot-wide fin of sugar. I was in trouble. Eventually I called for a drill. The drill was two pitches below. I anxiously waited for Glenn to bring it up while I stood softly on my fragile stance. Eternity passed before I sent a huge loop of the lead rope down and brought up the drill. Damn, the bit was too big. Oh God, both the hammerheads of my tools had worked loose. Job had it easy! I drilled a shallow hole and placed a 5/16" rivet in the 5/16" hole and beat the hell out of it. I pounded a nut halfway into the groove and equalized the weight between it and the rivet. I said a prayer, and Fly'n Brian lowered me down. I tried down-climbing, but the snow wouldn't hold my weight a second time. I reached the belay emotionally tattered.

Fly'n Brian took over the lead. He tension-traversed 40 feet right using my lower-off point and reached some ice-filled cracks. He yelled down that the cracks continued and that it looked like it would go. I had wasted a lot of time, and we had no more rope to fix. Snow was falling as I cleaned the pitch, and hope for the summit faded with the light.

Brian McCray on the steep end of the learning curve, pitch 26 on the upper headwall.
GLENN DUNMIRE

Brian Jonas, Flyn' Brian McCray, Jim Bridwell and Terry Christensen at the snow scoop bivy.
GLENN DUNMIRE

Back at the scoop cave, tempers were flying. I listened to each grievance with as much tolerance and understanding as I could muster after the day I had. After everyone had aired it out and felt a little better, I turned our attention to my other concern: the WEATHER. Clouds had been moving closer for a couple of days and that afternoon it had begun snowing. We'd had unbelievable luck with the weather so far, but I feared it was about to end. The top looked reasonably close from our high point, and, weather permitting, we agreed to try the next day. Glenn set his alarm for 4 a.m., which gave us almost four hours to sleep.

It cleared in the night and the sun was still on us when we reached the end of our ropes. I needed to rest my left leg after climbing the ropes, so Fly'n Brian took the first lead. The climbing was slow going: chop the ice away, try a piton, the crack bottomed, try something else. Fly'n Brian was doing the best he could, but everyone was anxious. We were all gathered at the belay, dodging falling ice. Eventually, the inevitable happened. A large piece hit me in the back. I wilted in pain. I was hurt, and I knew it. I tried shaking it off, but I couldn't lift my arms without intense pain. What now, I thought; this wasn't just my climb. Would Fly'n Brian be able to lead us to the top?

I cleaned the pitch to see how I felt. It was all I could do to follow, so Fly'n Brian heroically led on. The bear was showing his teeth again.

The upper part of the route was even more demanding than below. Fly'n Brian led on and on without a complaint. After five pitches, he called me up to hear my judgment of the route, but moreover of our situation. When I joined him, he told me he was spent and would lead no more. What looked like a few hundred feet had become ten pitches, and it wasn't over yet. I quickly surmised that, all things considered, we had to go down. There was enough light to keep climbing, but we were all tired, hungry, and getting cold. It had the makings of an accident. We

Brian McCray leading the Tension Traverse (pitch 33) on the upper headwall. GLENN DUNMIRE

had no ropes to leave fixed, which meant reclimbing the day's efforts (if we got another chance). There was nothing else to do. The next day, we sadly rappelled the route in perfect weather. Everyone was exhausted from the long days with little sleep, and we needed more food and fuel.

It was early when we got back to camp, and we decided to go back up the next day if the weather held. The barometer remained steady throughout the day while we packed our wall supplies and ate massive quantities of carbos. We turned in early and got up early. Glenn and Fly'n Brian started ahead with the goal of fixing two pitches. The rest of us would haul food, fuel and our last two ropes to the cave scoop. By late afternoon, we were melting ice for dinner. Glenn and Fly'n Brian came down in the evening with the good news that they had accomplished their mission.

Optimism was high in the morning. I led the ice pitch that Fly'n Brian didn't want to repeat. It had tested his ice experience above his comfort zone. Fly'n Brian then took us to our subsequent high point and brought me up. He lowered me down and around right into a corner of easy ice. We were moving well, I thought, as he came up. He started the next lead and I told him to take care passing a large flake perched in the overhang directly above the belay.

What looked like a routine pitch wasn't. Above the overhanging start, Fly'n Brian disappeared left, following a windscoop of snow. A long wait with nothing, then rushes of snow falling, covering me. Again and again the same reassurance, and then finally he called for slack, but slowly. After more than an hour, he called out, "Off belay!" I thankfully swung out into empty air and ascended the rope.

A tension traverse to the right across rock covered in sugar snow had taken us to yet another evil specter. The difficulty wouldn't let up. I was forced to climb up fragile ice over rock with shit for protection directly off a dubious belay. After the scary bit, I crossed over a ridge and found an easy snow slope. Another pitch up a narrow ice gully and I thought it was over. Wrong!

It takes too long to describe how two rope lengths of snow could take FIVE AND A HALF HOURS. For the sake of saving face for all of us, I'll say no more. I could feel frostbite setting in in my toes and I almost declined the summit, but the words "it's just a snow slope" didn't ring true. Glenn would not be denied and took us home. At 10:30 p.m., we stood five meters below the cornice summit, unable to stand on the tippy-top without tempting an incident.

The descent was long but orderly. I arrived last at the scoop at 4 a.m. It was obvious after removing my boots that I wouldn't be climbing for awhile. Who was the rookie?

We were finished, and so was the good weather. I was beaten up but happy—happy that the big guy hadn't pushed the "off" button. We'd be back.

SUMMARY OF STATISTICS

AREA: Ruth Gorge, Alaska Range, Alaska

NEW ROUTE: *The Useless Emotion* (VII 5.9 WI4 A4, ca. 4,700') on the east face of Peak 10,070' (a.k.a. the Bear's Tooth), May 3-21, Jim Bridwell, Terry Christensen, Glenn Dunmire, Brian Jonas, Brian McCray

Jim Bridwell was born in 1944 and began climbing in 1961. He first visited Yosemite Valley in 1962, quickly becoming one of its most instrumental characters. He started Yosemite Search

and Rescue in 1967, introduced the "a,b,c,d" sub-grading of the Yosemite Decimal System, ushered in America's first 5.11 with the route *New Dimensions*, and pioneered more than 100 first ascents, from *Sea of Dreams* on El Cap to the *Snake Dike* on Half Dome. His alpine ascents include the first complete ascent of the *Compressor Route* (southeast ridge) on Cerro Torre, the east face of the Moose's Tooth, and, with the *Sapphire Bullets of Pure Love* route, made the first winter ascent and first American ascent of Pumori. He lives in Palm Desert, CA, with his wife, Peggy, and son, Layton.

Jim Bridwell at the first portaledge camp. GLENN DUNMIRE

The Arwa Tower

An old-fashioned adventure

by Mick Fowler, *United Kingdom*

"**P**robably never photographed before," the caption said.

I peered closely at the photograph again. It showed a wild, ice-streaked, rocky spire that was beginning to give me quite an urge.

"Arwa Valley, India," the text said. The photograph was by Harish Kapadia. That man again. A promising sign. Harish lives in Bombay and has a commendable habit of exploring and climbing in the rarely visited parts of the Indian Himalaya that also attract the likes of me. It seemed that our paths were likely to cross once more.

But the Arwa Valley is a couple of days' walk north of the Hindu holy temple at Badrinath in the Garhwal Himalaya. This area is near the Chinese border and, as part of what the Indian authorities refer to as the "Inner Line," access can be as big a challenge as the climb. Expeditions here are only for those prepared to live with a fair amount of bureaucratic risk and uncertainty. There are, though, potential rewards that, to my mind, outweigh the risks. Just about all the mountains in this area are unclimbed. Harish's photograph showed two mind-boggling ones—the Arwa Tower and the Arwa Spire—but it seemed probable that there were other fine peaks nearby. There was no doubt about it: I simply had to go.

By April, 1999, four of us were ready to leave. I was to climb with Steve Sustad, a cabinet-maker based in Oswestry and my long-standing Himalayan climbing partner. We were to be accompanied by the delightfully named duo of Crag Jones and Kenton Cool. Crag has some sort of curious career analyzing sea life; Kenton is into cleaning buildings whilst hanging on an abseil rope. As a valuer of unquoted shares employed by the British Tax Service, I felt we were a good, diverse team, joined by little but a common urge to go climbing.

In retrospect, we put so much effort into getting a permit from the authorities that we had not focused sufficiently on finding out more details about the geography of the area. Our maps showed that Arwa Tal (Arwa Lake) was the obvious place to have a base camp—but where was it? In fact, where were the mountains we had come to climb? Naively, I had expected them to be obvious, rearing up in their full splendor above the Arwa Valley (the "Valley of the Ghosts" in Hindu mythology). But all we could see was one spectacular summit poking up over the bounding ridge. It didn't look like either of the photos we had seen, and we would have to cross the ridge to get to it. This was a serious problem; if the ridge was too difficult or dangerous on the far side, we could fail without even reaching the mountain.

Our two teams of two had somehow become separated. Steve and I felt that the lake must be further up and carried on. Meanwhile, Crag and Kenton had to cope with porters refusing to continue (they had run out of food). They decided that there was nothing for it but to stop at the only passable base camp site they could find. Steve and I, with a small group of porters, got ahead and out of contact with the others. It was delightfully disorganized. Tempers became frayed, and it was perhaps something of a miracle that the day ended with all of us and all of the gear in the same place. The porters still refused to continue and there was nothing to do but to pay them off and make the best of a bad job at Crag and Kenton's Base Camp site.

"What is this peak?"
Steve and I were standing on the ridge separating the Arwa Valley from the summit that we had glimpsed earlier. Much to our relief, the descent on the far side didn't look too bad.

I had feared that we might be heading for a boring peak capped with an interesting summit, but ahead of us was an orgasmic mountain that dropped sheer to the unnamed, snow-covered glacier below us. It bore no relation to either of Harish's photographs, but whatever it was, it was the one for us.

Somehow we convinced ourselves that it must be the Arwa Spire (it wasn't) viewed from a new direction. Retreating to BC, we formed a plan of action. Things were looking up after all.

It took us two days to get from BC to a relaxingly flat col at the foot of the north buttress of what we were ultimately to conclude was the Arwa Tower. Above us, the buttress soared to a forepeak, whilst to its right the northwest face was seamed with snow/ice streaks and looked to be our preferred option. It did, though, have several distressingly difficult-looking sections. This peak was not going to give up her virginity easily.

Crag and Kenton were also on the col. We had by now sorted out the location of the two peaks that we had come to climb, and they were off to attempt the Arwa Spire, which had previously been out of sight. The weather was perfect, but ground conditions were prompting considerable comment.

"What's going on here?"
Steve was voluble in his disapproval. I had to agree. Never before had any of us come across snow conditions quite like this. The surface layer was a three-inch-thick plate of ice, but every few steps this would collapse and we would fall into a bottomless sea of sugary snow. The sensation was not unlike I imagine it would be to fall through the surface of a frozen lake. The energy expenditure required to get back on to the hard surface was indescribable. Later in the trip, Crag and Kenton were only able to make progress by crawling on the surface, towing their heavy sacks behind.

Faced with such pleasures, Crag and Kenton made the wise decision to stay put until the morning, whilst Steve and I opted to crawl, fall and stagger our way across the short distance that separated us from the foot of the northwest face—which looked increasingly challenging the closer we got.

One good thing about the vast blank rock walls at the foot of the face was the minimal scope for disagreement over where to start. The north spur bounding the left edge provided the only feasible possibility—but not an easy one, as we were soon to find out.

"The crack has run out."
Steve was sounding uncharacteristically negative. We were less than five pitches up and he was climbing a horribly thin-looking crack—or rather he had been, but had now ground to a halt.

The sun was shining obliquely across the face, and I was feeling comfortably warm and relaxed and well able to offer the sort of moral support that stretched leaders find so completely useless.

"How about traversing to that bit of snow out to your left?" I suggested helpfully.

Unrepeatable rudeness came from above as I continued to soak up the Himalayan rays. Soon, though, blankness in all directions prompted a fresh assessment of the situation.

"I'll see if I can get a good peg in and then tension across."

There was a sound of heavy pounding as I lay back once more.

"Ahggh!"

The air was suddenly full of a falling body. There was a thump, followed by silence, and then a string of obscenities.

"****ing crack opened up."

I murmured sympathies whilst noting that in half an hour or so I would be in the shade and the temperature would plummet.

Ten minutes later, I was glad to see Steve back at the end of the crack with a peg in place. "I'm going to tension."

It all looked horribly precarious. I felt glad to have the soft option of simply holding the rope. Disturbingly, though, I noted that Steve had left his rucksack hanging on the tension peg—a problem for me to deal with at some stage, although in the circumstances I could hardly complain.

Much scraping and grunting started to come from above, interspersed with the occasional "Watch me."

It was clearly a desperate pitch and, following it with the security of a rope above, I used my usual Himalayan excuse of heavy sack (two in this case) and the need for speed to throw any ethical consideration to the wind.

"Pull!" I shouted as I dangled on the rope, gaining even more respect for Steve's efforts.

"A fine achievement, Stephen. A pleasure to second you."

We shook hands because that's what the English do in such situations. And Steve, American-born but living in Britain for many years, is nearly an Anglophile now.

He was his usual calm and philosophical self. "Your pitch looks nice, too," he said.

We almost always stick to alternating leads on long climbs. Sometimes Steve will take the lead out of turn on aid pitches and I on mixed sections, but by and large we are of much the same ability, and it suits our style to swing leads.

The pitch that Steve was pointing to looked to be a short but vicious and unprotected wide crack that led to what appeared to be a ledge of some kind. I was feeling tired, but try as I might, it was difficult to put it into the "aid" category and hand over to Steve. Also, it was getting late now and Steve's belay was a foothold on a steep slab. Unplanned Himalayan bivouacs are invariably cold and unpleasant and can easily result in rapid erosion of willpower and ignominious retreat. With such thoughts in mind and the lure of a ledge not far ahead, an extra-special effort was called for. I thrashed up in what was apparently an amusing, ungainly fashion into the gathering gloom.

It perhaps says a lot about Himalayan climbing that it is a real pleasure when a potentially atrocious night is suddenly replaced with the relative luxury of a ledge to lie on. In fact, this one was not quite five-star accommodation, but we could at least lie down end-to-end. I snuggled into a Gore-Tex bivouac bag whilst Steve managed to half erect the tent and began the evening's cooking efforts.

Our food requirements had arguably not been attended to thoroughly enough before leaving the United Kingdom. On our last expedition together, we had existed for 14 days primarily on mashed potato and noodles. It was not exactly the world's most interesting or varied diet, but Steve, who is much more of an expert than I in these matters, had assured me that it

The northwest face of Arwa Tower. The route starts on the left-hand spur and moves right to one-third height, where it continues up the center of the face. MICK FOWLER

A delicate start to the morning: Steve Sustad, pitch 1, day 2. MICK FOWLER

Sustad on day 2, with the unclimbed Arwa Spire above his head. MICK FOWLER

contained just about all the nutrients we might need. Being as we survived for a fortnight on it, I could only assume that he was correct. As such, there had been no need for complex discussions about dietary requirements for this trip. Mashed potato and noodles would be fine.

But we had hit a problem. Try as we might, we hadn't found any mashed potato in Delhi. Perhaps we had brought it out from England last time? In true disorganized fashion, neither of us could remember. On an expedition back in 1993, Steve and I had used baby food as one of our staple courses. That had worked well then, so the decision was made. Alternate nights of noodles and baby food it would be.

Over the years we have climbed together, Steve has increasingly recognized what Nicki, my wife, has always told him. I, for some inexplicable reason, appear not to be suited for work in the kitchen or the preparation of food of any kind. My mealtime responsibilities in the mountains now usually stretch to snow collection and melting whilst Steve takes on technical jobs such as hydrating noodles and mixing baby powder. And so I was able to lie in my sleeping bag and marvel at the stars as Steve labored over the stove and produced a truly disgusting "meal" of lurid orange "peach"-flavored baby food. I chewed the powdery lumps thoughtfully. Next time I would make a special effort to buy mashed potato in England.

Up above us, the rock looked disturbingly steep and blank. Perhaps with hot weather and rock boots it would give excellent rock climbing, but the morning dawned with a few gentle snow flakes, and our heavy sacks, big boots and ice climbing gear were clearly more suited to any ice streaks we could find. Steve had, in fact, brought his rock boots along, but the weather conditions and ground ahead convinced him that they would no longer be required.

Ever conscious of surplus weight, he tied them together and threw them down to be picked up from the foot of the face on our way down. Needless to say, they were never seen again.

The "snow/ice" streaks of the northwest face proved to be disturbing. The rock hereabouts was a smooth, sparsely featured granite. It rapidly became clear that what looked like fairly substantial snow/ice lines tended to be powder snow clinging to slight easings of the angle. My crampon points scratched and grated. I felt distinctly insecure.

"Can't you get any protection in?"

I obviously looked as insecure as I felt. . . or was it just that Steve was noting the long swing onto blank rock that he was facing if he should slip?

We persevered. Patches of ice occasionally provided security in the form of solid ice screws, but the rock was notably blank and the climbing unsettling and time-consuming. All the time I was very aware that we were moving out above very smooth walls and, if anything went wrong, it might be extremely difficult to abseil directly down the face. The adrenaline was slowly but inexorably building up.

As the hours ticked by, I began to wonder where we might spend the night. A repeat of the previous night's relative luxury looked unlikely. I must be getting old. I don't remember feeling this concern ten years ago. Then, I would just climb and trust that when dusk was approaching, we would be able to cut a bottom-width step in the ice and hold ourselves in place with a length of rope stretched taut between ice screws on either side. Perhaps, I considered, that was the problem: on this kind of ground there was no guarantee that we would be able to find a big enough patch of thick ice, and the thought of spending the night standing on a collapsing step in three-inch-thick powder snow with minimal belays did not appeal.

By late afternoon, little had changed. A couple of particularly exciting pitches up very thin ice streaks had necessitated sack hauling again, but we had now reached an impasse with no obvious way around it.

"Take care, Michael. Belays aren't very good."

Reluctantly, my eyes were drawn to the three tied-off ice screws to which Steve was attached. Half of their length was protruding from the ice. Backed up by the picks of his axes, they might hold a fall, but they hardly inspired confidence.

The impasse was a 20-meter exfoliating rock slab with an occasional smear of transparent ice. I teetered up on fragile edges, the points of my crampons grating unnervingly. Pegs behind insecure, exfoliating flakes did not exactly inspire confidence.

A bolt would solve the problem, but Steve and I have strong views on such things. Bolts can solve almost any protection problem. They do not require any weakness in the rock or any skill to place, and they destroy the traditional challenge of mountaineering. Once, after completing the first ascent of the Golden Pillar of Spantik in Pakistan, with Victor Saunders, a Spanish team actually contacted Victor and asked him if we minded them trying to repeat the route with bolts. Perhaps their misgivings sum up the sensitivities on the subject.

Either way, here on the Arwa Tower we had no bolts and no intention of using any. In retrospect, we would be able to say that we faced up to the full challenge of the face. At the time, it just felt downright frightening.

We were gaining height now and could see over the lower peaks to the north and on to the Tibetan plateau beyond. To the northwest in particular, exciting unclimbed objectives were coming into view. There will be plenty of potential in the Himalaya for a few generations yet.

Pulling out of the top of the pitch heralded a real change in the conditions. We were approaching the upper bowl of the face, and I could only assume that the wind howling over the crest and the lower temperatures at this altitude were responsible for the sudden change to bottomless powder snow. It was getting late, and I was feeling tired (completely knackered, actually) as Steve came up and headed off into the gathering gloom. The angle averaged perhaps 60 degrees, with numerous vertical rock steps. There was still no obvious place to spend the night.

By the time Steve had belayed and brought me up, there was nothing for it but to bivouac where we were. Overhangs above looked as if they might provide a bit of shelter, but the absence of any ledge promised some interest.

I hung forlornly in a shallow scoop in the powdery snow. Steve had somehow managed to excavate a better-looking ledge and set about preparing luke-warm baby food. I struggled not to retch while contemplating the gently falling snow and increasingly poor visibility. I was thankful that we were high enough on the face to be above any dangerous spindrift avalanches. There was a time when I would have been deeply concerned at the onset of a spell of bad weather, but years of doing this kind of thing have changed the old feeling of rising panic to one of resigned acceptance. After all, it would be naive to expect the weather gods to provide absolutely perfect weather for the full duration of something like a seven-day climb.

Things had improved slightly by the morning. Up above us, the sun intermittently caught the jagged crest marking the top of the face. We plowed on—literally. Even near-vertical pitches were plastered with a deep layer of useless powder snow. The climbing was precariously time-consuming, and it was not until late afternoon that we broke through the final difficulties onto the crest.

I had long anticipated this moment, and hoped that from here it would be an enjoyable scramble to the summit. It was, then, with some shock and dismay that we saw that, although it was probably less than 100 vertical meters to the highest point, the ridge was a complex knife-edge of overhanging towers. Some of them looked disturbingly blank and holdless.

By nightfall we had made little progress, although we had at least managed to cut a ledge in a small ice shelf, and were therefore able to spend our first night together inside the tent since we started on the face. Only a quarter of the floorspace hung off the ledge, but with sleeping mats down, it was easy to forget such minor problems. We slept soundly.

"What happens now?"

Steve was standing on the knife-edge crest of the ridge contemplating the way ahead.

"We could abseil down there."

"Mmmmmm."

We both stared thoughtfully down the far side of the ridge. A 25-meter overhanging abseil would place us on a steep snow/ice slope that we might be able to traverse and then regain the ridge beyond the tower. There was, though, the slight problem of how to reverse this maneuver on the way back. Climbing up ropes is my least favorite mountaineering activity. Here, though, we seemed to have no alternative but to commit ourselves if we were to stand a chance of making the summit. Leaving one of our two ropes in place, we slid down and started our summit bid.

My level of optimism was not high. It was one of those situations where I think we both felt that the weather and the apparent difficulty ahead were likely to defeat us. But we judged that it was not dangerous to continue and, having got so far, we felt that we owed it to ourselves to give it a go.

The snow/ice traverse was horrible. Rotten snow lying on hard ice made for difficult going. Steve then managed a desperate pitch on powder-covered rock, and suddenly we were

Fowler on the knife-edge ridge en route to the summit. STEVE SUSTAD

back on the crest.

"What do you think?"

It was difficult to suppress my growing elation. Neither of us could really believe that three rope lengths had changed the outlook so much. What from below had looked to be an impregnable final section now appeared passable. Even the weather was brightening up, with the odd ray of sunshine piercing the cloud. The summit spire was visible only 50 meters away.

It was, then, almost with a sense of surprise and disbelief that we were able to sit astride the summit knife-edge, marvel at the intermittent view, take stock of the situation and contemplate the forces that had driven us to focus so much time and effort in reaching such a place.

Back in the tent, our conversation turned to more everyday things. Steve enthused about the mass-market potential of a porch that he had designed, whilst I enjoyed shocking him with tales from the Shares Valuation Division. Our climbing aspirations are very similar, our ways of earning a living sharply contrasting.

We both stared out across the vast expanse of the Tibetan plateau.

Variety, we agreed, is most definitely the spice of life.

SUMMARY OF STATISTICS

AREA: Arwa Valley, Garhwal Himalaya, India

FIRST ASCENT: The Northwest Face (VI 5b A3 Scottish V/VI, 1000m) of the Arwa Tower (6352m), May 7-14, Mick Fowler and Steve Sustad (see Climbs and Expeditions, p. x, for a note on Crag Jones and Kenton Cool's attempt on the Arwa Spire)

PERSONNEL: Mick Fowler, Steve Sustad, Kenton Cool, Crag Jones

Mick Fowler

Born in 1956, Briton Mick Fowler, a valuer of unquoted securities, is married with two children, Tessa, 7, and Alec, 5. He started climbing seriously in 1976. With the route *Linden*, he was one of the first rock climbers to establish the E6 grade in Britain. His taste for the unusual has resulted in the dubious distinction of being the only climber arrested in both England and France for climbing on the chalk cliffs. Outside Britain, he has climbed a string of new EDsup routes, the most notable being the South Buttress of Taulliraju (Peru, 1982), the *Golden Pillar* of Spantik (Pakistan, 1987), the Northwest/North Face of Cerro Kishtwar (India, 1993), the Northeast Pillar of Taweche (Nepal, 1995) and the North Face of Changabang (India, 1997).

High Tension on Thalay Sagar

Straight up the north face

by Mikhail Davy, *Russia*
translated by Maxim Rivkin

May 31, 1999. It had been six hours since I started my way along the moraine toward Base Camp on Lake Kedar Tal. My backpack, full of climbing gear and wet clothes, was extremely heavy. We had not been to Base Camp for two weeks, and it was obvious. Before we left, we had to cut holes in the ice on the lake to fetch water. Now there was no ice at all. One could figure out with a glance at my feet that we had not had a single day of rest during the two weeks that we were away. When the trail went uphill, I had to slow down significantly and rest, leaning heavily on my ski poles. It was getting darker, and our trail, which had been barely noticeable in the daylight, was almost invisible.

Suddenly, I noticed that my mood was in sharp contrast to all the difficulties. I was tranquil and happy. We had made it.

It all started two years ago when we got our hands on an issue of the magazine *GHM* that had a review of the Garhwal mountain region in the Indian Himalaya. From the photos, it was obvious that the Garhwal is a very interesting area with monolithic granite peaks reminiscent of the Lailak and Karavshin regions of the Pamir-Alay, only much higher and often technically difficult due to the transition from solid granite to the unstable and dangerous schist bands in the upper parts of the mountains.

Two walls looked particularly steep and long: the west face of Bhagirathi III and the north face of Thalay Sagar. However, by the time we saw the magazine, rock routes on Bhagirathi had already been pioneered by others, and our friends and competitors Alexander Odintsov, Yuri Koshelenko and Igor Potankin were headed over to climb it as well. The only route that had been climbed on the north face of Thalay Sagar, meanwhile, passed through the ice couloir in the central part of the face; nobody had even tried to climb the rock buttresses.

At first, we planned the expedition for September, 1998. An Indian expedition permit was paid for at an exchange rate of 6.30 rubles for $1 U.S. The very next day—August 17, 1998—was the first day of the huge economic crisis in Russia. Inflation paralyzed the economy for many months, and in a matter of days the Russian ruble depreciated by a factor of four. We quickly ran out of money and had to reschedule the expedition for the spring of 1999.

In February of that year, in Chamonix, we witnessed two Australians receiving the Piolet d'Or for climbing the north face of Thalay Sagar. This only confirmed our opinion that our goal was a worthy one. On the other hand, we were not going to get the Piolet d'Or, since nobody would award two prizes for the same wall.

March and April passed by in turmoil as we looked for money and sponsors and worked on our gear. Finally, all of this was finished, and our small expedition boarded the plane to Delhi with a stopover in Tashkent. Our team was assembled of very strong climbers with substantial high-altitude experience. Victor Ostanin, who currently works as a principal in a

Thalay Sagar
Garhwal Himalaya
◊ 1999 ◊

sports academy for youth, was a champion climber of the USSR. Alexander Klenov, our captain, is one of the best climbers in Russian alpinism. Alexey Bolotov is a strong high-altitude climber whose resume includes successful ascents of Makalu via the west face, Everest, Khan Tengri and Peak Pobeda. Mikhail Pershin and a partner had just finished a winter ascent of an extremely difficult route on the north face of Ak-Su (See *AAJ* 1999, pp. 124-132).

Tashkent, as always, was warm and welcoming. We met with old friends and enjoyed strawberries from the local market at ridiculously low prices. After two days spent relaxing, we left Tashkent on the night of May 1. At 6 a.m. in Delhi, it was already too hot, with temperatures above 40° Celcius. We slept in a cool hotel room the whole day, letting Victor and Alexander take care of official business at the Indian Mountaineering Federation.

Early the next morning, we started our journey to the Himalaya. Three days of not-too-tiring travel by small bus, with nights spent in Rishkesh and Uttarkashi, passed by almost unnoticed, the effects of traveling in an unfamiliar, exotic country. Our main impression of India was that the country is a big trash dump with piles of garbage on the streets, even in Delhi. Sanitary conditions in little cafes along the road were far from satisfactory. We wished the cuisine were better: there was no beef at all, and everything was very spicy. Walls were covered with old, faded ads for Sony and Pepsi.

On the third day of our bus trip we entered Gangotri, a holy place for many Indians and the last town on our journey. Hundreds of people arrive here every day in overloaded buses and cars, and Gangotri is full of small hotels, motels and other places where one could spend the night. There are a lot of stores on the central street, almost all of them selling religious accessories. From here to Thalay Sagar, it is only 18 kilometers as the crow flies, but nevertheless, because of the mountain's steepness and inaccessibility, the first ascent was not made until 1979.

With a caravan of porters, we reached Base Camp on Lake Kedar Tal. A little earlier, an Indian expedition had taken the best tent sites, so we had to arrange our camp on the clay of the lakeshore. The sun was hot during the day, forcing us to cover every centimeter of our bodies to avoid sunburn. At night, it usually started to snow, covering camp in a white blanket. By morning, the snow would begin to melt, mixing with the clay to make a wonderful putty that stuck to our boots in thick layers.

In general, BC was not the best place for life, but our minds had already moved on to the beautiful gracious mountain that surrounded the valley. Depending on weather conditions and light, the mountain changed all the time. It could be snow-white, or red and yellow. It could be covered with clouds, or rise above them, lonely and majestic.

We did not have much time to spare. We needed to finish our acclimatization fairly fast. Our fourth or fifth night was spent at 6000 meters on the peak closest to camp. After two days of rest, on May 15, we started our approach to the wall. We had only five ropes with us; we planned to climb without extensive amounts of fixing. Nevertheless, our backpacks were nearly impossible to pick up off the ground, even though we made a number of carries and Victor, who was staying in BC, helped us put them on. Once we were on the route, though, even with most of the gear in our packs, they did not feel as heavy.

On May 16, Alexey and Mikhail went up to cross the bergschrund and prepare the first pitch while Alexander and I packed the portaledge. After lunch, we pulled it and the rest of the gear to the bergschrund. All day long, my eyes turned toward the wall above us. One could only assume how it was going to be up there. But, as we knew from past expeditions, the beginning is the most important part. We would find out more as time went on. The next day we would start our assault on The Wall.

Mikhail Pershin on A3 (80°) terrain, day 4. THALAY SAGAR EXPEDITION COLLECTION

Our spirits were great as we jumared the ropes that had been fixed the day before. We reached the rock under clear skies. Though the wall faces north, it is close to the equator, and around noon we could see the sun above our heads. Alexander took the lead and disappeared around the corner, finding solid granite but occasionally loose rock as well.

After 3 p.m., the weather started to worsen. At first, the snow was fairly light, but it soon changed to a severe storm. In a few minutes, the vertical wall was covered with snow, and the snow that collected above us came down in small avalanches.

We secured our "house," a portaledge designed by us and made by a Russian company in a hurry. When it was set up, we climbed in, plastered with snow. For several minutes, we caught our breath and defrosted under the roar of avalanches.

As we tried to cook dinner, we found out that our Primus stove did not want to work any more. At first we thought that it was because of the nearly 100 percent humidity inside the portaledge, but later we discovered that the problem had its roots in the very poor quality gasoline we were using. After it had burned, the gasoline left a thick, tar-like residue that plugged everything inside the stove.

We had had difficulties with fuel all along. At first, we were told that we could buy Epigas cartridges in Delhi, but when we arrived we found that just four cartridges were available, for $15 apiece. We were lucky to get a Primus that worked on gasoline instead. During our climb, we had to take it to pieces and clean it of tar twice a day.

The next morning, we moved very slowly: though it was not snowing, the rocks were still plastered. By 3 p.m., snow started to fall again as it had the day before. By this time, Alexander and I had managed to climb only about 90 meters up from where we had spent the

Day 5: Alexander Klenov on the sharp end (7a A3) at 6000 meters between camps II and III.
THALAY SAGAR EXPEDITION COLLECTION

night. Fortunately, Alexey and Mikhail had not taken down our portaledge. We rappelled quickly and sat there drying our clothes and listening to the sound of avalanches crashing on the roof. At 5 p.m., the snowfall ended and the sun appeared. We hoped that the weather would be better the next day.

I led. It is always more interesting to lead than to belay, because time passes more quickly. The weather pattern remained the same. At 1 p.m., it began to snow again. Using Russian cams, I climbed to the end of the crack, then came down to the portaledge, which had already been moved higher and set up by my friends. Tomorrow we would have to drill and then pendulum right to another crack system.

The next day Mikhail was on lead, working as the "woodpecker" while Alexey belayed. Alexander and I remained in the tent because the chances that Mikhail and Alexey would be able to use all the available ropes were not great, which meant that there was no need to move the portaledge. After lunch, as if on schedule, it snowed again. A couple of hours later, Mikhail and Alexey rappelled down. Mikhail was wet and mad: by the time they returned, the sun had reappeared.

Alexey and I went out for a second shift. I hooked on rock for some 30 meters (we had designed and built our own hooks) before switching back and forth from rock to ice higher up. Above, an inside corner looked like it would be possible to climb without hooks. I placed the last ice screw and rappelled down to the portaledge at dusk.

On May 21, our pace was a little bit faster as we jugged a few pitches fixed the day before, then pushed the route three pitches higher. The climbing was becoming less monolithic, but, as a result, we had to contend with more snow. Mikhail, meanwhile, was having strange problems with his eyes. He could not see straight ahead and had to rely on peripheral vision. Later, the doctors decided that it was the result of sunburn, but Mikhail had worked in sunglasses almost the whole time. We discussed the option of going down, but Mikhail insisted on going up, so we decided to continue our ascent. From then on, he always went third.

I led the first four pitches of the next day's climbing on snow-covered rock. Snowfall after noon was by now perceived as a regular thing, and it no longer put a stop to our progress. At the end of the day, I led an overhang of loose, frozen-together rock. We could tell we were at high altitude because the snow no longer stuck to the rock, falling instead in ceaseless powder avalanches.

On May 23, the snow started falling early in the morning, and visibility was down to about 30 meters. However, we could not wait for good weather: only half of our gas was left, and we had a long way to go to the summit. Keeping this in mind, we packed camp and started climbing up into the unknown. At the end of the day, we reached the top of the couloir that all the teams who tried to climb the north face before us had picked for their climb. For the first time, we saw signs left by other climbers. On the left of the couloir hung a medium-sized haul bag. When I finished jugging and unroped to move over to it, I found in the bag an almost new Hella Sport tent, probably left behind by an unsuccessful French expedition.

At night, the weather became slightly better, and visibility improved. The view of what lay ahead did not make anybody happy: above loomed a belt of black slate that formed a great roof. There was no good way up. It was clear now why so many teams had turned back here, while the ones who had made it had gone to the left or right.

It snowed the next day from morning to night. We were worrying more and more about our chances to reach the summit. The supplies were getting low. We could go for a few days longer without food, but without fuel—and therefore without water—there was nothing we could do at such an altitude. The climbing looked steeper ahead, and the weather was not improving. But as long as we could, we had to go on. We made it to the top of the couloir and, near nightfall, set up camp one pitch above its end.

May 25. Alexander and I worked three pitches up on bright red granite and by the end of day reached the black rock. Straight over our head, the overhang extended more than 20 meters out from the wall! It seemed that it might be possible to climb through the first roof farther to the right, but we could not see anything higher up.

This is where we wanted to set up our last camp before the summit. There were no more than four pitches of rock climbing left, but the question of whether we would be able to get through them or not remained.

May 26. We moved camp to the end of the route prepared the day before. By lunchtime, Alexander had climbed through the first roof. The rock was very unstable, and it was hard to find places for pitons. Alex mostly used cams for protection, often stuffing them between loose rocks. As I approached him, I could see that the edge of the roof above us was a giant lump of granite that must have weighed many tons. It had broken off, then miraculously jammed not too far from its original home. Right beneath it hung our portaledge. Thanks to the portaledge's great design and strong fabric, small rocks bounced off it—but we joked that "there would be no wounded" if the giant rock fell down on us.

The climbing immediately above remained about the same. We decided to traverse right on small ledges to make sure that camp and whoever was seconding were safe.

Until now, we had climbed in thick fog. But suddenly the clouds dropped, presenting us with a fantastic sight. We found ourselves beneath a bright sunset, looking out on a snow-white

plain of clouds. The nearest peaks were hidden in clouds, and only far away, probably in China, could we see mountains poking through. For the first time, confidence that we would reach the summit the next day arose in us.

Clear skies and cold greeted us the morning of May 27. We left the portaledge behind and started our summit bid. We had one rope left. In our backpacks were only still and video cameras and warm clothes. Or not—by this time we were wearing all the clothes we had. We had to reach the summit because there was no gasoline left, and we had only enough fuel in the Epigas cartridges for two more nights. And there was the long descent to keep in mind.

We jugged pitches fixed the day before, then climbed one more straight-forward pitch— and we were on the ridge! Strong winds greeted us and the route did not get any simpler. We had speculated earlier that we would find a snow slope on the ridge, but we were wrong. We had to go around a gendarme via a quite difficult chimney on the left and then climb back to our wall. For the first time we found a piton—probably that of the first ascent, because that team, too, had climbed this ridge.

At last, the summit snow dome appeared. It was impossible to determine how far away it was. Some believed that there were about 30 meters left, others, 300. In reality it was about 70 meters, but we could not climb those meters quickly. Indeed, we were up to almost 7000 meters, with ten days of work behind us, during which time we had not once stood on a flat surface.

But any journey ends sooner or later, and we were finally on the summit. Far below we could see our BC on the lakeshore. There was noticeably less ice on the lake than when we had started. We could see that Victor, our communication officer Sherma and the Indian cooks were watching us. We established a radio link and accepted their congratulations, but we did not feel any special joy. We were facing a descent via the same way we had come up. In twi-light, we rappelled down to our tent, but by the time we reached it, we had no energy to pull the ropes. We left them for the next day.

A few hours passed by in the morning while we retrieved the ropes and dismantled camp. We rappelled a few pitches down to the couloir and, instead of staying on our route of ascent, decided to drop into it. It was easier for the descent. After three or four rappels, we set up our portaledge on the side of the couloir. It was not a very safe spot, but the couloir was very steep and we did not expect too many flying rocks. However, we caught one. Everyone but me was inside the portaledge. Suddenly, a huge table-sized rock warmed by the late-day sun broke from the wall and with a roaring sound started its way down.

Screaming "rock!," I ducked, hiding under my helmet and backpack. The rock hit the wall and exploded. Only one four-pound piece reached us, stroking Alexey's leg through the tent walls. Once again, we thanked our good tent and the company that made it for us. If a rock like that had hit somebody's leg directly, one could almost guarantee a shattered knee. In our case, the rock did not even pierce the roof. To provide additional protection from falling rocks, we decided not to clean the snow from the roof, but fortunately, nothing more fell on us.

In the morning, we made tea using the last of our Epigas, then started rappelling. We wanted to spend the night on level ground, but we still had almost 20 pitches to go. Victor would have come to the ABC to bring us water and food, but he had no gasoline or cartridges, either. We had taken it all, leaving him only kerosene for the BC stove.

On the way down we saw loops, ice screws, ropes stacked between rocks and frozen into the ice. At one belay station hung an old bag. Inside (oh, miracle!), there were several Epigas

Day 9: Klenov at 6550 meters in the red rock beneath the shale band between camps VI and VII.
THALAY SAGAR EXPEDITION COLLECTION

Descent from the summit through the shale bands.
THALAY SAGAR EXPEDITION COLLECTION

cartridges. Unfortunately, they were all covered with ice. Mikhail started chipping the ice off the cartridges, puncturing almost all of them, but we recovered one undamaged. We were going to have hot food tonight!

At noon the next day, we noticed Victor. It looked as if he would reach ABC in less than an hour. We rappelled one, two, three pitches, but Victor remained in the same place.

The last rappel turned out to be a very long one. All the ropes were stretched and it was impossible to hear one another. Somehow we reached the snow and radioed Victor. He had walked on the glacier and found himself in between crevasses. The snow bridges over the crevasses were half melted and would not hold him anymore. He could move neither up nor down. We needed to go rescue him.

For the last few hundred meters to ABC, the bags rolled ahead of us as we held on to them with our ropes. Two of them cut loose almost simultaneously. One rolled straight ahead, while the other went left, disappearing into a crevasse. We would not be able to find it until the next morning. With the last of our energy, we brought our backpacks to the tent and, with inde-scribable satisfaction, took off our harnesses. We had not taken them off, even for a minute, for almost two weeks. It would have been nice to see Victor there with boiled potatoes and fresh bread, but there was nothing we could do.

Alexander and I roped up and went down, leaving Alexey and Mikhail to cook tea and food. Half an hour later, after falling to our waists in crevasses a couple of times, we reached Victor. He was frozen like a dog from staying in one spot for half a day. Hugs and congratu-lations made us feel a little bit better, but we still had to go back up to the tent, which took about an hour and a half. Our legs were unwilling to move.

It was dark when we reached the tent. Only there did it become obvious to us that we could finally congratulate each other. We had reached the goal toward which we had worked the whole time. On the north face of Thalay Sagar there is now a new Russian route: *High Tension*.

Later, there were many events: a difficult return to BC, a fun-filled party with a cappella international songs, dances and, of course, lots of whiskey. After that, there was the walk down to Gangotri, the trip back to Delhi, the worries at different airports. But all of this was mitigated by our return home and our thoughts of new plans and new mountains.

SUMMARY OF STATISTICS

REGION: Garhwal, Indian Himalaya

NEW ROUTE: *High Tension* (ABO, 7b A3+, 1400m) on the north face of Thalay Sagar (6904m), May 17-May 27, Alexander Klenov, Alexey Bolotov, Mikhail Davy, Mikhail Pershin

PERSONNEL: Alexander Klenov, Alexey Bolotov, Mikhail Davy, Mikhail Pershin, Victor Ostanin (BC manager)

Mikhail Davy at Camp IV (6250m) on day 7.
THALAY SAGAR EXPEDITION COLLECTION

Mikhail Davy, 34, started climbing in 1983 while attending the Sverdlovsk Mining Institute. He has been an International Master of Sport since 1994. His 25 Russian Grade 6 ascents include ten new routes. In the Russian championships, he has taken first place five times, second place five times, and third place twice. Many of his routes on peaks in the CIS remain unrepeated. He is currently ranked third among Russian alpinists in technical class and fourth overall. Since 1992, all his ascents, with the exception of one in 1995, were put up with Alexander Klenov. He lives with his wife, Olga, and their ten-year-old son, Serguei, in Yekaterinburg, Russia, where he owns a small real estate company.

Yosemite Speed, Patagonian Summits

Exploring Chouinard's maxim four decades on

by Timothy O'Neill

The imploring yell, "Go, go, go!" echoes from above. My jeans pockets bulge with keys, coins and paraphernalia; I've been in the Valley for one week. We have been simuling the last part of this route, but now the rope is stuck, so I hurriedly untie. I give the rope one last serious tug ("Come on. . ."), and surprisingly it pops free. I coil the cord while I climb the last 150 feet of 5-easy. As I tag the summit tree and collapse to the ground, I look over at Dean Potter, who drops the rope from his hands—my anchor—and stops the clock with a smile. Two hours and four minutes, a new record for the South Face of Washington's Column.

Though I have always climbed as if fire were nipping at my heels, this was my first experience using a watch to accurately record the time of an ascent. It was to become habitual in the coming months, and, like all good addictions, the first fix was free: Dean led the entire route.

As of late in Yosemite Valley, pure speed has been the subject of intense innovation, refinement and, to a lesser degree, competition. I landed in Camp 4 in early May, 1999, and already the ante in the speed game had been upped. Dean Potter and Miles Smart's ascent of *Tangerine Trip* (VI 5.10 A3) in a sub 12-hour time had knocked almost seven hours off the previous record. Cedar Wright and Chris McNamara were the next to smash an existing (18:05) speed record with their 10:57 ascent of the *Shield*. In the following months, dozens of routes would have their times slashed by teams that involved a revolving cast of characters employing a bag with a few new tricks.

Implementing new techniques to allow one to climb more efficiently and with less equipment is nothing new. Ever since Harding established the *Nose* only to have Robbins, Frost, Fitscher and Pratt complete the second ascent in 17.5 percent of the original time, we've been going faster. Our pursuit is driven by these goals, and the results can range from the discovery of the hidden knee bar in the crux sequence of the limestone sportfest to utilizing a lead system of three daisy chains that allows the soloist to forego the rope. But the recent speed ascents in the Valley utilize a number of techniques worth examining—and they also beg the question of what parts can be applied to objectives beyond Yosemite's borders.

The common strategy in the modern Valley speed ascents is to divide the route into leader blocks. A block can consist of several pitches or the entire route. The blocks are divided according to the relative strengths of each climber. For example, on their *Shield* ascent, Cedar "freeblasted" the first block (14 pitches) to Gray Ledges, then Chris led to Chicken Head Ledge (pitch 24), with Cedar leading to the summit. Generally, the leader is not able to retrieve gear placed during his block, and, with only one rope, the practice of hauling up spent pro is often times impossible. This requires that the leader back-clean long sections of aid and run it way out on the free climbing.

To achieve the fast times, both climbers must be constantly moving. Short fixing, introduced to the Valley by Aischan Rupp and Rolando Garibotti, has made this possible. The leader fires the pitch, gets to the anchor, immediately pulls up an amount of the rope sufficient to begin

Go! Chris McNamara and Miles Smart beginning a speed ascent of the Zodiac. COREY RICH

climbing, fixes it to at least two points on the anchor, shouts down, "Line fixed!," then launches into the next lead, often foregoing a self-belay unless climbing insecure aid. His yell sets the second into speed-jug mode.

The second's main objective is to get to the belay before his partner runs out of line and place him on belay. He needs to clean the pitches expediently and efficiently (leaving stuck gear behind is not an option when you only have a bare minimum to begin with) and also deal with lower-outs across traversing sections of rock where the leader can often only leave a few pieces of pro.

The intense pace of these climbs, while allowing for remarkable times, also magnifies the inherent danger that exists in climbing. There is less room for error. In June, I committed a nearly fatal mistake.

Dean Potter was busy getting handies in the Stovelegs during a speed ascent of the *Nose* on El Cap. Having fixed the line to the anchor, he yelled down, "Line fixed!" I began my lower-out off the top of Sickle Ledge, but failed to notice that I had not attached my ascenders. I realized something was wrong, but instead of checking, I released the rope from my hands and sprang more than five feet to the dihedral that led to the Stovelegs, bracing myself for a slight jolt. That was a gross underestimation.

I immediately began back-pedaling down an 85-degree slab until my body drifted away from the wall. As I started to free fall, I began egg-beating my arms and legs, desperately straining to remain upright. I was conscious of the fact that I was dropping to the end of the rope, more than 100 feet below, though I did not know why. I was weightless and waiting, wondering if the rope was going to arrest my fall.

As the rope finally began its maple-syrup stretch, I violently pendulumed across the face, hitting it several times before coming to a stop. Fortunately, I was relatively uninjured. This was my second speed climb, and my first (and hopefully last) speed descent. I slowed down and began paying close attention to every detail.

Speed climbing solo represents another realm of suffering and exposure, but recently, it, too, has evolved. Traditionally, the soloist relied on self-belays for an ascent, but the introduction to the Valley of the three-daisy-chain system has given climbers another option. The inspiration for this system is attributed to Bob the Aid Man, an eccentric climber who kept a rattlesnake for a pet, bringing it everywhere in a paper bag. In 1985, Bob

Pitch 11, hour 5, The Big Mac takes on the Witch's Tit (a.k.a. the Nipple, A2+) on the Zodiac.
COREY RICH

employed a two-daisy-chain system on the steep and committing West Face of the Leaning Tower, simply going piece to piece.

With the three-daisy-chain system, the solo climber steps up to the intended objective with a full rack and places his first piece of gear. He clips his daisy to it, then places another piece higher and clips that as well. When he has placed his third piece of gear and clipped it with his third daisy, he reaches down to the first piece, unclips that daisy chain, retrieves the pro, then progresses upward in the same manner. The technique ensures that he is anchored to the wall by at least two pieces at all times, and it allows him to seamlessly link pitches without the need to rappel, clean and jug the previous pitch. Although he must employ greater caution and rely on gear placement and intuition more than when rope soloing, he is able to conserve energy and time.

In 1999, Russell Mitrovitch's 12-hour, ropeless (save for ten feet) ascent of the *Zodiac* demonstrated the benefits of the three-daisy-chain system on the bigger walls. Since then, Dean Potter pushed it a little harder when he utilized a predominantly free solo and refined three-daisy-chain approach to became the first person to solo two grade VIs in a 24-hour period in July. He began by scorching up the *Nose* in 12:59 (record), ate some hotcakes with Chongo Chuck and José Pereyra at the Lodge Cafe, then cruised up to Half Dome and sent the Regular Route for a 23-plus-hour total. Two days later, Hans Florine awoke at the base of Half Dome and climbed the formations in reverse order. He blazed the Regular Route in 3:25 (record) and then the *Nose* with a total eclipsed time of 21:03.

Most parties do not really understand what's happening when they encounter speed climbers on a route. One moment they see a party at the base, and ten minutes and a puff of smoke later, some panting psycho is asking their name and apologizing for any inconvenience. The usual wall etiquette if you're moving much slower than an approaching party is to allow them to pass, when feasible. During a speed ascent, the pass usually occurs in mid-pitch. Communication between the two parties is essential and simple, and the process generally takes several minutes to pass the length of the rope. The slower leader temporarily suspends himself from his last piece of pro to facilitate the switch. I always thank the party and offer to buy them a beer when they get down. When we came upon Jon Blair as he was soloing *Eagle's Way* on El Cap's east face, we brought him a King Cobra to ease the pain of our passing.

It is an arguable point whether passing parties slows or quickens your ascent. You sometimes experience the need to wait for a leader who must get to a stance before you can continue, but you may also have an entire pitch, like the Great Roof, fixed for your aiders. Regardless, I find it to be one of the more enjoyable and random elements of a speed ascent. It's awesome to see a party get infused with energy and execute ten minutes of speeditude before remembering the weight of their two haul bags.

Stop—and a new record. Topping out on the Zodiac *some seven hours after beginning.* COREY RICH

The results of all the above-mentioned techniques, when coupled with the participating players, can get pretty dizzying. In August, Dean and I peddled a tandem bike to Mirror Lake with the intention of linking three Valley formations. We ripped up the Regular Route on Half Dome, simuling to Big Sandy, short fixing through the ZigZags, then simuling to the summit in 2:08, having climbed the route in two blocks. (Soon thereafter, Hans Florine and Jim Hearson shaved this record by 15 minutes, the first time a grade VI was climbed within the two-hour barrier.) We punched it down the Death Slabs, passing Miles Smart, who was on his way to solo the Direct Northwest Face (VI 5.10 A3) on the Dome. (He aviated an onsight time of 11:25.) We powered the bike to the Deli, where we onsighted some cola and Viking-sized cinnamon rolls. After tandeming to the Sentinel, we put in a 2:30 bike-to-bike free solo of the Steck-Salathé. More sugar onsighting at the Lodge store, a cruise down to El Cap Meadow and a night ascent of the *Nose*—7,000-plus vertical and 70-plus pitches, all in less than 21 hours.

The intensity, excitement and improved techniques fostered in last season's speed ascents force us to consider Yvon Chouinard's 1963 prediction of Yosemite as the training grounds for the alpinists of the future. The Valley provides months of perfect weather, miles of unsurpassed granite and the opportunity to initiate and master the craft of big wall climbing. Every climber out there knows El Cap and has either climbed it or one day plans to. Honing your skills here allows you confidence in your abilities elsewhere. The formula for success continues its evolution as more of us journey to the world's remote big wall and alpine arenas. And with the evolution of the formula, the style of ascent takes on as much significance as the objective.

In early January, Nathan Martin and I traveled to the Argentine Patagonia. I had met Nathan several years earlier and was aware of the strength and tenacity he had applied to his almost single-handed development of Telluride's first sport crag. We were on our way to climb El Cap when I asked him if he had a partner for his upcoming Patagonia trip. He said no.

"Dude, you do now," I told him.

Our goal was to bring our combined strength and speed to the *Compressor Route* on Cerro Torre. A season of almost 30 grade V and VIs in Yosemite still did not completely prepare me for the harshness of Patagonia. I was run over by talus, charred by the sun and beaten down by the endless hiking. Still, fortified by our recent speed pursuits, we had the confidence that, provided we got a weather window, we would use our Valley lessons to the fullest.

In our first week, climbing with Bruno Sourzac, we made an ascent of Innominata via the *Corallo Route* (V 5.11). The line was characterized by striking features and some loose rock. An incredible summit sunset provided the visual inspiration to endure the next month of storms.

As that month passed and we began to resign any hope of another summit, the weather indiscriminately opened, offering up three days of stability. We all grabbed at once. Utilizing a tip from Kevin Thaw, Nathan and I decided to try a line first attempted by Andy Perkins on Cerro Standhardt while waiting for the *Compressor Route* to come into shape. After negotiating the Torre Glacier, we simul-climbed 600 feet of 60- to 80-degree snow and ice to reach the col between Cerro Standhardt and Perfil de Indio. We then stowed our plastics for the next 14 pitches of Patagonia crack climbing. Since we had no photos or prior knowledge of the face other than the fact that Andy's efforts had reached about 400 feet, we were excited to find multiple crack systems lining the 2,000-foot face.

After two pitches of lower-angle simul-climbing, the wall steepened for 800 feet and provided the crux pitch of stemming and jamming out a series of overhangs. The route then kicked back considerably to allow for several pitches of simuling and rapid leads. The day was hot, with intense sun causing ice and rock to careen down to the left of our route. We arrived at the north mushroom at 5:30 p.m. A 40-meter rappel into the notch that separates the northwest face from the summit ridge brought me to an 80-foot face of 5.10, on loose flakes, with pro more questionable than Clinton's sexual ethics.

Three more pitches had Nathan placing one of our two ice screws at the base of the summit mushroom. With a running belay, he led up the northeast side of the "hongo," smashing his way up 45 feet of overhanging rime and ice. We topped out as the sun melted into the icecap, completing the route in about 12 hours. We chopped our first-ever ice bollard, simuled back to our packs and began the 12-hour descent, rappelling into the *Exocet* route.

The north and west faces of (from highest to lowest) Cerro Torre, Torre Egger, Punta Herron, and (far left) Cerro Standhardt. Routes are as follows. 1. the Northwest Ridge (Martin-O'Neill, 2000) (climbs to summit via final four pitches of Exocet, *which is shown); 2. Otra Vez (Giarolli-Orlandi-Salvaterra, 1989); 3. Spigolo dei Bimbi (Cavallaro-Salvaterra-Vidi, 1991); 4. La Giocanda (to the col "dei Falchetti") (Giovanazzi-Salvaterra, 1998).* ROLANDO GARIBOTTI

Nathan Martin on the first ascent of the Northwest Ridge of Cerro Standhardt. TIMOTHY O'NEILL

Having only four days left before we flew out of Santiago, Chile, we rested for 12 hours, then went for an attempt on the *Compressor Route* on Cerro Torre. We made it six pitches up before the weather collapsed. Heinz Zak, Peter Janschek and Elmar Sprenger, who had been forced to retreat after Peter snapped a piece of fixed webbing 50 feet from the mushroom, joined us in the descent. (Peter had sailed for 60 feet, pulled out a rivet and a copperhead and grazed the compressor, but was uninjured.)

Back at Norwegos, we decided to gamble with the weather and miss our flights. We rested a day to hydrate and refuel our fatigued bodies. The following morning, we left camp at 3 a.m. equipped with a few rivets, some heads and a drill that Heinz had loaned us. We reached the Col of Patience, brewed tea and soup and stripped our belongings down to the essentials.

I blasted off at 9:30 a.m., short-fixing the first three pitches. We then simuled the next ten. On pitch 14, I left my pack behind to negotiate an ice-filled chimney to reach the end of my block. We switched into our plastics and crampons and Nathan began his block, which would take us to the compressor. As the rope came tight, I began ascending one of Maestri's bolt ladders. Then, armed with only one ice axe, I simuled with Nathan through the Ice Towers. He next short-fixed his way up to and over the 15-foot icicle that hung from the compressor. I led the Bridwell pitch, replacing two rivets and the copperhead (apparently, a party the previous year had also ripped out some memorabilia).

We reached the snow mushroom at 8:30 p.m. I expected to find an unclimbable, unconsolidated horror show but was surprised to spot a relatively feasible passage on the east face. Sixty feet of lower-angle snow and rime led to a 20-foot overhanging section of two-foot-thick rime, with another 20 feet leading to the true summit of Cerro Torre. As the mushroom does not see many ascents, I assume most parties must expect to find an unpassable "hongo" and therefore end their ascents at the last anchor on the headwall, but with the constantly changing conditions of Patagonia it's always worth a look.

Nathan Martin on Cerro Standhardt. TIMOTHY O'NEILL

We rappelled through the night and were not surprised to find the Austrians starting up the route for their second assault. (They would summit the mushroom the following morning but would first endure five hours of Patagonia insta-weather inside a two-man bivy sack standing in the Notch.) Once at Norwegos, we collapsed, grateful for the weather, the summit and, most importantly, our health.

Our experience with simulclimbing, short fixing and our extensive aid background allowed us to make the most of the random and fleeting weather windows. Luck also factored in heavily. Timing can be the difference between touching the summit and brushing too closely to death. Speed is an invaluable ally when climbing among peeling ice patches, falling rock and horrendous weather.

It seems as if Chouinard's ideas have begun to manifest themselves in my climbing endeavors. Last season's regiment of speed climbing and constant practice of long easy solos helped carry me up a few of the torres of Patagonia. Although we did need to adjust our style to compensate for the heavy packs and double ropes that alpine climbing demands, we were able to employ the new techniques with excellent results.

I have learned many valuable lessons as well as techniques while climbing in Yosemite,and I plan on experimenting with them in other remote areas of the world. Regardless of whether I am an alpinist of the future or just one of the present, my personal evolution has brought me the desire to take less with the hope of retaining more.

SUMMARY OF STATISTICS

AREAS: Yosemite Valley, California, and Argentine Patagonia

ASCENTS: Various speed records established in 1999 in Yosemite Valley, Timothy O'Neill and others; the *Corallo Route* (V 5.11) on Innominata, January 12, Timothy O'Neill, Nathan Martin, Bruno Sourzac; the Northwest Ridge (V 5.11 WI5, 19 pitches) on Cerro Standhardt, February 15, Timothy O'Neill and Nathan Martin; the *Compressor Route* (VI 5.11 WI4 A1, 28 pitches) on Cerro Torre, February 18, Timothy O'Neill and Nathan Martin

Born in 1969, Timothy O'Neill has been climbing for more than ten years. He believes in freedom, laughter and the beauty of life on the edge. He currently makes his home in his 1977 Ford Econoline.

Timothy O'Neill on the Corallo Route, Innominata. BRUNO SOURZAC

Gyachung Kang

An alpine mentality in the Himalaya

by Marko Prezelj, *Planinska zveza Slovenije, Slovenia*
translated by Ana Perčič

"Have you noticed the mountain between Cho Oyu and Everest?" Andrej asked me in 1995.

"There are several interesting peaks east of Cho Oyu. I haven't observed any in particular."

"Well, I have. During acclimatization I spent the entire time watching the north face of Gyachung Kang. Look."

He showed me a photo he took during an attempt of Siguang Ri. Looking at it, I immediately warmed to the idea of an ascent from the Tibetan side. After we found out that the mountain is rarely visited and that it remained untouched from the north, the goal became even more tempting.

In 1996, we tried to organize a small expedition similar to the one we had used on the first ascent of Menlungtse in 1992: two alpinists, a doctor and a cook. The plan fell through due to the enormous amounts of money the Chinese required for expeditions to Tibet. It wasn't until 1998 that the Planinska zveza Slovenije (Alpine Association of Slovenia) actually showed some organizational interest in the idea. Our small expedition grew to become a PZS project: eight alpinists and a doctor. The enlarged team was intended not only to reduce costs, but also to transfer experiences to younger climbers. In this perspective, Andrej, the Himalayan veteran, was a real treasure, and he of course took over the post of leader.

In the spring, Andrej and Marko Car made a reconnaissance to Gyachung Kang, exploring the approach and examining the mountain's faces. They brought home a lot of useful information and photographs that only increased our enthusiasm. But we did not draw any specific routes on the photos; instead, we decided we would climb in roped parties of two, and that, depending on weather conditions and each individual's feelings, the routes would only be chosen once we arrived at the mountain. This was probably the key decision of the expedition. Relaxation and freedom of choice overwhelmed the monotony that can occur if a team is directed toward one goal only, especially during acclimatization.

Autumn came, and our departure with it. In Kathmandu, we devoted our time and money to food, equipment and packing. The weather was bad and remained so, even after our arrival in Tibet. We turned the acclimatization stay we had planned in Nyalam to our advantage. We all climbed in the nearby hills and reached higher than 5000 meters, which was enough for a carefree departure to Base Camp.

We camped by the road at the spot where the rivers from Everest and Gyachung meet, waiting two days for the yaks that would carry our loads to BC. We used the time to get acclimatized on the surrounding hills up to 5500 meters. On October 2, after lengthy negotiations about loads and prices, the yak herders directed their animals to the Gyachung River valley. Tomaž, meanwhile, realized he had forgotten his wallet and passport where he had eaten his lunch. This event, and Tomaž himself, became the source of jokes throughout the expedition. We proclaimed him the author of Seven Years in Tibet: Part II.

On October 4, we arrived at a little morainal plateau above the glacier where we pitched our nine tents. I shared a tent with Andrej and, as usual, we got along fairly well, complementing each other. We completely reduced superfluous talk about certain decisions. The younger team members often showed us how spontaneously well we understood one another when they brought us their own doubts and discussions.

The mountain we chose for our first acclimatization ascent—a 6700-meter peak neither mentioned nor named in Jan Kiclkowski's guide—had first caught our attention during the approach. Andrej, Marko Čar, Peter and I set off to climb it. The ascent, via the southeast ridge, was technically not demanding. Clouds covered the surrounding peaks, so we could not study any future climbs as we had planned. We descended via the east ridge, roping up for sections due to crevasses. The other four reached the top the next day.

The name for the peak came by itself. A day after our arrival at BC, we emptied the satellite phone account. Back home, we had been reassured that the account would be filled with all the necessary codes (which had not been entrusted to us). Unfortunately, this did not happen. Hoping that our problem would somehow be solved, we kept checking the account. Each time, a pleasant female voice said, "You have zero." Zero Peak, then, is the name we suggest for the mountain.

After two days' rest, we decided on another acclimatization ascent which would also allow us to assess conditions and study the north face of Gyachung Kang. We divided into four rope parties for the unclimbed Siguang Ri Shar (6998m). Janko and Blaž chose to go up the left side of the north face and then continue up the east ridge; Andrej and I started on the right side of the north face; Matic, Marko, Peter and Tomaž decided on the north face of the saddle between Siguang Ri Shar and Siguang Ri.

In the afternoon, we all set up bivouac tents at about 6000 meters, at the bottom of our intended routes. The next morning, we began our ascents. A strong wind blew, piling snow in drifts and launching small powder avalanches. The cold bit our toes as if we were at least 1000 meters higher. Andrej and I packed our rucksacks and started climbing near a poorly defined rock rib. We had no big difficulties; still, we found occasional hard ice beneath the snow, and we had to use both ice axes and touch the rock a couple of times to go on.

The wind followed us to the rib, where it forced us to make a long diagonal traverse to the right toward the saddle. The angle lessened as we waded through ankle-deep snow. In the middle of the traverse we saw the other four below, climbing right toward the rib. It seemed as if they were being strafed by powder avalanches even harder and making progress even more slowly than we were.

The fierce wind showed its true power on the saddle, where it literally blew away every thought of proceeding. We started preparing a place for the tent, putting pressed plates of snow around the tent as a sort of a windshield. The two other teams set up their tents next to ours. Though we were already feeling the affects of high altitude, the night was quite pleasant because of the attention we applied to setting up the tent.

In the morning, the wind was still blowing. Lightly equipped, we all decided to climb to the top of Siguang Ri (7309m), which looked easily approachable from the saddle. The only problem was the wind, which hampered the ascent and blew doubts into our heads.

We quickly climbed the first steep section, which was followed by a long plateau to the summit pyramid. Walking with the wind blowing in our faces was no fun whatsoever. Except for the beautiful view of Gyachung Kang and Everest, and the wish to get to the top, I had no

Siguang Ri and Siguang Ri Shar on the left, Zero Peak on the right. MARKO PREZELJ

real motivation to continue.

The final pyramid lured us for so long that we finally climbed to the top. The view would have been fully experienced only if the hurricane had stopped. We quickly turned to descend. Our doctor, Žare, told us over the phone that Janko had reached the top of Siguang Ri Shar the previous day. I thought it was great that we were climbing these mountains just like that. We were more experienced and no longer felt the fear and respect for the mountains that once kept us from climbing in such a way.

We descended quickly, reaching the saddle while it was still in the sun. The second night was less pleasant than the first. In the neighboring tent, Matic suffered from oxygen deprivation. We gave him first aid and reduced communication to a minimum. It appeared we were not yet acclimatized.

The night passed by slowly with little sleep, but when the morning came, I had to push the sleepiness away. Andrej, Marko and I decided to climb Siguang Ri Shar by its south face while the others descended to BC.

The strong wind weakened as we started a long traverse over the south face of the mountain. The sky gradually became completely covered by clouds. An unknown energy drove me on, and I led from the tents all the way to the top, through snow and short rock steps. Despite the sleepless night, I felt great. It seemed to me that with a pace like this we could visit all the surrounding peaks in two weeks. From the top we returned to the saddle, packed the tents and equipment and started a long descent to BC.

The next two days in BC were really nice. We were together again, ready to joke and tease. We celebrated my birthday. We infected one another with positive energy, not bothering our heads about the upcoming climb on Gyachung Kang. We felt pleased with the fact that we had already climbed three peaks with no major problems, something for which many people would have organized an independent expedition.

On the plateau before the summit of Siguang Ri. Siguang Ri Shar is visible below left and up from the col, Everest and Gyachung Kang on the right skyline. MARKO PREZELJ

Three days after Siguang Ri Shar, we hurried to the foot of Gyachung Kang. Curiosity and a wish to put up an Advanced Base Camp to allow fast access to the face would not let us rest. We marked our way on the rolling glacier with cairns and pitched two tents about half an hour's walk from the foot of the north face. Doing it together helped us get through some personal tensions that arose about the forthcoming ascent. In our minds, we looked for passages on the north face and at the same time "climbed" the east face, but we postponed making the final route decisions until later.

After we set up ABC, we had all the conditions to go to the top. We only needed to rest.

So we did, for two days, taking the rest seriously. Still, we did not raise the question about the route or how we would climb Gyachung Kang. On the third day, it started snowing. The snowstorm lasted for more than 60 hours and covered BC in almost a meter of snow. "We will get snowbound!," we joked at first. For three days, we shook the snow off the tents and cleaned the trails to the dining tent and toilet. The wind kept bringing new snow so that we could not think properly about the climbing.

On the storm's third day, the kitchen and storage tents collapsed under the weight of the snow. Gradually, we realized that our ambitious fairy tale was coming to an end. Or had it just begun?

"How are we ever going to return to the valley in all this snow?" Although it appeared on all our faces, it was the question nobody asked out loud.

In the afternoon of the third day, the snow stopped falling. The cold now became a visible fact. That evening, Andrej established the seriousness of the situation. We only had about 30 liters of kerosene left for cooking—and now, also for melting snow. This would hardly suffice for a week. In any case, we couldn't leave BC quickly because the yaks could not reach us in such conditions.

"So we will have to wait for the mountain to get rid of the snow and ascend just before we planned to leave BC."

Andrej's summary of the situation was so real that nobody dared doubt it, though we were all full of doubts. The thought of going back into the valley now lost its meaning.

We only had one option, and it quickly became a decision that we then turned into a belief. The cook promised to economize with fuel. Every day after the snowstorm we walked alone to the edge of the glacial moraine, looking toward the white valley like sailors over the endless ocean—and at the same time, watching conditions on the mountain.

Two days after the snowfall, Andrej and Tomaž went into the valley. The satellite phone—our connection with the rest of the world—kept informing us, "You have zero," and now was a good time to let our families in Slovenia know how we were. We also had to arrange for the arrival of yaks to BC. Tomaž worried about his lost passport. In the village of Cho Dzom, they found out that the snow had chased away all the Everest expeditions on the Tibet side. The only message Andrej and Tomaž were able to send home was the letter describing what happened, our determination to continue and the loss of the passport. The letter was personally taken to an agency in Kathmandu by a trekker, and from there it went to our homeland by fax. A substitute passport would be waiting for Tomaž on our return to the border of Zangmu.

Andrej made a deal for the yak herders to come to BC on November 3. The end was now determined.

While diligently shoveling snow during the storm, I had developed a mild case of snow blindness. The other five broke trail to ABC without me, walking through knee-deep snow to dig out the two tents below the face, then returning to BC in the evening. The trail was soon

The north face of Gyachung Kang. ANDREJ ŠTREMFELJ

Marko Čar on the north face of Gyachung Kang. MARKO PREZELJ

completely covered again by snow, but it still served as a directional later on.

The sun, which on our arrival had touched the north face for a short time, was by now low, with the face completely in shadow all the time. Wind and avalanches swept the snow from the face, which became more and more climbable.

Andrej and Tomaž returned from the village and told us that there were only nine days left to make the climb. Time pressures replaced the feelings of easiness. Again, Andrej had to make the final decision, because the uncertainty was greater for those who would go first. Andrej, Marko, Matic and I decided together to be the first to enter the face. The other four would follow the next day.

On October 26, the four of us eagerly (if slowly) waded through the snow-covered trail toward the two small tents below the face. If I missed a step, I sank in over my belt. Swearing did not help, nor did stepping carefully on the existing footprints. Marko waded through the first half; later, Matic and I alternated leads.

We came to ABC early enough to dig out the tents a little and dry the equipment. For the last time, we climbed the face with our eyes. I got into the real climbing mood; I no longer saw problems. While Marko and I cooked, Andrej and Matic went to make a short track in the snow toward the face, so that in the morning walking would be easier.

As the shadows covered the tents, we disappeared inside. I hung the cooker from the ceiling and opened the entrance to air out the tent as I cooked. I did not have much to do except light the cooker, which was constantly going out due to condensation on the pot.

We had already eaten the soup and rice when I started making tea. Andrej was napping in the corner, and I began falling asleep, too. The cooker went out again, and I lifted myself to light it. After a few unsuccessful attempts, I mumbled to Andrej, "Something's buzzing in my head," then fell back as if defeated by sleep. Andrej tried to light the cooker as well, but ended up like me.

When I came around, Marko was above me, saying "Breathe, breathe!" I bit for air, slowly realizing what was happening. Andrej threw up. Breathing deeply, I realized we had both been unconscious for some time. Marko and Matic had heard us rattle and hurried to help. We had been poisoned by carbon monoxide.

That night, we could not reach BC by radio, so Matic ran to get Doctor Žare. Meanwhile, Marko prepared something to drink and took care of us in a motherly way. In the morning, we concluded that the only option was to return to BC. After talking to Žare, we slowly went down. Halfway back, we met Janko, Blaž, Peter and Tomaž going up. It was enough to look at each other and say a few words before we each went our own way. Nobody knew whether we would be able to try again.

Žare examined us at BC. "No problem," he said. "Rest, and then you can try again."

The first four started climbing on October 28. We watched them from BC through binoculars and talked to them over the radio. They reported the conditions on the face were not bad and that they had put up two little bivouac tents on a snow crest at 6800 meters, the only real opportunity for a comfortable bivouac. The next day, a strong wind blew. Both rope parties decided to wait. Meanwhile, the four of us went up to ABC. We could not manage it without swearing this time, either. Andrej and I cooked in front of our tent that evening.

The wind did not stop in the morning. The rope parties, who had by now spent two windy nights at the first bivouac, faced a serious decision. Forward or back? Janko and Blaž decided to descend, Peter and Tomaž to continue.

Meanwhile, Andrej, Marko, Matic and I began our ascent. We soon met Janko and Blaž, who repeated what they had already told us over the radio. Some skeptical looks and encouraging words, and again we went in our own directions.

We progressed well, although the old steps were sometimes a worse option than kicking new ones. We pitched the tents on the snow crest where the others had dug ledges for their first bivouac.

Andrej and I took pains to enlarge the tent area, setting up the tent with care so we would be well-prepared for the night. After supper, we heard from Tomaž and Peter, whose tracks disappeared under a rock barrier above us. They had had quite a lot of mixed climbing, but, considering the heavy snowfall of the previous days, the conditions were good. They had pitched camp on a serac. Our efforts with the tent, meanwhile, had not been in vain: Andrej and I slept surprisingly well.

We started out early in the morning. Before we lost radio contact with them, Tomaž and Peter managed to tell us that they would try to get to the top that day. Gradually, I was gaining the self-confidence I had literally suffocated a few days before in ABC.

After 50 meters, we encountered the first sections of mixed climbing. Fortunately, it was not very steep, so we did not belay each other. In this way we gained time and energy. Before the serac where the angle broke, I looked up the slope leading to the top and saw two figures about 100 meters apart.

"Peter and Tomaž are descending from the summit," I thought.

But as we reached their tent, I realized they were slowly moving upward. They still seemed very close, and I got the idea that we could follow them. The summit seemed temptingly close as well. Only after we soberly estimated the situation did we decide to bivouac. I did not feel tired, but there was really no need to hurry. A rest would also save energy for the descent.

Andrej and I set up a tent on a large shelf. We dug deep into the snow. As the sun set behind the ridge, we went into the tents and cooked. While we melted the first container of water, Peter and Tomaž called during their descent from the top. They asked for some liquid. We were happy for them to have successfully summited, and we immediately made them some tea. The icy beard and shiny look as Tomaž came to get it were more expressive than all the congratulations and handshaking. His enthusiasm infected both of us and confirmed our determination to set foot on the summit the next day.

I slept well. In the morning I woke up motivated, got dressed and left the warm shelter of the tent. I felt great. We exchanged a few words with Peter and Tomaž, appealed to them to descend and went for the top.

Nothing spoiled my mood, not even the wind, constantly blowing but with less force than the day before. We quickly reached the northwest ridge. At such altitudes I often try to replace the monotony of the slow steps by counting them. Not this time. Filled with energy, I came to the front and after two and half hours of ascent, stopped below the summit.

I waited for Andrej, and we stepped on top together. We were sincerely happy to stand on the spot where everything turns downward, especially the view. After we shook hands and hugged in friendship, we relaxed and enjoyed the view with rapturous feelings caused by an old wish that had come true.

Soon, Marko and Matic joined us. Over the radio, we received congratulations and excitement from BC. For me, being there was a truly unique experience. Even the usual worry about the descent somehow dissembled to subconsciousness. I did not feel tired. It was an easiness I had never experienced before on any summit, intertwined with the joy of being able to share the moment with someone else.

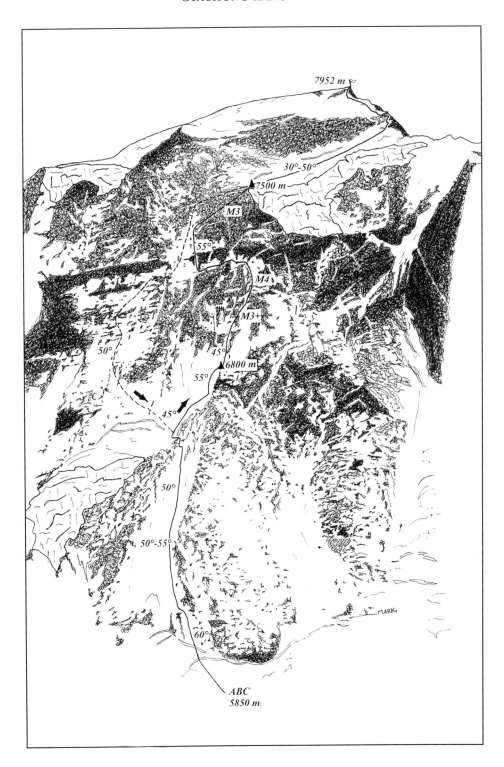

We reached the tents in an hour, where we realized that Peter and Tomaž were still there. We encouraged them to start descending, then struck the tents and packed our rucksacks. Andrej suggested descending independently as quickly as we could, and we all agreed. I thought we were hesitating too long, so I slowly began down. We descended somewhat to the left of our ascent route because it was less technical. In spite of the exposure, there was no need for belaying. At first I stopped to wait for the others, but the frequent waiting made me cold, and, after Janko confirmed the correct descent route over the radio from BC, I decided to descend to ABC without stopping. I noticed that Marko, Peter and Tomaž rappelled at two delicate parts, then I made my way quickly to ABC. The seracs hanging above the face in a certain way maintained my speed.

Arriving at the tents, I looked back with relief and saw Andrej and Matic at the foot of the face, Marko and Peter somewhere between the first bivy and the foot, while Tomaž was slowly descending near the first bivouac. Pleased to have escaped the area below the hanging seracs, I waited for Andrej and Matic.

They joined me, but our enthusiasm about the quick descent did not last long. Marko called us on the radio and said that Peter had slid the last 200 meters and stopped at the foot of the face, injured. His nose bled, he was rather confused and seemed incapable of moving on his own.

We all instantly went back up. Peter had to be moved from below the seracs. Marko radioed Žare, who confirmed the likelihood of concussion in addition to the visible wounds. We started a rescue that quickly proceeded on the avalanche cone under the face. As we walked, we sank deep in snow. We had been active all day, and our movement slowed down noticeably. Peter often simply collapsed and refused to move. Near midnight, when the trudging became unbearable and the serac danger was reduced, we stopped and pitched a tent, where we placed Peter and the exhausted Tomaž.

Concerned about Peter and Tomaž, we woke up early the next morning. Blaž and Žare came to help, followed by Janko and Kami Sherpa. With the first sun, we brought Peter, staggering, to ABC. Žare gave him and Tomaž additional medicine, and they immediately set out for BC. We cleaned and packed ABC, then descended, still sinking waist-deep in the snow when we weren't careful. Despite the heavy rucksack, I was not tired and reached BC at last light. By dark, we were all assembled, including Peter, who occasionally behaved like a child.

The doctor's diagnosis of Peter and Tomaž's condition was exhaustion and frostbite; Peter had also suffered a concussion with a possible skull fracture. This, and the fact that the yaks arrived at BC the next evening, spiked our happiness at the successful ascent with a great deal of concern. It would only pass in Kathmandu, where a careful hospital examination of Peter put our suspicions to rest.

At around noon on November 4, three days after summitting, the yak caravan left BC. We rushed into the valley, wanting to get to the village in one day. Upon arriving at Cho Dzom, we simply dropped onto the beds.

The quick pace from when we decided on the last ascent to when we left BC kept me from collecting my impressions until Pang La Pass, from which there is a wonderful view of the mountains from Makalu to Cho Oyu. We had spent exactly one month at BC, and, in spite of the bad weather, we had taken advantage of our stay. Although at first I looked at the fact that we had climbed four interesting summits, I realized that we had been through a lot, intensively gaining experiences that enriched us for good. Only there on the pass, four days after our descent from the summit, did I feel relief that the wish Andrej and I had shared for such a long time had come true, and that I was, at least for now, free from my exaggerated curiosity. The question of what it would have been like to have come there only with Andrej was no longer of interest. But in Kathmandu, I was leafing through books again....

SUMMARY OF STATISTICS

AREA: Mahalangur Himal, Tibet

NEW ROUTES: The east face/southeast ridge (III/2, 700m) of Zero Peak (ca. 6700m, first ascent), October 6, Čar, Meznar, Prezelj and Štremfelj, and October 7, Jost, Navrsnik, Jakofčič and Meglič, with descent via the east ridge/east face (III/2, 700m), October 6, Čar, Meznar, Prezelj and Štremfelj; *Trzic route* (IV+/4, 1100m) on the north face/east ridge of Siguang Ri Shar (6998m, first ascent), October 10, Meglič, with descent via the south face (III/3, 800m); the south face (IV/3, 450m), October 12, Čar, Prezelj and Štremfelj. The north face/east ridge (IV/3, 650m) of Siguang Ri (7309m) October 10, Prezelj, Štremfelj (to the saddle between Siguang Ri Shar and Siguang Ri); to the summit (II/2, 800m), October 11, Prezelj, Štremfelj, Čar, Jost, Meznar and Jakofčič. The Slovene Route (VI/4, 2000m) on the north face of Gyachung Kang (7952m), October 28-31, Jakofčič and Meznar; October 30-November 1, Čar-Jost and Prezelj-Štremfelj

PERSONNEL: Andrej Štremfelj (leader), Marko Prezelj, Marko Čar, Matic Jost, Peter Meznar, Tomaž Jakofčič, Janko Meglič, Blaž Navrsnik, Žare Guzej (doctor)

Marko Prezelj. MARKO ČAR

Marko Prezelj was born in 1965 and has been climbing since 1982. Trained as a chemical engineer, he now works as a climbing instructor, mountain guide and photographer. Among his many ascents around the world are Cho Oyu by a new route on the north face in 1988, Kangchenjunga South by a new route, alpine style, in 1991, the first ascent of Menlungtse's main summit, alpine style, via the east face in 1992, and a new route on the east face of Torre Norte del Paine in 1995. All these ascents were made with Andrej Štremfelj. In 1993, he made the fifth ascent of *Wyoming Sheep Ranch* on El Capitan with Silvo Karo. He is married and has two sons.

Trango Overview
Pakistan

Uli Biaho

Shipton Spire

East Hainablak

Great Trango Tower

Nameless Tower (EAST FACE)

UPPER TRANGO GLACIER

(Monk)

Trango Glacier

(WEST RIDGE)

PULPIT

SOUTH EAST FACE

DUNGE GLACIER

WESTERN BALTORO MUSTAGH

BALTORO G.

Great Trango Tower

"A" AMERICAN (1977 & 1984) & 1999
"CS" MORE CZECH LESS SLOVAK (1999)
"ND" NORWEGIAN DIRECT (1999)
"K" KOREAN VARIATION (1999)
"GV" GRAND VOYAGE (1999)
"NP" NORWEGIAN PILLAR (1984)
"J" JAPANESE VARIATION (1990)

Nameless Tower

"S" SLOVAKIAN (1987)
"PG" POLISH/SWISS (1988)
"J" JAPANESE (1991)
"BS" BOOK OF SHADOWS (1995)
"WF" WALL FICTION (1997)

Shipton Spire

"I" INSHALLAH (1996)
"BF" BALTESE FALCON (1997)
"SF" SHIP OF FOOLS (1997)

Uli Biaho

based on aerial photo by Galen Powell

The Trango Towers in Review

by John Middendorf

The impressive rock spires of Great Trango Tower and Trango (a.k.a. Nameless) Tower create one of the wonders of the Earth, capturing the imagination of everyone who travels on the Baltoro Glacier. Great Trango resembles a giant castle flanked by steep walls. On top of nearly a mile of sheer rock, four magnificent summit turrets comprise the East, West, Main (middle) and South summits. The sibling Trango Tower stands as a proud rook, the ultimate rock spire. The walls are among the largest vertical faces anywhere and have been the arena for the world's most impressive and historic big wall climbs. In his 1974 book, *Big Wall Climbing*, Doug Scott predicted, ". . . as the political situation improves [and access is eased], there will undoubtedly be a flood of applicants maneuvering to tackle these big wall climbs of the future. Here is the ultimate challenge of verticality, uncertain weather conditions and altitude." That challenge was met in 1999 by five teams on the Great Trango Tower alone. All five established new routes, providing inspiration for this introduction, which places the achievements in an historical context.

Great Trango was first climbed to the Main Summit in 1977 by Galen Rowell, John Roskelly, Kim Schmitz and Dennis Hennek from the alpine-esque west side, a long and serious endeavor that contained stretches of difficult rock and ice climbing. In 1984, the Norwegians Stein Aasheim, Dag Kolsrud, Finn Daehli and the visionary Hans Christian Doseth climbed the North Pillar of Great Trango Tower, by far the most striking and longest vertical buttress of the massif, in an ascent that stands as a momentous blend of spirit, human will and tragedy. (See Robert Caspersen's article in the pages that follow for a more detailed description of the climb.) The tragic Norwegian effort proved to be a milestone of style and commitment in big wall climbing that paved the way for future landmarks. The same year, Scott Wollums and Andy Selters put up a new route to the Main Summit via the Northwest Ridge. Their route requires very little technical rock climbing, has some serious alpine sections and is recommended by Mr. Selters.

In 1992, Xaver Bongard and I climbed a parallel route to the Norwegian's line to the East Summit. Our route, the *Grand Voyage*, is a 4,400-foot continuous vertical and overhanging wall capped by the 650-foot summit pyramid. On the final mixed rock and ice pitch, a short snow walk from the summit, we found one of the Norwegian pitons that had been used for a rappel. Despite the fate of the Norwegians, we too had committed to the route alpine-style with no fixed rope, and we realized what a serious endeavor it is to descend with only four 60-meter ropes and one 120-meter haulline from the massive peak. Our ascent marked the second ascent of the East Summit but the first successful round-trip to terra firma. It also set a new standard of length, style and commitment on remote big walls.

Despite the bounty of walls, no new routes were put up on Great Trango in the next seven years, though a variation was climbed on the lower Norwegian Buttress (two other variations to the route were put up prior to 1992). Several teams repeated the Northwest Ridge, including an Australian BASE jumping team. A notable attempt of the impressive unclimbed Southwest Buttress was made in 1990 by Jon Lazkano's four-man team, who climbed 61

The Trango Massif. From left to right: the Pulpit, the Main and East summits, Cruksunebruk, the Nameless Tower. ROBERT CASPERSEN

pitches before being turned back by storm some 600 feet from the Main Summit. In 1997, a four-member Korean team climbed a 12-pitch variation to the Norwegian Buttress route, which they then followed to the East Summit in an ascent that went virtually unreported in the West. The team included Youn-Jung Shin, the first female to summit Great Trango; Choi Seung-Chul also became the first to paraglide from one of Great Trango's summits.

In 1999, the West Summit and the summit of the Pulpit were both climbed for the first time. From the Trango Glacier, the strong American team of Mark Synnot, Jared Ogden and Alex Lowe climbed the impressive northwest face, 3,000 feet of steep slabs and ramps leading up to a 2,500-foot vertical wall. A new standard was set not in style of climbing but in expedition communications. Sponsored by the internet community, the team relayed daily messages, images and video through satellite-connected computers to civilization. Mike Graber and Jim Surrette climbed parts of the route to film the climbers. Conflicts that arose on the trip, the result of unprecedented e-mail journals that allowed the climbers to read what the others wrote to readers from around the world, created an indirect communication dynamic. The 28-day ascent was criticized by a Norwegian team strictly opposed to the use of motorized drills in the wilderness, but it is reported that the Americans cleaned the route extensively of fixed ropes and other equipment, which must be applauded, considering the magnitude of the project. Their route, *Parallel Worlds*, set new standards in location documentation. Sadly, it was also Lowe's last major climb.

Shortly after the Americans began their ascent, a team of Russians comprising Yuri Koshelenko, Igor Potankin, Alexander Odintsov and Ivan Samoilenko began a route just to the right of the Americans'. Climbing with less fixed rope, they established a new route in 20 days—an impressive achievement, particularly considering the dated quality of their equipment. It is interesting to read Odintsov's notes of conversations from the trip, in which he shows the strong bond made with Alex Lowe who, after using the Russian fixed ropes one day, carried a load up the wall for them. In his expedition report, Samoilenko is very careful to report the differences in their routes and styles, pointing out, for example, that despite a massive difference in budgets, the Americans did not have a doctor. Michael Bakin, the Russian expedition doctor, attended to all those in the area, including Lowe, to whom he gave stitches for a wound incurred in a fall.

At the tail-end of the media event, the German team of Thomas Tivadar, Gavor Berecz and Oskar Nadasdi arrived with the intention of establishing a new route of their own up the wall, only to find the obvious lines occupied. They climbed 35 independent pitches to the left of *Parallel Worlds* before joining that route. Some 39 days and 44 pitches into it, however, they were forced to retreat short of the summit after a storm had imprisoned them in their portaledges for three days.

Rising up from the Dunge Glacier, the east face of the Trango Pulpit is a 3,000-foot wall topped by a hanging glacier. Above that towers another 1,500-foot wall. At its top (6050m), a ridge continues via a long snow shoulder to the Great Trango's Main Summit (6286m). In July and August, a Czech-Slovak team comprising Michalem Drašar, Tomáš Rinn, Pavlem Weisser, Ivo Wondráček and the sole Slovak, Jaro Dutka, fixed 700 meters of rope on the Pulpit's Southeast Ridge, climbed to its summit, then continued onto the Main Summit in a 53-pitch effort they called *More Czech, Less Slovak*. At the same time, and summitting only several days later, the sheer northeast face was climbed by the Norwegian team of Per Ludvig Skjerven, Gunnar Karlsen, Robert Caspersen and Einar Wold in an impressive capsule-style ascent. Disdaining the use of extensive fixed rope and power drills, the team committed to lightweight style, planning for 25 days up and three to four days for the descent. After 38 days of technical big wall climbing, during which they reached the top of the Pulpit with no food, they set foot back on the Dunge Glacier, a full adventure behind them.

Of the new routes mentioned above, Yuri Koshelenko, Jared Ogden and Robert Caspersen relate their respective climbs in detail in the pages that follow, while Thomas Tivadar and Vlado Linek note the other two ascents in the Climbs and Expeditions section on pages 335 and 336. Combined with a number of fine efforts on nearby formations such as Shipton Spire, which saw a repeat of the 1997 route *Ship of Fools*, another new route on Nameless Tower, plus a flurry of applications for permits to the area peaks for the year 2000, it is becoming increasingly obvious that "the ultimate challenge of verticality, uncertain weather conditions and altitude" is being met in the Karakoram. What will the future behold for the mighty Trango Towers? The wonderful spirit captured by climbing bolder, lighter and faster will hopefully prevail.

The Trango Pulpit

A journey under the skin

by Robert Caspersen, *Norway*

W et snow entered the neck of my Gore-Tex. Looking up, my eyes stung with pain as the weather hammered down. I pulled up my hood. I couldn't help smiling. Out in the mist, ten meters horizontally to the left of me, Gunnar was swinging on the belay-seat, directly under the lip of a small overhang that seemed to be the draining point of the summit snow-fields. He would undoubtedly be soaked by the time I finished the pitch. Under his hood, I could clearly see two burning eyes and a big yellow smile. Between us there was a fine line of short knifeblades and bent RURPs. Above me, a 40-meter, perfectly compact dihedral led the way to the top of the Pulpit's headwall. It had been 33 days since we left the safety of our Base Camp on the Dungee Glacier and 13 days since our last decent meal. There was a 1400-meter drop below our feet. We were on pitch 41, an A3+ that forced me to dig deep into my bag of tricks.

Six hours after beginning, soaked to the skin but exhilarated by my progress, I watched Gunnar clean the pitch. We had made the top of the wall! A 300-meter ridge was the only thing separating us from the Pulpit's summit.

I tried to grasp the situation. How could this be? How had it been possible to endure so much pain and uncertainty? The list of good reasons for turning back had, during the events of the last three weeks, reached a substantial size. What kept us going? Where did we find the motivation?

My eyes swept the scenery and froze on the most dominating formation to be seen: the northeast buttress of Great Trango Tower. In the rugged landscape of my consciousness, this aesthetic and awe-inspiring line had always held a special place.

In the summer of 1984, four highly capable young Norwegian climbers—Hans Christian Doseth, Finn Daehli, Stein P. Aasheim and Dag Kolsrud—helped push Himalayan climbing to a higher level with their ascent of the buttress. Rock faces of nearly the same size and technical difficulty had been climbed in other venues of the world before, but never at such an altitude.

Two-thirds of the way up the climb, at the foot of the final headwall, reality came down on them. The lower buttress had taken far more time than anticipated, their food supplies were running low and they were making slow progress on the upper wall. With great difficulty, they decided that two people with the remaining food would stand a better chance of reaching the summit than if all four continued on the minuscule rations.

Aasheim and Kolsrud rappelled off, and, after reaching the safety of the Dunge Glacier, monitored their friends' further progress. After a week, they watched with tele-lenses as Daehli and Doseth topped out on the upper headwall and climbed the mixed terrain to the vir-gin (East) summit (6432m). A triumph. Aasheim and Kolsrud then watched as their two

Great Trango Tower and Nameless Tower, showing Norwegian Pulpit Direct on the Trango Pulpit.
ROBERT CASPERSEN

friends started their descent—surely thrilled, but just as surely in great fatigue.

Halfway down the lower buttress, Daehli and Doseth suddenly vanished from view. Later, their bodies were spotted on the glacier at the foot of the climb, but before anyone could bring them out they were buried by an avalanche. The triumph had turned into a total tragedy.

Though the deaths of Daehli and Doseth made a great impact on the small and intimate climbing community in Scandinavia, the memories of their personalities and their achievements as climbers continued to inspire many a climber throughout the years. Ever since I first started climbing, I knew that one day I, too, would stand beneath the Great Trango Tower and dwell on this beautiful, enormous and seemingly blank piece of gray-and-orange rock. After all these years, the Norwegian Buttress was still the most magnificent line I'd ever seen up a big wall. The Trango Massif stood out clearly as the ultimate venue for big wall climbing. I knew the others on our team felt the same. Somehow, we had all been planning this for at least ten years. Our motivation for being here was intrinsic and deeply rooted.

Though we had never climbed together as a team of four, Gunnar Karlsen, Per Ludvig Skjerven, Einar Wold and I knew each other well, and the sum of all our experience told us that we were ready for the challenge. Luckily, we were a great team. Now, however, the strain was starting to show. For one thing, there had been a change of topics in our conversations. Of course, we were always discussing our progress and the uncertainty of the terrain that lay ahead of us—that had not changed. But now we were also talking a lot about girlfriends, families, hot showers, beer, sport climbing and all the time in a context that involved food, good food and lots thereof.

The elastic had almost gone out of the rubber band. Living on minuscule rations for the last 12 days was getting to us. Our dialogues were often colored by the odd bark. But we never fought. Our goal was too well-defined. There were no options; we were in this too deeply. We always came out laughing. The whole situation was absurd. We were united by the seeming insanity of our situation.

Still, the last week had been tough on us, both mentally and physically. We wanted out. So what kept us going? I shifted in the belay sling, sent new blood to my numb feet and looked around. The answer seemed obvious. I had felt it all the time. The surroundings were breathtaking, our exposure immense. To this point, apart from four rope-lengths across a hanging glacier, there had not been one easy pitch. Eleven pitches of interesting free climbing and 26 pitches of sustained aid climbing had made every lead a challenge. Whether placing 35 knifeblades in a row in the depths of a perfect dihedral, skyhooking in an ocean of blank granite or trembling from a copperhead or a violated birdbeak in crumbling rock, the pure beauty of the climb kept us there. The continuity of our line was beyond our imagination. It was perfect. It felt as though we were about to create a masterpiece. But of course, it had been there all the time—we were merely discovering the treasure.

And what an exciting treasure hunt it had been. . . .

After dealing with the epic bureaucracy in Islamabad, the constant death threat of the Karakoram Highway and the chaotic organizing of the porters, we had been relieved to at last arrive at the deserted Dunge Glacier.

"When we leave the ground and pull up our ropes, we're safe," we told ourselves. For four young men, all beginners in Asian traveling, simply getting to BC had been quite stressful. Our biggest fear (after, of course, being stopped by an increase in the Kashmir conflict, spending weeks in Islamabad dealing with formalities or dying on the KKH), was being too weakened by the inevitable diarrhea to be able to climb. Fortunately, we escaped with only

"Skyhooking in an ocean of blank granite:" pitch 35 on the upper headwall. ROBERT CASPERSEN

minor problems.

Half an hour after arriving at our base at the snout of the Dunge Glacier, Gunnar, Per Ludvig and I hiked a further hour and a half to have a look at the face. From the start, our goal had been the Trango Pulpit, an enormous rock face to the southeast of the Norwegian Buttress. Since we knew so little about the face and couldn't be sure whether any climbable lines up it even existed, we had paid the peak fee for the Great Trango Tower—just in case. But we had not come all this way to try to repeat an old route. We wanted the unknown; we wanted virgin rock.

We were alone on the Dunge Glacier. The weather was calm, the view astonishing. It was just like I had imagined during my ten years of anticipation.

What the Pulpit lacked in beauty when compared to the Norwegian Buttress, it gained with its size, steepness and blankness. It consisted of two rock faces on top of each other divided by a hanging glacier two-thirds of the way up. The photos showing the upper wall had been what attracted us in the first place, but once we realized the size and the complexity of the lower wall, we felt assured that we had chosen a good project. The lower wall alone was the size of El Capitan. And above it loomed a steeper version of Half Dome.

In our opinion, there was only one line of weakness through the lower wall. Fortunately, it also looked to be the least avalanche-prone of the options. That it also happened to be the most direct and longest line on the wall was no drawback. The upper wall seemed very blank, but it was too far away to properly judge if it contained a feasible line. Time would soon enough tell. For now, we were in business.

During the next two days, we fixed ropes up the initial slabs. The first seven pitches were fairly low-angled and went free at mostly 5.10 with sections of 5.11. The slabs were compact and what existed of cracks were often filled with dirt. Although the climbing was easy, it was

The initial slab pitches, with the upper headwall visible above. ROBERT CASPERSEN

often run out, and I was glad the weather permitted the use of rock shoes. After fixing our seven climbing ropes, we spent the next three days organizing our gear and carrying it one and a half hours up the glacier to the foot of the climb.

On the morning of June 28, Einar having recovered sufficiently from intestinal problems, we quit BC and moved up onto the face, pulling the ropes and committing ourselves to the climb.

On the top of the seventh pitch, we established our first camp at the far right of a big ledge, our two portaledges hanging partly sheltered by a small overhang on the steepening wall. Snow provided all the water we needed. Just to the left, a constant stream of rocks fell down, caused by meltwater from the hanging glacier above. We immediately named the camp "Karakoram Highway," but, upon discovering that we were out of the target zone as long as we stayed close to the tents, soon learned to live with the sound of the passing "trucks."

Above us, two more pitches of slightly harder free climbing followed before we had to shift to aid. The rock became very compact and the protection intricate. We followed a huge left-facing dihedral for seven pitches. The "Dream Dihedral" required sustained nailing with extensive use of knifeblades and Lost Arrows and some sections of copperheading and sky hooking, the rock seldom permitting the use of nuts and camming devices. One expansion bolt was often placed by hand-drill at the belays.

After a long period of fine conditions, the weather turned unstable and what started out as light snow often ended in heavy rain in the afternoon. We were forced to spend one day in our tents at the Karakoram Highway, the cascades of water just increasing the "traffic" nearby. After a day of immobilization, the weather cleared and we were able to establish Camp II at the top of pitch 14. As there were no more snow ledges on the lower face, we hauled with us more than 100 liters of water from Camp I to supply us until we reached the hanging glacier.

Camp II also had its surprises, but only of the pleasant kind. Next to our portaledges, a small, one-meter by one-meter ledge was overgrown with beautiful flowers and big leaves of rhubarb. Yes! Rhubarb! I couldn't believe my eyes; I had to taste it, and yes, there was no doubt.

I had had my share of winter escapades in Norway, climbed two big walls in Antarctica and come to the Karakoram prepared for cold conditions. Being at more than 5000 meters above sea level, the mild weather surprised us all. But we did not complain. Only when it rained would we have preferred cold conditions and dry snow.

From the "Rhubarb" camp, the climbing got steeper and less straight-forward. The line passed through some roofs and sharp corners interspersed with blank sections. It was strenuous climbing in "rope-cutting country." The grades soon touched A3+ and A4, and our speed was reduced to that of a lazy snail.

On the 13th day, we could again erect our tents at a new camp. Above, we entered the "Guillotine," a beautiful yellow prow that turned out to be "the kingdom of anxiety." I was at the sharp end. I had climbed 15 meters of singing rock and above me hung the biggest and most dislocated piece of rock I had ever encountered on a climb. I searched in vain for the warning tag indicating its maximum weight load. Directly below me, Per Ludvig was pinned to the belay. One pitch further down, the rest of the family was resting in our homes. One miscalculation, Robert, that's all it takes. I got my hammer out and did a sound check, carefully tapping the monstrous block. This was rock 'n roll, alright! The pitch took me one and a half days to finish.

Immediately above followed another one of those time-consuming A4 pitches. For two hours, I hung from the belay, listening to Einar curse as he cleaned the pitch. Most of the metal was hammered into the rock with no thoughts for the seconding climber. Einar had hung motionless, belaying me for hours. When he finally clipped in next to me, I was prepared for some moaning, but instead he met my concerned expression with a broad smile. We were in this together.

Wet snow and heavy rainfall again cramped us in our tents for one-and-a-half days before we were able to establish Camp IV below the rim of the lower wall. Pitch 25 brought us up and onto the hanging glacier, which turned out to be easy, homogenous terrain, approximately 180 meters wide.

Our main goal had always been to climb the most direct and central line through the upper headwall. This was the grand prize: five to six hundred meters of overhanging and seemingly blank rock. Helped by vivid imagination, we were able to trace a thin continuous line of formations that cut through the middle of the face. But by the time we got there, we had already spent 20 days ascending the lower face, and what loomed above looked desperate.

There was another line on the left-hand side of the face that we had briefly discussed as a possible alternative if we were running short on time or food. It had far more features, bigger cracks, was less steep and shorter. It looked like it would go fast—and we were in great need of some fast progress, having only ten days' food left.

As Per Ludvig and I descended back to Camp IV, a huge rock-fall demolished the lower part of the possible "escape" line. The die had been thrown. We cut our daily rations to 1350 kcal per person, moved up and established Camp V at the foot of the Pulpit Headwall.

The opening pitches on the upper face gave us a taste of things to come. Flaky formations divided by compact sections made for interesting climbing, with several pitches going at around A3+/A4 as the route traversed diagonally to the right. When the weather deteriorated again, we climbed in perfectly dry conditions; the route was so steep, the curtain of heavy weather hung 15 meters out in space. Good. We deserved some luck.

On pitch 33 I ran out of luck (or had even more luck, depending on how you see it). I took a leader fall. I had already taken a handful on the climb, so this was no big surprise, but this time I landed upside-down onto a sharp flake. It felt as though my body had been cut in half. I screamed in shock, then almost fainted as the pain rose. I could not put any weight on my right foot. With great difficulty I finished the pitch, then retired to my sleeping bag, where I stayed for two days, eating painkillers.

The others had now arrived at a big section of blank rock and were bathooking at a snail's pace, so I wasn't missing out on much. The thought of being left with a stove and a bag of food while I waited for the rest of the team to pick me up on their way back down from the summit got me well in no time, and I was soon back up there with them, swinging the hammer.

Camp VI was established at the top of pitch 33, and again we hauled with us 100 liters of snow/water. It took us four and a half days to finish the two pitches of bathooking and reach more formations.

The slow progress was draining our reserves. The exhaustion of leading was obvious, but belaying for ten to 12 hours was even worse. On lead, your focus is zoomed in as you concentrate on the task of getting up the next few meters of rock. Passages might be scary, but having mastered them, you are rewarded with a great feeling of accomplishment. Belaying is usually a completely different story. You are in position to set your focus on wide-angle. And, given enough time to reflect on your situation, you tend to do so.

There were two different personality types who descended to camp in the evening. One had a gleam in his eyes. He babbled with enthusiasm, seeing only challenges. The other was filled with concern. He posed critical questions, saw only problems and had a long list of good reasons to get the hell out of there. That evening, coming down from a strenuous day of bathooking, Gunnar had the gleam. He truly enjoyed life on the big walls.

On day 30 we established our last camp on the climb, Camp VII, at the top of pitch 37. Directly above this camp, the climb followed a left-slanting line that we had hoped would be easy ground. Once again, hard and intricate nailing along loose flakes, expanding rock and small overhangs slowed us down. Things were looking grim.

Partly as a result of my own ruthless drive, Per Ludvig had too often ended up at the dead end of the rope, building a nest in his wide-angled world and slowly growing more defensive. Now, however, he had finally awakened. His focus had changed, and he was leading with great confidence, getting the most out of every day.

Pitches 40 and 41 climbed a dominating dihedral and finally put us on top of the actual rock face. The only remaining ridge led to the Pulpit's summit. On day 34 the weather again forced us to seek refuge in our tents. At this stage, we only had food for one more day, so we had to reach the summit the following day regardless of the weather.

At two o'clock in the morning on August 1, we left Camp VII in obscure and foggy conditions and jumared to the top of our ropes. From there we started up the ridge with two climbing ropes and a light rack. The first two pitches involved some moderate mixed climbing in a chimney and a slab section that felt desperate in plastic boots. On the ridge we found rappel anchors from the Czech-Slovak climbers who had summited a couple of days earlier via the Southeast Ridge. Our last six pitches were in common with theirs.

Four easy pitches of snow plodding along a thin ridge brought us to the Pulpit's summit. It was early in the afternoon on our 35th day. I was too emotionally moved to speak. We had pushed our mental and physical barriers to a new dimension.

Robert Caspersen, pitch 34. PER LUDVIG SKJERVEN

Gunnar Karlsen cleaning pitch 37 (A3+, day 31) above Camp VII.
ROBERT CASPERSEN

As we sobered up and reflected on our position, our big smiles were soon replaced by expressions of concern. Base Camp seemed awfully far away. Two weeks earlier, we had easily agreed that if we had to, we could manage without food on the descent. Other people had gone without food for more than three days. Now, however, reality came down on us. We had already been living on a less-than-appropriate diet for the last two weeks. We rested our eyes on the top of the Norwegian Buttress, thought about Hans Christian and Finn, doubled-checked one another and headed down.

Late at night, we were back in the vertical world of Camp VII, where we ate our last dinner and went to sleep. In the morning we started abseiling the Headwall with all our gear, reaching the hanging glacier at night. We had left three ropes in place on the steepest pitches so we could pull in and reach the anchors.

The next day we carried all our gear across the glacier with great difficulty. The muscle atrophy in our legs was serious, making it difficult to walk. We swung over the rim of the lower face and abseiled down to Camp II. The weather deteriorated again, but we didn't care. We were so close now.

On the 38th day, we abseiled the rest of the lower face in cascade conditions, setting foot on the Dunge Glacier late in the evening. We were very hungry and had some minor bruises from leader falls, but other than that we had suffered no major injuries, had not lost or left behind any gear apart from the rappel anchors and remained good friends all the way. The ropes no longer held us together, but there was something else, something else. . . .

SUMMARY OF STATISTICS

AREA: Pakistan Karakoram

NEW ROUTE: Norwegian Trango Pulpit Direct (VII A4 5.11, ca. 2200m) on the north-east and north faces of the Trango Pulpit (6050m), June 28-August 4, 1999 (plus two days of fixing), Robert Caspersen, Gunnar Karlsen, Per Ludvig Skjerven, Einar Wold

Robert Caspersen. EINAR WOLD

Twenty-seven-year-old Robert Caspersen started climbing in 1988. A three-time National Indoor Climbing Champion of Norway (1992, '94 and '98), he has onsighted 8a+ and red-pointed 8c. His first ascents in Norway range from big walls to crag routes. He has taken part in two expeditions to Antarctica, both led by Ivar Tollefsen. In 1993-94, he was part of the first expedition to Queen Maud Land, where he participated in ascents of Jøkulkyrkja (the range's highest peak), Gessnertind, Holtanna and Ulvetanna. In 1996-97, he returned to help make the first ascent of the Rondespire. A student at The University of Sport in Oslo, he is currently investigating free-climbing techniques.

Great Trango Tower's Northwest Face

Parallel worlds

by Jared Ogden

Our ledge, hanging cockeyed and dripping wet, was our only refuge from the tempestuous storm that had been lingering now for five days. Alex, Mark and I had tried three days in a row to lead one miserable pitch with no luck.

"I can't believe how big these snowflakes are," Mark said as he hung from the 27th belay.

"Yeah," I said in a chattering voice. "Look, our ropes are soaked—and if it gets any colder, we're screwed!"

Alex was on lead, again. This was his third time trying the pitch. It was cold and storming hard. Mark rappelled; he didn't have Gore-Tex on and was soaked. I watched him rap into the swirling void and heard frustrating yells all the way down. The ropes were icing up and he had to take out his knife to clear them—a dangerous endeavor, as he was on the verge of hypothermia.

"God damn," Alex moaned with a chuckle from above. "This sucks! You see the water flowing out of my jacket? I can't believe this!"

"You think we should bail for the day?" I begged from my frozen belay.

"Yeah. My hands are numb and I can't feel what I'm doing. Let's go down," said Alex.

Out of 15 days, only seven or eight hadn't been lashing, storm-ridden suffer-fests. We wondered if we had the determination.

In the history of the Trango Towers, there are grand successes and harsh failures. Legendary climbers have flocked to the area to make their mark in the world of alpine climbing and challenge themselves on the mighty walls. There have been bolt-free first ascents, demanding aid routes, all-free ascents of aid routes and all-free first ascents. Unlimited opportunities exist, and we had our sights set on Great Trango Tower.

In 1997, Mark Synnott and I were on our way to climb Hainablak Central Tower (a.k.a. Shipton Spire) when we first saw the massive northwest face. The wall is nearly 6,000 feet. The virgin West Summit is 20,415 feet high. It surprised me that no one had tried to climb the face over the 25 years that climbers have visited the area.

"When do you think we can do it?," I asked anxiously.

"Right now! I think we should do this instead of Shipton," Mark said immediately.

We realized we couldn't do that, because our porters were already three miles ahead in Base Camp, and our rack was really small, even for Shipton. But we knew we would be back before long.

For two years, we planned to return. Our proposed route combined all the elements of rock climbing: a long free climb up a 3,400-foot slab to a vertical and overhanging headwall that stretches over 2,000 feet, finishing on a knife-edge ridge for 1,000 feet to the West Summit. As with any expedition, however, we had problems with funding. Selling half our possessions and praying we'd be lucky had funded our Shipton Spire trip. With the same

WEST SUMMIT →

─ High Point: "LOST BUTTERFLY"

Approximate West Ridge

HEAD WALL

LOWER ICEFIELD

ENTRY SLABS

"THE RUSSIAN HAT"
(Camps Shown)
(July 15-Aug 10)

LOST BUTTERFLY
(July 17-Sept 5)
(Camps Shown)

PARALLEL WORLDS
(July 2-Aug 1)
(No Camps Shown)

"Harmless Caibir"

Great Trango
Northwest Face
⟡ 1999 ⟡

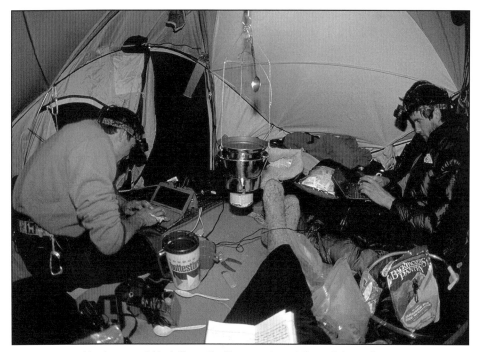

Alex Lowe and Mark Synnott with computers at Camp I. Jared Ogden

resourcefulness, we pulled together more than we had bargained for on Trango.

We were to make a film and host a live internet site. The logistics were horrendous, and we would have to make compromises to accommodate the media. I was struggling with my conscience. Was this unethical? Would we deface the alpine climbing world by using a powerdrill and fixed lines?

Indeed, these were some of the problems that we were facing as a team. We wanted to climb the wall as we have done many times in the past: committing ourselves to the highest standards of climbing practices and minimizing fixed ropes. But on this trip we would fix more than 3,000 feet of rope and spend a month on the wall, carrying computers and all assortments of cyberspace technology and video cameras on the climb. I saw this as an intrusion on what I had experienced in the past. What had happened to the solitude and silence of the Shipton Spire days? Wouldn't we be criticized? I became frustrated and wanted nothing to do with it.

At least, that's what I was thinking in the beginning. It all changed once on the wall. Solitude abounded. The silence was broken only by a solitary gorak soaring the mysterious thermals up high into the heavens or the distant rumbling of the glaciers buckling under their own weight. Once again, we were climbing in the magnificence of the Karakoram with the complexities of the world left behind.

While gazing out on this magnificence, I heard Mark shout, "That was amazing!" as he reached the top of pitch 16.

"A bit scary, though, running it out over pins placed single-handed on lead," he added when I met him at his belay. He was full of vigor and high on the experience. He later told me it was one of his favorite pitches.

A few pitches later, after reaching Camp II, we were relaxing in our ledge when we heard distant foreign voices.

"Did you hear that?" Alex asked, surprised. We thought we had lost it. We heard it again and made our way over to the edge to see what it was. Just a week earlier, we heard there was a four-man Russian team that had arrived to do the same climb. Could they be here already?

Moments later we were sharing a brew with Ivan Samoilenko, Igor Potankin, Alexander Odintsov and Yuri Koshelenko, talking about the Caucasus, mutual friends and how no one had yet broken Alex's speed record on Khan Tengri. When we saw the antique equipment they were using, we wondered how they had even arrived at this point. Alexander was wearing a leather carpenter's belt that held their pitons as Ivan jumared with legging straps that hooked into rings on his ascenders—something you would find on an arborist. When asked if they would lose their pins in a fall, Alexander simply replied, "Don't fall."

Ivan showed me their hand drill. Looking like a relic from the 17th century, it had a bit on one end, a rubber hand-pump mechanism in the middle like that on a stethoscope and a hardened butt to hammer on.

"Eye ave been using diss a drill for feefteen years!" he proudly announced. The bit was as blunt as a worn eraser, and they only had a few removable bolts, also from a long time ago. It was fascinating to watch them climb. We had a great time shouting across the wall to each other as we made progress.

We found the first headwall pitches to be featureless. Hooking, beaking and riveting linked up to a beautiful left-facing dihedral. Overhead, the wall reared up in a wave of golden granite, with dark roofs looming above.

Alex spoke of his family often. He carried photos of his three boys in his pocket at all times and occasionally brought them out to look at. He was a proud father, telling stories about them with longing and devotion. Mark, too, talked about his newborn son, William.

Looking across the valley to the southeast face of Nameless Tower and further up the glacier to the tiny summit of Shipton Spire, I could relive some of the greatest days of my life by recounting the experiences I had while climbing routes on these two formations. The mysterious energy and silence of the place brings tranquillity and humility deep into my heart and soul. Alex called it the Heartland. He was right.

The climbing was ethereal. Tapping and ringing of hammer and piton resounded through the thinning air. Our fears and doubts were being left behind with every inch we gained, giving each of us more confidence to push on in the face of deteriorating weather and dwindling food rations.

Camp III: The weather nearly shut us down. Mark and Alex were on a tightrope with their friendship. Caught in the middle, I tried to keep everyone focused on the objective, myself included. The stress of climbing all day and working more than three hours a night to type e-mails and download and transmit digital images for the internet was taking its toll. I kept thinking the intrusion was too much. It was going to break us apart. We all felt it. We could read it in each others' eyes.

I finished another long technical pitch, again with no drilling. Mark had run out a pitch on 15 beaks interspersed with manky blades and rivets to connect the blank sections. Alex avoided a deadly block by blading up a seam that ended on a blank wall. He faced a potential 150-foot fall as he resorted to hand-drilling 20 bat hooks in a row on a 110-degree wall to reach the end of his rope.

Following our ascent, criticism would circulate around how we drilled holes through blank sections. At the time, we were all struggling with the decision. Do we climb the wall without a drill? What if we fail as a result of a blank section? Do we leave the mountain as we found it? Or do we drill and climb to the top in the best style possible? We all agreed that we would place the least amount of holes possible to maintain a high standard and still make the summit.

The Great Roof

We always knew it would be dramatic. A horizontal roof 25 feet straight out to the lip on thin blades hammered straight up into a crusty seam. I tried to swallow my stomach out of my throat and managed to meekly spurt out a shout to Mark.

"Hey, watch me here," I yelled. "I had to back clean, so it's a little sketchy."

Alex (with a fever) managed to jug up to the roof to film Mark cleaning in golden sunlight. It was breathtaking. Uli Biaho was cloaked in a crimson blanket as the sun set over the distant summits of the Latok Group.

The route opened up to free climbing at this point. We would leave the next morning with a pack on our back and blast for the top. We carried two ropes, a small set of pitons, cams, slings and a little bivy gear.

The following morning, Alex leapt off the belay and didn't stop until he reached the ridge 800 feet higher. He was yelling incoherently about something. We figured he still had a fever. When we got to him, we understood.

It wasn't tragic, but it felt like it. Staring in disbelief, we all relished the splendor that the Karakoram has to offer. More and more, I remember that moment. I recall it all coming together right then. Everything that climbing is about happened at that spot.

All the walls had fallen away. The hard work and suffering had rewarded us with more than we had bargained for. Clear skies stretched out to distant peaks separating the Baltoro from the heavens. It was silent except for the ghostly rumble of the glaciers eating away at the mountains. The heavens had opened up and given us a brief spell of luck, just enough to make it to the summit. We knew we would succeed, and it showed on our faces. We were so far from home, but we all felt right there with everyone, as if everything was connected. It looked so much like a dream that we spent a long hour just staring out into it all and absorbing our accomplishment.

We made quick work of the remaining six pitches. Alex took a 50-foot whipper just below the summit but survived with a bad laceration to his right elbow. The summit was 25 feet away. We couldn't reach it because it was a blank slab and we had no drill. If you want it, go for it.

The skies closed back down and it stormed for another three days as we suffered through the most harrowing descent we have done. It was dangerous, but we made it. We came down to a BIG party. There were several more expeditions there, and some Germans even gave us a few beers to celebrate with. It was great to see all our friends.

We spent the next day retrieving our gear from the wall and packing loads. We left the next morning in a storm. Looking back up the wall, we could faintly make out our Russian comrades. They had a long way to go.

On the hike out, we all walked far apart from one another. We had gone through so much. It was very intense to be up there with all the world watching. We had more bad weather than

Alex Lowe cleaning pitch 30. JARED OGDEN

Alex Lowe jumaring on the headwall. JARED OGDEN

good, and it wore us thin. It wasn't the best trip we'd ever done, but we did finish our route.

Parallel Worlds was huge, perhaps the longest rock climb ever. I speak on behalf of our team in that we did it for ourselves first, then for all the masses to praise and slander. Who knows, in the future, we might see routes like this climbed in a day or soloed without a rope. In the end, the whole ordeal was really quite simple: it was about three climbers who wanted a challenge, a hard-earned adventure that would bring us all together. We hope it will stand as a tribute to Alex, who always put 110 percent into whatever he did.

SUMMARY OF STATISTICS

AREA: Pakistan Karakoram

NEW ROUTE: *Parallel Worlds* (VII 5.11 A4, 6,000') on the northwest face of the Great Trango Tower (20,415'), July 2-August 1, 1999, Alex Lowe, Jared Ogden, Mark Synnott

PERSONNEL: Mark Synnott, Alex Lowe, Jared Ogden, Darren Britto, Greg Thomas, Jim Surrette, Mike Graber

Jared Ogden

Jared Ogden was born in 1971. He has extensive professional experience working for companies such as The North Face, La Sportiva and Black Diamond, and his work as a photojournalist has been published in more than 20 publications. His climbing resume includes numerous first ascents, from mixed climbs such as *Cold Cold World* (M8+) and *Hardline* (M8+) to wall routes in Pakistan (*Book of Shadows* on the Nameless Tower, *Ship of Fools* on Shipton Spire) and Baffin Island (*Rum, Sodomy and the Lash* on Sail Peak). In 1997, he was the ice climbing champion in both speed and difficulty for the ESPN Winter X-Games. He currently lives in Durango, Colorado.

The Russian Way

Cameraderie and tribute on the Great Trango Tower

by Yuri Koshelenko, *Russia*
translated by Igor Politiko, with Henry Pickford

Parallel worlds: the American (left) and Russian teams hard at work on the headwall pitches.
YURI KOSHELENKO

I first heard the name Trango in 1992, when I had just begun climbing in competitions.* The very combination of the word's sounds evoked profound respect, eliciting associations with something fantastically monumental, inaccessible and distant, like the moon. The second stage of my growing familiarity with Trango occurred in 1996, when I agreed to participate in the project "The Russian Way: The Walls of the World." The Great Trango Tower, which would involve Alexander Odintsov as leader, Ivan Samoilenko as cameraman, Igor Potankin and me, was one of the objectives of the Project.

Time passed, and the mountain became a concrete goal, the center around which revolved our thoughts and deeds, our aspirations and emotions. I re-read "Grand Voyage," the article by John Middendorf, dozens of times, using it as a tuning fork with which to adjust my mental

---

*For an explanation of the climbing competitions of the former Soviet Union, see 1997 *AAJ*, pp. 108-111.

attitude toward the coming ascent.

Up until February, 1999, we lacked comprehensive information about all the aspects of the Great Trango Tower. We knew only that one wall had not been climbed. Things came into focus when, during the Piolet d'Or ceremony in Chamonix, we were helped by Bernard Domenech, who had found the book by Patrik Cordier, *Cathedrals de Trango*, in the inner vaults of the ENSA library.

This was the first time that we had seen the northwest face of the Great Trango. The impression it made on us was so deep that the decision to climb it came absolutely naturally. There was only one enigma. In spite of the relative popularity of the region, there had been no attempts made on the wall. This spoke indirectly of its great difficulty. The wall was so original and striking, both from the front and the side, that it couldn't be confused with anything else. The most exciting part of the wall was its steep, curved profile, which resembled the arched chest of a bird. The very thought that our route might lie here made my heart pound and the blood rush to my face, as though I were on my first date. All in all, the mountain's shape reminded me of a rocket hurtling upward that we would have to chase during our ascent. Everything about the photo of the wall moved, excited, and challenged us. During the following months, the pictures from Cordier's book became my treasure, my irrational bond with the future, the truth of my life, my goal, my dream.

But the aura of magic and poetry surrounding our future encounter with The Mountain dissolved in the prose of the preparations for the expedition. The pace of our planning and packing accelerated each day until our departure for Pakistan.

We arrived in Karachi on June 25 with the intention of crossing the entire country by train and auto. The reason for such a circuitous approach was simple: Russian Aeroflot flies only to Karachi, and only Aeroflot offered us the open-date return ticket for the money we had.

Inured to Central Asian trains during the rosy days of developing socialism, our team fearlessly occupied a compartment in the so-called "sleeping car" of the passenger train. The compartment consisted of a window replete with a grate, two fans of monstrous design, four berths hardly distinguishable from prison plank beds and a very hot and dense interior. Whenever the train moved, dust obscured our compartment, settling upon all the immovable objects in a uniform yellow-gray layer, allowing each of us to repeatedly marvel at the lifelike imprint of our bodies on the surface of the plank bed. This hallucination lasted about 40 hours. Nonetheless, it's probably worth it to take such a journey once in your life.

In Rawalpindi at the Ministry of Tourism, we were told about an American team that, to all appearances, had already begun working on the northwest face of Great Trango. We already knew about their expedition, and the news didn't worry us too much. The unclimbed wall of the Great Trango Tower was great enough to give both teams the possibility to test their skills and persistence. The question of who should start up first was not so important to us, because if both groups were successful, both routes would be put up in 1999.

On July 7, our team arrived at BC. The northwest face of Great Trango rose straight above our camp—about 40 minutes, and you are on the route. The Americans by now seemed like the old-timers there; they had climbed the lower part of the wall, and were shooting video and a film and making reports from the wall twice a day. If our arrival slightly surprised them, they nevertheless met us very cordially. Our meeting was consolidated by an evening party after the American climbers and film crew descended to BC from their preparations higher up.

We admired what the Americans had achieved on the Trango. They climbed the wall and at the same time brought the extreme energy of their ascent to the entire world via the internet. This made our common mission many-sided: alpinism, friendship and the grandeur of the mountain spirit had to triumph simultaneously and harmoniously.

From BC, the wall seemed like the nose of a warship with its prow cutting through space. After some consultation with the American team of Alex Lowe, Mark Synnott and Jared Ogden about their route, we planned our line to the right of theirs, along the left side of the overhanging "prow." We understood how difficult the main part of the wall was, but the desire to make a fine route and the requirements of safety ultimately convinced us that our decision was correct.

On July 14, Alex, Mark and Jared went up to finish what they had begun. Seven fixed ropes on the main part of the wall was not a bad start, yet all the same they spoke of the climbing on their route with considerable restraint: "very monolithic, smooth..."

Our team fixed all the static ropes we had on the 15th and 16th. After one final day of preparation, we started up. That day, Alex, who had descended the day before, was ascending the fixed lines parallel to us. We saluted each other warmly, which increased our good mood throughout the following sunny day.

Sleeping by pairs in portaledges on the vertical sections and in our one Bibler tent (all four of us together) on the ledges, our team reached the big ledge under the main part of the wall in four days. For the next three days the weather didn't pamper us: wet snow, water, sand and endless carries trashed half of our working ropes.

On July 21, after a morning carry in wet snow, Alexander Odintsov climbed the last two and a half pitches that separated us from the main wall and visited Alex, Mark and Jared. We set up our camp 100 meters below theirs. It seemed to me that the next period was emotionally the brightest time of the whole ascent.

The next day, after the obligatory descent for a load in the morning, Igor Potankin, Alexander and I, along with Ivan Samoilenko, our high-altitude cameraman, started climbing, and fixed our first rope on the main part of the wall. I dodged the falling stones that Ivan was sending down from the upper ledges, watching in horror as they ricocheted on the slabs close to the ropes pulled taut by my weight. Climbing up to the ledge and suffering nothing more than a slightly bruised shoulder, I was unexpectedly seized by the warm hospitality of the American team. I took huge gulps of piping hot tea from Alex's cup while thinking about the condition of the wet rock, in my mind selecting the gear I would need. On the whole, the evening was a success. While belaying me, Ivan told tales about Russian gear, and I climbed the pitch, took some photos and then descended to our tent via a route less prone to rockfall.

The schedule remained the same for the next few days. We carried loads from dawn onward, and toward evening fixed ropes and prepared the route.

Between the Americans and ourselves there developed genuine mutual assistance. They let us contact our doctor using their walkie-talkie, and we left our ropes for them so that they could descend for foodstuffs more quickly, for they had moved their ropes that had been closest to the ledge to the main wall. On his way back up, Alex brought along all our ropes and anchors, observing, "a dry run is a loss for the state."

On July 24, our teams said goodbye to one another. Alex, the very epitome of strength and skilled training, started ascending the fixed ropes first, in one go carrying a haulbag, a smaller haulbag and a portaledge, each tied to the next. Mark set off silently and Jared, radiating joy and mischief, turned 360s on his rope.

We had a veritably difficult, dangerous, hopeless section of climbing next: a consecutive series of roofs increased outwardly like an Archimedan screw as we climbed up. Unreliable vanishing cracks gave way to overhangs and "washboards," crumbling, out-sloping roofs and blind corners. We understood now what the Americans had told us: that no matter where we

Rock and roll, Russian style. YURI KOSHELENKO

tried to climb, there was no route. The terrain was of the utmost difficulty, terrible A3 and A4 sections, sometimes compounded by dangerous 5.10 to 5.11 free climbing. At times a tiny crack behind a roof would look promising, but then it would either disappear or end abruptly.

On July 26, Alexander, while climbing a roof, pulled off a huge block. For some time both rock and man flew together, before a jerk of implacable force tried to drag me through the eye of the nearest carabiner, my self-belay torn away. Alexander managed to part company with his dangerous granite companion; thanks to a stepped overhang, the block hurled downward without touching the wall, while Alexander, forsaking his deadly trajectory, was caught by a well-placed cam. But he hadn't cheated fate completely: the stone had injured his hip and shoulder. From a distance, the red webbing on his drill looked like blood stains on a smashed wrist. On this day, he fell two more times, but not as badly.

The tension of our ascent increased from day to day. On the 29th, having taken a minimum of food and water (60 liters), we left the big ledge and went upward into the unknown. Our hopes of finding less difficult terrain were fatally crushed each day. There was unstable weather: the new moon was approaching. And it was raining—at 5400 meters!

On the 30th, toward evening, we saw our American friends. They had done their work and, soaked by a downpour, were descending via their line of ascent. The ascent was over for them and the happiest time in a climber's life lay ahead: the victorious return. It was somewhat sad to feel that now we were alone with the wall; although we had competed a bit, for the most part we had encouraged and supported each other.

Each day on this wall was dramatic in its own way. We battled with all our might, opposing the severe and impersonal elemental forces of Trango with our will, experience and skill. Rain and wet snow interfered incessantly with our plans, but nevertheless, on August 3, we climbed between two roofs we called the "sickle" and the "eye." The next day—Ivan's birthday—we moved our camp, in the process getting ourselves soaked from head to foot. It was simply a miracle that nobody fell ill. I could virtually see the burning face of pneumonia before it was suddenly washed away by stronger emotions: Ivan incorrectly loaded the rope I had fixed and slid down over the edge of an overhang. It looked as if he had fallen. My feelings were so intense and powerful that it took me an hour and a half to struggle with them, during which time Ivan safely worked his way back to the platform and was already drinking tea, celebrating his birthday by himself.

On this and the next two days, although we did not advance much, we did solve a riddle composed of two roofs. Igor had finished the traverse begun by Alexander, and, after completing two pendulums one right after the other, found himself at the base of a beautiful crack and chimney system that led right to the ridge. It was a new type of climbing on the main wall, and after the terrible lower pitches, filled as they had been with fear and uncertainty, I simply reveled in climbing these outstanding cracks.

On August 8, we dropped our haulbag and two portaledges and made the spurt to the ridge but stopped one pitch short, spending the night in our Bibler on a small ledge that seemed as if it had been hewn out of the vertical for just this purpose. The ridge was moderately difficult, with individual cruxes. The accumulated fatigue and heavy loads (video and photographic gear alone weighed around 20 kilos) prevented us from reaching the summit that day.

The morning of August 10 didn't want to let us out of our tent. Mighty snow squalls and winds warned us plain and simple against climbing. The weather in the afternoon turned out to be somewhat better, but more guileful. After lunch, Igor and I began the assault on the summit tower; Alexander and Ivan were to strike and move our bivouac. From what we could see, there were two pitches of difficult rock and mixed climbing ahead. It required two attempts to climb the first pitch, which badly delayed us. Night was falling; it snowed intermittently. A snow and ice slope was partially punctuated by ice-covered rocks. Somewhere behind them lay the summit. I put my crampons on and climbed to the point where the top of this slope merged with the inky-gray sky. My crampons were gnashing on a few final meters of rock; only a straightforward section of snow remained to be climbed.

Suddenly, my ice axe started to buzz shrilly. Then it seemed like all around me was buzzing as well. The first lightning bolt struck somewhere in the distance; the second struck a rock on the ridge where I was planning to set up an anchor. The invisible howitzer gunner took aim. The next strike was behind me: I was bracketed by his shots. Grabbing all the gear, I made a few more obstinate steps toward the slabs I took to be the summit, in order to touch them with my hand. I don't know what it was, a direct hit from above or more likely an electrical discharge from below, but my desire to stick around yielded, finally, to my awakening instinct for self-preservation.

But our trials didn't end there. On August 11, during a moderate snowstorm, we were traversing a relatively complicated ridge after the summit. I should add that our supplies had largely run out toward the end of our climb. Our ration consisted basically of garlic and dehydrated potatoes, which several of us could not bring ourselves to eat.

Forty meters before the col between our summit and the central summit of Great Trango, something irreparable happened. During a difficult rappel, Ivan lost his balance and slid down along the ridge, dropping his haulbag that contained all the film and photo equipment as well as the film he'd already shot. As it later turned out, that haulbag also contained all his documents, money and credit cards, upon which we very much depended. In an hour, as though confirming the irreversibility of this event, the waning sun appeared from behind the clouds. It was a solar eclipse.

The image was surrealistic and terrible. If at that moment the mountains around us turned into an ocean or the heavens crashed upon the earth, I would not have been surprised.

After a short pause on the col, we continued our descent. True, we couldn't get by without another overnight bivouac. On August 12 at mid-day, we fell into the merciful hands of Doctor Bakin who, while waiting for us, had healed all the residents of BC in the best tradition of doctors, winning for himself love and esteem. On August 9, he even attempted to climb up to the col with an Austrian climber but was forced to turn back due to a bad bivouac and poor weather.

This story would be incomplete if I did not recount the two subsequent days of attempts to find the haulbag on the southeast slopes of Great Trango. Twice Ivan and I went in search. He was certain that the lost items awaited him at a certain point "x". Our second search attempt reminded us of an ascent. Reaching the col between the first and main summits of Trango, we climbed about 200 meters higher and traversed the slope. However, if there was anything there, the nightly snowfall and avalanches buried any hope of finding it. Someone joked that now all the film Ivan had shot belonged to posterity.

Our stay in Karakoram was coming to an end. We had made the ascent. Together with Alex, Mark and Jared, we, as it were, slipped through an ever-so-slightly-opened door of this wall. Each team, I think, rendered tribute to Trango in the form of joy, suffering, hope, persistence and exhilaration. The mountains always accept the tribute, though sometimes the price may seem excessive. But humanity cannot exist without extremes—such is the law of evolution.

SUMMARY OF STATISTICS

AREA: PAKISTAN KARAKORAM

New Route: *The Russian Way* (VII 5.11 A4, 2675m) on the "prow" of the northwest face of Great Trango Tower, July 15-August 10, 1999, Alexander Odintsov, Ivan Samoilenko, Igor Potankin, Yuri Koshelenko

PERSONNEL: Alexander Odintsov, leader; Ivan Samoilenko, high-altitude cameraman; Michael Bakin, expedition doctor; Igor Potankin; Yuri Koshelenko

Yuri Koshelenko, from Rostov-on-Don, Russia, began climbing in 1983. Since 1992, he has been a member of the Area Mountain Federation team, coached by Alexander Pogorelov.

Yuri Koshelenko. P. TOURNAIRE

Among his ascents are numerous Russian grade 5s and 6s in the Caucasus, Turkestan Gorge, Crimea, and Pamir-Alai, a new route on the Petit Dru (1998) and six ascents of 7000-meter peaks in the CIS. In the Russian national competitions, he has placed first in the high altitude class (1992 and 1993), the winter class (1994 and 1998) and the rock class (1997). He has been a Master of Sport since 1994 and an International Master of Sport since 1997. In 1998, he was rated the best climber in Russia according to that country's rating systems. In addition to his role in the Great Trango Tower climb, his ascents as part of The Russian Project include new routes on Peak 4810 (1996), Norway's Troll Wall (1997) and Bhagirathi III (1998).

Amin Brakk

A5 with a view

by Sílvia Vidal, *Spain*
translated by Christian Santelices

Pakistan, once again—its people, its streets, its odors and, why not, its bartering and characteristic discussions. Exhausting, yes, but very enchanting as well. Pep Masip and I had returned, this time with Miquel Puigdomènech, with a clear objective: to try to climb Amin Brakk, an immense granite massif without too many obvious crack systems.

Pep and I visited the country the year before with the intention of climbing Brakk Zang, a virgin needle 4860 meters high (see *AAJ* 1999, p. 398). We used our ascent to definitively study the Amin Brakk area as well. We took photos, looked for the most logical lines, the safest areas, observed the hours of the sun. . . and also tried to figure out the true size of Amin Brakk's west face, because there was not too much information on either Amin Brakk or the valley in which it is located. Our first trip was very important, for with it we were able to lay the groundwork for our future ascent.

Thus, at the beginning of June, 1999, we landed in Islamabad, the capital of Pakistan, with the intention of making our way to Amin Brakk Base Camp as quickly as possible. From the last town, which we arrived at by car, we looked for porters who would carry our barrels of gear to BC and also the two to three hours up the glacier to ABC (4575m).

We stayed in BC for 15 days, sharing it with Josh and Anthony, two Kiwi friends who helped us remember that climbing and traveling are a lifestyle. While we acclimatized, we climbed to ABC to stock it for when we would live there later. Then from ABC, we carried all of the gear and supplies to the base of the wall and fixed the first five pitches of the route.

Our route began with a 250-meter snow ramp that we had to climb many times while carrying a lot of weight (which is why it took us so long to get off the ground). To save having to carry water up the snow ramp, we filled our bottles at the first anchor, where there was a crack running with water. With a small plastic tube and a lot of patience we filled the 109 bottles we thought would be necessary for the climb. (Though there were no ledges on the line we took, we had no problems with water, as we were able to collect snow from the portaledge fly.) Twenty days after reaching ABC, we began living on the wall.

We calculated we would need 28 days for the climb. As it turned out, it took 32. Bad weather contributed to this, forcing our decision, after 12 days on the wall, to ration the little bit of food in our haulbags. And so we reached the point where all of our conversations took on a similar theme: food. "Hey! Have you been to that new restaurant downtown...?"

We decided to go up the center of the west face of Amin, because, although it looked like a difficult line, it was very elegant and at the same time appeared to be more protected from rockfall. Yet we still had an unfortunate occurrence. On our fourth day at midday, an avalanche of snow and ice fell, ripping the fly and breaking one of the ledge's tubes. We had to quickly fix it with some cord, duct tape and one of the aluminum steps of our aiders. The invention worked, lasting the rest of the climb.

Puigdomènech cleaning one of the A5 pitches. SÍLVIA VIDAL

The days passed, and little by little we began to realize the enormous number of days we were going to need to ascend the wall. But the truth is that you end up creating a routine that you can live with. In a month on the wall, there are moments of everything. Because we're talking about a lot of days with only two partners and above all living in a very reduced communal space, good relations with your partners are very important.

We only had one book, which we re-read many times, and some games that we used to pass the time in bad weather. It wasn't much, but we couldn't allow ourselves the luxury of carrying too much extra stuff. We figured that we were hauling at least 500 kilos with us up the wall. Of that, only 218 kilos were water.

The days passed, some faster than others, and we slowly kept progressing. There were pitches—the majority of which were very technical and 70 meters long—that took us three days to put up. Two A5 pitches demanded all my imagination to finish. One of them, an open corner with no cracks, took up many hours. Besides a lot of small copperheads, I had to use leadheads (seldom used on granite but typical on limestone routes) because the corner was too open for the copperheads to stick. A lot of smoke escaped from my head for every small advancement.

But the hours were worth the effort. Because that's what aid climbing is all about, right? To figure out how and where to put the gear.

Another pitch that also took a few days to climb was the tenth, a smooth slab without any natural protection where Pep had to place 27 bolts. We placed only 31 bolts on the entire route. The three of us don't believe in drilling bathook holes, because once you begin to use bathooks, you're already modifying the natural grade of the wall. For us, it would been like chipping holds on a free climb. We understood that to place solid bolts takes more time than to drill bathook holes. But our goal wasn't to move rapidly. It was to remain faithful to the style we believe in. There are no bathook holes on the whole route, because I believe that the rock and your climbing ability determines a route's grade. When you can no longer advance with what you have in front of you, it's important to recognize this point and surrender to the reality. But this is just one opinion, a very personal one that the three of us happened to share. Everyone has their own philosophy.

Climbing capsule style, making camps on the wall, means that when you change camp you gain altitude. You change the location of your home and get a new panorama. This is what fascinates me about big wall climbing: discovering, day by day, the landscape that surrounds you.

So that's how we climbed until we had made a total of four camps. We fixed three pitches above Camp IV, then climbed three more to arrive on the summit of Amin Brakk the afternoon of August 6.

A lot of people ask what you feel when you arrive at the top after so many days and so much work. The truth is that I suppose I didn't feel much on the summit, as our minds were occupied with the descent. Really, the summit awaits you down in Advanced Base Camp, not up on top where the climb is far from over.

Yet the descent remained. It took us a couple of days to carry it out, because the day we came down from the summit to Camp IV, our rope got stuck on one of the rappels. We could have cut the rope and descended with our remaining ropes, but we didn't think that was very appropriate. Since we had been cleaning everything on the route and we didn't want to leave any trash on it (we took out all of the copperheads and pitons, leaving only bolts and slings for the rappels), this meant that the following day, we devoted ourselves to climbing the pitch again to the point where the rope was stuck, then returning to Camp IV to sleep. An extra day.

The thirty-first.

On August 8, we rappelled to the ground, finally arriving at our tent in ABC. We found it very much changed, because it is on a glacier and they have a life of their own.

Now we were tired but satisfied, because we had achieved our objective of climbing this wall. And we had done it on our terms, without any type of outside assistance. We didn't bring radios or telephones or any other apparatus to communicate with the outside world. We only used whistles, with a code that we invented, to communicate with each other on the wall.

And that's our story, a story which, like all others, is very personal. Pep and Miquel will probably have their own versions. But what is certain is that we all lived our climb very intensely and were each deeply influenced by the experience.

SUMMARY OF STATISTICS

AREA: Pakistan Karakoram

FIRST ASCENT: *Sol Solet* ("Sun, Little Sun") (VII 6c+ A5 60° ice, 1650m) on Amin Brakk (5850m), July 8-August 8, 1999, Sílvia Vidal, Miquel Puigdomènech, Pep Masip

Sílvia Vidal. PEP MASIP

Sílvia Vidal, 29, from Barcelona, Spain, taught physical education until climbing caught her attention. She began climbing seriously in 1994 and a year later began aid climbing for the first time. In 1995, she traveled abroad, visiting Yosemite, where she climbed *Mescalito* with a partner (her first time on granite), then soloed *Zodiac* without fixing. The next year she soloed *Principado de Asturias* (A4) on el Naranjo de Bulnes, the biggest wall in Spain. At the same time, she began traveling and climbing further afield, climbing *Sea of Dreams* and *Reticent Wall* on El Capitan, establishing the route *Sargantana* on the Porcelain Wall and making the first ascent of Brakk Zang in Pakistan, the latter two with Pep Masip. She is currently "surviving" on her mountaineering, traveling and having fun.

Amin Brakk, showing 1. Sol Solet *(Masip-Puigdomènech-Vidal, 1999). 2.* Czech Express *(Holeček-Silhan-Šťastný, 1999; see page 344 for note).* SÍLVIA VIDAL

1

2

The Ship's Prow Solo

Learning to breathe on Baffin Island

by Mike Libecki

On the frozen ocean near the Ship's Prow. MIKE LIBECKI

May 6, 1999, 4:27 a.m. It has been 17 hours since the violent wind started its attack. I can't sleep. I lie on the frozen sea ice. So far I have fixed three pitches in between storms. I can't concentrate on this novel. I can't even hear the bell signal system for the polar bears anymore, ringing like a frustrated alarm clock over in the cook tent.

The wind's attempt to destroy my tents and freeze me continues and seems to be getting stronger. I wonder if the poles in my tent are going to break or if the seams are going to rip open. Did I secure my tents well enough? Are my fixed ropes being slashed? The attack of the wind is so incredibly loud and violent, it sounds and feels like a parachute has been constantly opening since the start of the storm. I tried my communications radio: only static, no one to be heard. Breathe in—"the time isss... ." Breathe out—"nowww... ." Don't worry: what happens, happens.

Off the coast of Baffin Island, just north of the Clark and Gibbs Fjord in the mouth of Scott Inlet, lies a small dot of land known as Scott Island. At its northernmost point is the aptly-named Ship's Prow. Just less than 2,000 feet high, this overhanging wall of granite rises directly out of, and over, the frozen ocean. For three years it had enticed me, but the opportunity to climb it only arose after other Arctic plans fell through.

In the spring of 1999, two partners and I had planned to climb what is possibly the biggest, most demanding wall on Baffin Island—almost 5,000 feet of north-facing sheer granite. We had planned to travel to this wall by traditional dog sled, something no climbers we were aware of had done here before. At the last minute, due to lack of funding and other technicalities, both partners suddenly withdrew from the expedition. Rather than give up, I decided to go solo.

The original objective had to be replaced with one that was more realistic for a soloist, especially because I had only a few days to plan my journey to go completely alone. Given its hold on my psyche, the Ship's Prow was the natural choice. I planned to climb its north wall. The ascent would entail an extraordinary 50-day adventure of harsh Arctic weather, complete with dog-sledding over the frozen ocean and hunting seal with the local people.

I arrived in Clyde River on April 23, early enough in the season for the dog teams to have plenty of time to travel on the six-foot-thick sea ice. Upon my arrival, I joined Jaycko Ashevak, his nine-year-old grandson Benji and Imosy Sivugat, the three Inuit guides who would escort me to the base of the Ship's Prow, roughly 150 miles away. We visited the six unsheltered pens that contained a couple of hundred dogs out on the open snow. Together, we fueled the dogs with raw seal meat, their main staple. They would pull our qamutiiks (long sleds used for hunting) on the journey—no small task, as each sled required 17 healthy, well-fed dogs to pull the hundreds of pounds of gear and food I brought for the climb.

After feeding the dogs, we waited for just more than a day while they digested their food and slept. I came to learn that the dogs live in their pens 365 days a year without shelter. Even more interesting, they are only fed every two to three days, no matter the situation.

The four of us traveled over the frozen ocean for the next several days. The surface ice and snow resembled shavings of glass, reflecting little sparkles of light that shone at me from every direction. It was like being inside a snowy Christmas ball decoration, the kind that you shake to set in motion all the little glittery snowflakes.

In the Arctic morning twilight of our fourth day, the distinct point of the Ship's Prow came into view through the fog. We were now just a day away from the wall. We set up camp after 14 hours of travel just as the temperature plummeted to -22° Fahrenheit.

The next day, instead of immediately taking me to my goal, the guides wanted to take advantage of the unusually clear and cold weather to hunt for seal. I was invited to join them and gladly accepted. It was a welcome interruption to the daily routine. It also allowed me to stall for time: in just a couple of days, they were going to drop me off and leave me alone for five weeks. I must admit, I was a little nervous about being alone out here. It didn't help that they mentioned there was a 50-50 chance of a polar bear coming to see what I was up to or how I tasted.

Four days became six as we hunted, ate seal and bannock (local homemade bread) and took care of the dogs. At feeding time, we watched the 51-strong pack devour ten seals in just minutes. The dogs consumed everything except the blubber, which is too tough for them to chew. They even crunched down the bones. Blood and guts flew everywhere while we drank tea and watched the ten-hour sunset roll across the horizon.

The next afternoon, after a week or so on the sleds, we reached our destination. While I set up base camp, my Inuit friends left to go back to Clyde River. As I watched them disappear around the corner of the Ship's Prow, I was instantly slapped in the face with utter solitude and total silence.

I remembered a day in high school when my biology class tried a small experiment to demonstrate the sense of hearing. We closed our eyes and, without making a noise, just listened. We heard breathing, cars in the distance, the air conditioning, maybe a bird singing outside. That first night at camp on my own, I did the experiment again. Silence. For the first time in my life, I heard no wind, no people, no voices, no cars, no airplanes, no animals—nothing. In the end, in a great meditation, I could hear only one thing: my pulse. I was literally alone, at a place on Earth that is still truly wild.

I quickly fell into a well-remembered rhythm of duties that would allow me to survive in this environment and climb this amazing wall alone. I started melting snow, setting up tents, sorting gear and scouting the wall. I had forgotten how much I enjoyed tending to camp and chores, and work reflexively became play. But as much as I embraced my temporary home, the seriousness of the project I'd undertaken slowly sank in. The once gray, dismal wall of the Ship's Prow now radiated neon-peach in the alpenglow, the overhanging objective peering down upon me with a bright invitation for its first ascent. Beneath the magic glow, I was reminded of the task I would attempt to claim solo and hoped that somewhere on the wall hid a weakness that would be my route to the top.

To get a better perspective of the wall, I walked a couple of miles out over the frozen ocean, crossing two sets of polar bear tracks on the way. (I patted my 12-gauge loaded with slugs as I stepped over the tracks.) Looking back toward Scott Island, I spotted what looked like a clean line just a couple of hundred yards to the right of the Prow's point. At least 70 percent of the route would be overhanging. With capsule-style climbing—alone—2,000 feet would turn into 30,000 feet of ascent due to the necessary hauling, fixing, jugging and cleaning of all the pitches.

I prepared myself and my gear to spend the next few weeks climbing the wall. As with chopping my iceberg chunks into fist-sized pieces (a perfect fit for my hanging stove), I did as much on the ground as possible to make it easier for myself later on. Meanwhile, as expected, the weather changed for the worse. On the way to Base Camp with the Inuit, we had had remarkably stable weather, but now the temperature dropped and the snowfall was steady. These changes weren't of enormous concern, but they were accompanied by a violent, relentless wind that stormed through camp like a herd of elephants. Unable to sleep through the constant battering wind and worried that the tents wouldn't hold, I nervously scrawled in my journal with stiff, frozen limbs. Aside from the wind, this little book and my novels were my only companions.

May 6, 1:16 p.m. The wind has gotten worse. I must admit, I am quite concerned. Meditation helps, but it doesn't mean that my tents aren't going to rip apart at any moment. The wind blows so hard that the tent ceiling reaches down and scratches my sleeping bag.

A huge explosion just came from my cook tent; the main vestibule on my cook tent was ripped away, and now the fragile door to the tent is all that defends its inner peace. At least I secured the tents well, using ice screws to lash them down to the frozen sea. I just got into

The Ship's Prow, showing The Hinayana. M<small>IKE</small> L<small>IBECKI</small>

Looking down on wall camp, with the Base Camp tents visible on the sea ice below. MIKE LIBECKI

my bivy sack; in case the tent rips open I shall go into the fetal position, wait, meditate, and hope that I don't freeze.

Still only static on my communications radio. I am definitely on my own. More M&Ms. My thermos is empty. Good God, I wonder how my fixed ropes are. I wonder if the cook tent is ripped open. Breathe in—"the time isss...." Breathe out—"nowww...."

The violent, angry wind lasted for 43 hours, during which time I did not sleep at all. When I went outside to check my cook tent for damage—and for needed liquids, hot liquids—I walked against the wind at a 45-degree angle, as if trying to hold up a wall against the wind (80 m.p.h.? more?), to get to the tent 15 yards away. My fingers were numb by the time I got there. Just the vestibule had been ripped away; the inside was still protected. I managed to make some hot chocolate and fill my thermos.

Before the treacherous wind started, the sea ice had been covered with snow. Now, blue sea ice surrounded me. All traces of snow had been scoured and blown away. The only snow to be found were three-foot ramps that were crafted around my tents by the wind.

Several days later, I finished fixing about 1,000 feet of rope. After rhythmically moving up and down the first five pitches to haul gear and take photos, I finally set up my first portaledge camp on the wall. I then retreated to Base Camp for several more days of rest and warmth to let the remnants of the stormy weather settle. With not much else to do—all of my gear had been sorted, organized and repaired—I read the last two of my paperbacks in restless anticipation.

I witnessed the ebb and flow of the sun's movement across the sky. Its golden radiance at midday would become a maroon inferno by evening, entwining aurora purples and paradise pinks. Then, just as it dipped halfway into the ocean's horizon, the colorful light show reversed itself, and the sunrise again blessed the land with light and warmth. A new appreciation for the cycles of nature grew within me. I felt, as I watched these sunsets, that I was experiencing the natural world at its purest; I thanked God for where I was, for allowing me to experience what I was seeing. I needed to write about this beauty, and the lead in my pencil quickly consumed the paper in my journal.

The weather became good enough to climb again. I hauled the rest of the wall gear to the portaledge and took residence. This contraption would be my home for the next three weeks. It seemed much colder up here—I was more exposed to the wind—and temperatures in the below-zero range were common. As I jugged up the fixed lines, I had to stop and shake my hands and feet every few minutes to get the blood back into them. Because this had to be done the entire time I was on the wall, the process used up a significant amount of time and energy. Cold ate into my fingertips and toes, causing discomfort that would last far beyond the duration of the expedition; even weeks after the trip, my toes were still numb.

Despite the cold, for the next week and a half, the weather favored me and remained stable. Every day, I'd fix one pitch, clean it, set an anchor for the next day, then wake up the next morning and repeat the process. I made steady progress until a heavy, driving snowstorm began just a couple of pitches below the summit. But I continued climbing, and in a few days I finally stood on top. Tired but elated, I snapped a few photos and congratulated myself on another first ascent. But I was also nervous; the snow and wind grew fierce and the temperature dropped. Shivering as I began my descent back to the portaledge, my body froze up like an engine without oil. I quickly rappelled the fixed lines to the portaledge camp, feasted on Clif Bars, beef jerky and hot chocolate, then fell into a deep sleep.

The storm was violent but short-lived, and in two days, thinning clouds revealed the sun once again. Now that the storm was over, I wanted to go back to the summit to see the view I had missed earlier, so I jugged back up the fixed lines to the top of the wall. I spent a couple hours on the summit taking photographs, lost in the view. I marveled as I gazed out over the white-frozen sea. There were icebergs as big as apartment buildings. Greenland was out there somewhere. The sun dissolved into the infinite

Stellar cracks. MIKE LIBECKI

ocean. It seemed like only days ago that I was traveling with the dog teams over the sea ice.

Two days later I stood on the frozen ocean, back at Base Camp, pulling the ropes through my last rappel anchor. I still had at least a week before my scheduled pick-up would arrive. Time always seems to go too slow and too fast at the same time. I was pretty anxious to get back to the States and end the worries of my loved ones, who didn't understand why I had gone on this journey alone.

Within just a few days, I found myself at home in a garden with ripe tomatoes and basil. I knew I had to indulge on the fresh pesto while I had the chance, because in just a month, I would be climbing huge granite domes on the other side of the world in Madagascar's warm sunshine.

Why ration passion?

SUMMARY OF STATISTICS

AREA: Scott Island, Baffin Island, Nunuvat Province, Canada

FIRST ASCENT: *The Hinayana* (VI 5.8 A3+, 600m) on the north face of the Ship's Prow, April 23-June 3, Mike Libecki, solo

Mike Libecki

Mike Libecki, 27, has a passion for grass-roots, from-the-heart adventure. He satisfies this appetite from a menu of wide variety, such as bike touring solo across Japan, climbing Denali in a week, and big-wall first ascents in the Northern Arctic. A favorite adrenaline-producer is climbing cutting-edge first ascents in remote areas. In the last three years, Libecki has established four first ascents in Baffin Island, one in Greenland, and four in Madagascar. He currently makes his home in Utah.

Rock Peaks of the Siguniang Region

New routes, anyone?

Photographs by Tamotsu Nakamura, *Japanese Alpine Club*

"Mt. Siguniang, the highest peak of the Qionglai mountains, has become so famous and popular within China itself that the southern side of the mountain, access to which is very easy from Chengdu, is now congested with hundreds of tourists and trekkers, domestic as well as foreign. However, if you were to look north, you would note many lofty granite peaks towering toward the sky. These peaks, which range from 5300 to 5900 meters in height, encircle two beautiful valleys as if to form a grand coliseum. Although approaches are not very difficult and a 1:50,000 Chinese topographical map indicates the relevant position and altitude in detail, the peaks remain little-known—and in many cases, untrodden."

—Tamotsu Nakamura

The Siguniang mountain region in the Qionglai Mountains of the Hengduan Shan, Sichuan Province, China, is home to a concentration of granite peaks that will be of interest to both the modern free climber and the aficionado of new routes. Indeed, longtime readers of the *AAJ* might recall an article in the 1984 volume by Ted Vaill describing the first ascent of Celestial Peak. The article included a photo of Celestial Peak that depicts a pyramidal granite tower so symmetrically precise it might have been cut by laser. A 15-member American Alpine Club party led by Peter Woods that was in the area at the same time made the first ascent of Bok'ra and attempted a circumnavigation of Mt. Siguniang. Their comments gave further indication that here might be an area worth further exploration: "From the summit [of Bok'ra] we could see dozens of unclimbed granite peaks to the north, west and south which would rank with the finest rock climbs on earth."

The highest peak of the area, Mt. Siguniang ("Peak of Four Daughters," officially given 6250 meters but perhaps as much as 330 meters less), inspired America's globe-trotting Charlie Fowler to call it "certainly one of the most beautiful 6000-meter peaks in the world." It was first climbed in 1981 by a Japanese team over a period of 16 days with the aid of ca. 2000 meters of fixed rope. Their route climbed snow and ice on the right-hand side of the south face to a prominent shoulder, then continued up the east face/ridge to the summit. The same year, the American team of Jack Tackle, Jim Donini, Kim Schmitz and Jim Kantzler attempted the steep 6,000-foot north face, reaching ca. 5300 meters after 11 days above high camp, six days of which were spent on the final push.

The second ascent of the peak came in 1992, again by a Japanese party and again on the south face, this time via an elegant rock buttress left of center to a snow-and-ice finish on the west ridge. This ascent took 23 days and used 600 meters of fixed line.

The south face of Siguniang, showing 1. 1981 Japanese route (Iwata-Takahashi). 2. Charlie Fowler route (solo). 3. 1992 Japanese route (Yoshimura et al). Tamotsu Nakamura

Two years later, Charlie Fowler visited the area for the first time. Transfixed by Siguniang's beauty, Mr. Fowler climbed an independent line on the right side of the south face to the shoulder, then more or less followed the line of first ascent up the east ridge. His three-day solo ascent included a top-out late in the day in deteriorating weather and a descent of the same line that he described as "epic."

The history of Celestial Peak shares parallels with Siguniang in its evolution of styles. The 1983 first ascent had the dual goal of climbing the mountain and making a film of the climb.* Wrote Vaill, "With a nucleus of strong Yosemite climbers, we hoped to do the entire route in EBs, Fires or equivalent rock-climbing shoes, to push the route as high as possible with 3/8-inch polypropylene fixed lines and then go for the summit. Fixed lines were to be placed on the route primarily to allow the team access to the face for filming purposes." In 1985, American Keith Brown took a considerably lighter approach when he made the second ascent via a three-day, 26-pitch line on the southeast ridge, solo.

Further activity in the area has been rather limited. In addition to his solo of Siguniang, Mr. Fowler has made a number of other ascents in the region. Also in 1994, he soloed a 5383-meter peak to the west of Celestial Peak, and another 5484-meter peak north of Siguniang. In 1997, he made another first ascent, this one of a 5666-meter mountain, again north of Siguniang. All his ascents have been carried out on predominantly alpine terrain. In 1997, Jon Meisler, an American who lived in Chengdu for seven years and now runs the mountaineering and trekking company High Asia, brought his friends Jeff Hollenbaugh and Mike

---

Tower of Challenge is available as a ten-minute video, narrated by Hoyt Axton, for $10 (including shipping) from Edward Vaill (DVaill@aol.com).

The north face of Siguniang. CHIHARU YOSHIMURA

Pennings to the region. Strong American free climbers both, Hollenbaugh and Pennings put up *Grand Theft Oreo*, a ten-pitch 5.9, on a rock peak to the southwest of Celestial Peak.

In 1998, the Japanese explorer Tamotsu Nakamura, whose photos are represented here, crossed a 4644-meter pass north of Mt. Siguniang that separates the Bi Pung from the Chang Ping valleys. He found the crossing to be, as he notes, "the highlight of the tramping indeed. I found myself in the center of countless magnificent rock peaks. . . (s)ome spiky, while others . . . were big masses of formidable rocks." His camp, pitched at the source of the Chang Ping Valley, saw him in a "palace of a huge rock garden in harmony with vivid green trees and meadows."

There are three main valleys in the Siguniang region. The Bi Pung Valley is an adjunct valley north of the area of main interest to the climber. The Chang Ping Valley features Celestial Peak on its west side and Siguniang on its east. According to Mr. Meisler, the Chang Ping Valley "is full of interesting walls, especially further up (north). The next valley west, the Shuang Qiao Valley, is also full of walls." A road has been built up the Shuang Qiao Valley. (It is, notes Mr. Meisler, "horrific.")

What might the visiting climber expect to find? Culturally, he or she could experience a land more reminiscent of Tibet than China. In his 1984 article, Mr. Vaill noted, "The valley in which Siguniang and Celestial Peak are situated has strong ties to Tibetan culture, although it is not geographically part of Tibet today." In terms of access, the area, which is being pushed by Sichuan tourism authority as a point of interest to Chinese and foreign tourists, has a series of trails that would allow the climber easy access to a number of peaks.

ABOVE: *The ca. 1000-meter south face of Peak 5513m. Unless otherwise noted, these and the peaks depicted in the following photographs are unclimbed.* TAMOTSU NAKAMURA
BELOW: *The northeast faces (ca. 800m) of peaks 5422m and 5466m.* TAMOTSU NAKAMURA

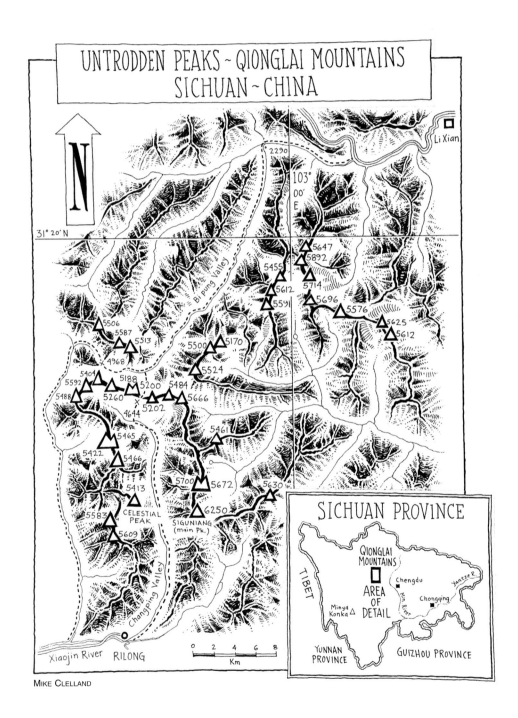

MIKE CLELLAND

ABOVE: *The north face (ca. 1300m) of Peak 5666m. This peak was first climbed by Charlie Fowler in 1997.* TAMOTSU NAKAMURA
BELOW: *The ca. 1000-meter east face of Peak 5465m.* TAMOTSU NAKAMURA

The ca. 900-meter east face of Peak 5260m. Tᴀᴍᴏᴛsᴜ Nᴀᴋᴀᴍᴜʀᴀ

"Bear in mind," cautions Mr. Hollenbaugh, "that the Siguniang area is somewhat sensitive in that it is one of the last remaining homes to the panda and red panda. Publicity toward conservation could benefit the area, as the Chinese government only wants to [profit from] tourism."

The range has a "granite plug" of good rock that begins on the south side with Siguniang and Celestial, and ends on the north side before Bok'ra. At each end, there is an abrupt transformation to worse rock. Though Mr. Vaill recalls "Yosemite-quality" granite from his team's ascent of Celestial Peak, a recollection born out by photos from the climb, Mr. Hollenbaugh's assessment is more reserved. He notes, "The rock is good (this from a desert and Black Canyon climber). It ain't Yosemite, Patagonia, or Pakistan, but it's good. Our route was clean and we felt comfortable doing a majority of our raps on slung horns. With some effort you could do a ton of good climbs, most (outside of those on the Siguniang massif) on the slabby side."

Spring and autumn would best suit the free climber, with the rainy season falling in July and August. As Mr. Fowler pointed out in his note in the 1999 *AAJ*, "In the future this whole area should become very popular with climbers, as there are unlimited possibilities for rock and alpine routes on fairly low-altitude peaks, and with very easy access from the city of Chengdu."

EDITOR

AAJ references:

1982, pp. 285-286, Siguniang (6250m), first ascent, and p. 286, north face, attempt.

1984, pp. 43-48, Celestial Peak, first ascent, and p. 309, Bok'ra, first ascent, and attempt at circuit of Siguniang.

1986, p. 303, Celestial Peak, second ascent.

1993, pp. 277-78, Siguniang, second ascent.

1996, p. 310, Siguniang, third ascent, and first ascents of three other peaks.

1999, p. 211, first ascent of a ca. 5700-meter peak.

Tamotsu Nakamura. CHRISTIAN BECKWITH

Tamotsu Nakamura was born in Tokyo, Japan, in 1934 and began climbing with the Hitotsubashi University Mountaineering Club in 1953. In 1961, he traveled with the first Japanese expedition to the Peruvian and Bolivian Andes, making the first ascent of Pucahirca Norte (6050m) in the Cordillera Blanca and three first ascents and several second ascents in the Cordillera Apolobamba and Pupuya. He lived abroad from 1967–1994, in Pakistan, Mexico, New Zealand and Hong Kong and has made 18 exploratory treks in southwest China and southeast Tibet. He is auditor of The Japanese Alpine Club, a member of The American Alpine Club and The Himalayan Club and an International Fellow of The Explorers Club. He published his book, *East of the Himalaya*, in 1996.

Supplemental Oxygen and Mountaineering Deaths

O$_2$: the extra breath of life on Everest and K2?

by Xavier Eguskitza, *United Kingdom*
Raymond B. Huey, *The University of Washington*

The higher one climbs, the harder one works to climb. The increasing scarcity of oxygen with altitude is the reason, of course. One way to compensate is to breathe supplemental oxygen, an idea first suggested in 1878 by the French physiologist Paul Bert. Supplemental oxygen was first used in the Himalaya just after the turn of the century and extensively by British Everest expeditions in the 1920s. It is currently used by most climbers on Everest.

Right from the beginning of its use, however, supplemental oxygen has provoked debates, and even today it sparks passionate exchanges (for example, between A. Boukreev and J. Krakauer). Several issues have received the brunt of discussion.

Does supplemental oxygen enhance overall performance? Given the widespread use of supplemental oxygen on Everest today, this may seem like an odd question. However, in the early 1920s and even into the late 1940s, this question was serious and unresolved. At issue was whether the physiological "benefit" of supplemental oxygen would outweigh the "cost" of having to carry heavy and cumbersome backpacks (some weighing more than 30 pounds) and of having to deal with high-resistance masks and unreliable regulators. Observations by G.I. Finch on Everest in 1922 showed, however, that climbers using supplemental oxygen not only climbed considerably faster than those not using supplemental oxygen but also slept better. Many later studies, as well as the experiences of mountaineers themselves, reinforced the conclusion that supplemental oxygen does enhance overall climbing speed and performance.

Do climbers need supplemental O$_2$ to reach the summit of Everest? For decades, this issue was hotly debated, both by mountaineers and by medical physiologists. In 1978, Reinhold Messner and Peter Habeler dramatically silenced the debate by summiting Everest without supplemental oxygen, thus proving that at least some individuals had the physical and mental capacity to reach the summit and return safely on ambient air alone.

Is the use of supplemental oxygen aesthetic or ethical? This was—and still is—a question that each climber must answer personally. Although he himself used supplemental oxygen on Everest, G.L. Mallory disliked its use in part on aesthetic grounds "…When I think of mountaineering with four cylinders of oxygen on one's back and a mask over one's face—well, it loses its charm."

H.W. Tilman argued in 1948 that climbing with supplemental oxygen use was not climbing by "fair means," a theme that later became Messner and Habeler's famous motto. Messner's opposition to supplemental oxygen is cogent: "By reaching for an oxygen cylinder, a climber degrades Everest to the level of a 6000-meter peak...."

Should supplemental oxygen use be required for guides? This new debate has been prompted, of course, by the recent rise of guided expeditions to Everest and especially by the tragedies on Everest in 1996.

Does supplemental oxygen enhance safety? The positive effects of supplemental oxygen on a climber's speed and performance suggest that supplemental oxygen use might well enhance climber safety, as G. Pugh argued in 1957. Yet, despite all the debates over supplemental oxygen, this issue has not previously been studied directly. We begin such a study here.

To explore a potential link between supplemental oxygen use and safety, we decided to investigate whether death rates on K2 and Everest differed depending on whether or not a climber had used supplemental oxygen. Any impact of supplemental oxygen on safety is likely to be most conspicuous in an analysis of death rates of mountaineers descending from these summits: such mountaineers are often near their physical limits and thus should be especially vulnerable to accident, medical emergency or mental error during their dangerous descent. So we decided to begin by focusing on death rates during descent from the summit of these peaks.

The basic data were obtained by interviews with climbers (primarily by Elizabeth Hawley for Everest and by X. Eguskitza for K2). Most of these data are readily available in standard books but were corrected and updated through December, 1999. For Everest, we analyzed data from 1978 (first ascent without supplemental oxygen) through 1999. For K2, we analyzed data from 1978 (first ascent without supplemental oxygen) through 1997 only, as no climber reached the summit of K2 in 1998 or 1999. For all climbers known for certain to have reached the summit, we determined whether they used supplemental oxygen at any time on the mountain (during either ascent or descent, or while resting or sleeping) and whether they died during descent. We then used formal statistical analyses to search for an association between use of supplemental oxygen and death rates during descent (for statistical details, see Huey and Eguskitza, *Journal of the American Medical Association, 2000,* **284**:181).

We first computed the overall death rates of all climbers reaching the summit. The danger of reaching the summits of these peaks is clearly evident. On Everest, one in 29 climbers (3.4 percent) who reached the summit during the survey period died during descent. On K2, one in seven (13.4 percent) died (Table 1). Sadly, K2's lethal reputation is accurate.

Next, we compared death rates during descent of climbers based on use of supplemental oxygen. Death rates for climbers not using supplemental oxygen were significantly higher than for those who did (Table 1). On Everest, climbers not using supplemental oxygen had death rates more than double those using supplemental oxygen (8.3 percent vs. 3.0 percent). On K2, the difference is overwhelming (18.8 percent vs. 0 percent). Essentially, one in five climbers who did not use supplemental oxygen died during descent from the summit of K2.

Because Himalayan mountaineers usually climb in groups and sometimes die in groups, the above statistical analyses of death rates of individual climbers are potentially suspect. In particular, the high death rate on K2 is undoubtedly inflated by the simultaneous deaths of many climbers trapped by huge storms (1986, 1995). As a precaution, we did an additional analysis of "summit teams" rather than of individuals, where a summit team is defined as a group of climbers who reached the summit on a given day via a given route. In effect, this second analysis asks whether teams using supplemental oxygen were more or less likely to suffer the death of at least one team member. Thus this analysis counteracts the bias induced in individual death rates by multiple deaths in storms. For each summit team, we determined whether climbers had used supplemental oxygen and whether anyone died during descent. A few teams had mixed use of supplemental oxygen, and we split such teams into two.

Teams not using supplemental oxygen were significantly more likely to suffer a death during descent than were teams using supplemental oxygen. The difference on Everest is small (12.5 percent vs. 7.5 percent), but the difference on K2 is again overwhelming (34.3 percent vs. 0 percent): one in three K2 summit teams not using supplemental oxygen suffered the loss of one or more climbers during descent. Thus, the high individual death rate on K2 (above) is not only an inflated consequence of a few deadly storms that each killed many climbers.

These analyses validate a fact that Himalayan mountaineers already appreciate, namely, that reaching the summit of Everest and especially of K2 is dangerous (Table 1). However, these analyses show for the first time that reaching these summits without supplemental oxygen is suggestively even more dangerous (Table 1). We emphasize that these analyses cannot prove that mountaineers using supplemental oxygen had lower death rates because they used supplemental oxygen. Perhaps such mountaineers have lower death rates instead because they are more cautious in general and take fewer chances. For example, mountaineers using supplemental oxygen might be more likely to have better equipped their high camps, and access to these crucial supplies during storms (rather than supplemental oxygen) could have been the actual reason for their enhanced survival (L. Reichardt, personal communication).

Nevertheless, two reasons suggest that supplemental oxygen does have a direct impact on death rates. First, by enhancing climbing speed and performance, use of supplemental oxygen will almost certainly enhance climber safety as well. Second, because those few climbers able to reach these summits without using supplemental oxygen are likely to be on average relatively fit, skilled and experienced, they should have lower—not higher—death rates than climbers using supplemental oxygen, all else being equal. Consequently, the direct impact of supplemental oxygen on death rates during descent might be even greater than suggested in Table 1, were we able to standardize climbers by skill and experience.

Although our analyses suggest that use of supplemental oxygen directly lowers death rates of individual climbers (or of summit teams) who have reached the summit, they do not address a separate and important question: Does supplemental oxygen lower total deaths on an expedition? Potentially, use of supplemental oxygen could indirectly lead to more total deaths for two reasons. First, because porters are normally used to ferry oxygen canisters to high altitudes, an expedition using supplemental oxygen will necessarily be large and thus expose more people to risk. Second, use of supplemental oxygen undoubtedly enables more climbers to attempt and reach the summit, where risk of death is high. [Note: these two arguments apply principally to Everest, as porters and oxygen are rarely used on K2.] Ultimately, a more comprehensive analysis will thus be necessary to address the issue of total death risk.

Himalayan mountaineers make many decisions that require them to balance adventure against acceptable risk. One key decision is whether to use supplemental oxygen. The decision to climb with supplemental oxygen appears to promote an individual climber's chance of survival, at least during descent from the summit of Everest or K2. However, whether the use of supplemental oxygen itself is the direct cause of that higher survival cannot be determined conclusively. But we hope these patterns will encourage further discussion of factors that influence survival and success on the high peaks.

The authors would like to thank E. Hawley for generously sharing data; C. Bonington, T. Hornbein, C. Houston, L. Reichardt and J. West for constructive comments and discussion; and the J. S. Guggenheim Foundation for support.

Table 1. Use of supplemental oxygen is associated with lower death rates of mountaineers descending from the summits of Everest (1978-1999) and of K2 (1978-1997).

Everest

Use of Supplemental Oxygen	Number of Ascents	Number of Deaths	Percentage of Deaths
yes	1077	32	3.0
no	96	8	8.3
Total	**1173**	**40**	**3.4**

K2

Use of Supplemental Oxygen	Number of Ascents	Number of Deaths	Percentage of Deaths
yes	47	0	0
no	117	22	18.8
Total	**164**	**22**	**13.4**

Raymond B. Huey

Xavier Eguskitza is a mountaineering historian who lives in England and who has been compiling data on mountaineering on the 8000-meter peaks since 1974. He has frequently contributed reports on Himalayan expeditions to the *AAJ*.

Raymond B. Huey is a professor of zoology at the University of Washington. He normally studies the evolution of physiology in fruit flies and lizards but is also fascinated with analyses of factors influencing success and death of mountaineers on the Himalayan peaks.

The Earth's Changing Glaciers

by Dr. Andrew Klein, *Texas A&M University*

The retreat of the world's glaciers was thrust into the American public consciousness in September, 1997, when Vice President of the United States Albert Gore stood in front of Grinnell Glacier in Glacier National Park, Montana, and declared, "It's retreating before our very eyes."

The Vice President went on to conclude that the rapid retreat of the world's glaciers is one of the most tangible signs of the global warming that has occurred over the last century. While his assertion that the recent glacial retreat is attributable to the so-called "greenhouse effect" is still under debate, the fact that glaciers worldwide are currently in a state of retreat is not.

The declaration comes as no surprise to mountaineers, who have observed the retreat first-hand. Where last century's climbers walked over snow and ice, alpinists at the beginning of the twenty-first century may encounter rocks and loose rubble. Why is this happening? The following article presents a brief synopsis of our current knowledge about the world's glaciers: their retreat, the unique relationship between glaciers and climate and the effects of past and current climatic conditions.

THE EARTH'S GLACIERS: JUST THE FACTS

Before we begin examining glacial retreat, a basic overview of the global distribution of glaciers is in order. While glaciers currently exist on six continents (presently, Australia alone has none at all), it may come as a surprise to many mountaineers that the total number and area of the world's glaciers are poorly known. Ignoring the large Antarctic and Greenland ice sheets, which account for the vast majority of the Earth's ice cover, the best estimates are that there are about 160,000 glaciers and 700 ice caps covering an area of 240,000 and 430,000 square kilometers, respectively. (Ice caps differ from glaciers in that they have no confining rock walls.) Of the total number of glaciers and ice sheets, only a quarter have been cataloged, and an even smaller number have been extensively studied.

Through empirical observations, the volume of a glacier has been found to be proportional to its area raised to the 1.36th power. Based on this relationship, the total volume of the Earth's ice caps and glaciers (excluding the Greenland and Antarctic ice sheets) is estimated to be 100,000 and 80,000 km^3, respectively. To put this into perspective, if all these glaciers were combined into a single ice cube, it would be 56 kilometers on a side. This total includes glaciers and ice caps in alpine areas, as well as those bordering the Greenland and Antarctic ice sheets.

Figure 1 shows the distribution of the world's glaciers. It can be seen that, although glaciers exist almost everywhere in the world, not all areas of the world are equally glaciated. For example, glaciers cover a much higher percentage of Europe than they do South America. Generally, the lowest altitude to which glaciers descend increases toward the equator, so glaciers in the tropics are found only on the highest peaks, while glaciers near the poles descend to sea level.

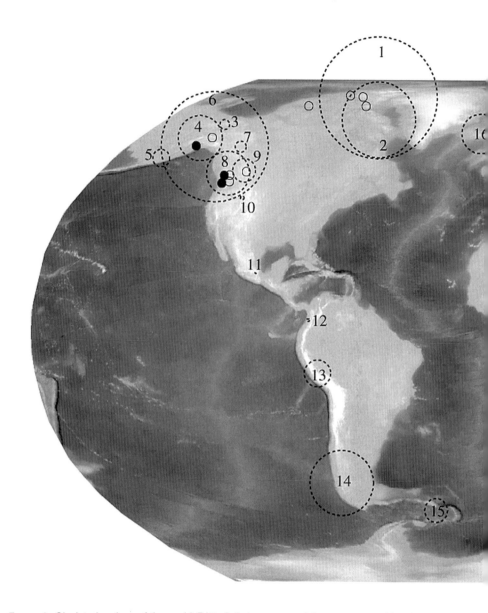

FIGURE 1. *Glaciated regions of the world. Dotted circles represent the area covered by glaciers in different regions (excluding the Greenland and Antarctic ice sheets). The circles are scaled in proportion to the total glacier area they represent. The circles are centered on the geographic center of each glaciated region and may or may not encompass the extent of all the glaciers in the region. The dots indicate whether glaciers with long mass balance records had positive (filled) or negative (empty) mass balances over the period from 1968-1989. Glacier areas are from Meier and glacier mass balance measurements are from Dyurgerov and Meier.*
     Numbers and corresponding regions*: 1: Canadian Arctic-North. 2: Baffin and Bylot Islands, Labrador. 3: Brooks Range, Kigluaik Mountains. 4: Alaska Range, Talkeetna, Kilbuk Mountains. 5: Aleutian Islands, Alaska Penninsula. 6: Coastal Mountains, Kenai Penninusula to 55°N.*

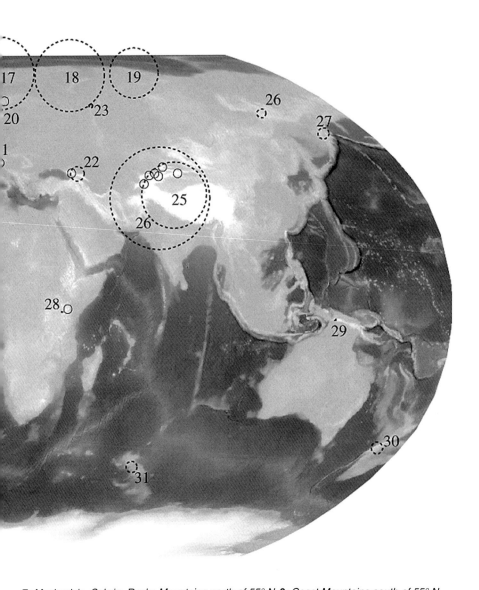

7: *Mackenizie, Selwin, Rocky Mountains north of 55° N.* 8: *Coast Mountains south of 55° N,
Cascades, Olympics.* 9: *Rocky Mountains south of 55° N, Selkirks (Canada), Northern Rocky
Mountains.* 10: *Middle and Southern Rocky Mountains, Sierra Nevada.* 11: *Mexico.* 12: *Andes (10°
N to 0°).* 13: *Andes (0° to 30° S).* 14: *Andes (30° S to 55° S).* 15: *South Atlantic Mountains.*
16: *Iceland, Jayen.* 17: *Svalbard.* 18: *Franz Josef Island, Novaya Zemlya.* 19: *Severnaya Zemlya
and other CIS Arctic islands.* 20: *Norway, Sweden.* 21: *Alps, Pyrenes.* 22: *Caucasus, Turkey, Iran.*
23: *Ural Mountains, Byrranga, Putorana.* 24: *Hindu Kush, Pamir, Alai, Karakoram, Himalaya,
Nyainqentangla.* 25: *Tien Shan, Kun Lun, Altai, Qilian Shan, Dzungaria, Sayan.* 26: *Kodar, Orulgan,
Chersky, Sun-Kho, Koryasky.* 27: *Kamchatka.* 28: *Africa.* 29: *West Irian.* 30: *New Zealand.*
31: *Kerguelen, Heard Island.*

Out of all the world's glaciers, only 250 (or 0.15%) have their mass balance measured. (A glacier's mass balance refers to the amount of ice gained or lost over a period of time, usually a year.) Out of these 250 glaciers, only about 50 have mass balance records stretching back over 20 years. As seen in Figure 1, glaciers with long mass balance records are clustered in Europe, the United States and Canada. Other areas with considerable glacier area, such as the Southern Andes, have few or no long-term mass balance records. Although the number of extensively studied glaciers is small, they do provide a strong indication that glacial retreat has been pervasive across the globe over the last half century. Unfortunately, even this limited glacial monitoring network is threatened by continuing government cutbacks, both in the United States and beyond.

GLACIERS AND CLIMATE

While it is easy to observe a casual relationship between glacial retreat and climate changes, understanding the exact physical mechanism linking glaciers and climate is much more difficult. Why is it, and how is it, that glaciers respond to changes in their immediate climate?

Simply put, glaciers are mass balance systems. At any time, glaciers are either gaining (accumulating) or losing (ablating) mass. This net gain or loss of mass over the glacier surface results in changes in glacier shape and size.

During at least a portion of the year, glaciers accumulate mass through snowfall, avalanche activity, wind deposition and a host of other processes. While accumulation occurs during the winter months for glaciers in the European Alps and North American Rockies, the timing of accumulation is more complicated in other parts of the world. For example, the tropical glaciers in the South American Andes receive most of their accumulation during the wet season, which coincides with their warmest time of the year. Portions of the Himalaya, meanwhile, may have two distinct accumulation seasons: winter and the monsoon.

Because glaciers do not continue to grow unchecked, there must be a process that counteracts accumulation. Enter ablation. Ablation includes melting and sublimation (the transformation of H_2O directly from solid to vapor form). Glaciers terminating in lakes, rivers or the ocean also lose mass by calving (the breaking-off and drifting-away of ice from the terminus—i.e., the end of the glacier). Ablation is not only affected by air temperature but also by the amount of radiation absorbed at the glacier surface, which in turn is affected by cloud cover and the albedo (reflectance) of the glacier's surface.

If a glacier is in equilibrium, the amount of ice added by accumulation over a year is exactly balanced by the amount of ice lost to ablation. When a glacier is in equilibrium, its size (though not necessarily its shape) remains unchanged. If there is net accumulation, the glacier will thicken and the additional mass will be transferred by glacial flow to the glacial snout, causing it to advance. Thinning and retreat will occur if the glacier loses mass. Because a glacier's mass balance is affected by both accumulation and ablation, glaciers are very complex indicators of climatic change. It is possible for a glacier to experience ablation due to higher air temperatures but still advance if ablation is offset by increased accumulation.

The intricate relationship between glaciers and climate is further complicated by the fact that climatic changes may not be immediately manifested in changes in the glacier terminus. The exact time it takes for a climatically induced change in mass balance to translate into a terminus position is a complex function of the length, geometry and thickness of the glacier itself, as well as the slope of the terrain beneath the glacier. Generally, small glaciers respond more quickly to climate changes than larger glaciers. Small cirque glaciers may respond to a climate variation within a year or two, while larger valley glaciers may take decades to react. In a single area, then, some glaciers may be advancing while others are simultaneously retreating.

Alpine environments are characterized by an inverse relationship between temperature and elevation: as elevation increases, the temperature normally decreases. The rate of this temperature decrease with elevation is termed the lapse rate, which, for most mid-latitude mountain ranges (such as the Rockies and the Alps), is approximately 6.5° Centigrade per kilometer. Thus, ablation typically decreases with altitude.

Over the course of a year, a glacier's lower reaches are commonly characterized by a net ablation and the upper reaches by net accumulation. The altitude at which ablation and accumulation are equal—that is, the elevation at which the net balance is zero—is termed the equilibrium line. The area below the equilibrium line is termed the ablation zone, while the area above the equilibrium line is the accumulation zone.

An easy way for mountaineers to detect the transition between the ablation and accumulation zones is to look for the transition between bare ice and snow. This is termed the transient snowline. The transient snowline is not an immobile delineation, but rather moves up and down the glacier in response to snowfall and melting over the course of a year. At the end of the ablation season when the transient snowline is at its highest altitude, it is often very close to the position of the equilibrium line (which is determined using mass balance measurements described below). Year-to-year variations in the snowline through field observations, aerial photography or more recently by satellite images can give glaciologists an idea of the relative year-to-year health of a glacier.

MONITORING GLACIER HEALTH

Glaciologists have developed several methods to monitor "glacier health." The ideal method is to make mass balance measurements—to directly measure the ice gained or lost over the glacier's surface over the course of a year. This is typically accomplished by installing a network of stakes over the glacier surface and then revisiting them at periodic intervals. Changes are measured in the distance from the glacier surface to the top of the stake, which is a measure of the amount of ice gained or lost (Figure 2).

To determine the total mass balance of the glacier, it is divided into a series of elevation bands and the glacial area (square kilometers) in each band is determined. The total mass balance of the glacier is calculated by multiplying the area of each band by the amount of ice gained or lost at that altitude from the stake measurements. Summing these values for each band produces the net mass balance for the glacier. If this value is positive, the glacier experienced a net gain of ice over the year. If it is negative, the glacier experienced a net ice loss.

The difficult, laborious, expensive and occasionally dangerous field studies (which are being supplemented by newer technology such as satellite remote sensing) are conducted because they provide the information necessary to compare year-to-year changes in glacier mass balance with various climate records (usually temperature and precipitation). This enables glaciologists to understand relationships between the glaciers and their immediate climate.

Unfortunately, these mass balance records are often of limited term. The oldest records extend back only into the 1940s. Longer-term records of glacial change are available from other sources such as glacier terminus positions, which are probably the most familiar to mountaineers. In addition to being a fairly simple measurement to make, glacier terminus positions have an added advantage: there exist numerous sources of information about them,

FIGURE 2. *Field glacial mass balance measurements. Glaciologist Bernard Francou prepares to install a stake on Zongo Glacier in Bolivia using a vapor drill.* ANDREW KLEIN

including direct measurements, photographs and sketches. A mountaineer taking a photograph of the terminus of Gangotri Glacier on Bhagirathi III can unknowingly be contributing to glaciology. Figure 3 shows such photographic documentation for a small Andean glacier.

Former positions of glaciers are marked by the locations of moraines (deposits of unsorted and unstratifed sediments produced during glacial advances and left behind as the glacier retreats). The age of the deposits can be determined through a variety of methods, including radiocarbon dating (for older materials), lichenometry (which uses the size of lichens grown on rocks found on moraines to infer the moraines' age) and dendrochronology (which uses tree rings to determine the age). The moraine record can be incomplete, because later glacial advances can wipe away the record of earlier, less extensive advances. However, it is still possible to construct a detailed picture of glacial changes using moraines. One of the most famous records of terminus positions is for Grindelwald Glacier in Switzerland and is illustrated in Figure 4.

Inferring climatic changes from terminus position records can be difficult because of the varying response time of the terminus to climatic changes, difficulties in precisely dating moraines and the multitude of non-climatic factors that can affect the position of the glacier snout. The terminus position of some types of glaciers, most notably tidewater and surging glaciers, are primarily influenced by non-climatic factors.

Still, the fact that glaciers are directly affected by their climates cannot be ignored. The present state of worldwide glacial retreat, even if it not irrefutably tied to the greenhouse effect as Vice President Gore suggests, does offer proof that the world is warmer today than it has been in the past.

FIGURE 3. *Recent retreat of a small Andean glacier on Cerro Wila Llojeta in the Cordillera Real, Bolivia, from 1989 (upper photo) to 1993 (lower photo).* ANDREW KLEIN

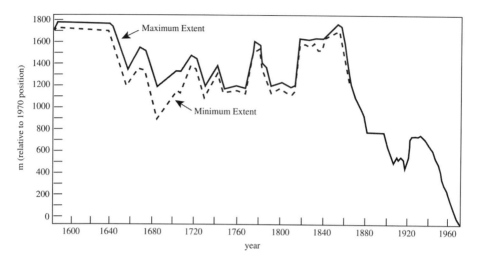

FIGURE 4. *Terminus positions of the Grindelwald Glacier from 1600 to 1975 as measured relative to the 1970 position. There is some uncertainty in the actual position, hence the maximum and minimum boundaries. Adapted from Messerli and others.*

GLACIAL CHANGE FROM THE LAST GLACIAL MAXIMUM TO THE PRESENT

Placing today's current glacier retreat into its appropriate climatic context requires some understanding of how the Earth's climate has changed over the past 20,000 years. Somewhat paradoxically, many of the features we associate with glaciated alpine environments are actually indicative of the largely deglaciated world we currently inhabit. The characteristic U-shaped alpine valleys familiar to today's mountain travelers were carved by numerous advances of glaciers that have long since melted; the moraines upon which many alpine trails run are composed of material deposited by glaciers along their former edges. The picturesque tarns that dot the glacial landscape were originally formed beneath many meters of glacial ice.

Some 14,000 to 20,000 years ago during what is termed the Wisconsin glaciation in North America and the Würm or Weischel glaciation in Europe, ice sheets as deep as two kilometers covered large areas of North America and Eurasia. Alpine glaciers were much larger than at present. In fact, while ten percent of the world is currently covered with ice, at the time when the extent of the large North American ice sheets were at their maximum, the coverage was more than 25 percent. Sea level was also 120 meters lower then, because much water was frozen in the large ice sheets.

Within the last 10,000 years—a period scientists term the Holocene Period—the appearance of the world's glaciers and ice sheets has changed dramatically. Scientists have constructed a detailed picture of the Earth's climate over the Holocene Period by piecing together different sources of paleoclimatic information, including ice cores from ice sheets, ice caps and glaciers around the world; the landforms evidence left behind by retreating glaciers; and analysis of tree rings and ocean sediment cores. The picture that emerges is not one of monotonic glacial retreat since the last global glacial maximum but one of abrupt climatic changes that have witnessed repeated expansion and contraction.

About 6,000 years ago, most of the extensive glaciers and ice sheets of the Wisconsin period were gone. The last remnants of the once-extensive Scandinavian Ice Cap and North American Laurentide Ice Sheet had finally disappeared, and sea level had risen to within a few meters of its present level. Since then, the earth's climate has seen numerous climate variations, though of much smaller magnitude than the large climatic change between the Wisconsin and today's inter-glacial period.

Between 6,000 and 3,000 years ago during what is known as the Hypsithermal Interval, many regions of the world were warmer and/or drier than at present. At this time, glaciers in many regions of the world were smaller than they are today. Cirque glaciers in the United States and Canadian Rockies and the European Alps disappeared, and larger valley glaciers retreated sub-stantially.

Many of the glaciers we see today are not simply remnants of much larger glaciers left from the Ice Ages, but are glaciers that shrank and then readvanced, or in some cases were reconsti-tuted entirely. This regenerated glaciation during the Holocene is termed "Neoglaciation." There is considerable evidence that, during the Holocene, many regions of the world experienced repeated glacial advances and retreats, though (with a few notable exceptions) evidence for glob-ally synchronous glacial advances is lacking.

The most recent of these Neoglacial events, and for many regions of the world the most extensive, occurred from ca. 1450 to 1850 A.D. Termed the "Little Ice Age," it is well docu-mented in Europe. Looking back to Figure 4, one can see the advances and retreats of the Grindelwald Glacier during the Little Ice Age. Evidence is also mounting for other glacial advances in other regions of the world during this time. Figure 5 shows a recently reconstructed

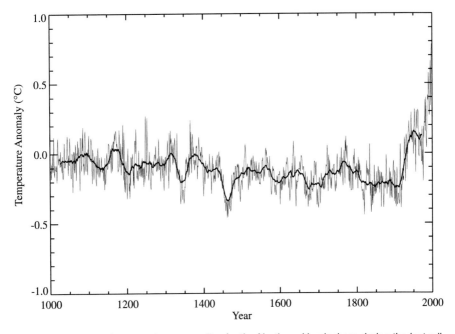

FIGURE 5. *Reconstructed temperature anomalies for the Northern Hemisphere during the last mil-lennium. The anomalies are plotted as departures in degrees Celcius from the 1902-1980 mean. The thin line is annual temperatures and the thick line shows averages for 25-year periods. The period from 1905 to 1998 is from the instrumental record and the period prior is from paleoclimate reconstructions. Adapted from Mann and others.*

Northern Hemisphere air temperature record for the past millenium. Temperatures during the Little Ice Age are a few tenths of a degree Celsius lower than the 1902-1980 mean. The 1800s were especially cold—the coldest period, in fact, of the last millenium.

The glacial advances that accompanied the rather small temperature decrease during the Little Ice Age stand in marked contrast to the pervasive glacier retreat that has marked much of the 20th century. Given the temperature history illustrated in Figure 5, it is not surprising that glaciers have recently been in a state of marked retreat. In particular, the Northern Hemisphere temperature record shows the latter half of the 20th century to be the warmest period in the last 1,000 years. The past decade has continued the trend, and the 1998 temperatures exceeded all annual temperatures in the past 1,000 years! Evidence from ice cores extracted from mid- and low-latitude mountain glaciers suggest that temperatures in the latter half of the 20th century have been warmer than any other 50-year period in the past 12,000 years. Over the course of less than 200 years, alpine glaciers have experienced the most prolonged cold period of the last millenium, followed by the warmest in the millenium and perhaps even of the entire Holocene.

Given that a very small (a few tenths of one degree Celsius) drop in temperature caused large glacial advances during the Little Ice Age, it is not unreasonable to expect that current glacier retreat is related to the warmer conditions that have prevailed during the latter half of the 20th century. During this time, air temperatures have been consistently above those during the previous 950 years of the millenium. However, is it actually the case that increased global air temperatures are leading to worldwide glacial retreat?

The answer is an unequivocal yes. Figure 1 illustrates whether the best-studied glaciers in the world have gained or lost mass, and Figure 6 illustrates the annual mass balances for a few select glaciers. It is interesting to note that glaciers from around the world have witnessed an increased loss of mass between the late 1970s and early 1980s. These data, while scarce, do demonstrate the pervasive nature of the current state of global glacial retreat, and the best recent estimates place the global loss in glacial mass on the order of about 130 mm of ice per year. For the 1961-1990 period, for which the world's mass balance record is the most complete, this is equivalent to the loss of nearly four meters of ice from the surface of the world's glaciers.

The Future

While mountaineers may be most interested in the consequences of glacial retreat in alpine environments and its effect on, say, the ice routes of the Cordillera Blanca, potentially the most serious repercussions of alpine glacier retreat are felt far afield and at much lower altitudes. Mountaineers might not have asked the question, "What happens to all the glacial meltwater?" But this question has serious ramifications.

As the world's alpine glaciers melt, the water they stored is returned to the oceans. While this melting will not cause a 120-meter change in sea level as did the melting of the large Northern Hemisphere ice sheets, the consequences are still significant. Current estimates place the current rate of sea level rise due to glacial melting at between 0.25 and 0.5 mm per year.

The Intergovernmental Panel on Climate Change represents the consensus opinion of the scientific community on climate change issues; its conclusions are meant to be the standard guide on the subject. As the 1995 IPCC estimates place the current rate of global (eustatic) sea level rise at 1.8 mm per year (± 0.1 mm), current glacier melting is contributing somewhere between 14 and 28 percent of the current sea level rise.

While glaciologists lack a crystal ball that would enable them to predict the future of alpine glaciers, if the current warming trends continue (as is expected), then the world's glaciers will

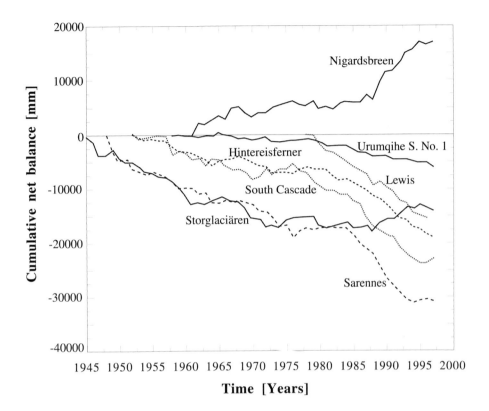

FIGURE 6. *Cumulative mass balance records from selected glaciers around the world. (Data is from the World Glacier Monitoring Service.) The locations of the glaciers are as follows: Nigardsbreen: Southern Norway; Urumqihe S. No. 1: Tien Shan, China; Hintereisferner: Austrian Alps; Lewis: Mt. Kenya, Kenya; South Cascade: North Cascades, USA; Storglaciären: Northern Sweden; Sarennes: French Alps.*

undoubtedly continue to retreat. Thus, as Al Gore said, the future does look bleak for the glaciers in Glacier National Park, and alpine enthusiasts can expect to be witness to continued glacial retreat and the disappearance of some individual glaciers. Still, mountaineers do not need to fear a glacier-less future, as there is no threat that all the world's glaciers will disappear in our—or our children's—lifetimes.

Acknowledgments. The author wishes to acknowledge Baker Perry for encouraging me to write the paper, Bernard Francou and Pierre Ribstein of IRD (ex-ORSTOM) and Geog Kasser of the University of Innsbruck for teaching me much about tropical glaciers, and Joan Ramage of Cornell University and Austin Post for their thoughtful comments on the manuscript.

Further Reading

Dyurgerov, M. B., and Meier, M. F. "Year-to-year fluctuations of global mass balance of small glaiers and their contribution to sea-level changes." In *Arctic and Alpine Research.* 29: 392-402. 1997.

Dyurgerov, M. B., and Meier, M. F. "Mass balance of mountain and subpolar glaciers: A new global assessment for 1961-1990." In *Arctic and Alpine Research*. 29: 379-391. 1997

IAHS(ICSI)/UNEP/UNESCO. "Glacier Mass Balance Bulletin No. 5 (1996-1997)." In *World Glacier Monitoring* Service and ETH Zurich. 1999.

Callender, B.A., Harris, N., Houghton, J.T., Kattenberg, A., Maskell, K . and Meira Filho, L.G. (Eds.) "Climate Change 1995: The Science of Climate Change." *IPCC Second Assessment Report.* Cambridge University Press, UK. 1995.

Mann, M. E., Bradley, R. S., and Hughes, M. K. "Northern hemisphere temperatures during the past millennium: Inferences, uncertainties, and limitations." In *Geophysical Research Letters*. 26: 759-762. 1999.

Meier, M. F. "Contribution of Small Glaciers to Global Sea-Level." In *Science.* 226: 1418-1421. 1984.

Meier, M. F., and Bahr, D. B. "Counting glaciers: use of scaling methods to estimate the number and size distribution of the glaciers of the world." In *Glaciers, Ice Sheets and Volcanoes: A Tribute to Mark F. Meier.* S. C. Colbeck, Ed. 89-94. Hanover, New Hampshire: U.S. Army. 1996.

Messerli, B., Messerli, P., Pfister, C., and Zumbuhn, H. J. "Fluctuatons of climate and glaciers in the Bernese Oberland, Switzerland, and their geological significance, 1600-1975." In *Arctic and Alpine Research*. 10: 247-260. 1978.

Thompson, L. G., Mosleythompson, E., Davis, M., Lin, P. N., Yao, T., Dyurgerov, M., and Dai, J. "Recent Warming—Ice Core Evidence From Tropical Ice Cores With Emphasis On Central-Asia." In *Global and Planetary Change*. 7: 145-156. 1993.

Andrew Klein

Dr. Klein is an assistant professor of geography at Texas A & M University, where he applies remote sensing to the cryosphere, including global snow cover and Andean and Himalayan mountain glaciers. He is currently collaborating with other Texas A&M researchers to develop an environmental monitoring program for McMurdo Station, Antarctica. Previously, Dr. Klein was a visiting scientist in the Hydrological Sciences Branch at NASA/Goddard Space Flight Center. He received his Ph.D. in 1997 from Cornell University, where he conducted remote sensing of glaciers and glacial landforms in the Central Andes, an area in which he has a continuing interest.

Commercialization
and Modern Climbing

Three views

by Pavel Chabaline, Will Gadd and Steve House

Editor's Note: Climbing has been accepted as an activity worthy of popular media attention for some time now. Good news: we as a body are traveling in larger numbers to farther-flung crags and mountains than we have ever done before. Sponsorship seems within the reach of every expedition able to provide a resume and a business plan and a few extra dollars await the climber able to capture the crux moves of the latest V10 in the crisp resolution of Velvia 50. The heroes of climbing report back from Antarctica, Baffin Island and the wilds of Africa live on the internet. Ever more remote places and difficult routes form the backdrop, and the craziest dreams are realized and celebrated in the pages of *National Geographic*, *Outside* and *Men's Journal* magazines. None of this would be possible without the extensive financial support brought by mainstream recognition.

But to go mainstream in such a culture as ours does not come without strings attached. What are the hidden costs of the "free" expedition? What effect does sponsorship have on the objectives we choose and the resulting style we bring to those climbs? What happens when the popular media hold up perfectly documented climbs and climbers for emulation—with certain details that might make for a slightly harder sell edited out in the final cut? It seems this is an appropriate time to examine all the influences that commercialization exerts on climbing as it weaves itself ever more intimately into the various branches of our pursuit.

Problematically, the very nature of commercialization in climbing curtails its discussion in mainstream forums. Most public presentations of climbing, be they traditional print periodicals, modern web sites or film and video productions, are commercial in nature, and as a result a discussion of their effect, whether positive or negative, is not readily forthcoming. The reasons behind this vary, but the sentiments are perhaps best summed up by one American climber contacted for the purposes of this article: "I don't think my sponsors would like it if I talked about their influences on my climbing."

Climbing is evolving today in ways influenced by commercial interests. More and more climbers work the angles, putting together climbs and trips the primary interest of which may be less the objective than it is how that objective will be presented upon return home. The selective representation of details from sponsored climbs is becoming more common. While some truly great ascents that would not be possible without sponsorship are being made, many others that mean little in a historical context come to us dressed in robes of grandeur on web pages, in centerfold spreads, and on the 8 o'clock cable shows. Invoking a host of superlatives ("extreme" is a perennial favorite, but "highest," "longest," "hardest," "farthest" are in constant contention for the adjective of choice), these productions often blur the line between reality and a slick sale to an uneducated public. In the end, we can be presented with lavish expeditions etched so deeply into the public consciousness that they are eventually accepted as the Great Climbs of the day.

In order to grow in balanced and healthy ways, we must examine the influences shaping our evolution. With this in mind, we sent out a series of questions to climbers around the world in an attempt to bring a candid discussion of the effects of commercialization on modern climbing into the conversations of the community. The questions were as follows:

How have commercial interests helped you as a climber, and climbing in general? How have they hurt? How do commercial interests today influence climbing objectives, style and/or climbing decisions? How do they influence the reporting of climbs? How is commercialization influencing the evolution of climbing in your country in areas such as modern-day expeditions, access and outside regulation? What role, if any, does the popular press play in commercialization? What do you think would constitute a healthy relationship between commercialization and climbing in the future?

Certainly, the three responses that follow here are not a definitive statement on the matter. We hope that they will help generate some thought—and talk—about the issue within the community. How you understand them and what role they play in your own climbing, of course, is up to you.

The editor would like to thank Kitty Calhoun, Lynn Hill, Yasushi Yamanoi, Alex Huber, Mick Fowler, Eric Simonson, Phil Powers and Michael Kennedy for their comments and feedback. In addition, special thanks go out to Marko Prezelj, whose hard work on the Slovenian perspective was invaluable.

Barbie in the Mountains

Pavel Chabaline, *Russia*

There is a great difference between Russian (Soviet) mountaineering and that of other countries. I'll try to explain in a few words the history of Soviet mountaineering in order to help readers understand the Russian point of view.

We have had mountaineering competitions for about 50 years. In these competitions, there was no commercial interest, no prizes, no money. There were only the expenses, which had to be covered by the competitors. But still, for competitors it was very important to win, because the basis of communist ideology was collectivism, and Soviet society's appreciation of a climber's success was equal to sponsorship in other countries.

In the final years of the Soviet Union, our government gave winners the opportunity for future climbs by covering expenses incurred during competitions. It was impossible to get money from professional mountaineering (guiding, advertising, sponsorship, etc.) because there were no (and there still aren't any) rich consumers. Outdoor equipment and gear manufacturers were not as popular in the Soviet Union as they are in the United States or France, for example. But if you were a winner, it was possible to climb without paying for your own expenses.

There were many kinds of competitions (rock, ice, mixed, high-altitude, traverses, new routes, winter classes) and many levels of championships (of the Soviet Union, the republics, the regions, trade unions, military, mountaineering camps, etc.). Obviously, the lower the level of the competition, the less the expenses. At the highest level (the Soviet Championships), climbers had the possibility to mount serious, helicopter-supported expeditions. This was the reason the best climbers participated and tried to win. And it was a serious reason for different sport clubs to form their own teams, because the earnings of the clubs' clerks depended on the quantity and quality of the successes of the clubs' climbers. And the best climbers became real professionals: they had to climb the whole year, not for money, but for the possibility for future climbs.

The elite Russian mountaineers today are, in general, climbers from the Soviet period: Babanov, Ruchkin, Odintsov, Koshelenko, Pogorelov, Klenov, Davy, Tarasov, Tukhvatullin. The only young climber who has developed after the days of Soviet mountaineering that I can point to is Mikhail Pershin. These are the elite, the "knights" of mountaineering, and for them, the process is more important than the result. They can't stop climbing because it is their life, and now they work hard and pay their own money, mainly for expeditions. But in Russia, we don't have rich mountain equipment companies like the ones in the West, and those Western companies don't like international heroes. If they have to choose from two climbers of similar levels who need sponsorship for expeditions, they will help the climber from their own country first. The climber from another country has a chance only if he is *legendary*, more than famous, or if he is a great showman. I think that in Russia, without such sponsors, the elite climbers will never be troubled by the problems of commercialization.

But we have two groups of climbers today in Russia: the old, strong climbers and the young but not very strong climbers. Commercialization today influences this latter group. Climbers from the first group are very famous, and they want to prolong their mountain life. The second group of climbers likes mountaineering, but they are afraid to choose the same level objectives as the elite.

Both groups are able to find sponsors for their expeditions, because the first are very famous and the second are very active. But the latter climbers have to prove that their expeditions are not just ordinary, but really great expeditions. And they must have success. For this reason, they organize high-altitude expeditions to 8000-meter peaks by normal, standard routes. But they say to sponsors that such ascents are great events! Or they make crazy but unusual projects, such as driving a Land Rover to the summit of Mt. Elbrus, etc.—and they get money for it. They write a lot of articles in magazines, make films and cry a lot about their "great" successes to validate all the expenses paid for by their sponsors. In this ocean of "Barbie" mountaineering, the voices of the really strong climbers are drowned out. And the new generation of climbers learns not how to solve the world's mountaineering problems, but how to advertise their mundane events. Perhaps this is very nice for the popularization of alpinism, and a lot of younger people will begin to climb as a result, but the problem is that mountaineering then becomes like the rest of sports and is no longer an exceptional, extraordinary activity.

Fifty years ago, our climbing academician, Delone, said, "Alpinism is an injection of heroism into the whole nation." Now it is not the same. Alpinism was exceptional and sacred because it was closed to the masses. And now it finds itself in the same historical situation as is love. When love was poetry, it was exceptional and sacred. When mass media put love in TV and magazines, it became pornography. You see that year to year in the mountain world there are fewer and fewer really great events, but more and more Barbie expeditions.

To my mind, to save the spirit of the extraordinary in mountaineering, we need to think about competitions in alpinism, as we had in Russia until recently. There are two types of high-level mountaineering. One is when you climb only for yourself, and only the process is interesting for you, nothing more. Another is when you try to prove to everybody and anybody your importance and your strength. It is not good, not bad; both mindsets have the possibility to exist. But for the young climbers, the second mindset is (usually) more important than for the elite climbers. In the latter case, it is necessary to have the estimation (but a fair and honest estimation) of your peers. Famous, well-known climbers have more chances for support, and young alpinists need objective estimation of their ascents. Nowadays, your importance usually depends on your ability to self-promote, not on your climbing. If we were to have competitions with defined rules, everybody would be able to see who is really strong.

We must outline definitively the real problems in world mountaineering, judge the truly great ascents once a year and put this information into the serious mountain publications (something akin to the Piolet d'Or in France, but international).

Maybe, maybe…

Pavel Chabaline was born in 1961. He has climbed more routes on Ak-Su North (5217m) than any other climber. His nine routes on that peak include five new routes and the first winter ascent. In 1998, he led all the aid pitches on the *Lightning Route* on the north face of Changabang, and in 1999 he attempted the north face of Jannu. He has taken first place in the Russian Championships (Technical Class) in 1990, 1992, 1993, 1994, 1998; first place in the Soviet Championships in 1992; and first place in the CIS Championships in 1995. He lives in Kirov, Russia.

Pavel Chabaline. CARLOS BUHLER

Selling Out by Selling Climbing and Other Myths

Will Gadd, *Canada*

Climbing is undoubtedly more mainstream than ever; you only have to look at the advertising in *Rock & Ice* or *Climbing* to see that climbers are both advertising targets for major companies such as Ford, Subaru and Rolex and the models used to sell product for those companies in the media. The *X Games* put climbing in front of more people than perhaps any other TV broadcast, and the *Outdoor Life* and *Discovery* channels regularly broadcast climbing stories. Each climbing "story" in any medium is ultimately paid for by advertisers. Because more people are interested in climbing, advertisers will pay to reach those people. For the climbers involved in the production of each story, this in turn pays for climbing trips that would be financially difficult or impossible to manage on their own. I'm not independently wealthy (more independently poor!), so for me and many other climbers, selling our stories to the media makes the climbs possible.

I personally have absolutely zero problem with this form of commercial climbing. In fact, I whole-heartedly support it. Try as I might, I can't find a problem with the public watching climbing, or climbers using the money that generates to further their own climbing aims. The Puritans claim that having cameras involved in the sport takes the soul of climbing away. I think the soul of climbing is actually quite robust and can most likely stand a little scrutiny without withering. In fact, a little public scrutiny of climbing is probably a good thing for both the climbers and the mountains.

Those who deride media-supported climbing trips are usually either jealous ("How did those guys get the cash? Man!") or trying to stay true to some sort of historical myth that climbing didn't used to be commercial. Climbing is exploration. Exploration costs money. When Admiral Byrd set out to "explore" the South Pole, he raised huge capital on everything he did (some of it in the midst of the Depression). He was an amazing promoter, transmitting evening radio programs live for the duration of the events, endorsing Grape Nuts and pretty much everything else he could hawk. In fact, Byrd's use of that era's internet-equivalent to publicize his cause and satiate sponsors puts most modern commercial exploration/climbing efforts to shame. Mallory and Irvine didn't go to Everest on wages earned waiting tables; they sold stories to the newspapers back home. So when the

Puritans start decrying the increasing role of commerce in exploration in general and climbing in particular, I have to laugh. In a historical context, today's climbers are plainly poorly paid amateurs.

Does the media attention ruin climbing? Media attention to anyone else's climbing certainly hasn't ruined my own personal climbing experience (has the media circus surrounding commercial climbing on Everest affected you at all?), nor has being involved in sponsored climbs. In fact, some of my best mountain trips have involved cameras or the moments after the trips when I sit and think and write for a magazine or web site. So I'm left scratching my head: If commercial climbing doesn't detract from anyone else's experience of climbing on a personal level, and nobody is making anyone climb with a camera or pen in hand, then what's the problem? I'm not a psychologist, but there's plainly something wrong with the motivation of the critics.

Participating in competitions and selling my story to the public also allows me to do what I want to do more of: climb. Every minute I spend working at a non-climbing-related job is one less minute that I can climb or be in the mountains. I've had a (very) few climbers tell me I've sold out by accepting money from sponsors or competing in televised events. They usually feel I should work at a non-climbing job and only climb on the weekends like them. I ask you: Who has "sold out," the climber following his or her dream 250 days a year all over the world, or the person so sunk into debt and other perceived obligations that they can only manage the odd day out? This same climber will often bitterly lament to anyone who will listen that his job has ruined his climbing, or disparage the efforts of full-time climbers with, "well, I could do that, but they're sponsored and I have to work for a living."

If you truly care about climbing, you find a way to do a lot of it. If you're not climbing enough because of your job, then obviously your job or what it affords you is more important. If you're an artist, you should damn well do your best to practice your craft. Please don't construe this as an attack on weekend climbers, for it's not: the man or woman who holds a 50-hour-a-week job and busts a move on the weekends is often doing climbing every bit as meaningful to them, something I support from the bottom of my heart. But don't tell me I've sold out because I live to be in the mountains and have found a way to do so.

Some proponents of "self-supported" climbing also make the argument that being paid to climb "taints" a trip because the money came from a sponsor. Climbing is not immaculate conception; the money always comes from somewhere. It is paid for by work, and there is no difference between commercial climbing work and any other kind of work. If you work selling stocks and then use that money to go climbing, aren't you "sponsoring" yourself? Some might point out that you're beholden to a sponsor, but playing with other people's money actually takes some of the pressure off, at least for me.

Commercial sponsorship from Black Diamond, The North Face and many other companies also pays for a large percentage of the Access Fund budget. Should we kick them out and make the members pay because money from "sponsors" is tainted? I think responsible companies should support climbing and wilderness advocacy; if they also support climbing and climbers through either direct sponsorship or advertising on climbing programs (as Salomon and The North Face have both done), then I think it's good business and good climbing.

As a climber, I look at the public's willingness to support climbing through watching or reading about it as a supreme compliment. If someone sees a TV program that I've worked on and gets excited to climb or empathizes with the climbing experience, then that's a good thing. It's good for the people who get inspired and then learn to climb, because climbing, to quote another climber, "soothes the soul." It's good for the environment, because climbers are usually staunch defenders of wilderness, and climbing is a very low-impact form of mountain use compared to ski areas, roads, hotels and the other commercial ventures one finds in our national parks and wilderness areas. More climbers means more defenders of space free from commercial development.

There are a few good arguments to be made that increasing the number of people in the mountains through climbing or any mountain sport is bad for the mountain environment, and that therefore exposing the public to climbing will harm the environment by increasing the numbers of climbers. But the argument that televised climbing dramatically increases the number of climbers is both wrong and elitist. It's wrong in the same way that Formula One racing doesn't inspire everyone to have a go, and it's elitist in saying that John Q. Public doesn't have the right to climb or use the environment in a non-damaging way.

My mother once commented that the only environonmentally responsible thing to do is to immediately kill yourself. Although she was speaking in jest (I'm here), there is also a grain of truth to her statement. But since we are here, I think it's worth showing the general public that mountains and wilderness are worth preserving, and the best way to do that is to show people their beauty and the experiences that they offer. The more public and compelling the message, the mo' better. Ansel Adams' photos hang in plenty of people's houses who don't own hiking boots, but who see the content and find it moves them. Images of mountains and wild places in the media alert the public to the fact that these places are special. With any luck, it might actually encourage them to want to preserve the wilds, instead of paving them for another RV park.

I do think there are a few issues in commercial climbing (or any climbing) that need to be examined, and this is where the public scrutiny that media exposure can bring comes in. Would the Everest Base Camp ever have begun to be cleaned up without the gross images in magazines and on TV? The media exposure helped create a public awareness of the problem, which in turn helped create a P.R. opportunity for companies such as Nike to kick in for the clean-up. And when things went bad on Everst in '96, an IMAX film crew was instrumental in providing assistance. If you're on TV or a public figure in the climbing world, then you're also more likely to know that what you do is being examined, and act accordingly. Some say that commercial climbing encourages "summit at any cost," and this may be true with some climbers. But to me, this is an issue for those climbers and their consciences. I'm not their dad or a cop, and I don't feel compelled to tell anyone how to climb as long as what they do isn't environmentally criminal. I've also noticed that sponsors prefer that their climbers return alive, so a summit-at-any-cost argument doesn't hold water for me. A lot of the anti-money climbing arguments sound suspiciously like sex-ed editorials in far-right newspapers, a "don't do it or you'll go blind" sort of mentality.

I look at each "commercial" climbing experience and try to answer the question, "Can I sleep at night if I do this?" My form of commercial climbing doesn't kill anybody, does very minimal environmental harm and may in fact be good in the long run if it inspires more people to care about wild places. Plus, I get to climb a lot. I sleep fine at night. May all your climbing days end safely.

Will Gadd spends as much time in the mountains as possible. He is sponsored by Black Diamond, Scarpa, Red Bull, Hard Corps, Gin Paragliders, Superfly and Ball Instruments. He has worked on numerous TV programs about mountain sports and written extensively about the mountains for many magazines, but feels that his soul is still in good shape.

Will Gadd

Divided Interests and
the Hope for American Alpinism

by Steve House

Author's note: Passing judgments about the worthiness of other's accomplishments goes against the grain of the anarchistic pursuit we call "climbing." That being said, we all make judgments as part of the process of assimilating information to our own personal experience; indeed, I make judgments in the following article. But these judgments are only important within the context of my own values and experience, and I ask that readers of this article recognize them as such.

Do you remember where you were when you heard that Mugs Stump climbed the Cassin Ridge in 15 hours, that Messner and Habeler used pure alpine style to summit Hidden Peak or that Hillary and Norgay climbed Everest? These climbers affected us with accomplishments that set the benchmark for their age in mountaineering. And where is that benchmark today? The definition is perhaps most easily stated in terms of what it is not. In the year 2000, the cutting edge in alpinism is not fixing ropes, placing bolts, using oxygen or using high-altitude porters. I could go on, but suffice it to say that these are concepts that stylistically belong to decades of the past. It was a long time ago now that Messner summarized these tactics as "the murder of the impossible."

As an introduction to the coming century, I feel compelled to add that cutting-edge alpinism is also not: re-leading pitches for the camera, making e-mail dispatches from the bivouac or climbing with partners whose only purpose is documentation. These are ideas that according to some will define cutting-edge climbing in the future. I think that these ideas will simply define a new specialty within climbing that I'll call "business climbing." Business climbing will divide our talents and degrade the amount of cutting-edge climbing that will be accomplished.

Historically, the best barometer of the state of climbing has been alpinism. And the last stylistic climax in alpine climbing came in the mid- to late 1980s when many of the 8000-meter peaks were climbed in single-push style, often by new routes. Such climbing was termed "night-naked" by Voytek Kurtyka; he, Jean Troillet, Pierre-Allain Steiner and Erhard Loretan were at the center of adapting this bivouac-less style to the peaks of the Himalaya.

More recently, the "night-naked" or "single-push" approach has been applied successfully to more technical routes in the Himalaya by the Slovenians. But the Alaska Range and Patagonia are also important crucibles for this expression of light and fast. In 1999, Silvo Karo and Rolando Garibotti climbed a 900-meter direct start to the only existing route on Fitz Roy's formidable 2300-meter west face. This was the second ascent of the Czechoslovakian Route which was climbed with extensive use of fixed lines over two seasons in 1982 and 1983. Karo and Garibotti climbed nearly 50 pitches (VI 5.10d 65°) with "some crackers and one and a half liters of water"; glacier to glacier, their ascent took 35 hours. This is an excellent example of what is "state-of-the-art" in alpinism today.

The fact is that big walls climbed using drill bits and static line, and expedition-style climbs of 8000-meter peaks, do not stretch our collective experience anymore. But these are the objectives that business climbing will push people toward. It is a matter of logistics that sponsorships involving heavy use of cameras, web sites and films are incompatible with modern lightweight tactics.

Then there is the issue of finances. How many of the people that followed the American ascent of Great Trango Tower last summer realized that the trip had a seven-figure budget? That the climbers, cameramen, and technical support were all being paid to do their respective work? Is this kind of expedition "bad" or "wrong" for climbing? I'd say no; they were climbing and, I hope, having fun. Furthermore, it seems that the media attention showed the climbers in a more favorable light than some media events of the past.

However, it begs some questions. Was the 1999 American Great Trango Tower expedition a milestone in the history of climbing? No. Were their accomplishments equitable with the amount of publicity it garnered? Absolutely not. Cast in those terms, the aforementioned attempt on Fitz Roy was a greater contribution—and it was never reported in climbing's mass media, let alone discussed.

I am not proposing that one team's effort is worthwhile and the other's is worthless. Rather, these examples illustrate differences in the visions of the climbers. We the climbing public need to understand the competing visions of climbing the hardest route with the most style versus that of combining a paycheck with an expedition.

Business climbing is not going away; there seems to be a growing demand for it. Good news for the thousands of people who excitedly followed Lowe, Synnott and Ogden's ascent of Great Trango Tower last year. And fortunate for the sponsors who likely made a return on their investment.

Luckily for the progress of alpinism, people like Karo and Garibotti aren't going away, either. Neither are the road-tripping life-style climbers in Camp 4 who are the living roots of climbing. However, it is extremely important for the climbing community to understand how important dollars are to an expedition. To state the obvious, having enough money is absolutely crucial to an attempt.

Here we owe a debt of gratitude to the organizations that grew up with our sport. Several of these companies have created an infrastructure for helping climbers fund their personal visions of how and what to climb. Companies like Polartec, Patagonia, Black Diamond, *Climbing* magazine, Gore, and recently, the American Alpine Club have created competitive climbing grants. The more well known are: the Mugs Stump Award, the Lyman Spitzer Climbing Grant, the Helly Hansen Mountain Adventure Award, the Shipton-Tilman Grant and the largest of them all, the Polartec Challenge Grant.

These grants are available to anyone who calls up and requests an application form. They are typically distributed annually, and they award up to $10,000 to a single team. To motivated teams with good objectives that can win several grants, it is possible to fund the majority of a lightweight expedition's budget to all but the expensive 8000-meter peaks.

These grants help climbers whose climbing objectives rule out heavyweight film and web site productions. It also solves a dilemma for the many people who simply don't want to have their climbing publicized in any way.

I believe that it is very clear that these grants have been, and will continue to be, instrumental in helping alpinists define what the state of the art in climbing will be in the coming years. Not only do they provide the crucial dollars for airline tickets, but they also force teams to focus on developing their objectives. The grant applications require maps, route photos, and an explanation of why theirs is an important objective.

The great tragedy of modern business climbing is that the energies of talented and accomplished climbers will inevitably be divided. Just as we have seen guiding jobs on 8000-meter peaks draw talent out of the core of alpinism, so too will these newly popular industries of climbing films and web sites. The lure of notoriety and the reliable paycheck will draw those hardcore weary of the hand-to-mouth lifestyle, and their vast talents will go with them.

Modern mountaineers, both armchair and active, need to understand the differences among sponsorships. Everyone with a TV can enjoy the result of a well-documented adventure. But as an educated group, we need to ensure the continued support of the organizations that are committed financially to these grants. Specifically, I want to call upon the membership and the directors of the American Alpine Club to do more to help mountaineering efforts at the top levels of development. These trips provide the greatest return to our community by way of inspiration—and without our collective inspiration, climbing would be just another ball-sport instead of the incredible force that it is on our lives.

Steve House

Steve House was born in 1970 and began climbing in 1984 with the La Grande, OR, chapter of the Boy Scouts. In the Alaska Range, he established three new routes on Denali in three years and put up *The Gift (That Keeps on Giving)* on Mt. Bradley. In Canada, his new routes include the Southwest Face of King Peak and *M-16* on Howse Peak. He lives in Mazama, Washington, with his wife, Ann, and is a professional mountain guide.

High Altitude Pulmonary Edema

New horizons

by Robert B. Schoene, M.D., *The University of Washington*

Over the last three decades, increased awareness and education have lessened the instances of high altitude pulmonary edema (HAPE) encountered by otherwise healthy, active sojourners to high altitude. HAPE had been described in Europe as early as the late 1700s and in South America in the late 1800s and 1900s, when it was thought to be pneumonia and/or fluid in the lungs from heart failure. But it was not until the 1950s and 1960s in Peru and the United States that HAPE was recognized as a distinct disease unrelated to infection or heart failure that could afflict otherwise healthy, young and middle-aged individuals. Although not nearly as common as acute mountain sickness (AMS) and occurring more commonly at slightly higher altitudes (3000 meters or above), HAPE, unlike AMS, can be fatal.

The purpose of this article will be to review what is known about HAPE and its underlying pathophysiology. We will also provide an update on the latest research and insight into the underlying mechanism of the disease, which results in a potentially fatal leak of fluid into the lungs. References are provided for more exhaustive reviews, but this piece is intended only to tantalize the reader about the current research—research that will one day lead to better understanding as well as better prevention and treatment of HAPE.

BACKGROUND

Clinical presentation

The primary predisposing factor to developing HAPE is not allowing enough time for acclimatization. Rapid ascent, as in all altitude illnesses, is the primary predisposing factor to becoming ill. Recognition of the signs and symptoms of HAPE by the victim and his/her group members should lead to proper decision making that optimizes the chance for survival and quick recovery. Unless trauma or weather conditions prevent a victim's descent, no one should die from HAPE.

How rapid an ascent is too rapid? The question is difficult to answer, because there is tremendous individual variability in the time course of acclimatization. In this modern world of fast travel, everyone tries to get to their destination as quickly as possible. Unfortunately, this can lead to HAPE in people who, if they had ascended more slowly, would not have become ill.

Climbing, trekking or recreational parties traveling to high altitude must be educated regarding the risk and signs of developing HAPE. Any time a party member can not keep up and develops signs of inordinate shortness of breath, exercise intolerance and cough with a rapid heart rate, HAPE must be suspected. Pulse oximeters, which are now available, accurate and inexpensive, can provide guidelines for people who are having trouble oxygenating their blood, a condition that may be a reflection of early or evolving HAPE. As the disease progresses, coughing may produce pink, frothy sputum, which is accompanied by very low oxygen saturation levels. It is at this point that the disease can progress rapidly to death.

Over the past decade, the guidelines for treatment of HAPE for recreational and climbing parties have changed. For instance, in high altitude resort areas such as in Colorado, it used to be routine for physicians to evacuate individuals at great expense and inconvenience by ambulance or helicopter to a low altitude hospital. Experience has shown that in most cases, evacuation is not necessary. In these communities, healthcare facilities are usually available. If the patient's oxygen saturation level can be elevated to 90 percent or higher with portable oxygen, and if they have friends or family with them, they can be sent back to their accommodations with portable oxygen. As long as they can be observed by friends and a physician is available in case the condition worsens, there is no need to evacuate. If, on the other hand, it is the physician's clinical judgment that the patient is critically afflicted with HAPE, then evacuation is mandatory. If the disease is recognized quickly enough, most individuals recover quickly from HAPE, and they can often return to climb or ski again on the same trip.

On the other hand, in the field setting of a climb or trek where medical care is not available, evacuation to a lower altitude while the victim is still able to walk on his or her own is essential to prevent progression of the disease and possibly death.

PATHOPHYSIOLOGY

Pulmonary Hypertension

The first description of HAPE in the English medical literature was made by Charles S. Houston in a *New England Journal of Medicine* report in 1960. At the same time, Herbert N. Hultgren, Chief of Cardiology at Stanford University Medical School, was adventuring in the high altitude mining towns of Peru, where he observed and described a number of cases of HAPE. Over the next 15 years, Dr. Hultgren did some landmark research studies of the cardiopulmonary characteristics of people with HAPE. These studies, which have subsequently been confirmed on numerous occasions, demonstrated that individuals with HAPE did not have congestive heart failure. They did, however, have accentuated pulmonary artery pressures compared to healthy individuals at high altitude.

These findings remain a seminal characteristic of HAPE-susceptible individuals. They suggest that upon ascent, such individuals develop higher pressures in the blood vessels of the lung. The pressures may stretch and damage these fragile blood vessels in such a way that fluid leaks from the intra- to the extravascular space in the lung tissue. This fluid leak then enters the alveolar space, and the ability of the lung to obtain oxygen from the air is impaired.

The Campaña Margharita hut sits on the summit of Monte Rosa (4800 meters) in the northern Italian Alps. In an insightful and bold clinical study in 1991, Bartsch and colleagues tested the hypothesis that HAPE-susceptible individuals, who have high pulmonary artery pressures when they go to high altitude, could avoid developing HAPE if the rise in pressures was minimized. The drug nifedipine is a calcium-channel blocker known to attenuate the sharp rise in pulmonary artery pressures. Nifedipine was used to treat HAPE-susceptible subjects before and during the ascent to the Monte Rosa hut. Bartsch and colleagues evaluated the subjects after the ascent with clinical exams, chest x-rays and a Doppler ultrasound estimation of pulmonary artery pressures. The results showed that nifedipine minimized the rise in pulmonary artery pressures and prevented the development of HAPE in these individuals, many of whom would have been expected to become sick.

This elegant field study, based on previous research and sound physiologic principles, resulted in a practical clinical application. It is now recommended that HAPE-susceptible patients be prescribed nifedipine upon and during their stay at high altitude resorts or regions of climbing and trekking. Good studies, however, have not been done to prove the efficacy of nifedipine to treat HAPE once it has developed.

Using the same physiologic principle of the relationship between pulmonary vasoreactivity and HAPE, this same Monte Rosa group used nitric oxide (NO) to look at its effect upon pulmonary gas exchange of oxygen and carbon dioxide and distribution of perfusion of blood to the lungs of individuals with HAPE. Although this intervention is not practical in high altitude settings, NO selectively decreased pulmonary artery pressures. The study showed that nitric oxide increased perfusion of blood to areas of the lung that were not edematous, thus improving oxygenation. It also furthered the understanding of the physiology of the gas exchange, ventilation and perfusion of blood to the lung in HAPE.

In this regard, it is important to acknowledge that each person's reaction to stress from a physiologic and biochemical standpoint is different. These differences make each individual's ability to adapt unique.

The biochemistry of nitric oxide is no different. Nitric oxide, the focus of intense research in medical science, is produced in many vascular beds of the body. Researchers have recently found that in rats taken to simulated high altitude, the adhesion of white blood cells and subsequent inflammation in tissue capillaries, which may lead to further edema formation in the tissues of the body, are decreased with three weeks of acclimatization. This process appears to be mediated by an increase in NO synthesis. The study suggests that NO plays a role in the acclimatization process.

A breakthrough in the understanding of HAPE occurred in the 1980s under the directorship of Peter Hackett. With the use of bronchoscopy in climbers with HAPE, studies at the Denali Medical Research Camp at 4300 meters characterized the nature of the edema fluid. These studies gave further insight into the mechanism of the leak in the lung. They showed a very high protein content in the alveolar fluid, suggesting a large pore leak into the lung tissue and alveoli. In fact, the values were higher than any other patients previously described. The studies also found evidence of inflammation, which can also contribute to loss of integrity of the endothelial lining of the small blood vessels in the lung. The question then became: "Is the leak in HAPE secondary to damage of the pulmonary small blood vessels by very high pressures, or is it secondary to violation of the integrity of the blood vessel lining by inflammation?" The logistics and nature of the studies in the field at high altitude did not allow investigators to answer this question.

Inflammation

Although high pressures are the primary mechanism of edema formation in the lung, inflammation may be a confounding factor. In a recent study on Monte Rosa, bronchoalveolar lavage was performed at the onset of HAPE. No inflammatory mediators were found. The findings suggest that high pressures create the break in the vascular wall, leading to subsequent leak in the tissues. The inflammation that was found in earlier studies are probably a response to the initial leak.

In Summit County, Colorado, at little less than 3000 meters, the inflammatory mediator leukotriene E4 was found in the urine of HAPE patients, a discovery that goes hand-in-hand with the lavage studies. But what is more interesting is that about two-thirds of

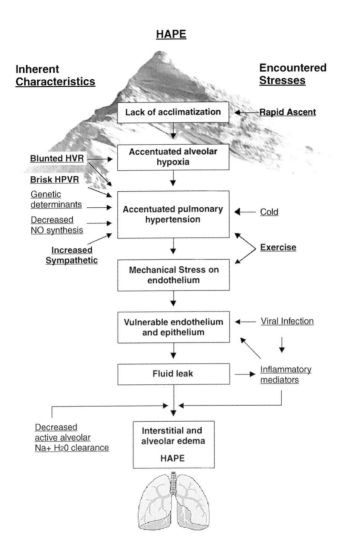

HAPE Schema. *The diagram represents a proposed mechanism for the development of HAPE. HAPE-susceptible individuals may have some or all of the* **inherent characteristics** *or* **encountered stresses** *that lead to the leak of fluid from the blood vessels to the tissue of the lung. For instance, some of the genetic traits include a blunted breathing response upon ascent to high altitude, which leads to lower levels of oxygen in the lungs and blood; a stronger vasoconstrictive response in the pulmonary circulation, which leads to higher pressures and stress on the endothelial lining; slower clearance of fluid from epithelial lining of the alveolar airspace; and a lower production of the natural vasodilator nitric oxide (NO) during acclimatization. Some of the encountered stresses include the common denominator, high altitude; rapid ascent without time to acclimatize; cold, which accentuates the pulmonary vasoconstrictive response; exercise, which increases stress in the blood vessels; concomitant viral illnesses, which may impose some degree of weakness on the lining cells of the lung; and other inflammatory mediators, which are a result of the initial leak of proteins from the blood. Of all of these, high pressures in the pulmonary vasculature appear to be the most important factor in initiating the leak.*

the patients had a history of a viral upper respiratory infection before or during their development of HAPE. One could speculate that the viral infections resulted in an increase of inflammatory mediators, which make the endothelial lining of the blood vessels more vulnerable to the subsequent increase in pressures that they will experience upon ascent.

Ventilation

Another physiologic response that is essential to acclimatization to high altitude is an increase in breathing. Although this response is generally predictable, everyone experiences it to a greater or lesser degree, and the response is probably inherent. Studies on Denali and in Japan and Europe have shown that individuals whose responses are more blunted than healthy controls upon ascent are more susceptible to developing HAPE. By not being able to increase ventilation adequately, one can not optimize the obtaining of oxygen from the air at high altitude where the oxygen availability is less. Individuals with a blunted response, therefore, do not have as much oxygen in their lungs or blood. Subsequently, they may have a more intense pulmonary vascular response and higher pulmonary artery pressures. One could then speculate a mix of physiologic characteristics: a blunted breathing response and a more intense pulmonary pressure response, which act in concert to make the likelihood for developing HAPE greater (see HAPE schema on right).

Fluid Clearance from the Lung

Another area of recent HAPE research has dealt with the ability of the epithelial lining of the alveoli in the lung to reabsorb fluid that has developed there. This process, requiring moving of fluid across the membrane with energy from sodium-potassium (ATPase), appears to be slower in HAPE-susceptible individuals. This response is probably linked to genetic factors. One could speculate that those whose capability to clear fluid from the alveoli is impaired have prolongation of their clinical course.

FUTURE DIRECTIONS

Based on what is known from previous research in the field of HAPE, investigators still have an exciting array of questions to ask to understand the mechanism of HAPE and thus develop better preventative and therapeutic interventions.

Questions for ongoing research are as follows:

- What are the sequence of physiologic, cellular, and biochemical reactions that precede HAPE?
- Are there interventions that can mitigate these accentuated reactions and thus prevent HAPE?
- What more can we learn from the HAPE-susceptible victims?
- Do they have characteristics that are identifiable as genetic markers of physiologic responses?
- What is the role of NO in acclimatization and how does it pertain to HAPE?
- What is the role of alveolar clearance of fluid in the predisposition to and prolongation of the course of HAPE?

SUMMARY

HAPE is fortunately an uncommon, albeit potentially fatal, altitude illness. Some individuals are predisposed to developing HAPE, particularly if they do not allow time for adequate acclimatization. Each individual undergoes the process of acclimatization differently and thus may be more or less susceptible to the development of all altitude illnesses. Allowing time for acclimatization is still the best preventative measure; recognition of symptoms early should minimize the chance that anyone becomes gravely ill or dies from HAPE. Enough clinical and practical information is available to develop even better educational programs for the sojourner to high altitude and to his/her physicians, travel partners, or high altitude guides. Awareness and prevention are certainly the best ways to attack HAPE.

Medical research, begun by great pioneers such as Charlie Houston, Herb Hultgren and others, has led to further insight into the mechanism of this non-cardiogenic form of pulmonary edema occurring in otherwise healthy individuals. Understanding at the physiologic, cellular, molecular, and genetic levels will be forthcoming. When it does, it will be another example of the human will to understand the mechanism of diseases and thus prevent the unnecessary loss of people who enjoy the many wonders of the high altitude environment.

Suggested References

Bartsch, P., Maggiorini, M., Ritter, M., et al. "Prevention of High Altitude Pulmonary Edema by Nifedipine." In *The New England Journal of Medicine*. 325:1284-1289. 1991.

Houston, C. "Acute Pulmonary Edema of High Altitude." In *The New England Journal of Medicine*. 263:247-480. 1960.

Hultgren, H., Grover, R., and Hartley, L. "Abnormal Circulatory to High Altitude in Subjects with a Previous History of High Altitude Pulmonary Edema." Circulation. 44:759-770. 1971.

Kaminsky, D., Jones, K., Schoene, R.B., and Voelkel, N. "Urinary Leukotriene E4 Levels in High Altitude Pulmonary Edema: Possible Role for Inflammation." *Chest*. 110:993-945. 1996.

Schoene, R.B. "High Altitude Pulmonary Edema." In *High Altitude* (Hornbein, T.F. and Schoene, R.B., eds.), from Lung Biology in Health and Disease Series (Lenfort, C, exec. editor). Marcel Dekker, Inc. Publishers: New York. In press.

Schoene, R.B., Swenson, E.R., Pizzo, C., et al. "The Lung at High Altitude: Bronchoalveolar Lavage in Acute Mountain Sickness and Pulmonary Edema." In *The Journal of Applied Physiology*. 64:2605-2613. 1988.

Suzuki, S., Noda, M., Sugita, M., et al. "Impairment of Trans-alveolar Fluid Transport and Lung Na-K+-ATPase Function by Hypoxia in Rats." In *The Journal of Applied Physiology*. 87:963-968. 1999.

Ward, M.P., Millidge, J.S., and West, J.B. "High Altitude Pulmonary Edema." In *High Altitude Medicine and Physiology, Second Edition.* 388-407. Chapman and Hall Medical: London. 1995.

West, J.B., and Mathieu-Costello, O. "High Altitude Pulmonary Edema is Caused by Stress Failure of Pulmonary Capillaries." In *The International Journal of Sports Medicine.* 13:S54-58. 1992.

Robert Schoene

Dr. Robert "Brownie" Schoene began climbing in the Shawangunks while in medical school 30 years ago. As a pulmonologist at the University of Washington in Seattle, he was a climber-scientist on the 1981 American Medical Research Expedition to Mt. Everest. Also in the 1980s, he conducted research on Denali with Peter Hackett, participated in the high altitude chamber study Operation Everest II and studied high altitude dwellers in Chile and Peru. His particular interests in high altitude are physical performance and HAPE. He is a professor of medicine at the University of Washington.

Climbs and Expeditions, 1999

A ccounts from the various climbs and expeditions of the world are listed geographically
from north to south and from west to east within the noted countries. We begin our coverage with the Contiguous United States and move to Alaska in order for the climbs in the
Alaska's Wrangell Mountains to segue into the St. Elias climbs in Canada.

Unless noted otherwise, accounts cover activity in the 1999 calendar year (January 1-
December 31). First-person accounts from winter 1999-2000 activity and shoulder-season
areas (e.g., Patagonia) are included when possible. Climbers returning from the southern
hemisphere can help us in future volumes by submitting accounts as soon as they return
home. We encourage climbers to submit accounts of other notable activity from the various
Greater Ranges to help us maintain complete records.

A chart on page 447 gives a useful comparison of the various rock climbing ratings
readers will find in the accounts below. For conversions of meters to feet, multiply by
3.28; for feet to meters, divide by 0.30.

The UIAA Expeditions Commission is attempting to compile first ascent information on
routes established in the Greater Ranges. In addition to recording ascent information, the purpose of the project is to give contact addresses of the climbers involved to facilitate access to
more details by interested climbers. Information on the project, as well as results from the
past records, are available at the UIAA web site: http://www.mountaineering.org.

NORTH AMERICA

CONTIGUOUS UNITED STATES

CALIFORNIA

SIERRA NEVADA

Mt. Ritter, South Ridge. As we climbed the Southwest Ridge of Mt. Ritter, Ben Craft and I
were amazed at the dramatic ridges dropping off to the west and south from the summit.
After doing some research, it appeared that the section from Ritter Pass to the summit of
Mt. Ritter—i.e., the south ridge—had not yet been traversed. On October 2, 6 a.m. found
us at Ritter Pass just as it was light enough to climb without headlamps. Four hours of
simul-climbing over fourth- and fifth-class rock on the crest of the ridge got us to the
prominent tower that looms over the Southeast Glacier. After this, the ridge doglegs west
and hooks up with the last part of the southwest ridge. Most of this first part of the ridge
was classic Sierra ridge climbing, with long exposed fourth-class catwalks broken up by
steep steps and gendarmes.

The technical crux of the route came with the high tower that connects the south ridge and
the southwest ridge. The climbing was typical of the area: smooth (sometimes slick) rock

with many razor-cut edges, and a bit runout in places because of the lack of continuous crack systems. After climbing the tower, we downclimbed its west side (fourth class) to the site of our bivy a few weeks earlier on the southwest ridge, then continued over familiar ground to the summit of Mt. Ritter. We summitted at 4:30 p.m. and got back to camp just as it was getting dark.

The South Ridge (V 5.8) of Mt. Ritter is a less serious climb than the Southwest Ridge, with less continuous exposure and more third-class terrain. Still, it was long enough that we thought it deserved a grade V, as we climbed almost non-stop for ten and a half hours simul-climbing most the way. A party using standard pitch-by-pitch climbing techniques would be hard pressed to complete the route in a day.

CRAIG CLARENCE

Kings Canyon National Park

North Dome, My Own Private Idaho. During June 21-23, Matt and Jennifer Pollard and I established a line on North Dome in the unexplored territory between *Freak Show* and *North to the Bone. My Own Private Idaho* (V 5.10 A2) uses the big right-facing dihedral on the apron to gain the base of the main wall. The line then goes up a black streak to small ledge with a flake, where it follows superb cracks up and right to a long ledge. The rest of the climb has mixed aid and face climbing. An old rusty bolt with a bail sling 30 feet up the main wall indicated there was an earlier attempt on this line.

BRANDON THAU

Yosemite Valley

Yosemite Valley, Various Activity. (An excellent overview of the new Valley speed ascents appears earlier in this journal in an article by Timothy O'Neill. The information provided there supplements the routes and times described below.—Editor)

In 1999, Yosemite Valley was the scene of an unprecedented number of speed climbs with records being broken almost daily, sometimes on the same route. Many of these climbs were made by a newer, younger and most often faster generation of climbers. Some routes that had periodically seen minutes shaved off their times by successively faster teams had their times practically halved by this upstart crowd. In the process, huge risks were taken by climbers whose "style places a premium on speed and audacity—but mostly speed." (*Outside* magazine, Feb. 2000)

Not to be overlooked, however, were the valiant efforts of Tommy Caldwell, who not only free climbed all the pitches consecutively on the *Salathé* (VI 5.13b), becoming the first American to do so, but took only one fall on the entire climb. Caldwell had climbed the route in 1998, vowing to come back and free it, which he did last spring in three days with his friend Mike Cassidy. His one fall came on the Teflon corner pitch above El Cap Spire, which also thwarted Yuji's onsight effort of 1998. As with all subsequent ascents since the Piana/Skinner free ascent, Caldwell avoided the first crux of the right double crack (5.13b) by linking to *Bermuda Dunes*—the left double crack—via 5.12a face climbing.

Scott Burk and Sam Shannon were also active near the *Salathé*, making the third ascent of *Freerider* (VI 5.12d) in June. This easier variation of the *Salathé* was pioneered by the

Huber brothers in 1998.

And now, onto the speed section. The *Zodiac* was the scene of intense activity. Chris McNamara and Miles Smart made a new record with a 7:04 showing in March, breaking the old record of 8:40 by Russ Mitrovich and José Pereyra the year before. Cedar Wright and Ammon McNeely then made another quick ascent of the *Zodiac* in 8:42 in May. This record was especially memorable as it was onsight and hammerless. Their secret was a lot of camhooking—up to 50 feet out from good pro. Next up was Russ Mitrovich, who soloed the route in 12 hours last August, smashing Steve Gerberding's 1993 record of 17:52, using eye-raising tactics. Except for a mere ten feet of belayed free climbing at the base of the White Circle, Mitrovich did the entire route with the rope on his back while clipped in with daisy chains to various gear placements. At one point he was clipped in to only three fixed copperheads.

Miles Smart soloed the Regular Northwest Face of Half Dome in 5:57 in September. Hans Florine did the same in June with a 6:59 showing. Dean Potter had done it the year before in 4:17. On July 26, Potter started up the *Nose* at 5 p.m. in his notorious style, incorporating bold free soloing with spurts of roped climbing, then ran down El Cap and up the Regular Northwest Face of Half Dome in a combined time of a little over 23 hours. On the *Nose*, he free soloed classic pitches such as Boot Flake, and aid-soloed (clipped into two or three pieces with daisy chains) the last two and a half pitches after abandoning most of his rope when it got stuck in a flake below. On pitch 14, a classic and glassy 5.9 lieback, while passing a two-person party, Potter free soloed below the leader, said "just don't fall on me, dude," and climbed on past. This was the first time the two outstanding monoliths of Yosemite Valley had ever been linked in a day by a solo climber. Before the dust had settled, Hans Florine linked the two-in-a-day solo the very next day, but in reverse order, climbing Half Dome first and the *Nose* second, and, like Potter, also incorporating lots of free soloing on the routes. Florine's combined time was 20:43, about two hours faster than Potter's. Florine did not know about Dean's climb until after climbing Half Dome. While Han's record Half Dome time of 3:57 beat Potter's 5:17 Half Dome time, Potter's record-breaking *Nose* solo of "13 and some change" would seem to beat Han's 13:41 time. It's going to be hard to one-up these two outstanding solo bifectas!

In September, Miles Smart and Tim O'Neill started up the *North American Wall* at first light with no headlamps and topped out later that evening with a sub-ten-hour time of 9:36. They absolutely devastated the previous record of 21-plus hours by Florine, Conrad Anker and Mark Melvin. Smart and O'Neill's time was mostly onsight, as the pair did a lot of free climbing to speed things up. The pair also made a record-breaking ascent in September of *Lurking Fear* in 5:17, which was entirely onsight.

O'Neill teamed up with Dean Potter to make the first triple linkup of Half Dome, Sentinel and El Cap—in about 22 hours (see article). Florine and Jim Herson broke the Half Dome Regular Route record in October with a time of 1:53. Herson also teamed up with Chandlee Harrell to grab the *Salathé* record in 6:32. Their July ascent went up the free-climbing variation above Long Ledge and is considered to be a faster variant.

Also in July, *Mr. Midwest* saw a record ascent by Chandlee Harrell and Peter Coward of 13:39. The pair also made a record on *Realm of the Flying Monkeys*, taking just 9:59. The same month, Hans Florine, Mark Melvin and Steve Schneider made the first one-day ascent of *Sunkist* in 19:24.

Tim O'Neill, Miles Smart and Cedar Wright broke the *Eagle's Way* record, climbing the route in 10:40 in August. In November, Hans Florine and Tim O'Neill made a record 1:56

ascent of the West Face. Jim Haden, Sean Leary and Eric George climbed *Kaos* in 27:50 in December, the record for that route. The greater Half Dome routes—that is, routes to the right of the Direct route—saw their first speed-climbing activities ever. In August, Peter Coward, Chandlee Harrel and Greg Murphy climbed *Tis-sa-ack* in 31:45, the first-ever push on this classic testpiece. The very next day, Steve Gerberding, Steve Smith and Scott Stowe climbed the same route in 26:15. They noticed an unusual amount of chalk on the climb, not realizing that they had been beaten to the first push of the route by a single day. Well to the right, *Jet Stream* was climbed by Eric George, Russel Mitrovich and Jared Ogden. This was a part of a five-wall, three-week binge by George and Mitrovich, in which they broke the record on four El Cap routes. This included an awesome taming of the *Wyoming Sheep Ranch,* still one of the Captain's hardest aid routes, in 29:31. partnered by Sean Leary. For more details on this and other speed climbing records, or to report your own speed ascent, go to Hans Florine's website at www.speedclimb.com.

El Capitan saw three new lines established in 1999. In May, Mark Bowling, Steve Gerberding and Scott Stowe made the first ascent of *Every Man For Himself* (VI 5.8 A3) on El Capitan. The line starts right of *Gollum* and "weaves itself through the *Pacific Ocean* and *North American* walls." *Allied Forces* (VI 5.9 A3) was put up in September by Mark Bowling, Steve Gerberding and Al Swanson. The line starts left of *Mirage*, joins *Mirage* for 100 feet high on the route, and then busts straight up to the top and right of *Mirage*. Also on El Capitan, Jim Bridwell and Groaz Giavanni made the first ascent of *Dark Star* (VI 5.10 A5), a ten-pitch route in between *Chinese Water Torture* and the East Buttress route. The first pitch is the crux and has one rivet that is "kind of hard to see." They made their climb in November.

STEVE SCHNEIDER

Yosemite Valley, Various Activity. On El Cap, Leo Houlding, assisted by José Pereyra, established the dynamic *Passage to Freedom* (runout 5.13c/d A0), a free variation of *New Dawn* to the top of El Cap Tower (see below). Meanwhile, Michael Mayr and Richard Schipflinger made the third ascent of the free route *El Niño.* 81-year-old Gerry Blach jumared the 25-pitch *Aquarian Wall* in 11 days with Mike Corbett. Beth Coats, who has no use of her legs, did *Zodiac* in four and a half days with Russ Mitrovich and Steph Davis, while paraplegic Mark Wellman spent 11 days on the *Nose* with Corbett. A sobering event was the big rockfall on Glacier Point Apron, which killed a climber and damaged existing routes.

El Capitan, Passage to Freedom. I wanted to find a way to free climb the *Dawn Wall* and decided to attempt a line built around the aid climb, *New Dawn*. Andrew McAllum fixed ropes to the fourth belay. I spent several days on these pitches, closely inspecting all the free lines on offer. After climbing pitch 1 of *Mescalito* and conducting a few wild pendulums, I found a way through the initial polished, blank slabs into the corner and crack systems of *New Dawn*. However, about 40 feet below the fourth belay, the crack became an unclimbable knifeblade seam. This enforced a desperate move out right, leading to a traverse across thin ledge systems to ten feet of completely blank rock, before the ledge systems picked up again and led easily to an old bolt belay. This pitch became known as the "Alfa Slab" (5.13b). I red-pointed the first three pitches: a bold 5.12b, a fun 5.10+ and a really pumpy, long 5.12c that finished at a natural belay placed from the only available hands-off rest.

More ropes were fixed and before long an umbilical cord trailed from "Lay Lady Ledge" 1,000 feet down to Mother Earth. We retreated to the Valley floor. José Pereyra had just arrived in the Valley and agreed to join me. We hauled gear for two days. José went up the pitch above the Alfa Slab, an easy-angled, grass-filled corner. With a good knowledge of climbing in the jungle, José awarded the pitch 5.10+/J2. The next pitch was hard 5.12d.

At this point the line split into two distinct routes. The right-hand corner looked climbable, but only if there was a way to cross the featureless rock between the two lines to get to it. The way was a huge sideways dyno between two hollow flakes. With only a week left in the Valley, I needed to decide whether I wanted to aim for the top, knowing I didn't have time to free it all, or focus on getting to El Cap tower totally free. I decided the top could wait until next time. Above the dyno pitch, a super to uselessly thin crack in the back of an acute groove had to be overcome. I tried it onsight. Several large, gear-ripping falls later I'd reached the belay "French free" (known to me as cheating). This was a really long, really pumpy, super technical 5.13b. Forced to rest for a couple of days by a strained tendon, my mind became fixed upon the Alfa Slab. I was struck by an idea. To make the route totally free (if A0), we would bolt a four-inch Alfa Romeo badge in the middle of the blank section of rock on pitch 4. I borrowed a drill and bore a quarter-inch hole in the appropriate place and riveted the Alfa badge to El Cap forever. Having never placed a bolt before, I didn't do a very good job, so when it came to climbing this section I would have to contend with a spinning hold! I also persuaded Kevin Thaw to come visit us on the ledge and place a bolt I'd omitted earlier on his way up.

I began my first redpoint on the groove at 7 a.m. After an epic day of failed efforts, I finally reached the belay, having got there from the tight chimney stance at the bottom of the pitch without falling off, at 8 p.m.

I then returned to the Alfa Slab. I took a belay at the hands-off rest by the bolt that Kevin had placed for me. An imaginative reverse mantle, then tiny holds led to a balancey reach for the Alfa badge. A fantastic double dyno off the badge to the start of the ledge systems and the hardest climbing of the route was over. The way I climbed it created a long 5.13b and a short 5.13c pitch. Now all that remained were the three corner pitches from Lay Lady Ledge onto El Cap Tower.

My plan had always been to climb as free as possible a route up the *Dawn Wall* to the top. I had failed. But in this failure I think I learned more about myself, people and climbing than in any success. The three 5.11s to El Cap Tower gave José and I a sweet and lasting reminder of what it is we climb for in the first place: the experience, not the achievement.

LEO HOULDING, *United Kingdom*

Lower Cathedral Rock, The New North Face, Previously Unreported. The north face of Lower Cathedral Rock has arguably the shortest approach of any wall in the Valley. It is blissfully cool in the summer and overhangs ominously over South Side Drive, yet it hadn't had a new route in almost 40 years! Indeed, the original route—done by Royal Robbins, Chuck Pratt and Joe Fitschen in 1963—was rendered unclimbable when a three-pitch feature known as the Gong Flake fell off in 1981.

After establishing many fine free climbs along the base of the wall, Steve Gerberding and I recruited Mark Bowling in August, 1998, to probe the black hole of the upper north face in the hopes of once again finding a passage through this dark puzzle. The first three pitches, known as *Pilgrimage* (5.11b), are a nice free outing in their own right. They lead to the Crow's Nest, a lofty perch below white roofs. Two serious aid pitches provide the key to the final bulging headwall. Steep and loose mixed climbing leads to the very summit, where a piton dropped from the summit lands 1,400 feet later, ten feet out from the base of the wall. *The New North Face* (V+ 5.11b A3+) has fixed rappel stations. Take lots of beaks and draws; the fifth pitch must be left fixed in order to rap the route.

AL SWANSON

Camp 4, Celebration. This gathering was one of the finest occasions ever held in Yosemite. After several years of rumors and heated discussions about nearby construction changes that would have altered our walk-in climbers' camp beyond recognition, the NPS announced Camp 4 was eligible to become a national historic register site. As a result, a unique celebration happened on September 25 to recognize Yosemite climbing, climbers and this sacred campground.

We assembled from around the world on a few weeks' notice—easily 650 people in all. Tom Frost and Dick Duane, who organized this event with the help of the AAC, were so overwhelmed with the response, last-minute appeals were made to discourage more from coming. No way. "We're coming!" was the unanimous response.

The initial festivities took place next to Big Columbia Boulder in Camp 4. Old friends gathered. Pictures were taken. Chuck Pratt, Steve Roper, George Whitmore, Yvon Chouinard, Warren Harding, Royal Robbins, Chris Jones, Sibylle Hechtel and on and on were there. Lots of hugs and handshakes all around. Climbers active in every decade since the Forties posed in front of the shutter. Allen Steck could have stood in all of the decade records but chose not to, as his grandson wanted to play.

Then to the Camp 6 amphitheater, for a free catered dinner, thanks to Tom Frost and the AAC. Next, the main event. It was standing room only. As I looked around, I noticed NPS and NFS employees and concessionaires joining in. Something really special was happening here. Groups from around the world were represented. This first-and-last-time-in-this-millennium event was not to be missed.

AAC President Alison Osius presided as the Mistress of Ceremony. She started by introducing Tom Frost, who explained why we were there. This was to be a form of climbers' "coming out" party. Tom thanked the NPS officials prominently in attendance, and told them we were joining up to preserve Camp 4. But he also asked everyone in attendance, whatever our differences in the past, to go legit. Out-of-bounds camping: OUT. Breaking the rules: OUT. There is simply too much at stake. This was a celebration of the traditions of climbing in Yosemite, and due to our growing numbers, climbers desperately need the NPS (and vice versa) to preserve, protect and manage future climbing activities. Camp 4 is to be the symbolic centerpiece of the new relationship.

Next followed attorney and climber Dick Duane. Dick was largely responsible for our NPS discussions and he described what had transpired to bring us all together. Eloquent responses were given by Chip Jenkins and Russ Gallipeau on behalf of the NPS. The presentations were inspirational. The NPS and the audience were one.

Some of our heroes were introduced. There was Steck about Harding, Harding about Robbins, Robbins about Harding, Herbert and Chouinard about Frost. Frost's leadership was recognized by his climbing partners. One person *can* make a difference.

Others joined in: Galen Rowell, Doug Robinson, Sibylle Hechtel, Jim Bridwell represented by his son Layton, John Bacher, Mark Chapman, Kevin Worrall, Hans Florine, John Yerrian, Steph Davis, Mike Corbett…. So many moving appreciations were shared. And it just kept getting better, until long after nightfall, Jules Eichorn, one of the pioneers with Norman

In very broad historical terms, we present four decades of Valley Regulars as photographed by JOHN MIRELES *at the Camp 4 Celebration, September 25, 1999.* ABOVE: *the '60s.* BELOW: *the '70s.*

ABOVE: *the '80s.*
BELOW: *the '90s.*

Clyde when roped climbing was introduced to climbers in the West, read a letter describing his fond memories of climbing in Yosemite and the High Sierra from early in the century.

Our last speaker was worth the wait. David Brower, at age 87 an honorary member of the AAC and the climbing archdruid, described his first visits to the Valley and his early Yosemite climbing days, and then brought his history of preservation and environmental advocacy into the present. His appeal for activism by future generations could not have been received by a more favorable audience.

The legacy of the efforts behind this event are far reaching. The old Sunnyside Campground is no more. Camp 4 is the sign, and it will remain. In the new Yosemite Valley masterplanning process, the NPS preferred alternative will expand Camp 4; add more walk-in and walk-to sites in the Valley; emphasize public transportation, day use and recreational uses in the Park to accommodate the summer and holiday visitation bulges; and convert the North Park Highway from Camp 4 to El Cap into a walking/bicycling path. All worthy improvements for preserving the quality of the Yosemite climbing experience.

There is a granite bench next to Big Columbia. It is there in memory of Raffi Bedayn, who in 1976 was the first recipient of the AAC Angelo Heilprin Award. It was Raffi and others like him who, working with the Yosemite NPS in their day, did so much to enable the climbing traditions of ours. There is continuity here. The climber John Muir created national parks. After Raffi Bedayn, David Brower and Tom Frost, new chapters will be written, and new heroes will be needed. But on this one occasion, we became joined in a wide-open, unabashed climbers' sharing of appreciation for the past, present and future of Yosemite climbing and Camp 4. And as the next day dawned under clear skies and the crisp fall fragrance of pine and bay blowing gently across a sea of vertical granite, a chorus of "on belays" rang throughout Yosemite Park.

R.D. CAUGHRON

Half Dome, New Routes. Eric Coomer, Bryan Law and I developed some new aid lines on the far right side of the northwest face of Half Dome in 1999. I began solo in late May, carrying several loads of wall gear up the *Bushido* gully while it was still filled with snow. I started climbing on flakes and splitters just right of the *Jet Stream* and continued into the far right corner in a 300-foot high section of layered dihedrals. The corner got quite thin near the top, requiring many beak tips and #1 copperheads. Above the corners, the route follows various smaller and sometimes fragile features linked with hooks and the occasional rivet. The weather deteriorated as I passed the point of easy retreat, and it began raining as I was finishing the fifth pitch. I woke up the next morning to winter conditions. My rack and ropes became completely encased in ice. The storm continued for two days. At this point the route sort of named itself: *Solitary Confinement.* After the storm, another long pitch of aid and a short free section took me near a bolt ladder on the *Bushido* route. I placed a rivet and tried to pendulum into the ladder. After numerous unsuccessful tries at different heights, I jumared back up to the rivet to find my lead line almost cut by an edge I hadn't noticed. I immediately drilled two more rivets to reach *Bushido* (23 new holes for the route). I finished the last couple of pitches of *Bushido* with a knot tied in the lead line.

Eric Coomer and I returned to Half Dome in mid-June. We started at about the same place as *Solitary Confinement,* sharing belays and a few moves but mostly climbing new features for the first two pitches. We then continued independently, through incipient and fragile features, until running out after pitch 5. Eric Coomer executed a successful pendulum ("the Airstream Penji") into a rivet ladder on the *Jet Stream*, saving us a couple of rivets (14 new holes for the route). Inspired by Hunter S. Thompson and Eric Coomer's recent move to a low-rent apartment complex in Colorado, we called the route *White Trash Vacation*. We finished the wall via *Jet Stream* and enjoyed a bivy on the summit under a brilliant full moon.

ERIC GEORGE, *unaffiliated*

Porcelain Wall, Strange World. In August, Bryan Law and I climbed a new route, *Strange World*, on the Porcelain Wall. We began with a few moves of *When Hell Was In Session*, then headed right, across *Sargantana*. The first four pitches wander on and off of *Sargantana* on low-angle mixed free and aid. After leaving *Sargantana* on the fourth pitch, the route is independent to the top. We kept a laid back one-pitch-a-day pace after the initial fixing effort. The weather was perfect and there was plenty of food, beverages, music, etc. We had the amenities to travel in comfort and style, and even with an extra haulbag we barely had room for it all.

Bryan led "the Lawnmower Pitch," which took us through dense vegetation to the base of the headwall. After a couple of tree moves on the next pitch, the route is mostly steep and clean from there on, and we were surrounded by some of the most colorful rock I have seen. The headwall gets progressively steeper toward the top, and in places the moves are quite physically demanding. We found many sections of hard aid but overall, most of the climbing is moderate. The line is surprisingly natural for a modern Yosemite nailing route (about 30 holes in 1,700 feet of new climbing) and we both felt it was one of the nicest routes we have done. I am still amazed it was unclimbed until last year.

In spite of an initial scare and the ample evidence of fresh rockfall everywhere near the base, we saw no significant rockfall while we were on the wall.

On all of our ascents last year, we decided not to rate the routes. I personally have found the A1-A5 system to be useless. It has been redefined so many times that no one really even knows what the ratings are supposed to mean. And even if everyone did, exaggeration and sandbagging would persist. I don't expect everyone to agree, but for me, not rating at all is a simple and liberating solution.

ERIC GEORGE, *unaffiliated*

Half Dome, Peripheral Vision. On July 17, Karl McConachie and I completed the first traverse of Half Dome's northwest face (VI 5.11c PDH). It is a line we had talked about since our ascent of *Same as it Never Was* in 1986, but just never got it together. Karl, however, knew it was a great line and wasn't about to let it slip away. He was so inspired, in fact, that he completed a reconnaissance of the first six and a half pitches solo during the summer of 1994. With a tremendous amount of scoping, he had pieced together a very aesthetic and natural start, linking features few people could perceive that required minimal drilling. Only five pendulums exist on the entire route, three of which are on pitch three, the "Buku Haiku Traverse." One of the pendulums takes place on an overhanging wall—for sure, one of the most technical swings in Yosemite, 60 feet down, wildly bouncing in space to a series of hook moves followed by beaks and heads. Of course, all must be back-cleaned to regain that 60 feet. Later in the pitch, Karl spent nearly one hour trying to get a single placement—a #0 RP, hook and blade tip equalized—from a fully stretched horizontal position that he had managed during his recon. He refused to drill and eventually succeeded. This will certainly get drilled by

Half Dome's Northwest Face, showing new routes and variations to Jet Stream *(J) and* Bushido
(B) established in 1999. 1. Peripheral Vision *(McConachie-Smith).* 2. Repo Man *(George-Law).*
3. White Trash Vacation *(Coomer-George).* 4. Solitary Confinement *(George).* JAY SMITH

future, less capable parties, but it will be a shame.

Spurred on by the recent girdle traverse of El Capitan, I teamed up with Karl to complete
the route. It begins on *Bushido* and finishes on the northwest shoulder, where one can walk
off to the cables. It is a truly outstanding climb of 18 near-60-meter pitches with all but a few
feet being new ground. We spent nine nights on the wall and a total of 12 days. Fifty-five
holes were drilled, of which 20 were for belays. It follows for the most part a very prominent
line that is quite visible from the Valley floor. The route involves excellent climbing that can
be just as exciting for the second as for the leader. In fact, I took numerous 20-footers cleaning pitons, which were easiest to remove while standing on. Very little gear was left fixed.
This is a grand tour, especially if you want to see all the routes on the Dome.

JAY SMITH

SIERRA NEVADA

Sierra Nevada, Various Activity, Previously Unreported. Although there was little coverage
in the 1999 *AAJ*, route development and freeing of old aid lines continues at a frenetic pace
in the California High Sierra. Unreported from August, 1997, Craig Harris and partner
completed *Milktoast Chimney* on the south face of Peak 12,960'+, a stunning 1,200-foot
line starting just five feet east of Beckey's *Red Baron Tower* route. In spite of its intimidating visage, the pair found the classic eight-pitch chimney system surprisingly easy at

5.8. This route ranks as one of the best and most continuous chimney climbs in California outside Yosemite Valley.

In August, 1998, Em Holland and partner completed the first free ascent of the old Hechtel Southeast Face route on Columbia Finger, climbing a steep offwidth/stem problem to free the aid pitch at 5.9. They found several of Hechtel's old aid pitons on this pitch, some of which they were able to remove by hand, belying the current view that such items are "permanent installations."

Also unreported from August 1998, Bob Harrington and I completed the first free ascent (and second overall ascent) of *Planaria* on Temple Crag in the High Sierra, first climbed 21 years earlier by Gordon Wiltsie and Jay Jensen. The first two (aid) pitches were bypassed by establishing a two-pitch variation to the right of the original line. Higher, we climbed the left side of "The Flatworm" via the same offwidth that had ejected Wiltsie and Jensen with a 30-foot fall during the first ascent. After climbing the route, we continued to the summit via the upper buttress, rating the entire climb V 5.10R.

BRUCE BINDER

Peak 12,600'+, Direct Northeast Face, Consolation Prize, Previously Unreported. In August, 1998, Bob Cable and I climbed the large pyramid-shaped unnamed peak half a mile north of the twin summits of Seven Gables. The peak, as seen from the Seven Gables Lakes Basin (i.e., from the east), is separated from the Seven Gables summits by a large col that intersects the long north ridge and east face. Our route began directly below the summit at the base of a slightly bulging column that runs straight up the center of the northeast face. Due to a steep snowfield, we traversed in from the left across a face to reach the column about 100 feet above its base. We climbed cracks on the left side of the column, which eventually took us onto the center, then the right side of the column. From here, an arête arched up and left for four more easier pitches to the summit. We descended the snow slopes, dropping east from the notch that separates this peak from Seven Gables. This was a quality route with good rock and steep climbing. Using a 60-meter rope, we completed *Consolation Prize* (IV 5.9) in 11 pitches.

ERIC TIPTON, *Rim of the World Climbing Club*

Temple Crag, North Peak, The Crystal Way, Previously Unreported. The Crystal Way (IV 5.10a) provides a day-long adventure up the 1,500-foot wall of North Peak (upper buttress) on semi-difficult ground. Scott Scully and I climbed the route in June, 1996. Find two crack systems immediately left of the Northwest Couloir. Climb the right one for two pitches. Here the route crosses the lower buttress descent route. Climb up 400 feet on fourth-class ground. On the right is a 300-foot tower that is detached from the upper north face. Traverse right to the base of the tower and climb a vertical jam crack, avoiding an obvious loose alcove on the right. Belay on a large ledge, then climb a left-facing corner and traverse up and right onto the right edge of the tower. Belay in a sandy gully between the tower and the north face. Continue up the arête of the tower to its top. At this point you are at the base of the arête that forms the prominent left-facing dihedral (*Mendenhall Route*) on the left side of the north face. Ascend directly up the arête (5.10a) and gain a shallow dihedral just right of the prominent dihedral. Climb this to its top and move right onto the face of the upper buttress. There are many crystal pockets in this area of the face; please leave them in place. A final pitch leads to the summit ridge of the north peak. A few fourth-class pitches lead to the summit of Temple Crag.

MICHAEL STRASSMAN

Temple Crag, East Face of North Peak, Mediatrix, Previously Unreported. Heather Baer-Schneider and I climbed *Mediatrix* (IV 5.8, 2,500'), which takes a straight line up the center of the face as seen from Second Lake. Begin climbing left of *26th Of July Arête* and gain the gully. Easy solid climbing leads up for six pitches to the base of the upper east face of the north peak. Continue straight up a slightly left-leaning crack system for six more pitches to the top of the north peak. Fourth class takes one to the top of Temple Crag.

MICHAEL STRASSMAN

Aiguille Extra, South Face, Previously Unreported. Peter Noebels and I climbed the South Face (IV 5.10c, 1,400') of Aiguille Extra in July, 1993. This route is a beautiful climb with excellent crack climbing and clean rock. The climb begins on a ramp right of the snow chute. It ascends crack systems just left of a large diagonaling overhang. Climb the ramp and ledges to the base of a right-facing book.

MICHAEL STRASSMAN

Ruby Wall, Don't Take Your Love To Town, Previously Unreported. Don't Take Your Love To Town (IV 5.10, 1,200') is the most direct route to the top of the Ruby Wall. It climbs between the *Rowell Arête* and *Wide Sargasso Sea*. Charles Byrne and I made the first ascent in August, 1997. Begin on a ramp that leads to a gully between those two routes. Before entering the gully, climb straight up on discontinuous flakes to a broad ledge. Climb a wide crack from the center of the ledge (5.10). Leave the crack and follow flakes right past a small overhang to a nice small ledge. Ignore the flaring overhang above you and traverse right to another ledge with a detached pillar on it. Climb the pillar and step off it (5.10) and ascend cracks and dihedrals around the corner. The summit dihedral is above you. Remain on the arête left of the dihedral until able to traverse left to a ledge. A gold wall (easily visible from the ground) split by cracks is above. Climb the hand-sized crack for a full pitch (5.10) to easier ground below the summit.

MICHAEL STRASSMAN

Mt. Dade, North Pillar, Previously Unreported. Paul Linaweaver, Ron McTarque and I climbed the *North Pillar* (IV 5.10, 1,200') of Mt. Dade in September, 1995. The route ascends directly up the north pillar. It is unclear if ours was the first ascent, as this is a very prominent feature in one of the Sierra's most-visited valleys.

MICHAEL STRASSMAN

Mt. Morrison, South Ridge of South Peak, Previously Unreported. Kirk Schultz and I climbed the South Ridge (IV 5.9+, eight roped pitches in 2,000' of climbing) of South Peak of Mt. Morrison in November, 1995. Not much needs to be said about the rock quality on this route; however, it is a thrilling and exposed climb. Climb a dike at the base of the east face to gain a large ledge 100 feet off the ground. From the ledge, scramble about 800 feet up gully on the left side of the east face to gain the south ridge. Climb a wall of sandstone, then a wall of limestone behind it (both 5.8) to a ridge of shit rock. This puts one in a large notch between the south ridge and the main ridge. Ascend a low-angle dihedral to the top of the east face. Climb into a notch and ascend a very loose rock to an arête that leads to a steep thin crack (crux). Scramble down to a gully that forms the left side of the south ridge, then 300 feet up to the top of the south peak, which is apparently the true summit of Mt. Morrison.

MICHAEL STRASSMAN

Mt. Muir, South Face, Previously Unreported. Charlie Byrne and I climbed the South Face (IV 5.9, 1,600') of Mt. Muir in June, 1997, in a single day from Whitney Portal. Begin climbing at the toe of the lowest point of the south face. Ascend a clean dihedral to a ramp. At the top of the ramp, go up cracks in a right-facing corner to a step-off on a pinnacle, then up a crack on the left wall. Climb up ramps and cracks through a small overhang. Climb up and right on third-class ledges to a clean, right-facing corner. Above this, more third class leads to the base of a chute (snow-filled in early season). Cross this to the base of a beautiful right-facing corner with a wide crack and climb the wall to its left. Go straight right to reach the summit ridge.

MICHAEL STRASSMAN

Lone Pine Peak, Windhorse. In August, Em Holland and I established a new route on the South Face of Lone Pine Peak. *Windhorse* (V 5.10 A3) ascends the huge, left-facing crescent dihedral several hundred feet west of the Direct South Face route. After 16 pitches, the route crosses the Direct South Face and finishes via five free pitches climbed in the late 1970s but never reported. Six days were required to complete the route, which ascends 2,400 feet of some of the most varied and spectacular climbing we have ever encountered.

BRUCE BINDER

The south face of Lone Pine Peak, showing Windhorse.
BRUCE BINDER

Third Recess Peak, Northeast Buttress, Previously Unreported. Third Recess Peak is the unnamed peak on the right as you hike up into Third Recess. Lara Wilkinson and I climbed the Northeast Buttress (IV 5.10, 1,600') in June, 1994, in 11 pitches. The route offers a variety of climbing challenges in a remote location. Begin climbing on slabs to the right of a prominent right-facing dihedral (this dihedral may offer a more direct way up the lower section). A small chimney is followed by thin seams (5.10) leading to a large ledge. From the left side of the ledge, climb blocks to a left-facing corner. At the top of the corner, traverse left into the top of the prominent dihedral. Follow the dihedral to a beautiful ledge on the buttress. Traverse to the right of the first tower and ascend a corner to the prow of an arête. Follow the prow of the narrow arête past towers to the base of a large tower. Climb a beautiful hand crack/corner around the left side of the tower. From here the climbing is mostly fourth class, with a few fifth-class sections.

MICHAEL STRASSMAN

Michael Minaret, West Ridge, The Crescent, Previously Unreported. After the *Minaret Traverse* and the South Face of Clyde, the West Ridge (IV 5.8) is the longest route in the Minarets. It was first climbed by Lynn Bowering and me. Approach via North Notch or Amphitheater Col between Michael and Adams Minaret. The ridge is shaped liked the crescent moon: low angle at the start, steepening to vertical in the middle and overhanging at the top. Begin at the base of the ridge and climb unroped for 300 or 400 feet (look for Norman Clyde's cairn that marks Clyde's ledges on the way up). Stay directly on the ridge, climbing easy cracks and a series of low-angle roofs, then skirt left past horror show detached blocks on the ridge. A giant ledge provides a perfect view of the superb next pitch, where a series of ceilings capped by a 30-foot overhang blocks the way to the summit ridge. From directly on the ridge, ascend a finger crack in a corner to the first roof. Skirt this on the right and step back over the lip to gain a crack leading to the final overhang. Either jam underneath or pass the overhang on the left by stepping on the lip of the overhang beneath it. This is one of the finest pitches I have ever climbed in the High Sierra. Two more arête pitches, past the pinnacle that resembles the profile of Walter Starr, lead to the summit. Descend via four rappels straight down to Amphitheater Col.

MICHAEL STRASSMAN

Seven Gables, The Golden Thread Arête. The north side of Peak 12,840', the northernmost point in the Seven Gables Massif, bears a strong resemblance to Temple Crag in the Palisades, 20 miles to the southeast. Six major buttresses and arêtes drop steeply away from the summit ridge for over 1,500 feet. On September 5, Stuart Polack and I made the first ascent of the most aesthetically pleasing line on the north face of this peak, the curving arête immediately west of the summit. We began climbing in a large recess low on the left flank of the arête. Three pitches up an ever-steepening ramp and crack system (some 5.8) took us to its crest. The first pitch along the arête is a very rude eye opener. What appeared from below to be a gentle slab is a steep face split by a poorly protected 5.8 finger crack. Although most of route is moderate scrambling (5.5-5.7), the steep flanks and narrow crest of the arête force commitment early on. The ninth pitch is the crux, a flared 5.8 corner at the top of which you stem left into a 5.9 lieback. At the end of the 12th pitch, our noses not so gently bumped into the end of the arête, a nearly featureless headwall barring direct access to the summit. We traversed into the couloir to our right, climbed a steep ramp to a large ledge, then followed disconnected 5.7

cracks to the summit ridge 100 feet below the top. Back in camp that evening, we watched rays from the setting sun paint a slender thread of golden light along the path of our route, *The Golden Thread Arête* (IV 5.9, 14 pitches).

WALT VENNUM

NEVADA

Red Rocks

Rainbow Wall, Sauron's Eye and Emerald City. Brian McCray and I had eyed the most obvious feature of the Rainbow Wall, a huge arch in the center of the wall that expands up half the wall, for some time. Mike Ward had started a route on the right side of this arch. In February, Brian added a new aid line, *Sauron's Eye* (5.10R A4), up the left side of the arch. The fourth pitch, the crux (A4), climbs out the top of the arch on knifeblades and through a 25-foot roof. Warren Hollinger took an unfortunate 50-foot fall and broke his back while participating in the first ascent of this route.

Emerald City was an old aid line (5.10 A2) that had (probably) not been climbed in years; it looked like the next possible free line on the Rainbow Wall. On June 12, I climbed the first pitch, an easy but interesting 5.10, using everything from a #2 tcu to a #5 Camalot. The next pitch was a thin crack, coming in at 5.12a, which led to ten to 15 feet of completely blank corner. Brian and I aided it and then worked the moves on top rope. They were very difficult, and although we could do it on top-rope we were unsure about doing it on lead. We started trying, each vying for the first ascent of this pitch. We'd get our nerve up, grab the gear and then head out. With hands perspiring, toes aching and sores on our palms, we'd try one more time to get through this blank section of rock. We'd fall and then come down and let the other try. I was sure I had perfected the move and now only had my mind to blame for not completing it. This time I did it (5.12d) and we moved on. The next notable pitch was the fifth (5.12a). It climbed a thin, technical face and arête and required a smear move on mossy, smooth rock at the crux. Although pitch 6 was only 5.10, it would have been the most difficult pitch on the route for me. It climbs up an extremely loose pillar with little gear. It then traverses a ledge with much loose rock. Brian styled it and set up a solid belay on the huge bivy ledge. When I reached the anchor, we were struck by the sound of what had to have been a swarm of bee creatures and sat silent for a moment as they passed below us. The next several pitches were nice 5.11 and 5.10 cracks. These led to a classic dark offwidth. We finished the route on 200 feet of #4 and #5 sized crack. We completed the route in just under 24 hours. We added one bolt to the route on the .12d pitch and actually removed a bolt (not there on the first ascent) on the first pitch. *Emerald City's* 13 pitches were free at 5.10, 5.12+, 5.10-, 5.10, 5.12-, 5.10, 5.11, 5.10, 5.11, fourth class, 5.9 (OW), 5.6 (OW).

ROXANNA BROCK

UTAH

The Desert, Various Activity, Previously Unreported. Utah 95 passes through Comb Ridge, a dramatic, deep cut in the Navajo sandstone. In March, 1997, Mike Baker and Leslie Henderson put up *Magic Man*, a five-pitch, 250-foot 5.10+ route on the Prayer Stick, a column that leans against Comb Ridge. The route climbs the right side of a prominent pillar. Baker also established *The Dark Side* (5.9, 250') solo up the left side of the tower in September, 1998. In the Valley of the Gods, in 1997, Chris Rowins, Mark Fleck, and Marco Constant put up *Cape Town Caper* (5.8 A3, three pitches) on the south face of *Lady in a Bathtub*. In the popular Hatch Wash south of Moab, in the Rims Recreation area, Jay Miller and Andy Roberts climbed the *Big Liebowsky* (C2+, four pitches) in October, 1998.

ERIC BJØRNSTAD

The Desert, Various Activity. Jeff Achey and Irene Bloche made the first free ascent of the giant hoodoo Mexican Hat. The climb, which they called *The Frito Route* (5.12), begins ten feet left of the *Bandito Route*. The first two or three bolts are stick-clipped, giving the overhanging ascent an upper belay.

In the Moab Area, *The Full Monty* (5.11 A0, three pitches) was climbed on Super Chimney Tower by Paul Ross, Jimmy Dunn, and Billy Rothstein in November. The tower is located up the Moab Rim Trail off Kane Creek Boulevard. The first two pitches were climbed solo by Todd Madaux and named *Arnold Ziffle*. In the popular Sunshine Wall in the north Salt Wash, just north of Arches National Park, several new lines were established. Among them was *Burning Shoes* (a.k.a. *Shattered Illusions of Love*) (5.9 A3, three pitches) on Tower 143, climbed by James Garrett, Pete Keane and Brad England. The tower is the most prominent tower at the right end of Sunshine Wall.

In the Hurrah Pass area south of Moab, the spectacular Amazon Tower saw its first ascent by Andy Roberts, Dave Mealey and Matt Vanosdell. The route (5.11 A2, four pitches) climbs the west face of the spire. In the same area, Soltice Tower (5.10 C2) was climbed by Ted Rummings and Roberts in June.

ERIC BJØRNSTAD

Arches National Park

Organ Rock, Pilon's Pillar. On Organ Rock, *Pilon's Pillar* (V A5a 5.10) was soloed in November with three bolts. The route starts up *Pele Nubian Sacrifice* and goes straight up the overhanging east pillar. Although the crux has a 60- to 65-foot runout on beaks, it is the most straightforward and safe A5-minus I have done.

JIM BEYER

Valley of the Gods

Valley of the Gods, Various Activity. In 1999, with various partners, I visited the Valley of the Gods in southeastern Utah five times. While the bulk of my time was spent racing around Valley of the Gods Loop Road like a maniac (trying to set a new time record and a new dust-plume-height record), I also managed to climb five major towers that were previously unclimbed. Drivers/climbers/lunatics also involved included Jesse Harvey, Jon Butler, Benny Bach, Lefty Angus Burns and Jeff Widen. First ascents were as follows. January 2: *Putterman in A Bathtub* (II 5.9 C1, 450'). January 3: pitch 1 variation to Forrest-Hurley, Petard Tower (5.9 C1). January 9-11: *Putterman on The Throne* (III 5.9 C1, 450'). March 6: *The Putterman*

Residence (II 5.8 C1, 300'). March 7-8: *The Hand of Puttima* (II 5.9 Al, 300'). December, *McYetta's Loaf* (II 5.8 C1, 300').

CAMERON M. BURNS

San Rafael Swell

Mexican Mountain Area, Lone Rock, South Face. We had long had our eyes on the prominent right-facing dihedral system working its way up the south face of Lone Rock. Despite Eric's guidebook and all the hoopla about it, the tower known as Lone Rock still had no additional routes. We saw more bikers and four wheelers than usual but no other climbers. On March 13, John Sweeley and I made the first ascent of the South Face (III 5.9+ A1)

The rock is generally superb. For the offwidth master, the free rating would be harder, the C1 would be minimal and the nailing may be necessary to protect only a brief rotten section. By no means, however, should it be considered only a wide climb. Fun finger and hand cracks predominate. Three long pitches take one to the south summit intersection with Owls Eyes. Here one may continue to the higher north summit via the last 5.7 pitch of the other route or descend by rappel to the west.

JAMES GARRETT

Canyonlands National Park

Dabneyland, Various Ascents. This area is just outside and south of Monument Basin. It is named after Walt Dabney, who began the Canyonland's "No New Fixed Anchor" policy in 1995. The policy was designed to stop any new climbing development, but I reckon it just adds to the fun. There is more commitment when the pins and bolt kit have been left at home, and it is very satisfying to leave no trace.

The Pixie Stick is the only tower previously climbed in the area. During 1999, three new towers were climbed. In January, Kath Pyke and I climbed *The Intemperate Bass* (5.11a) on the furthest tower east, which we named Captain Pugwash. Nigel Gregory and I climbed Captain Bird's Eye via the route *This Is The Place* in October; the route involved three excellent 5.10c pitches on perfect Cutler sandstone, with mostly face climbing on pockets and edges. In November, Ralph E. Burns and I climbed *Captain Collywobble.* This involved four pitches to produce *Dottyback Deamo Daydream*, another 5.10c free climb. The descents from these fin-like towers involved simul-rappelling. Two 60-meter 9-mm ropes pulled fine each time. On *Captain Collywobble*, the tallest of the group, we used one 60-meter and one 70-meter rope.

STEVE "CRUSHER" BARTLETT

Soda Springs Basin, Yum Kipper, Toad Rage. In the basin south of Candlestick Tower, and below the White Rim Trail, Fran Bagenal and I attempted the obvious large tower, which we called Yum Kipper, in April, climbing two pitches. We retreated, encouraged by a vicious sandstorm screaming through the imposing slot of the third and final pitch. I returned a couple weeks later with Strappo Hughes,Tony Herr and many large Friends. We each took turns on the slot. Strappo eventually summitted after freeing the crack with one hang. He sat on top, untied and dropped the ropes so I could attempt a redpoint. I too hung once, though in a different spot. The rumble of approaching thunder told us we'd better call it quits. Tony followed, entirely free. We proclaimed the pitch 5.11c, and the climb *Toad Rage*.

Yum Kipper is about 250 feet high; the top layer is squared off, and composed of a very coarse, abrasive sandstone/limestone. Simul-rappelling was out of the question. Plan B involved a piece of lumber and a small saw. A nice piece of redwood 4 x 4 cut down to 4' 6" straddled the chimney. We hoped that after rappelling from this, we could walk out from the cliff and pull sideways on the lumber and yard it off. It would not budge. I jumared back up, the sky now black, while raindrops whipped around. Better hurry up with a Plan C. I duct-taped a three-foot 2 x 4 under one end of the 4 x 4 to make a "T." One end of the 2 x 4 hung over the edge about a foot, and enough rope was tied to this end to reach the ground. I rappelled, pulled on the ropes tied to the 2 x 4 and the whole anchor pivoted over the edge and came crashing down.

STEVE "CRUSHER" BARTLETT

Fisher Towers

The Titan, Sun Devil Chimney, First Clean Ascent. On March 20-21, Andy Donson and I made the first clean ascent of the *Sun Devil Chimney* (5.9 A3) on the Titan. We used tri-cams, small Aliens and hand-placed pins in existing scars and gave the route the clean grade of 5.9 C4.

KATH PYKE, *United Kingdom*

Arch Canyon

Cathedral Arch, Bats in the Belfry. In June, I got a call from Jeff Lowe asking if I would film and photograph an attempt on a new route in remote Arch Canyon, 25 miles west of Blanding in southeast Utah. I hardly ever turn down a job that pays me to go climbing. The team consisted of Jeff Lowe with his wife Teri Ebel, my assistant Deborah Nbozny and myself.

Jeff Lowe is famous for picking out classic new routes. Here he did not disappoint, taking us past probably a dozen or so unbelievable towers on the way to his prized route on Cathedral Arch. This tower, complete with an arch in the bottom left-hand corner, was reached after four hours of four-wheeling. Our campsite was situated in a beautiful grove of trees. We even had a stream and a pool for cool and frequent dips!

Arch Canyon's Cathedral Arch, showing Bats in the Belfry *(V 5.10 A3).* FREDDIE SNALAM

Now followed two days of technical climbing in 100-degree heat and 250 feet of gain in three pitches. We had 350 feet to go, but Jeff and Teri had to return home for a Fourth of July family reunion. On July 11, the team returned. Jeff and I ascended the fixed ropes and after three more days and one bivouac 95 feet below the summit, we emerged to the cheers of our base camp team of Teri and Deborah. We had climbed *Bats in the Belfry* (V 5.10 A3), but all we could think of was that cool swimming hole 650 feet below!

This region is Hopi Indian land. Ruins from the mid-1800s line the high valley walls. Visiting and exploring the sites is allowed. Signs of graffiti and vandalism were non-existent—a truly wonderful feeling. What an adventure!

FREDDIE SNALAM, *unaffiliated*

Zion

Kolob Canyon, Paria Point, Experimental Earth, Previously Unreported. In September, 1998, Jim Bridwell, Ron Olevsky and I climbed *Experimental Earth* (V 5.10 A3, ten pitches) on the south side of Paria Point. The route follows the continuous crack systems about 100 feet left of *Wind, Sand and Stars*. Most of the route was aid climbing and all belay stations were fixed, enabling us to rappel the route after summiting.

MARK BOWLING

The Temptress, Ascent, Previously Unreported. In April, 1998, while exploring one of Zion's many backcountry canyons, Andrew Nichols and I stumbled onto a gem of a wall. "The Temptress" is 800 feet tall, sleek, sheer, and straight as a rail. From the ground, the most distinguishing feature is a massive, double-tiered roof, each tier totally horizontal, 40 feet across and ten feet deep. The roofs are inset between opposing corner systems, the left coming up from below and the right ascending out to the sheer headwall above.

The approach starts with 1,000 feet of gain, first in a wash and then up fourth-class slabs. The slabs lead to a saddle. This is the head of a few different canyons, the largest splitting the East Temple and the Twin Brother formation. From the saddle, we scrambled down into the wash bottom for about a quarter of a mile until we came to the first rappel. We fixed a rope to the single-bolt rap station for our later return. The rappel left us in a beautiful, rarely traveled hanging canyon less than 200 feet wide with a proud stand of giant ponderosa pines. An open meadow right below the wall made an excellent base camp.

The first two pitches cross rightward up a series of right-facing dihedrals. With nightfall coming, but still not high enough for our belay, Andrew drilled one 3/8-inch bolt and lowered off. By morning it was pouring, and we hastily exited the canyon, ascended up our rope and went back to the car. Between weather and schedules, it took us three weeks to return.

Before long, Andrew was back at his high point, 50 feet below the roofs. After four reachy bathook moves, he was back into cams and soon drilling our second anchor. The next pitch was the roof. All of the edges of the roof had cracks up the sides, making its only true bond that from directly above. Scary. About 40 feet above a traverse, I drilled a hanging two-bolt belay under a nicely protective roof. With the next pitch, Andrew broke through three or four more roofs out onto the headwall above, then lashed a large and very loose boulder that we dubbed "the Protozoa" (and which we trundled the next morning) to the wall. We rapped back down to the ground at dusk.

Early the next morning, we ascended our 520 feet of fixed ropes. Our high point was in a transition of the rock's layers. The softer, lighter-colored rock ahead deteriorated in quality. One more steep section, then the angle began to kick back. Barely able to see and wearing only hiking boots, I freed up pancake-stacked ledges and gritty corners for 110 feet to a large tree. The slabs got easier above. With a large tree-covered ledge in sight, we quickly fifth-classed up 300 feet of slab to the top of the buttress. With only half a liter of water and an ocean of slabs between us and the summit of the East Temple, we called it good and rappelled the route in five raps, adding one rappel station on a ledge 120 feet above the ground to facilitate the descent. In the morning we thanked the Temptress for her gracious hospitality and began hauling loads up out of the canyon the way we had come in, leaving only one set of anchor slings and footprints as visible evidence of our adventure.

DAVID LITTMAN, *unaffiliated*

Kolob Canyon, Nugget Mesa, Sheehe Buttress. In October, Kathy Dicker and I made the first ascent of Kolob Canyon's Nugget Mesa (the buttress left of the waterfall). Our climb, *Sheehe Buttress* (V 5.10 A3), takes the obvious, most central line up the 1,200-foot southwest face. The climb is moderate, enjoyable and on quality rock. On the summit, we placed a small cairn and a summit register. The descent is made down the route and is quick, easy and safe. However, the final pitches are runout on moderate rock with questionable anchors. These pitches can be avoided if one wishes to forego the summit. The climb took a total of nine days over two attempts, the first attempt in frequent snowstorms and the final push in searing 100° temperatures. We named the route in honor of our friend, Sean Sheehe, who died earlier in the year. The route is easy to locate and requires a standard wall rack. It is a probable two- or three-day climb for most parties, although it could certainly be done in a day by a strong team. An all-free ascent might be possible at mid-5.13.

SCOTT COSGROVE

Paria Point, South Face, The Futura Wall. Troy Anderson, Todd Stephens and Nathan Brown put up *The Futura Wall* (V 5.10 A3) on the south face of Paria Point from March 25-27. The climb begins 100 feet to the right of *Wind, Sand and Stars*. Descent was made by rappelling the West Face route.

CLIMBERS' TOPO BINDERS, *Zion National Park Backcountry Permits desk*

Mt. Kinesava, The Jolly Green Jam Crack. In early November, I climbed a new ten-pitch route, The Jolly Green Jam Crack (IV 5.10 C1), on the southeast face of Mount Kinesava. The route ascends the face of a fairly distinct buttress about 200 feet to the right of *Arakis* and 300 yards to the left of *King Korner*. It follows a continuous and rather wide crack system until it joins *Arakis* for the last pitch. Rope soloing, I free climbed up to about 5.10. That took care of 75 percent of the climbing; the rest was easy and clean aid. This route would best be done as a free climb. To descend, *Arakis* has bolted rappel anchors, some of which are still only one bolt.

KIRBY SPANGLER, *unaffiliated*

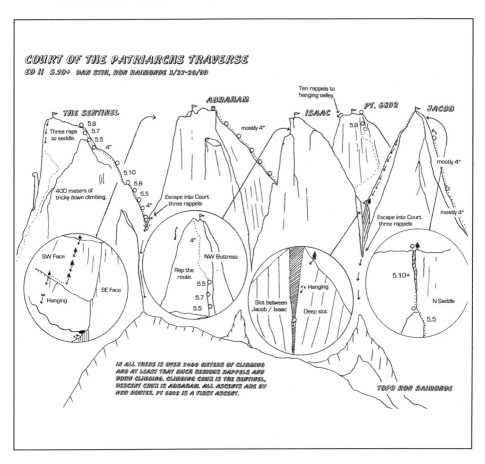

Court of the Patriarchs, Enchainment. During three days in late March, in Zion Canyon's Court of the Patriarchs, Dan Stih and I climbed all three of the Patriarchs and the Sentinel in one push. This traverse also included a possibly unclimbed formation known only as point 6,892'. All five towers were climbed by new routes. No holes were drilled on any of the routes, but one fixed pin was left on the Sentinel's north ridge at the 5.10R crux. This was the only pro on the pitch of near-vertical white cap slab. We did, however, drill two hanging rappel stations, the first in the 150-meter deep slot between Jacob and Isaac, and the other on the descent of the massive southwest face of Abraham. Besides the one pitch on the Sentinel, the climbing is fairly low key. There is nothing over 5.9, though long and serious "if not deadly" falls were in no shortage, especially on the descents. We simul-climbed almost all of Abraham and Isaac. The descents were far more intense and committing than the climbs, the one of Abraham taking more than six hours, and the Sentinel taking about four. The descent from point 6,892' was no picnic either, requiring at least ten rappels. All of the routes went completely free and clean. Most of the rock on the traverse is poor, and all of the routes offered little in the way of protection. We climbed alpine style with a light rack, melting snow for water and going without food for the last 25 hours. We gave the traverse a high adventure level rating and an Alpine rating of EDII, as this best describes it.

RON RAIMONDE

Chris McNamara on the "Tsunami" pitch of Los Banditos, Right Twin Brother. JERRY DODRILL

Red Arch Mountain, Wigs In Space. In March, James Garrett, Chris Eng and I climbed a new route on Red Arch Mountain called *Wigs In Space* (IV 5.9 Al/Cl, nine pitches). The route climbs a flat-faced pillar on the southwest buttress of Red Arch Mountain. Begin 100 feet left of *Bits and Pieces.* The rack is highly specialized and required several high fashion wigs. The first ascent was made with less than eight piton placements; the route was freed several months later at 5.11 by Cameron Tague and Jeff Hollenbaugh.

CAMERON M. BURNS

West Temple, Southeast Face, Full Steam Ahead. From February 11-24, Ammon McNeely soloed the route *Full Steam Ahead* (VI 5.10 A4) on the southeast face of West Temple. Gabe McNeely belayed him on the first pitch. The first and sixth pitches have deck potential. The eleventh and twelfth pitches have many (35-40) holes that need bolts. For the descent, rappel *Back Where It All Begins*; fix the thirteenth pitch and bring extra rope to pendulum the triple-roof pitch, or pendulum without bags.

CLIMBERS' TOPO BINDERS, *Zion National Park Backcountry Permits desk*

Temple of Sinawava, The Not So Secret Show. In October, Todd Stephens, Tyler Philips, and Troy Anderson climbed *The Not So Secret Show* (IV+ 5.10 A3, seven pitches) on the Temple of Sinawava. Descent was made by hiking the ridge west toward Angel's Landing, then catching the West Rim trail. Further details are lacking.

CLIMBERS' TOPO BINDERS, *Zion National Park Backcountry Permits desk*

Right Twin Brother, Los Banditos. In May, Luke Miller and I climbed a new aid line on the Right Twin, 100 feet to the right of *Peyote Dreams.* The independent line, *Los Banditos* (VI A4 5.8R), climbs three 60-meter free pitches of varying quality to six 60-meter pitches of mostly steep and clean aid. Highlighting the route is a 400-foot long beak and blade seam splitting an overhanging, clean headwall that our photographer Jerry Dodrill christened "The Dreamcatcher." The crux came on the first pitch of this feature and required 20-plus beaks and as many blades above a large ledge. Luke led some sketchy free-to-aid-to-free moves on the second to last pitch. Lots of rope drag and poor gear made this pretty exciting. We finished the route on the most spectacular top-out to a climb I have ever seen. Dubbed the "Tsunami," the last 40 feet ascend a perfect cresting-wavelike formation. Top-stepping the last bolt, I cut my feet from my aiders until they were dangling three feet from the wall, then threw a leg over the top and pressed a 5.9 mantle. The route was named after some bandits who stole camping gear from our photographer and his assistant before the climb. We placed 17 stout bolts at belays, 34 on lead and enhanced no placements.

CHRIS MCNAMARA

ARIZONA

Oak Creek Canyon, Arizona Boneless Chicken Ranch. In early November, Dan Stih and I established a new wall route in Oak Creek Canyon, high in Counterfeiter Canyon, just north of Sedona. The route, *Arizona Boneless Chicken Ranch* (IV 5.11 A3+) climbs a steep 175-

meter-high wall of fairly compact Coconino sandstone. The route, a continuous line from ground to summit, starts up an incredibly clean open book (C2) to the base of a five-meter roof. At this point the routes quality begins to deteriorate rapidly; the only reason we continued climbing was the combination of the enticing cracks we saw higher up and the distorted cognitive thought process one gets with repeated desert epics. Pitch 2 climbs over the "Chicken Ranch Roof" (A3+) and up some of the most horrifically loose sandstone either of us had ever contemplated climbing. Dan led the roof and part of the rotten overhanging seam above before lowering off a junk rivet and handing me the rack.

After jugging past the worst of the climbing and seeing the garbage Dan had placed, I arrived at his high point with my heart in my throat. The thought of falling on the rivet I was jugging on, let alone the mess below, encouraged me to start nailing in anything that looked remotely feasible as protection. Finishing the pitch I realized that, for the first time in nearly 15 years of aid climbing on sandstone, my heart was beating so radically I feared I might actually have a heart attack. Hand-drilling two half-inch by four-inch Rawls calmed me down. Pitch 3 climbs excellent rock (A2) to a semi-hanging belay. Pitch 4 starts out an overhanging 5.11 offwidth and finishes up another steep, rotten A2+ seem. Pitch 5 finishes the route free to the top. There doesn't seem to be any mediocre rock on the wall; it's either excellent or garbage.

RON RAIMONDE

Baboquivari Peak, Various Ascents. In March, I soloed a new route on the east face of Baboquivari Peak. *Freak of Nature* (VI 5.10 A5a) starts 40 feet left of *Cradle of Stone* and climbs straight up a blankish golden wall left of the black water streak in the center the face. The fifth pitch (A5a) has 22 A3/A4 placements in a row, producing a 45- to 50-foot runout. The route finishes with a 5.10 A2+ variation to the *Spring Route* aid corner. Pasted quarter-inch aluminum heads protect 5.10 face climbing. No bolts were drilled and all free climbing was led free onsight.

JIM BEYER

NEW MEXICO

Navajolands

Shiprock, Various Ascents. In January, I soloed *Parallel Reality* (IV A5+) and *On a Tear* (VI A5+) on the south face of Sextant Spire. Both routes are extreme aid routes that went in without bolts, and both have excellent groundfall potential.

On the west face of Shiprock, I soloed *West Sanctum* (VI A5+ 5.10) from December 1-11: fat solo action with eight bolts in 11 days and ten nights and three A5 pitches in a row.

For *West Sanctum*, I tried to get a permit from the grazing permit administrator at the Shiprock Chapter House but was declined. A climbing accident on Shiprock involving a woman and a broken leg four years ago resulted in a big rescue. The grazing-permit administrator informed me that Shiprock Chapter House passed a resolution as a result of the accident encouraging the Window Rock Chapter House not to give out permits.

JIM BEYER

COLORADO

Rocky Mountain National Park

Longs Peak, East Face, The Casual Route, First Solo, and Other Activity, Previously Unreported. I soloed (what is now called) the *Casual Route* on Longs Peak on July 14, 1980, all free; it took me two hours something. My girlfriend walked up and met me on top. I always assumed it had been done before until I read the guidebook recently, which credits the first solo to Charlie Fowler in 1984. I also soloed the Regular Route on the northwest face of Half Dome that same summer on September 27 in six hours something—which is not quite as fast as Dean Potter's ascent last year, but was done almost 20 years before! My ascent was mostly free but with a backrope on two bolt-ladder pitches down low and on the pitches above Big Sandy. I met up with Steve Bell (and Roger Mear, I think) on Big Sandy.

STEVE MONKS, *United Kingdom*

Longs Peak, East Face, Gear and Clothing, Previously Unreported. In August, 1998, Cameron Tague and I did the second ascent of *Gear and Clothing* (IV 5.9 A4) on the Diamond. The ascent itself is not significant; however, the amount of free climbing on the route is worth mentioning. We freed several of the aid pitches at 5.10-ish. One pitch, an A2 corner, was freed by Cameron at 5.12 and was excellent. The A4 pitch might go free as well, as would the pitches on the upper headwall, to a patient party. Watch out for the death flake on the pitch below Table Overhang; it could take out your belayer and all those slow starters in the North Chimney.

KENT McCLANNAN

Keyboard of the Winds, Various Ascents. In early July, Nigel Gregory approached me with a gleam in his eyes. "Are you up for a little new routing?" he asked. Nigel's British upbringing made me immediately suspicious. I hesitantly said, "I don't know; maybe." He took that for an enthusiastic "yes," and before I knew it we were off to explore a beautiful group of small, unclimbed spires in Rocky Mountain National Park.

Perched on the ridge between Longs Peak and Pagoda Peak are five independent spires called the Keyboard of the Winds. Although they look a bit slabby when viewed from Black Lake, they are quite steep and offer interesting climbing. The spires range from 250 to 700 feet tall and we found the rock to be fairly solid, despite the occasional loose block and some thick lichen. It all made for a marvelous adventure! However, the climbs were not without incident. Nigel fell from the first pitch of *Mr. Stubbs*, and one of his double ropes was severed two-thirds of the way through by the gate of a carabiner. Unconcerned by the event, he simply pulled out a knife, cut off the damaged bit and carried on to the belay.

In total, we climbed a new route on the northwest face of each of the five towers. At least two of the spires had never been summitted, and four of the towers had never been climbed by a technical route. Generally, we followed the path of least resistance up obvious crack systems. Starting from Pagoda Peak and heading northeast, the towers and routes are as follows. *Picking Plums* (5.10c) on Sievers Tower; *Brass in Pocket* (5.11b) on Jackpot Tower; *Cools the Burning* (5.10a) on Mrs. Stubbs; *Stubbs Fights Back* (5.11a) on Mr. Stubbs; and *Step-in-stein* (5.10a) on The Dark Tower. It is easiest to descend off the back of the spires via one mandatory

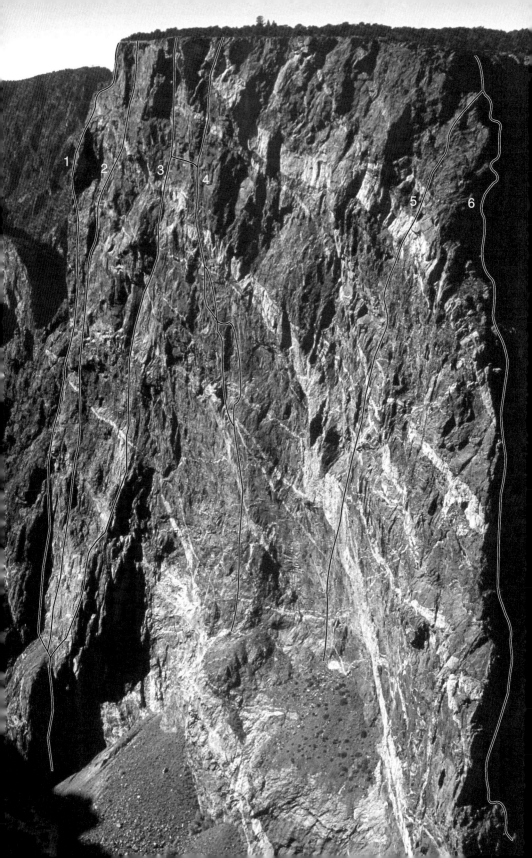

rappel or some easy scrambling.

DAVE SHELDON

Rocky Mountain National Park, Enchainment. In August, Mike Pennings and I left the Longs Peak parking lot at 3 a.m. and climbed *Pervertical Sanctuary* (5.10) on the Diamond. We then dropped over the west side of Longs and soloed the North Ridge of Spearhead (5.6) before traversing around to climb the Petit Grepon's South Face (5.8). From there we kicked steps up Andrew's Glacier onto the Continental Divide and continued north to where we could glissade Tyndal Glacier to reach the north face of Hallet's. We started up the classic Northcutt-Carter (5.7), but found a massive rockfall had eliminated the second pitch just days before. We were able to do a variation to the right, which was runout and 5.10. The rest of the route is the same as before, but the first two pitches could be unstable; finding an alternative is recommended. We summitted on Hallet's and continued along the Divide to where we could glissade Ptarmigan Glacier to reach the south face of Notchtop. There, darkness caught us and we climbed the *Spiral Route* (5.4) by headlamp. We reached the Bear Lake parking lot at 1:30 a.m.

Our effort bagged 5,000 feet of climbing in about 20 miles of cross-country hiking but, as Pennings pointed out, our climbathalon was just the beginning of possible enchainments in the Park. Add Mt. Alice, Chief's Head and Shark's Tooth to the package for a full day.

TOPHER DONAHUE

Chief's Head, The Headdress. Following a wet summer, a cold September caused ice to form in unusual places in RMNP. Eli Helmuth and I climbed a smear originally found by Duncan Ferguson on the north face of Mt. Meeker. A week later, Helmuth was guiding Longs Peak and saw a much larger flow on Chief's Head. We went in with Simon Fryer and climbed the feature at the end of September. To the right of the rock climb *Much Ado About Nothing*, we found five pitches, including the crux 60-meter pitch, which inspired the name *The Headdress* (M5+ WI5+). At the end of October, I returned to try another line in the area and *The Headdress* was gone.

TOPHER DONAHUE

Black Canyon of the Gunnison

Painted Wall, The Serpent. In mid-October, Kennan Harvey and I climbed an all-free variation to the *Dragon* route on the Painted Wall. We climbed in classic wall style, with the leader free climbing and the second following on jumars. A "true" free ascent is left for future European rock stars. We followed the original *Dragon Route* (Baillie-Baxter-Lovejoy-Karlstrom, 1972) for 600 feet to Kor's Cave, a huge overhang sheltering what was once a spacious bivy ledge that has since fallen off. From the remnants of this ledge where the *Dragon* goes right, we went left under the roof, climbing three complex pitches diagonally up and left to rejoin the *Dragon* in its "Stygian Traverse." At the end of this traverse, we continued left

The Painted Wall, showing 1. Southern Arête (Dalke-Goss-Kor-Logan, late 1960s). 2 Journey Through Mirkwood (approximate) (Newberry-Pearson-Pulaski-Rosholt, late 1970s). 3. Forest-Walker (1972)/Stratosfear (Coyne-Leavitt, 1984) (Forest-Walker finishes direct to the rim; Stratosfear traverses right to connect with the Dragon Route. Traverse shown). 4. Dragon Route (Baillie-Baxter-Karlstrom-Lovejoy, 1972). The Serpent variation (Achey-Harvey, 1999) takes the leftmost paths (shown). 5. Beyer route (Jim Beyer, solo, date unknown). 6. Northern Arête (Disney-Kor, 1962). JEFF ACHEY

onto new terrain, joining the *Dragon* again a pitch higher, just beyond a rotten yellow band that forms the original route's aid crux. Easier free climbing led to the *Dragon* exit chimneys and juncture with the *Stratosfear* route, with four more moderate crack pitches to the top. The free route involves about 600 feet of new climbing in 1,800 feet overall.

We took four days car-to-car, most of which was spent hauling, carrying loads or drinking wine on our portaledge. The main challenges lay in route finding and sparse protection on the steep, intricate wall and in protecting our ropes from the sharply fractured rock. I had climbed the original *Dragon Route* in winter three years earlier with Mark Synnott; Kennan had never been on the Painted Wall before. Other than what I remembered from my previous ascent, we climbed all pitches onsight, using no aid for progress, inspection or placing protection. We placed no bolts. Seven pitons were left fixed and about ten 5.11 sections were encountered. This being a wall climb, we suggest a Yosemite-style rating of new wave 5.9+.

Although we left all our pins fixed, future parties are advised to carry a few knifeblades because the Painted Wall sheds flakes, ledges and fixed gear. The rock that is not loose or fractured is generally flint-hard and excellent for climbing. A good selection of modern micro-gear, wired nuts and long slings is advised; the Kor's Roof pitch requires several four- to five-inch pieces. We led on double 10-mm lines and though we had no serious mishaps, by the end of the climb we had cut or damaged three of the five ropes we carried. A detailed topo, full of helpful beta and gratuitous names for prominent features, is available by sending your firstborn daughter to Kennan Harvey.

JEFF ACHEY, *unaffiliated*

The Serpent, Second Ascent. In November, Jeff Ofsanko and I were looking for adventure about a week after Jeff Achey and Kennan Harvey did the first ascent of a free variation to the *Dragon* on the Painted Wall. With Achey's topo, we found our way to the top in four days of wild climbing. The climbing is excellent although a bit more serious than they noted. Even relative to other climbs in the notorious canyon, we felt it deserved an "X" rating. Harvey and Achey placed the existing pins from tricky free stances, so not all the placements are perfect. Carrying a few pitons is mandatory. Getting dangerously offroute would be easy, so putting a bolt kit in the bottom of the bag is good insurance.

TOPHER DONAHUE

WYOMING

GRAND TETON NATIONAL PARK

Grand Teton, New Routes, and Other Climbs. On the east face of the Grand Teton, in July, Zac Martin and I climbed *The Golden Arête* (V 5.11d AI2) with 15 bolts and *Offspring* (III 5.11 A1) with four bolts and three points of aid. Both routes are located to the right of the *Smith Otterbody Route.* The routes went in ground-up with a hand drill. *The Golden Arête* was pushed to the summit in 16 hours via the *Otterbody* and Ford Couloir routes after spending two short days on the first three pitches. In August, I soloed the *Crystal Tower* (III 5.10) on the Grand Teton. This overhanging tower of golden rock with a white serrated summit is located at the base of the Underhill Ridge. This six-pitch route is similar in quality and difficulty to *Caveat Emptor* and is located in the heart of the Tetons. In September, I soloed a new route on the west face of the Exum Ridge of the Grand Teton. *Got to Kill Captain Stupid* (III 5.9+) climbs the steep wall above the Wall Street Couloir to the left of the Jackson-Rickert at a surprisingly moderate 5.9, joins the West Face of the Exum for its 5.7 offwidth, then finishes in the chockstone-capped chimney just right of the Pownall-Gilkey exit.

In Death Canyon, Zac Martin and I climbed *Braeburn's Corner* (5.11a, five pitches) on the Omega Buttress across the gully from *Ship's Prow Pillar*. Also in Death Canyon, Zac and a partner put in a long Grade V on the south side of the canyon in a two-day effort.

JIM BEYER

WIND RIVER MOUNTAINS

Cathedral Peak, South Tower Direct. The spectacular 1,200-foot face of Cathedral Peak rises above Cathedral Lake, just seven miles from the Dickenson Park Trailhead on the Lander side of the range. Until Chris McNamara and I climbed the South Tower of this 12,166-foot peak in a long day, the only route on it was *Orion's Reflection*, a Grade V 5.10 A3 done by Fred Beckey and Jim Kantzler in 1979 with one bivy, during which they saw, guess what, Orion's reflection in the lake below. Our route took several tries in the vain hope of freeclimbing a line somewhere up the perfect Wind River gneiss, but the lack of vertical crack systems and frequency of horizontal ceilings made us resort to a fair amount of aid on the upper wall. Our *South Tower Direct* (V 5.11b A2) starts up the center of the left of the two towers that are split by a massive couloir on the upper face. Near the top, we veered toward the left side to avoid more overhangs after a strenuous pair of pitches with multiple ceilings. We topped out just as a thunderstorm was closing in.

Spending a week camped at Cathedral Lake, Chris and I also climbed a Grade III 5.10 free route up the lower-angle, 800-foot South Buttress of Cathedral, as well as a four-pitch 5.10 new route with Randy Spurrier up the 500-foot south face of what we called Isthmus Dome, just north of the narrow isthmus between Cathedral and Middle Lakes.

GALEN ROWELL

Mt. Hooker, Brain Larceny, Second Ascent, and Buffalo Head, East Face, The Skeptic. Cameron Teague and I made the second ascent of *Brain Larceny* (Donahue-Harvey, 1994) free in one day on August 25. The grade was confirmed at V 5.12R. The line follows good rock with pitches fairly consistently at 5.11 and 5.12 and contains no fixed gear. We used no route info other than a matchbox-sized, multi-xeroxed photograph from *Rock & Ice* No. 82.

Buffalo Head is the northernmost tower of the ridge between South Fork Lakes and

Kath Pyke on pitch 5 of The Skeptic.
CAMERON TEAGUE

Wasakie Pass. Cameron Teague and I made the first ascent of *The Skeptic* (IV 5.11, seven pitches, 900') on September 27. The route takes a line up the center of the east face that gains a major left-facing dihedral before following a 200-foot featured wall to the summit. The route was completed with no prior scoping in one day. Descent is via slabs to the southwest and a short rappel into the gully.

KATH PYKE, *United Kingdom*

Point 12,612', East Face, The Illness. In August, 1988, Franziska Garrett, James Garrett and Fred Beckey traveled to the seldom-visited St. Lawrence Basin of the Wind River Range to attempt the east face of Point 12,612' on the Wolverine. James and Franziska spent the night at the top of pitch 5. They climbed two pitches in the morning and then descended. The three of them then climbed the beautiful ridge (complete with a gendarme rappel) on Saddleback's north face (5.8, 1,800') the next day.

Then, in the summer of 1997, Franzisca Garrett, James Garrett and Kris Pietryga returned to Wolverine. This time, equipped with ample aid gear and portlaledges, James and Kris made it to pitch 8, whereupon the weather turned bad just as Kris pulled off a huge block, nearly hitting James. They descended.

Finally, in August, 1999, James Garrett, Fred Beckey, Ryan Hokanson, John Chilton and Kris Pietryga traveled to the St. Lawrence Basin once again. Kris and his friend, Fisherman Sam, fixed the first two pitches and carried huge loads for us. In the next two days, Ryan, James and Johnny made the first complete ascent of *The Illness* (IV 5.10 A3, nine pitches) on the east face, with Fred providing spiritual advisement at camp. The route consists of nine full 200-meter pitches, and requires some thin nailing and a few heads. We used a horse packer to get our stuff to within three miles of the wall, well worth the exorbitant prices charged; contact the Ft. Washakie Chamber of Commerce. This climb exists on the Wind River Indian Reservation so restrictions may apply.

RYAN HOKANSON

Squaretop, AC/DC. To the left of the great bay in the east face of Squaretop, the wall forms a long fin that ends in a tower. From Granite Lake our route and the formation are quite obvious. We called the tower "Squaretower" and our route on the face *AC/DC*. It is an excellent, varied and difficult route. I first tried it with Mike Weis and Carol Kacza about a million years ago, then returned with my son Dan last summer for another attempt. He and I were stormed off, but we climbed gullies and short headwalls left of the tower and reached the summit in a fun way.

In general, the route ascends the south face of the tower, starting from an obvious grassy ledge at the base of the steep upper wall. The approach is not trivial, and we roped up both times prior to reaching the ledge. Careful route finding and better climbers might avoid that necessity.

From the right end of the ledge, follow cracks and chimneys on the right side of the formation, then trend left across the middle of the tower, aiming for the crack and corner on the left edge of the wall capped by an enormous triangular roof. At the base of the roof, traverse right about half a rope-length out to the east edge, and from there, follow cracks to the summit. By the way, the triangular roof has a very wide crack splitting its right side (five or six inches?) that will make a very exciting pitch, which we were fortunately not prepared to tackle.

I would recommend this climb, and future parties should be very aware of the loose block on pitch 2 if they choose that crack. One can climb over it or do the crack/flake system to the left (which is what we did the first time) but the right crack is outstanding and hard, and the second should definitely honk that deathblock.

I lost my watch with wedding ring attached somewhere on the third pitch. Maybe it will turn up one day. Ten pitches (some short) to the summit, an 80-foot rap to the notch, two pitches to summit plateau (some 5.7 on the first pitch). We'd rate the climb IV 5.10. Good pro, recommended. Harder variations are quite apparent. Descend east gullies to Granite Lake. Catch trout, eat dinner.

ANDY CARSON

MONTANA

Glacier National Park

Glacier National Park, Various Activity. The 1998-'99 ice climbing season was largely a feast of leftovers in Glacier National Park. Routes that had been on the table for years but were not as choice as the rest finally got devoured. Many of these routes were done early season and are included in last year's journal. Later in the season, I skied in to the southwest face of Cannon Mountain and soloed *A Walk in the Park*, a nice 900-foot WI3 just to the right of *Lost in a Crowd*. I returned to Cannon with Julie Vance to establish *Sunken Battleship*, a 350-foot slabby mixed line to the left of *Cannon Barrel*.

On the south side of Cannon Mountain lays the Hidden Creek drainage. Through a series of scouting missions, local climbers discovered a reasonable approach (only five hours) into this narrow valley. Just below the level of the lake, the canyon opens into a virtual cornucopia of water ice. Here, partnered with Blase Reardon and later with Jim Earl, I climbed a total of eight WI3s and 4s up to three pitches long. Due to the high density of routes and the relative lack of climbers in Hidden Creek, thinking of names for all of that ice seemed pointless. Suffice to say that there are still plenty of hidden morsels for the FA-starved ice climber.

KIRBY SPANGLER, *unaffiliated*

Mt. Edwards, Various Activity. On the left side of Mount Edwards' north face is a large triangular buttress. At mid-height, this buttress is dissected by a distinctive snowy ledge. From this ledge, water ice seems to ooze from deep within the mountain to form spindly 'sicles and thin curtains that descend the steep rock to the snow slopes 500 to 800 feet below.

In the winter of 1996-'97, Jim Earl, Kelly Cordes and Chris Trimble began the quest to reach this ledge. They climbed three pitches up the rightmost (and longest) line on the buttress but failed to attain the ledge. They named their incomplete route *Baby Semler* in honor of one of Glacier Park's finest. For three years, this was the extent of activity on the buttress.

With Y2K, fat ice and motivation returned. Earl and two others attempted a line just to the left of Baby Semler. Again they climbed three pitches but fell short of the elusive ledge. Sticking to the theme, Jim dubbed this line *Holy Moses* after another park ranger. Two days later, Jim was again making the four-hour slog to the bottom of the buttress, this time accompanied by me. We climbed two pitches up yet another line, but due to heavy snowfall and increasing avalanche danger, we opted to retreat. (We refrained from naming this incomplete route because we knew that another party had been attempting it as well.)

After that first trip up to the buttress, all of those almost-done routes were all that I could think about. With Jim gone to Ecuador for a month, I was left scrambling for a partner. I con-

Climbs of the Bureaucrat Buttress. Rule Book Roger *(née* Baby Semler*) is on the right,* Holy Moses *in center. The big flow on the left remains unclimbed despite five attempts by various parties in the winter of 1999-2000.* KIRBY SPANGLER

vinced my friend Blasé Reardon to join me. I was looking for the easiest way to reach that snow ledge, and I reckoned *Baby Semler* would be it. Three moderate pitches brought us to the route's previous high point. Here I followed a narrow snowy traverse 100 feet to the left. This brought me to a steep continuous curtain of ice. A few feet up, it was thick enough to install a hanging belay. One more pitch landed us on the snowy ledge that signified the end of the route. Finally, success on the buttress. We began referring to it as the "Bureaucrat Buttress," and changed the name *Baby Semler* to *Rule Book Roger* (IV WI5). The reference remains the same.

Almost immediately I began seeking a partner to attempt *Holy Moses*. Two weeks and many logistical snafus later, I was back, this time with Ryan Hokanson and Mike Jobeck. Again we cruised the first three pitches. The fourth and final pitch remained hidden from view around a corner. From the ground it had looked rather difficult, so as I started the lead, I was anxious about what awaited me. As I worked out the moves, the pitch revealed itself section by section: sustained and technical, but not especially strenuous. At mid-pitch, a snow blob collapsed under my weight and sent me for a short ride. This was but a minor setback, and soon I found myself once again at that not-so-elusive-anymore ledge. *Holy Moses* (IV WI5+) was now whole.

I wish that could be the happy ending to the story of Bureaucrat Buttress, but soon enough Jim was back. There was still a line to be done, and he wanted it bad. I had a funny feeling that morning and was glad when Jim offered to lead the crux third pitch. As I belayed the first pitch, I began to relax. As the rope paid out, I prepared to climb. Glancing up to check Jim's progress, I saw a bright flash, accompanied by a loud thunk. Instantly I was on the ground and bleeding badly. I had taken a chunk to the face. The game was up. Poor Jim got turned back again.

KIRBY SPANDANGLER, *unaffiliated*

ALASKA

BROOKS RANGE

West Maiden, North Prow. On August 1-2, Lorna Corson, Randy Farris, Mike Menoloscino and I climbed a possible new route on the north side of the West Maiden. We began our climb by traversing left across the wide ledge that is a prominent feature on the lower right side of the face. We then climbed up from the ledge at a couple of small patches of snow and ice below the second major weakness on the face above. After talking with John Markel, I believe this is where their original Markel-Duggan North Buttress route heads straight up. Our route angled up and left for four pitches and led to a corner system near the actual prow of the buttress. These pitches were wet, exposed to rockfall and not entirely enjoyable. From this point on, though, the climbing and rock improved dramatically. We climbed on, or just to the west of, the crest of the actual prow for the next 16 long pitches. The climbing was rarely easier than 5.7 and never harder than 5.9 or easy 5.10. While most of the climbing involved good crack climbing, there were also several pitches of very runout face. The last pitch avoided a chimney by climbing a perfect one-inch crack through a roof with the whole route dropping away below. We called our climb *The Maiden Voyage* (V 5.9+ R). A true classic.

For descent, we had planned to rappel the gully to the east of the East Maiden. However, as we arrived at the summit at 2:15 a.m. in a gathering storm, we were forced to descend into the Ayagomahalla Valley and suffer through a rainy and foodless 15-mile bushwhack back to our camp in Arrigetch Creek's south fork. We climbed 20 60-meter pitches, used no pitons or bolts and left the route in the same pristine shape that we found it.

NORM LARSON

Arrigetch Peaks, Various Ascents. In early August, Stan Justice, Dean Justice, Ian McRae,

Michael Williams and I flew into the Arrigetch Peaks of the Western Brooks Range. We cut our flight costs in half by flying from Graying Lake (near Prospect on the Dalton Highway) to Takahula Lake. We avoided mosquitoes by choosing to climb in August but paid the price with rainy, cold weather.

Most of the higher (above 6,000') peaks in the area have been climbed. We spent two lazy days bushwhacking into a valley south of Shot Tower. After making base camp in a high meadow, we split into two teams. Ian, Michael and I chose the first peak that caught our eye as our (only) objective. We climbed the North Arête of Coolage Tower (IV 5.9 A1) after two failed attempts due to rain. The climb consisted of one crack system that steadily rose for 1,500 feet. The crack size varied from offwidth to knifeblade and back again. Surmounting the final bit involved some tricky free climbing and overhanging aid. We rappelled down the east face to avoid the traversing nature of our line of ascent. The rock on our route was the best any of us had seen in Alaska.

JEFF APPLE BENOWITZ

ALASKA RANGE

Mt. Crosson, South Ridge, Previously Unreported. In May, 1996, Paul Ramsden (UK) and Andrew Brash (Canada) made the first ascent of the South Ridge of Mt. Crosson before continuing up the Sultana Ridge to the summit of Mt. Foraker. We climbed in a super lightweight style and had a great time. The South Ridge provides 6,000 feet of elevation gain and was climbed over two nights due to the high daytime temperatures. The main difficulties were found low on the ridge, where the shale pinnacles were covered in unconsolidated snow. From the summit of Mt. Crosson, we continued to the summit of Foraker over two days. Conditions on the ridge were excellent and the weather was very good. We returned to Crosson before descending the usual Southeast Ridge. The round trip took a total of five days; we gave the outing an Alaskan Grade 4 for the whole thing.

PAUL RAMSDEN, *United Kingdom*

Denali National Park, Mountaineering Statistics. This past climbing season is the second time since 1991 that the mountain did not claim any lives. Unrelenting high winds contributed to a summit rate of less than 20 percent during the month of May. Later in the season, stretches of moderate weather allowed more mountaineers to reach the top of McKinley. This raised the overall summit percentage for the season to 43 percent. The historical summit rate dating back to 1903 remains at 51 percent.

The 1998-'99 winter season on Denali saw intense cold weather and high winds. This led to an early retreat for three expeditions. Although no climbers summitted Mt. McKinley this past winter, one climber summitted Mt. Foraker, although not in time to be considered a winter ascent. (See below.)

Mountaineering in Denali National Park and Preserve has increased dramatically over the years. In 1984, 695 climbers attempted to climb McKinley; this past year, that number almost doubled to 1,183 climbers on the mountain's slopes. In 1995, the National Park Service started a three-pronged approach to attempt to reduce the number of accidents and deaths and to support those efforts using funds paid by climbers. This program consists of a 60-day pre-registration requirement, a climbing special-use fee and a preventative search and rescue and education program. From 1990 through 1994, Denali averaged 12 mountaineering rescues per year. After the implementation of the 60-day pre-registration requirement and with an aggressive education program, the average number of major rescue missions decreased by 23.2 percent. The number of climbers on the mountain increased by ten percent during the same time frame. Fatal accidents also decreased from an average of four per year to two per year. Since the implementation of the current program, a dramatic reduction in the number of foreign rescues and fatalities has also occurred.

There were nine major mountaineering incidents in 1999 involving 15 mountaineers. The National Park Service spent $101,223 for mountaineering-related search and rescue activities. The military spent an additional $115,604 assisting in these incidents.

Denali National Park initiated a fuel can monitoring system this past season to record the number of fuel cans being used and illegally discarded on the mountain. The ultimate goal of this project is to ensure that all fuel cans used on expeditions are removed from the mountain. While some data collection took place in 1998, this year's concerted effort to track the cans met with considerable success. During the registration process, expeditions were assigned a can number which was then written on every gallon of white gas carried out of the Kahiltna Base Camp where fuel is stored. We hope climbers will assist us in these efforts in the years to come.

DENALI NATIONAL PARK REPORTS

Mountain/Route	Teams	Climbers	Successful Teams
MOUNT MCKINLEY			
Cassin	4	8	2
East Face	1	1	0
Messner Couloir	3	4	3
Muldrow Glacier	5	26	1
Muldrow Glacier Traverse	1	3	1
Northwest Buttress	1	2	1
Orient Express	1	2	1
Pioneer Ridge	1	4	0
West Buttress	263	996	141
West Buttress Traverse	5	34	2
West Rib	18	60	7
Upper West Rib	13	40	6
Wickersham Wall	1	2	0
Total	318	1183	164

Statistics for Foraker and Hunter were missing from the web site. However, the Denali National Park Ranger's station was kind enough to pass on the following. On the Foraker front for 1999, a total of 22 climbers attempted the mountain, with 12 climbers reaching the summit via the *Sultana Ridge*. For Mount Hunter, out of the 48 climbers that voluntarily registered with us, there was one reported summit by two climbers via the West Ridge.

DENALI NATIONAL PARK REPORTS

Mt. Foraker, Sultana Ridge, Notable Ascent. Japanese soloist Masatoshi Kuriaki attempted a winter ascent of Mt. Foraker. He spent 57 days on the *Sultana Ridge* before attaining the summit, which was achieved after the official end of winter. Further details are lacking.

Mt. Foraker, South Face. New Englanders Steve Larson and Joe TerraVecchia established a new route, the South Face (Alaska Grade 6, 9,400'), on Mount Foraker (17,400') from June 4-20. The route ascended the 3,500-foot diamond-shaped wall between the *Infinite Spur* and the French Ridge. A full account of their climb appears earlier in this journal.

Mt. Hunter, North Buttress, Attempt. Flying in with Talkeetna Air Taxi, I could see that Mt. Hunter's north buttress was in condition. I had visited Alaska in 1998 and had a variety of stuff to go at. I set up base on the now-familiar glacier and skied up to do a recce. Everything was there. The night was clear, the 'schrund went well enough, and I was soon moving up to somewhere near *Deprivation*. To its right was an intriguing line. I self-belayed for once in my alpine life, enjoying the feeling of security and the hard sketchy climbing. All went well, though frustratingly slowly. My plan had been to fix my two ropes and go down. I had every bit of gear I needed, though, so I carried on. The plan was simple: climb the first, second and third rockbands, then carry on directly to finish as for the *Moonflower*. Leave the heavy stuff and go for the summit, returning to descend the partly equipped *Moonflower* line.

It took two days to get to a junction with *Deprivation* at the top of the second band of rock, having been dusted by a huge powder and serac avalanche while aiding up a corner below the top of the first band. . . . The good buzz changed to one of electric danger when I realized I was on a windslab slope. I was looking up to my last obstacle: the rock above, then open slopes to the exit off the wall. I just could not push it. Lots of rappels, v-threads, nuts, pegs, more threads, then down the lower section of *Deprivation*. The last throw of the rope off a bollard and I was staggering, dragging ropes back to my skis as the mountain became active.

For a while, the weather hung in the balance; it stormed, people left. The weather changed; it became cold, but not too cold. I decided to climb at night and sleep in the mid-afternoon when the face caught the sun. So no sleeping bag—a bivy sac and down jacket instead, three days' worth of food and gas. I opted for two 5.5mm Dyneema ropes and no self-belaying. On the aid, I'd just put in as many pieces as I could, attaching slings and back-cleaning as I went. I could hang the sack on a fifi hook and pull it up without having to go back down. The system works: I recently fell off while free soloing on the Grandes Jorasses. Tends to send the heart rate up a bit, that's all.

Climbing like this, I reached the foot of the second rockband in only the first day. It being too warm, I stopped to await the night. An all-night, full-bore storm plastered the face in rime ice and new snow. I bailed, battling with frozen gear, clearing the bergschrund as the face woke up.

I went up again a couple of times, but each time it snowed so much that slowly the reality dawned on me that it was finished. I'd lost, failed yet again, but what an experience to be totally at one with my ideal. The second time up, I took real pleasure in the fact that I was evolving my style to that of a purer one. I had some great climbing on one of the world's mythical mountain faces. What more can one wish for?

ANDY PARKIN, *United Kingdom*

Mt. Hunter and Thunder Mountain, Various Activity. From late April to late May, Dan Donovan and I (leader) based ourselves on Thunder Glacier on the south side of Mt. Hunter. In 1998, I had spotted a potential new variation to Mt. Hunter's West Ridge route, so as soon as camp was established, we made the five-mile trek to below the south side of the west ridge and the foot of an icefall protecting a glacier basin. On April 28, we climbed a straightforward 1,500-foot couloir, traversed around a little, dropped 500 feet into the basin, then walked about one mile up the basin to below the first of a series of rock and snow ribs that lead to the west ridge. We spent the remainder of the day camped at just below 8,000 feet.

The central section of the west ridge has a long, flattish corniced section that is very rocky on its south side. It then climbs steeply to an icy shoulder, after which easier snow slopes lead to the plateau. The couloir gains the ridge at the top of this shoulder, thus avoiding all of the difficulties of the ridge and making a two-day ascent to the North Summit very reasonable, with full descent on the third day. On our ascent, we gained the ridge at 11,250 feet after four hours in soft snow. We then continued on to the plateau at 13,000 feet, arriving at approximately 2 p.m. Lacking the fitness to summit that day, we made our camp, only to have a storm arrive during the afternoon. We spent April 30 in the tent. The storm abated late in the afternoon, though visibility was not sufficient for a summit attempt. On May 1, we headed off for the summit in a cool wind (-30°C), but turned back at approximately 13,800 feet due to windslab conditions. We returned to our tent then descended the ridge, continuing into the basin, where we waited for the remainder of the day, as a British party camping on the ridge at 11,300 feet had decided to follow us out. On May 2, we climbed out of the basin and returned to camp. (Subsequently, several parties climbed to the summit from a camp at 11,300 feet via this variation, which we named the *Ramen Route*.)

On May 13, we headed off to the north face of Thunder Mountain. We reached a highpoint of approximately 8,100 feet, barely 950 feet above the bergschrund, before very poor (or no) protection forced a retreat.

On May 15, we made an early start and, with reasonable snow conditions, traveled around to the adjacent glacier and gained the foot of the rock buttress on Mt. Hunter's west buttress by 10 a.m. We climbed a short distance up the right side to gain a snowy traverse that angled back left to the foot of a corner system on the front of the buttress. From this point, we climbed six hard 60-meter pitches (one solid Scottish 6 pitch). The last two pitches were serious climbing on steep, exfoliating slabs; one fall was taken. Some easy snow/ice then led to a snow band at half-height, which we reached at midnight. Light snow fell on and off during the climb, continuing into the night. We made a late start the next morning in heavy snow. The only feasible way ahead looked to be hard rock climbing, and with snow continuing to fall heavily, we decided to retreat.

We next decided to climb the Southwest Ridge of Mt. Hunter, bringing snowshoes so we could complete a traverse of the mountain if weather permitted. We left camp at 3:20 a.m. on May 20, arriving at the top of the ridge around noon, having only needed to belay the leader on two short sections high on the ridge. We traversed onto the plateau for a quick brew, then summitted the South Summit at 2 p.m. By this time, the weather had deteriorated considerably. We decided to continue and by 5 p.m., we were underneath the North Summit. We were too tired to continue to the summit. With the weather looking very threatening, we opted to descend, which we began to do in white-out conditions with steady snow falling. We eventually camped at 11,300 feet near the top of the *Ramen Route*. On May 21, we left quite late, but cloudy conditions, initially with light snow falling, meant that the slopes of the *Ramen Route* were in surprisingly firm condition, only getting soft in the lowest section. Upon reaching the basin in the afternoon, we rested and enjoyed a leisurely dinner while waiting for the sun to leave the lower couloir. We started off at 7:30 p.m., but deep soft snow still made progress into the main descent couloir extremely slow. Once gained, however, the snow was considerably firmer and the descent rapid. We returned to camp in steady snowfall, arriving at 1:30 a.m.

DAVE WILLS, *United Kingdom*

Thunder Mountain, Attempt and Air Time. On May 12, Jim Donini and I flew into the Tokositna Glacier to attempt a route on the south side of Thunder Mountain. The climb, which splits two huge rock buttresses, is a 3,000-foot alpine gully capped with a beautiful 600-foot ice ribbon leading to the summit snowfields.

On our first attempt it was still dark when we got to the base of the initial icefall, a pillar of overhanging choss that wouldn't take any protection and barely held tools. Donini found a traverse to the left that in seven pitches took us around the icefall and deposited us 150 feet above the start of the icefall. A few pitches of steep gunbarrel-type gullies led to the icefield below the ribbon, and by 5:30 p.m., we were looking up at four pitches of incredible ice. Unfortunately, it was dumping heavily on us, the descent was going to be an exploration and Donini had broken a crampon. So we bailed, leaving a fixed rope over the rotten ice so we could cruise it on our return.

The next time up, I was belaying Donini in the gunbarrel when a chunk of something came down and whacked me in the arm. Bailed again.

Finally on May 21, we got ourselves to the ribbon at a decent hour. It was 8:30 a.m. when I swung my tool into the start of 600 feet of perfect Alaskan ice. Donini got the next pitch, a stepped, rampy kind of thing that ended in a hanging belay below the final steep pitch. The first 80 feet was another section of perfect plastic, and I protected it with three bomber screws. Then it ramped back to 50 feet of névé and snow and was capped by the final 15 vertical feet that led to the summit snowfields. The ice here was rotten, though, and a stubby screw that barely held its own weight was about ten feet below me when I fell. It pulled, of course, so there was about 80 feet of slack in the rope when I went flying by Donini, harpooning him with my crampons on the way past.

When I came to, I realized that both my feet were hosed. I put in a couple of screws, equalized them and tied in, and Donini rapped down to me, discovering on the way that I had chopped the rope almost in two. We splinted my feet with an ice tool and two rolls of tape and self-evac'd to the top of the icefield. The splint didn't work and I started to bleed a lot, so we made the difficult decision to go for help. Donini chopped me a ledge, tied me in, then rapped and downclimbed the gully to base camp. By some miracle, our pilot, Paul Roderick of Talkeetna Air Taxi, decided to do a late evening fly-by, and Jim was able to flag him down. By 9 p.m., a rescue was underway.

Bad weather kept them from short-hauling me on the 22nd, but they were able to get me off early on the morning of the 23rd. I was admitted to Providence Hospital in Anchorage with two frostbitten feet, a compound fracture of my left tib/fib, hairline fracture of my left talus, a shattered right talus and a broken left pinky. The route still awaits an ascent.

MALCOLM DALY

Mt. Huntington, East Face. Paul Roderick of TAT dropped off Alex Lowe and me on the West

The east face of Mt. Huntington, showing the 1983 Kimbrough-Tuckey line and the camps and high point of the direct attempt by Doug Chabot and Alex Lowe. BRADFORD WASHBURN #8196

Fork of the Ruth Glacier under perfect skies. A high pressure had settled into the Alaska Range, and we were psyched to take full advantage of it. We unloaded the plane at noon on May 12, left our base camp gear in the haul bag and immediately started climbing. Our objective was to climb the East Face, which was done in 1983 (Kimbrough-Tuckey), but to try and finish via the large rock buttress guarding the top. Alex had tried this route with Steve Swenson a few years prior but got hit with a rather prolonged storm that made retreat from the Rooster Comb Col quite terrifying.

We climbed up and over the Rooster Comb Col. Ankle-deep snow with a firm base and some easy-angled ice made climbing quick and enjoyable. Within four hours, we set up our first camp on a shelf directly across from the East Face (which looked awesome). The next day, we climbed the 1983 route, which consisted of long snow ramps with rock bands and ice steps. It was a beautiful line. We veered off the '83 route near the base of the buttress and set up our first camp at 10,030 feet. The following day, the 14th, I led up the buttress. The first pitch was mixed climbing up a granite corner that steepened to a 5.10 hand crack for pitch 2. I couldn't believe our luck: no gloves, no loose rock and climbing in rock shoes. Unfortunately, after a few more rock pitches we got shut down. I tried in vain to push up through a corner system that ended in a blank slab with overhanging snow. Alex tried too, but had no luck. This was the obvious way to go, as there was no other weakness that we could

The east face of Barille, showing 1. Cobra Pillar *(Donini-Tackle, 1992), 2. East Face (Bonapace-Orgler, 1988) 3.* Forever More *(Valeri Babanov, 1999).* BRADFORD WASHBURN #7160

find. So we admitted defeat with the buttress, rappelled down and set up camp.

Once again we awoke to perfect skies and took off to finish the East Face via the '83 route. The climbing on the upper part of the route was stellar. The rock steps, serac band and ice runnels reminded me of the clean, beautiful climbing on the Cassin. The last pitch was an overhanging, loose, ice/snow step that capped off the summit ice serac. Alex led this surprise crux fluidly and quickly. We summitted by 1 p.m. and then started down the west face. Downclimbing the upper face with the aid of a photo, we were able to find the top of the Nettle-Quirk Route, which we then rappelled. At the bottom of the route, just like clockwork, Paul zoomed overhead in the Cessna 185, checking up on us. At 8:30 p.m., we were on the Tokasitna, and Paul landed shortly thereafter to pick us up. We shuttled over to our still-packed base camp, threw it all in the plane, cracked open the celebratory Foster's Oil Cans and flew back home. Two nights on the mountain, a summit and traverse on the most beautiful 12,000-foot peak in the world. It was our last climb together, and one of my best. Thank you, Alex.

DOUG CHABOT

Ruth Gorge

Mt. Barille, Northeast Buttress, Forever More. I arrived on the Ruth Glacier on May 21. A 12-day storm kept me in my tent until June 2. The next day, I undertook an attempt of a new route on the south face of Mount Dickey, but the granite was so greatly affected that it would in no way allow me to get any safe protection or set up a secure anchor. Though there already existed two routes on the east face of Barille, the northeast buttress—2,700 feet high and 1,200 feet of it a sheer buttress cut by several roofs and ledges—still remained unexplored. On June 7, I passed over the heavily torn glacier at the foot of the peak and then reached the rock itself. Starting in a dihedral system, I managed to climb 300 feet that day and fix the rope. I spent the night in the tent and the next day continued the ascent. Using the same technique, I reached a big roof that stuck out six feet beyond the face. I climbed it precisely with cams and reached the headwall. Fifty feet higher was the beginning of a wide crack almost 300 feet high. I had to use sky hooks. The whole next day was devoted to climbing that long stretch of offwidth. On the fourth day of the ascent, when I was already in the upper part of the buttress, I came across a small sloping ledge that turned out to be a stretch of pulpy rotten granite. This ledge cost me a lot of nerves.

On June 12, I finally reached the top of the rock buttress. Above was a series of simple rock and big ledges. Climbing it, I encountered loose stones and blocks. That relatively easy part of the face was followed by another buttress that was not so sheer as the previous one. I spent the fifth night of the ascent in the middle of the buttress. The sixth day was the longest. After climbing another 450 feet, I reached the snowfield. To get to the summit, I had to climb the 300-foot snowfield, two moderately difficult rocky stretches, and about 900 feet of snow slope that smoothly transformed itself into the ridge. I decided to leave the tent behind. It took me four hours, sticking deeply in the molten snow, before I reached the summit of Mount Barille.

The sky turned black with storm. Descending cost me an hour and a half. I reached the tent in the company of strong wind and heavy rain. Such dreadful weather lasted until midnight. The entire next day, June 14, I retraced my way down. At 10 p.m., I crawled into the lonely tent on the glacier, very tired. I called the route *Forever More* (ED+ VI 5.10 A3, 900m).

VALERI BABANOV, *Russia*

Mt. Johnson, East Buttress, Attempt. Flying into the Ruth Glacier, it's hard not to notice the sweeping expanse of rock that forms the east buttress of Mt. Johnson. A strong team composed of Jim McCarthy, Yvon Chouinard, Henry Barber and several others made the first attempt on the route in 1971. The group was stymied about 1,000 feet up where a few small ledges ended beneath a smooth, steep wall. The following year, Barber returned again with Chouinard and two other climbers, determined to push around to the south from the ledges and then up the buttress. Their attempt again failed to go much beyond the ledges at 1,000 feet. In the 1980s, Mugs Stump began his long fascination with the route, making at least four attempts, once with Renny Jackson in 1991. But even though the route is spectacular looking, the quality of the rock leaves much to be desired.

Paul Roderick of TAT flew Renny Jackson and me onto the Ruth Glacier below Mt. Wake on June 23. It rained the next morning but cleared in the p.m., allowing us to fix the first three pitches. The first pitch off the glacier was one of the cruxes: wet, thin 5.10+ crack climbing. We launched June 25. Climbing in the 5.7-5.8 range got us to a small ledge atop pitch 7, where Barber et al went further left along the ledge. We went straight up a few pitches that had been previously climbed by Mugs and Renny in 1991—the key to the whole climb. It had three 5.10 pitches, with two of them traversing straight right into a hidden corner system. Renny had the sharp end on "Mugs's Traverse," and as he climbed, our respect for the MAN increased sharply.

It started to rain again as Renny finished the ninth pitch, so we descended to the ledge (too marginal to pitch the Bibler on). The next day, the weather never improved so we left our haulbag on the ledge and rapped the route, leaving the last three pitches fixed. The route dried by June 30. We made good time to the ledge and Renny finished the "Traverse" and then continued on 5.9-5.10 terrain in a dike/corner system. Swapping leads, we led well into the night. At around 2 a.m., we called it quits and got some shut-eye while hanging in our harnesses at a belay station.

We started July 1 with a full blown, six-and-a-half hour aid pitch (A3+) that once again had me in awe of Mugs. Another pitch brought us to a bivy ledge, where we decided to leave the haulbag. On July 2, we fit everything we needed into one pack and climbed from pitch 18 to pitch 33. The climbing was easier, but the rock was really starting to deteriorate. At the top of the "Slip-Slide Slab" pitch, Renny, having a personal moment, dry-heaved from the ridiculously scary and desperate climbing. And the rock continued to get worse. At the top of the 33rd pitch we found a protected flat spot to set up the Bibler. We were now under the prominent tower on the ridge.

On July 3, in five pitches of absolutely hideous climbing, we reached the top of the tower. On one pitch Renny had to climb a crumbly slab of rock that could only be crossed by chopping steps in it with his hammer (*piolet desperate*). The desert-style method of protection was the only available option for the next several pitches. Once on top of the tower at the top of pitch 38, we could see that the climbing continued for quite some time on this horrible rock. At the tower we had a short discussion about going on, but we both felt as though we were surviving on luck and that we should leave while we had the chance.

On July 4, we did 28 rappels down the route to our base camp. Luckily, we left a rope to aid on the descent on the "Mugs's Traverse" pitches. On July 5, we skied the five miles up the Ruth Glacier to the Mountain House, where Paul picked us up that afternoon.

DOUG CHABOT

Mt. Johnson, showing the line taken by Jackson and Chabot to high point on the east buttress. The Elevator Shaft *(Chabot-Tackle, 1995) is the cleft down and right from the summit.* DOUG CHABOT

Hut Tower, Southeast Face, Boy's World. From June 12-13, Bob Semborski and I climbed a new route on Hut Tower in 30 hours round-trip from base camp. To the best of our knowledge, this is the fourth line on the formation and has the same approach as for the South Ridge. From our base camp directly between Mount Barille and the Moose's Tooth, we started down-glacier at 12:30 a.m. on the 12th. By 6 a.m., we had reached the col between Hut Tower and the unnamed formation to the south (P. 5,700'?). This section involved a prominent couloir of steep snow that gained about 1,300 feet of elevation. At the col, we rested and waited for warmer temperatures. Our original intention was to climb the South Ridge, but we decided that easier terrain lay around to the right (east).

The climb ascends from left to right through mostly moderate terrain, overcoming short sections of difficulty separated by longer, easier sections. Routefinding was fairly straightforward, even though the route zig-zags a fair bit due to tremendous looseness and wetness. We were convinced that this was virgin terrain because of the level of vegetation, loose rock and the complete absence of any apparent traffic. The climbing difficulty never exceeded 5.9 with the most memorable pitches being the second and seventh. The second pitch involved a stem around a huge loose flake followed by a squeeze chimney. The seventh pitch was an eight-foot-wide chimney capped by an enormous chockstone that created a five-foot roof. This section was exceptionally wet and loose, and reminds me of the roof pitch of *Syke's Sickle* on Spearhead in Rocky Mountain National Park, only choked with ice. Two more pitches brought us to the summit, where the view of Broken Tooth was breathtaking.

The descent was via seven double-rope rappels back down to the col, requiring tension traversing from right to left. Except for the ropes getting stuck on the second-to-last rappel, the entire experience went remarkably epic-free. Rock fall was a constant hazard, but fortunately no one got hit. We walked (no, stumbled) into camp at 6 a.m. on the 13th and slept for two days. Out of respect for those hardmen who have gone before, we named this route *Boy's World* (a much more difficult route called *Men's World* lies around the opposite side of the formation).

SHANE WAYKER, *unaffiliated*

Peak 10,070' (a.k.a. The Bear's Tooth), East Face, The Useless Emotion. In May, Jim Bridwell, Brian McCray, Brian Jonas, Glenn Dunmire and Terry Christensen established a new route on the east face of Peak 10,070' (a.k.a. The Bear's Tooth). *The Useless Emotion* (VII 5.9 WI4 A4, ca. 4,700') was established over two weeks in May, with the route being fixed to the top of the rock pillar before the headwall above was climbed capsule-style. It was McCray's first alpine climb; he led more than half the climb. A full account of their adventure can be found earlier in this journal.

Moose's Tooth, Ham and Eggs, Second Ascent and Trade Routification. A picture of the 3,000-foot south face of the Moose's Tooth in a recent *Climbing* magazine article about the Ruth Gorge caught my attention. There was a narrow steep couloir on the right side of the face that led straight up to the summit ridge below the true (east) summit. A note explained it was the *Ham and Eggs* route (Davies-Krakauer-Zinsser, 1975). In May, my partner, Harry Hunt from Anchorage, and I decided to attempt it. We flew to the Ruth Gorge with Talkeetna Air Taxi on May 8 in unsettled weather, but the 9th dawned clear and beautiful. Within several hours, we packed and were making the five- or six-hour approach through the icefall to the plateau below the south face of the Tooth. By mid-afternoon, we caught up with a pair of climbers from Seattle/Fairbanks who were also gunning for *Ham and Eggs*. The next day the weather was unsettled, and the other climbers said they didn't have enough food to wait out the weather, so we could attempt the route first.

We started up around 7 a.m. on the 11th. The climbing was straightforward, and very fun. It consisted mostly of 50- to 55-degree snow interspersed with several WI3 steps and one mixed WI4-ish crux. We simulclimbed the snow sections and belayed all steep pitches. There were roughly 17 60-meter pitches to the col. We made it to the summit ridge around 9 p.m. and made the true east summit at 11:57 p.m. After heading down, we took a couple of hours' break near the top of the couloir in a strange, hoar-frosted natural cave. We started rapping down the couloir around 4:30 a.m. By 9:30 a.m., we were back at the tent. We note the approach route from the Ruth Glacier to the plateau below the Tooth can entirely avoid the icefall if one takes the very avalanche-prone gully to the right (south) side of the icefall. This should not be attempted if the snow is not frozen.

Subsequent to our ascent were numerous (reportedly as many as ten) additional ascents in May and June. Among them were Kelly Cordes and Scott Decapio, Dan Gambino and Pete Tapley, the Fairbanks/Seattle pair (Dale Remsburg and friend Kristy), Mike Davis and a partner, Hunter, from Truckee, and Dave Hart and Brad Gessner. Hart and Gessner managed to forego the Ruth-to-the-Tooth icefall because TAT flew them onto the plateau at the base of the Tooth. Also, Joe Reichert and Rob Hancock repeated the original West Ridge route to the East Summit and descended via the newly-established rap route in the *Ham and Eggs* couloir. For the record, Carl Tobin and Brian Teale attempted *Ham and Eggs* back in 1984, got quite high on the route but turned around short of the top of the couloir. In my opinion, *Ham and Eggs* is deserving of its new-found "insta-classic" status. It's a fun, challenging, sustained route to one of the major summits in the Alaska Range without an inordinate amount of danger, in the right conditions.

PETER HAEUSSLER, *unaffiliated*

Overview of the south face of the Moose's Tooth. The east (true) summit is the rightmost of the four rocky summits. Ham and Eggs *takes the couloir to its left.* Shaken Not Stirred *climbs up between the first and second summits from the left. Peak 10,070' (a.k.a. the Bear's Tooth) is the snowy peak on the far right.* PETER HAEUSSLER

Moose's Tooth, Shaken Not Stirred, Various Ascents. In May, the *Shaken Not Stirred* route on the south face of the Moose's Tooth received its second, third, and fourth ascents over the course of three days. Kelly Cordes and Scott DeCapio, Topher and Patience Donahue and Dan Gambino and Pete Tapley all climbed the route in one-day pushes. The route was reported to be in ideal condition, with a shoulder-width ice runnel for seven or eight pitches providing a groovy outing.

Little Switzerland, Various Ascents. It was reported in a *Climbing* magazine article that the team of John Mattson and Josh Zimmerman, with photographer John Burcham, was active in Little Switzerland. Numerous photographs of the area document the team's efforts, which include *The Jester* (5.10b, seven pitches) on the east face of Royal Highness and *The Blade* (5.10d), a variation to *The Jester.* Reference is made to ascents of "roughly ten routes, both new and existing, ranging from 5.7 to 5.12." Other climbs appear to have been made on the Plunger, the Throne and the south face of the Middle Troll. Further details are lacking. (*Climbing* 196)

Little Switzerland, Various Ascents. On June 20, Rob Feeney and I flew into Little Switzerland and set up a base camp on the Pika Glacier. After a 24-hour rain storm, the clouds

parted and we had mostly good weather for the next ten days. We spent several days cragging at the base of the Royal Tower and the Throne. We repeated some great routes and climbed some new lines as well. On June 24, we climbed the south face on the Middle Troll at 5.8 in seven pitches. On June 26, we climbed the east buttress of the Royal Tower in 13 60-meter pitches, joining *The Chase* for the last pitch. The climb took nine hours, two of which were spent on a ledge at the top of the ninth pitch waiting for a snow squall to let up. The climbing was primarily mid-fifth class on excellent rock. We called the route the *Gargoyle Buttress* (IV 5.10) for the distinctive boulder at the top of the route. Retreat slings from previous parties were found to the top of pitch 6. We rappelled the route in 15 pitches and left solid rappel anchors with descending rings. On June 29, we free climbed The Plunger, a small spire to the east of the Throne. The last pitch has an amazing overhanging thin hand crack that goes free at 5.12a/b.

Rob Feeney on the south face of Middle Troll.
DAVE ANDERSON

Although there are few crack systems that continue to the top of the peaks in Little Switzerland, the individual pitches contain high-quality crack climbing.

Dave Anderson

Mt. Deborah, Northwest Ridge, First Alpine-Style Ascent. In May, during a relatively stable period of weather, Matt Porter and I flew into the head of the Yanert Glacier on the west side of Mt. Deborah. From the 6,200-foot landing area, we left a cache and traveled to the north icefall at the head of the glacier. This is referred to (appropriately) by Fred Beckey as the "Frozen Hurricane." The icefall can be negotiated on the far north side with some climbing under loose blocks. This is one of the greatest objective hazards of the route. Once in the basin above, some route finding will bring you to the base of the route at 9,000 feet. The next morning, we left early and climbed over the bergschrund and ascended a 45- to 55-degree slope to the ridge. Once on the ridge, the climbing increased in intensity, and soon the ridge was climbed as low to the rock ridge as possible in order to stay off the cornices. Protection was good, and running belays made the climbing go fast. Once over the crux ridge section, the terrain backed off for the last 500 feet to the summit. This took eight hours to climb from the tent. Matt broke the summit cornice off (Not Recommended), and we began to rappel directly down the west face. After 20-some-odd rappels on a 100-meter rope, we were over the bergschrund and back in camp. We were climbing and descending for 15 hours total. The weather turned nasty on the summit and descending in the wind and increasing spindrift was

The Northwest Ridge of Mt. Deborah, looking down on William Glacier.
Mike Wood/Matt Porter Collection

a drag. We holed up the next day before descending through the Frozen Hurricane. We spent the next four days skiing and hiking out the Yanert Valley to the Parks Highway.

MIKE WOOD

CHUGACH MOUNTAINS

Mt. Amulet, North Face. Heading east on the Glenn Highway, there is a great clump of peaks to the south across the Matanuska River opposite the Victory Bible Camp. The Spectrum Glacier that Monument Creek flows from has been visited often in the past by climbers, and this year it saw an increase in ascents. In May, Josh Sonkiss soloed the north face of Amulet (8,290') to gain the summit. This new route was a beautiful line that has long been coveted by locals. In March, 2000, Matt Porter and Carl Oswald climbed the north face on snow with ice at the very top for the route's second ascent. This beautiful peak has been climbed for years via the east and south ridges and continues to offer great climbing opportunities.

MIKE WOOD

Mt. Awesome, North Face. Mt. Awesome (8,645'), an attractive peak on the west side of the Spectrum Glacier, saw an ascent in April. During the spring crust weeks, Matt Porter skied in to snag a solo ascent of the impressive north face. The route is reported to have snow climbing to 50° with some nice ice sections up to 70° for short sections.

MIKE WOOD

The Ice Cream Cone, Southwest Face. Known by local Matanuska Valley residents as The Ice Cream Cone (8,675') and by Anchorage locals as the Sky Buster, this peak was climbed in April by Carl Oswald, Chris Flowers and Matt Porter. Some tenacious scouting on a couple of different occasions led to a great climb on the southwest face on a super spring crust.

MIKE WOOD

Peak 8,680', Ascent. On August 26, Kelly Bay of Wrangell Mountain Air flew Mike Loso and me to the 4,500-foot level of the upper Bremner Glacier. We spent the 27th and 28th checking out peaks in the area for routes and moving camp five and a half miles to the west. On the 29th, Mike and I ascended Peak 8,680' as a warm-up climb. Our warm-up climb ended up being a full 13-hour day to ascend the icefall that flows west and then south from the summit. We first climbed up the lower icefall, only to be turned back by huge crevasses. So we down climbed, then climbed back up the left-hand edge of the icefall through the "moat" between the ice and rock. Some rock scrambling brought us to 6,000 feet, where we skied up and around the upper icefall on the left (north) side before circling back to reach the southwest ridge of the peak. Extremely sticky snow made this a torture ski across the upper snow slopes. A large bergschrund with a "hairy" snow bridge required some delicate tiptoeing before we reached the easier ridge beyond. A short steep pitch found me on a short, thin corniced ridge, where I proceeded to kick off the cornice and send Mike a small avalanche. After a short stay on the summit, we headed down and reached camp just before dark. Peak 8,680' is the highest peak in the group of peaks bounded by the Bremner, Middle Fork Lobe and Fan glaciers. It may have been the first ascent.

Although we did move camp up to the base of a beautiful ridge of one of the larger peaks, three days of rain and snow ended our chances of doing any further climbing. When we reached the original landing site, it was covered in ten inches of new snow, and we spent five hours shoveling and packing a runway so that Kelly could land and pick us up the following morning. Luckily, it was clear that night, and our runway froze hard as a rock.

DANNY W. KOST

FAIRWEATHER RANGE

Mount Fairweather from Glacier Bay. On April 8, Mark Jefferson and I left Gustavus in two double kayaks with gear and supplies for an ascent of Mount Fairweather. We paddled 60 miles up Glacier Bay to its northwest terminus at Tarr Inlet. Tarr Inlet ends at the Grand Pacific, a tidewater glacier east of Fairweather. We switched to skis and sleds and skied up this glacier to the Grand Plateau Glacier and eventually climbed the mountain via the normal Northwest Ridge route on April 29. It was a 58-mile ski from Tarr Inlet to high camp on Fairweather. We intercepted the normal route approximately 42 miles from Tarr Inlet. We could have gained high camp by two other shorter routes, but each of these has a lot of objective hazard, though they would make an interesting future approach. We returned to our boats by the same route and paddled back to Gustavus after 35 days. We believe this was the first time anyone had climbed the mountain via an approach from Glacier Bay along the Grand Pacific Glacier.

MICHAEL P. DZIOBAK, *unaffiliated*

Burkett Needle, Voyage of the Celestial Tramps. From May 6-31, Sébastien Foissac and I put up a new route capsule-style on the southeast face of the Burkett Needle. Drop-off and pick-up by boat was made from Thomas Bay. We spent 41 days in the Coast Range, without any radio or assistance. The approach took us six days to ferry more than 200 kilos, first by foot (triple portage) and after with skis and two pulkas each. At first, we went to have a look at the northwest face of Devil's Thumb, but it was really out of condition. So we decided (and did not regret) to go to the Burkett Needle. A blizzard destroyed our tent on Baird Glacier while we were inside, and we had to dig a snowcave in a hurry. Our pulkas disappeared, taken away by the wind, despite the big stones we put on them. Nevertheless, we started the climb, living from then on in our portaledge. The climbing, mostly free, was sustained and committing. Moreover, we felt it was harder due to the snow and cold. After a 300-meter buttress, we followed a very aesthetic snow ridge to the bottom of a forbidding gendarme, from which we escaped via two long rappels. The junction was made later after having hauled our gear to the little col between the needle and the gendarme. We kept on hauling our stuff to the middle of the needle, traversing snow bands. We even did a tyrolean. We spent 14 nights in the Negresco Bivouac (named after a very famous five-star hotel in Nice). After a few days of excellent climbing, the weather, which was not very good at all, became really bad. We stayed several days "portaledge-bound" in a continual snowstorm. We had to evacuate the snow around the portaledge in order not to be buried. On May 29, the weather finally improved and we passed the headwall. Unfortunately, storms came back in the late afternoon and we stopped 50 meters below the top, covered by ice. We were incredibly motivated to reach the summit, which we did the next day. The pitch I completed was one of the hardest I ever did, due to the weather conditions (terrible wind, snow, ice). After six or seven hours of fierce fighting, a gift awaited us at the top: no wind! The way down was hellish: ten centimeters of ice on a fixed rope I left on the headwall. We finally reached our portaledge at 2 a.m. We had very little time to return (we could not miss our meeting with Dieter and his boat), so we walked 15 to 17 hours a day, using our haulbags instead of our lost pulkas. *The Voyage Of The Celestial Tramps* (VI 7a+ A3+, ca. 1200m) took 41 days in total. A special thanks to Dieter and Ken for their hospitality. (A complete account of the voyage appears earlier in this journal.)

LIONEL DAUDET, *France*

WRANGELL MOUNTAINS

Peak 10,091' and Other Activity. On May 10, Tracey Becken, Bill Drake and I were flown by Kelly Bay of Wrangell Mountain Air into the 8,300-foot level of the upper Chisana Glacier some seven miles north of Frederika Mountain. On May 11, we skied up to the base of Peak 10,091' before kicking off our skis for the last several hundred feet. This was our warm-up peak. On May 12, we skied up to Peak 9,310' to check out snow conditions on some steeper slopes. The winter of 1998-'99 created a bad snow layer throughout much of Alaska. We found an unconsolidated layer some two feet down that forced us to reconsider the climbs we would do from here on out. On the 13th, we climbed Peak 9,500'+, which lies just two miles east and south of Peak 10,522'. On the 14th, we retraced our steps from the previous day, then turned up another Peak 9,500'+ just west of the previous day's summit. We then climbed Peak 9,400'+, which is only half a mile to the south. This summit was special to Tracey and Bill, as we left some mementos in honor of a sick friend of theirs (Sarah Freney) and named it "Sarah's Peak" in her honor. On the 15th, Tracey wanted a rest, so Bill and I skied to the south to attempt either Peak 10,630' or Peak 10,565'. We went up the glacier between the two peaks to a saddle at roughly 9,500 feet. Here the weather started to deteriorate, but we continued up toward Peak 10,565'. We climbed up steeper slopes to Peak 10,300' before deciding to turn around due to the weather. After we retreated, the weather then cleared off. On the 16th, we all skied up toward Peak 10,522', which I had soloed in 1998. The 17th found us moving camp to the west through whiteout conditions to the base of Peak 9,230' at 8,400 feet. We spent the 18th in our tents due to weather. On the 19th, we skied up to a pass at 9,000 feet, just south of Peak 10,200'+. We then went up the southwest ridge of this peak to within only a few feet of the main summit. The ridge was too thin and unconsolidated to safely continue. On the 20th, Bill and I attempted the widely corniced east ridge of Peak 10,200'+ and reached a high point of around 9,800 feet. This peak is volcanic in origin, and Bill and I enjoyed some beautiful rock formations, including black obsidian. On the 21st, we were picked up and flown back to McCarthy. This region was once along the glacier route to the Chisana gold fields. We believe these were the first ascents of the peaks.

DANNY W. KOST

Regal Mountain, Peak 12,454', Parka Peak, Rime Peak. On May 9, Paul Claus of Ultima Thule Outfitters flew Dawn Groth, Ben Still, Kathy Still, Wayne Todd, Cory Hinds, Elena

Hinds and me to 9,000 feet on the upper Nabesna Glacier below Regal Mountain (13,845'). We established a high camp at 10,800 feet, from which we made an ascent of Peak 12,454' (first ascended in June, 1955) via its east ridge (Alaska Grade 1). The next day, we climbed Regal Mountain up its southern slopes (Alaska Grade 2) after retreating from its striking southwest ridge. We then spent two days skiing 15 miles west over Mountaineers' Pass to an 8,000-foot camp below the north face of Rime Peak (12,741') and Atna Peak (13,860'), scrambling up Peak 8,560' en route. Cory, Wayne, Ben and Cathy then climbed the northwest face of Parka Peak (13,280') (Alaska Grade 1) via Mountaineers' Pass, only removing their skis for the final 700 feet. Cory, Elena, Wayne and Cathy then attempted the east ridge of Rime Peak (Alaska Grade 2) from the Atna/Rime col before turning back at 12,500 feet. Exposed snow and ice climbing up to 60 degrees made for exciting climbing. Future parties should be aware that all routes up Parka, Atna and Rime Peaks from the north are exposed to sometimes considerable serac avalanche danger. Our group also made ascents of Peak 10,060', Peak 8,500'+ and Peak 7,280' before our pilot returned for us on May 22, after 14 sunny days in the Wrangells.

DAVID HART, *Mountaineering Club of Alaska*

CANADA

ST. ELIAS RANGE

Northwest Cook to Mt. Cook, Traverse. Climbers Greg Brown (Canada), Bertrand Eynard (France), Dave Hildes (Canada), and Alun Hubbard (leader, UK) and crew Chris Barnett, Armel Castello, Tobyn Ross (all from Canada) left Vancouver on June 14 aboard *Gambo*, a 46-foot steel ketch, to sail the Inside Passage up the west coast of North America to Yakutat Bay, Alaska, in 12 days. After a successful drop at the toe of the Hubbard Glacier, we ascended the 40-kilometer, heavily crevassed Valerie Glacier for four days and, by July 5, had established Base Camp at 1650 meters on the Seward Glacier by the foot of Northwest Cook. Carrying seven days of food and fuel, we climbed the 2000-meter north ridge of Northwest Cook using two daytime bivies at 2100 meters and 2700 meters to rest. The climbing was of moderate difficulty, mostly on poor, crusty snow and rotten ice of 30 to 75 degrees with the occasional chossy rock section. We summitted Northwest Cook on our third night in ideal conditions; at the higher elevation, snow was firm. The weather had remained exceptionally stable (but very hazy) throughout.

We then followed the unclimbed ridge to Mt. Cook, with Bertrand leading through the crux of the route, a steep rock notch, during the fourth day. The next morning saw us finish the ridge, and we managed to locate ourselves at 4150 meters, immediately below the summit, at 10:45 a.m. on July 9 in rapidly deteriorating conditions. We set up camp in the lee of the summit ridge to wait out the blizzard. After 15 hours of being buffeted by severe winds, a promising clear patch appeared in the sky at 2:30 a.m. We emerged from the tent at 4 a.m. and jaunted up to Mt. Cook's broad summit to enjoy a glorious sunrise on July 10. For the next three days we were frustrated by short weather windows and hunger, but on July 13 we were back on the Seward Glacier at our BC. Our plan to descend by the Valerie was quelled by the amount of snow-melt on the tenuous snow-bridges on which we had ascended. Instead, a 50-kilometer ski down the Seward Glacier to where it meets the Malaspina allowed VHF

Mt. Cook (center) and Northwest Cook, showing the traverse taken by the team. DAVE HILDES

contact with Gulf Air Taxi pilots and we arranged for a pick-up. Return to Vancouver was made in ten days aboard *Gambo* with (mostly) favorable winds on the outside waters of Alaska and BC.

Sadly, David Persson, a good friend and original expedition member, fell to his death in late May while attempting to telemark down *Liberty Ridge* on Mt. Rainier. In memory of David, we have applied for Northwest Cook to be named after him.

DAVE HILDES,* *Canada*

*Supported by a grant from the Shipton-Tilman Fund, Mount Everest Foundation, the British Mountaineering Council and the Polartec Performance Challenge.

Mt. Vancouver, Attempt, and Mt. Seattle, Ascent. On June 1-4 during a prolonged spell of unsettled weather, we had a minor epic trying to approach the East Rib of Mt. Vancouver (4812m) through the complex icefall guarding the route. We escaped in a dubious weather window with the aid of GPS waypoints. Cutting our losses, we opted to attempt Mt. Seattle (3069m), a complex mountain bigger and more serious than its height would indicate. The first and only previous ascent was by Fred Beckey and party in May, 1966, via the South-Southwest Ridge. We opted for the East Ridge to the North Summit, which forms the Alaska-Yukon boundary. This is the most direct route on the north side of the mountain, but the way is barred by a huge serac band near the summit ridge.

On June 7, we ascended from the glacier at 1100 meters via several unconsolidated snow mushrooms to a large 'schrund on the main ridge at ca. 1865 meters. On the ridge, facing the rising sun, snow conditions became dangerously slushy after about 8 a.m. and only consolidated after 1 a.m. The following day, we continued up exposed slopes with unnerving wind-slab that required snow stakes for upward progress to a second camp at 2480 meters. On June 9, we tackled the nerve-racking traverse below the seracs on mixed rock and hard ice. From the distinctively shaped North Summit, it was apparent that the South Summit is perhaps 30

Mt. Seattle from the north. The North Summit is the highest point visible. Most of the east ridge, including the serac barrier at the top, is visible as the left skyline. PAUL KNOTT

meters higher. The intervening ground was not technical, but we had insufficient time for the three kilometers or so of undulating snow ridge. After a camp on the summit ridge, we reversed the route without mishap, reaching the glacier on June 11. Ours was a new route, the first ascent of the North Summit, and the second ascent (and first British ascent) of the mountain as a whole.

PAUL KNOTT, *United Kingdom*

Wrangell-St. Elias, Various Ascents. During the 1999 season only three trips other than ours (see above) resulted in ascents that were recorded in the climbers' log in Yakutat. Apart from a glacier skills course, we were the last climbers approaching from this side to leave the range. This information obviously excludes parties flying in from Kluane. The West Ridge of King Peak was climbed June 4-9 by a Colorado team. A May 18–June 6 attempt on Mt. Kennedy from the Cathedral Glacier by an Idaho team failed on Hubbard due to weather. First ascents of four peaks from 9,300 to 10,700 feet in the North Watson area of the Fairweather Range were made from April 17-30; the hardest was 2,500 feet of 60-degree ice on the north face of Peak 10,700'.

PAUL KNOTT, *United Kingdom*

Kluane National Park Reserve

Mountaineering Summary and Statistics, 1999. This year, even with the unusual weather conditions, there were 46 climbing expeditions comprised of 176 people that accrued some 3,005 person-days within the Icefields of Kluane. Overall, this was one of the busiest years on record for the Icefields.

There were 31 expeditions and 107 people on Mt. Logan this year, representing 61 percent of the persons in the Icefields. The *King Trench Route* (standard route) saw 18 expeditions and

65 people; the East Ridge had ten expeditions and 35 people. Other routes on Mt. Logan attempted this year were the *Catenary Ridge*, South Face and *Hummingbird Ridge*. Nine expeditions were successful to either the East or West peak of the mountain, putting the success rate at 30 percent for all expeditions on the mountain. Once again, climbers reported some large crevasses opening up on the upper *King Trench Route* above 15,000 feet, but these posed no major problems.

The major complaint this year was the weather. Storms forced long delays in getting in or out of the Icefields. Temperatures into the -40°s were common in May and some frostbite problems were reported. On the positive side, there were no search-and-rescue operations or fatalities within the Icefields, although some falls into crevasses were reported.

Other mountains that were attempted included Lucania, Steele, Kennedy, Queen Mary, Vancouver, Seattle, McCaulay, King Peak, Walsh, Pinnacle, Hubbard, Augusta and Mt. Baird. Interesting climbs included a believed first ascent of Mt. Seattle to North Peak (see above), and a route up the Northwest Ridge of King Peak.

A new activity within the Icefields this year was the establishment of the Icefield Discovery Lodge in the Divide area near Mt. Queen Mary. This camp is a trial commercial venture to allow more people to experience the true heart of Kluane National Park: the Icefields. Approximately 35 people flew into the area during the summer and spent at least one night in a comfortable heated camp on the glacier.

Park wardens spent some time in the King Trench area this summer monitoring use. Some of the climbers contacted expressed concern over latrines and human waste, especially at King Trench Base Camp and Camp I. Wardens noticed that the lower *King Trench Route* gets excessively wanded by the end of the summer as most parties do not remove wands upon completion of their trip. The onus seems to be left to the last team on the mountain. One group on a late season trip on the East Ridge of Mt. Logan reported quite a bit of older fixed line surfacing on parts of the route.

Of note is the use of satellite technology. More climbers are showing up using GPS units for navigation in the Icefields. And the satellite phone, especially the Iridium phone, seems to work very well in this environment and is a great improvement over the heavy HF radio system.

Anyone interested in climbing within Kluane should contact Mountaineering Warden/Kluane National Park/Box 5495/Haines Junction/ Yukon, Canada, Y0B 1LO or visit the Kluane National Park web site at http://www.harbour.com/parkscan/kluane/climb.htm for a mountaineering registration package.

RICK STALEY, *Mountaineering Warden, Kluane National Park Reserve*

Mt. Slaggard, Mt. Macaulay, Southeast Macaulay, Northwest Steele, Mt. Strickland, Ascents and Attempt. On April 16, Paul Claus of Ultima Thule Outfitters flew Paul Barry, Jim McDonough, Shawn O'Donnell, Kirk Towner and myself to 10,500 feet on the upper Anderson Glacier in Kluane National Park. After placing a high camp at 13,300 feet, we repeated the 1959 first ascent routes up the east ridge of Slaggard (15,575', Alaska Grade 1) and the south ridge of Macaulay (15,400', Alaska Grade 1) (see 1960 *AAJ*, p. 132). We then moved camp three miles southeast over Southeast Macaulay (14,500') to 11,900 feet on the ridge toward Northwest Steele (13,845', Alaska Grade 1). Our hopes of making its first ascent were dashed when we discovered faint crampon imprints in the ice on the northwest ridge just below the summit. Rangers later confirmed an earlier party had climbed Northwest Steele the prior summer—could their tracks have lasted that long? We descended back to Base Camp where Paul and I attempted the unclimbed east ridge of Mt. Strickland (13,800', Alaska Grade 2). We reached 12,500 feet before turning back due to dangerous snow conditions and steep ice. Our pilot returned for us on May 2 after 17 days in this seldom-visited corner of the Canadian St. Elias Range.

DAVID HART, *Mountaineering Club of Alaska*

Fairweather Range

Northern Fairweather Range, Various First Ascents and Descents. On April 18, our group of seven climbers and skiers (Jim Earl, Tiffany Scrymgeour, Chris Erickson, Anne Sherwood, Brendan Cusick, Chris Trimble and Hjoerdis Rickert) were flown from Yakutat to our Base Camp in the northern Fairweather Range. This was located about 12 miles north and very slightly west of Mt. Fairweather itself, at 8,000 feet on a small side lobe of the glacier that runs north from Mt. Watson toward Mt. Lodge. (This glacier eventually becomes the Grand Pacific Glacier). Immediately after setting up BC, Brendan Cussick and I headed up to climb the ice face to the saddle between Peak 10,620' and Peak 10,891'. This climb was always between 60° and 75° and always icy—a classic alpine calf pumper (IV 75°, 2,800'). We reached BC the next morning at 7 a.m. after a night of rappeling, downclimbing, and postholing around the backside of Peak 10,620'.

Two days later, Tiffany Scrymgeour and Hjoerdis Rickert made the first ascent of "Cerro Solo" (Peak 9,400'+, II low fifth class). The same day, Chris Trimble and I climbed the north

Peaks of the Fairweather Range. From left to right: 1. "Cerro Solo," showing line of ascent. 2. "Ski Peak." 3. "Little Debbie." 4. Peak 10,620'. 5. Cussik-Earl route to saddle. 6. Peak 10,891'. JIM EARL

face of "Mt. Dan Fox" (Peak 10,891', III 80° 5.4), which is one and a half miles immediately south of Cerro Solo. We named the peak after Dan Fox, a counselor and climber who died of lung cancer in Missoula, MT, two years ago.

Several days after this, Brendan, Tiffany, Hjoerdis and I climbed the east buttress of Point 10,397', which is a sub-peak of Peak 10,755' one mile to the northwest. This climb involved 1,600 feet of climbing on 5.6 rock, iced-up corners, and 60-degree snow. The same day, Chris Trimble, Kris Erickson and Anne Sherwood climbed, then skied and snowboarded the south face of Cerro Solo. Following this, the weather changed and it dumped six feet of snow on our camp.

Kris, Anne, Brendan and Chris did a variety of other serious ski, snowboard and telemark descents, including lines on the south face of Little Debbie (Peak 10,590') and the 60-degree southeast face of "Ski Peak" (Peak 9,200'+, located half a mile west-southwest of Cerro Solo), of which Kris, Chris and Brendan made the first ascent.

Everyone except Chris Trimble and myself left on April 30. The two of us remained, waited out several days of bad weather and approached the north face of Mt. Watson (12,500'). We began climbing this face at 4 a.m., reaching the north ridge after 12 hours on ice and snow up to 80 degrees. The summit ridge, about one kilometer long, was not straightforward: it involved 1,000 feet of 75-degree traversing on the knife-edge ridge. We summitted just before dark and scurried down the East Ridge (line of original ascent by Walter Gove and party in 1974). After one rappel on a rocky part of the ridge past a serac barrier, we stopped and brewed up some hot liquids. In an hour, it was light enough and we were rested enough to continue descending across the plateau just east of Mt. Watson, then back west to our camp at the base of the mountain by mid-morning. We each suffered slight frostbite on our toes from the cold temperatures, which we estimate to have been -15°F. It was the first ascent of the North Face and Ridge (V 80° 5.7, 4,500').

JIM EARL, *unaffiliated*

NORTHWEST AND YUKON TERRITORIES

RICHARDSON MOUNTAINS

Richardson Mountains, Traverse. In August, we completed the traverse of the Richardson Mountains above the 68th parallel. Peak 5,550' at the western rim of the mesa highlands was our mountaineering focal point. Our route proceeds from the Mackenzie River southeast of Mt. Gifford to the Bell River headwaters and across the western perimeter ridge to Bonnet Lake above the Porcupine Flats. Dioramic displays of tundra wildlife were witnessed, with wolves and grizzlies in extraordinary abundance. An impressive natural arch was found and explored above the Almstrom headwaters.

DENNIS SCHMITT

LOGAN MOUNTAINS

Vampire Peaks, New Routes. Pike Howard and I flew to Summit Lake in the Vampire Peaks area on July 8. Our intentions were to explore the peaks west of Mount Mulholland on the

Moraine Hill Glacier and continue the exploration of the Vampire Peaks. We established Base Camp at the foot of the Phoenix in rainy weather near the terminus of the Moraine Hill Glacier. The rain continued for seven days and deposited several inches of snow on the glacier and nearby faces. Hoping that time and good weather would stabilize conditions, we headed up to the Vampire Spires, which had escaped much of the snow. A window of good weather opened as we hiked and for the first time we saw blue sky. Not wanting to waste the opportunity, we rushed toward the Canine, an 800-foot, free-standing granite tower, and glassed a line for the next day.

The Canine had been attempted by the Childers party in 1998 (see 1999 *AAJ*, pp. 269-271), but they were forced to retreat in the face of poor weather. We found predominantly moderate climbing, although loose and unsavory at times, on our route, *Rabies Shot* (IV 5.10 C2+). A long (180'+), loose, and lichenous offwidth was the first major obstacle. Having grunted our way up that, Howard battled a bizarre corner formed by the convergence of two plates of rock (5.10 C2+). Protection in this section was difficult as cams would hopelessly umbrella in a chimney behind the façade of an otherwise normal-looking crack. A final pitch that included 5.10 face and crack climbing ended on a spacious ledge 15-18 feet below the true summit. Alas, the summit block was composed of rotten, vertical, and decomposing stone. I tried to lasso the summit, but that trick ended when the flake I snagged nearly chopped the rope after it peeled off the wall. We decided against a bolt ladder, and I drilled a single bolt for a rappel. This was the only bolt or piton used on the climb. Considering that fact and our alpine location, we felt justified in our restraint.

After a rest day, we started up the Vampire Spire. Our route took a direct line up the center of the south face on clean, golden rock. The first three long leads (5.9, A2+, 5.10/A1) follow a large dihedral before meeting *The Infusion* below a difficult (5.10+) offwidth. No bolts were used on the direct start, which we called *The Undead* (IV/V 5.10+ A2+). After a day off due to rain, we headed back up, hoping to summit via the final pitches of *The Infusion*. Sleet and rain once again sent us fleeing for the tents just before a pendulum onto easier ground. The next morning, we awoke to six inches of snow. Having only one day's food left, we headed down to our food cache to eat and dry out. To our surprise, our metal bear box containing two weeks of provisions and our radio was gone. "Into Thin Air" was a fitting title to that chapter of the trip as we searched fruitlessly for our provisions. A large grizzly had eaten our canned goods and simply walked away with a 60-pound food box. Seven days of rain, snow and hunger followed until a break in the weather allowed us to hike back up to the Vampires and retrieve our gear. Luckily, our bush pilot Warren LaFave flew in to drop off a crew from Colorado. On the fifth day of good weather out of 23, we wished the newcomers good luck and flew away. I wish only that Mother Nature had been more hospitable. Future parties are warned against the unpredictable weather.

JACK CHILDRESS*

*Recipient of the Boyd Everett Fellowship Grant

Vampire Spire, New Routes. During the first three weeks of August, Colorado climbers Pat Goodman, Nan Darkis and I traveled to Canada's Northwest Territories to the Vampire Spires. Located 25 miles north of the Cirque of the Unclimbables in the Logan Mountain range, this group of steep granite peaks was rumored to offer excellent potential for new routes. This proved to be true and we established Base Camp in a plush meadow, a 30-minute hike away

from the spires, and immediately scoped a new line.

Taking advantage of 75° weather, our team succeeded on a seven- pitch line during the first three days. *The Lair of the White Worm* (V 5.11 A2+) ascends an obvious, continuous crack system on the east face of the 1,200-foot Vampire, 150 feet to the right of the 1995 route, *The Infusion*. The climbing involved everything from face to thin nailing to offwidth and chimney, with one bivy on a good ledge at the top of the fifth pitch. *The Lair of the White Worm* will go all free at around 5.12c; however, it took five days of perfect weather to completely dry some crucial sections.

After regrouping for one day and still in the midst of unbelievably stable weather, we began work on another great-looking line conveniently on the same spire. *Sanguin Solution* (V 5.11 A2+) added 500 feet of new climbing to *The Infusion*, and the three of us again summitted after three days. We finished just as the weather deteriorated into an exciting electrical storm.

Both the Vampire Spire and its towering neighbor, the Fortress, still have potential for new lines, especially hard nailing. Located three miles south is the Phoenix, an interesting, steep, 2,500-foot formation with only one existing route and potential for several hard nailing routes. Golden Wing Buttress, a steep, clean-looking 800-foot wall, stands two miles to the east of the Phoenix and is also relatively untapped.

BRAD JACKSON, *unaffiliated*

BUGABOOS

North Howser Tower, Armageddon. "That shifty, nibbling sonova...!" The sun wakes us instead of the watch we had set for our alpine start. A nearby pika must have had a midnight snack of my salty watch wristband. A full-moon approach brought us here to Applebee Campground in the heart of the Bugaboos, the Hounds Tooth erupting from the glacier, purple shadows dancing.

The morning opens clear, August 25. Snowpatch Spire lights up with alpenglow, its golden snow-cup precariously perched. We decide the pika was right and continue our leisurely morning. Coffee jump starts and we make our way across the glaciers, over crevasses, through notches and up and down drainages. The toe of the mammoth tower finally comes into view in early afternoon: the west face of the North Howser Tower. We climb 1,000 feet of granite to a fine bivy perch. Then night moves in, windless. An endless horizon of purple peaks poke into the pink, gliding clouds. Mike and I wake with staring smiles. The headwall looms above. Our path continues up a soaring right-facing dihedral with a few roofs splitting it, the first dihedral to the right of the *All Along the Watchtower* corner. The yet-unascended terrain bounces back thoughts of impossibility. The idea of climbing it is hellishly evocative, the other options creating only a pale when compared to the *Armageddon* (our name for the route). We figured we packed just enough in our one backpack to keep us alive through the worst, through an Armageddon event.

We look up. Finger locks—it's gotta be, all the way, until that roof anyhow. And, oh yeah, that shellfish, scalloppini-looking pitch. Oh, and, can you see... Ahhh! Let's go, whose lead?

It's going. It's going. Fingies, flares, arm bars, your lead, my lead.... Arghh! A pecker and

The Southeast face of Vampire Spire, showing 1. The Undead *(Childress-Howard, 1999).*
2. Sanguin Solution (Darkis-Goodman-Jackson, 1999). 3. The Infusion *(Benge-Epperson-Hollenbaugh, 1994). 4.* Lair of the White Worm *(Darkis-Goodman-Jackson, 1999).* BRAD JACKSON

a blade; damn, we have to aid climb ten feet of the thousands that we've freed. No problem though. Our goal is to go up, so we do.

The sun's angle lowers with the route's. Mike's final block of pitches leads us to a devilish horn of rock protruding from the wall. It's dark. The moon is silenced by the advancing army of clouds. As the wind picks up, the bivy sacks and sardines come out, no sleeping bags of course (just enough to survive Armageddon, remember). Lashed to the horn, we sit inside our sacs.

"Sacreman!" we yell, trying to communicate over the wind's howl. French-Canadian blasphemy comes in handy when trying to laugh through a sleepless night. Armageddon has come.

Morning arrives all too slowly. Hail is now surfing the currents of wind. The bivy sacks are hard to leave, but sitting on our numb butts doesn't entice either. We go! Snow falls; fingers numb. We continue up dihedrals, around corners and over some ice. A bit of gendarme navigation and some ridge-work finally takes us to the summit. It clears, and we get the views. Good God! *Armageddon* (VI 5.11+ A2) has ended. The feeling that comes to mind is flight. Great! Now we have to get off this thing.

JONATHON COPP, *unaffiliated*

Snowpatch Spire, South Face, First Free Ascent. With true and conscious minds, Micah Jessup and I entered into the realm of the mighty Bugaboos, bent on exploring new pathways in the vertical world. After brewing in the rain for several days, attending Kain Hut yoga classes and developing bad symptoms of cabin and wet-tent fever, blue finally chased away the white. Several masterpiece routes were climbed following standard early- to mid-afternoon starts, but then ambition reared its dominating head.

"We must challenge ourselves. We must explore. We must go where no one has gone before. We must try the complete South Face of Snowpatch Spire!" Assuming white rock is of the best quality (not so true in the Bugs), and after being blessed by a mountain goat on the approach, Micah drew the first pitch. We could not see an obvious line past the first pitch on the lower half of the face, but… there appeared to be potential.

Micah struggled for a full 55 meters on the first pitch, ignoring the rope drag, runout and little bit of moss. The second pitch had me searching three different options before I cut out right and up an open corner. New England Boy almost needed a puff on his pipe to figure out the third pitch; dropping down and underclinging the blocky roof was not apparent until he was committed. Three more *largos*, only the last of which was obvious, and we plopped onto the mid-way ledge.

Finally, after a full day of route finding up runout and quite featureless rock, we arrived at the start of the Upper South Face, the Tom Gibson and Rob Rohn extravaganza, six pitches directly above where we started. We continued up the upper part of the route the following day. We were surprised at how stout and sustained the Rohn-Gibson is—definitely a masterpiece of the era.

No pins nor bolts were placed, though we certainly wished we had them at the time, and they may be a good idea for any future ascentionists. Grading? On the lower half, Australian 24 with a capital R. Bump up the Rohn-Gibson part to French 7a+ and add an extra pitch to the topo in the guide book.

GUY EDWARDS, *noncorporate and independent*

Bugaboos, Various Ascents. On July 6, Todd Offenbacher, Jay Sell, Bob Schultz and Nils Davis arrived at the CMH Lodge. The four of us met Paul Bingham, a British friend of Todd's living in Vancouver, who joined us for the first four days. The group chartered a helicopter and flew in to the west side of the Howsers, a.k.a. the East Creek Basin.

The first afternoon and following day it snowed one foot. The subsequent five days provided incredibly clear and dry weather, allowing two teams of two to complete a significant amount of climbing. Jay Sell and Bobby Schultz scoped and began fixing on a line on the South Howser Minaret between the *Italian Pillar* route and the Southwest Pillar route. We could hardly believe this line had not been done and spent much time studying the guide and the Minaret to discern this possibility. One pitch up, they discovered rap slings and nothing further. Prominent crack systems proved to be bottoming runnels and seams, providing aid climbing up to A2+. They fixed five ropes, at which point they were stopped by weather for approximately four days. The two then jugged to their high point, climbing 600 feet of new ground (in which lay the crux A3 pitch) to join the Southwest Pillar route. They finished on the last three pitches of this route. *Doubting the Millennium* (VI 5.10 A3) is seven new 50- to 60-meter pitches.

Todd and I completed a new line on Pigeonfeather's Southeast (right) Peak in three days of climbing over four days. The route is eight pitches, mostly 60 meters in length, with extremely high-quality rock, cracks and free climbing. *Wide Awake* (V 5.10+ A2) is virtually all clean and would possibly go all free in drier conditions. There was a significant amount of snow and ice on the routes, with water running copiously from the cracks due to the huge amount of precipitation in 1999. The route was characterized by a 220-foot, four-inch crack reminiscent of Indian Creek on the fourth pitch.

Very unstable, cold, wet weather predominated for the latter two weeks of our stay. Todd and I (nearly) completed a new route on the west face of the Central Howser Tower in this poor weather over six days. We encountered moderate free and aid climbing; the route is mostly clean, with three large pendulums and a long section of hooking on the seventh pitch that gave it the A3+ rating. The initial three pitches are comprised of a large corner/chimney system. The main wall is gained on the fourth pitch and with it came exposed, clean, quality aid and free climbing.

We backed off 20 feet from the summit in a blizzard, in the middle of the night, with no bivy gear and one functioning headlamp. *Fear and Desire* (VI 5.10 A3+) is nine 50- to 60-meter pitches.

NILS DAVIS

Central Howser Tower, West Face, Chocolate Fudge Brownie. In early August, Brian Webster and I slogged over to the backside of the Howser massif to add another route to the west face of Central Howser Tower. We missed out on the first ascent of this remote and neglected face by one week. Our line begins by climbing the first three pitches of *Fear and Desire* (Offenbacher-Davis, 1999), then, where it doglegs left to gain the center of the wall, our route continues straight up the right-hand pillar. *Chocolate Fudge Brownie* (VI 5.9 A2) climbs nine long pitches of easy aid to reach the south ridge, one pitch from the summit. The main excitement occurred on pitch 5 when I encountered a five-foot by 15-foot "floating flake" precariously pasted to the wall. Not wanting to even breathe on it for fear of scraping both of us off the face, I copperheaded thin seams and riveted blank rock several feet to the right for the route's only A2 section. We named the intimidating feature "The Pillar of Despair, Touch if

You Dare." The route is named for the huge one-foot by one-foot chocolate fudge brownie a baker friend of Brian's gave us. It kept us sugar-buzzed for the whole trip.

SEAN ISAAC, *Canada*

CANADIAN ROCKIES

Canadian Rockies, Various Activity. The summer of 1999 was a frustrating one in the Canadian Rockies. From sport climbs to big alpine routes, wet rock was the norm through mid-August. The Front Ranges were somewhat dryer and saw the most activity. The Ghost River area continued to be the focus for the development of long rock routes on impeccable limestone, with Andy Genereux and Keith Haberl being the main activists. New route activity in the Ghost encompasses a variety of styles, from bold onsight ground-up ascents to rap-bolting, with the majority of routes being put up on lead with a power drill. This style has yielded some of the finest multi-pitch rock climbs in the Rockies. While the 1999 season saw mostly shorter routes go up, unreported from the summer of 1998 is *The Ardent Heart* (5.10d, 300m) by Haberl, Brian Spear and Ken Wylie, the first route to top out on the impressive formation known as The Prow in the Waiparous Creek area north of the Ghost proper. In the best tradition, it was put up onsight, with all bolts drilled by hand and with Haberl leading the last 5.10 pitch in a downpour.

In the Bow Valley, Raphael Slawinski and Rodger Debeyer made the first free ascent of *Orient Express* (5.11d, 510m), the original 1976 route on the North Face of Ha Ling (formerly known as Chinaman's) Peak above Canmore. Slawinski also teamed up with Eric Dumerac to make the likely first free ascent of *Remembrance Wall* (5.11b, 555m) on the same face. The latter route in particular is highly recommended, offering sustained and varied climbing. Further west, unreported from the summer of 1998 is a 12-pitch route (IV 5.10R) on the Stanley Headwall, put up by Slawinski and Marcus Norman. It is the first route to top out on this impressive rock wall, better known as a destination for hard ice/mixed climbing on routes such as *Nemesis* and *The Day After Les Vacances de Mr. Hulot.*

An extended period of high pressure in late August/early September made up somewhat for the summer that never was. The visiting Salt Lake City climbers Chris Harmston and Seth Shaw timed their road trip perfectly with the weather. They warmed up with a rare ascent of the serious *Above and Beyond* (5.11c R A0, 305m) on Mt. Yamnuska. Moving on to the Icefields Parkway, bolting on-lead with a power drill, they put up the stellar *Salt Point* (5.11+, eight pitches, 400m) on the vast expanse of perfect rock next to the Weeping Wall.

Indian summer also brought some alpine routes into condition. Classic north face routes such as the Greenwood-Locke (V 5.9) on Mt. Temple and the Beckey-Chouinard-Doody (IV 5.7) on Mt. Edith Cavell were climbed, with the latter seeing multiple parties on a single day! In the Columbia Icefields, the *Andromeda Strain* (V M5+ WI4) received at least two ascents by Scott DeCapio and partner, and Dumerac and Slawinski. This superb alpine mixed route is now routinely freeclimbed, with the crux 5.9 A1 going at well-protected M5+ drytooling. The short but stout *Sidestreet* (III M6) nearby also received a number of free ascents in the spring and fall (neither route is particularly recommended mid-summer).

Winter seemed to arrive early, and by early October new ice routes were going up in the Front Ranges. However, by the end of the month, unseasonably warm weather descended on the range. With rain falling high up in the alpine, many routes fell down. Several spectacular lines formed on the 500-meter high face of the East End of Rundle above Canmore. They were attempted, but rapidly melting ice forced retreat before they could be completed.

The 1998-'99 ice climbing season was highlighted by several multi-pitch mixed testpieces going up, the work chiefly of Kefira Allen and the tireless Dave Thomson: *The Real Big Drip* (V M7+ WI6+, 200m) in the Ghost River area, *Nightmare on Wolf Street* (V M7+ WI6+, 185m) on the Stanley Headwall, and *Rocket Man* (V M7+ WI5+, 350m) on Mt. Patterson (home of *Riptide*). (Note that while both alpine and ice routes are given commitment grades denoted by Roman numerals, the two use different scales.) Unfortunately, this season none of these spectacular routes formed up, and no comparable new ones went up. Perhaps it was the initially poor ice conditions that set the tone for the season of 1999-2000, which was marked by an explosion in technical standards, fostered chiefly on short, often bolt-protected, drytooling testpieces. With many locals climbing at a high standard, friendly rivalry led to a frenzy of activity, with routes up to M9+ going up, the work chiefly of Ben Firth, Will Gadd, Sean Isaac and Slawinski.

The skills acquired at the crags were also applied to "traditional" routes. Rob Owens and Patricia Deavoll put up *Stuck in the Middle* (V M7- WI5+, 145m) on the Terminator Wall. After a pitch and a half of sustained mixed climbing, it joins Alex Lowe's *Troubled Dreams* at the crux of that route. This excellent variation received several repeat ascents. Dave Marra and Eamonn Walsh climbed the often-looked-at ice in the gully above *Ice Nine* on Mt. Wilson on the Icefields Parkway to produce *Eh Spring Chicken Named Logan* (V 5.8R WI5, 500m). Also on Mt. Wilson, Cory Balano, Dave Edgar and Marra made a likely first ascent with *Suntori* (VI M6+ A2 WI6), spending two nights out on the route. Linking ice smears and mixed gullies, *Suntori* gains 1500 meters in elevation to top out on spectacular white quartzite towers. Edgar and Marra also put up *The Ice Cream Man* and *The One-Eyed Kid* (V 5.9R WI5+, 500m), a long route in a big setting on the east side of Mt. Stephen near Field.

In April, Blanchard, Steve House and Joe Josephson made another attempt on a new line on the Emperor Face of Mt. Robson. Described as "the big daddy of faces in the Rockies" by Sean Dougherty, author of *Selected Alpine Climbs*, the Emperor Face has only two established routes, the Logan-Stump (1978) and the Cheesmond-Dick (1981), neither of which has been repeated. They reached a point some five pitches below the *Emperor Ridge* before being forced down by a storm. Their previous attempt three years ago was cut short at the same point when they dropped the pump to their stove. After coming down, Blanchard and House attempted the rarely climbed *Sphinx Face* on the northeast side of Mt. Temple, but bad weather once again shut them down.

On the solo front, the prolific Guy Lacelle enchained the *Weeping Pillar* (V WI6, 315m) and *Polar Circus* (V WI5, 700m) on one of the shortest days of the year. Mike Verwey later duplicated this feat. *Slipstream* (VI WI4+) remained a popular solo objective, but lived up to its reputation with hazards ranging from cornice fall on the route to crevasse danger on the descent.

Two ice routes with a big reputation came in unusually thick this season and received numerous ascents: *Riptide* (V WI5+, 200m) sported only short sections of its trademark "weirdness" and was nowhere near its original grade of WI6+/7 R. Similarly, *Gimme Shelter* (VI WI5+, 300m) has yet to be repeated in the thin conditions of the first ascent. Nevertheless, the sustained vertical ice and dangerous serac barrier overhanging the route made it an exciting outing. Most parties climbed the waterice in several hours and rappelled from below the seracs, but near the end of the season Dumerac and Sean King, after a comfortable bivy in a sheltered cave several pitches up, continued over the seracs in another four pitches, including a difficult pitch on glacier ice.

RAPHAEL SLAWINSKI, *Canada*

Howse Peak, East Face, M-16. On March 23-27, Barry Blanchard, Scott Backes and I climbed a new route that follows the exciting-looking ice formations on the east face of Howse Peak in Alberta, Canada. The route consisted of about 15 pitches and we ended at the top of a striking couloir, some distance below and to the south of the summit.

The adventure began with a three-hour ski approach. We soloed up about 1,000 feet of steep snow and easy ice to the base of the first difficulty, a WI6 pitch that Scott led. This pitch introduced us to the unique brand of "snow-ice" that we would find on much of the face. This material, while fairly good for climbing, was bad for protection and anchors, which caused us to use rock gear almost exclusively throughout the climb. We climbed some fourth-class snow and ice to the base of a WI7 pitch that spindrift erosion had left overhanging and concave. The first night was spent in a narrow, two-pronged snow cave of the "torpedo tube" variety that Barry, Joe Josephson and I had perfected three years earlier on Robson.

The second day we climbed only five pitches, of which one was very difficult. I led that pitch in three and a half hours. It consisted of an easy mixed traverse to a very narrow, thin, steep and delicate ice runnel with reasonable rock gear every ten feet or so. We bivouacked in a second, somewhat longer torpedo tube two pitches above that crux.

The next day it was snowing considerably and the face was running with spindrift all day. We waited it out in the cave. The morning of the fourth day we saw stars at 6 a.m., but by the time we were out of the cave at 8 it was snowing and avalanching again. After a brief trip back into the cave to discuss options and eat the last of the food, we decided to go for it with minimal gear because we knew the major technical challenges were behind us. The weather improved briefly and Scott led the incredibly spectacular "Peruvian Traverse," which climbed horizontally for 800 feet in and out of snow runnels and ridges. The traverse ended above the couloir that George Lowe had incorporated into his variation of the Northeast Ridge some 30 years earlier. We rappelled into the "Lowe Couloir" and left a rope fixed there for our return. We then climbed approximately five pitches of entrancingly beautiful grade 2 and 3 ice to the top of the couloir.

The exit from the couloir was blocked by a large cornice, but a traverse out and under it looked feasible. After some discussion of whether to exit the face and traverse the peak, or reverse the route with rappelling, we decided to rappel. We quickly made eight or ten 100-foot rappels and, combined with some down climbing, regained our fixed rope. During this descent we heard a helicopter, and with Barry's VHF radio we were able to talk to the park wardens, who had been concerned about us being on the face during such weather. We assured them we were OK and on our way down.

After Scott re-led the Peruvian Traverse in reverse, we were on our last rappel to the snow cave when the hazard caught up to us. Scott was inside the snowcave and I had just arrived and called "off rappel" when a cornice or snow mushroom from the face collapsed and hit Barry. Barry was clipped into a screw in the snow-ice, which was tied to a piton driven just underneath a small overhang. When Barry was hit with the snow blocks, the ice screw pulled out and he was swung below the piton. This probably saved his life, since more snow came down and continued to work him over. He lost his pack and had snow forced into all the openings in his clothing as he got repeatedly pummeled. It took me some time after the snow had subsided before I contacted Barry. He slowly rappelled down under his own power. When he arrived at the cave he was quite shocked, sore and scared. Inside the cave he got into a sleeping bag with Scott and a hot water bottle, which I used the last of our fuel to make. After an hour, we were able to ascertain that his injuries were in fact mostly minor, with his chief

The east face of Howse Peak, showing M-16 *(Blanchard-House-Backes, 1999).* STEVE HOUSE

complaint being a sore and unflexing right knee.

The next morning the storm had subsided and we began our rappels at first light. I led first, Barry came second with help from Scott and Scott rapped last. Sometime during the first rappels, Barry called the park wardens on his radio to ask for assistance on the trip from the base of the face to the car, a distance of six miles in variable snow conditions. By late morning we had gained the lower part of the face when we heard the helicopter approach. Barry's radio was no longer working properly because it had become wet during his accident. We had no way to communicate with them and a park warden named Mark was soon getting slung onto the face. When he came in, we clipped him to our final rappel anchor, a spare pick driven behind a flake. Solid, but unconventional. Mark assumed that we all wanted to go out but upon explaining the situation to him, we decided it was best for him just to take Barry out and allow Scott and me to continue under our own power to the roadhead, which is what we did.

That day was not without significance as it was also Barry's 40th birthday and his wife Catherine had planned a wonderful party with nearly 100 people in attendance.

We named the route *M-16* in reference to its difficulty and seriousness and in allusion to Barry's experience of being "under the gun," and also partially in objection to the "new" sport of mixed climbing on bolted crag routes, which alpinists have been doing for centuries, just not at the crags and without the bolts.

STEVE HOUSE

Baffin Island

Stewart Valley

The Citadel, The Endless Day. Mike "Twid" Turner, Louise Thomas, Jerry Gore and Shaun Hutson made the first ascent of "The Citadel" in Stewart Valley via their 900-meter route, *The Endless Day.* (The climbers note that the peak may already have an official name.) The climbers were gobsmacked at the potential of the arctic valley; all members thought it was as impressive as Yosemite. The 25-pitch route was climbed in some of the worst weather the team had experienced anywhere else in the world. The climb took from midway through May to the middle of June. After fixing 500 meters of rope, the team moved up in capsule style to establish a hanging portaledge camp at half-height. Eight nights were spent living in portaledges during freezing conditions; it snowed most days. From the portaledges, the team climbed up an impressive corner to the summit of The Citadel. Fate was on the team's side: as they climbed over the top of this impressive wall, the clouds cleared and the sun came out. The breath-taking view rounded off a very successful expedition. The final push took a 36-hour day to climb to the summit and return to the camp. The endless light of the arctic allowed sun on the wall from 8 p.m. to 8 a.m. This was the first all-British team to make a new route in the frozen fjords of Baffin's east coast.

Mike "Twid" Turner, *Wales*

Scott Island

Ship's Prow, Solo Ascent. From April 23-June 3, Mike Libecki made the first ascent of the north face of the overhanging Ship's Prow via *The Hinayana* (VI 5.8 A3+, 600m). An account of his solitary adventure can be found earlier in this journal.

Scott Island, Ascent and Attempts. Three of us arrived in Clyde River on a Monday afternoon and waited two days for one member (the first to leave) to feel up to the trek. We left Clyde with two snowmobiles and komatiks. About ten hours later, we arrived at a hunter's cabin on the Clark Inlet, across from Scott Island (or Piliktua, as the Inuit call it). The view from here is great, but belies the distance between the formations quite well. There are about ten peaks in the area with 3,000- to 4,000-foot walls boasting natural lines. Many more peaks have stunning 2,000- to 3,000-foot walls. Most of the formations in the area require some form of alpine approach.

We decided on a 4,000-foot south face of a formation on the east shore of the mouth of Clark's Fjord that faces the widest section of the Clark Inlet. After we set up camp, a small storm blew through and the first member of the expedition left with the guides when they returned to Clyde.

We spent several days scoping the wall, trying to pick out the easiest way through the mixed-up lower section to the spectacular overhanging pillar above. We opted for the more stable left-trending ramps that led through the "Airplane," then back right to the main wall under the pillar. After I led two climbing days and fixed 400 meters of rope to the beginning of the rock climbing, my partner said he did not want to continue. We cleaned the ropes as we retreated, leaving the anchors in place.

After some rest days, we summitted "Lone Wolf Point" (named for a wolf that visited our camp) on April 29 via a 600-meter couloir topped with 2,000-foot-plus vert of second-class talus on the peak's western flanks. I built an Inukshuk (a large cairn) on the summit. In the following days we decided that we should pick a smaller objective. The guides were not able to move us for a week, so we decided to start a route on the formation's west buttress. We finished two pitches on the fantastic white granite before Qullikkut guides moved us ten kilometers to Piliktua's 2,000-foot formations. We set up camp below the wild geology of the 1,800-foot "Raven," which we named for a couple of ravens that roosted on the formation. After I led the first two pitches in three climbing days, my second partner felt he couldn't go on. We had been there three weeks and had started three routes. I was determined to complete a route with or without a partner. I decided to stay and solo my route.

I hauled all my rack and ropes to the high point and continued to about 750 feet (four pitches) before taking to the wall. I continued up the wall to a high point of 1,600 feet before losing momentum and my psyche. After ten days of living on the wall, I retreated, fixing 460 meters of static line back to the ice. The route is currently rated 5.7 A3, with the difficult aid involving many thin pins on an exfoliated and expanding headwall at the high point.

JON FOX

Gibbs Fjord

Jushua Tower, Zen and the Art of Leadership. On May 14, Steph Davis, Brandon Kannier and I arrived in the small village of Clyde River. The next three days were spent traveling by snowmobile with Jushua (our Inuit guide) across the six-foot-thick frozen ocean to the Gibbs Fjord. We estimated our objective to be more than 2,500 feet tall; it sported many large roofs and a sizable ledge a quarter of the way up with snow on it.

The journey began with 600 feet of moderate free and aid climbing. From a big ledge, I led a 60-meter A1 pitch that landed us on a small snow- and rubble-strewn shelf. This ledge would become Camp I as we committed to a capsule-style ascent. From the small snow ledge, Steph led a very loose and dangerous free pitch (5.11) that ended under a small roof. Over the next four days we aided and free climbed through small roofs and thin knifeblade cracks. Snow, strong winds and very cold temperatures were our constant companions for the 22 days that we spent on the wall. Day 6 was spent hauling our massive amounts of water, gear, food and living quarters 800 feet to CII. From CII, Steph gracefully floated up a very steep and difficult face climb with tricky and marginal protection. On the next pitch, we encountered some of the infamous red loose rock for which Baffin is known.

With only 600 feet of rope fixed, we moved home again to establish CIII. On the next pitch above CIII, Brandon had the wretched luck of blank rock. Steph and I agreed this would be a good day to polish off the rest of the whiskey. Sixteen hours later and only 100 feet of vertical gain, Brandon at last arrived at a feature. He was so exhausted from drilling that he called it a day, drilled some more for the anchor and rappelled back home.

By day 14 everyone was beginning to feel the effect of a poor diet, lack of drinking water and uncomfortable sleeping conditions. Brandon and Steph ascended a short 40-foot pitch to a large ledge. From the ledge, the wall was severely overhanging and sported a large thin flake in the center and a very thin corner on the right. With a big ledge below, this pitch definitely looked like hard aid. I was forced to climb the overhanging A4 head seam with a busted chisel.

The following day we moved the camp; we were now 2,500 feet up the wall. The next pitch saw Steph free and aid climbing through large roofs and even larger chimneys. The next day, Brandon and I ate a quick breakfast, jumared up and I began my lead. Three hours later I was yelling with joy to be on the summit. When Brandon and Steph arrived, we hiked the 300 yards to the true summit. Once there, we broke out the cigars and began flying the kite that we had hauled up this 2,700-foot cliff. Brandon rappelled back down to the portaledge while Steph and I cleaned the fixed ropes. After a long sleep we got up and organized the 18 rappels back to the sea ice. Eighteen hours later we were at last down on the scree ledge. We called the route *Zen and the Art of Leadership* (VI 5.11 A4).

With six days still left before pick-up, we took a hike to some surrounding walls and relaxed around camp. On our 35th day in the Gibbs fjord, our Inuit guide arrived. On the ride out, one of my Baffin dreams came true. I saw a polar bear. Jushua said it wasn't a large bear, but it was quite impressive in my eyes.

RUSSEL MITROVICH, *unaffiliated*

NEWFOUNDLAND

Blow Me Down Provincial Park, Ice Routes. On January 1, Arthur Haines and I took the ferry to Port-aux-Basques, Newfoundland. Our plan was to climb ice routes rumored to be located above the large inland fjords within Gros Morne National Park. However, severe weather and poor snow conditions prevented us from reaching this area. Instead, we concentrated our efforts around the city of Cornerbrook. On January 3, we climbed a 1,000-foot snow-and-ice route (WI4) located in Blow Me Down Provincial Park. This area lived up to its name with gusts up to 70 m.p.h. and temperatures in the teens.

On January 5, we followed the north side of the Humber River to the base of a large cliff called The Old Man. We climbed a steep ice flow that splits the cliff (WI 5-) for 500 feet. Temperatures rose to 45° F and a strong southern wind blew the melt water up the flow, making for poor visibility and extremely wet climbing. We climbed several shorter flows to the west of Marble Mountain Ski Area on January 5-6.

Although we found no evidence these routes have been climbed, they are the most striking lines and I'm sure, because there are ice climbers living in the area, they have been climbed. I did not find any record of ice climbing in Newfoundland in any of the *AAJ* or some *CAJ*s I looked through, but I know climbers have visited the area. Overall, this area has a fair amount of easily accessible ice; however, climbing later in the season would provide longer days and potentially better ice conditions.

DAVE ANDERSON

GREENLAND

ROOSEVELT RANGE

J. V. Jensen Land

Avanarsuasua, Exploration. Our exploration of extreme north Greenland continued in July. Our interests were once again broadly based. Dr. Ko deKorte and Peter Baldwin completed their study of the region's bird populations. Dr. Lawrence Hacquebord observed for archeo-logical sites (discounting the Skafte site for the 1998 expedition). Our major mountaineering objective was the twin-peaked summit (1300-1400m) above the polar trunk glacier at the bend of the Ulvehojene Valley. Dr. Miki Rifkin, Cindy Liebeck, Dr. Frank Landsberger, Jerry Weidler, Chuck Stielau and Vic Bradford and I circumnavigated the three-kilometer terminal face of the glacier to its west side and five of us proceeded up the north face to a partially ice-free plateau at 1100 meters. Vic Bradford and I climbed further west, unroped up the exposed ridge, traversing class IV rock steps and pinnacles and steep ice to the north summit. The higher (south) summit required body belays on its final exposed pinnacle. We returned to our Advance Base Camp after 22 hours of climbing. The week to follow brought us to what we determined to be one of the two most northerly lakes in the world, which lies above a coastal canyon ten kilometers west of Kap Jesup. It is unmapped. From this lake, Vic Bradford and Chuck Sielau climbed to Hammaken Point and Ikiorti, the world's most northerly summits, by new routes on the north side.

Concerning the Skafte site (see 1999 *AAJ*, pp. 288-289), arctic small-tool culture sites are already proven to exist in Independence Fjord. Eigel Knut's discoveries include the north side of Frederick Hyde Fjord. The Skafte site, if valid, would only prove a migration route around the north coast.

DENNIS SCHMITT

Northeast Greenland

Louise Boyd Land, Various Activity. Team Members Helen Bostock, Andrew Bostock, Matt Tinsley, Dave Mills and Neal Hockley were in the field (centered on 73°30' N, 28°00' W) from July 2-August 26. The majority of the climbing was done during July, with no major climbing taking place after August 8. The weather was generally stable due to large arctic high pressures sitting over the region. Occasional snow was received but never for more than two days in a row. The wind was rarely noticeable and never really strong. Twenty-four-hour daylight was enjoyed throughout the trip.

In total, 15 first ascents were made on formations over 2000 meters high, three granite rock spires and a granite wall were discovered and climbed and two new routes were put up on the previously unclimbed northwest face of Petermann Bjerg.

First, we ascended all the significant peaks in close proximity to our Base Camp. These were mainly ski ascents with little technical difficulty. It was usually possible to ascend the majority of the mountain on skis, just removing them for the final narrow sum-mit ridge. The rock in the area around BC was very broken and not suitable for climbing. The routes we took up all these mountains were the obvious ridges. All these routes were PD or below.

We then journeyed north and managed to gain entry to a very secluded high glacier. This contained a chain of nice triangular peaks and some excellent granite rock climbing. This appeared to be the only area in Louise Boyd Land with rock suitable for climbing and, although we were only here for four days, we managed to get some interesting mixed climb-ing in. We climbed all the mountains surrounding this glacier. Three of the most southerly ones formed an easy horseshoe of grade PD-. In this valley there were also three granite teeth that would provide some excellent rock climbing and some interesting couloirs. We ascend-ed all these via the most accessible routes, which we graded PD+ but which involved some mixed climbing, generally following ridgelines. The final mountain in this valley is the largest and has the most scope for technical mixed climbing. The group took a line up the center of a rock band separating the lower snowfields from the summit snowfield. This initially involved an ice gully that led into a rock corner which, after a tricky lead, led onto more broken ground. A large gully was then followed onto the summit snowfield. This route was graded at PD+ III.

The final part of our mountaineering program was undertaken on the ski south for pickup. It included the two most noteworthy of our first ascents at the southern boundary of Louise Boyd Land. These two mountains were the highest in the region by some way and provided some interesting ice routes, though the rock was again rather poor. We ascended the first directly up the south face via two gullies (they were numerous to choose from). One gully was straightforward, but the other narrowed in the middle to give some vertical ice for about ten meters. Once overcome, it was just steep snow to the summit. From this top, we descended the ridge southeast to the col and carried on to the summit of the second. The ridge is broken but relatively easy.

As well as first ascents, we put up two new routes (the 6th and 7th ascents) on the unclimbed northwest face of Petermann Bjerg, the highest mountain in the High Arctic. These routes were both ice routes up the 1000-meter face. The climbing was not particularly difficult, but the size of the face made the routes seem more daunting. One party went directly up the northwest face via the main gully (60°+ ice) in four hours, and the second party went up the ridge separating the northwest face from the northeast face, initially reaching the ridge via a 55-degree ice couloir. The ascent took four and a half hours.

All the climbing was carried out during the night when it was colder and the snow was in better condition.

ANDREW BOSTOCK, *United Kingdom*

Rignys Bjerg Mountains, Various Activity. Expedition members Brinley Mitchell, Peter McEwen and Ian MacDonald are part of a group of gay men who believe that the twin activities of sailing and climbing assist with building health and vitality. We had as our objective to establish physical and mental well-being through the dynamic of exploring a remote area of east Greenland while living under the threat of AIDS.

We led an expedition into the Rignys Bjerg Mountains from July 3-25. From Base Camp at 1600 meters, we made three first ascents. We climbed a 2000-meter peak (69° 18.120' N, 26° 46.257' W) by its south ridge (PD) in three hours; a 2320-meter peak (69° 18.120' N, 26° 46.257' W) by its northeast ridge (PD) in five hours; and a 2020-meter peak (69° 17.901' N, 26° 45.704' W) by its southwest ridge (PD, technical) in two and a half hours. We also carried out six two-day exploratory ski tours on a glacier at the edge of the ice-cap located at 69° 18.180' N, 26° 43.587' W. The mountains in the area were up to a height of 2500 meters. Most ascents were between 400-600 meters.

The condition of the rock was extremely friable and all ascents were on snow slopes and ridges. The greatest objective danger was rockfall and crevasse crossing. The weather was clear, sunny and calm with a maximum daytime temperature of between 20- to 30°C with about seven days of snow storms and Gale Force 8 winds (unsettled weather).

The equipment and provisions were shipped in on one Twin Otter flight. We withdrew all refuse from the field. One of our party developed pneumonia with pneumocystis carinii but made a full recovery three months after the end of the expedition. The area was reached from

Akureyri in Northern Iceland.

BRINLEY MITCHELL, *United Kingdom*

Rignys Bjerg Area, Various Activity. The Rignys Bjerg mountains lie some distance east of the Watkins Bjerge and Ejnar Mikkelsens Fjelde areas at approximately 69° 5' N, 26° 30' W. In late May, Nigel Edwards and three others were flown into the area. Due to a misunderstanding, their pilot set them down at the location used by British groups in 1998 rather than their intended, more easterly site. Despite this mix-up, the team made a total of ten first ascents in this mostly unexplored region before being picked up by the flight taking the Scott Umpleby/Jim Gregson group into the Watkins Bjerge (see account below).

JAMES GREGSON, *Alpine Club*

Lindbergh Fjelde, Various Activity. On July 25, Paul Walker of Tangent Expeditions International flew a team comprising Ralph Atkinson, James Berry, Luke Francis, David Howe, Phil and Anita Jones, Malcolm Minchin and Owain Turner into the Lindbergh Fielde. At 69° N, 31° W, this area lies 60 kilometers northeast of the Lemon Mountains and a similar distance northwest of Gunnbjørns Fjeld. Apart from a visit to its southern edge by a British group in 1992, it had never been explored or climbed in. Walker's group reported some poor-quality rock but large numbers of very attractive snow and ice peaks. Over a period of 16 days, the team made 20 first ascents of mountains between 2600 and 3200 meters high; the weather was perfect throughout this time. The group was flown back out to Iceland on August 11.

JAMES GREGSON, *Alpine Club*

LEMON MOUNTAINS

Lemon Mountains, Various Activity. The Lemon Mountains are one of Greenland's geological freaks; their spiky peaks sit uncomfortably between the usual Greenland domes on either side. You can find them on the map at the northern end of Kangerdlugssuaq (68° 30' N, 32° W), a large fjord halfway between Ammassalik and Constable Pynt on the east Greenland coast.

Our group of eight "youngsters" (Rupert Gladstone, Rupert Finn, Dr. Sarah Walmsley, Andy Parker, Tim Harvey, Dan Haywood, Tom Chamberlain and I) spent four weeks climbing 18 routes (including 12 first ascents) on the Hedgehog Glacier, including several peaks opposite the Cathedral, the highest mountain in the region. The Lemons are only 2000 to 2500 meters in height, but from a base at 1100 meters we had climbs up to 1000 meters long. We were delighted to find sound rock and ice, and climbed routes from F- to TD+.

We reached the area by a ski-equipped Twin Otter directly from Iceland with an airdrop of supplies by a Piper Chieftain. As a group of eight, we made most efficient use of the planes, although the trip still cost £2000 a head. The expedition report can be found at www.wayupnorth.clara.co.uk

RICHARD PASH, *United Kingdom*

SCHWEIZERLAND

Schweizerland, Various Activity. From July 22-August 22, Britons Al Powell, Kenton Cool,

Pete and Andy Benson, Andy MacNae and Richard Spillet achieved ten free climbs and much sun bathing on south-facing walls at the head of the 16th September Glacier in the Schweizerland Mountains of east Greenland. Eight of the climbs were first ascents. On July 23, Powell and Cool arrived in Kulusuk, traveled by boat to the Knud Rassmussen Glacier and skied to Base Camp (66° 16' N, 36° 26' W) below Tupilak over three days. The rest of the team arrived by helicopter on the 28th. The following routes were then climbed during a three-week period of stable weather (all are first ascents unless otherwise noted).

Powell and Cool climbed Rodebjerg (2140m, 66° 21' N, 36° 25' W) via the South Pillar (D+, 1100m) for the route's second ascent on July 30. It was a stunning line, and an easy descent was made down the glacier below the west face. On August 3, Powell and Cool climbed the south face of the west summit of Tupilak (2264m, 66° 19' N, 36° 32' W). It was a tricky approach: the left-hand icefall is very dangerous, the right-hand one slower but safer. Their route, *Big Air* (ED1 VII+, 870m), starts at a gray tower directly below the summit, eventually breaking out left near the top. The route was climbed in 40 hours round-trip to BC. On August 10, Benson and Benson climbed the south face of the east summit. Their route, *Ulysses* (ED1/2 VII+, 950m), takes a large sustained corner system below the east summit.

The Red Wall (Pt. 2070m, 66° 20' N, 36° 22' W) is an immaculate south-facing cirque with an easy descent via the east ridge. The South Ridge (D+, 800m) was climbed by Benson and Benson on July 30. They took a gully left of the icefall to gain the ridge. The pair also climbed *Red or Dead* (ED1 VII, 580m) on August 5. They started at the left-hand snow patch and took the right-most of four prominent grooves in the center of the face. *The Baron* (ED1 VII+, 620m) was climbed by Powell and Cool on August 9. The route climbs the next groove left of *Red or Dead*.

Fallen Star (ca. 2040m, 66° 19' N, 36° 16' W) is a prominent, clean-cut summit. On August 13, Powell and Cool climbed *Vidal Soupspoon* (ED1/2 VII+, 850m) on the southeast face. Approach was made from the north via the 1550-meter col below the east ridge. The route takes the immaculate corner on the right-hand side of face, eventually joining the east ridge.

The south face of Little Midi (ca. 1650m, 66° 21' N, 36° 15' W) is reminiscent of its namesake. MacNae and Spillet climbed the Southeast Face (TD VI, 260m) in seven good pitches; descent was made down the south flank to the left of the face.

Beacon (ca. 1600m, 66° 17' N, 36° 17' W) is the striking pyramid five miles east of BC. MacNae and Spillet repeated the West Ridge (D+ 800m) on July 31. The climb took six hours for the ascent and another six for the descent, which involved a couple of rappels.

Viewed from Slangen Pass, the Devil's Thumb (1587m, 66° 14' N, 36° 25' W) appears to come straight out of the movie *Close Encounters*. The South Face (TD VI+, 300m) was climbed by Benson and Benson on August 14. The route follows a groove system in the center of the face. Descent was made via the east ridge. Finally, on August 16-18, the whole team descended the Knud Rasmussen Glacier on foot and retired to Kulusuk for tea and medals.

AL POWELL, *United Kingdom*

Schweizerland, Various Ascents. It was reported that an Italian expedition of Luigi Airone, Paolo Cavagnetto, Fabio Jacchini, Ercole Passera, Allessandro Quagliolo and Cesare Racaschietto skied from Tasilaq with 100-kilo pulkas to the mountains around Tupilak in June, making three possible new routes. On June 13, they climbed *Dia Pero* (TD+, 6c), a 600-

meter route on an unnamed pyramid (ca. 1700m). On top the remains of a German tetropack were found. On June 16, *Pilastro del Centenario* (TD, 6a, 900m) on the east-southeast ridge of Rodebjerg (2140m) was climbed in ten pitches; an empty aspirin bottle was found on top. On June 18, the team climbed *Sedna* (ED2 6c A2+) in 15 pitches during three days. Ropes were fixed to the top of pitch 9; the route appeared to be the first ascent of an unnamed pyramid (ca. 1700m). (*High Mountain Sports* 210)

OFJORD REGION

Tsavagattaq, South Ridge, and Other Activity. It was reported that Bengt Flygel Nilsfors, Magnar Osnes and Odd Roar Wiik (Norway) with Micke Sundberg (Sweden) visited the Ofjord region near the head of Scoresby Sound Fjord south of the Staunings Alps in 1998. Wiik and Sundberg unsuccessfully attempted the striking Tsavagattaq via the south ridge. Nilsfors, Sundberg and Wiik returned to the area in July, 1999, with Patrik Fransson (Sweden), this time climbing the south ridge of Tsavagattaq in two and a half days. The route involved more than 30 pitches at up to 5.11a interspersed with long sections of scrambling. Descent was made via 32 rappels and a lot of downclimbing. A small cairn was found on top, probably accessed via the southwest face. Wiik commented that it was the best alpine rock climb he had done.

Also in the fjord at the same time was a group of seven Swedes who focused on the Grundtvigskirken Peaks. Anders Granål, Johan Hansson, Mads Homgren and Mike Wright climbed the middle summit of Grundtvigskirken Spire via the East-Southeast Pillar (ED1). The descent was made via rappel by the same route. Magnus Lindberg and Mike Wright then climbed the south face of the south summit of the Spire via a 25-pitch line up to 5.10c/d. Descent was made by the East-Southeast Pillar anchors established earlier. (*High Mountain Sports* 210)

WATKINS BJERGE

Watkins Mountains, Various Ascents. Just after midnight on June 16-17, a Twin Otter skiplane of Air Iceland lifted off from Isafjordur, Iceland, to take a group of five Britons—Scott Umpleby (leader), Dr. Jon Dallimore, Gordon Downs, Sandy Gregson and Jim Gregson— into the Watkins Mountains. En route, the plane set down in the Rignys Bjerg area to pick up another group of four Britons who had been climbing in that district. At 3:30 a.m. on June 17, we touched down in bright sunshine at 2560 meters near the head of the Woolley Glacier at 68° 50.569' N, 29° 23.77' W in the Watkins Mountains, which hold the highest peaks in Greenland as well as a multitude of other unclimbed summits. On June 18, a day of light snowfall and mist, my group opened its account with the first ascent of Forefinger (3367m) by its north ridge. On June 19, in an attempt to switch into a nighttime climbing regime, we left camp at 10:30 p.m. to make a very interesting traverse over the twin summits of Terra Nova Peak (3020m) then continuing along the arête to Flash Point (2960m) (both first ascents) with a descent by another ridge to form a two-horseshoe outing. The next night, we made an attempt on Julia (3455m), skiing up the eastern flanks to a high point of 3200 meters. The onset of very high winds and fierce spindrift caused us to abandon our attempt and descend to camp, where we had bad weather for three days.

Descending the northeast ridge of Dome. JIM GREGSON

On June 24, we were able to make a successful ski ascent to the summit of Paul-Emile Victor (a.k.a. Mound, 3609m) from where we could look across to Gunnbjørns Fjeld piercing the cloud layer and at the huge reservoir of unclimbed mountains stretching in all directions. In the evening of June 25, we skied northeast from camp to the toe of a strikingly sharp snow/ice arête, by which we made the first ascent of Midnight Peak (3249m). Sandy and I continued over the summit to complete a traverse by downclimbing the steep eastern arête. We now decided to ski and haul pulks around to Gunnbjørns Fjeld, so we struck our camp on June 26 and made a ten-hour overnight journey of 25 kilometers down the easy grade of the Woolley Glacier, then back up a tributary ice-stream to make our final camp at 2220 meters at 68° 54.942' N, 29° 43.738' W.

After a rest day, we pulled out of camp at 7 p.m. on June 28 to ski up toward Gunnbjørns Fjeld (3693m, highest Greenland summit; 3693.65m the most recently surveyed altitude). We left skis at ca. 3300 meters, then climbed the southwest ridge to the summit in very good conditions to spend an hour in splendid calm. A fantastic ten-kilometer ski run back to camp completed a 13-hour round trip. According to our research, it was probably the 25th ascent of Gunnbjørns Fjeld; Gordon, a 64-year-old, was delighted.

In the evening of June 30, the five of us set off to ski up the side glacier that separates Dome and Cone (second- and third-highest peaks in Greenland). We then made an attempt on Dome along its northeast ridge but gave up our try at ca. 3600 meters, where we ran into very unstable windslab on a steeply convex arête flank. After descending, Sandy and I went briefly to look for a route onto Cone, but gave up on that also and followed the others back to camp. We passed July 2 in packing up, and on July 3 headed out toward Isafjordur to close another interesting trip.

JAMES GREGSON, *Alpine Club*

TASERMIUT FJORD

Ketil, West Face. Jon Allen, Doug Byerly, Jim Funsten and Mike Wood visited the spectacular granite climbing mecca of Greenland's southern fjord country in July. European climbers have climbed fairly extensively in the region in the past 20 years but curiously, few American teams have visited the area. Funsten and Wood hoped to establish a new Grade VI wall climb on the enormous 1400-meter west face of the Ketil, while Allen and Byerly hoped to make the first alpine-style ascent of the face via the brilliant 1977 French Route. Ketil, meaning a "pot of mussels," was named by early Norse settlers who established a monastery in the area in 1200 A.D. The face has four routes to date, all established in fixed-rope, big-wall siege style. Due to typically poor weather and imminent exposure to the frightfully dangerous Fohn wind, a gale every bit as fierce as a full-blown Patagonian tempest, fixed ropes are utilized to provide a quick, efficient escape route. It is not surprising that very few alpine style ascents have been made in the region.

The 1977 French Route (Barrard et al) had been repeated three times, all by large teams fixing the first 22 pitches to the top of the prominent gray pillar. On July 19, Allen and Byerly climbed the majority of the gray pillar in 12 hours, finding sensational granite free climbing up to 5.11 that featured sustained offwidth cracks still clasping on to the 20-year-old wood bongs placed by the Barrard party. The following day brought colder, blustery conditions to the shady wall while the pair climbed the remaining 20 pitches, including the crux pendulums and the notoriously exposed and loose black dike that diagonals for six pitches across the top

The 1400-meter west face of Ketil, showing 1. 1977 French Route. 2. 1981 Catalan Route. 3. Piola Route. 4. the West Pillar. DOUG BYERLY

of the face leading to the fourth-class terrain below the low-angle summit ridge. Cold, exhausted and facing darkness, the pair decided to bivouac and complete the 50 meters of fourth class in the morning. That night the first major Fohn storm of the season descended upon them from the northeast. By morning, the storm was raging with full force as the pair attempted to gain the summit ridge. Realizing they would surely be blown off the mountain if they left the more sheltered west face, they decided to call it good, having climbed all the difficulties of the giant wall. In plummeting temperatures and wind gusts exceeding 100 m.p.h., the two began the long, arduous descent back down the route. Eighteen hours and 40 rappels later, having employed all the Patagonian rope management tricks, the pair hit the ground with two chopped ropes and frazzled minds. No summit, but the face had been climbed in 36 hours, 60 hours round-trip with no fixed rope or trash left on the face. The route was not free climbed but would go free at mid-5.12 with some rehearsal and cleaning.

After two weeks of wind and rain, the weather improved, and Allen and Byerly loaded up 90-pound packs and hiked 15 miles down the rugged fjord to the famous Ulamertorssuaq peak, home to at least six fine 850-meter routes, three of which are entirely free up to 5.13. On August 1, the pair climbed the first 17 pitches of the beautiful *Moby Dick* route (VI 5.13) via very difficult and circuitous face climbing in 12 hours to the base of the 1,200-foot overhanging headwall crack. Once again the weather deteriorated, and, fearing another epic Fohn wind storm, they reluctantly retreated. Out of supplies, they were forced to hump the big loads back up the fjord. Two days later, Byerly, Funsten and Wood repeated the epic coastline trek with even larger packs. Poor weather prevented another attempt on Moby Dick, but they did manage to climb the 500-meter Swiss Route (IV 5.10 A2) on the south face of Pyramiden peak. One day before being plucked out of the fjord, Byerly and Funsten raced up the elegant West Ridge (III 5.9) of Pyramiden just before another Fohn wind blew in from the inland icecap.

Doug Byerly

Kirkespiret, North Face, Previously Unreported. It was reported that Danes Christian Illum and Asmus Nørreslet made the first ascent of the north face of Kirkespiret during a four-member expedition to the Ketil region in August, 1998. The 11-pitch route, *Gold Fever* (TD+, 6b A1, 400m), was climbed in eight and a half hours. Descent was made down the northeast face to a high plateau. A piton was found at the top of the tenth pitch, suggesting an earlier party had climbed up the shorter, easier northeast face to join their route. (*High Mountain Sports* 199)

MEXICO

BAJA CALIFORNIA

SIERRA JUAREZ

Cañón del Tajo

El Gran Trono Blanco, The Millennium. May brought the completion of the first new major route on El Gran Trono Blanco in a decade (see AAJ 1991, pp. 189-190). Several years in the planning and "construction," *The Millennium* (*El Milenio*, IV 5.11b or 5.10c A1) was conceived as a long free route linking the *Happy Hooker* to the Southeast Buttress route with several new pitches. The result is an enjoyable and securely protected route with a 50/50 mix of crack and friction climbing.

Gary Anderson and John Smallwood made the first continuous ascent on May 22. The approach down the canyon along the base of the south face was a one-hour boulder scramble. From the extreme right (east) end of the third-class bench underlying the south face, begin in a left-facing dihedral. Follow 5.8 cracks for two pitches. Pitch 3 leaves the *Happy Hooker* route by frictioning right (5.10b). A good ledge is reached by continuing up and right on 5.8 friction to a short crack. Traverse right to a large flat ledge. Friction up to and then

The east and north faces of El Gran Trono Blanco. WERNER R. LANDRY

over a small overhang. Friction traverse left (5.11b), then up to a good stance. Eleven bolts protect this crux pitch and an extra 3/8" hole was drilled for those needing to aid and tension traverse. Pitch 7 (5.10c friction) also has 11 bolts and leads to a crack and sheltered flat ledges. Traverse right 60 feet, then up (5.6) to a tunnel on the left. Here the route meets up with the original Southeast Buttress route for the next three pitches. Pitch 9 enters the tunnel and exits onto a steep face (5.10b) to a semi-hanging belay below a 5.11 (or A1) roof. Ascend the roof to a strenuous 5.10 squeeze chimney where tying off natural chockstones provides additional protection. After traversing left to a large right-facing dihedral, continue up (5.9) to brushy ledges. Third-class 200 feet to a gully on the *Happy Hooker* route. Traverse left across the gully on a fourth-class ledge to its end at a 5.5 crack, staying left of the gully weakness. From the small ledge atop the crack, the new exit pitches (13 and 14) follow bolts up 5.8 friction to lower-angle friction above. The May 22 ascent took nine hours. The third-class descent and return to the vehicle required another hour. Belay anchors have a minimum of two 3/8" x 4" stainless steel bolts with rappel rings, and most belays have good ledges. The tops of pitches 5, 7 and 11 have flat bivouac sites for parties choosing to overnight. For leaders who opt out of the 5.11 crux, adding a 3/8" removable bolt and a cheater stick to the gear rack provides the option to lead at 5.10c A1. Bring nuts and cams from small wires to four inches, one tube chock (Big Bro) and 11 quickdraws. Climbers who assisted with developing *The Millennium* were Andreas Met, Shaun Standley and Monte Swann.

JOHN SMALLWOOD, *unaffiliated*

El Gran Trono Blanco, Leaving On A Jet Plane. Mark Richards and I finished a new route,

Leaving On A Jet Plane (VI A3+ 5.10, 13 pitches), between the *Giraffe* and *Pan Am* in early October. The route is non-stop exposure with a big-wall feel all the way. Lots of hooking, thin placements in seams and even some good crack and face climbing characterize the route. It meets *Giraffe* at Poncho Villa ledge and goes right across blank face (hooks and bolts) to a big ledge, then follows a crack system to the top.

The climbing and the views make for a great wilderness experience. Plan for three days on the route; bring portaledges and stick to small gear (the route is mostly clean, but bring some knifeblades and baby angles).

WERNER R. LANDRY

CHIHUAHUA

Basaseachic Waterfall National Park

El Gigante, Yawira Batú. During the first days of May, Cecilia Buil (Spain) and Carlos Garcia (Mexico) made the second ascent of El Gigante in Chihuahua, Mexico. Their initial plan was to attempt a first ascent in the canyon of La Sinforosa, located in the same region as El Gigante. They had heard that even higher walls than those of El Gigante could be found in La Sinforosa, but an aerial reconnaissance showed that although 1800 meters high, the walls were not as steep and challenging as those of El Gigante (1300 meters). For this reason the team turned its interest to a corn-yellow vertical strip they spotted the year before on El Gigante, when they made the first ascent of the wall. (American photographer Chris Giles accompanied the team, scoping the route from the base of El Gigante with them, then going to the top on his own, guessing the approximate location of their route and rapping down to photograph their ascent. He fixed lines to the bottom, but Buil and Garcia did not use any of his anchors or gear.)

The yellow strip was reached by a traverse to the right for several pitches. On that section, the rock quality varied from good (pitches 1 and 2) to bad (3 to 6). Large, loose blocks were frequent and the terrain was consistently overhanging from pitch 3 on. The fourth pitch required heavy aid climbing and took almost a whole day. After fixing pitch 5, the team had to leave the wall due to problems with the drill. After a quick trip to Chihuahua, the lower end of the yellow strip was finally reached by passing a big roof on pitch 6. The change of color also brought better rock.

Pitches 7, 8 and 9 were characterized by dirty cracks populated by lots of plants. A diving mask proved to be a useful weapon to fight against the dirt blown into the eyes by the wind while cleaning the cracks to place protection. Between pitches 7 and 13 the average advance per day was two pitches. By pitch 13 the work of prior days called for an "evening off duty." The day was still not over, though. A weak link on the belay setup suddenly broke, and instants later climbers and gear were hanging all messed up a couple of meters further down. Fortunately, the incident had no major consequences.

The next day, pitch 14 followed a left-facing roof to a cave, close to which the belay was established, and pitch 15 was the best one of the whole route. Pitch 16 followed an overhanging crack to the right. Although it appeared to be an offwidth, the V-shaped crack allowed for the use of small protection inside. The last bivouac was established on the following belay, just one rope length below the top. After a somewhat technical final pitch, the climbers topped off the wall by noon. The route was named *Yawira Batú*, which is Tarahumara for "the rising corn."

Carlos Garcia and Cecilia Buil atop El Gigante after the first ascent of Yawira Batú, *with the walls of Basaseachic Waterfall National Park behind them.* CHRIS GILES

This note is based on a report written in Spanish by Cecilia Buil. Translated and adapted by Christian Oberli. No specific grading of the route is indicated in the original report.

Rolando Larcher on the sixth pitch of Rest Day alla Pagoda. MARCO CURTI

NUEVO LEON

El Portrero Chico

Milesky Wall, Rest Day alla Pagoda. In January, Rolando Larcher, Fabio Leoni and Marco Curti, all from Trento, Italy, established a new route, *Rest Day alla Pagoda* (7c+) in the Milesky Wall sector in three days. The route has six pitches which range from 25-40 meters each. With the help of a battery-powered drill, they climbed from the ground up, placing bolts while hanging from hooks. They wanted to create a route with a high degree of difficulty that presented notable mandatory difficulties and that asked of future ascensionists a certain commitment to climb it. The team climbed all the moves free during the first ascent, then redpointed it. On January 30, Rolando Larcher and Fabio Leoni made a one-day redpoint ascent. The individual pitch difficulties are 6b+, 7a, 7a, 6c, 6c+, 7c+. *Rest Day alla Pagoda* is a wonderful overhanging climb. Descent was made with double ropes.

Larcher and Leoni repeated onsight the gorgeous *Time for Living* (8a) in the La Infamia sector. The six pitches (7a+, 7a+, 7b/c, 7b/c, 7c/8a, 7c) are all overhanging. In the Virgin Canyon sector, they bolted four one-pitch routes: *El Balota* (7b), *Mr. Patacca* (6b), *Jesus* (6a+) and *Gil* (6a).

ERIK SVAB, *Italy*

SOUTH AMERICA

PERU

CORDILLERA BLANCA

Alpamayo and Santa Cruz, New Routes. On June 15, Kenzo Suzuki (Japan) left Base Camp (4850m) at 11 p.m. and climbed the 1979 Tomo Cesen route on the southeast face of Alpamayo until he reached the *Andes* route. The next day, he climbed original ground to the top, then downclimbed the *French Direct* route on the southwest face. With Toshiyuki Hirose, Suzuki then established a new line on the southwest face of Santa Cruz. On June 24, they left ABC (5000m), reaching the summit the next day. They graded the route TD+.

KAZUYUKI SASAKI, *Editor, Run Out*

Shaqsha, South-Southeast Face. On May 23, Xavier Carrard, Abel Calana, Juan Morales, Marcos Niño, Franco Obando, Hector Reyes, César Vargas and Aritza made a possible first ascent with their route *Feliz Cumpleaños Momo* (85° IV+, 700m) on the south-southeast face of Shaqsha (Shacsha, 5703m). From a camp at 4990 meters in the Quebrada Rurec, the group climbed the route and returned to Base Camp in a 17-hour push.

ANTONIO GÓMEZ BOHÓRQUEZ, *Spain*

Nevado Rúrec, Brevete Seguro. On May 23, Koki Castañeda, Williams Dávalos, Saúl Angeles, Chinchilla Zárate, Toni Ortiz and Félix Vicencio made a possible first ascent on Nevado Rúrec (5700m) via the southwest ridge of the south face. The route, *Brevete Seguro* (max. 60° ice and snow; 90° to reach the summit), took 14 hours round-trip from a camp at 4600 meters on the moraine of the Quebrada Rurec.

ANTONIO GÓMEZ BOHÓRQUEZ, *Spain*

Huantsán, North Face, New Route. Slovenian climbers Grega Lačen, Matej Flis and Iztok Mihev climbed a new route on the north face of Huantsan (6395m). They entered the face on June 29 at midnight and reached the top at 8 p.m. the next day. They arrived back at Base Camp one day later in the afternoon. The route, *Koroska* (VI 6a+ M4/5 85°, 1400m), was named after the climbers' province. The climbing was carried out under huge seracs and was very dangerous. They did most of the climbing at night. During the day, they stayed in a snow hole. Rock pitches were surprisingly compact, but the snow was very loose. They wanted to rappel the route, but serac fall forced them to traverse to the north summit and descend down the North Ridge (TD-, Booij-Egeler-Terray).

GREGA LAČEN, *Slovenia*

Ishinca, Northwest Face, Magic Mushrooms. On July 6, while still acclimatizing in the Ishinca valley, Vasja Kosuta and I established the new route *Magic Mushrooms* (IV 80°, 500m) on the northwest face of Ishinca (5530m). We started early in the morning from our Advanced Base Camp at the lake near the Ishinca Glacier. We were very close to the beginning of our climb. After approximately half an hour's walk over the moraine, we started climbing. We began with about 150 meters of not very steep ground (40-45°). Then, somewhere in the middle, it became steeper and we had to climb a steep slope with a little snow, in some places mixed (70°). After that we reached a big barrier of overhanging seracs (quite scary!) and started a long traverse to the left under the seracs on a slope the angle of which was 50 to 60 degrees. We wanted to climb vertical ice at the left end of the seracs, but the ice was very bad, so we decided to climb the rock to the left (initially 80°, then IV- for 15m). From there, we continued over the upper snow field (50°) to the top of the mountain (after digging through the snow cornice, 70°). It took us seven hours to reach the summit and another two or three to return to camp.

MATIJA KLANJSCEK, *Slovenia*

Churup, Northwest Face, Primorska Smer. On July 11, Simon Markocic, Vasja Kosuta, Borut Golja and I established a new route, *Primorska Smer* (V+ A0 80°, 500m), on the northwest face of Churup (5493m). We started at 2 a.m. from a base camp at the lake. As for the other climbs on the left side of the main wall of Churup, we went to the beginning of the glacier, then up, then made a long traverse to the right (first we tried to climb directly to the line of our route, but there was no snow in the gorge and the rock was very slick and crumbly). We started to climb early in the morning. At first it was not too steep (45°), then it became steeper (50-60°), then we encountered some mixed parts (III+, 80°). After two hours, we reached the first big rock barrier with a small cave on its left. Vasja climbed the barrier (V-, 30m) in very bad conditions. The snow didn't give any purchase and protection was bad, though the rock was very good granite. This pitch ended up in deep snow (60°). Luckily there were four of us, so we managed to "dig through" this steep slope, which ended with the next (bigger and overhanging) rock barrier. Simon started to climb with one hand free, one ax and crampons. He aided with a piton over one overhanging section (A0), but otherwise climbed it free (V+, 20m). The next slope was about 60 degrees. After that we continued to the right. The main difficulties were over. We only had to climb one steeper "chimney" (70°); otherwise, it was a 50-degree snow slope. We ended on the ridge on the right side of the mountain. We planned to traverse it to the top, but it was very warm and began to snow heavily so we decided to descend. We made seven rappels with double ropes (50m), four times on pitons, three times on snow stakes. We downclimbed the bottom section. All together it took us 16 hours.

MATIJA KLANJSCEK, *Slovenia*

Pisco West, Southwest Face. Gustavo Montalvo and Alejandro Pérez Rayon (México) made a possible first ascent on the southwest face of Pisco West. *Pinches de Güey* (TD, 90° mixed, 60-70° snow) involved six pitches with 50-meter ropes and was climbed in ten hours.

ANTONIO GÓMEZ BOHÓRQUEZ, *Spain*

Chacraraju, East Face, The Shriek of the Black Stone. 1999 was an El Niño year in Peru, and climbing conditions were very poor. Andrej Markovic and I were members of a Slovenian expedition. Our main goal was to open a new route on the east face of Chacraraju East (Huaripampa, 6001m). After finishing our acclimatization on Ishinca (5530m) and Urus (5495m), and after Andrej soloed his 1996 route on Ranrapalca (6162m) (see *AAJ* 1997, p. 232), we set up Base Camp under Chacraraju East. Ten days later (unstable weather, running out of food), we started climbing.

We needed two carries to transport all our gear, food and equipment to beneath the face. Each of us had 30 to 35 kilos in his rucksack. On July 28, we slept under a great overhang; just after we started to climb the next morning, a big piece of ice fell where we had been sleeping. The first day of climbing was the hardest, especially for the second, who had almost everything in his rucksack. The leader had just the equipment necessary for the pitch he was climbing. We climbed the main snow slope on the right followed by a snow ledge to the right (55-70°), then some rock and mixed pitches (V to VI) and 60- to 70-degree snow in the dark. We reached an overhang and started digging a ledge for our first bivy. We were exhausted and fell asleep soon after drinking some hot tea and eating tasteless soup. We did not hear the alarm clock the next morning and overslept. The day before we had been climbing beneath seracs; when we woke, we heard them breaking and falling down. We decided to wait a day and rest.

The following morning we reached the main rock section in the middle of the face, the hardest part of our route. We climbed some rock and snow pitches as well as the first pitch of aid (A1), which was combined with a 70-degree powder snow slope. When we woke the next day, the mountain was covered in clouds, and snowing now and then. We climbed one very long pitch (VII- A2) and a 70-degree powder snow slope beneath the seracs. We spent the night in the middle of the seracs digging a snow hole from midnight until 4 a.m. during a snow storm. It was my turn to cook, but as I was trying to convince Andrej to eat I noticed he was already asleep. The next morning it had stopped snowing and was pretty sunny. We decided to dry all the gear. A very big piece of granite fell a few meters from our hole. We were terrified, but we came up with a name for the route: *The Shriek of the Big Stone*.

The next day we started climbing early in the morning with just the climbing equipment and one thermos of warm tea. We had a lot of unnecessary equipment for extreme technical climbing, but still, we were able to climb faster. We climbed rock, snow and ice pitches up a snow ramp toward the small ridge on the left side of the summit. There were two hard pitches, first with aid (A2+) followed by a pitch of free climbing (VII–), then 70- to 90-degree ice (we had left our ice screws in the snow hole and climbed that pitch without a belay). We reached the small snow ridge in the dark; a strong wind had started blowing after sunset. We called the upper section of the mountain "the pyramid." It offered easy to very hard rock climbing (from III to VII) and also snow/ice climbing (50-90°). We reached the summit around midnight or 1 a.m. in even stronger wind and a few minutes later started to descend. After five long rappels we downclimbed the snow ledge to the right, made one more rappel and soloed another pitch down to the snow hole. We retrieved the equipment we had left behind that morning, made two more rappels to the great snow field/ledge in the middle of the face, then soloed left along the ledge to the main snow slope and serac. We continued descending, moving right along the snow field until we reached the crevasse and the glacier. It was August 3; we had completed our route, *The Shriek of the Black Stone* (Krik̆ Srnega granita) (VI/VII A2 90°, ca. 950m, 25 pitches) in six days alpine style.

JURE JUHASZ, *Slovenia*

Chopicalqui, West Face, Piece of Happiness. In July, I climbed a new route on the west face of Chopicalqui with Bostjan Perse. The name of the route is *Piece of Happiness* (D 80°, 500m). We started to climb at about 5400 meters and finished at 5900 meters. The snow conditions were good. The last 200 meters were climbed on hard black ice.

ANDREJ ZAMAN, *Slovenia*

Yanawaka, Attempt and Possible First Ascent. On July 1-2, Pedro Arias, Juan Padilla and I attempted Yanawaka (La Peña Negra de Parón, ca. 4900m) via a line up the center of the peak's vertical north face. (The locals of Paron that I asked in 1985 used three names to refer to this mountain: Yanakawa, El Cerro Negro [the Black Peak] and La Peña Negra [the Black Cliff]. In the Quechuan language of Huari and Huaraz, "waka" means "a cliff with the form or design of a person or animal" [although it also means "ancient tomb" in Huaraz and Tarica] and "yana" means "black.") After 200 meters, we abandoned the route due to an abundance of moss and other vegetation in the cracks which required too much time to clean and created dangerous rockfall.

At the Laguna de Parón, we told two South African climbers, Mike Cartwright and Malcolm Crowans, of our attempt. Three days later, they climbed the mountain by an easier route that eventually gained the northeast ridge. They named their route *Solar Shield* (5.9, 650m). This may have been the first ascent of the mountain.

ANTONIO GÓMEZ BOHÓRQUEZ, *Spain*

Unnamed Peak, Mission Control. Kent McClannan and I climbed a new route on an unnamed peak west of Shaqsha in the Cordillera Blanca. The granite wall, which tops out at ca. 16,000', is clearly visible from a base camp midway up the Rurek Valley and can be identified by the low vegetation-to-rock ratio. On this wall's east face, *Mission Control* (IV 5.11+ A2+) was completed over three days between periods of unsettled weather in June. The route follows an obvious right-leaning, right-facing dihedral system for four pitches, then follows the ridge for an additional eight pitches. Most of the harder climbing was encountered in the first half of the route, with the crux (the "Jules Verne Simulator") coming at the end of pitch 2. We rappelled the steep yet shorter section of the wall just south of the summit. There was no sign of previous route activity elsewhere on the peak.

CAMERON TAGUE

Ranrapalca, Scandinavian Direct, Solo. On July 24, Pavle Kozjek (Slovenia) made a solo ascent of *Scandinavian Direct* route (ED inf) on the north face of Ranrapalca (6162m). It took him three hours to climb this ca. 1000-meter mixed route (the topo of the first ascensionists indicate 12-15 hours for their ascent). He couldn't get information about the other ascents of this route, which seems to be a little bit overgraded. He descended the Northeast Face route.

FRANCI SAVENC, *Planinska zveza Slovenije*

Paron Valley

La Esfinge, Dion's Dihedral. On June 23, after two weeks of effort, Larry Dolecki and I climbed to the 5325-meter summit of La Esfinge, completing the first ascent of a big wall aid route on the mountain's east face. La Esfinge is a beautiful alpine tower of orange granite that hosts four previously established routes on its east and southeast faces.

Our original objective was to add a second route to the cold 900-meter southeast face, but due to lack of time (only 16 days total to acclimatize, ferry loads, climb and descend), we focused on the shorter right side of the east face. Although only 500 to 600 meters in height, this area of the wall had the steepest, cleanest rock on the mountain. We set our sights on a soaring orange-streaked corner that dominated the upper part of the face, which was separated from the ground by 200 meters of thin features and seemingly blank sections.

After a couple of easy free pitches, the tricky aid began with three pitches of hard nailing and heading interspersed with some rivets. The crux (A3) arrived on the fourth pitch, which took two days to climb due to intricate route finding and long sections of copperheads with ledge fall potential. During these initial days, the weather wasn't the perfect Peruvian blue sky that we had heard about, but at least it was consistent: sunny, warm skies in the morning would last until about 3 p.m., when clouds would build up, resulting in an evening snowstorm. The

Larry Dolecki on the first ascent of Dion's Dihedral.
SEAN ISAAC

following morning would then be back to clear skies.

After four days of fixing, we committed to the wall with food and water for five days and our double portaledge. We had hoped for free climbing, but the huge orange corner turned out to be more aid, taking everything from birdbeaks to #5 Camalots. Luckily, route finding was zero in the laser-cut dihedral and the pitches went quicker than expected, allowing us to top out three days later. We rappelled the route the same day we summitted, reaching the ground well after dark and in yet another swirling snow storm.

The 11-pitch route was named *Dion's Dihedral* (VI 5.9 A3) in memory of young Canadian alpinist Dion Bretzloff, who tragically had been killed on Yerapaja three weeks earlier.

SEAN ISAAC*, *Canada*

*Supported by a grant from the Canadian Himalayan Foundation

La Esfinge, East Face, Papas Relleñas. Cedric Cruaud, Gired Devernay, Benoit Peyronnard and Pierre Plaze made the first ascent of the route *Papas Relleñas* (ED 6c+ A3, 600m) on the east face of La Esfinge (5325m) from July 20-25. The route appears to go to the right of Bohórquez's 1985 route.

ANTONIO GÓMEZ BOHÓRQUEZ, *Spain*

CORDILLERA HUAYHUASH

Siula Grande, West Face, Avoiding the Touch. On June 16, Carlos Buhler and I completed a new route on the west face of Siula Grande in the Cordillera Hauyhuash of Peru. This was the same mountain face on which the British climbers Joe Simpson and Simon Yates endured the great survival epic described eloquently in Simpson's book *Touching the Void.* Our route followed the Simpson/Yates ascent until approximately the middle of the face, at which point we climbed up and left into a gully that went directly to the summit. In 24 pitches of climbing, the route was constantly technical with sections of thin ice up to 80 degrees. Our attempt to descend the north ridge proved to be terrifyingly tedious. Slow progress on the dangerously corniced ridge prompted a decision to rappel a line to the left of our ascent. Twenty rappels (two on rock, 18 on ice) put us on the glacier, having spent three and a half days on the ascent with another two and a half on the descent. We called our route *Avoiding the Touch* (WI4, ca. 1000m).

MARK PRICE, *unaffiliated*

BOLIVIA

CORDILLERA REAL

Carlos Buhler avoiding the touch while descending the north ridge of Siula Grande. MARK PRICE

Cordillera Real, Various Activity. From July 5-July 19, a group of students and faculty from Appalachian State University's Geography Department engaged in field studies and research on the Altiplano and in the northern Cordillera Real in Bolivia. Undergraduate geographers Louisa Gibson, Jordan Hill, Mark Isley, Shannon Higgins, Alisa Fisher, Trey Schweitzer, Paul Turner, Daniel Ezell, Patrick Kennedy and Dave Hammerman, and graduate students Breece Robertson and Scott Cecchi were led by Department Chair Dr. Mike Mayfield, recent masters graduate and instructor Baker Perry and graduate student and ASU Outdoor Programs Coordinator Joe Quinn. The group was joined in La Paz by Dr. Andrew Klein of Texas A&M University. After completing a rural mapping project related to access to primary health care in the village of Puerto Acosta on the northeast end of Lake Titicaca near the Peruvian border, the group traveled to Sorata to stage for the glacier research segment of the course. Research Base Camp was established in the col between Illampu and Ancohuma at Laguna Glacier at 16,500' after a two-day trek from Sorata (8,500').

Under the direction of Dr. Klein, the glacial lake perimeter, the extent of the ice on the lake and the headwall above it were mapped using a GPS unit. Data collected will be analyzed to compare and quantify the rate and amount of change at Laguna Glacier. Dr. Klein will incorporate this information into an overall world snow cover and global climate change model.

During the research phase, Perry, Mayfield, Hill, Isley, Schweitzer, and Kennedy, joined by Fred Bahnson, who accompanied the group to BC, and Bolivian Pablo Chugar, attempted Ancohuma, spending the night at Campo Alto (ca. 18,600') before being forced to descend with moderately severe AMS.

JOE QUINN

CORDILLERA APOLOBAMBA

Sunchuli Pass Area, Ascent. On June 9, Yossi Brain (U.K.) and I climbed the northwest face of an unnamed peak just northeast of the Sunchuli Pass. This face is located between what are named Cuchillo II (5450m) and P. 5450 on the 1993 Paul Hudson map. We climbed the glaciated face directly through a rock band up to a large, well-built miner's cairn just 100 meters south of the summit and then traversed the summit ridge to the true summit at about 5400 meters. This involved a 300-meter ascent on well-consolidated snow up to 55 degrees with a 50-meter mixed pitch (M3) in the middle.

DAKIN COOK

El Cuchillo, New Route. On June 10, Yossi Brain (U.K.) and I climbed a new route on El Cuchillo (5655m). We started up a difficult, 250-meter, narrow (20-30m) icefall on the south side of El Cuchillo that involved short sections of technical 90-degree-plus alpine ice. This initial section (250m) took almost ten hours with one fall through a seemingly bottomless hole in the icefall and the breaking off of a large triangular block of ice on a 90-degree-plus move. The aforementioned block of ice was significantly slowed by the quick response of my nose, which blocked its downward path. The last 350 meters of the climb was accomplished more rapidly in a light snowstorm on up to 60-degree snow to the summit. The descent was made down the Northeast Ridge route.

DAKIN COOK

Soral Este, Southwest Face. On July 24, Fred Bahnson, Baker Perry and I climbed the southwest face of Soral Este to its lower, southeast summit (5460m). Our approach was made up through the moraine just southeast of the obvious rock pinnacle that divides the long-tongued northwestern glacier from the wider but shorter southeastern glacier tongues. After a short two-hour roped climb through icefall and seracs, we reached the southwest headwall and proceeded unroped up 60- to 65-degree snow directly to the lower summit. The descent was made via the route of ascent.

DAKIN COOK

Pico Integral, Southwest Face. On August 24, Joe Stock and I left La Paz at 3 a.m. for the southwest face of Pico Integral, a "small" satellite peak of Huayna Potosi. The southwest face of Pico Integral (18,640') may have been climbed in earlier years, but the rapid recession of snow and ice on many of Bolivia's peaks gives routes such as ours an essentially different character. After a quick two-hour drive, we made the approach and were at the base of the face at 7 a.m. After an initial grunt and heave-ho, we were over the bergschrund and on route, ropes still in the packs. We made quick work of the initial climbing, mixing it up at 5.7 rock and 60-degree-plus ice. From there, the ground steepened and we roped for the following nine pitches, with the crux coming three pitches below the top. The first was a traverse pitch of M4-: clean a time bomb of rocks from the vertical terrain, mantle, repeat four times. From there, Joe led a stunning two-hour pitch through a gully of M4+ climbing interspersed with unconsolidated snow. This led to a quick 5.7 pitch to the top of Pico Integral at 4 p.m.. We opted not to continue onto the summit of Huayna Potosi and arrived at Zongo Pass at 8 p.m.

No name for the route, which we give the Bolivian grade of two llamas and a chicken.

BRENDAN CUSICK

Apolobamba, Various Activity. Team members Simon Cooke (leader), Toby Spence, David Gerrard, Andrew Naslas and Kate Ackroyd arrived in La Paz on July 26. Traveling through Charazani, Lagunilla, Jatunpampa, and Incachani, we reached Sunchuli on the 31st. Base Camp was established next to a small lake where the watercourse is diverted for the mining village.

On August 3, all members had an acclimatization day up the "small rocky summit" (Pt. 5490m, a.k.a. the Nubbin) next to Pt. 5680m. The ascent was made by a gully formed between the rock of the south side and the snow slope, with an escape made from deep powder onto rocky ramps, before returning to finish with a wade up the gully. All members reached the ridge; Simon and David carried on up the 100-meter ridge via a scramble to the summit. On August 5, Toby and David climbed a new route (AD) on Cuchillo 1 (5560m) via the southeast buttress/face (initially III rock then mixed) to join Simon and Kate (who had climbed up the normal route) at the top of the buttress. All four then continued up snow patches to the summit. On the 7th, all members made an easy plod up the glacier on scree and snow slopes to the top of Pt. 5600m southeast of Cavayani. On the 10th, Toby and David made a first ascent (PD+) of the rock needle (which we called the "Aiguille de l'Index Finger") east-northeast of Pt. 5680m. The route involved a glacier slope to the ridge, rock (III) to avoid seracs, then Scottish II to the ridge. The needle was III+ and loose. On the 12th, David and Andrew climbed Cuchillo II (5450m) via the south ridge (PD) from Paso Sunchuli. On the 13th, Toby, David and Andrew attempted Corohuari (5668m) along the west ridge from Paso Sunchuli (PD), but failed due to bad rock. On the 15th, Toby and David made the first ascent of Pt. 5680m (we'd suggest the name Huay Huari). The route went up a gully and buttress via the west face (rock III, ice Scottish II). They then continued to traverse over Pt. 5600m and Cavayani (D). The team left BC the next day.

The area is definitely worth further visits with several possible unclimbed lines and a few virgin tops.

SIMON COOKE, *United Kingdom*

Various Ranges, Various Activity. Luke Aspinall, Toby Johnson, John Marsham and I planned a three-month expedition to Bolivia, with the intention of climbing in the Cordilleras Apolobamba, Real and Quimsa Cruz. However, things very rarely go to plan.

After establishing ourselves at the usual Condoriri Base Camp on July 8, we ascended Pequeño Alpamayo (normal route), Illusion (normal route), Ala Izquierda (west to east traverse) and attempted the southwest face of Piramide Blanca. On approaching Cabeza de Condor, I was hit by rockfall, which resulted in a severe skull fracture and a two-week stay in the hospital before returning home with Toby. Luke stayed in La Paz working, while John climbed with non-expedition members for the remaining two months.

On August 28, John, Sam Maffett (Australia) and Gina Tent (U.K.) took the bus to Pelechuco in the Apolobamba and set up BC east of Chapui Orco (6044m). Over two days, they climbed two peaks on the ridge extending east from Chapul Orco Norte (PD and D-). They then failed to climb Chapul Orco by its east ridge due to poor snow. After moving BC to the lake shore on the west side of Chapul Orco, "Flora de Roca" was attempted by its south ridge; the party came within 15 meters of the summit. Finally, Chapul Orco was climbed by the west ridge (PD).

All these routes with the exception of "Flora de Roca" were probably new routes, but only Chapul Orco is a peak large enough to be marked on the Paul Hudson map. It should be noted, however, that there is a color topographical map of the Apolobamba, though the IGM insisted it either did not exist or was not available.

On August 21, John and Sam set up a high camp at the foot of Pico Schulz and ascended it by the southeast ridge. The following day they climbed Illampu by the Southwest Face route and Huayna Illampu by the Northeast Ridge. With unseasonable snowfall during mid-September that made rock climbing almost impossible in the Quimsa Cruz, John and Dana Witzel (Canada) managed to climb nothing in these splendid Aiguilles.

MARK CRAMPTON, *Edinburgh University Mountaineering Club*

Cordilleras Quimsa Cruz, Various Activity. In July, after a visit to the Cordillera Apolobamba, I joined Scotsman Russell Small and Australian Sam Maffett in La Paz for a trip to the Cordillera Quimsa Cruz. We took public buses to the village of Rodeo and backpacked up the jeep road to Laguna Altarani at 4850 meters. (The summit UTM [1000-meter] grid locations mentioned below are as shown on the Bolivian IGM maps "Mina Caracoles" and "Yaco.") Russ and I climbed the previously unclimbed east ridge (PD) of Cerro San Luis (5620m) [678,000m E, 8120,400m N] by hiking around the north side of Laguna Altarani, then climbing northeast up a glacier to its head at the low point of the east ridge. We followed the ridge west on moderately steep snow and loose rock to the summit. We descended by the south and southwest ridges.

After an ascent of Cerro Santa Fe (5210m) [677,300m E, 8116,900m N] via the northeast ridge, Sam, Russ and I climbed a peak shown as "Cumbres Khasiri" [678,900m E, 8119,300m N] on the Yaco map (5410 meters on the map, 5320 meters by altimeter). This peak is 0.9 miles southeast of Cerro San Luis, and 1.3 miles east-northeast of Cerro Monte Blanco (Don Luis). We hiked around the north side of Laguna Altarani, and climbed the left

side (AD) of a moderately steep (30-50°) glacier on the west face of the peak. This is a distinctive and attractive peak, which I had thought might be the "Altarani" of other expeditions, but there was no evidence of a previous ascent. We built a cairn and descended the south edge of the same glacier that we had ascended.

I returned to La Paz, while Maffet and Small climbed Gigante Grande (5748m) via the glacier north of Laguna Congelada and the south ridge, and Jacha Cuno Collo (5800m).

CRAIG PATTERSON

Cerro San Luis, showing the route on the east ridge climbed by Patterson and Small. CRAIG PATTERSON

Cerro Presidente, Attempt and Tragedy. On September 25 at 8:30 a.m., Yossi Brain and a young Canadian woman, Dana Witzel, were killed in a slab avalanche on Cerro Presidente (5700m) in the Apolobamba range of the Andes. Four of us, Yossi, Dana, Eric Lawrie and myself, had gone into the range, near Pelechuco, the day before and set up a high camp on the long flat glacier below Cerro Presidente, Cerro Apollo 11 and Cerro Radioaficcionado. We had planned to attempt two or three new routes on these peaks during two days at high camp. The week before we had had an unseasonally long period of rains and snow in the high mountains, but the snow conditions on the glaciers were relatively good.

Yossi and Dana set out on one rope about five minutes before Eric and I and reached the base of the 300-meter headwall before us. They started up the lower low-angle wall on the right-hand side, encountering knee-deep snow some 50 meters up; at this point the wall had an inclination of some 30 to 40 degrees. Meanwhile, seeing the snow conditions, Eric and I circled around the small bowl at the base of the wall on firm snow to attempt the left-hand side. I yelled to Yossi our intentions. He then started moving to his left; I think that he was looking for firmer snow on steeper ground, both to make climbing easier and to avoid avalanche danger. About ten steps to the left, as I was watching him, he kicked into the still-deep snow and a large horizontal crack, about 50 meters above him and some 100 meters long, appeared suddenly. A slab avalanche engulfed them both and carried them some 50 meters down to the bowl below the wall. As the avalanche settled, we saw Dana's lower leg rise up once and fall back down. We immediately headed for that spot and uncovered Dana within 15 minutes and started cardiopulmonary resuscitation until we were unable to continue. We were unable to resuscitate her. After resting, we followed the rope and uncovered Yossi, who was buried under one and a half meters of snow in the heaviest part of the avalanche. We moved the bodies further down the slope, covered them well to protect them from birds and descended the mountain.

The next day, a group of guides taking an annual course under the direction of two French guides from Chamonix arrived to effect the body recovery, which went as smoothly and efficiently as anything I have witnessed in Bolivia. Yossi's remains are to be cremated in La Paz and his ashes scattered on Illimani, the mountain that is the symbol of La Paz and which rises majestically over the city. Dana's remains are to be returned to Canada, accompanied by her brother.

DAKIN COOK

CORDILLERA DE COCAPATA

Cordillera de Cocapata, Exploratory Climbing. My attention was drawn to the Cordillera de Cocapata near Cochabamba by Evelio Echevarría's description of its granite peaks as a potential "rock climbers' playground" (see "Cordillera de Cocapata, Bolivia" in *The Alpine Journal* 102, pp. 154-160). The temptation to play proved irresistible. Ignoring dismissive remarks from Yossi Brain ("No snow, shite rock, why bother?") and relying on first-hand accounts such as 1911 visitor Herzog's "bizzarely formed peaks," "steep rocky horns" and "extraordinarily impressive black tower" and Echevarría's "excellent gray granite" and "long, steep slabs," the Yorkshire Ramblers' Club mustered five climbers (David Hick, Tim Josephy, Duncan Mackay, Rory Newman and Michael Smith) to visit the range. We spent two weeks among the 5000-meter peaks as one part of a larger, six-week trip encompassing Peru, Bolivia and Chile. We were the first climbing team into the Cordillera de Cocapata since 1911.

Ten hours' driving from La Paz, an overnight roadside camp and two hours spent skirting the range saw our small group at Peñas on the northern side of the central group with all requisite

Cerro Willpanki I seen from the south across Poma Apacheta and an intervening low ridge. Willpanki's slabs are unclimbed. Josephy and Thellache ascended the left skyline. MICHAEL SMITH

food and fuel. Within the hour, our fixer-cum-climber, Javier Thellache, had a local family providing horses and porters for the several kilometers' pull up toward the lakes below the Jatúncasa-Sankhayuni group. There is no local infrastructure to support mountaineering, so the family was convinced we were seeking gold or gems, hunting, poaching their trout or intent on making a film. Camped by Lago Chacapata (4450m) on alpaca grazing ground, we enjoyed good weather with only a few hours of snow in two weeks. The 12 hours of daylight invariably saw the sun shining throughout to raise the temperature well above freezing (though the light to moderate winds were chilling, especially in the shade). Excellent meals were prepared using much better quality food than I had been able to find on previous visits. Distractions from climbing included passing alpaca herds and herders, condors and caracaras squabbling over a pony carcass and a small earthquake.

Jatuncasa provided easy angled slab climbing (40°) for 500 meters with poor protection but was probably not Herzog's Incachaca as previously supposed. The descent, as with most of the climbs, was loose and involved abseils. Sankhayuni's main top was probably Herzog's peak and was gained via two chimney gullies. The second summit was climbed in four unprotected pitches while the fifth gave the soundest rock in the area and a contorted route to find the true top on this serrated ridge. Willpanki required a small camp distant from our base and yielded interesting conversations with a local hunter and farmer. The attractive long steep slabs to the east await another visit. We pioneered routes on the southwest ridge of the main peak (despite considerable amounts of poor rock, so OK, Yossi, you were right) and the obvious cold, shaded southwest ridge on Willpanki II. Mountain scrambling over new ground was found on Malpasso and unnamed peaks south of Willpanki and Pututini in the north. The area provided easily accessible exploratory climbing unlikely to give anyone a world class reputation. Andean Summits provided excellent logistical support and are aware of other "off the beaten track" areas.

MICHAEL SMITH, *Yorkshire Ramblers' Club*

SANTA VERA CRUZ

Pico de la Fortuna, Ascent, and Cerro Santa Vera Cruz, Ascent and Discovery. The Santa Vera Cruz is the smallest range in Bolivia. With an extension of only 20 kilometers between the villages of Huanacota on the north and Ichoco on the south, these mountains, which carry the south-

The southeast face of Pico de la Fortuna, home to
Khespicala *(Gonzalez-Martinez-Navarro, 1999).*
JAVIER SÁNCHEZ MARTINEZ

ernmost glaciers in Bolivia, rise rather inconspicuously. Henry Hoek, who first wrote about them when describing his 1904 trip, devoted a whole chapter to the Santa Vera Cruz. However, he only traversed it on his way to the Quimsa Cruz range, without ascending any peak.

Thirty-five years had to elapse before another German, Josef Prem, undertook to explore those unknown nevados. Prem was no doubt one of the pioneers of Bolivian mountaineering. In 1939, he soloed Cerro Santa Vera Cruz (5560m) along the north ridge. A few years later, his fellow countryman, Federico Ahlfeld, followed the same route.

Then again, there was a lapse in the history of this range: 40 years later, Evelio Echevarría, a mountaineer who came to know this range best, climbed the small ridge peak of Cerro Calacala (4600m), situated north of the lake of Huariananta. He returned on two occasions, attempting Cerro Chupica (Aimara: "blood red"), some 5100 meters high, but failed, climbing to a few meters below the summit, the second needle of the five that crown the peak.

On May 8, Javier Navarro, Isidro Gonzalez and I accomplished the first ascent of Pico de la Fortuna (5493m). This difficult mountain demanded 17 hours of continuous effort, on a flank averaging 50 degrees, but reaching 70 degrees in some stretches. We christened this route *Khespicala* (Aimara: "precious rock"). The last pitch (unstable rock) brought us to the summit of this beautiful mountain, which, this year, thanks to "La Niña," was plastered with heavy snow. Had it been done a year earlier, this same climb would have been a mixed route, and a very exposed one.

Two days later we headed for Prem's mountain, having decided to attempt it by a new route we named *Jenecheru* (Aimara: "unending fire"). We avoided the crevasses by climbing up the western slopes (max. 55°). At the summit we made two discoveries steeped in history: one, Prem's card, conserved inside a little tin box for some 60 years. And two, an archaeological find, which, according to the Bolivian archaeologist Oswaldo Rivera, dates back to the last or

Acheological items from the Tiwanaku culture found on the top of Cerro de Santa Vera Cruz.
JAVIER SANCHEZ MARTINEZ

expansive period of the Tiwanaku culture, that is, some 800 years ago. It must have been an offering to Pachamama (Mother Earth). A cloth called aguayo was wrapped around all the ceremonial objects: a small wooden container, two altar vases with geometric drawings, also wood, a thorn needle and a human clavicle bone used as a tool, and a small spoon. Also included were some teeth, probably of a small rodent, and some silver cloth pins called tupus. This was all that we found on this high shrine at 5560 meters. It is astonishing that some 800 years ago, some Andeans literally climbed (there is no easy way up) this sacred mountain. They may have had goals different from ours, but perhaps they carried the same belief as those of us who go to the hills do: that peace and inner calm are found only in the heights.

Pico de la Fortuna (Peak of Fortune) gave us good luck and the achachilas (mountain genii) opened before us in the Cerro Santa Vera Cruz what they had kept hidden for centuries. A great paradox for us now is to try to understand why these mountains, so accessible from La Paz (four hours by bus) may have been forsaken by climbers who nowadays always seek first ascents. Lack of information is very likely a major reason, but perhaps we must also think that at present there is no real spirit of exploration, but a fear of what is not well known. At the gates now of the 21st century, we have been conditioned to consume only what is offered to us, including mountains, and we have been losing sight of the value of the adventure of climbing a mountain about which there exists no history and no information. Today, there are places, not too far away, still undiscovered and summits still untrodden.

JAVIER SANCHEZ MARTINEZ

Additional Note: Besides the two great peaks mentioned by Sanchez, this small range has a few more rock peaks, among which are cerros Trinidad and Huariananta, both around 5400 meters. Aside from short scientific and geographic notes, this range had received to date no other detailed mention except one that appeared in the article "Climbing in the Bolivian Andes" by Josef Prem (1945 *AAJ*, pp. 322-332).

EVELIO ECHEVARRÍA

CHILE

Monte Trinidad, Northeast Face. Pablo Pontoriero and Diego Cannestraci put up a new route on the northeast face of Monte Trinidad (ca. 1700m) on February 10-11. The route, *Vamos con Peto* (6b+, 450m), follows a crack system in the center of the face. Due to the prevailing humidity in the area, one encounters moss and lichen on new routes. Despite this character-istic, the rock is an excellent granite. They set up Base Camp on the bank of the Cochamó River, a five- or six-hour walk from the village. From there, they made the approach to the base of the route in four hours. This final part was made easier because of the trail opened by Simon Nadin (U.K.) the previous season.

On February 10, they climbed the first seven pitches and bivouacked on a ledge. The next day, they climbed the last two pitches and descended to the base of the route. They left only two bolts at the end of the seventh pitch. At the moment of writing this account, there was a group of Brazilian and Italian climbers in the valley working on new routes. The place holds an enormous potential, with granite walls of 700-800 meters.

FACUNDO JOSÉ, *Club Andino Bariloche*

CHILEAN PATAGONIA

"Dos Hermanos," First Ascents. The team (six Chileans and two Argentines), met at Puerto Natales, Chile, in early February, 1999, and after receiving the necessary permits from the national authorities, sailed north toward Puerto Eden in Isla Wellington. The ferry, which had Puerto Montt as its final destination, took two days to reach the small Alacaluf village. Some days later, we continued through the channels in an small fishing boat. We spent three more days in heavy seas to reach the bottom of Fiord Falcon, where we established Base Camp at 49° 34' 35.8" S, 73° 50' 26.2" W. The boat left immediately to avoid the icebergs; the plan was for it to return in March. The camp was well above sea level so as to be protected from the big waves that would come from time to time from a large nearby icefall. Two other camps were established, allowing us to reach four virgin summits with mixed difficulties in rock and ice in a range we called "Dos Hermanos" at 49° 33' S, 73° 47' W. (Dos Hermanos lies to the west of Risopatron, right over Fiordo Falcon.) Peaks climbed are as follows:

• Primera (1250m) (49° 33' 36.1" S, 73° 47' 25.8" W), February 28.
• San Jorge (1560m) (49° 34' 01.3" S, 73° 45' 05.0" W), March 1.
• Escondida (1750m) (49° 34' 04.3" S, 73° 44' 58.2" W), March 2.
• Punta Chilena (2100m) (49° 34' 01.0" S, 73° 45' 03.0" W), March 9.

Weather conditions were poor and only Punta Chilena was climbed on a sunny day. There are other interesting summits like Punta Argentina in Dos Hermanos, Risopatron Sur and P. 3018 (unnamed and the last unclimbed 3000-meter peak in Patagonia) awaiting future expeditions. Also in Isla Wellington, well above Puerto Eden, there are several virgin mountains.

An unclimbed mountain of the Dos Hermanos Range. CARLOS COMESAÑA

Our small fishing boat had problems picking us up in March due to the icy seas; we had to wait until wind conditions settled down enough before we could leave the area. By mid-March, we finally returned to Puerto Eden, from where a coast guard of the Chilean Navy took us to Puerto Natales.

The region is still an adventure paradise for traditional exploratory mountaineering and probably will continue to be so due to the extremely harsh weather conditions (mainly winds and heavy snow fall) together with the absence of any human presence.

CARLOS E. COMESAÑA, *Centro Andino Buenos Aires*

Hornopiren National Park, Exploratory Mountaineering. In January, 2000, I led an exploratory mountaineering expedition to climb a group of unnamed, unvisited peaks located within the boundaries of Chile's Hornopiren National Park (latitude 42° S; topo map H-73: Rio Traidor). The peaks surround an extensive glacier area in the northeast quadrant of the Park, ten kilometers southeast of Lago Pinto Concha. The team of five North Americans included Randy Earlywine, Daniel Collins, Susan Detweiler, Rich Henke and myself. We spent 25 days in the area and made the first known ascents of several peaks and numerous minor summits ranging in elevation from 1859 to 2342 meters. The long complicated approach, thick temperate rain forest, and, more than anything, stormy weather have discouraged most andinistas from exploring this area.

We approached the peaks from the east by small boat via Lake Tagua Tagua and the Rio Puelo and then on foot with pack horses up the Rio Traidor Valley. Fortunately, we had good weather early in the trip while we were scouting out the approach and climbing routes. Once above timberline, all climbs had glacier approaches with rock scrambles or climbs to the summits. The rock was granitic (decent to good quality), though sometimes capped with a schisty metamorphic rock (friable). Provisional names and elevations of the peaks we climbed are as follows: Peak 2186, Cuernos de Pirén (Horns of Snow); Peak 2080, Banded Peak (striped geology); Peak 2033, Cerro Improbable (Improbable Peak); Peak 2342, Morning Star Peak; Peak 1890, Vizcacha Peak; Peak 1859, Florentina Peak.

After a delightful climb of Morning Star Peak, the highest in the park, we got hammered by a three-day storm that, at its peak, kept us in the tents for 36 hours straight. Note: not all summits are clearly marked on the topo map due to 50-meter contour intervals. If you are interested in a more detailed summary of the expedition, please contact me directly: gperless@yahoo.com

GARY PERLESS, *Washington Alpine Club*

Tierra del Fuego

Monte Sarmiento, South Face, Attempt. Sergio Echeverria and I had the honor to meet Mr. Jack Miller, the person who knows more about the amazing Cordillera Sarmiento and the Canal de las Montañas than anyone else. He came to Patagonia to try to preserve this cordillera and canal as a National Park. In a five-day trip to explore the area (March 1-6), we (Jack Miller, Christian Regenhard, Sergio Echeverria and I) tried to make the second ascent of the South Face on Monte Sarmiento (2123m). After three days on the mountain with an advance camp at 1300 meters, 90 m.p.h. winds and a lot of snow forced us to go down.

SERGIO ECHEVERRIA *and* HERNAN JOFRE, *Chile*

Grupo la Paz, Various Activity, Previously Unreported. We met up with Andy McAuley and Vicky O'Malley in December, 1997, in Puerto Natales. Our plan was to make a first ascent on a mountain from the Grupo la Paz (a.k.a. Torres del Diablo). We waited a day until a fisherman could take us the 50 sea miles with him. He passed the Canal Kierke and took the next channel to the right, dropping us off in the Canal Santa Maria. The peninsula between the Canal Santa Maria and the Canal de las Montañas is called Peninsula Roca or Cordillera Riesco. The kayaks made us independent and helped us to discover untouched virgin climbing from the fjords and the shores. After two days of seeking a sheltered base camp, we were lucky to find an overhanging rock with enough room for two tents and a kitchen-place all in a row. The main problem in this region is the ever-pouring rain and the soaked ground— extreme conditions for clothing and man's motivation.

Carsten and Andy found a way over the two passes to the easternmost of the Grupo la Paz. After we transported all the material to the bottom of the mountain, the waiting period started. We made one try to climb up, getting to the snow field, but the weather was not stable, so we had to return. While waiting for the day without rain, we paddled in the fjords, went fishing, crossed heaps of rivers and enjoyed being alone with nature.

Punctual with the full moon (in accordance with the Indians' belief), the weather changed and we had two days of sun. On January 12, Carsten and Andy climbed the 900-meter east face of the easternmost Grupo la Paz in seven hours. The rock quality is poor compared to the typical Patagonian granite. It seems to be a young granite with a lot of loose rock. Nevertheless, the south faces have quite a lot of demanding climbing possibilities. The established route has 14 pitches and is called *Cuando Cambia la Luna* (V 6a). The following day, Carsten, Anke and Vicky went to the summit of a mountain east of the Grupo La Paz via the southeast face. The route follows a ca. 50-degree ice field in the lower part. In the upper part, the rock climbing is quite easy (fourth class).

CARSTEN VON BIRCKHAHN *and* ANKE CLAUSS, *Germany*

La Dama Blanca and Grupo La Paz, East Summit, Ascents. Jose Carlos Tamayo and I left Puerto Natales on November 13 in our sea kayaks, pointing our bows toward Resi Fjord. The Cordillera Sarmiento de Gamboa was our final destination. Meanwhile, our climbing partner, Jesus Martin, got under way on the fishing boat La Katita with all of the equipment to survive for two months at the foot of the virgin mountain called La Dama Blanca (the White Lady), the highest summit of the range.

The objective of this expedition was to try to arrive at the summit of the mountain, filming the entire endeavor for the Spanish television program, "Al Filo de lo Imposible." For that, the film team, made up of Sebastian Alvaro, Esteban Velez, Manolo Rojo and Daniel Salas, intended, aside from surviving the climate, to film the kayak crossing, the set-up of Base Camp and the approach to the mountain. Fortunately, the weather did not prove to be too severe, and, after some intense experiences, we managed to accomplish this objective.

On November 15, the film crew made the return trip, leaving the three of us with everything ready for the climb. We had the luck of living through a spell of very adverse weather

La Dama Blanca. The Quesada-San Vicente route climbs up the glaciated slopes from the left to the summit. IÑAKI SAN VICENTE *(courtesy of* DESNIVEL *magazine)*

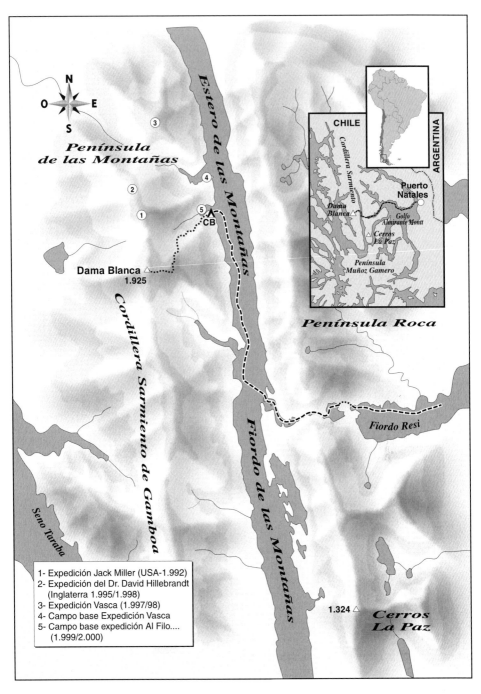

1- Expedición Jack Miller (USA-1.992)
2- Expedición del Dr. David Hillebrandt
   (Inglaterra 1.995/1.998)
3- Expedición Vasca (1.997/98)
4- Campo base Expedición Vasca
5- Campo base expedición Al Filo....
   (1.999/2.000)

Fiordo de las Montañas is actually Canal de las Montañas. Map courtesy of Desnivel *magazine.*

that did not leave us the slightest possibility of trying the route. After various attempts at setting up intermediate camps, the severity of the conditions made it clear to us that it did not make sense to fight against the great elements.

At this point, the day arrived when Jose Carlos and Jesus had to leave. On December 28, we abandoned the Canal de las Montañas aboard La Katita. We left a tent installed at BC in anticipation of new reinforcements. On January 18, with a new climbing partner, Rafael Quesada, we left Puerto Natales aboard a fishing boat. We used a local ferry to arrive at the Canal de Las Montañas. With our kayaks, we soared up the canal in two days and were able to paddle right to BC. The weather continued without respite and was so cold that we were only able to explore the lower surrounding areas and paddle around in the kayaks.

On February 8, we left at 3 a.m. from a bivouac at 715 meters above sea level. A calm night of high clouds permitted us to climb to the plateau at the foot of La Dama Blanca to see a beautiful sunrise at 1330 meters. The route was obvious; a spur that begins between the south and north summits kept us safe from the sunbathed seracs. The north summit is the higher of the two, and only the last 120 meters were difficult. After numerous bergschrunds, we arrived at a 60-degree scoop with more vertical sections. The final 80-degree couloir put us on the secondary summit eight hours after leaving our bivouac. The summit and the landscape were worthy attributes of the savage, Patagonian beauty. The reading we got at the summit (1925m) was a bit higher than our map from the Chilean Maritime Geography Institute, but this inspired more confidence in me in view of the rapid atmospheric pressure changes.

In a few hours we had put an end to the excuse of occupying this peninsula. After gathering up BC, we left, towing our equipment to the Grupo La Paz on the rock peninsula—rock towers that had accompanied us in this country for so many days. The barometer reached its highest point on the trip and on February 15 we climbed the east summit on the first splendid day of the whole season. In a twisted landscape, an easy climb permitted us a lovely view of the panorama of these savage mountains. One more time, the exacting governess of Patagonia invited us to return.

IÑAKI SAN VICENTE, *Spain*

Cerro San Valentin, Ascent, and Hielo Patagonico Norte, Traverse. Two of us, Tomasz Schramm and Andrzej Smialy, had as our goal to make a traverse of the northern part of the Hielo Patagonico Norte as well as to climb the highest mountain in Patagonia, Cerro San Valentin (4058m). We were asked many times if we were mad and were informed, by the way, that there are better ways to commit suicide.

After landing on the shore of Laguna San Rafael, we started our pilgrimage toward San Valentin on November 23, 1999. Because of nasty crevasses in the lower part of the San Rafael glacier, we proceeded on the rock of the glacier bed. This took six days, at which point we were welcomed by the crevassed surface of the glacier. We had heavy loads, so we were forced to walk the same distance several times, which is why it took us until December 4 to reach the main plateau. Our pulkas helped to turn our walk on the glacier into a pleasure. After we survived on a huge, steep, fog-covered, crevassed ice field, the way to the top of San Valentine was open. So we used it. We hugged one another on a summit after a nine-hour climb in a blizzard. Then we headed toward Cerro Cristal on the main ridge of the Andes. Unfortunately, "El Respiro" (our name for the blizzard on Hielo) had the same plan. We quickly made one another's acquaintance and in six days of struggle we walked just over ten kilometers. In very poor visibility, we got lost a bit (our GPS was helpless—there *are* white spots on a map) and at last we stood on a pass between Mocho and Cerro Fierro (perhaps the first to do so). During the next two days we struggled with blizzards and gravity on steep snow slopes, ice and rock cliffs, making seven rappels en route. When we set foot on the flat surface of a glacier, we called our newly opened route down from the Hielo "Desperado Pass."

A week-long trek back to human settlements led us through the rough and hazardous terrain of the Fiero and Leon river valleys. We crawled over house-sized rocks, through the green hell of Patagonian bush and across the Rio Leon at the end. Berries are common there, and we fed ourselves on them during the last days when our expedition food was gone. We spent 35 days on this walk (from Laguna San Rafael to El Pedregal farm) instead of the 26 we had planned.

ANDRZEJ SMIALY, *Polish Alpine Club*

Hielo Patagonico Sur, North to South Traverse. Mostly unknown territory, the Hielo Patagonico Sur, 400 kilometers long by 80 kilometers wide, is the third-biggest ice plateau in the world. Its weather is the worst in the world and in the middle lies the infamous Reichert Fault.

Many have tried to cross it from north to south, but all met with failure due to the complex logistics, the extreme conditions and the commitment of walking 400 lonely kilometers. The most noteworthy attempts have been that of the Spanish team in 1992 and Arved Fuchs et al (German) in 1995. In 1996, Pablo Besser and I made an unsupported attempt with Jorge Crossley (Chile) but failed due to inexperience. After climbing down the Reichert Fault, we left the Ice after 54 expedition days.

On October 24, 1998, Pablo Besser (expedition leader), Mauricio Rojas, José Pedro Montt and I stood at the starting point of the Ice Cap, the Jorge Montt Glacier. Without mechanical help or human contact, we began an almost-unsupported expedition (we had one cache in the middle) walking day by day, carrying 100 kilos each, combating humidity, crevasses, storms, wind and a stark landscape.

Fifty days later we arrived at the Reichert Fault, the most important obstacle in the traverse. We down-climbed to the bottom of the Fault, took our loads and made the first (and obligatory) ascent of East Bastion, climbing it because it stood in our way. Near the summit, we spent nine terrible days in a snow cave waiting for good weather. Finally we were able to rappel 620 meters (150 overhanging)

The north face of the unclimbed Paredon Peak (2256m) as seen from East Bastion.
RODRIGO FICA PÉREZ

down the virgin south face. We were the first humans to cross the Reichert Fault, which in itself took 30 days.

Low on rations and really weak, we walked the last 160 kilometers across broken glaciers in 21 days to finish on January 30, 1999, at Seno Ultima Esperanza, the Pacific Ocean, after 98 days on the Ice Cap.

RODRIGO FICA PÉREZ, *Chile*

Torres del Paine National Park

Escudo, North Ridge, Previously Unreported. Ralph Thäusing and I climbed the North Ridge of Escudo in March, 1993. It had already been climbed by Jerry Gore and Andy Perkins three months before (see 1993 *AAJ*, p. 197); however, we didn't know this. We climbed to the col as for the existing route, then, on the second day, went right where they went left to finish below the summit on the schist band (as they did). Bad weather was coming in, so we went down. Our variant was 6b A3.

ANDY PARKIN, *United Kingdom*

Almirante Nieto, East Face. Chad Peele and Jeff Brandner attempted a route on the east face of Almirante Nieto. The pair reported poor rock with no protection; the snow crossing was fine. From Las Torres Camp (820'), it took them 17 hours to reach 7,200 feet. They did not summit.

SERGIO ECHEVERRIA *and* HERNAN JOFRE, *Chile*

Cuerno Norte, West Face, Nacimientos. On February 13, Andre Labarca, Claudio Retamal and Luis Ortiz (Chile) finished a new route on the west face of Cuerno Norte. *Nacimientos* (V 5.10 A1, 15 pitches) was climbed in 18 hours from Advanced Base Camp. (Base Camp was in the Valle del Frances, 15 minutes from the British Camp; ABC was a three-person cave, 20 minutes from the base of the wall and a one-and-a-half hour hike up toward Cuerno Norte.) The route goes straight to the col between Cuerno Norte and Mascara (a.k.a. the Mummer) on easy slabs in seven pitches (5.5). They climbed this section unroped. From the col, the southwest edge of Cuerno Norte was climbed on excellent granite in eight pitches, at which point they reached sedimentary rock. All the granite was climbed clean except pitch 7, where Andre made the only aid move (A1) of the route. Once on the sedimentary rock, they hiked to Cuerno Norte's principal summit in 20 minutes. They rapped the route of ascent, using pitons for the anchors. The party reported no sign of another route on this ridge.

A UIAA report of a 1998 route by Andre Labarca and Claudio Retamel on the southwest face of Cuerno Principal was incorrect. Though attempted, the route was not finished.

SERGIO ECHEVERRIA *and* HERNAN JOFRE, *Chile*

Mascara, East Face, Attempt, Cuerno Este and Cuerno Chico, New Routes. We were in Paine National Park from December 11-January 21. The aim of our stay with Robert Tanner (Germany) was to climb Cerro Mascara from the Bader Valley. The Welsh Camp, which is in perfect condition, was the chosen starting point. Depending on loads and snow conditions, it takes between two to four hours to hike to Mascara. Out of the 15 days that we hiked to the small nameless glacier near Mascara, we could only climb on six. Three hundred meters of rope were fixed in three climbing days to the col between Mascara and Cuerno Norte. We wanted to climb *Duncan's Dihedral* (IV 5.11 A1), but the cracks were icy and the rock full of snow. Instead, we climbed six new pitches that we called *Kurz vor Knapp* (5.10 A2) before connecting with *Duncan's Dihedral*, but at about 200 meters below the summit, the boys were forced to turn back because of the bad conditions. (Anke had remained at the col.) On January 10, Robert had to leave to go back to Germany.

After a goodbye party for Robert in Puerto Natales, we returned to the Refugio los Cuernos (where the Rio del Valle Bader enters the Lago Nordenskjöld), the site of our new camp. The weather was incredibly good and we had three good days of climbing on the Cuernos. On January 14, we opened a new route on Cuerno Este which we named *Condorito* (6b+). It is a 300-meter line on the east face in very good granite; after two pitches of slabs, it follows a perfect crack system. The climb starts at the steeper part of the wall where the slabs drop down to Valle Bader (until recently referred to as the Valle Pingo; see *AAJ* 1999, pp. 330-332).

Three days later, on January 17, Cuerno Chico (a.k.a. Cuernito) awaited us. We started to the left of the yellow-reddish rock and continued after the third pitch in the steeper part to the right. *Pluma del Condor* (6b) is 300 meters long. Both routes end just before the black sedimentary rock starts.

Back from climbing, we waited another two days for good weather and then decided to leave the park. Since we had planned to climb in alpine style, we had just a minimum of climbing gear with us, and on January 19 we left in kayaks from the Refugio, crossed the Lago Nordenskjöld and got a ride to Natales from the Podeto. With kayaks, even coming to the Refugio was very simple because you can enter the Rio Paine near the Laguna Amarga and then paddle down the river and cross the lake, which takes about two hours.

CARSTEN VON BIRCKHAHN *and* ANKE CLAUSS, *Germany*

Espada, Chilly Willy. From January 21-February 8, Thierry Bionda and Jean Michell Zweiacker (Switzerland) put up a new route on the west face of Espada in the Valle del Frances. *Chilly Willy* (VI A3 5.8, 250m) was reported to have excellent granite. The day of the ascent was February 2.

SERGIO ECHEVERRIA *and* HERNAN JOFRE, *Chile*

Central Tower of Paine, Macaroni-Porridge Junction. Our team was composed of three members: Filip Šilhan, Marek Holeček and David Šťastný. We left for Patagonia on January 26 with the aim of climbing one of the routes on the 1200-meter east face of the Central Tower of Paine as free as possible. We arrived at Campo Torres on January 31 in typical Patagonian weather. There was only one climbing team at the camp and two more in the Japanese Camp higher in the valley. Everybody was waiting for a bit more bearable weather. Within the next week we got our material to Advanced Base Camp beneath the towers. The weather improved quickly on February 7, so the next day we set out on our climb.

With our first experience of Patagonian weather, we put off our original plan of climbing the 1991 German route, *Riders on the Storm*. Instead, we started on the right side of the wall, mostly following the line of the 1974 South African route, where we found old fixed ropes, all of them severely cut. For the first three pitches we shared the belays of this line, then

David Šťastný on Macaroni-Porridge Junction, *trying to find a link to* El Regalo de Mwoma *some 100 meters above. (The team was forced to pendulum.)*
FILIP SILHAN

moved slightly to the left. After having climbed 12 pitches, we got to a dead end. We had to decide whether to turn back and continue more to the right or to make a pendulum to the left and join the 1992 British route, *El Regalo de Mwoma*. We chose the second option and found ourselves in a thin crack about 50 meters above an obvious spire. The terrible weather stopped us for the next two days, which we spent in our portaledges. We continued on February 13, when the weather improved slightly. The free climbing was over. Up to this point, the hardest pitch was about 8 (5.11d).

Our progress slowed down to 50 to 100 meters a day. We started to discover what "British aiding" is all about. There were no bolts on belays and in some places even no pitons. We had to admire the boldness of the Britons.

On the eighth day of the climb, we got to a tiny ledge. From this point we set out on our summit push. We took just our sleeping bags and light food for two days. It seemed to us that the crack would never end. We still had to aid all the pitches. Suddenly, the gradient of the wall broke off. We continued on a starry night, hoping to reach the summit. At 2 a.m. we decided to make a bivy and continue in the morning. It was a beautiful sunrise and we saw that we were almost at the top. It took us four pitches to get to a false summit. For the last couple of meters we untied from the rope and soloed to the correct top. On February 17 at 10 a.m. we reached the highest point of the Central Tower of Paine and enjoyed the excellent views. We stayed for about 30 minutes and then started to descend. By evening, we reached the spire at the beginning of the crack with our haulbags and portaledges. It took us the next day to get down on the glacier. The last four days we suffered from terrible thirst because we had no water. We named our variation *Macaroni-Porridge Junction* and graded it 8 A3+. We placed ten bolts and about 30 pitons.

FILIP ŠILHAN, *Czech Republic*

South Tower, Southeast Buttress, Hoth. On December 22, 1999, Sean Easton and I arrived at the entrance of Torres del Paine National Park with four porters. In three days, with the help of the porters, we managed to move most of our gear to our chosen Advanced Base Camp at the base of the glacier.

The south face of the South Tower of Paine, with the Central Tower on the right. Notes Conny Amelunxen, "After seeing and hearing the winds blast around the edge from the south face, it is very clear to me why it is unclimbed." Hoth follows the right skyline; Lungo Sogno (Leoni et al, 1987) follows the left skyline. CONNY AMELUNXEN

Sean and I continued moving gear up the glacier to the base of the South Tower of Paine. With all our equipment at the base of the wall and one pitch fixed, we descended for the New Year's celebrations. The day we went back to Puerto Natales, the closest town to the park, the weather turned and storm after storm started coming in. When we returned to the park a week later, one of the transfers had to negotiate two and half feet of water over sections of the road.

After another week of waiting at Base Camp, the weather improved marginally, allowing us to reach our Advanced Base Camp. Four days of impeccable weather followed. We climbed to our first wall camp site over two days, then returned to the ground, leaving five 60-meter lines fixed. After a day of hauling, we blasted, pulling up our ropes. As we went up the fixed lines, we watched an enormous storm materialize around us. The storm lasted four days. Originally we left the ledge only to accommodate bodily functions. On the last several days, we didn't even leave the ledge for this. Five days later we rappelled. We had eaten a third of our food without advancing and had to go down for more.

On January 25, we committed ourselves to the wall. The afternoon looked promising; however, on the two-hour hike from ABC to our fixed lines, the temperature dropped more than 25 degrees to -15° C. We jugged iced ropes, skidding all over verglas. Over the next two weeks, the temperature might have risen above freezing once or twice.

Within the first five days, we fixed and hauled the next three pitches to establish Camp II.

The east face of the South Tower of Paine, showing 1. Hoth *(Amelunxen-Easton, 2000). 2.* En el Ojo del Huracán *(Piola-Sprungli, 1992). 3.* Italian Route *(Aiazzi-Aste-Casati-Nusdeo-Taldo, 1963). A South African team climbed 22 pitches on the east face in 1985. An accident turned them back 150 meters from the summit.* SEAN EASTON

The weather went spiraling downward quickly. The inverted spindrift avalanches imprisoned us in our portaledge, where we were hammered by ferocious gusts of Patagonian wind. With our supplies being steadily depleted, we were forced to climb through conditions that were less than hospitable.

Thirteen days later, the alarm went off and I peeked outside. Thinking I was dreaming, I went back to sleep. When I woke an hour later, the day was calm and cloudless. I started up the first fixed line at 9 a.m.; Sean followed shortly after. When he finished the last aid pitch, we screwed together our ice tools and changed to alpine mode. We were on the summit of the South Tower of Paine at 7:40 p.m. From the summit, we were able to see the Patagonia ice cap, Fitz Roy, Cerro Torre and the never-ending pampas disappeared into the east. Seven rappels later we were at the top of our fixed lines. It was dark. The wind had picked up again. Over the next four hours, we battled for our lives to get down those fixed lines. The first two got stuck when we tried to pull them. We had no option but to go down. The next pair got hung up. We were forced to rap our last two ropes to camp and wait for better conditions. At 2 a.m. we arrived at CII, exhausted. Hour upon hour, the wind persisted and our paranoia mounted. Our last two ropes were fixed above us, being tormented by a wind that is famous for cutting ropes. The next evening the wind slowed. Without wasting a moment we jumped out of the ledge to rescue the lines. We had climbed the entire route in 60-meter pitches. Our dilemma was that one of the last two ropes was only 50 meters. Although we had to make several extra rappels, the descent went smoothly. After rescuing our haul bags from a few crevasses, we were in town on February 12, having established *Hoth* (VI 5.10+ A4 WI2/3, 1100m, 27 pitches) on the southeast buttress of the South Tower of Paine in 24 days, including 19 nights in a portaledge, in a capsule-style ascent of the wall with an alpine-style summit push.

Conny Amelunxen, *Canada*

Argentine Patagonia

Fitz Roy, Supercanaleta, Attempt, and Aguja Poincenot and Aguja Guillaumet, First Winter Ascents. Paul Ramsden, Jim Hall, Nick Lewis and Andy Kirkpatrick were in Argentine Patagonia from June 20-July 20, 1999. Setting off at 2 a.m. on July 1, we found deep unconsolidated powder in the initial section of Fitz Roy's *Supercanaleta*. As height was gained, this changed to powder-covered rock slabs before eventually thin ice was reached after 300 meters. There then followed pitch after pitch of very thin ice.

At half-height, the gully opens and gradually peters out. We climbed several steep rock pitches in order to reach the obvious chimney line above. This was quite hard with difficult route finding. What followed were many pitches of extremely hard (Scottish VII) and uncompromising climbing before the first half-reasonable ledge in a basin was reached at 2 a.m. From the basin, we climbed straight up and were treated to many pitches of excellent mixed climbing, with ice smears, snow-filled cracks and nasty offwidths all adding to the fun.

We broke out onto the ridge proper at about mid-afternoon. Beneath the so-called Second Pinnacle, we found a reasonable ledge and decided to stop for the night. The weather by this time had deteriorated considerably, but we hoped it would blow itself out over night as many of the previous storms had.

Unfortunately, it did not. Several times our bivy tent was actually picked up off the ground with all four of us in it. (In Chalten, the Ranger Station recorded winds up to 120 m.p.h., and that's in the valley). Dawn eventually arrived with no improvement in the weather, but we decided to stay where we were as we still had plenty of food and fuel and still felt roughly in control of the situation. Unfortunately, the roof blew out of our bivy tent around mid-day and sitting it out was no longer an option.

What followed was a rather grim 16-hour descent back down the couloir. We eventually emerged out of the spindrift maelstrom much relieved in the early hours of the morning. With thoughts on tea and biscuits, we descended to the tent, only to find it gone. We had left the tent well secured, but now all that remained were the snow stakes anchoring down a few tatty guy lines.

Unfortunately, the tent contained our passport, credit cards and cash, as well as all our camping equipment. We spent the rest of the night crammed in the ripped bivy tent making brews and getting thoroughly soaked as the temperature on the glacier seemed to be hovering around an abnormally warm 0°C.

Dawn brought no relief in the weather, and with little food or fuel, no tent and saturated sleeping bags, we had no option but to make for Chalten in a day. The route back was now avalanche-prone, but there was little choice.

Now distinctly lacking in gear and running short of time, we decided to opt for something with a shorter walk and the possibility of good snow hole accommodation. We decided to head on to the Paso Superior and check out Guillaumet, Mermoz and Poincenot.

We dug a snow hole at the col, which made an excellent base for our last week in the mountains. What is more, the weather appeared to have settled down, so we were hopeful of ticking a few routes. We made the first winter ascent of Guillaumet via the excellent *Amy Couloir* and North Ridge. The weather was excellent and the climbing on good granite was very enjoyable, though the gloves did stay on.

We left the hole early the next morning for the Whillans Route on Poicenot. The first half of the route followed the obvious ramp line and was fairly straightforward, if unprotected and very exposed. The transition from snow to mixed also involved a considerable increase in difficulty. From the shoulder, things looked steep and intimidating and we were unsure of the feasibility of our proposed alpine dash. In the end, though, the blank granite walls and overhangs were passed and we found ourselves on the summit.

The next day we descended to Chalten, well content with our first trip to Patagonia. In conclusion, we would say that the winter offers longer periods of good weather, but with the huge drawbacks of little daylight, very cold temperatures and relatively little ice build-up. Winter may well be the key to getting up some routes, but not all of them.

PAUL RAMSDEN, *United Kingdom*

Cerro Torre, West Face, Winter Ascent. In July, Thomas Ulrich, David Fasel, Stefan Siegrist and I climbed the 1974 West Face route of Cerro Torre. Rumors of more stable weather conditions and the fact that we would avoid summer crowds motivated us to go to Patagonia in winter. We had two three-day spells of good weather during the five weeks we were there, conditions that wouldn't be exceptionally good in Patagonian summer. If there is an advantage to Patagonian winter weather, it's that you can see the storms developing for a full day, which is much different than the summer, when it can go from deep blue windless skies to raging storm in less than six hours. But the fully developed winter storm is just as fierce as its summer counterpart with two added complications: the days are much shorter and the temperatures are much colder. My personal conclusion: the Patagonian winter is no picnic (thank God) and is certainly as grim as Patagonian summer climbing and in some ways, grimmer.

On the first winter ascent of the West Face of Cerro Torre. THOMAS ULRICH

We approached via Paso del Viento with much arduous slogging. We made two attempts on the West Face, the second successfully. Ice conditions on the route seemed good, but because I haven't been on the West Face in summer I can't truly compare. We climbed to the summit plateau beside the last summit mushroom, but unfortunately not to the absolute top—the second time I've failed to complete those last few meters. It took us two and a half days to get to the top from an advanced camp at the base of the Filo Rosso and 16 desperate hours to get from the top back to camp (the usual atrocious winds complicated descent). After a successful descent, we left the ice cap through Paso Marconi and made all haste for La Casita, the only bar/restaurant open in Chalten at the time. The summit party with the English winter expedition (Kirkpatrick, Lewis, Ramsden, Hall) in La Casita was classic post-expedition debauchery. The hardest load I carried during the whole trip was lugging the utterly inert Thomi and David from the bar back to the sleeping bags. Without the help of the four Brits, Stefan and I would not have been able to do it.

GREG CROUCH

Argentine Patagonia, Various Activity. Between October 28, 1999, and January 23, 2000, Laurence Monnoyeur and I had 18 days of good weather overall. From October 28-November 11, we traveled on the Hielo Continental from Marconi Pass to the Refugio Fuerza Aerea and back with skis, pulkas and sails (these were very, very good for heading south). On October 31, we attempted a line of ice on the west face of Cerro Marconi Sur. It started with a long snow couloir, then two pitches of thin ice (max. 85°). The third pitch was too difficult (funky, with rime and ice), and the sun began to warm up the face a bit too much: large chunks of rime detached themselves from it. I had broken two teeth a few hours earlier while crossing a bergschrund. We stopped and returned to the tent in three rappels. On November 6, we climbed Cerro Cristal (2105m) and on the 7th, Cerro Campana (2459m) by the route of first ascent. It was a very beautiful summit, with a 70-meter pitch (90°) in the summit mushrooms. We descended in two rappels, then skied to the Fuerza Aerea. We then spent three windy days horizontal in the tent at the foot of the Cerro Murallon, and on November 17-18 hiked south toward the Refugio Pascal and bivouacked in the forest (how good it was to see the green!).

Bruno Sourzac trying to piece it all together on Cerro Murallon. LAURENCE MONNOYEUR

From November 20-24, we made an attempt at a new route on the east face of Cerro Murallon (2656m). There was a 50-degree snow shoulder, then mixed terrain (90° A2 M5). The wind blew too strongly. There must have remained just 350 meters to the top of the wall. We made seven rappels in the eye of the cyclone! It was a marginal and trying descent: we left ropes, pitons and Friends and, drenched and numb with cold, were happy to find our tent that same evening.

On November 28, we made an ascent of Cerro Mariano Moreno (3536m) from the Nunatak Witte via the route of first ascent. We skied to the summit and had a beautiful descent. On December 4 and 5, we attempted a new route on the north face of the Domo Blanco (2315m) following the pillar west of the obvious serac. The beginning of the route (250m) faces west. We climbed 150 meters of terrain at A2 6a (90 percent aid), and then stumbled: there was too much aid, too much ice in the cracks and we were too slow!

On December 21, I climbed Aguja de l'S from the Polacos Camp with Dean Potter and Rolo Garibotti. Laurence climbed it with Stephanie Davis. On January 8, Laurence climbed Cerro Solo (2248m) with Tommy Bonapace. On January 9, with Bruce Miller (U.S.), I climbed a 120-meter "drip" on Cerro Solo ("*Las Lagrimas del Solo*"). We encountered an ice waterfall (90°, then 75°, then 80°) at the summit ridge/band of Cerro Solo on the east face. (Two waterfalls form on a steep, black rock wall on the upper tier of the east face of this peak. *Las Lagrimas del Solo* is the left-most of the two icefalls.) We descended via the regular route.

On January 11, Laurence and I climbed St. Exupery (2680m) via the beautiful Kearney Route. The next day, I climbed Innominata (2501m) via the *Corallo Route* with Timmy O'Neill and Nathan Martin (U.S.). It was a very beautiful line, but we found bad rock in the central dihedral. On January 13, Laurence and I climbed El Mocho (1980m) via the Voie des

Benitiers. It was a very beautiful route. We accessed the route at pitch 3 via ledges to avoid the bottom. On January 14, I climbed Punta Inti, the smaller tower of "Cordon" Torre, with Laurence in six pitches. We siesta'd beneath the summit on the lichen "lawn"! On January 17, I soloed Aguja Guillaumet via the *Amy Couloir* on the east face.

BRUNO SOURZAC, FRANCE

Argentine Patagonia, Various Activity. In late 1996, Italians P. Cavagnetto, R. Giovanetto, M. Motto, G. Predan and C. Ravaschietto attempted to climb Punta Filip (the northwest gendarme of Aguja Bifida) from the western flank, but they retreated some 20 meters short of the summit at the top of a significant foresummit, because they considered that climbing the gendarme of the summit itself would require extensive bolting. They named their route *Su Patagonia.*

On November 22, Silvo Karo (Slovenia) and Rolando Garibotti (Argentina) completed the first ascent after climbing a new route on the east face. They climbed a line that involves five mixed pitches on the lower part and seven rock pitches on the upper pillar. They followed a series of ramps and dihedrals leading to the col between Punta Filip and the southernmost tower of the Triologia Inca. They managed to overcome the summit pinnacle by lowering 25 meters on the north side of the pinnacle from the col on its eastern side, and climbing a very exposed slab (no bolts).

Silvo Karo on the east face of Punta Filip during the first ascent of Amigos Perdidos *(Garibotti-Karo, 1999).* ROLANDO GARIBOTTI

They named the route *Amigos Perdidos* in honor of Aischan Rupp and Janez Jeglič, two close friends tragically lost in the mountains, and also as a humorous reference to the fact that they lost two Friends on the route. They christened the tower Punta Filip to honor Janez Jeglič's son, who was born a few months after the disappearance of his father on Nuptse in late October, 1997.

On the east face of Punta Herron, the obvious ice/snow runnel and chimney leading to the "Col dei Sogni" was attempted by Ermanno Salvaterra (Italy) and José "Pepe" Chaverri (Spain) in early 1994. They attacked just left of *Motivaciones Mixtas* but were forced to retreat after 300 meters when Chaverri was injured by falling debris.

On November 28, 1999, Karo and Garibotti completed this line. After the first few easy pitches they were faced with the difficult first pitch of the obvious left-leaning line, which involved some tricky aid climbing, after which a long difficult chimney/ice/rock system leads to the easier middle section. The climbing proved to be a bit harder than expected, and it required 15 hours to reach the Col dei Sogni. Their original intention was to continue on from the col along the route *Spigolo dei Bimbi* (Salvaterra-Cavallaro-Vidi, 1991). In the morning they found this route impractical due to large quantities of verglas covering the rock and therefore decided to retreat. They called the 23-pitch line *Tobogan* (ED- 85° 5+ A2, 900m), a direct reference to the fact that this line leads to the *Spigolo dei Bimbi* ("Pillar of the Children").

On December 5-6, 1999, Karo and Garibotti managed to climb alpine style the Slovak* Route on the southwest face of Cerro Fitz Roy starting from the Torre Glacier. The Slovak Route was first climbed in January of 1983 by Slovaks Michal Orolín, Vladimír Petrík and Robert Gálfy. The Slovak climbers had attempted the route one season earlier starting from the Torre Glacier but were not successful. They eventually completed the ascent by climbing from the Hombre Sentado Ridge, thus avoiding the lower 800 meters of the face. They climbed with extensive use of fixed ropes, which were placed to where their route joins the 1968 Californian Route 400 meters from the summit. The whole face starting from the Torre Glacier had been attempted on many occasions.

Karo and Garibotti started from the Polish Camp in the Torre Glacier at 4:15 a.m. and were at the base of the 2300-meter face some 45 minutes later. The lower 800 meters involved easy snow ramps and some tricky mixed climbing, half of which required roped climbing. The base of the prominent dihedral one-third of the way up was reached at 10 a.m. This involved some of the hardest climbing on the route, which proved to be fairly dangerous due to loose rock. By 6 p.m., Garibotti and Karo had joined the Californian Route, where they had some difficulties finding the proper line of ascent (due to fatigue?). Just before 10 p.m., they gained the ridge of the *Supercanaleta*, where they decided to bivy. They had intended to climb the route in one push and did not carry any bivy equipment or stove. After a cold night out, the morning of December 6 saw them negotiating the gendarme ridge, and eventually they reached the summit a little after 11 a.m.

After the de rigueur photos and other summit affairs, they descended the Franco-Argentinian Route and continued on to Rio Blanco. As they did not have any bivy gear and had not had any food for most of that day, they decided to continue to the "De Agostini" Camp, where they had their base camp. This three-hour hike involved some of the most exciting moments of the whole ascent: halfway there, they were surprised by a wandering puma (mountain lion). The rest of the hike produced some sore necks, as they kept looking over

---

*Though this route, a.k.a. the Czech Route, was established when Czechoslovakia was still an integral country, the first ascensionists were of Slovak ethnicity. Garibotti suggests it is more appropriate to refer to the route as the Slovak Route. Barring that, it should accurately be known as the Czechoslovakian Route.

their shoulders in fear of another unwanted guest. At 2 a.m. they arrived at Campo de Agostini, where they collapsed into the depths of a big pot of spaghetti before eventually crawling out of it and into their sleeping bags.

They were full of praise for the fine effort of the Slovak climbers in 1983, who, considering the objective dangers, were very brave to undertake fixing ropes on such a long line. Although the vertical gain is 2300 meters if one starts from the Cerro Torre Valley, the first 1000 meters is actually easy terrain and should be considered part of the approach. There are a few sections of bad rock, but overall the climbing is very easy, rarely more difficult than 5+. They considered the route to be ED- 6b/A0 65°, 2300 meters. With the exception of four pitches that were jumared by the second, both climbers climbed the entire way.

ROLANDO GARIBOTTI, *Club Andino Bariloche*

Aguja Saint Exupery, South Face, Petit Prince, Variation and South Face, Attempt. Etienne Fine and Philippe Driel (France) completed the third ascent of *Petit Prince* between January 12-25, 2000. They fixed ropes on the lower half of the face and then completed the ascent climbing alpine style. From the top of the 14th pitch, instead of climbing left to the col between the two summits to join the Austrian South Pillar route, they climbed a four-pitch direct variation to the summit (A3). They thought the route was superb and fairly well protected from the strongest winds.

Marcelo Galghuera and Horacio Gratton (Argentina), with support from Jorge Garcia and Fernando Garmendia, made an attempt on the south face in early 2000. They attempted a line to the left of *Petit Prince*, climbing 60 meters of ice to 60°, followed by 80 meters of poor quality rock (black basalt band) and 130 meters on the wall itself (A2). They used fixed ropes on their attempt.

ROLANDO GARIBOTTI, *Club Andino Bariloche*

Aguja Poincenot, East Face, Patagonicos Desperados. Italians Giuseppe Comino and Cesare Ravachietto attempted to make the second ascent of the 1989 Anker-Piola route, *Patagonicos Desperados* (6c A3, 550m), which takes a magnificent line straight up the east face of Aguja Poincenot above the start of the Whillans route. On January 16, they climbed the first seven pitches and bivouacked. On the following day, they climbed a further six or seven pitches, completing almost all the hard climbing, but bad weather forced them down three pitches short of the summit.

On the first ascent of this route, D. Anker and M. Piola climbed the upper section of the route by slanting up right from a point halfway up the Whillans Ramp and returned two days later to add the lower seven pitches. The route still awaits a continuous ascent.

ROLANDO GARIBOTTI, *Club Andino Bariloche*

Aguja de la Silla, West Face, Attempt. In January, 2000, Tommy Bonapace and Christian Zenz (Austria) attempted the west face of Aguja de la Silla in alpine style, spending six days on the wall. They retreated 300 meters from the summit. Bonapace had previously attempted this line between February 16-24, 1995, with Toni Ponholzer (Austria). The two had climbed alpine style and retreated after 23 pitches, some 450 meters from the summit.

ROLANDO GARIBOTTI, *Club Andino Bariloche*

Cerro Fitz Roy, Diedro Directo. Ben Gilmore and I completed a new variation to the Casarotto Route on the North (Goretta) Pillar of Fitz Roy. *Diedro Directo* (VI 5.10 A3, 32 pitches) has 12 new pitches of climbing before joining the old Casarotto line. We fixed ten pitches and then summitted in three days on February 20, making the sixth ascent of the peak from the North Pillar. (The route follows a big dihedral that splits the base of the North Pillar between the Casarotto and the Polish route, *Devil's Dihedral*).

BRADY ROBINSON, *unaffiliated*

Fitz Roy, Czechoslovakian Route. In February, 2000, Alan Mullin (Scotland) and I began the Czechoslovakian Route on the west face of Fitz Roy from the Polish Camp, a bivy site situated just above the Torre Glacier in its lateral moraine. This site is roughly 45 minutes from the couloir we used to access our climb and five hours above the Campamento Bridwell (a.k.a. Campo de Agostini) Base Camp. A prior lull in the weather had allowed us to stash gear and food on the first rock buttress 280 meters into the couloir. No fixed lines were employed on our climb, just a cache left at the beginning of the technical climbing. With the advent of good weather we moved together, simul-climbing the initial mixed ground (mainly easy mixed with two short 85° sections) to the prominent feature of Sitting-Man Ridge. We then continued along the ridge in simul-style (easy rock, 5.7) until the face proper, which begins with three chossy 5.9 pitches. This deposited us below the big gray overhanging dihedral. Here was the only snow-melting possibility en route as well as a flat ledge that provided a perfect bivy opportunity. Though we were only about 30 percent (and 11 hours) into the journey at this point, we stopped, drank and ate while filling seven liters of water for the remaining mission.

The next day's breakfast pitches through the overhanging dihedral proved to be the technical crux (hard 5.11). The Czechoslovakian Route branches right above the dihedral. Our initial plan was to do some new climbing directly into another large dihedral, but many offwidth pitches thwarted our psyche, and free climbing the remainder of the Czechoslovakian route became the goal. The climbing stayed mainly in the 5.10 range with occasional 5.11 pitches; ramps, steep cracks and chimney/offwidths characterized the route. The fine weather we had enjoyed during the previous days slowly deteriorated, with the bright moonlight we had counted on never breaking the cloud's veil. Wind became our plague while climbing through the second night. Our junction with the Californian route in the morning brought respite: conditions on the other side of the southwest arête were dramatically different. Everything was verglassed yet windless. We continued above the junctions of *Supercanaleta* and the Californian routes, opting to stay on the south side in a continuous dihedral (the Californian Route's descent) rather than weather the north side. Conditions continued to deteriorate. After 25 hours' climbing beyond our bivy, the second tower, above the Czechoslovakian Route's climbing conclusion*, became our high point. Strong wind and rime ice prevented us from traversing the final 250 meters across the north side to the summit. Even after a substantial amount of simul-climbing and short fixing, we still roped around 30 pitches (VI 5.11, 85°). Descent was made down the Californian Route, with continued descent down the west side back to the Campo Polaco bivy.

KEVIN THAW, *United Kingdom*

---

*It should be noted that this route as defined by its first ascensionists finishes on the summit. The Slovaks reached the Californian Route on one occasion and on another occasion a high point similar to Mullin's and Thaw's, and both times they returned, as they did not consider their ascent finished.

Cerro Fitz Roy, showing 1. Northwest Ridge (Abert-Afanasieff-Afanasieff-Fabre, 1979). 2. Supercanaleta (Comesaña-Fonrouge, 1965). 3. Czechoslovakian Route (Orolín-Petrík-Gálfy, 1983). 4. Californian Route (Chouinard-Dorworth-Jones-Tejada Flores-Thompkins, 1968). Other features shown are 5. Aguja de la Silla. 6. Aguja Desmochada. 7. Aguja Kakito. 8. Aguja Poincenot 9. "La Brecha de los Italianos," a col just south of Fitz Roy's south shoulder first reached by Italians in 1937. 10. La Silla ("the saddle" between Fitz Roy and La Brecha). 11. French Route (Terray-Magnone, 1952). JOSE LUIS FONROUGE

Cerro Fitz Roy, Various Activity. From November 29-December 1, Joe Reichert and Sue Nott climbed to the end of the difficulties on the Californian Route, but strong winds forced them to traverse over to the Franco-Argentine descent route without reaching the summit. They made one bivy in La Brecha while going up and another one on the ridge of *Supercanaleta.*

The pair also attempted a new line on the east face of Cerro Fitz Roy, just left of the East Pillar (Ferrari) route. They fixed five 60-meter ropes at the top of which they placed their portaledge, where they spent 15 nights. The first five pitches were slabby (5.9, A2) and the last four above the camp were A3-A4. Bad weather forced them to retreat.

There were countless attempts on the Franco-Argentinian Route in early January, most notably a solo attempt by American Clay Hall, who, on January 16, 2000, climbed to the top of the fifth pitch where he bivouacked. He was forced to retreat the following day due to lack of water and strong winds. Ascents were as follows: Kurt Albert and Bernd Arnold (Germany), January 13; Franz Baumgartner and Mario Rubin (Switzerland), January 13; Nicolas Benedetti and Leonardo Viamonte (Argentina), February 16.

Carlos Garcia and Carlos Suarez (Spain) climbed the *Royal Flush* route from December 2, 1999 to February, 2000. They completed the route after fixing the first 23 pitches, retreating at the juncture of the *El Corazon* route, 300 meters from the summit. This was the fourth ascent of the route, which has been completed only once to the summit (Treppte-Gälbe-Schafroth,

1998). On December 27, while recovering their many fixed lines, Carlos Garcia suffered a 30-meter fall when he slipped through the ends of his ropes while rappelling. He was lucky enough to land at the base of the route itself, three pitches above the bergschrund. He was towing several ropes, and as he fell past a prominent flake, one of them got caught and slowed him down considerably. He suffered many torn ligaments.

ROLANDO GARIBOTTI, *Club Andino Bariloche*

Aguja Mermoz, West Face, and Guillaumet, Northwest Ridge. Zlatko Koren and Klemen Mali (Slovenia) came to Piedra del Fraile Base Camp on January 28, 2000. The first ten days it rained a lot, and there was even snow in BC. In bad weather, we managed to bring our gear to Paso del Cuadrado. Our main aim was to climb *Tehuelche* on Fitz Roy's north face. But after the rainy days, all the cracks on the lower part of the route were filled with ice and snow.

On the first beautiful day we changed our plan and noticed a nice line on Mermoz's west face. We didn't have any information about the line or whether it had already been climbed. The same day that we brought the gear to the base of the wall (February 7), we climbed the first 120 meters and fixed the rope, then rappelled down and bivied at the base of the wall. During the night, the weather changed for the worse and we left for BC.

In the first four pitches we found old pitons and bolts at the belays. After the fourth pitch there was nothing. The information that Rolando Garibotti gave us was that two Swiss climbers, Vicent Banderet and Paul Maillefer, tried to climb the line in 1985 but retreated after completing eight pitches when faced with a steep offwidth. (Notes Garibotti, "Banderet and Maillefer descended a different way, which is why the Slovenians found no equipment higher than the fourth pitch.")

After a few days, the beautiful weather started. On February 12, we started from BC at 2 a.m. At 8 a.m., we started to jumar the 120 meters. After the comfortable ledge, we found the hardest climbing on the route: offwidth cracks mixed with aid and free climbing. During the day, the weather changed and in the afternoon, it started to snow and blow. In the middle section, where we found the hardest climbing of the route, we also had a lot of bad rock in wide cracks. In bad weather, we managed to climb to the top of the wall at 11 p.m. or so and quickly started to rappel. After two rappels the weather cleared up, and we had a cold but clear night for the descent. We descended our route of

The west face of Aguja Mermoz, showing Barriga Patagonia *(Koren-Mali, 2000).* ROLANDO GARIBOTTI

ascent, which we called *Barriga Patagonica* (6a+/A1- V+, 650m). At 6 a.m., we stood at the base of the wall. We took a rest at the bivy for three hours, then left for BC with all the gear.

Four days later we left for Guillaumet, thinking to climb a new line on the west face. The weather was bad again. In bad weather, we climbed the Northwest Ridge (V A0, 400m) (Comesaña-Fonrouge) in three and a half hours. We departed BC on February 20, 2000.

KLEMEN MALI, *Slovenia*

Aguja Guillaumet, North-Northwest Ridge, Free Ascent and Other Activity. Bruce Miller and I arrived at Chalten at the end of November with the intentions of trying the *Supercanaleta* on Fitz Roy. After our first and only attempt on December 3, we decided against it, for it was in poor shape. During our seven-week "super-expensive camping trip," we refined our camping techniques, bouldered much, got fat and managed to get some hand jams on the lesser summits of this proud range. We climbed the North-Northeast Ridge on Guillaumet for possibly the route's first free ascent, for Bruce sent the A2 pitch at .10+ tight handies. The climbing was excellent, but the summit was not obtained; high winds forced us to retreat. We rapped the route.

We tried to climb the Franco-Argentine Route on Fitz Roy for several weeks with no great height gained because a four-week storm did not give us a window of opportunity. During our last days in, we managed to climb the Kearney Route on St. Exupery (IV 5.10), the Anglo-American Route with the Kearney Variation on Innominata (IV 5.11-), *Medialuna* (III 5.11), and Bruce and Bruno Sourzac linked up and climbed a new route (III WI4) on Cerro Solo.

KENT McCLANNAN

Aguja Guillaumet, East Face, Attempt. Dave Hesleden and I went to attempt the West Face of Fitz Roy in November and December, 1998. In actual fact it was quite snowy and icy, so we switched to the east side. After one attempt at the Franco-Argentine Route on the big Fitz (all the cracks were full of ice), we realized that we would be better off trying to climb on mixed routes. We did 450 meters of good climbing on the [400-meter] east face of Guillamet, abseiling off two to three rope lengths from the top due to constant spindrift. The climbing was good and hard: Scottish VI/VII-ish with poor protection on the second half.

ANDY CAVE, *United Kingdom*

Torrecita Tito Carrasco, First Ascent, and Cerro Pollone, West Pillar, A Fine Piece. In November, 1999, I went back to Patagonia with Jim Donini with no fixed objectives but hopeful of finding some good unclimbed terrain above the Marconi Glacier. Armed with info provided by my hero, Rolando Garibotti, and after some reconnaissance, we settled on a pair of decent prospects.

At our first opportunity, we climbed a beautiful virgin tower that is the first peak on the ridge north of the main summit of Cerro Pollone and named it "Torrecita Tito Carrasco" in honor of a friend of Jim's wife, Angela. Tito died in Angela's arms after he was struck by rockfall while sport climbing at El Portrero Chico, Mexico, in 1997. We followed the path of least resistance with sections of snow, ice and mixed, capped by a few nice pitches of moderate rock. The last few meters of rime and rock to the absolute summit were spicy. In all, an excellent day outing.

Torrecita Tito Carrasco is the small pillar on the left. The Crouch-Donini route roughly follows the sun/shadow line. The prominent formation in the center is the west pillar of Pollone. A Fine Piece ascends the sun/shadow line. The sun-lit formation to its right has no known routes. GREG COUCH

A week or so later we got a second opportunity and went after the West Pillar of Cerro Pollone, which had been attempted by Michel Piola and Daniel Anker of Switzerland some years before. We took two days and 16 pitches to get to the top of the pillar, which featured tons of high-angle free climbing on superb rock. The summit view from the top of the pillar is astonishing: all the peaks of the Fitz Roy massif, an incredible angle on Cerro Torre, both the east and west faces of Piergorgio, and stunning views out over the ice cap—probably the best I've had in Patagonia.

After limited discussion over a quart of whisky decanted into a plastic Coke bottle, we decided to name the climb *A Fine Piece*, as revenge for the gruesomely politically correct name *Greenpeace*, a nearby route that an Italian team did up the nose of Piergorgio's west face. I whole-heartedly recommend *A Fine Piece* to anyone interested in an alternative to the madding crowds on Cerro Torre's *Compressor Route* or on Fitz Roy's Franco-Argentine route. *A Fine Piece* has a very straightforward approach, much less objective hazard than that found on the approaches to those standard routes on Fitz or Torre, lots of quality freeclimbing, several killer bivy ledges and a better summit view. I think the whole route would go free with just a few short sections of 5.11 (and maybe not even that). The right team should be able to peel the whole thing off in a single day.

GREG CROUCH

Cerro Piergiorgio, West Face, All You Need is Love. Michel Bordet and I put up the tent at the foot of Piergiorgio: 600 to 900 meters high and two kilometers wide, one part facing northwest, the other, west. Both aspects had only one route.

A brief look at the west face and our route is traced, beginning with a small, 50-meter pillar beneath a large, 200-meter dihedral. Two hundred meters of compact slab lead to the dihedral, then 150 meters on an oblique, right-trending ramp and a 100-meter easy slope to the summit. The small pillar is quickly devoured, followed by an evening of hauling. The next four pitches on the compact slab are not of the same type; rather, they are high-angle industrial work.

A small, 5-mm hole, a 5-mm rivet. Toc toc toc. . . 60 meters of progress, six hours of work.

Four consecutive days, and all of it the same. The dihedral that follows is the reward: classic, very steep A1/A2 or 6a/6c/7a. The only catch in the dihedral story is the ice waterfall coming from the upper névé that melts on nice days and comes down on us at about 2:32 p.m. Without neoprene suits, we ring in our retreat, and we cry; it's surreal. The weather is beautiful, not a breath of wind (very rare in this area) and we're not climbing. Seated at the foot of this immense wall, we look up at the only trail of running water—right in our route. Who can have it in for us like that?

Another day passes despite everything, and Mich climbs under cover while I am in a shower at the belay. Two hours later, he leaves the dihedral behind; I, not far from hypothermia, join him. My companion warms me up with big slaps on the back. It is gorgeous out; the sun sets slowly. At 10 p.m., warmed up, I tackle the next pitch, which leads to the final slope. A few meters of IV and I go for a 25-meter traverse on rivets. At 2 a.m., I put in an anchor piton. At 6 a.m., after a "really great" night without bivy gear, Mich rotates his arms vigorously and embarks upon the next pitch, which should go quickly. This evening, if the weather holds, we'll get out.

As regards the easy pitch, we find ourselves on a bobsled run; the rock is completely iced over.

Let's go, one last effort, find the energy. . . 11th, 12th, 13th pitch. . . . At 3 p.m., the weather is still splendid, and we have left the difficulties behind. Our behinds in the air, we lap up water like two thirsty dogs (it's been 40 hours since we last ate or drank) and laugh about our

David Autheman on the "high-angle industrial work" of the lower slab pitches. The route's defining feature, the dihedral, can be seen above. MICHEL BORDET

great luck.

We set down all of the gear and leave for the last sprint up the easy snow slopes. With a very professional hand, Super Mich carves out the last steps beneath the col. Summit. No, no, I don't kiss him.

Hey, put on a little rimmel, and I'll take a photo of you with Cerro Torre in the background. Go on, turn around. . . .

And already, it's time to descend.

(The route, *All You Need is Love* [ED+ A3 5+, 700m], was finished on November 11, 1999; it lies to the right of the *Greenpeace* route. It involves two very distinct sections, the lower portion involving compact slabs that required lots of drilling [bathooks, rivets and bolts for five pitches] and the upper part that follows a very distinct dihedral. The pair fixed ropes to within 80 meters of the easy terrain leading to a col on the summit ridge, located some 80 meters below the summit itself, from which they descended.)

DAVID AUTHEMAN, *France*

Cerro Standhardt, Northwest Ridge, Aguja Innominata, Corallo Route, and Cerro Torre, Compressor Route. Timothy O'Neill and Nathan Martin climbed the *Corallo Route* (V 5.11) on Innominata on January 12 with Bruno Sourzac; the Northwest Ridge (V 5.11 WI5, 19 pitches) on Cerro Standhardt on February 15, a new route; and the *Compressor Route* (VI 5.11 WI4 A1, 28 pitches) on Cerro Torre on February 18. On both Cerro Standhardt and Cerro Torre, the two men climbed the summit mushrooms, which involved unprotectable climbing on inconsistent rime ice. A full account of their Patagonia adventures can be found in an article by O'Neill earlier in this journal.

Cerro Torre, Various Activity. Beside the ascent mentioned above, the *Compressor Route* saw only one other repeat this season: Heinz Zak, Peter Janschek and Elmar Springer (Austria) climbed it on February 21. The Austrians as well as the Americans climbed the summit mushroom. See the article by O'Neill for more details on these climbs.

In October, 1999, Ermanno Salvaterra and Mauro Mabboni (Italy) established a new variation to the *Compressor Route*. From the base of Maestri's infamous 60-meter bolt traverse, they continued straight, following the obvious line of weakness up the edge of Cerro Torre's southwest spur. This line had previously been attempted by Jose Luis Fonrouge (Argentina), Pete Crew, Dougal Haston, Martin Boysen and Mick Burke (UK) in early 1968. The Anglo-Argentinean team had managed to climb one and a half pitches from the bolt traverse and were on their second pitch where Haston dropped the bolt kit, a mistake that forced them to give up their attempt. Salvaterra and Mabonni climbed five new pitches before rejoining the *Compressor Route* at the base of the so-called Ice Towers (at the height of the prominent rightward ice traverse). The climbing involves some A2 and aesthetic free climbing along the spur's edge (6a+). They spent nearly seven days on the mountain and were forced to retreat not far from the summit due to bad weather. They climbed alpine style with a portaledge.

The West Face (Ferrari) route saw a number of fine efforts. Miyasaki Motohiko and Suizi Mikio (Japan) repeated the route on November 7, 1999. They climbed from their camp at Filo Rosso (Hielo Continental) to the formation known as the Helmet. The following day, they

The top of Cerro Torre, showing 1. South Face (Karo-Jeglič, 1988). 2. 1999 Mabboni-Salvaterra variation. 3. Compressor Route (Maestri et al, 1971). DAVID NEILSON

climbed to the vicinity of the last rime formations below the summit mushroom, where a wide crevasse proved impassable. Forced to retreat, they returned back down to the Helmet the same day. Then a fierce storm moved in and for four days they were unable to descend, having to bivouac without sleeping bags or food. It was not until the November 12 that they managed to descend to Filo Rosso, but upon arriving they were unable to find the entrance to their snow cave due to the large amount of new snow and were forced to bivouac outside one more time. This was, according to them, a "death bivy," and they suffered some frostbite in their hands and feet. The next morning they managed to dig out their cave, where they rested for more than a week before they moved out.

Jimmy Surrette and Charlie Fowler made an ascent of the route on January 13. Unlike other parties for this climb, they made their Base Camp at Campo Bridwell in the Torre Valley (the east side), rather than at the Filo Roso (below the face to the west). They retreated from the foot of a steep rime formation, 40 meters below the plateau at the base of the summit mushroom. Mick Poynton and Leigh McGinley (U.K.) climbed the route from the Circo de los Altares in February, 2000. Leigh went snowblind on the descent, thinking he had lost his glasses, when in fact they were still in his pack! They retreated from the same place as had Surrette and Fowler.

ROLANDO GARIBOTTI, *Club Andino Bariloche*

Hielo Continental Norte, Traverse, and Cerro Pared Norte and Peak 2970m, Ascents. Between November 26, 1998-January 5, 1999, Paolo Cavagnetto* and Lorenzo Nettuno (Italy) and Nigel Topping and I (U.K.) traversed on skis with pulkas a ca. 200 kilometer, north-south route (mostly following the route of Shipton's 1963 expedition) across the Hielo Continental Norte from Laguna San Rafael to the Baker Channel, exiting via the Steffan Glacier. Of our five weeks on the ice, we got just four days of decent weather; the remaining days sat (more toward the latter half as we gained elevation) on a spectrum with moderate winds, low visibility and rain on one end and full tempestuous conditions with driving, frozen sleet or snow on the other. Despite challenging conditions, we completed the traverse and our scientific objectives, failed in an attempt on Cerro Largo and made two first ascents, which were snatched in the only weather window available: Cerro Pared Norte (3005m) (Shipton's original objective), and an unnamed 2970-meter peak* some two kilometers to the south. Neither peak (both involved snow and ice up to 60°) was overly challenging from a technical perspective, but the latter peak was climbed in fairly hostile conditions (on the summit, we were bombarded by coffee-table-sized airborne windslabs ripped up from the windward slopes) marking the onset of a storm that had us pinned down on a nearby col at ca. 2000 meters for five days (up to and including Christmas Day) with an accompanying snowfall in excess of three meters.

The delay put pressure on the final 45 kilometers out via the long and arduously broken and crevassed Steffan Glacier, which was concluded successfully but, in fine epic tradition, without food. From the end of the glacier, which terminated in a large berg and brash-strewn lake with two large rivers flowing from it, we waited for a further three days (living off the "fruits of the forest" and expending much energy waving ice axes and chasing any local wildlife that had the misfortune to chance upon us) for our pre-arranged boat to show up and take us on to Tortel via the glorious Baker Channel.

During the traverse, we took 55 radio-echo sounding measurements of ice thickness and

---

*Paolo Cavagnetto died in a rock fall along with two aspiring guides on Mt. Blanc in July, 1999. The team has applied to the IGM, Chile, for the unnamed peak that was first climbed on December 21, 1998, to be named after him.

snow cover to compose a climate change/glacier retreat modeling investigation and gathered samples for analysis of persistent organic pollutants (POPs) in the region. To conclude (and with the added luxury of hindsight) all I can say is that Wilfred Noyce's 1969 quote from *The World Atlas of Mountaineering* seems as true as ever: "Most of the glaciers are still untrodden and the area offers a splendid field of new mountaineering possibilities to anyone willing to face the severe weather conditions which prevail."

ALUN HUBBARD, *Wales*

ANTARCTICA

Antarctica, Overview. The 1999-2000 season was the busiest season ever for tourism in Antarctica. This popularity was reflected in the relatively high number of mountaineers active on the continent, particularly in the Peninsula area. Most yacht-based climbers reported generally good weather, and in the Sentinel Range the extremely poor weather of the previous season did not materialize, heralding a return to the traditionally high success rates on Vinson Massif and Mt. Shinn.

DAMIEN GILDEA

ANTARCTIC PENINSULA

First Ascents in the Behrendt Mountains and Bean Peaks, and Other Activity. In December and January, the British Antarctic Survey (BAS) Field Assistant Phil Wickens again made a number of ascents with his party in the course of their geological work. They were working in the Orville Coast region, an area never visited by non-government climbers but which has seen some previous ascents in the Latady Mountains by American scientists (reported in this journal). This area is at the extreme southern end of the Peninsula, on the eastern side, which is not accessible by yacht.

The party started in the Behrendt Mountains in early December, where they summitted five peaks, the highest being Mt. Hirman (1200m). They then moved to the Mt. Hassage area, summiting Mt. Hassage (1100m). Both these areas had previously been visited by scientists but no ascents have been recorded. The party then moved to the Bean Peaks in late December, where they climbed five peaks and nunataks, the highest being Carlson Peak (1289m). They also did some climbing on Cape Zumberge.

In mid-January, the group visited the Hauberg Mountains, where they climbed three peaks, the highest being Novocin Peak (1304m). This peak had been climbed by Americans Carrara and Kellog in November 1977, by the north ridge. Wickens' group also made an interesting traverse of a six-kilometer long ridge in the northern Hauberg Mountains, which contained many peaks, the highest at 1300 meters.

Finally, in early February, the group visited the Wilkins Mountains, where two peaks were climbed, and then the Latady Mountains, where three peaks were climbed, the highest of them being McLaughlin Peak (1700m).

DAMIEN GILDEA

Mt. Scott, North Summit, Ascent, and Other Activity. From December to January, an Australian party aboard the yacht *Tooluka* visited the Peninsula. All the climbers aboard attempted to make the probable first ascent of Mt. Zeppelin (1265m), southeast of Eckener Point. Starting from an ice landing in Graham Passage to the north, they camped at 500 meters but eventually retreated due to deep snow, poor visibility and heavy snowfall during the one and half days they were on the peak. Lucas Trihey, Chris Jewell and Keith Tuffley then made an ascent of an unnamed pyramid-shaped peak (1320m) above Neko Harbour in Andvoors Bay. After landing by inflatable boat, the group skied to half-height, then followed a 45-degree ridge over moderate ground with only a few crevasses posing any real difficulties, before reaching the summit in a whiteout and strong winds. Following this, the *Tooluka* party undertook a three-day ski traverse on Wiencke Island. From the northern tip of the island, they followed the eastern coast, over the Thunder Glacier to Port Lockroy, mostly in bad weather. This party also skied various slopes on Enterprise Island, Hovgaard Island and Doumer Island.

As a finale, *Tooluka* then visited the popular Mt. Scott (880m) above Lemaire Channel and made what was probably the first ascent of the north summit of this peak via a ridge on the west face. Trihey and Jewell climbed about 35 pitches straight out of the water in a 29-hour push to the summit. They encountered ten pitches of rock up to grade 5.7 and in Trihey's words, "mega-exposure, hideous, Andean-style, razor-edge ridge climbing, an awkward gendarme and excellent ice gullies." Ascent required abseils, which would have made retreat difficult. A fast descent was made in good conditions down the glacier to the north of the peak.

DAMIEN GILDEA

Wiencke Island, Ascents. On January 11, New Zealanders Mike Roberts, Lizzie Craddock, Richard Craddock, Amber Chisholm, Anton Woperis and Steve (last name unknown) started climbing from an anchorage near the Chilean base of Gonzales Videla. A long glacial traverse south and east took them to a col near Mt. Hoegh (890m). The whole party then ascended a smaller 805-meter peak to the southeast of Hoegh. Upon returning to the col, Richard Craddock, Steve, Woperis and Chisholm climbed Mt. Hoegh, while Lizzie Craddock and Roberts climbed another peak (730m) to the southeast. On January 13, the whole party made an ascent of Jabet Peak (545m) on Wiencke Island, a climb first done in May, 1948, by the Britons Pawson and Richards and climbed a number of times since.

January 17 saw the Craddocks, Woperis and Roberts make a probable new route on Janssen Peak (1085m) on Wiencke Island. This peak forms the southwestern end of the popular Sierra du Fief range in southwestern Wiencke Island. The climb involved 12 and a half pitches of 45- to 50-degree snow on the obvious and aesthetic east face. The party finished their trip with Steve, Woperis, Roberts and Chisholm making a ski-traverse of Doumer Island on January 18.

DAMIEN GILDEA

Cape Renard Tower, Attempt, and Pt. 3,600', Ascent. Our goal was to attempt the first ascent of the north face of Cape Renard Tower (747m) located on the west side of the Antarctic Peninsula. Cape Renard Tower has been climbed twice before, once by a Canadian team who climbed a mixed route to the lower east summit and in 1999 by a German team who climbed the west face to the main summit. We were aboard the yacht *Pelagic* (Latin: "of the sea"), a vessel with a seven-ton steel-encased lead lifting keel built by Captain James "Skip" Novak for the purposes of sailing and mountaineering in this region. The team comprised Julian-Freeman Attwood, Skip Novak and myself. Jules and I had made a previous attempt on the Tower in 1996.

After an aborted attempt to land at the base of the Tower on February 19, we moved to the northeast to the one spot where the collapsing ice wall is breached by a tenable line of ascent. A long pitch up this enabled us to fix a rope for the next morning. We returned, then climbed back up the rope and hauled 20 loads up the wall on to the top of the seracs. We set up camp on the top. We then established a traverse across the glacier to the lip of the 200-foot ice cliff from where a narrow ledge system led across the rock face to join our original "direct start" from the cave site of 1996.

From the ledges, there followed two more days of steep and difficult rock climbing to reach the toe of the massive couloir that cleaves the face. We established fixed ropes on all this section so that we could both return to camp and re-ascend to our high point as soon as possible with the plan of establishing a camp high on the mountain. However, after various discussions, it was decided to make a single alpine-style attempt from above the fixed ropes.

After some bad weather, Skip and I climbed back to the toe of the couloir by 7 a.m. on our big day. We climbed this in about a dozen pitches and then followed the ramp line that cuts across the upper walls up rightward. As night fell, we prepared for a cold bivouac without sleeping bags. The first pitch the next morning proved to be an awkward grade V piece of ice. We were forced to continue up the ramp line for another two pitches. The climbing became increasingly difficult until we ended up faced with a blank wall leading into a blank corner that stopped us in our tracks. Our high point was three-quarters of the way up, at the end of the ramp across the headwall on the summit tower, two pitches short of the easier summit ground. It took 15 rappels to return to the top of the fixed ropes, then three more rappels back to the ledge line as darkness fell. A weary plod with heavy loads back across the glacier and we reached base camp by 11 p.m.

I also made a solo ascent via a new route (with Freeman-Attwood in support) of the highest point of the Wall Range on Wiencke Island. This is Point 3,600' (1097m) on the chart at a position of 64° 49.5' S, 63° 23.0' W. The route was a technically straightforward line up a broad couloir opposite Jabet Peak to the crest of the north ridge. I then hung a right for an hour's ascent along the crest via a series of rounded elephants' backsides to the summit. Along the way I experienced rough weather with high winds and poor visibility. Subsequent checks have revealed that this summit had in fact most likely been climbed at least once before by members of the well-known Italian climbing group Lecco Spiders in 1976. They had christened it Monte Italia (1097m). It appears they had traversed to it from the neighboring summit, which they had climbed using siege tactics under difficult weather conditions.

CARADOC ("CRAG") JONES, *Wales*

Mt. Demaria, Ascent, and Other Activity. In early February, a British party visited the Antarctic Peninsula aboard the yacht *Shantooti*. On February 23, Luke Milner and Roger Haworth made an ascent of Mt. Demaria (635m) with Vladislav Timofeyev and Pavel Silin, the latter two being Ukrainians from the Vernadsky base. This steep peak was first climbed in July, 1979, by a BAS group and has received a number of ascents since. On February 28, Richard and Roger Haworth then attempted the unnamed highest peak of the "Seven Sisters," a feature in the Sierra du Fief on Wiencke Island. Their attempt via the northwest ridge was unsuccessful due to poor snow conditions. On March 4, this pair then ascended to the highest point on the ridge between Jabet Peak and Noble Peak (720m) via the west ridge. This summit had been reached by British in 1948 and again by Italians in 1976.

DAMIEN GILDEA

Arctowski Peninsula, Port Lockroy/Wiencke Island, Paradise Bay and Cuverville Island, Ascents and Descents. Doug Stoup, Stephen Koch, Hans Saari, Kris Erickson, Rick Armstrong, Jared Stackman and Rick Hunt were on the Antarctic Peninsula for an exploratory adventure from February 11-25. The team fired out a nine-day ski blitz, basing out of the ritzy *Akademik Shuleykin*, an ice breaker complete with sauna and a five-star chef. Utilizing Zodiak rafts to access remote islands and bays, the team notched seven first descents, ranging from cruiser fun runs to desperate icy chutes.

With little photo documentation of the Antarctic Peninsula to work with, the expedition came armed for the worst, not knowing what the terrain would be like. They found Alaska-style terrain beyond their wildest dreams. Three of the descents—"Tina Point," "The Shuleykin" and "Lowe Peak"—were first ascents as well. The 2,000-foot Lowe Peak was named in honor of legendary climber Alex Lowe, who was killed with Saari and Erickson on the Shishapangma Ski Expedition in Tibet last fall. The team also skied *The Honey Bowl*, *Sunshine Daydream*, *The Whale's Tail* on Mt. Demaria and the horror show *Zeiss's Needle* on the Arctowski Peninsula. *Zeiss's Needle* sported some of the most technical skiing, with the top sliver nearing 60 degrees and barely 180 centimeters across.

HANS SAARI

Notes Damien Gildea, "Many of the peaks in these areas would have had previous ascents by BAS personnel based at Port Lockroy over the years, but it was almost certainly the first time snowboarding had been conducted here and almost all of the peaks would never have had ski descents."

SENTINEL RANGE

Mt. Bentley, Northeast Ridge, Ascent. The most notable ascent in the Sentinel Range this season was on Mt. Bentley (4145m), well north of Vinson Massif. Americans Wally Berg and Bob Elias were installing weather beacons and surveying on the Embree Glacier, visited for the first time in the 1998-'99 season. The north face of Mt. Anderson (4157m), the highest unclimbed peak in the Sentinel Range, is accessed from here, but was not considered feasible this season by Berg. On January 12, Berg and Elias spent eight and a half hours ascending, unroped, the northeast ridge of Mt. Bentley. This is a stunningly aesthetic direct line rising around 1800 meters straight out of the Embree Glacier. The pair did not visit the summit, stopping about 60 meters short due to high winds and the difficulty of a precarious ice ridge. They made a point of not claiming the second ascent of Mt. Bentley. The first ascent of Mt. Bentley was made via the south ridge in January, 1998, by Veikka Gustafsson and Patrick Degerman of Finland.

DAMIEN GILDEA

HEARD ISLAND

Mawson Peak, New Route. Mawson Peak (2745m) is the highest point of Big Ben, the volcano on Heard Island. The peak received its third ascent when Australian climbers Robb Clifton, Stuart Davies, Matthew Rogerson and Tim Curtis journeyed to the island by fishing boat from Perth, Western Australia, and climbed the mountain via a new route from the west. They reached the summit on January 10 after an attempt two days earlier was beaten back by the island's notoriously harsh weather. The party found generally poor climbing conditions with many crevasses and noticed that both sulphur and steam were emanating from a vent near the summit. The first ascent of Mawson Peak was from the Gotley Glacier to the southwest in January, 1965. The second ascent was from the east in February, 1983.

DAMIEN GILDEA

AFRICA

MALI

Kaga Tondo, Croatica, and Other Ascents. From mid-January to mid-February, an expedition of Croatian climbers was active in Mali. Boris Cujic and Ivica Matkovic led the team, which climbed a new line on Kaga Tondo. *Croatica* (F6c+, 650m) was established from the ground up with electric drill and bolts. The route took four days to be established. The team experienced an average temperature of 30°C.

They also climbed (traditional style) four new routes with difficulties from V+ to VIII up to 650 meters in length. (Further details are lacking.) Finally, they repeated the French Route (Guy Abert et al) on Suri Tondo (F7a, 580m).

EMANUELE PELLIZZARI

Kaga Tondo, Various Ascents. It was reported that in December, 1998, Claus Obrist, Helmut Gargitter and Pauli Trenkwalder put up the 600-meter *Inshallah*, which follows an obvious crack system to the left of *Garmi Airlines* (Griso-Lucas, 1985). Three attempts were necessary to reach their high point, some 60 meters below the summit, where heat and lack of water forced a retreat.

In February, 1999, Polish climbers Bogdan Fic, Tomek Samitowski and Krzysiek Zielinski, with Waldi Niemiec and Michael Zielinsk in support, put up the 19-pitch route *The Last Beer in Hombori* (7a+ A0). The route takes possibly the last logical unclimbed line on the east face, to the right of the right-facing corner system of *Marabu Loco.* (*High Mountain Sports* 205)

Suri Tondo, Veus del Desert and BMW. It was reported that Spanish climbers Sílvia Vidal and Pepe Masip established *Veus del Desert* (6b+ A4+, ten pitches) on the middle of the southeast face of the south summit of the 400-meter Suri Tondo. The first five pitches were almost entirely aid, while the remainder of the route went free at 5 to 6b+.

Meanwhile, Bernard Marnette and Salvador Campillo made the first ascent of the Suri Tondo's west pillar with the seven-pitch route *BMW* (6a+). (*High Mountain Sports* 205)

CAMEROON

MANDARA MOUNTAINS

Zeuvu Tower, South Face, New Route. On December 3, our team met in Douala, the capital of Cameroon. We had come to climb in an obscure area called the Mandara Mountains that lay along Cameroon's northern border with Nigeria. Our climbing team included South Africans Ed February and Andy Deklerk and myself. We were also joined by Simon Boyce, Greg Child and Robin Freeman, on assignment to document the trip for *National Geographic Television*. We were eager to keep moving toward our objective, but unfortunately Cameroon lacks reliable travel by air and at this time of year, many roads are impassable from weeks of heavy rain.

On December 7, we finally caught a flight to Garoua (one of the larger cities in the north) and the next day we took a bus to Maroua, the northern capital. The local Kapsiki people are incredibly poor, but the landscape in which they live is very beautiful, with craggy orange-colored outcrops set against lush green fields of peanuts, sorghum, millet and corn. After some last-minute shopping in the local market, we loaded two four-wheel-drive jeeps for the four-hour drive to the village of Rhumsiki.

With our first view of the Mandara Mountains, I breathed a huge sigh of relief. The horizon was riddled with fangs of rock poking into a hazy sky. There were dozens of towers clustered into an area of roughly 100 square miles. The spires looked steep, even overhanging, and up to 1,000 feet high. A quick reconnaissance determined that Zeuvu Tower (a tower we had seen in a French film called *Chocolat;* pronounced Zivi by those of Rhumsiki) was indeed the best objective, so we established a camp at its base just outside the village. We hired a local man named Koji who spoke good English to be our cook/guide. We would now have the companionship of nearly all the village children for the rest of our time in Rhumsiki.

We knew from our research that the first recorded ascent of Zeuvu Tower was in 1961 by a group of French volunteers who followed a jungle mountaineering route on the north face. However, the holds on this route were so polished that it was obvious it had been climbed by locals long before the '60s. We were initially guided up this 5.7 route by school children who had soloed it many times before. In fact, historians believe that hundreds of years ago, frightened villagers likely sought refuge on the tower during the frequent slave raids by tribes from Sudan.

We decided to attempt the tower's south face because it was close to 1,000 feet high and very steep. Unfortunately, the dense volcanic rock (which we believed to be syenite) was glassy smooth and lacking in hand holds and crack systems. We decided a ground-up ascent would be a bolt ladder, so instead we decided to approach the route on rappel. We spent the next several days cleaning off loose rock and vulture feces, as well as placing bolts in sections where natural protection did not exist. It was scorching hot to be on the face in the sun, so we tried to climb during the morning shade as much as possible.

Finally, we began our attempt to free climb the tower from the ground up. We ascended our ten-pitch route a couple of different times, but we had trouble getting it to go all free. Low down, Ed mastered a 5.11d offwidth coated in vulture piss, but Andy and I took whippers on

The south face of Zeuvu Tower. MARK SYNNOTT

the back-to-back crux pitches. On the final day of the expedition, we split into two teams (Andy and Ed and Greg and myself) for a last try. This time, Andy and I both completed the route with no falls. We called the climb *The Great Technical Adventure* (5.12d) (named after the local kids, who Greg and Andy nicknamed "the technicals"). Ours was the sixth route on the tower and the second on the south face. Andy Deklerk made two base jumps off Zeuvu Tower, which he believes were the first-ever base jumps in Cameroon.

We would like to extend our thanks to the National Geographic Society and specifically the Expedition Council for their generous support of the 1999 Rhumsiki Tower Expedition.

MARK SYNNOTT

KENYA

NDOTO MOUNTAINS

Poi, East Face, True At First Light. In December, Todd Skinner, Steve Bechtel, Scott Milton and I flew to Kenya with the east face of Poi (6,562') as our objective. Strengthening the team were Peter Mallamo, Nic Good, Sandra Studer and Bobby Model, who joined as a film crew. Our trip was greatly facilitated by the Kenyan member of our team, Saba Douglas-Hamilton, our translator, bush camp wrangler and knower of things Kenyan.

A month before our team's arrival, Todd convinced Jeff Bechtel, who was climbing Mt. Kenya with Bobby Model, into reconning Poi for us. After all, Todd wiled, "On a map, Poi is only an inch north of Mt. Kenya...." Jeff rented a Land Rover and drove north. The inch became three days each way along horrid roads and partially dry riverbeds. The recon yielded good still photos and video footage from all sides.

Using Jeff's photos, we guessed that Kenyan gneiss would be similar to the stuff in Wyoming's Wind River Mountains. We were wrong. Flying in to a camel-crowded dirt strip allowed a glimpse of Poi from the air. Observing the mountain from the air confirmed what Jeff's photos indicated: that there was one truly great line on all of Poi and that line was directly up the middle of the central east face.

We arrived expecting discontinuous crack systems, which we planned to link by face climbing. However, the gneiss formed less like our familiar Wyoming rock and more like the syenite of Hueco Tanks, Texas, and was often scabbed by fingertip flakes. Beginning at one-third height, huecos appeared, but unlike the Texas variety, these African huecos are big enough to crawl inside. The largest are more than 100 feet high and 40 feet deep! There were no crack systems on the great line we had selected, so we agreed that the finest route would result by establishing our climb from above. We spent several weeks finding, equipping and preparing the line for an ascent. The rock was, for the most part, of good quality and provided an abundance of incut edges. Numerous pitches were composed of bullet-proof, marble-like rock. A long traversing section down low forced us along a section of poor mica schist, which did clean up nicely and allowed reasonable passage. We were very pleased that the great face of Poi was yielding a fantastic and fun route.

Early on, I had been solo aid climbing to get a close look at a band of huge overhangs. A hook popped and I took a 50-foot fall directly onto my belay anchor. After righting myself, I was very scraped up and sore, but relieved that everything seemed to be okay. (Back home in Wyoming, x-rays confirmed that my kneecap had been cracked in the fall.) Other than being demoted to the team's slowest, I thought I was fine.

Ten days later, on Christmas Eve, I developed incredible pain in my knee. The next day, with help from Saba and Nic, I walked down off the mountain to recuperate. The rest of the crew kept at work, establishing our climb. When I felt strong enough, I slowly made my way back to the shoulder camp. That day, the team free climbed the first five pitches. The next day, we moved onto the wall for the remainder of the ascent. All of the 21 pitches feature outstanding face climbing that requires every technique from classic thin slabs to wild and dynamic overhanging sweeps. The difficulty is mostly in the 5.11 range, with a few of 5.12. Pitch 6 and pitch 20 were the 5.13 cruxes of the climb. We called the route *True At First Light* (5.13b, 21 pitches).

PAUL PIANA

Poi, North Face, Dark Safari. In the early 1980s, Andrew Wielochowski (a Brit based in Kenya) did the first climbing on Poi. After several attempts, he got up a line on the right-hand side of the east face, climbing ground up over three and a half days. His was basically a free climb with one short aid section (six or seven pitons) up an overhanging groove and a lot of bold 5.8 to 5.9+ climbing. Andrew also made two attempts on the south face, getting halfway up, and a notable attempt on the left side of the east face, doing 500 feet of hard climbing before having to retreat when his second was hit by a rock.

In 1992, I went out to try the north face but, due to poor route finding in the bush, failed to reach the base! We ended up making the second ascent of Andrew's East Face route, eliminating the aid. I was full of respect for the first ascent, which involved face climbing on fragile flakes 40 feet above any pro, and I was really fired up about Poi, which seemed to me about as adventurous a crag as you could ever find.

In January, 1999, Steve Sustad, John Barry and I tried the 2,000-foot north face via a huge curving corner line toward the left side. We got about halfway (eight pitches up to British E5/6) when John pulled a guano-plastered flake off onto his foot, causing a nasty gash. John was out of commission, and because risk of infection was so high, we decided to head back to civilization.

In February, 2000, we went back with the same team plus Jan Rowe, a mate of John's. Jan knew he probably wouldn't be up to the climbing, but we thought he could act as support, jumaring with supplies, etc., so he was persuaded to come on the route "for the experience." After climbing and fixing to our 1999 high point, we cut loose from the base and spent three days and two nights on the face, sleeping in hammocks. Retreat would have been very difficult due to the overhanging and slanting nature of the upper part of the route. With no pegs or bolts with us, failure was always a possibility and in fact in several places it seemed we had reached an impasse. The climbing was always challenging, with a lot of bold and serious 6a (5.12) and the easiest pitch British E2, 5b (5.9+). The route was climbed all free apart from one short section that was overcome with a very dicey lasso move (we later spotted an alternative to the left that should go free). We named the route *Dark Safari* (E6, 17 pitches).

Just before our trip, the North American team (see above) spent a month establishing a new route on the east face (left of the original Wielochowski East Face route). Both our team and the Kenyan climbing fraternity were somewhat shocked by the tactics used, which included:

• Using 42 porters to establish a base camp on top of Poi and working from abseil ropes for two weeks cleaning and bolting the line.

• Using a generator at the base for re-charging cordless-drill batteries.

• Making no contact with the Mountain Club of Kenya to find out about established ethics/traditions of climbing on Poi (and Kenyan bush crags in general).

As far as I know, there was previously just one hand-placed belay bolt on Poi and the MCK are not impressed that their prime bush crag has now been bolted from top to bottom. No doubt the climbing on the American route will be good and hard, but it raises issues as to how the wilderness crags of Africa should be treated. What I find unsavory is the "raid-like" approach and complete disregard for local climbers and the ground-up ethic established by the people who pioneered climbing on Poi. How would Skinner and Piana react if a Kenyan team arrived in Yosemite and bolted their way up *Salathé*? So far in Kenya, bolts have been used on a handful of single-pitch sport climbs on outcrops near Nairobi. Routes on the big bush crags have been ground-up adventures. It's the most adventurous rock-climbing arena I've ever come across and it would be a tragedy if it became just another bolted-up area like

The south and east faces of Poi, showing 1. True At First Light *(Bechtel-Milton-Piana-Skinner, 1999). 2. East Face (Corkhill-Wielochowski, 1983).* PAUL PIANA

Mali or Madagascar. On the *Dark Safari* route, we took no pegs or bolts.

PAT LITTLEJOHN, *United Kingdom*

MADAGASCAR

Andringitra National Park

Andringitra National Park, Various Activity. The French team of Thierry Giginot and Patrice Glairon-Rappaz spent several weeks repeating quite a few of the classics from last year and making a greatly criticized second ascent of *Fantasia* that involved new bolts and holes for hooking. Meanwhile, Gerard Thomas and Jacky Sananes put up the highly recommended and praised seven-pitch *Pectorine* in May. The climbing is exceptional on perfect rock with an incredible pitch on knobs and chicken heads (V+); difficulty is moderate with most pitches in the 6a/b range. The line is on the very wide wall right of Karambony, at the opposite side of *Tsaky-tsaky* and *Ebola*. Descent is made via the classic Karambony gully.

Two Swiss brave hearts who were present at the same period as the *Bravo Les Filles* team (see below) applied a different approach, working very hard and hand-drilling the 16-pitch *Norspace*. Stephane Salur and Walter von Ballmoos spent nearly a month in June and July on their project. Difficulties were consistently around 6b/c; two pitches had single 7a moves. The line is directly right of *Gondwanaland* and exits in the gully between Tsaranoro Be and Kely.

Michel Piola came back with his family and friends and repeated quite a few of the now-classics from his 1998 expedition. They spent ten days on the northern limestone cliffs in the Diego Suarez area, where they bolted a dozen single-pitch routes up to 7b. They also put up a fun ten-pitch route on the right-hand side of Karambony's north face, which goes up slabs just left of the gully. It is actually two routes: *Alien I* goes for the first four pitches to a big slanting ledge and finishes on top of the protruding pinnacle (above a characteristic yellow roof) with two more pitches (5c/6a max). *Alien II* starts from the ledge, has a common pitch with *Alien I*, then goes straight up for five or six pitches (6b max). The 350-meter route was opened on August 3 and 5 by Piola and Fabian Pavillard.

September turned out to be very busy with the visit of two impressive Spanish mutants. Francisco Blanco and Toti Vales opened a bold line of 12 pitches (plus 150 meters of III-IV climbing to the summit) named *Via Mora Mora*. Francisco bolted this incredibly hard and continuous route over six days in September, including a 150-meter, totally continuous 7b/c+ groove in the upper part. Although not redpointed, pitch 7 implies a long 55-meter 8b/b+ pitch. It is possibly the hardest route to date and seems to be quite engaged climbing. This 700-meter line lies just right of *Mai Piu Così* on Tsaranoro Atsimo. This was also the first route of such difficulty opened from the bottom with a Ryobi gas-powered drill.

Mike Turner, Louise Thomas, Steve Meyers and Grant Farquar (UK) repeated many routes in September and opened the much-sought-after north face of the Karambony. From September 15-22, they established *Always The Sun*, which lies between the *Rainboto* pillar and *Aliens* gully. Difficulties up to 7c+ were unexpectedly concentrated on the second half of the climb.

Probably the last major route of the season was opened from October 8-17 by another Swiss team of Dennis Burdet, Régis Dubois and Damien Ruggieri. *Taoka Gasy* (the local Malagasy ethyl alcohol, heavily absorbed by locals and some visitors) has 15 pitches plus 130 meters of climbing/scrambling to the top. Seven of the pitches are 7a or harder, with a crux of 7b+. The same Swiss team put up *Le Catta Marrant* on the west face of Pic Dondy on the other side of the valley facing Tsaranoro; they were accompanied by Christian Delaroche, who had already made an attempt on the face (nine pitches, V+ max) in 1998. Despite some lichen, they found very beautiful friction slabs and some impressive grooves on the upper part. They confirmed the quality of the face and the big potential of the large western face of Dondy. *Le Catta Marrant* is

Francisco Blanco on pitch 4 (5.12c) of Mora Mora.
CRAIG LUEBBEN

a very beautiful 23-pitch route of moderate difficulty with only a few 6a sections. However, protection is scarce.

In 1998, with my daughter, Badria (Baba), I put up *Baba Kely* to the right of *Alien I*. The route has four pitches up to V+.

GILLES GAUTIER, *France*

Tsaronoro, Bravo Les Filles. Nancy Feagin, Kath Pyke, Beth Rodden (who had never placed a piece of pro or climbed a big wall) and I, along with Greg Epperson (photographer) and Kevin Thaw (film team rigger) and Michael Brown and Rob Raker as the film team arrived at our base camp, located within an hour's walk of the Tsaranoro massif, on June 23. We noticed one particularly nice-looking wall with a separate summit to the right of the main formation that didn't have a single route up it, so we set our sights on climbing this wall. On June 24, we began the first pitch of the route. Since we were four climbers, we split up into two teams of two. Kath and I formed one team and Nancy and Beth formed the other. The lower part of the wall started out fairly low angle, but after the first few pitches, the angle of the wall gradually became steeper and the climbing more difficult. Since there were very few cracks in which to place natural protection, our main forms of protection were bolts placed on the lead.

By the time we reached pitch 6, the climbing went from 5.10d to 5.11c. Pitch 7 (5.12c) was even steeper, the climbing was more difficult and it was harder to find edges of rock to hang my sky-hooks on and drill the protection bolts. By the time we had reached pitch 8, Beth had to leave for a competition back in the States, so Kath, Nancy and I continued to equip the last five pitches to the top. Our goal was to climb the entire route from the ground up while placing all the protection bolts on the lead. Once the route was equipped, we would try to free climb the entire route from ground to top.

As it turned out, we finished equipping the route with only one day left before leaving the Tsaranoro area. Up to that point, I had free climbed every pitch of the route except pitch 8. On the last day, Nancy and I rappelled down to pitch 8 and I began the process of working out a complicated sequence of moves. This pitch starts out on thin face holds, then follows up a finger crack until the crack peters out into a steep, shallow groove. After

Nancy Feagin on pitch 7, Bravo Les Filles. KATH PYKE

The Tsaranaro Massif, showing 1. Bravo Les Filles (Feagin-Hill-Pyke, 1999). *2.* The Zoze Wall (Haden-Koyogagi-Libecki, 1999). Life in a Fairy Tale *(Luebben-Luebben, 1999) takes the left-hand skyline.* MIKE LIBECKI

trying every possible solution I could imagine to get past this blank section of rock for over two hours, I finally found a way to free climb past the crux. After working out each move on the pitch, I tried to link the whole sequence together twice, but both times, I ran out of strength on the last few moves before the end. After having spent nearly 15 days climbing, hauling, jumaring, rappelling and drilling more than 50 protection bolts, my body was thrashed. Nonetheless, during the remaining hours of daylight, Nancy and I continued free climbing up the last five pitches of the route (5.12b, 5.11b, 5.10c, 5.10d, 5.10a). At the end of the day, Nancy, Kath, Rob and I free-soloed up the last 300 feet to the summit of the Tsaranoro formation. While watching the sun set over the vast desert highlands of the Andringitra mountains, we all felt a great sense of peace and satisfaction at having climbed such a superb route, *Bravo Les Filles* (5.12c/AO or 5.13d, 13 pitches), probably the most difficult rock climb ever put up by a team of women.

LYNN HILL

Karambony, Sakay, Tsaranoro, The Zoze Wall, and Other New Routes. On July 8, Jim Haden and I arrived in Antananarivo, Madagascar. Within 20 minutes we were slapped in the face with the fact that we had no agenda or local contact. I had planned to have us take on the improvised adventure to add some spice; it started the moment we stepped through the Customs doors. We thought about contacting Tana Des Lezards, a local outfitter and guide service (partly owned by climber Gilles Gautier in Madagascar) who had taken most climbers to the destined climbing areas. Instead, we thought we would find a local with a nice 4 x 4 vehicle to take us there. After several days driving south and getting a local's point of view (amazing), we arrived in the last civilized town of Ambavalao, where we stayed for a couple days, as it happened to be Madagascar's wine capitol.

After stocking up on wine ($1 a bottle at most), we headed toward Mt. Tsaranoro. On the way in, we stopped for a couple of weeks at some nice domes about 11 miles north of Tsaranoro. Here we completed two nice first ascents on unnamed formations: *The Eyes of the Owl* (5.11+, 700'), and *Devil's Dust* (5.9 A1, 1,200'). The free climbing was fun, but we really we wanted to do some awesome longer routes near the amazing Tsaranoro.

About this time, Misako Koyonagi, one of Japan's top women climbers, arrived to meet us, and we proceeded to complete some top-notch new routes. First we made the first ascent of the northeast face of Mt. Karambony, a huge tombstone-like formation to the right of Tsaranoro, with the route *Sakai Wall* (VI 5.10 A3+, 1,400'). (Sakai is a Madagascar special hot sauce.) This route contained one of the best pitches I never imagined, a 190-foot pitch of knifeblades, beaks, rurps, heads and spice. After the pitch was fixed, it was so steep you had to lower out 100-plus feet to jug up. The three of us also completed *The Zoze Wall* (VI 5.10 A3+, 1,800') on the right side of Tsaranoro (Zoze is the name of a local who became our friend, mostly because of our pancakes and coffee). This route offered a variety of beautiful climbing from vertical chimneys and hard face climbing to splitter finger cracks. Jim and I ended our climbing venture with an attempt of *Norspace* (5.11c/d), which goes almost up the center of Tsaranoro. We bailed just a few pitches from the top, as my fingers were close to igniting (Jim didn't want to hear me cry anymore) after having enjoyed its best pitches.

Our same guide who showed up to take us back to the airport several hundred miles to the north had us stop by his house. No wonder he had a brand new, totally loaded 4 x 4 safari vehicle (the nicest vehicle we saw the whole time on the island). He was Madagascar royalty with a mansion, servants, guards, 400 rose bushes, a prize-winning garden, silver and gold attire for his home, feather beds, you name it. We even drank 15-year-old bottles of French Bourdeax with our lobsters. Never did ask how he got his money.

MIKE LIBECKI*

*Supported in part by a grant from the AAC

Tsaranoro Atsimo, Southeast Spur, Life in a Fairy Tale. In September, Mark Wilford, Silvia and Craig Luebben and non-climbers Lane Ahern and Dhasa Bishop traveled to the Tsaranoro Massif in southern Madagascar. The climbers ascended three classic Tsaranoro routes, including the fabulous 1,800-foot *Out of Africa* (6c+). Unfortunately, Mark had to leave after only two weeks, but the Luebbens stayed and began equipping a new 1,600-foot route up the Massif's southeast skyline, drilling bolts on lead. Though they carried a large rack, they found placements for only three stoppers on the entire route. Most of the pitches were long, often requiring the full length of their 200-foot lead rope.

Using a Bosch drill with a solar panel to recharge their batteries, the two drilled more than 140 bolts in seven days, using fixed ropes to regain their high point each day. Though some claim there can be no adventure with so many bolts on a route, putting up the route turned out to be quite an adventure. Each placement was drilled from sketchy stances or hook placements, which is extremely strenuous work, and 30-foot falls were often possible with the drill in hand. Plus, there was constant doubt that the pitches above would go. The lack of crack systems in the Tsaranoro has forced almost all the free routes to require many bolts.

While camped at the base of the wall, the group was serenaded by drums and chants from the tribes in the valley below and lemurs in the surrounding forests. After the route was drilled, they took a reprieve, visiting nearby rain forests and the powerful Indian Ocean. Then they returned, hoping to free climb the route, with only one day remaining before their departure. The climb, which they named *Life in a Fairy Tale* for their surreal experience in the beautiful valley, turned out to be very continuous, with seven pitches out of ten being 5.11+ in difficulty (later verified by a British team that made the second ascent). The route was mostly fun and thoughtful slab climbing, with a few bulges to keep the climbers honest. The Luebbens freeclimbed their route to the top, then cleared their fixed ropes and headed home. In a touching moment, as they left the Massif, the villagers they had camped beside early in the trip came out to say goodbye.

CRAIG LUEBBEN

COMMONWEALTH OF INDEPENDENT STATES (C.I.S.)

Our special thanks to Vladimir Kopylov (http://mountains.tos.ru) of the Russian Mountaineering Federation for his invaluable help on this section.

RUSSIA

CAUCASUS

Kiukiurtliu, Northwest Face, Lukashvilly Route. From August 21-27, a team of the Moscow Mountaineering Federation led by Alexander Abramov and comprising N. Vlasov, L. Dorfman, O. Milenin and I. Turchaninov climbed the 1981 Lukashvilly Route on the northwest face of Kiukiurtliu (4639m). Kiukiurtliu is situated in the Elbrus group; the ascent is one of the most difficult routes of the Caucasus. The team climbed during bad weather with a lot of snowfall, fog and cold. The route goes along the left part of the headwall on completely vertical terrain. The rock face is about 1000 meters high with a very steep average incline. The problem of this face is that the rock is not very hard and in order to make good belay points it is necessary to use long, specially-made pitons of 15 or even 20 centimeters.

The same team had tried to climb a new route on the face in December, 1999, but the weather conditions were very terrible. The team spent more than a week waiting for better weather, but received only deep snow and fog.

VLADIMIR SHATAEV, *Russian Mountaineering Federation*

Mt. Western Doppah, Northeast Face/Northeast Ridge. From July 21-27, a team from the Moscow mountain club Strannik ("pilgrim") comprised of V. Zadokhin, leader; V. Doolnev, M. Borschev, V. Polivko, A. Filipov and P. Yatsenko established a new route via the right part of the northeast face/northeast ridge of Mt. Western Doppah (4389m). The route goes along the right-hand side of the 600-meter buttress, where the climbers encountered a lot of small waterfalls and wet rock. Mt. Western Doppah is in the Digoria region; it is part of the Suganskiy range of the Central Caucasus and is part of the Kabardino-Balkaria Republic (the Besengi region is to the west). The area has not been visited much in the last ten years.

VLADIMIR SHATAEV, *Russian Mountaineering Federation*

Mt. Karatosh, showing the 1999 Salin-Slobodchikov-Ziatkov route. Photo courtesy of VLADIMIR KOPYLOV

Mt. Karatash, North Face, New Route. Mt. Karatash is situated in the northeast part of the North Chuyskiy crest in the Aktru Valley of the Altai range. Organized by the sport committee of the town of Biysk, a team led by A. Afanasiev and comprising N. Ziatkov, A. Salin and I. Slobodchikov put up a new route (6A) in the center of the north face of Mt. Karatash. The route was 1030 meters long on a steep rock face. Ropes were fixed from May 3-4, and the route was climbed from May 6-10. The route is composed of three almost vertical rock buttresses. The mountain still has the potential for about five more hard new routes.

VLADIMIR SHATAEV, *Russian Mountaineering Federation*

Mt. Shkhara, North Face, New Route. Mt. Shkhara (5068m) lies in the Besengi region of the Central Caucasus. Valery Shamalo and Robert Krymskiy from St.

The north face of Shkhara, showing 1. J. G. Cockin (5A, 1888). 2. A Sheynov, solo (1988). 3. I. Kraynov (5B, 1983). 4. The Bottle Route (Shamalo-Krymskiy, 1999). 5. Unknown (to West Summit, 5057m). 6. A. Blankovskiy (6A, 1980). Photo courtesy of VLADIMIR KOPYLOV

Petersburg climbed a new route via the north face through the so-called "Bottle" from July 22-27. The route on the 1500-meter snow/ice face climbs along very steep rock and ice slopes in the shape of a bottle. During the climb, in the lower part of the face, a small avalanche caught the group, but they were not hurt. They took a few short falls on the fixed rope and were hit a few times by rockfall. The beginning of the steep rock face had a waterfall section that soaked the climbers.

VLADIMIR SHATAEV, *Russian Mountaineering Federation*

KYRGYZSTAN

KYRGYSKY ALATAU

Ala Archa National Park

Korona, North Face of First Tower, Solo Dream. From May 6-9, Alexander Ruchkin established the route *Solo Dream* (Russian grade 5B, or 6a A4, 600m) on the north face of the First Tower of Korona (4810m) in the Ala Archa National Park. Korona lies at the highest end of the Aksay Glacier. The north face is very difficult, and the First Tower dominates the others. There are now six routes on the First Tower; three, including *Solo Dream*, have had only one ascent. Many brave men tried repeating the Kalugin Route to the top. But all of them were unsuccessful. Indistinct crack systems and the steepness of the wall turned back all climbers.

The route *Solo Dream* consists of 12 pitches on the top section of the wall (600m), which is steep enough so that after snowfall it is not covered by snow. The average steepness of rock was 74 degrees. The steepness of the main part was 86 degrees. The starting weight of the rucksack was 30 kilos. Small thin hooks and technical Friends were very popular on this route because there are many incipient cracks.

ALEXANDER RUCHKIN, *Russia*

Korona, North Face, New Route. The north face of Korona ("the Crown") Peak (4855m) is a 900-meter wall with no routes easier than 5 on the Russian scale. The wall stretches east to west for 1.5 kilometers and has seven routes. On January 22, Alexander Ruchkin, Dmitry Grekov and Andrey Puchinin put up another route, in winter. The 900-meter route was given 5B on the Russian scale (5.10 A1) and has an average steepness of 74 degrees.

We wanted to establish a new climb and make a film. To save weight, but at the risk of making an open bivy in winter, we didn't take sleeping bags, stoves, portaledges or extra food. We took pitons and a small drill kit just in case. We found ourselves under the wall after a 40-minute walk from the Nauka Hut (3700m) in the Ak-Say Gorge. We started climbing at dawn. Dima and I climbed together, resting only when Andrey, the videographer, climbed up the fixed rope. Sometimes we gave him advice about how and when to make the film. This made him cross, and he would threaten to give us the camera. Mixed climbing together with steep 75- to 95-degree ice in narrow goulottes make the route impressive and interesting. In comparison, this route is more difficult than the 1976 (Henry) Barber route on Free Korea Peak. We climbed the route in a day, then made our descent under the bright full moon. The route was called the *Mobile Route* (V 5.10 A1, 900m). And we were called the mobile guys,

The 900-meter north face of Korona, showing 1. The Col Route (two variants, both 4A). 2. F. Popov (5B, 1976). 3. I. Plotnikov (5B, 1995). 4. I. Smirnov (5B, 1962). 5. Mobile Route (Grekov-Puchinin-Ruchkin, 5B, 1999). 6. Solo Dream (Ruchkin, 5B, 1999). 7. K. Kaliugin (5B, 1982). 8. I. Plotnikov (5A, 1995). NIKOLAI CHTCHETCHNIKOV

for the risk of spending a winter night on the wall.

ALEXANDER RUCHKIN, *Russia*

Free Korea Peak, North Face Direct, Previously Unreported. From February 23-27, 1997, Alexander Ruchkin and Andrey Puchinin established the North Face Direct route (6A A3 +, 900m) on the north face of Free Korea Peak (4740m). The route takes a direct line up a weakness in the wall between the Bezzubkin and Mishljaev routes, and then along on narrow 90-degree ice. It is interrupted by two rock sections in the center with vertical walls and roofs. There is a lot of ice, but on the rock there are few cracks for reliable protection. Bad weather delayed us under the beginning of a steep section for two days.

ALEXANDER RUCHKIN, *Russia*

Free Korea, North Face, New Route. The north face of Svobodnaya Korea (Free Korea Peak, 4740m) holds ice and mixed routes of more than a kilometer in length. Under the leadership of Michail Michailov, our team of four (including Andrey Puchinin, Alexander Gubaev and Vitaliy Akimov) decided to attempt the first ascent of a difficult route on Free Korea. We

The 900-meter north face of Svobodnaya Korea (Free Korea Peak), showing 1. Zaharov (6A, 1992). 2. A. Shvab (5B, 1982). 3. B. Studenin (6A, 1962). 4. A. Kustovskiy (6A, 1962). 5. S. Semiletkin (6B, 1988). 6. J. Popenko (6A, 1975). 7. V. Bezzubkin (6A, 1969). 8. A. Ruchkin (6A, winter 1997). 9. L. Myshliaev (5B,1961). 10. V. Bagaev (5B, 1974). 11. Henry Barber (US) (5B, 1976, solo). 12. G. Andreev (5A, 1959). 13. George Lowe (US) (5A, 1976, solo). 14. Akimov-Gubaev-Puchinin (1999). 15. Unknown. ALEXANDER RUCHKIN

attempted this new route from November 15-27, during the time of the coldest freeze. Summer is a dangerous time to climb on this face as there is much rock and ice fall. The very coldest temperature during the climb was -32°C. Each evening the condensation in the portaledge would grow to two to three centimeters and each morning when we lit our stoves we were given a most unwelcome shower. For the entire climb we were faced with very bad weather and, not by design, ended up staying on the wall for a total of 14 days. The last three days, we were very hungry because our food had run out and we only consumed hot water and sugar tablets. All of us lost between five and seven kilograms during the climb.

In the beginning of the year 2000 we felt prepared to attempt a fast climb of a new route on the north face of Peak Korona (see above). The winter climbs of our team show that on these walls there exist many new routes that still have not seen a first ascent. We believe that there is not one climbing team that can't test their mettle to the utmost on these kilometer-long walls and perhaps even establish new routes of their own. Good luck to all future climbers!

ANDREY PUCHININ, *Russia*

Peak Semionova-Tienshanskogo, New Route. Peak Semionova-Tienshanskogo (4875m) is the highest peak of the Kyrgyzskiy Alatau. From July 24-25, Elena Nagovitsina, Tamara Zueva, Alexander Afanasiev and Dmitry Aliadvin put up a new route (5B) via the left spur of the west face.

VLADIMIR SHATAEV, *Russian Mountaineering Federation*

PAMIR-ALAI

Lailak Region

Ak-Su North Peak, North Face, New Route, Previously Unreported. From August 4-12, 1996, Alexander Ruchkin and Alexander Odintsov established The Direct North Face (Russian Grade 6B, 5.11 A3+) on the north face of Ak-Su North (5217m). Practically nobody believed an ascent up the center of the wall was possible. That's why our win was so pleasant. It seemed that the wall was absolutely smooth, without any relief. Micro-relief was observed only after multiple and detailed examinations. The idea was born a long time ago and we thought it over many times. After we had climbed five different routes on the wall, we collected real experience and a kind of data base.

Big wall strategy was used during the ascent. Eight nights were spent on the wall and one on the top. There were no ledges on the route. The climbing was very precise, almost jewellering, because there were many "live" stones on the route, and at any moment we needed to think about our friend below. We climbed what cracks we could find, which were hardly any. We ascended the center of wall by sky hooks, sometimes drilling holes for them. If we were lucky and found a crack, it was flaring and shallow. Bolts could hold only body weight but not a fall. All protection points were made with Petzl 12-mm screws. We wanted to live badly. Thank you, Petzl. The route is logical and beautiful.

ALEXANDER RUCHKIN, *Russia*

Karavshin Region

Karavashin Region, Various Ascents. After a frustrating visit to the neighboring Lailak region where poor weather stopped us from attempting any big objectives, Mark Pretty and I travelled to the superb granite towers of the Karavashin region. Here we set up camp on August 1 in the Ak-Su Valley with John and Anne Arran, the other half of our British team. Among the four of us we made nine new routes in the valley up to 1300 meters long (all figures are the total sum of the climbing) and 5.12 in difficulty. Of particular note was John and Anne's route *The Philosopher's Stone* (5.12b, 1200m), which takes the quartz veins and overlap right of *The Great Game* (Pritchard-Green, 1997) on the "Wall of Dykes." The first 250 meters of this was fixed over three days and included the two crux pitches, which involved long runouts above sky hooks. The remainder of the route took one and a half days of sustained climbing, including a junction with *The Great Game* for its crux pitch.

While participants in the Russian championships taking place in the area suffered on 12-day repeats of existing routes, Mark and I climbed numerous new routes in conventional, fast, one-day style. We also made two more ascents spread out over one and a half days with *The Big Joke* (5.12a, 1000m), which climbs the Central Pyramid (Pik 3850) 400 meters left of the

Slesova (left) and the "Wall of Dykes," showing 1. The Last Laugh *(Parnell-Pretty, 1999)*. 2. The Great Game *(Pritchard-Green, 1997)*. 3. The Philosopher's Stone *(Arran-Arran, 1999)*. IAN PARNELL

upper section of *Black Magic* (Harvey-Donahue, 1997) and *The Last Laugh* (5.12a, 750m), just to the right of the waterfall on the left-hand side of the "Wall of Dykes."

After Mark departed early due to illness, I free soloed *The Isolationist* (5.10, 1300m) on the east face of Kotin in five hours of climbing (13 hours camp-to-camp). For the nine first ascents, we placed a total of four pegs and one hand-drilled bolt, a contrast to many of the recent routes by European visitors. The team eventually departed on September 1, a week earlier than planned, due to an invasion by Taliban guerillas from Afghanistan who kidnapped a Japanese party trekking in the area.

IAN PARNELL, *United Kingdom*

Peak 4810, East Face, New Route. Alexander Pogorelov and Vitaly Polohov from Rostov-on-Don established a new route (6B, 1100m) on the east face of Peak 4810, fixing the initial pitches of the route from August 4-11, then climbing it from August 14-22. All four routes on the east face of 4810 (Vedernikov, 1989; Sitnik, 1989, Klionov, 1993; Odintsov, 1995) are on the right-hand side of the face. The Pogorelov Route takes a line close to the center of the face.

While we were preparing the route, we noticed that the most dangerous part of the face is

The east face of 4810, showing 1. Southeast Ridge. 2. A. Pogorelov (6B, 1999). 3. A. Odintsov (6B, 1995). 4. A. Klionov (6B, 1995). 5. M. Sitnik (6B, 1989). 6. V. Vedernikov (6A, 1989).
IVAN SAMOYLENKO

on the left-hand side, where the face is not as steep and there are some shelves with snow. Snow melting on these shelves results in stone fall. We spent several days scoping the face with binoculars, looking for a possible route with the maximum number of cracks but without success. We decided to start in the center of the east face in an inside corner, then move left from the overhanging rocks traversing toward a series of roofs. It was very inconvenient to fix rope diagonally in the overhanging part, but it was the only hope to climb the route. In the upper part, overhanging rock protected us from rock fall.

Andrew Zavgorodniy and Anatoliy Popov helped fix the initial pitches. After fixing 350 meters (seven pitches), we experienced two days of extremely bad weather with snowfall. For this reason, we came down, as we did not think it would be possible to climb this face in such conditions. The first part of the route is a combination of vertical and overhanging rock with only a few cracks. We used a lot of skyhooks. It was difficult climbing (VI, A3-A4). The second part of the route was climbed free (IV-VI). In the lower part at the edge of the inside corner and face there were very loose rocks—too loose to use skyhooks or get good gear. We had to move the loose rocks before we could get any protection.

As with the two previous years, the weather was very unsettled. During our climb, it rained every day in the afternoon, after which the entire face was covered with verglas. When the sunshine warmed the face, the ice would fall down. We spent nine nights on the route (one night during fixing). On August 22 at 6 p.m., we reached the ridge. By this point, there were no longer any climbers in either the Ak-Su or Kara-Su valleys.

ALEXANDER POGORELOV, *Russia*

Asan, Stars and Stripes Forever, and 4810, West Face. Roxanna Brock and Brian McCray brought home the bronze, placing third in the International Mountaineering Trophy big wall climbing competition. The event, hosted by the Russian Mountaineering Federation from July

The north and west faces of 4810 and Asan. Routes on 4810 are as follows: 1. M. Sitnik (descent route) (5B, 1986) 2. A. Kritsuk (6A, 1988). 3. V. Igolkin (6A, 1990). 4. A. Rusiaev (6A, 1988). 5. A. Voronov (6A, 1988). 6. G. Kopejka (6A, 1988). 7. S. Ovcharenko (6A, 1988). SERGEI KOVALOV

25-August 20, took place in the Karavshin region. The pair was the only American team to compete with many of Russia's best big wall climbers. Also present were teams from France, Slovenia, the Ukraine and Kyrgyzstan. It was necessary for each team to climb two routes chosen from a list of approximately 20. Scores for each route were based on altitude, difficulty, number of repeats and length. The judges evaluated and scored new routes. Final scores were primarily based on the route scores and speed of ascent.

For their first climb, Roxanna and Brian established a new route, *Stars and Stripes Forever* (a.k.a. *Free Willy*, 5.9 A4). It ascends a dihedral system on the right side of Asan (4230m). A small, bottomed-out seam exits the dihedral and leads to the 70-meter, A4 crux, diagonalling up and left across a golden headwall. The 15-pitch route took the team four days to complete (with one day waiting out bad weather) and follows a crack system its entire length (900m). Only two bolts were added at belays.

The nine-day ascent of the Sakharov Route* on Peak 4810 involved 47 pitches and the climbers were inundated with rain and snow daily. The route climaxed in a snowstorm, which stranded the pair in their portaledge for 40 hours.

Radios were provided as part of the competition, allowing the team to report daily to base camp and the judges. After the storm, the pair was told, via the radios, that they were only three pitches from the top. With renewed psyche they were up early the next morning in below-freezing temperatures, peeling frozen ropes off the rock and hammering iced carabiners open. Seven pitches later the storm, lack of ice tools, fatigue, heavy haulbags and altitude caught up with them. Although they were able to see the summit only three pitches away, they gave in and descended the route. A two-day descent, culminating with ten rappels down an icy couloir, left them with a feeling similar to the intestinal funk they experienced often during their stay.

Winnings from the Moonstone Mountain Equipment People's Epic Contest primarily funded the trip to Kyrgyzstan. Being notified only three weeks prior to the competition, the couple initially thought the "epic" involved planning such an expedition on such short notice. As the trip progressed and more hurdles were added, the two joked about winning an epic. At 14,000 feet in a serious blizzard, they struggled to speak with Russian judges who spoke little English. Each day of climbing was a race to finish as many pitches as possible before the rain, sleet and/or snow hit them. Immodium dosing was a daily ritual. The pair carried their entire iron pin rack up less-than-vertical terrain because they were not provided a gear list. Because the routes followed no crack system and no topos were supplied, the team was continually lost while climbing. They dropped their haulbag off the wrong side of the mountain because they didn't have any trail information. On Asan, they climbed an extra 500 feet up and back down fourth-class terrain with haulbags because they had vague descent information. The descent rappel followed a 2,000-foot waterfall of snowmelt.

The two consider themselves lucky to have survived the experience and say they came back to America with a renewed sense of patriotism. Brian summed up the adventure well: "We were really psyched; it was the first epic that had ever been given to us."

ROXANNA BROCK *and* BRIAN MCCRAY

Slesova, West-Southwest Face, Fiamma d'Oriente. Andrea Zanetti, Cristoforo Groaz and Giorgio Pancheri (Italy) opened a 1300-meter route, *Fiamma d'Oriente* (7 A3+), on the West-Southwest face of Pik Slesova (Russian Tower, 4240 m) in the Ak-Su Valley. The climb had 33 pitches, and the team spent a total of 12 days on the wall, topping out on July 17. They

---

*It is traditional for routes in the CIS to bear the name of the leader of the first ascent party. It appears this route is known as the Kritsuk Route in the CIS (see topo on page 313).

rapped the route of ascent. The route was dedicated to the alpinists Alessandro Chemelli and Dario Bampi, who died on Mont Blanc on July 18, 1999.

ANTONELLA CICOGNA, *Italy*

Slesova, Fiamma d'Oriente, Second Ascent. Three weeks after the establishment of the *Fiamma d'Oriente* by an Italian group (see above), the route was repeated by I. Pekhterev (leader), D. Vlaznev, I. Vlaznev, V. Kazartsev and V. Lavrenenko in six and a half days, from August 1-7. After climbing the route, the Russians and Italians conferred and found that their respective ascents varied at two points in the center of the route. Apart from its difficulty, this face has another characteristic: lack of water. The first snow is found only near the summit. Therefore, the Russians fixed the route for several days prior to launching.

VLADIMIR SHATAEV, *Russian Mountaineering Federation*

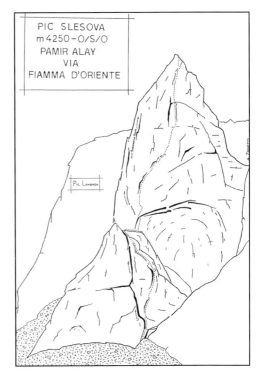

PIC SLESOVA
m 4250 – O/S/O
PAMIR ALAY
VIA
FIAMMA D'ORIENTE

Pic Lambada

Asan, Forever Yak, Previously Unreported. In July, 1998, Martin Waldhör and I spotted an obvious dihedral and crack system that leads above an initial slab straight through the south face of Asan to finish high up on the southwest arête left of the summit. It looked impressive and it was unclimbed* so we moved our small tent onto a nice meadow about an hour's walk below the bottom of the face. On July 17, we started our first attempt only to be stopped on the second pitch when we were forced to hand-drill bolts on a very wet slab. We reached a crack system in the afternoon and rapped off. After a rest day, during which we were visited by a herd of hundreds of yaks, we climbed the route in ten hours and returned to our tents nearly 17 hours after leaving. *Forever Yak* (IV 5.10, 600m) has excellent sustained 5.9 to 5.10 climbing, though at times a bit runout. We removed the eight bolts on pitch 2 to use for belays higher up. We descended the normal route on the other side of the mountain.

JÖRG STRASSNER, *Germany*

WEST KOKSHAAL-TAU

Kotur Glacier Region, Various Ascents. Guides Pat Littlejohn (U.K.), Alan Delizee (France) and Vladimir Komissarov (Kyrgyzstan), with Dr. Jane Whitmore, Alan Dunworth, Richard Smith, Ingrid Crossland, Christopher Clarke and Joanna da Silva, approached the Kotur

---

*The Ak-Su and Kara-Su valleys have seen extensive climbing for nearly two decades. It is unclear whether this was in fact a new route.

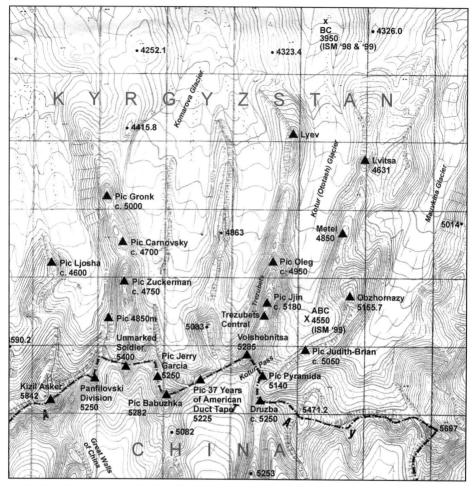

Peaks of the western end of the West Kokshaal-Tau. Peak 37 Years of American Duct Tape is correctly called Peak 52 Years of American Duct Tape. Map courtesy of PAT LITTLEJOHN

Glacier region by six-wheel-drive vehicle (an ex-Russian army vehicle) and set up Base Camp at 3950 meters on a flat, grassy spot below the snout of the Kotur (or Ototash) Glacier. Advanced Base Camp was established at 4550 meters some four hours up the glacier and from here, peaks were attempted alpine style in three climbing teams. Going clockwise around the head of the glacier from east to west, summits climbed were:

• Pik Obzhornazy (5155.7m). This peak had been climbed by Russians in the 1980s. We took the same route via a shallow spur on the west side (PD).

• Pik Judith-Brian (5050m). Possibly climbed before, but we made a new route via the east ridge (AD+) characterized by a big leaning gendarme (which proved too hard to re-ascend, forcing a descent by the north face).

• Pik Pyramida (5140m). This peak had been climbed by Russians in the 1980s. It is an elegant but straightforward snow peak at the head of the glacier, left of the Kotur Pass; we climbed it via the northwest ridge (PD).

• Volshebnitsa (White Witch, 5285m). The queen of the group. A stunning, technical peak that we climbed by the north ridge (D+) via ice runnels up to 75 degrees, then a spectacular knife-edged crest for the mountain's first ascent.

• Pik Jjin (5180m). Highest of the Trezubets ("Three Teeth"). There are in fact four "teeth," one of which was climbed by Russians in the 1980s; one remains unclimbed. Pik Jjin was tackled by a prominent ice ramp on the east face followed by a corniced ridge (AD).

• Pik Oleg (4950m). This was the most northerly peak of the ones we climbed and the lowest point of the Trezubets. We climbed it via the north flank (PD); it had probably been done before.

PAT LITTLEJOHN, *United Kingdom*

PAMIR/TIEN SHAN

All Four 7000ers and Khan Tengri in One Season. I departed Italy on July 2 and returned August 28. The following peaks were climbed in sequence. In the Pamir, Andrey Molotov, Denis Urubko and I summitted Pik Lenin (7134m) on July 15 four days after arriving at Base Camp. It was the first ascent of the season. Pik Korzhenevskaya (7105m) was then climbed on July 27 in three days (Moro, Mario Curnis, Molotov, Urubko). It was the first ascent of the season. On August 8, after four days of climbing, Moro, Curnis, Molotov and Urubko reached the summit of Pik Kommunism (7495m). It was the first ascent of the mountain in two years.

After a move to the Tien Shan, Moro, Curnis, Molotov and Urubko climbed Khan Tengri (6995m) on August 19 in 48 hours. Then, on August 25, Molotov and Urubko climbed Pik Pobeda (7434m) in four days. Moro came down with dysentery and abandoned the climb the day before the summit.

This was not the first time that the four 7000ers and Khan Tengri were climbed in one season by one group. A Russian group in the days of the former Soviet Union managed the same feat. I don't remember the names, but I met one of the team members. He told me that they had been sponsored by the Communist government and their military club and that their climb had been easier than ours because the five mountains were at that time in one country (USSR) and they used helicopters to go to each base camp. We used cars, helicopters, buses, jeeps and foot to climb the five mountains that are now in three different republics (Kazakstan, Kyrgyzstan, Tadjikistan). In Tadjikistan there is a war (both civil and with Afghanistan) and it is very difficult to move around. Ten years before us, Anatoli Boukreev and Rinat Khaibullin climbed four of the five in one season, but this, too, was in the days of the USSR.

SIMONE MORO, *Italy*

PAKISTAN

8000ers, Increase of Royalty Fees. The Pakistan Ministry of Tourism announced that for the year 2000, the fee for 8000-meter peaks would be raised, from US $7,500 for five members and $700 dollars for every additional member, to US $9,000 for seven climbers and $3,000 per additional member. For K2, the royalty was raised from US $9,000 dollars for five climbers and $1,000 dollars per additional member to US $12,000 for seven climbers plus

$3,000 per additional member

Aziz Ahmed Khan, the Director of Operations for the Ministry of Tourism, said the Ministry now ensured that all the expedition requests should be finalized in 90 days.

ASEM MUSTAFA AWAN, *The Nation, Pakistan*

HINDU RAJ

Hindu Raj, UIAA International Expedition Training Camp. The 23 young participants from 13 different countries (and all five continents) of the UIAA International Expedition Training Camp started their expedition on September 3. The expedition was organized by Jean-Claude Marmier, then-President of the Comité de l'Himalaya et des Expéditions Lointaines of the FFME. Taking into account the number of participants, a suitable area was needed that could accommodate a dozen rope teams on a large selection of varied and unclimbed objectives. With his great experience of the mountains of the world, Bernard Domenech knew where to find such an area: the Hindu Raj massif, lying to the east of the chain of the Hindu Kush. A rarely visited massif, it is today one of the rare areas where there remain many unclimbed summits of 5000 to 6000 meters. Big granite pillars, couloirs and great narrow ridges were present in the dozens, allowing for something for all tastes and all levels. The area is also very attractive because access is only three days from Islamabad to Base Camp.

The young mountaineers were on their first expedition. The objectives of the Camp included the organization, techniques and logistics of an expedition in a distant country as well as alpinism itself. The climbing teams, most of which had been agreed upon by advance e-mail exchanges (vive l'internet!), opened up a "véritable festival de premières": 14 new routes in total, which were as often on rock as on ice or mixed terrain. The mountains carried little snow—last winter was dry. The weather was exceptional: three perfect weeks, almost without interruption. The conditions became difficult, very different from those that Domenech experienced the year before. The main couloirs quickly became very exposed to stonefall.

Everyone chose the route that suited him/her. At Base Camp, Emmanuel Pellissier, supported by Bernard Domenech and Victor Gryshchenko (Ukraine), orchestrated the climbing. Everyone, then, could rely on the counsel of experienced guides. Thus conditions were right so that all could acquire experience on virgin terrain—remote, but with an acceptable level of safety.

Ascents achieved during the camp were as follows (all routes are new except Pashchoshi):
• Pt. 4980m via the Northeast Couloir (Couloir du Grand-Père) and East Ridge (ADinf., 1000m), M. Peloquin (CND) and G. Coubat (F), September 12.
• Pt. 4380m (first point on the northwest arête of Pt. 4980m) via the northwest arête (Dsup 5c A0, 350m), B. Drouillat and O. Mansiot (F), September 25.
• Col 4800m (between Pt. 5250m and Chikari) via the couloir on the north face (D 45° 3, 800m), M. Peloquin (CND) and G. Coubat (F), R. Wesley (NZ) and C. Argo (CND)
• Col 4800m (between Pt. 5250m and Chikari) via the icefall on the north face (VI 5 ice 4c, 900m), Ildi Kiss (H) and E. Pelissier (F), September 25.
• Pt. 5400m (forked point of the northeast ridge of Chikari) via the north face (TD 75° VI, 1400m), W. Dvorak and R. Liemerth (CZ), September 17-18.
• Breche 5500m (on the north ridge of Chikari) via the east couloir (TD, 1500m, very exposed), Breserk, Kovak and Bevjk (SLO), September 16-17.

The north and east faces of Chikari and Makutchum (6191m, on the far right) as seen from Base Camp on the left bank of the Ghalsapar Glacier. The routes of the Oriental Col lie to the left; the Breche 5500 couloir lies to the right of the imposing 1800-meter pillar that reaches the principal summit (5928m). This was climbed via the well-defined col Coup de Sabre to the left of the northern peaks and via the opposite face (hidden). BERNARD DOMENECH

• Coup de Sabre (5350m) via the East Couloir (D 50°, 400m), Breserk, Kovak and Bevjk (SLO), September 12.

• Chikari (5928m), West Face (TDinf, 1200m), by two routes, one on the Coup de Sabre and another on the point to the left of Coup de Sabre, Breserk, Kovak and Bevjk (SLO), M. Peloquin (CND) and G. Coubat (F), R. Wesley (NZ), September 21-24.

• Pt. 5620m (right of Coup de Sabre) via the South Ridge (TD 5c, 300m), R. Jarvis and S. Ashworth (GB), September 21.

• Pt. 4850m ("Amman Chhish") via the North Face (AD 45°, 100m), R. Jarvis, S. Ashworth (GB) and C. Staunton (IRL), September 22.

• Breche ca. 5500m (on the east ridge of Makutchum) via the South Couloir (AD 45°, 650m), Ildi Kiss (H), E. Pellissier (F), B. Drouillat (F) and A. Norreslet (DK), attempt stopped at 5850m on the east ridge by bad rock (TDsup/EDinf mixed, 12 pitches, 350m), September 17-18.

• Pt. 4300m ("Jute Chhish") via the South Ridge (D 5c, 300m), B. Drouillat and C. Gardien (F), September 22.

• Pt. 4400m ("Nanar Peak") via the East Ridge (TDinf 5c, 400m), Ildi Kiss (H), E. Pellissier (F), Jawed Ali (PK) and O. Mansiot (F), September 22.

• Pt. 5415m via the Southwest Couloir (Dsup, 65° at exit, 1200m), C.Argo (CND) and R.Wesley (NZ), September 12-14. Repeated in one 18-hour day by Ildi Kiss (H), E. Pellissier (F), B. Drouillat (F) and A. Norreslet (DK) Pashchoshi (5508m) (from the Borum Bar Glacier) via the North Arête (AD, 600m). Repeated by V. Gryshchenko (UKR), E. Von Delft

Chushubalstering II (ca.6000m). The northwest pillar takes the main line in the center of the photo. The northeast arête of Chushubalstering is visible on the upper left skyline. BERNARD DOMENECH

(SA), S. Darmach (P), G. Quercia (I) and Ch. Rother (D) September 23.

On "la Pierre d'Orthaz," a large block on the moraine, several difficult traverses up to 6a were established, while at Base Camp, about ten top-roped pitches from 5c-7a were put up.

Numerous photographs and maps prepared the previous year by Bernard Domenech (now president of the Comité de l'Himalaya et des Expéditions Lointaines) can be found at www.expe.com.

JEAN CLAUDE MARMIER, *France*

Areri and Chuchubalstering, Various Ascents. Also in the Hindu Raj massif (see above) was a group selected from previous members of the Jeunes Alpinistes FFME. Accompanied by Emmanuel Guy, they profited from the logistics of the UIAA expedition which allowed them to explore the northern aspects of the virgin peaks Areri (5700m) and Chuchubalstering (Thui Zom, 6158m). Based out of the Aghost Bar Glacier, they accomplished a number of fine climbs. On Pt. 5560m a little to the north of the main summit of Areri, Marcel Dumas, Brice Lefèvre and Erwan Le Lann established the route *Entre l'Areri* (VI 5+ 5c, 36 pitches, 1150m) on the northeast face from September 18-23. The route followed a steep 1200-meter ice and mixed line next to a spur on the north face. The three brought a small bivouac tent but no sleeping bags with them; descent was made via a separate line. On Pt. 5800m, D. Boitard, M. Kalisz and A. Ravanel made a 23-pitch attempt (V 4+, 800m) to the right between September 21-23.

The most beautiful route taken last summer in the Nialthi Valley, and also one of the most difficult, was the Northwest Pillar of Chuchubalstering. Jérôme Thiniéres, Stéphane Benoist and Bruno Ravanat established the route *Yakamoneye* (VII 6, 1500m) to the top of the previously unclimbed West Summit from September 19-22, forgoing the main summit due to exhaustion and diminished food supplies. Their route followed thin, difficult ice to ca. 5000 meters on day 1. The main rocky section of the wall was encountered the next day, with another bivy established at a comfortable ledge at 5400 meters. On day 3 of the climb, a committing pendulum was followed by increasingly difficult ice that culminated in a 40-meter snow and ice wall up to 95 degrees with no gear. That night was spent at 5800 meters near the top seracs. The next day, the team began their descent, making 30 rappels, mainly from Abalokov threads, throughout the night.

On Chuchubalstering II (6000m), the west summit of Chuchubalstering, Y. Ponson, E. Guy, B. Jacquemot and S. Empereur climbed the west-northwest face from September 15-18. The 1600-meter effort stopped two pitches from the top and included 1300 meters before it met the west arête, which it

The north face of Chuchubalstering. JÉRÔME THINIÈRES

Bruno Ravanat and Stéphane Benoist on day 4, Yakomoneye, the northwest pillar of Chuchubalstering. JÉRÔMETHINIÈRES

joined at around 5700 meters. The northwest pillar was climbed as well. On September 21-24, the northwest face (VI 5+, mixed 6a, 800m, 26 pitches) of the northwest pillar was climbed by H. Qalizza, G. Sauget and S. Montaz-Rosset.

BERNARD DOMENECH, *France*

HINDU KUSH

"Cima Asso," First Ascent. For the third year in a row, the Club Alpino Italiano—Asso supported an expedition to Pakistan. The leader was Angelo Rusconi. The aim of the expedition was to reach an unknown valley in the mountain chain of the Hindu Kush. The people selected to the team were Luciano Giampi, Simone Rossetti, Cristian Cattivelli and Davide Valsecchi.

We started on July 28 from Gilgit driving two 4 x 4 cars to Gakuch along the Gilgit River, then passing through Iskoman towards Gugulti with the Iskoman River on the right-hand side. After choosing the porters, we started our journey on the morning of the 29th. We passed through the Handis Valley, following the Iskoman River to where it joins the Mathan Ther River. Always keeping the Mathan Ther River on the right-hand side, we walked through the valley, noticing impressive granite walls more than 1000 meters high, all easily reachable.

Crossing a bridge, we arrived at Mathan Ther village, located on a green plateau at the junction of two rivers, one from the Suncighi Valley, the other from a western region called Bhari. From the locals, we learned we were the first foreigners to have reached their village.

On July 30, we walked through the west valley to Bhari, a medium-sized village in a field close to a big green lake overlooked by two big mountains. We placed our Base Camp near the lake, at 3850 meters. Our BC was in a good position to observe the numerous peaks around us. At the lowest level of these mountains we could see widespread gravel fields beneath vertical granite walls. Many of these mountain had crests and edges covered by ice and snow. Among these was the 5100-meter peak straight above the right-hand side of the lake. We named it "Cima Asso," the name of our home town in Italy. All the members of the expedition made it to the top on August 5.

The locals showed us Kampur and Gharmush peaks, the only known peaks over 6000 meters. All the members who took part in the expedition agree that the valley is ideal for expeditions and trekking. It is possible to easily reach a comfortable base camp surrounded by granite stone walls and untouched peaks.

CLUB ALPINO ITALIANO—ASSO

BATURA MUZTAGH

Karambar Glacier Area, Various Ascents, Previously Unreported. One of the least-visited regions in the Karakoram is the northwestern part of the Batura Muztagh. After extensive investigation in Alpine and Himalayan journals, we decided on the Karambar Glacier area where there are a lot of interesting 6000-meter peaks, most of them unclimbed until our trip. The highest peak in this area (and the only 7000-meter peak) is Kampire Dior (7143m) at the head of the Karambar Glacier. First climbed in 1975 by a Japanese expedition (1976 *AAJ*, p. 549), it was the only summit of interest for many years in spite of the fact that it is located in an area with hundreds of interesting possibilities.

Dieter Rüelker, Frank Polte, Joerg Ehrlich (leader) and I started on July 28, 1998, from Berlin. We established Base Camp on August 3 on a sunny grass plateau in Karambar Ilag (3300m), where the local farmers live during summer time. The inhabitants of this small village were very friendly, and the oldest of them even remembered the last mountaineering expedition that had been here in 1977.

We spent two days in reconnaissance trips along the Karambar Glacier and the side valleys, taking photos and drawing a sketch map of the area, which is not covered by good maps and is sometimes even shown wrong on the available maps. After more reconnaissance on August 11, we established one high camp at about 4300 meters near a small glacial lake at the head of Kutshkulin Valley. East of this beautiful camp site, the main Kutshkulin Glacier turns toward an ice-covered wall that rises to a prominent summit of ca. 6000 meters (which we would later, in agreement with the local people, name Kutshkulin Sar). After some hundred meters of easy approach from our camp, the Kutshkulin Glacier becomes heavily crevassed and rugged; the first attempt by Frank and me failed at about 4600 meters after hours of crossing, climbing and traversing. Dieter and Joerg tried it the next day, reaching about 4900 meters at the north side of the glacier very close to the steep rocky walls of the neighboring mountain ridge. After one rest day, we started in the early morning and reached a platform on the glacier at about 4900 meters, where we established our second High Camp.

The weather changed completely, forcing our descent to BC in heavy snow. On August 18, we started again from Karambar Ilag to reach High Camp I and, one day later, High Camp II. We started our attempt at 2 a.m. on August 20. We crossed the bergschrund roped up, then climbed the first 200 meters on ice up to 60 degrees before reaching a snowy ridge on the icy northwest face. We climbed about 12 pitches, belaying from deadman anchors because of insecure snow conditions and the absolute pre-dawn darkness. Four more pitches over crevassed terrain led us to the saddle, a big snow plateau just below the final summit pyramid, which we reached at 8 a.m. and where we left our bivouac gear. It took us about two hours to climb the last two pitches on unconsolidated snow up to 60 degrees, with the snow conditions getting worse with every step. Breaking through a one-meter cornice, I reached the summit at about 2 p.m. Celebrating this probable first ascent, we named the mountain Kutshkulin Sar. Our altimeters showed its elevation to be between 5860 and 5990 meters— just inside the permit-free category. Due to rapidly worsening weather, we hurried to descend.

Kutshkulin Sar, with the line of first ascent (Ehrlich-Polte-Rüelker-Walter, 1998) marked. The line by Woods-Jeffrey and Keller-Thomas (1999; see below) lay more to the left on the same face.
MARKUS WALTER

We were back at camp after 19 hours of continuous climbing and one hour of searching for our snow-covered tents. We descended to BC the next day, leaving the high camps for another summit attempt at the head of Kutshkulin Glacier.

We rested at Karambar Ilag for three days of bad weather before ascending to High Camp II again. There we had to wait one more day for somewhat acceptable weather before ascending further up the Kutshkulin Glacier on August 28. We carried rock gear for the expected summit pitches on our next mountain but were surprised to gain altitude without any technical difficulties. Snow and ice up to 50 degrees led to the corniced summit, where we had a great view of the whole mountain range in beautiful weather. We rested a long time on the summit before descending to our camp. We named the peak Sax Sar ("Saxon Spire") after our home region. Though some maps show its altitude to be between 6100 and 6432 meters, we registered its altitude at 5999 meters.

Though our time was nearly over, the weather still seemed to be good, so Dieter and I tried to make a speed ascent on another nice mountain in the upper Kutshkulin area. Starting at 4 a.m., we reached the ca. 5980-meter summit at 10 a.m. after having climbed about 15 pitches of straightforward 50- to 55-degree ice. Just as we climbed onto the broad corniced summit ridge to reach the very top, the whole cornice broke off five meters away from us. We profited from this by getting a spectacular look northeastward down onto the far glacier through the new hole. The weather was incredibly good, offering a view of the High Pamirs (peaks Marx and Engels) in the far northwest to Nanga Parbat in the far southeast. To the west, the massive Koz Sar dominated the scenery. Before descending the same route, we named this third summit Yeti Sar (who knows who broke the summit cornice just before we reached it?). Then we climbed down, removed our High Camp II completely and reached

Yeti Sar (as seen from the descent on Sax Sar), with the line of first ascent (Rüelker-Walter, 1998) indicated. MARKUS WALTER

Camp I the same evening. The next day, Dieter and I carried loads from Camp I down to BC, from which we descended on August 31 with the help of the local farmers and their donkeys.

MARKUS WALTER, *Alpinclub Sachsen, Germany*

Kutshkulin Sar, Ascent. In August, a six-man international team visited the Karambar Glacier region of northern Pakistan. We were entirely self-funded. The Karambar Glacier lays at the northern limit of the Ishkoman Valley with the surrounding mountains forming the extreme western boundary of the Karakoram range. The whole region has received little attention in comparison with the widely traveled eastern Karakoram and was chosen for its new route potential on sub-6000-meter peaks.

Members Simon Woods, Jock Jeffrey, Walter Keller, Bryan Godfrey, William Cadell and Adam Thomas used Gilgit as a base from which to explore the upper reaches of the Ishkoman Valley. After organizing transport and cooks, they left Gilgit for a three-day drive to the road-head at Bad Swat. A two-day walk in gave access to Base Camp on the true right bank of the Karambar Glacier. From here, two weeks of exploration and reconnaissance of the Kutshkulin Valley (which runs due north from Karambar Ilag) ensued, the result of which was a decision to concentrate on the peaks at the head of the Kutshkulin Glacier, which runs north from the Karambar itself.

After many days reconnaissance and acclimatization, the team attempted a mountain known as Kutshkulin Sar (ca. 5900m). Following a two-day approach to the mountain via Advanced Base Camp, Camp I was established high on a ridge above a tributary of the Kutshkulin Glacier. From here, two teams comprising Woods and Jeffrey and Keller and Thomas climbed the initial slopes beyond camp to the start of the large and heavily crevassed west face, one team electing to place an intermediate camp here, the other continuing on. This face was found to be the technical crux of the ascent with much route-finding through seracs and climbing up to 80 degrees. A col to the north of Kutshkulin Sar was reached and a high camp established at the foot of the final summit pyramid. From here it was a short and relatively easy ascent for both parties, following a line over a serac barrier, across a small plateau and finally joining the upper section of the east ridge, which led quite steeply to the summit. The summit was reached on August 29.

Descent to high camp was via the same route, but a more direct line to intermediate camp was found through the seracs of the west face. From here, one team retraced the initial approach, with the other descended more easily via a small glacier to reach a point just below CI. First climbed in 1998 by a strong German team (see above), this represents the second ascent of Kutshkulin Sar via a new and completely independent line.

Although access throughout the region was generally difficult due to lean snow conditions and large and very active icefalls, much potential exists for further exploratory climbing in the Karambar Glacier area, albeit of a high standard.

SIMON WOODS, *United Kingdom*

Koz Sar, First Ascent. Ichiro Yamagata led an eight-member team from the Sendai Ichiko Alpine Club of Japan that made the first ascent of Koz Sar Peak (6677m) via a small ridge in the south face. From 5000 to 5900 meters, the climb offered a crumbly rock slab with an average angle of 70 degrees. In the last 300 meters of the route we found good rock on a few vertical sections that we were able to overcome by free climbing. But we couldn't use rock shoes due to bad conditions. Instead, we climbed the steep rock gully and slab using ice axes and crampons. Other expedition members were Takashi Ota, Manami Takahashi, Toru Nagasawa, Kazuhide Watanabe, Katsuyuki Kuriyagawa, Yasufumi Saito and Kotaro Takami.

We left Islamabad on July 13, arriving at Gilgit the same day at 11 p.m. On the 17th, we left Giligit by jeep and reached Bad Swat. The next day, we started trekking from Bad Swat to Mahtran Dan. Base Camp (3800m) was established at the foot of south ridge on July 20, Camp I (4500m) at the upper end of right-hand side of the moraine of the west glacier on July 24, Camp II (5000m) just below the snow plateau at the bottom of the south face on August 4, Camp III (5600m) on the small ridge located on the south face on August 10 and Camp IV (5900m) on the southwest ridge on August 14. We used a total of 1400 meters of fixed rope from 5200 to 6200 meters. Nine hundred meters of 9- and 10mm caving rope was fixed from 5200 meters (just above the bottom of the face) to 5850 meters (the crest of the southwest ridge). It took five days to fix this part of the route. Two hundred meters of 9mm caving rope and 300 meters of 9mm climbing rope were used for fixing the route from Camp IV to 6200 meters. It took only one day to fix this part. Takashi Ota and Katsuyuki Kuriyagawa reached the summit from CIV on August 17. For the anchors, we used approximately 100 pitons, ten bolts, ten ice screws, five snow stakes and one set of nuts. The team left BC and descended to Mahtran Dan on August 21.

TAKASHI OTA, *Sendai Ichiko Alpine Club, Japan*

Batura I, Attempt and Tragedy. Atsushi Inenaga led a team in an attempt on Batura I (7785m) via the south face. Team members were Seki Tsuyoshi, Sugiyama Hirota, Takasaki Wataru and Fujita Yasunobu. Batura I was first scaled by the German climbers in 1976. Polish climbers made the second and third ascents in 1983 and 1988, and for the past 11 years the peak remained unclimbed. Prior to its departure from Islamabad, the team planned to have Base Camp at the Muchichul Glacier at 4000 meters and then fix the route from Camp I at 5000 meters to CII at 6000 meters with 800 meters of ropes. The area is infested with crevasses, and a little higher a moderately steep climb begins which has an avalanche danger above 6000 meters. The last 300 meters near the top offer mixed terrain.

Fujita Yasunobu, Seki Tsuyoshi and Sugiyama Hirota were moving toward the summit from CIII (ca. 6500m) when they sent a radio message to BC saying that they had decided to descend due to bad weather. An avalanche caught the climbers as they descended, sweeping them down 1200 meters to the base of the mountain. The fall was witnessed through binoculars by the two remaining members in BC. No signs were found of the three men.

ASEM MUSTAFA AWAN, *The Nation, Pakistan*

NALTAR MOUNTAINS

Shani Peak, Various Ascents. From July 25-September 4, Andreas Amons, Elwin van der Gragt, Benno Netelenbos and Melvin Redeker (the Netherlands) operated with a leave-no-trace objective from a 3920-meter Base Camp in the Upper Shani Valley. Our goal was to establish new routes alpine-style on one of the huge faces of Shani Peak (5885m).

The Northeast Spur (alpine TD+, 1000m) on the northeast buttress of Shani Peak was climbed by Andreas Amons and Melvin Redeker on August 19-22. Though the buttress appears to offer one of the closest climbs from BC, it is actually one of the most remote. The bottom icefall of the Shani North Glacier denies a direct approach; instead, the pair reached the base of the climb after a ten-hour approach from BC by climbing the grassy slopes toward Pakhor Pass, then, at 4400 meters, crossing the scree slope toward Twins East Glacier. They then climbed up this to the second plateau (North ABC, 4600m), crossed the crest of the middle *rognon* in its saddle via steep ice and finally traversed the Shani North Glacier to the northeast buttress.

The route starts in a broad gully directly above the icefall of the Shani North Glacier. After finishing the

The Northeast Spur (Amons-Redeker, 1999), which reaches the East Summit (5610m) of Shani Peak.
MELVIN REDEKER

gully, the line links the snow/ice fields around the edge of the buttress via mixed ground. Then, where the edge sharpens toward the "false summit," the route continues up the rock crest on rather poor rock. Protection is sparse. Due to bad weather, the party spent four days on the face with two days of food. On August 22, after completing the Northeast Spur climb, they set out from their 33-hour bivouac at the false summit in whiteout conditions to make the first ascent of Shani Peak's East Summit, the easternmost of Shani's triple summits. The climb consisted of a two-hour, straightforward, crevassed, 50-degree snowclimb. The altitude at the top was ca. 5615 meters (as measured by a wrist altimeter). Descent was made by down-climbing and rappelling the same route. The poor rock added extra thrill to the rappels. The original plan—to traverse all the summits and descend via the west ridge—was, under the circumstances, impossible.

A new route, the Southeast Face Direct (TD+, 1600m), which takes a direct line straight to the main summit, was also established. Approach was made via the upper Gulupur Glacier (South ABC), less than three hours from BC. The route follows the rock pillar to the left of the 1989 English route, then passes beneath the "fortress" halfway up, through the central snowfield and through the steep ice gully to the summit. The bottom half of the route consists of sheer Chamonix-like granite rock climbing, while the top half is closer in character to the north faces of the Bernese-Oberland. Steep snow, ice and rubble sections added juice to the climb. The bonus was found at 5650 meters in the form of a short, thin, 80-degree ice ramp that is hidden from the eye below. The route was first attempted on August 20 by Benno Netelenbos and Elwin van der Gragt, who reached the top of the pillar at 5050 meters before being caught by the same weather as the party on the other side of the mountain. On their second attempt, on August 30, Benno and Elwin rushed to the summit after 15 hours of climbing and one bivouac at 5220 meters. The climb was repeated the next day by Andreas Amons and Melvin Redeker, who added an important variation to the climb by avoiding the crux of the pillar and the horrible wet sneak-through "Tang-gila-gufa" passage high on the rock section. Descent, which provided the full scope of horror offered by the glaciers, was made via the West Ridge route in a 12-hour struggle back to BC.

While acclimatizing, other climbs made included Sentinel Peak (5345m), via the south face; Snowdome (5360m), via the north ridge; and a peak, measured and verified at 5322 meters, climbed on August 16 by Elwin van der Gragt, solo (AD, 500m). Believing it to be unclimbed, we dubbed it "Pointe Paula." We later found that, in the account of the successful 1989 English Shani expedition, a peak (probably the same one) named "Sentinel North" in a table of peaks in the area, was listed as having been previously climbed. The climb is not registered anywhere, and we do not know where they got their information.

ELWIN VAN DER GRAGT, *The Netherlands*

Pt. 5520m, Dedo De Galupour and Bubulimotin, Ascents. It was reported that Spaniards David Larrión and Ager Madariaga made perhaps the first ascent of the east ridge of Pt. 5520m in early August. The peak lies on the watershed between the Sumaiyer and Nagar valleys; incorrectly dubbed "Sumaiyer Peak" by the pair, it was originally named "Peak Dawson" by the British first ascensionists who climbed it in 1979. Larrión and Madariaga then traveled to Naltar, where, on August 17, they made the first ascent of the northeast couloir/north ridge of "Dedo de Galupour." The 800-meter route involved 60-degree snow and ice and rock up to IV+. On August 21, the pair made a possible first ascent of a 5002-meter peak via a 1000-meter mixed route (50° IV). (*High Mountain Sports* 212)

HISPAR MUZTAGH

Sakar Sar, First Ascent. Akira Miyazawa, Makoto Ishikawa, Kanji Kamei and Teruaki Suzuki, along with two high-altitude porters, were in the area from July 19-August 30. Base Camp was made at 4500 meters. From BC to Camp I (5100m), the team encountered moraine and snow slopes. From CI to CII (5700m), we climbed a snow face with hidden crevasses, then another snow slope. We climbed from CII to the summit on August 13, reaching it at 12:30 p.m. Snow and ice faces led to a snow ridge, which was followed to the top of Sakar Sar (6272m) (36° 54' N, 74° 15' E). All members and both porters reached the summit. We were blessed with good weather.

MAKOTO ISHIKAWA, *Alpine Club of Yokosuka*

RAKOPOSHI-HARIMOSH MOUNTAINS

Shel Chakpa and Barbachen Peak, First Ascents. I had noticed Shel Chakpa (Balti for "white broken rock") during a 1995 trip to Haramosh II, and on subsequent visits the following two years. Though a handful of parties pass it each year en route to Spantik and the other Chogo

Lungma peaks, the local men all agreed that foreign parties had never been anywhere near Shel Chakpa. As the mountain is not over 6000 meters, and in an "open area," no permit, peak fee or liaison officer was required.

Stew Muir, Bill Church, Gus Morton and I traveled to the valley of the Basha River that drains from the Chogo Lungma Glacier in July, arriving at Base Camp on the 18th. We hoped to climb Shel Chakpa via the north- and west-facing slopes. From July 19-22, we experienced intermittent rain while we made various acclimatization walks. Stew, Bill and Gus made a reconnaissance to the site of Camp I on Shel Chakpa July 23. All members went up to camp on the Barbanchen Glacier the next day, where we hoped to climb a peak that looked lower and easier than Shel Chakpa for acclimatization and also to give us another view of our main objective. Poor weather during the next two days forced a return to BC. No sooner had we got down than the

Shel Chakpa, showing the Northwest Face route (Church-Morton-Muir-Wilkinson, 1999).
DAVE WILKINSON

weather improved. We climbed to Camp I, then, the next morning, went down a loose gully to a basin and climbed snow and ice couloirs through the mixed face to regain the ridge above the towers near our CII site. The climbing was technically reasonable, but the recent mild weather had stripped much of the snow to leave the slopes in very icy condition. We returned to BC, leaving the gear in place for next time.

We then had a frustrating period of poor weather, including one more plod back to CI, to try our patience. On August 6, we climbed back to CII. On the rocky ridge above this camp, we were surprised to find not only ibex tracks, but also a well-built cairn. Either someone had sneaked up, or more likely, the cairn had been built by an enterprising hunter. The route above CII had no in-situ gear or other signs of previous ascent. We rose before midnight the next day and set off at around 1 a.m, climbing in pitches with ice-screw belays. At one-third height, a flat area gave a rest, then a couple of hundred feet of snow allowed faster movement to the foot of the mixed ground. We started this section at first light, taking a meandering line up icy ramps and gullies between rock ribs at about alpine TD, but with fairly good rock belays. A rock shoulder gave a welcome rest, then an open ice slope led to the top, which was reached at about 9 a.m. We abseiled from rock anchors, taking a more direct line in descent than we had in ascent. We staggered into camp at 5 p.m. after 16 hours on the go. After a day off, our abseil descent continued in the dark with another pre-dawn start that saw us back to BC. The weather worsened.

Bill and Gus left for home August 14, but Stew and I had an extra week, so we sat out a few days of snow, then went back to our previously tried "training peak." This time the weather was kinder. The ascent was almost entirely on glacier terrain, with two bergschrund pitches that required a rope, and summit provided wonderful views of Shel Chakpa and K2.

DAVE WILKINSON, *United Kingdom*

Panmah Muztagh

Choktoi Glacier Area, Various Ascents. The team was composed of Luca Maspes, Emanuele Pellizzari, Massimo Sala and Gianni Zappa, plus geologist Paolo Biffi. We explored the Choktoi Glacier, which lays on the north side of the Latoks and ends at the foot of the east face of the Ogre. The approach is via the Panmah Glacier, taking a left (as one walks) just before the confluence with the Chiring Glacier. The area offers many climbing opportunities, but the weather was found to be from poor to bad. Very few sign of previous expeditions were noted on the glacier. Two spots for Base Camp were found at the beginning of the glacier, with rock and water, but quite far (from two to five hours) to the main climbable faces. The area offers great mountaineering but not really great rock climbing.

The team stayed on the glacier for 18 days. It snowed on nine of these, and on another three days we experienced bad weather. Massimo Sala and Gianni Zappa climbed an unnamed pillar about one hour from BC, experiencing difficulties up to 6a+. The descent was made with three rappels in an east-facing couloir, then with easy walking on a steep moraine. The ascent and descent was done in a day. Nothing was left behind beside the anchors for abseils. Maximum difficulties were up to UIIA VI+.

Emanuele Pellizzari, Luca Maspes and Gianni Zappa made an attempt on the Indian Face Arête, a prominent rock face about one hour from BC. The route ends on a pinnacle short of the summit of Latok III. The climb took three days. The team climbed three pitches on an afternoon, fixing the line for a successive attempt. Then it snowed for three days. On day one

The Indian Face Arête, with the summit of Latok III in the distance above. The Scott-Allen route follows the boundary of light and shadow, with the south wall in shadow. PAUL SCHWEIZER

of the real climb, the team added another eight pitches before bivying on a poor and extremely rotten and dangerous snowy ledge. The day after, the team climbed another six pitches and bivouacked on a steep and snowy ledge (after day 1, we had no food). On the last day we climbed one pitch, then made the descent.

The climb is very hard, sustained and sometimes dangerous and difficult. Except for the first 70 meters and two short pitches in the middle, all the pitches are at least UIAA VI and A1. The team placed four bolts on the ascent: two at belays, one for protection on a very rotten part of rock (A2+ and VI) and one because the leader was caught by dark (subsequently, the hanger to this bolt was removed). About two nuts, one sling (for a pendulum) and five stuck pitons were left on the route. We found nasty snow conditions.

The descent on the blank wall is a serious undertaking via rappels that are never shorter than 50 meters and as long as 59.8 meters. Most belays were made with two pitons or one single bolt. The overall difficulties involved 18 pitches up to UIAA VIII- and A3.

On the fifth pitch, we found a Wild Country #3 Friend with a carabiner and tied-off sling. At home, we discovered this was left by the Doug Scott/Sandy Allen party. After that piece, on the same pitch, we found difficulties up to VIII-. We found no further traces of climbing (pitons, scars, etc.). We feel the previous team did not do our line but took a crack toward the left (where the Friend was found) and did another line from then on. On the rappel, 50 to 60 meters from our high point, we found a piton with a sling at a bivouac site plus an empty gas cartridge. Via private correspondence, we determined that this piton was the high point of the Scott/Allen team.

Although the Scott/Allen party claimed a new route, and even though we went higher than they did, we feel our route remains a strong attempt but cannot be claimed as a new line or a summit. The next pitch after the Scott/Allen high point was rated VII and A3 (aid crux of the route).

Part of the team had to return home, but Luca Maspes, before moving into another valley and joining another team (see below), put up a new route (V, 400m) on a peak christened Simo Peak. Descent was made via an easy rock couloir.

EMANUELE PELLIZZARI

Biacherahi Tower, Hanispur South and Indian Face Arête, Ascents. The expedition was comprised of Muir Morton (leader), Tom Bridgeland, Sam Chinnery, Alasdair Coull, Neal Crampton, Dave Hollinger, Dan Long and Paul Schweizer. We set up Base Camp in early July on a strip of moraine on the north side of the Choktoi Glacier, directly across from the Indian

Biacherahi Tower from high camp. Hollinger and Schweizer ascended the right skyline.
PAUL SCHWEIZER

Face Arête on Latok III. The first quarter of Latok III's north spur was found to be seriously threatened by unstable seracs, especially to the right. When a huge serac avalanche from high on the north face, to the left of the spur, came very close to wiping out several members of the party, we decided to abandon the north spur and focus on some objectively safer alternatives.

On July 19, Hollinger and Schweizer climbed Biacherahi Tower (5800m), the striking shark's-fin-type formation directly across the Choktoi Glacier from Latok I. We climbed it from near the col linking the Choktoi and Nobande Sobande Glaciers. Ascending Biacherahi Tower took about four and a half hours from high camp; we left around 5 a.m. and attained the high col between the Tower and its neighboring peak (a Snowdome-type formation of roughly equal height) by about 7 a.m. After ascending the north ridge for several hundred feet, we decided to rope up and encountered ice up to 65 degrees. We rappelled the route with ice threads to get back to the col.

On July 28, Hollinger and Schweizer made an ascent of Hanispur South (a.k.a. Harpoon Peak, 6047m), the prominent triangular summit directly behind BC (see *AAJ* 1999, pp. 386-389). On July 27, we established a high camp in the col between Hanispur and Trident (or Choktoi) Peak and the next morning ascended a steep névé face to the north ridge, which we followed over sections of steep, rotten ice and mixed ground to a false summit. Here we rappelled 40 feet into a notch in the ridge and continued for two more pitches to the actual summit.

On Hanispur, ascending the route took about eight and a half hours from high camp. The north ridge was fairly jagged and heavily corniced, with some very rotten ice. The first difficulty was a rotten snow mushroom which we traversed under to the left. This was followed by a pitch of reasonably engaging mixed climbing (probably hard Scottish 4). The crux was a pitch of totally rotten 75-degree ice. We reached the summit at about 2 p.m. Descending took some time, because we had to reverse the rappel from the false summit. We then rappelled into a long northeast couloir which led straight to high camp after maybe 15 rappels and a lot of down-climbing. We didn't get back to high camp until midnight, then returned to BC the next day.

Chinnery, Coull, Morten and Hollinger also did the first ascent of the West Wall (A3, 800m) of the Indian Face Arête. The main arête line was first climbed by Doug Scott and Sandy Allen in 1990. The new variation climbs an obvious groove that runs up the left side of the vertical west wall of the spur. It starts 80 meters up the central couloir and reaches the Scott/Allen route at about half height. On the Indian Face Arête, the wall was climbed during five days using fixed ropes and returning to the comfort of BC each night until the final push.

On July 27, Coull, Chinnery and Morten followed the fixed line to the ridge, cleaning all fixed gear as they went. The original Scott/Allen route was then followed, with one bivy, to reach the summit of the arête on July 28.

PAUL SCHWEIZER, *University of Edinburgh Mountaineering Club*

Ogre, South Buttress, Attempt, and Latok IV, South Summit, Ascent. Alexander Huber, Toni Gutsch and Jan Mersch reached Islamabad on May 31. Thomas Huber arrived on June 3. Our lost equipment (24 out of 37 pieces) finally arrived on June 9. We reached Skardu on June 11 and Askoli on the 13th. After a four-day walk-in, we reached Base Camp on June 17. We established Advanced Base Camp (5000m) June 26 and three days later began up the south buttress of the Ogre, establishing a portaledge camp at ca. 6000 meters. We chose the south buttress, an intimidating bow of rock which, due to its protruding nature and steepness, is not exposed to avalanches, rock- and icefall. The pillar was first climbed by the Frenchmen Fine and Vauquet 15 years ago. High on the mountain, the two were hit by a storm and had to give up just below the summit. In 1997, Jan Mersch and Jochen Haase reached the top of the pillar in just six days from BC, but were hit by a storm and didn't reach the top either.

We then changed our objective to Latok IV (6450m). After exploring the route and after several days of bad weather we started our first attempt, but this attempt ended at ABC in bad weather.

On July 10, we started our next attempt, which ended at approximately 6300 meters in the col between the double-summitted Latok IV. On July 16, we started another attempt on the Ogre, ascending from BC to the portaledge camp on the buttress. The next morning we were offended by a cloud barrier only 50 kilometers away from us. In view of the need for another four days of good weather, we canceled our attempt and rappelled down to BC. On July 18, we had another day of unexpectedly good weather, but the barometer was falling and

The south face (with the southwest ridge following the sun/shadow line) of Latok III and the southwest face of Latok IV (right). Latok V is just out of the picture on the right. Huber and Huber took a line on Latok IV on the left side of the face; Motomu Omiya and Tsuguo Tsuchida attempted the right-hand skyline (see below). MOTOMU OMIYA

snow began to fall the night of July 19. Another week of bad and unstable weather bound us to BC. During the night of the 27th, it suddenly began clearing and we immediately started to climb up to the portaledge camp again, where we bivied. The next morning we canceled the attempt due to a heavy storm and health problems in the team. Jan left the expedition after the attempt and started to travel back to Germany on July 29. All further attempts ended in snow or rain, so we canceled the Ogre attempt on August 4. Toni left BC on August 6.

On August 8 at 11 p.m., Alexander and Thomas stumbled up 12 kilometers of rubble-covered glacier toward the base of Latok IV's southwest face, which comprises mainly steep ice fields quite similar to the Spider on the north face of the Eiger. We climbed them without belaying to get up and down the hill in a day, only roping up when the angle became steep just below the ridge. We both reached the (lower) south summit (6450m), then made it back to BC 22 hours after leaving. The porters came on August 10, which marked the end of the expedition.

ALEXANDER HUBER, *Germany*

Latok IV, Attempt. Motomu Omiya and Tsuguo Tsuchida (Japan) attempted the south ridge of Latok IV*. The pair arrived at Base Camp on August 4. They reached their high point of ca. 5700 meters at 2 a.m. on August 14. Heavy snow and a lack of time stopped the attempt. They departed BC on August 21.

*There is some confusion regarding the name of the peak Omiya and Tsuchida attempted. Mr. Omiya personally handed a photo of Latok IV to the Editor of this journal and indicated the line they tried, but referred to the peak as Latok V. He also gave an altitude for the peak as 6190 meters. This does not correspond to the altitudes for any of the Latok group as noted by the Swiss Foundation for Alpine Research *Karakoram* map. We can say with confidence that the photo captioned Latok IV on page 333 is the one attempted by Omiya and Tsuchida. The confusion may be the result of the Italian measuments of the Latok group, a matter investigated on pages 320-321 of the 1998 *AAJ*.

BALTORO MUZTAGH

Shipton Spire, Ship of Fools. Anders Lundquist, Mattias Jakobsson, Karl Ljung and I reached Base Camp on June 21. After organizing the equipment and admiring what is probably the most beautiful Base Camp in the Karakoram, we started ferrying equipment to Advanced Base Camp. Eighteen days later we established our first portaledge-camp. We climbed in capsule style and established three camps. On July 23, Karl and Mattias reached the summit after 21 days of climbing. Anders and I reached the summit the day after. The route we climbed was Mark Synnott and Jared Ogden's wonderful 1997 route, *Ship of Fools* (VII 5.11 A2 WI6, 1350m).

LUDWIG QVARNSTROM, *Sweden*

Great Trango Tower, Korean Fantasy, Previously Unreported. From June 21-August 19, 1997, expedition members Sang-Jo Lee (leader), Youn-Jung Shin (f), Choi Seung-Chol and Hyung-Jin Kim established a variation to the Norwegian Buttress Route on the North Pillar of Great Trango Tower. The team arrived in Islamabad on June 22, and reached Base Camp on July 2. On July 10, they transported equipment to the start of the climb and fixed the first pitches.

Their variation, which they called *Korean Fantasy*, is located at the separating point of *The Grand Voyage* and the Norwegian Buttress Route (see topo on p. 86). The next day, an avalanche swept away food and equipment, forcing the team to spend the next four days searching for lost supplies and carrying loads again. During their climb, they bivouacked at the second, sixth, ninth and tenth pitches. They began the climb proper on July 21st, climbing some 12 new 45- to 50-meter pitches, including one A4+ and three A4 pitches, before joining the Norwegian Route. This they followed to the east summit, which they reached on July 28. Choi Seung-Chul paraglided down to BC; the others rappelled the route. On August 1, they reached the base of the route and withdrew the fixed ropes. They departed BC on August 7.

KIM WOO-SUN, *Korea*

Great Trango Tower, Northwest Face, Parallel Worlds. From July 2-August 1, Alex Lowe, Jared Ogden and Mark Synnott, with Darren Britto, Greg Thomas, Jim Surrette and Mike Graber operating as film crew and internet coordinators in Base Camp, established *Parallel Worlds* (VII 5.11 A4, 6,000') on the northwest face of the Great Trango Tower (20,415'). A full account of their climb appears earlier in this journal.

Great Trango Tower, Northwest Face, Russian Direct. Alexander Odintsov, Igor Potankin, Ivan Samoilenko (high-altitude cameraman) and Yuri Koshelenko arrived at Base Camp on July 7. From July 15-August 10, the team established *The Russian Way* (VII 5.11 A4, 2675m) on the "prow" of the northwest face of Great Trango Tower. Three of the team led by turns; Ivan Samoilenko made a film. It was a rule to climb each day, even if the weather was bad and they could only climb ten meters. On the big ledge beneath the headwall, the Russians shared time with the American team (see above) for several days. The story of their climb appears earlier in this journal.

Great Trango Tower, Northwest Face, Lost Butterfly. Our expedition was planned to be a first ascent of the (presumed) highest big wall on earth, the nearly 2000-meter northwest face of the Great Trango Tower. With this project we garnered the Polartech Challenge Prize. In addition, we had strong support from the German Alpine Club (DAV), as well as from brand-name mountaineering gear companies. Unfortunately, we also had a rival for the wall. An American trio (Lowe, Ogden, Synnott) who knew our plan in detail hurried to the mountain a month before us in order to secure a first ascent for themselves. They were supported by a million-dollar (!) budget from the internet company Quokka, and they were "on stage" day and night. At the last moment, a four-person Russian expedition was also added. Our team for the wall climb was Gabor Berecz, Oskar Nadasdi and Thomas Tivadar, along with Peter Schäffler. Rita Bürger and Stephan Huber accompanied us to climb the standard route via the north shoulder.

We started from Munich on July 14 and reached Base Camp at 4200 meters on the Trango Lake on July 25. Here we were received by, among other expeditions, an American high-tech village, as well as trash and fields of fecal matter. The Americans had occupied the most logical line on the face, the only large system of dihedrals. The Russians chose a series of small crack corners to the right of that line. So what was left over for us was the left side. We started on the flatter, lower part of the wall on July 27 and climbed 25 pitches (maximum 5.10 A3) to the middle of the wall (5200 meters), hauling with us ten sacks and barrels. It had taken us ten wall days to this point, along with a few bad weather days in BC. Unfortunately, we found massive amounts of trash here (especially Russian candy wrappers, packaging materials and gas cylinders) and thrown-down gear (lots of US ropes). Later, the Russians even threw their portaledge down, which barely missed us. Even their line did not take a pretty end: about 200 meters under the exit they could go no further with their spartan gear and had to traverse about 100 meters to the left.

Rita and Stephan left us on August 13 after their summit attempt failed at 6000 meters due to weather. After the Americans and the Russians ended their routes (both supposedly VII 5.11 A4), we started our final push on August 14. We climbed for a number of rope lengths on an almost continuous series of corners and cracks that moved to the left. Since most of the formations were polished and compact, we had to climb mostly on tied-off hooks, beaks and copperheads. The passage between 5300 meters and 5600 meters thus became the key to the route (A4+, A3, A4, A3, A4-, A3, A4- clean, new-wave pitches).

Unfortunately, the weather was bad and very cold nearly throughout. A number of times, we were forced to wait idly through storms and snow for many days in the portaledge. After August 25, it turned into downright winter in the upper part of the wall (-10°C in the tents). On August 28, P. Schäffler finally gave up and descended.

Because we were only a threesome from that point forward and we had too few days for an independent line, we decided to climb into the American route, only ten meters away, in order to make more rapid progress. So on the 36th pitch we climbed over and repeated from that point forward all the rope lengths judged as difficult by the "Quokka Route." Unfortunately, we found a climbing style that showed only one thing: when you have a million dollars backing you up, you have to get up no matter how! Next to "normally" climbable fine cracks, corners and hook areas, we found drilled rivets and copperheads, as well as rows of bathook holes (25 holes in the 26th pitch alone). We also often found the ratings exaggerated (the most difficult US pitch, pitch 28, was actually A3+). Had these pitches been, for example, on El Cap, then these three top men would have lost face.

From the 40th pitch on, the wall laid back a bit, but on the other hand the icing up of the cracks increased dramatically. Thus our "winter ascent" was made more difficult. Renewed storms stopped us once again for three days. At this point, time became too tight, but we wanted to continue until the last hour. We stopped about 60 meters before the exit (at about 6000 meters) in the 44th pitch, which would offer fantastic free climbing in the summer.

We rapped down and broke down all of our equipment in three days, cleaned up and transported all of the trash that could be burned to BC, where our porters were already waiting. During the night, everything was packed into porter loads and the next morning we were allowed to begin our three-day walk out after 25 wall days. The result: *Lost Butterfly* (VII 5.10 A4+), new plus ten pitches of the American route, *Parallel Worlds*.

THOMAS TIVADAR, *Germany*

Trango Pulpit, More Czech, Less Slovak. In July, the Czech/Slovak expedition consisting of Ivo Wondráček, Tomáš Rinn, Pavel Weisser and Michal Drašar (all Czech) left Prague June 18. Jaroslav Dutka from Slovakia had problems with his transit visas to Great Britain and joined the expedition in Base Camp on July 2. The approach to the face of the Trango Pulpit was grade 4-5 climbing in itself. The team established Camp I at the base of the wall. The face is composed of three pillars separated by big snow fields. There were already climbers from Norway to the right of their proposed route. The Czech climbers had food for 20 days.

Great Trango Tower, with More Czech, Less Slovak *(Drašar-Dutka-Rinn-Weisser-Wondráček) on the Trango Pulpit indicated.* Ivo WONDRÁČEK

The climbing itself was more or less cracks in solid yellowish granite. They climbed left to a unique rock formation, the Guillotine, which stuck up from the face.

On July 8, they reached the first snow fields at 4900 meters, where they established CII. From July 11-13, the weather was very poor and the climbers waited in their portaledges. On July 16, Dutka and Weisser reached the second snow field some 1500 meters above the base, where they established CIII (5400m). They also found signs from a previous attempt to climb the Pulpit via this line at this point. Above the snowfield the rock was untouched.

On July 17, Rinn and Wondráček climbed almost to the final ridge. Dutka and Drašar reached the summit of the Pulpit (5800m) the next day, then descended to CIII late in the evening. On the 19th, the weather deteriorated. Dutka, Wiesser and Drašar decided to descend to BC to wait for better weather. Rinn and Wondráček stayed in CII for the next six days.

On July 26, the weather improved. Rinn and Wondráček started to climb from CII to the summit of the Pulpit. They reached the final ridge at dusk, where they slept. In the morning, they summitted the Pulpit. Wondráček felt sick and decided to descend to BC. Rinn stayed to wait for Dutka and Weisser. They wanted to continue with their climbing to the top of Great Trango. The three slept on the top of the Pulpit on July 28, then, in perfect weather the next day, they traversed to Great Trango via the 1977 American Route, climbing 13 pitches to the summit, which they reached at 5 p.m. They then descended to the Pulpit, spending the night there once again. On July 30, the weather deteriorated again. The next two days they cleaned the route of all ropes and gear.

Their route, which they named *More Czech, Less Slovak* (VII 7- A2, 53 pitches, 2100m), was the first ascent of the Trango Pulpit on the Great Trango Tower. The team hand-drilled all bolts at the belays.

VLADO LINEK, *Slovakia*

Trango Pulpit, Norwegian Trango Pulpit Direct. From June 28-August 4 (plus two days of fixing), Robert Caspersen, Gunnar Karlsen, Per Ludvig Skjerven and Einar Wold established the *Norwegian Trango Pulpit Direct* (VII A4 5.11, 48 pitches) on the Trango Pulpit (ca. 6050m). The Trango Pulpit is a secondary summit on the Great Trango massif. Climbing capsule style, the team linked together the lower wall, which faces northeast, and the upper wall, which faces directly north. The two faces are divided by a 180-meter hanging glacier. The team found reports of two other attempts on the wall, one by a Spanish team, who reportedly turned back after only five or six pitches on the lower face, and another by an Australian team that tried a slightly shorter, not-so-direct (but more feasible-looking) line up the right side of the lower face. It is said the Australians turned back after reaching a section of very hard aid on the 12th or 13th pitch. The Norwegian route takes the central line on both the lower and upper face. They used hand drills on their route and brought food for 30 days. The climb took 38 days. A full account of their journey appears earlier in this journal.

Nameless Tower, Claire de Lune. Gabriel Besson, Claude-Alain Gaillan, David Maret and I arrived at Base Camp on the Dunge Glacier at the beginning of July. The route we opened, *Claire de Lune* (VI 6b A3, 1230m), lies between that of Michel Piola (*Gran Diedre Desplomado*) and the Spanish Route (*Insumisoa*). Approximately 900-1000 meters of our route was new. We started on the left side of the base of the Tower's southwest face at 5000 meters with the first three pitches of *Insumisoa*, at which point we made our first camp. We then opened a new line on the slab directly above. The route followed the gray rock through a rock scar and a system of cracks to the summit (6230m). At midnight on July 28, under a magnificent full moon, we arrived on top. We used two sets of Camalots up to #4. We placed one bolt at each belay. Eight days were spent on the rock. We made two fixed camps with portaledges, one at the base of the slab and another one at the base of the gray rock. From the base to the camp, we fixed rope and then climbed in capsule-style to the top. The hardest pitch (A3) is two pitches after the gray rock and has a little bit of ice.

FRÉDERIC ROUX, *Switzerland*

Nameless Tower, Yugoslavian Route, and Nanga Parbat, Kinshofer Route. Alberto and Felix Iñurrategi, Jon Lazkano and Jose L. Tamiyo climbed Nameless Tower (6245 metres) via the Yugoslavian Route, summiting on June 26 at 3:30 p.m. The four then traveled to Nanga Parbat; Jon Lazkano left the team early. After reaching Base Camp (4200m) on July 15, the three remaining team members carried out a rescue to save the Columbian expedition leader Volker Stallbohm, who was injured at 6600 meters above Camp II on the Kinshofer Route on July 13. Jose L. Tamiyo, speaking on behalf of the expedition, said, "We were a little acclimatized after climbing the Nameless Tower, so we pushed from BC at 4200 meters to Camp II at 6000 meters on July 16."

After assisting in the rescue, the three climbers went from BC to CII on July 27 in one push and then made CIV at 7300 meters the next day. From CIV, they climbed to the top and back to Camp II on July 29, reaching the summit on July 29 at 7:30 a.m. from the Diamir side.

ASEM MUSTAFA AWAN, *The Nation, Pakistan*

Gasherbrum IV, Northwest Ridge, Ascent. Jae Soo Kim (expedition leader), Young Tae Kim (climbing leader), and expedition members Oun Bea Kim, Seong-Sang Kim, Min-Gi Jo, Yong Gun Kim, Il-Oong Jung, Dong-Ho Seo, Seong-Cheol Kim, Chi-Won Yun, Yeon-Ryong Kang, Jung-Hun Han and Jin-Ok Park departed from Seoul on May 8. On May 22, the team set up

Looking toward the Main Summit of GIV from the North Summit. CHI-WON YUN

Base Camp at 4900 meters. Other camps were established as follows: Camp I (5400m), May 27; CII (6400m), June 3; CIII (6800m), June 8; CIV (7400m), June 15. On June 28, the first summit attempt failed due to bad weather. On June 31, CV was set up at 7800 meters. We left CV for the summit at 4 a.m. July 1, and at 4:15 p.m. Chi-Won Yun and Yeon-Ryong Kang set foot on top.

As a whole, Gasherbrum IV's northwest ridge has a route as long as that of other 8000-meter mountains, which is why we planned our climbing style as a mix of polar (expedition) method and alpine style. The terrain between camps I and II comprised a lot of snow and ice; this section required 14 hours of work a day for four days to fix the rope and set up CII. The wind between camps II and III was very strong. There was a moderately difficult rock face between camps III and IV. In particular, the lower part of the summit section was without snow and ice, and camming units were very useful here. We found two carabiners with something like the words BEDAYN CALIFORNIA on them. I hope that I can find the owner of these two carabiners.

We had enough rock climbing gear to climb the south face as well when we were finished with the northwest ridge, but the weather didn't allow us to do that.

CHI-WON YON, *South Korea*

Gasherbrum IV, Southwest Ridge, Attempt. Steve Swenson, Charley Mace, Steve House (U.S.) and Andy DeKlerk (South Africa) made an attempt on the unclimbed southwest ridge of Gasherbrum IV (7925m). The intent of the expedition was to climb the route above 7000 meters alpine style without the use of fixed rope. In addition to climbing objectives, we also installed several new toilets at popular campsites on the Baltoro Glacier. Our expedition also succeeded in collecting and carrying out more than 500 pounds of trash from Gasherbrum Base Camp.

We arrived at Gasherbrum BC on July 1. By July 7, we had established our Camp I at around 6000 meters on the South Gasherbrum Glacier below Gasherbrum IV and the Italian Icefall. We spent a couple of days carrying loads and acclimatizing by skiing up to the base of the face below the southwest ridge. On July 9, a storm forced us back to BC for five days. We returned to CI on July 14, and on July 15 we skied up to the base of the route and climbed 700 feet up the lower snow face. The initial snow slope led to difficult mixed climbing on very rotten rock. It was our intent to fix rope up this face to where it reached the crest of the southwest ridge at 7000 meters.

A storm on July 19 lasted until July 26, so that it wasn't until the 27th that we were able to return to our Camp I. On July 28, we continued to fix rope up mixed climbing with rotten rock. The climbing was to the right of a prominent rock tower on the ridge. Below the ridge crest, much of the climbing was thin unconsolidated snow over loose rock that presented few opportunities for placing gear. The weather changed for the worse again on July 31, so after only three days of fairly good weather, we returned to BC in a storm. The storm kept us in BC from July 31-August 4.

On August 5 we returned to CI. On August 6, CII was placed on two very small platforms in a notch in the southwest ridge crest at 7000 meters. On the morning of August 7, we climbed a few hundred feet to the first rock band on the ridge at about 7200 meters with the intent of trying to find a better location for CII. The ridge crest consisted of more unconsolidated snow over bad rock, and a better campsite could not be found. The weather began to deteriorate again, so later that same day we descended to CI. On August 9, the entire team left for BC in this storm.

August 9-15 was another period of bad weather, but on August 16 it cleared, so all four of us returned to CI. At CI it was clear, but above 7000 meters it was extremely windy. On August 19, the wind seemed to abate, so we climbed up to CII only to return due to high winds up high and deteriorating weather.

On August 20, all members returned to BC in overcast conditions and light snow. The section of the ridge above CII looked to be difficult rock climbing and we thought it might take as long as three days to reach the summit from our CII and another day to descend. Faced with this kind of difficult climbing up high, we did not want to commit to alpine-style climbing unless there was some indication that a more stable weather pattern had been established.

We waited at BC from August 21-August 24. We were running out of time, so we returned to CI on August 25 to wait for a break in the weather. The next day a storm dropped two feet of new snow at our CI. The storm continued until midday on August 28. On the 29th, we climbed to CII and spent the night there, hoping to continue upward the next day.

On August 30, a combination of the unsettled weather and some poor health led to a decision to descend from CII and abandon the climb. On August 31, all the remaining gear was carried down from CI to BC, where the porters were waiting for us to leave. On September 1, the expedition left BC. The weather closed in again and it snowed heavily for several days.

STEVEN J. SWENSON

MASHERBRUM MOUNTAINS

Charakusa Region, Various Ascents, Previously Unreported. Giangi Angeloni, Angelo Carminati and Ennio Spiranelli traveled to the Charakusa Glacier (Hushe Valley) in August, 1997. Various ascents were made: Sulo Peak (6000m) by the South Couloir (55°); The Dog's Knob (5400m) via *Andrea Son* (5.10d, A1, 200m) on the southwest face of this short and perfect rock tower. Also attempted was a route on the third rock spur of K7 (4900m). The climb ended on the great ledge after two days (5.10b A1, 16 pitches).

GIANGI ANGELONI, *Club Alpino Italiano*

Charakusa Area, Fathi Brakk, Parhat Brakk and Beatrice, Ascents. Jimmy Chin, Evan Howe, Brady Robinson and Doug and Jed Workman, guided by Ibrahim Zahid of Hushe, base-camped in the Charakusa (Tsa'racksa) Valley. The team climbed three significant new routes over a period of 55 days, as well as throwing their fair share of disc, bouldering and cragging.

Jimmy and Brady entered the valley in late June ahead of the others, anxious to get on the rock. As the others hiked into the valley in early July, Jimmy and Brady were finishing up a new route on Fathi Brakk. This 3,000-foot monolith was first climbed in the summer of 1998 by an Italian team from the southwest. Jimmy and Brady's committing and direct line up the north face was completed in three days and entailed a variety of climbing including face, crack, ice and aid. Success was attained in a 24-hour push after two other attempts to complete the route. Future parties can be assured an adventurous time navigating through loose death blocks and sleeping on sloping, wet bivies. Some weeks later during very wet weather, the team was appalled to watch rockfall scour the bottom of the route.

Brady and Jed then teamed up for the previously unclimbed Parhat Brakk (5300m). The

Fathi and Parhat Brakk. The Chin-Robinson route on Fathi Brakk and Tavis Ridge *on Parhat Brakk follow the vague shadowed dihedrals visible on the left-hand skylines of both formations.* EVAN HOWE

twin tower to Fathi, Parhat was attempted by Americans Angela Hawse et al in the summer of 1995. In contrast to the loose stone on Fathi, Parhat proved solid with exquisite crack climbing. Over two weeks of climbing and extensive gardening, they were able to free much of the route up to 5.11, including a stout bombay fist crack through a roof that Brady floated. After 360 meters, the weather deteriorated and they aided four pitches, foregoing the all-free attempt. After excessive coffee on day 10, Jed, determined to fire a dyno, whipped into a corner three times. Upon completing the sequence, the two continued up the final four pitches, leaving the redpoint for the future. Perched upon the summit needle far above the glaciers, their cameras buzzed with electrical current, prompting a hasty rap back to wall camp. Their adventure was not over, however. Upon reaching the base of the wall, a catastrophic serac avalanche deposited 30 feet of ice upon their imminent descent route. The airblast pasted Robinson with ice and sent their haulbags careening down the glacier. Back in BC, the rest of the team was assembling makeshift probes and rescue gear before a radio call put their minds at rest. Considering the luck they had had, Jed and Brady named their route *Tavis Ridge* (VI 5.11 A3, 850m) after the luck charms (tavis) Zahid had given them at BC.

Meanwhile, across the valley, Doug, Evan, and Jimmy were climbing a new route on the southeast face of Beatrice (5950m). This 800-meter wall was first climbed by a 1998 British expedition in two teams by separate routes. Doug, Evan, and Jimmy ferried 250 kilos of gear 1000 meters to the base of the wall over a period of nine days. An advanced camp was established on the glacier at 5150 meters. Over five days of wet weather, they fixed 300 meters of rope and established a wall camp before descending to BC for respite.

During this hiatus, both climbing teams and Greg Mortenson of the Central Asia Institute convened at BC. Mortenson, acclimatizing for the Gondagoro La and a service project on the Baltoro, was accompanied by Little Karim and his son. A goat was sacrificed for the festivities that followed and the next day everyone departed for their respective projects.

Committing to the wall, the Beatrice team moved into wall camp and continued linking cracks toward the summit. Low pressure continued to tease them until the temperatures dropped and snow began falling in earnest. Wet snow rimed to the face as a meter of snow buried tents in ABC. They quickly found themselves cowering in their portaledges. Warm daytime temperatures sloughed snow down the face. As the avalanches bombarded the flies, the team supported the structure of their homes by pushing out with their feet. Two days later, the skies cleared for Doug's birthday and his lead. The following day they jugged 180 meters of fixed line and climbed another 200 meters to the top of the wall. Snow-draped loose blocks guarded the summit, which has yet to be reached by any wall climbers. They called their route *Wanderlust* (VI 5.10+ A3).

The southeast face of Beatrice, showing 1. Hatija *(Thomas-Huxter-Pyke, 1997). 2.* The Excellent Adventure *(Farquar-Myers-Turner, 1997). 3.* Wanderlust *(Chin-Howe-Workman, 1999).*
EVAN HOWE

Also of note was the expedition's desire to help the Balti people, who were incredibly hospitable to us throughout our stay. Jimmy and Brady, prompted by Greg Mortenson of the CAI, performed skits at the local elementary school in order to teach "Leave No Trace" ethics to the children. Doug, Evan and Jed helped the residents of Hushe haul grass out of the hills to store for winter feed for livestock. The locals enjoyed seeing Americans be porters for once.

Considering the war in Kashmir, a mere 100 kilometers away, and death threats toward Americans from Islamic fundamentalists, we were pleased to experience nothing but hospitality and enthusiasm from the Pakistani people. We all left regretfully, very anxious to return to our new-found friends and mountains.

EVAN HOWE, DOUGLAS *and* JED WORKMAN

King Brakk, Allah's Finger, Ibrahim Peak, First Ascents. A team of three Italians and one Swiss carried out a massive campaign of exploration in unknown valleys and peaks of the Hushe area. The team was composed of Maurizio Giordani, Lorenzo Lanfranchi (Switzerland), Luca Maspes and Natale Villa.

They first went to Khridas Valley, close to Hushe. The valley entrance is about one kilometer beyond Kande, the starting point for the Nangma Valley. In two days of steep walking plus occasional climbing (V/V+), they got to Base Camp. Because of the serious approach, the porters carried 15 kilos instead of 25, so supplies were limited.

During ten days, they climbed two new peaks that they christened King Brakk and Allah's Finger. The east- and northeast-facing route (VI+ A2, nine pitches, 400m) on King Brakk (ca. 4800m) was climbed in a day. The route was rappelled. The second line took the team four days for 760 meters. It was VIII- compulsory free climbing plus some sections of A2/A3. Some bolts were placed at belays. The route was rappelled. This valley offers great opportunities for rock climbing on unknown and unclimbed summits

Later, Giordani and Villa had to return home. Maspes and Lanfranchi went to the Honbrok Valley. They climbed a peak called Ibrahim Peak, which lies about two days' walk from Hushe. Rotten rock and easy scrambling led to the summit. The valley offers little possibilities for rock climbing. Cigarette Peak (local Hushe name) at the end of the valley appears interesting for ice climbing, but only above a nasty and dangerous, very broken glacier crossing. The local guide Little Karim was with the team in both valleys.

EMANUELE PELLIZZARI

Amin Brakk, West Face, Attempt. The team members of the Korean Alpine Club Amin Brakk Expedition were Young Soon Hwang, Jung Ho Bang, Dong Chul Shin, Myoung Rae Kim and Ihn Soo Park. The team departed Seoul May 22 and established Base Camp at 4200 meters on May 30. The first portaledge camp was set up on June 13 at 5250 meters. On June 18, the second portaledge camp was established at 5450 meters, and the next day, all members bivouacked at 5700 meters. On June 20, Young Soon Hwang, Jung Ho Bang and Ihn Soo Park reached 5800 meters. They had climbed 24 pitches to this point, fixing rope from the start of the climbing at 4800 meters to the bivouac point at 5700 meters. The most difficult pitch had been a five-tiered roof (A4) above the first portaledge camp at 5250 meters. At 5650 meters, they found a blue haulbag and a 35-liter rucksack from the 1996 Spanish team's attempt in which a 10.5mm rope, Friends, belay seat, climbing clothes and a 16mm video camera were packed. Mr. Hwang asked their Pakistan cook, Ssadic, to give the video camera to the Spanish team's leader. But the other equipment in the bag was left where it was found. The team also found several carabiners clipped to pitons below 5650 meters that they exchanged for their Korean Trango carabiners.

On June 21 at noon, they decided to descend because of heavy snowfall and strong winds. Mr. Hwang said it was very hard to decide to descend, but one of his members, Jung Ho Bang, was in too poor condition to attack the summit. Mr. Hwang said, "When I decided to give up on the summit with only 100 meters to go, it reminded me of a phrase from Joe Tasker's book, *K2*. Tasker wrote, 'Though we could not ascend the summit of K2, we knew that the most important thing is not [the] peak but the long distance traveled [. . . toward] K2 itself.'" At 5800 meters, they left a bolt and a cam nut. On the descent, they left 20 Trango carabiners, taking the Spanish (Bonati) carabiners in their place. They also left a hanging cook set (because it was cracked) at 5700 meters. The team did not retrieve their ropes after their descent. BC was closed on June 22, and the team arrived home in Korea on June 29.

On the way out, they met three Czech climbers (see below) and showed them their climbing video from Amin Brakk. But the Korean team's English was too poor to explain detailed things.

KIM, WOO-SUN, *South Korea*

Amin Brakk, Czech Express. Based on the experience of previous groups, we arranged to arrive in the Amin Brakk area at the end of June. The unclimbed west face of Amin Brakk, situated in the Nangma Valley, was the object of our interest. Our climbing team was composed of three members: Filip Šilhan, Marek Holeček and David Šťastný.

We arrived at Khande, the village that serves as the starting point for Base Camp, on June 22. We met the Koreans in the lower valley as they were descending from BC. We exchanged a couple of simple words. They looked like Napoleon's soldiers after the Battle of Waterloo. I asked them about their ascent; one of them answered that they hadn't been successful. We never saw the video showing the Korean attempt. I saw the camera (Sony DV1000 3CCD), but the Koreans were too tired to keep [up a] longer discussion. There were also communications problems.

With the help of five porters, we established our BC on June 26. At BC, we discovered a serious problem. We forgot our carabiners at home. We had just three single carabiners, three quickdraws, 80 bolts, 15 Friends with 'biners, two figure 8 rappel devices, three sets of stoppers and many slings. Fortunately, we found some 'biners hanging on our backpacks as well as on my photographic gear. Later, on the wall, we found more 'biners and many Friends.

Troubles with a locally purchased kerosene stove forced us to go back to Hushe in the main valley. The trip turned to be an excellent acclimatization. After getting geared up, we bivouacked beneath the wall on June 28, ready to make a serious attempt on the west face of Amin Brakk. At this time there was already one team of Spaniards who were attempting to climb the blank face at the far left. We were ready for a more obvious line on the wall, which was originally attempted by Spaniards in 1996 (see *AAJ* 1997, pp. 312-13, and *Desnivel* #114, 1996, pp. 53-58) and most recently by a South Korean team (see above).

On the first day of climbing we discovered that previous parties had left much fixed rope on this line. At that moment we didn't even dream that the ropes were fixed up to pitch 26. It was a bit disappointing to climb just a couple of centimeters away from fixed ropes, but there was no other way. We used the old ropes to descend and I used them twice for taking the photos. We never used the ropes for the ascent. From the base of the route to the very end, we climbed only under our own power. We used old bolts at the belays, which saved us a lot of time. There was no sense to place new bolts ten centimeters away from old ones.

On the second day, David dropped the bolt bag containing 70 bolts. He rappelled down on the glacier to look for them but found only seven. At that point, we had ten bolts and about 40 pitons.

The first third of the wall is a rotten slab with many features on it. It took us four days and 12 long pitches to get to an obvious ledge. Mostly vertical to slightly overhanging climbing started from this point. Deteriorating weather trapped us in the portaledges for two days. After one night's snowstorm, the wall turned to a big icefield, so we decided to descend back to BC. We used old fixed ropes (probably from the Spanish '96 attempt) for rappelling down as well as for jumaring back onto the ledge two days later when the weather improved. We nicknamed the ledge "Cracked Bucket Ledge," because of the leftovers of our predecessors. (The cracked bucket we found on the first bivy ledge was obviously too old to belong to the Korean climbers.)

The upper two thirds of the wall looked really challenging. The climbing was on solid gray, almost featureless granite. About half of the wall is dissected by huge overhangs. The distance between the ledge and the overhangs is about 300 meters and the wall is clearly divided by a continuous crack. The climbing demands a lot of jamming and liebacking with good possibilities for protection. We freeclimbed six long pitches, the hardest one rated IX- (5.12b). The seventh pitch above the Cracked Bucket Ledge is mostly overhanging and the most difficult technical pitch on the route. David started this pitch, but after placing a couple of pitons in a shallow crack, he fell and ripped out some of the gear, cutting his face. Marek finished this ugly overhanging section and graded it A4. (After our experience on the *El*

Marek Holeček on the west face of Amin Brakk.
FILIP ŠILHAN

Regalo de Mwoma route on the Central Tower of Paine [see page 272], we had to downrate the most difficult technical pitch on Amin Brakk to A3.)

Above the overhangs is a quite comfortable ledge, though not as good as the Cracked Bucket Ledge below. We found a broken A5 portaledge, so the name of this place was pretty clear. A tricky greasy crack that led from the ledge took us almost half a day to climb. It was the 20th pitch; we had spent nine days to this point on the wall. We climbed five more pitches that day, mostly crack climbing, until an evening snow storm stopped us. It snowed during the night and the next morning the weather looked about the same. In spite of that, we decided to go for the summit. We took just the necessary gear, with sleeping bags and food for two days, and jumared to our highest point. We found the blue haulbag full of gear [at 5700m], but we didn't use any of it.

The 26th pitch, climbed the day before, was the most difficult free climbing pitch on the route. Below the overhang, the thin crack gets greasy and loose; it's overwhelming climbing at IX (5.12c) with just a little space and a little time for protecting. All the moves on this pitch were done free, but with rests. There was no time to try a redpoint attempt, but it would be possible. We did one more pitch and reached the high point of the South Koreans.

At this point it was already snowing hard and after two more pitches, the snowstorm became outrageous. The visibility lowered to eight or ten meters. We barely knew where to climb. A couple of meters of crawling in the snowy couloir took us to a rocky projection on the far south part of the west face. In the frozen snow, we dug a poor bivy site and spent one night—the longest one of all. It was snowing all the time but the next morning, the weather looked pretty stable.

It took us a short discussion to decide to continue. We started at about 5 a.m. With crampons on, we traversed a bit to the right and climbed up a long snowfield on the south side of the summit pyramid in 300 meters of mixed climbing. The gradient of the wall was up to 70 degrees. We didn't use a single ice screw on this section. We reached the top on July 12 at 1 p.m. just between two snowstorms. There was unpleasant electrical tension up on a snowy bulge, which is actually the summit. Because of a poorly functioning altimeter, we did not get an accurate height. The visibility was pretty low, but it was clear that this bulge is the true summit. From the rocky outcrop, which is about 20 meters beneath the top, we rappelled down to the saddle from where we had started our push for the top that day. It took four 50-

meter pitches to reach the traverse.

On the descent, there were a couple of tough moments (we left two 9mm ropes on pitch 29 because they got stuck), but at the end of the summit day we reached the camp at the broken portaledge. It was still snowing. The following day, the 13th of the climb, we rappelled down on the frozen fixed ropes. With the heavy pigs on the rope, it was more than an adventurous performance. During the descent, one of the Spanish climbers looked out of the portledge. It was Pep Masip. He was asking me something. I shouted "yes" to him, as I thought he was asking me if we had reached the top. Later on, I realized that he asked me if we were retreating as well. Anyway, we survived even this descent down the west face. Back on the ground, we named the route *Czech Express* (9 A3 70°).

FILIP ŠILHAN, Czech Republic

Amin Brakk, West Face, Sol Solet. Spaniards Sílvia Vidal, Miquel Puigdomènech and Pep Masip traveled to the Pakistan Karakoram, where, from July 8-August 8, they put up the route *Sol Solet* ("Sun, Little Sun") (VII 6c+ A5 60° ice, 1650m) on the west face of Amin Brakk (5850m). An account of their climb can be found earlier in this journal.

Changui Tower, East Face, Ludopatía. Fermín Izco, Mikel Zabalza and I left Pamplona on June 18 for Islamabad. Our objective was to climb in the Nangma Valley, which Fermín and Mikel got to know when they opened a new route on the Nameless Tower in 1995 (see *AAJ* 1996, p. 294).

We left Islamabad quickly on our way to Skardu in a van followed by a jeep to Kande, a village from which we started our two-day walk to Base Camp (4300m). We did some acclimatization and looked at walls. We decided on the east face of Changui Tower (5800m), rejecting the south face of Amin Brakk because of avalanche danger. Furthermore, we tried to find a route that would be predominantly free climbing rather than aid.

Our ascent began with numerous one-and-a-half-hour carries to the foot of the wall from BC. The next day, we fixed the first three pitches and went back to the tents. We returned to the wall with the intention of not descending until we had stepped foot on the summit.

We used two ledges, 300 meters of static line, a 10.5mm 60-meter rope, another 9mm 60-meter rope and a 6mm auxiliary cord that we used to haul the bag. We climbed capsule style.

After six days on the wall, a sudden change in the weather forced us to descend using all of the ropes that we had. We just made it to the start of our route. Three days later, we returned to the wall and had "laughs" to see who would be the first to jumar the 6mm cord. Luckily, it held.

Back on the climb, we found granite of exceptional quality, good weather and a multitude of cracks and dihedrals with many sections at grade 6. Marvelous. There was little work for the aiders and much less for

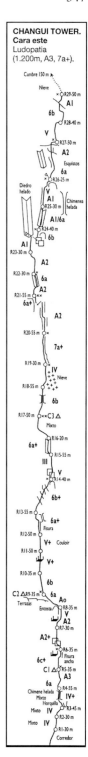

the drill (we only placed the occasional bolt at the occasional belay when we couldn't use Friends or nuts). We made the fourth camp on a big ledge at the foot of the final 350-meter vertical pillar, which ended up being the most technical part of the route. We finished the rock climbing and attacked the last 200 meters of snow, which gave access to the summit. This we reached on July 16. We rappelled the final pillar of the route and descended via a corridor that gave access to the valley, dragging all of our gear and trash, which saved us from rappelling the entire wall. We called our route *Ludopatía* ("Compulsive Gambling") (A3 7a+, 1200m).

After two days of rest back in BC, we proposed to try an ice wall of more than 1500 meters, but the persistent bad weather in all of the Karakoram at the end of July made us desist and return home.

RUBÉN ARAMENDÍA PÉREZ, *Spain*

HISPAR MUZTAGH

Pumari Chhish, South Face, Attempt. The south face of Pumari Chhish (7492m) rises 3000 meters from the Jutmal Glacier. This complex face is threatened on most aspects by high hanging seracs, and the line Julie-Ann Clyma and I took followed an obvious spur on the left side.

From ABC (ca. 4570m), a day was spent reaching the lower part of the spur (ca. 5400m). This involved an approach on easy but threatened snow slopes and then technical rock climbing (HVS) followed by 55-degree ice slopes. After a day stopped by snowfall, a traverse across the lower part of the face and an ascent of a hanging face (60° ice) led to an open bivouac at ca. 5900 meters. A further day in very bad weather led to a precarious camp at ca. 6200 meters. This was the maximum height reached before a descent was made back down the route.

The weather conditions were extremely unstable throughout the expedition. Snow fell on all but five days. Retreat from the highpoint was necessitated by the weather and extreme avalanche conditions. Thirty-six hours were spent with avalanches passing around and over the tent. There were no accidents to expedition members or support staff.

We were very fortunate to obtain a permit within one month of applying

The south face of Pumari Chhish. ROGER PAYNE

to the Ministry of Tourism. They were very accommodating to our tight time schedule, and with the help of our agent, Nazir Sabir Expeditions, we were able to arrive in Islamabad and leave for the mountains on the same day.

ROGER PAYNE, *British Mountaineering Council*

SPANTIK-SOSBUN MOUNTAINS

The north branch of Snow Lake, as seen from Advanced Base Camp at the bottom of Tarci Peak.
GIANGI ANGELONI

Snow Lake Area, Cornice and Tarci Peaks. Seven members of the Bergamo section of the Club Alpino Italiano spent July 19 to August 4 in a base camp (4700m) where the Biafo merges with the Sim Gang Glacier. The original project was the second ascent of Solu Tower (S. Venables and partner, 1987) by a new route, but the bad weather persuaded us to change our objective.

The weather broke for only two days and on July 23, Giangi Angeloni, Angelo Carminati, Giorgio Carrara, Gigi Rota and Ennio Spiranelli climbed the central spur (A1 60°, easy mixed, 800m) of the west face of Cornice Peak (5882m). Four days later, on July 28, Giangi Angeloni, Gigi Rota and Ennio Spiranelli made the first ascent of Tarci Peak (ca. 5800m), located on the north side of Snow Lake, in a day from Advanced Base Camp, via the south ridge/west face, a route we called *Imperial Rabbit* (5.9 AI 55°, 12 pitches, 600m). The proposed peak name is in memory of Tarcisio Fazzini, our mountain-climber friend who died in 1990. Skis were used to access all the peaks.

GIANGI ANGELONI, *Club Alpino Italiano*

Peaks above the Snow Lake area. Tarci Peak is the pointed peak in the center of the photo.
GIANGI ANGELONI

Sosbun Tower, Attempt, and Nameless Peak, Ascent. Even if they are "veterans" of the Karakoram, few climbers know the name of the Sosbun Tower. These rocky towers are located in the Sosbun Glacier. Taeko Yamanoi and I were with Daisaku Nakaga, with whom we became friends in our Lady's Finger expedition in 1995. Since then, we have looked for beautiful unclimbed walls like the Lady's Finger and found these hidden rocky towers at last.

In the glacier, as we expected, there were a lot of unclimbed needles. This isolated place, detached from trekkers and climbers, made us feel as if we had found our own paradise. The wall we attempted to climb was so large (more than 1000m) that we approached it with a pure capsule style.

We spent four days trying the main tower and couldn't help but give up in the end. First, the rock was so loose that we were scared that our ropes would be cut by rock fall. Flakes piled up like scales screeched beneath my feet in the aiders and loose blocks also made me feel gloomy. Secondly, the morning sunshine melted the upper snowfield and a huge waterfall would appear, usually around 8 a.m., in the center of the wall. What we enjoyed there wasn't a comfortable vertical cruise but rather a survival of the terrible rock fall and bad weather.

Needless to say, after coming back to Base Camp we weren't satisfied with this climb. We decided to try another tower, the Jannu-shaped "Nameless Peak." What we needed to prepare for it was a little equipment, that is some pitons, a small stove and a cooker for tea breaks. Our tactics were also simple, dashing for the summit and coming back immediately.

"Nameless Peak," showing the line of ascent (Yamanoi-Yamanoi-Nakaga, 1999). YASUSHI YAMANOI

In fact, the "Nameless Peak" provides ideal geography for alpine style.

Leaving BC at 6 p.m., we passed 60-degree snow slopes with some effort because of some solid icy sections. Furthermore, the fatigue we had gotten in the Main Tower also slowed down my climbing. As a result, we reached the crest at 10 a.m., spending more than 15 hours to reach it. For the summit, we dealt with a final three or four pitches of rock (V A2). My first sight of the Biafo Glacier flowing like a highway and the scenic Baintha Brakk strongly impressed me.

At this moment, we should confess that we didn't reach the real summit. About 45 feet beneath the it, cracks disappeared in the darkness. We were not so discouraged. However, Daisaku was snoring, hanging from a rope, and Taeko was listening to someone who was not even there. I had also spent more than 30 minutes putting up the anchors. It was about time to descend. It was 42 hours of restless work before we made a landing on the safe earth.

The Sosbun Towers could be climbed despite the rock quality. The climbing would basically be the same as that in the Alps and Patagonia. I hope many climbers will visit and try the exciting work in such a "nameless" land.

YASUSHI YAMANOI, *Japan*

INDIA

GARHWAL

Mukut Parvat East, Correction, and First Ascent. The 1998 expedition from South Korea led by Oksun Hong (see 1999 AAJ, p. 355) claimed the first ascent of Mukut Parvat East (7130m) in the Garhwal. The expedition claimed to have reached the summit and provided photographs and details that were published in various journals. In 1999, an Indian team from the Nehru Institute of Mountaineering led by Col. Ajit Dutt attempted the same peak by an almost similar route in June and July. They found a Korean snow stake on a dome below the summit. The Indian team proceeded further and climbed another higher snowy point which was at least 80 meters higher; it took them almost one hour. From this higher snowy peak they could view the main peak of Mukut Parvat I and the Korean high point below them. Thus, they concluded that the point they climbed was the true main summit of Mukut Parvat East and the Korean team had reached a subsidiary point 80 meters below.

The photographs, route details and timings from the Korean ascent and the Indian team were compared by J. C. Nanavati, adviser to the IMF. All the pictures, reports and details were sent to the Korean leader for their studies and comments. The Korean leader in a letter confirmed that they were on a lower summit and had mistaken the true summit as Mukut Parvat I and not proceeded to it. Thus the Koreans had not climbed the main summit of Mukut Parvat East. Hence it is now placed on record that the first ascent was made by NIM-Indian team in 1999, while the Korean made the first ascent of Mukut Parvat East II.

DR. M. S. GILL, *President, The Indian Mountaineering Foundation*

Arwa Tower, First Ascent and Arwa Spire, First Attempt. From May 7-14, Britons Mick Fowler and Steve Sustad climbed the Northwest Face (VI 5b A3 Scottish V/VI, 1000m) of the Arwa Tower (6352m), making the first ascent of the peak in the process. An account of their

The unclimbed Arwa Spire. MICK FOWLER

climb appears earlier in this journal. Meanwhile, Crag Jones and Kenton Cool attempted two lines on the north side of the unclimbed Arwa Spire (6193m) in May. Firstly, an attempt was made via the icefield leading up to the left of the summit tower, but deep powder on very hard ice caused a retreat. An alternative mixed line further left was then tried. Deep powder overlying steep smooth rock slabs again led to a retreat.

CARADOC "CRAG" JONES, *Wales*

Panch Chuli III, Attempt. The virgin Panch Chuli III (6314m) was attempted from May-June by a young IMF team selected from all over India. The leader, S. Bhattacharya, was an experienced mountaineer from Delhi. They attempted the peak from the eastern approaches through Meola Glacier. After overcoming the icefall they reached the final ridge directly from the icefall instead of traversing to the col between Peak II and III. They had to stop about 80 meters before the main summit due to steep ice. A second attempt was not made.

HARISH KAPADIA, *Honorary Editor, The Himalayan Journal*

Shivling, East Ridge, Third Ascent. When my boss, Captain Bolo, asked us to suggest an expedition for the spring, I immediately remembered a picture of Shivling and proposed to him the east ridge. Our small team was made up of Doctor Pascal Urbain and four climbers: Frédéric Gentet, Laurent Miston, Philippe Renard and myself. On April 30, a bus brought us from Delhi to Gangotri. Two days of trekking were necessary to reach Base Camp (4300m). The East Ridge of Shivling, a.k.a. the Ganesh Ridge (VI 6 A3), was climbed for the first time in 1981 by Doug Scott, Greg Child, George Bettembourg and Rick White. It was considered, at that time, to be one of the most technical routes ever climbed in alpine style.

On May 14, we decided to try the original South Ridge route of Bhagirathi III. We had the authorization and moreover it would improve our acclimatization for Shivling. The day after, we walked seven hours around the Bhagirathi range to pitch a camp at 5300 meters. The South Ridge contains grade 4+ climb and 55-degree slopes. On May 16, after seven hours, we reached the icy and sharp summit ridge.

On the 19th, good weather incited us to leave for Shivling's East Ridge. Philippe and Laurent stayed at BC. An easy beginning was quickly followed by the crenellated part of the ridge. Some very old fixed ropes reminded us that Doug Scott and his friends were here 18 years ago. We stopped before the night, having climbed 1300 meters from BC. The next day, we encountered the first hard part of the ridge. The weather changed very quickly and the snow came. We had not worn our rock climbing shoes for a long time! At 4 p.m., Frédéric climbed up to fix a rope for the morrow. He put a 40-meter Tyrolean traverse across a little pass beneath us. May 21 was cloudy; above the Tyrolean, we free climbed an A1 pitch. With climbing shoes, it's 6b.

The fourth day, I climbed a strenuous pitch with large cracks and arrived at the first pendulum. The haulbag made a nice flight! Then we climbed a difficult chimney; it was snowing a lot. May 24 was summit day; it was snowing and the wind was strong. Frédéric climbed three pitches and I did the last rocky pitch. The wind was always strong when we did the 200 meters of the ice cap in deep snow. After a small serac, we reached the summit. We went down on an icy 45-degree ridge. Approaching the great serac of the normal route, the fog was still present. So, we preferred to make a sixth bivouac.

ANTOINE DE CHOUDENS, *Groupe Militaire de Haute Montagne*

Thalay Sagar, High Tension. Russian alpinists Alexander Klenov, Alexey Bolotov, Mikhail Davy and Mikhail Pershin established a new route on the north face of Thalay Sagar (6904m). *High Tension* (ABO, 7b A3+, 1400m) takes a line up the rock buttress to the right of the prominent couloir first climbed in 1997 by Andrew Lindblade and Athol Whimp. The climb was established from May 17-May 27. Davy's article on the ascent can be found earlier in this journal.

Dunagiri, North Face, New Route and Attempt, Previously Unreported. It was reported that in 1998, Spaniards Xabier Guembe and Jon Beloki completed a new route (80 degrees, IV, 1900 meters) alpine-style on the previously unclimbed north face of Dunagiri from May 15-21. A second Spanish group of Fermin Izco and Mikel Zabalza attempted a more difficult line on the face to the left of the Guembe-Beloki route but were forced to retreat 300 meters below the summit ridge after climbing 1000 meters of 60- to 80-degree ice. Guembe and Beloki descended the west ridge. Beloki was ill and Guembe was too exhausted to assist him; the pair had gone three days without food or water when Izxo and Zabalza came to their rescue at 6400 meters. (*Desnivel*)

HIMACHAL PRADESH

Gya, Second Ascent. Gya (6794m), at the tri-junction of Himachal, Jammu and Kashmir and Tibet, had received eight expeditions but had no ascents, either due to misidentification or bad weather. The Indian Mountaineering Federation organized its second expedition to Gya from May to June. Expedition members were Chewang Motup Goba (leader), Nadre Sherpa, Cyrus Shroff, Lobzang Tsering and Amrish Jha. The team left Delhi on May 18, was in Leh until May 21 and reached Chumar on May 25. Base Camp was finally established on May 27 at 4800 meters at the head of the glacier. For two days, loads were ferried to the Advanced Base Camp (5350m), which was established on the 31st in bad weather.

In Leh we had heard of a three-member Bombay team who were attempting Gya ahead of us. On May 31, the Bombay team's local helper came to our camp to inform us of the help-less conditions of their team, who were unable to descend due to exhaustion and no food. Team members and Sherpas were sent despite the terrible weather to rescue the two mem-bers, who were brought back safely to our ABC. One member had suffered frostbite and we were also informed of the death of Arun Samant on his return from Gyasumpa.

The snowstorm did not deter our team from continuing the work of establishing Camp I and ferrying goods on June 2-3. The route was opened to Camp II, which was established on the col above Lingti Valley at 6200 meters. With photographs from past expeditions, it did seem that this route from the southeast would be the most viable. However, though the team and Sherpas worked hard at fixing ropes to open the route for four days, on June 9 we were stopped 80 meters short of the summit by a necklace of smooth hard rounded overhanging rocks that seemed impossible to cross. We traversed halfway across this rocky necklace to look for an opening but were unsuccessful. The particular route from the southeast that we attempted was technically very challenging and 1500 meters of rope had to be fixed. Tired but not defeated, we returned to BC and rested for another four days before deciding to attempt the peak again by the northeast ridge.

On June 13, the team again pushed back up the mountain to Camp I. The following day turned out to be perfect weather. According to past expedition reports, it is rare to see such weather on this mountain. As planned, all members and Sherpas ferried loads with the first summit party to Camp II which was on a ramp, but safe under a huge rock below Gyasumpa at 6250 meters, where two tents were set up. The remaining team returned to CI.

Taking turns from here, the summit team worked extremely hard at leading and belaying as they traversed the steep slopes to fix ropes below Gyasumpa as far as the ramp between Gyasumpa and Gya North. The first summit party consisted of Nadre Sherpa and Lobzang Tsering with two Sherpas. Dawa Wangchuk and Nima Thendup, though exhausted after a long day's work of fixing ropes, felt that they would be able to work fast along the pitches with fixed rope and get to the summit the next day. The summit team returned to CII at 6:30 p.m.

On June 15, another perfect weather day, the summit team left at around 5 a.m. and traversed the slopes between Gya North and Gyasumpa by 11 a.m. The route ahead was totally exposed and impossible to negotiate without fixing ropes up to the summit. By 12:30 p.m., the summit team had done the gully which from CI looked difficult and steep. Here they found a rope probably left by the Army expedition.

At 2:24 p.m., Nadre Sherpa stood on the summit of Gya, informing us by radio. He was followed by Dawa Wangchuk Sherpa, who was on the summit at 2:30 p.m., Lobzang Tsering at 2:36 and Nima Thendup at 2:42. On the summit they found a piton! (See below.) After the success of the first party, it was decided that the second summit party should move to CII.

On June 16, another day of perfect weather, the second summit party of two members (Cyrus Shroff and Amrish Kumar Jha) with three Sherpas (Pasang Tenzing, Pasang Nurboo and Chomber Sherpa) left at 3 a.m. and summitted at 8:10 a.m. All team members and Sherpas were down at CI by 5 p.m.

On June 17, everyone moved down to BC. An Indo-Tibet Border Police team was waiting for us, as they had failed to bring down the body of Arun Samant and were hopeful that the IMF team would help them to bring the body down. The next day, two members with four Sherpas were sent up with three ITBP members to bring down the body. After handing over the body to the ITBP team at ABC, our Sherpas brought down all the equipment from ABC.

On the evening of June 19, our horses arrived from Chumar and on the 20th the whole team with all the gear arrived at Chumar.

MOTUP CHEWANG GOBA, *India*

Gya, Correction. The Indian Army Expedition to Gya organized by Three Infantry Division during July-August, 1998, was scrutinized by Shri J. C. Nanavati, adviser to the Indian Mountaineering Foundation. Mr. Nanavati concluded that, on the matter of the lack of sufficient evidence, the Army Expedition may have instead climbed Gya North instead of Gya Main. This was complicated due to the fact that the expedition had not taken unobstructed views from the peak, misidentified the immediately connected peak of Gya North in summit photos, etc.

On June 15-16, the IMF-sponsored expedition led by Mr. Chewang Motup (see above) climbed Mt. Gya and brought the vital summit photographs from various directions. Mr. Nanavati, the adviser, again scrutinized the photographs and other details provided by the leader of the aforesaid Army Expedition vis-à-vis the details brought by the leader of the IMF Expedition and came to the conclusion that the Army Expedition indeed climbed the then-virgin Gya (6794m) in August, 1998. The IMF Expedition brought additional evidence in the form of a Stubai piton left by the Army Expedition, along with a piece of cloth with the names of the summiters dated August 12, 1998. The conclusion is clear that the Army Expedition were the first to climb Gya on August 12, 1998. The IMF is only too happy to correct the previous IMF findings and to acknowledge the achievement of the Army Expedition.

DR. M. S. GILL, *President, The Indian Mountaineering Foundation*

Peak 6553m, Attempt, and Peak 6222m, Ascent. Peak 6553m (a.k.a. Dibiboikri Nala) is an unclimbed peak on the Dibiboikri Glacier. A three-member British expedition led by Anthony Ewan Mecleran attempted it from September-October. However, only the nearby Peak 6222m was climbed via the west ridge by team member Bowden on September 30.

HARISH KAPADIA, *Honorary Editor, The Himalayan Journal*

Peak 6118m, Ascent. Peak 6118m (near Yunan Tso, Baralacha Pass) is an unnamed peak on the Manali-Leh highway and is easy to approach. A Snout Adventurers Association, Calcutta, led by Ujjal Roy, established a base camp on August 17. Seven members climbed the summit on August 23 and 24. Exact location of the peak (and valley) is not known.

HARISH KAPADIA, *Honorary Editor, The Himalayan Journal*

Dhhun, First Ascent. Dhhun (6200m), which means "guardian," was first climbed in August via the north face by a Japanese expedition led by Tsuneo Suzuki. The top was thought to have been reached on August 6 by three members and three high-altitude porters; on August 8, four members along with four porters realized the earlier group had only reached a subsummit and continued the one-kilometer walk to the main summit.

HARISH KAPADIA, *Honorary Editor, The Himalayan Journal*

MIYAR NALA

Thunder Peak, East Ridge, Previously Unreported. In 1998 and 1999, a small Italian expedition visited the Miyar Valley in India. The team was composed of Gianluca Bellin and Diego Steffani. In 1998, they climbed a tower christened "Thunder Peak" (ca. 6100m) by the obvious east ridge. The ascent involved climbing up to VII, occasional points of aid, mixed up to M5 and ice up to 85 degrees; it was done in the purest alpine style without porters or fixed ropes and in a single push with open bivouacs. The name was given for the massive storm that caught them while they were abseiling.

The team returned again to the same valley the following year with the intention of first doing an easy 5000- to 6000-meter peak for acclimatization and then going for the massive south face of an unnamed rock tower. They were only able to do the acclimatization scramble before Diego Steffani exploded his knee and had to return home.

EMANUELE PELLIZZARI

KUMAON

Burphu Dhura South Peak, Ascent. The IMF expedition to the virgin peak of Bhurphu Dhura

(6210m) in Kumaon was led by Lt. Commander Satyabrata Dam of the Indian Navy and consisted of six members. The team left Delhi on September 12 and arrived at Munsyari on September 13. The walk in started on September 15 and the team established Base Camp (3845m) at the snout of Sankalp Glacier on September 19. It took another three days to establish Advanced Base Camp at an altitude of 4630 meters. ABC was ideally located on a rock bed close to a glacial lake, a little short of the Kalabaland Icefall. Based on earlier studies and an initial reconnaissance of the mountain, the team decided on the south ridge approach. The team split into three pairs and carried out extensive reconnaissance, primarily to discover a route that would preclude traversing the cascading icefall on the southeast face. The weather, which had been deteriorating, took a turn for the worse. A scree-filled gully with gigantic boulders balanced delicately all the way up was selected as a probable access to the upper reaches of Burphu Dhura. A day's climbing with several heavy loads of equipment brought the team to a dead end, beyond which the formidable icefall gaped. The next day a gully further to the south was identified that seemed to clear the icefall and lead to a snow ramp beyond. Following the gully, Camp I was established on a snow rib a little south of the bottom of the first gendarme at an altitude of 5505 meters.

On September 30, the team climbed Burphu Dhura South (5815m), a virgin subsidiary peak of Burphu Dhura Main. From the summit, the entire south ridge of Burphu Dhur aMain could be studied in totality. Though the unsettled weather did not provide much opportunity, it was decided to place CII (summit camp) on a shelf atop an ice caves. The shelf was located around 50 meters higher than a prominent notch above the second gendarme. The next three days, which were punctuated by extremely bad weather, were engaged in fixing pitches to CII and load ferrying. Nearly 500 meters of rope was fixed over steep and difficult snow and rock.

On October 5, five members occupied CII. The next day, leaving two members at CII, the rest of the team was forced to descend to CI due to extremely inclement weather. The night of October 6 was the worst that the team encountered, with thunder and lightning raging all around. On October 7, CII was wound up and the full team gathered at CI to consider alternatives.

Finding a brief window on October 9, the team made a definitive attempt from CI, gaining the top of a "shark's fin" at 6115 meters. Finally, a long paper-thin corniced ridge with several gaps in between and fully exposed drops on either side brought the team to an unexpected halt. All the equipment, ropes, etc., had already been exhausted and the objective danger was considered far too hazardous to continue the ascent. Further attempts were ruled out due to continuing bad weather and dwindling rations. The team returned to BC on October 11.

The whole expedition was marred by stormy weather. Incessant snow, blinding blizzard, plunging temperatures and technical climbing of the highest order challenged the team every day and almost at every step. Four of the members suffered from exposure, contracting severe chilblain and minor frost bite. The members took every opportunity to photograph and sketch the surrounding peaks and ridges, since many of the summits in the area remain virgin.

LT. CDR. S. DAM, *India*

LADAKH

Umdung Kangri, West Ridge. Umdung Kangri (6643m) is a high peak seen in the south as one descends from Parang La pass. It is near the watershed with the Lingti Valley in Spiti and Ladakh. A Japanese Alpine Club—Tokai Section, expedition led by Tatsumi Mizano made a successful ascent of this peak; nine people reached the summit on August 6, 8 and 9 via the west ridge.

HARISH KAPADIA, *Honorary Editor, The Himalayan Journal*

NEPAL

Pre-Monsoon in the Nepal Himalaya. Seven climbers died this spring in the Nepalese Himalaya, all during descents from 8000-meter summits. Two had no previous success on any 8000-meter mountain and used artificial oxygen during the final hours of their climbs to their summits, while five had been to the tops of 8000ers in previous years and did not use oxygen at all this spring. The seven were:

• Pascal Debrouwer, a 29-year-old Belgian organizer and guide of travel in mountain regions of the world who before this year had scaled the least difficult 8000er, Cho Oyu, on Everest's north side. He used no bottled oxygen.

• Tadeusz Kudelski, a 44-year-old Polish teacher with no summit success on any lower 8000er, on Everest's north side. He did use artificial oxygen.

• Michael Matthews, a 22-year-old British securities trader also with no previous 8000-meter summit experience, on Everest's south side. He too used supplemental oxygen.

• Vasili Kopytko, a 34-year-old Ukrainian doctor who had scaled Cho Oyu and now was part of a three-man summit party who were the first Ukrainian citizens to reach the summit, on Everest's north side. He used no artificial oxygen.

• Miss Ji Hyun-Ok, a 33-year-old South Korean fine-arts teacher who had summited Gasherbrum I and Gasherbrum II in recent years, on Annapurna I's north face. She became the first Korean woman to reach the highest peak of Annapurna I, but she and her Sherpa companion fell to their deaths the same day. She used no bottled oxygen.

• Kami Dorchi Sherpa, 33, who scaled both Annapurna I and Manaslu last year. He accompanied Miss Ji to the top of Annapurna I and died with her. He also used no bottled oxygen.

• Michael Knakkergaard-Jorgensen (better known by a simplified version of his family name, Jorgensen), a 31-year-old mountaineer and tour operator who had scaled Everest and Lhotse in recent years, on Makalu's northwest side. He was the first Dane ever to summit Makalu. He used no bottled oxygen.

ELIZABETH HAWLEY

Post-Monsoon in the Nepal Himalaya. In the post-monsoon in the Nepal Himalaya, the summer monsoon rains and snowfall continued throughout September and into early October, several weeks beyond the normal end of the rainy season, only to be followed by a few mid-October days of more heavy snowfall resulting from a cyclone nearby in India. Many teams on Cho Oyu, Ama Dablam, Baruntse and other mountains with very limited time at their disposal had to retreat from what they considered unsafe avalanche conditions or simply from snow too deep to manage to get through.

There was very little success on Nepal's eight 8000ers. Even on Cho Oyu, where success rates are often high, 21 expeditions did some climbing but just nine of them sent anyone to the top and all followed the normal route on the northwest side. The other 12 teams—including cautiously-led commercial ones—withdrew well below the summit because of dangerous snow conditions. And those who were successful were able to reach the summit only from September 26-October 1; before and after those dates, snow conditions were very bad.

One Japanese mountaineer, Toshiyuki Kitamura, tried to solo Cho Oyu's seldom-climbed southwest face but had to abandon his attempt at 7400 meters in soft snow under a hot sun that defeated him. He moved over to the standard route and followed teammates to the top five days after their ascent.

No one even attempted Annapurna I. Only one team out of seven (a predominantly American group that included Ginette Harrison; see below) had any summiters on Dhaulagiri I. Everest had no summitters at all, and the same was true for Kangchenjunga, Lhotse and Makalu, which had only one team each, and for Manaslu with four parties.

On Everest, there were only four expeditions this autumn (one Spanish party for Nepal's Southeast Ridge route, one Spanish and one Italian group for the North Col in Tibet, though they were not there at the same time, and a South Korean group on the seldom-attempted 1983 American Route on the east face, also in Tibet). None were successful. The last previous autumn season in which only four teams came to Everest was in 1985.

There were surprisingly few fatal accidents in the Nepalese Himalaya this season despite the very dangerous snow conditions. But five climbers did die in Nepal, and all were killed by avalanches. The American climber Alex Lowe died with his teammate David Bridges on Xixabangma (Shishapangma), which is entirely in Tibet and covered accordingly later in this journal. The 41-year-old Briton, Mrs. Ginette Harrison, the only woman ever to summit Kangchenjunga, was caught in a danger zone around 6500 meters on Dhaulagiri I on October 24. She was highly experienced in Himalayan climbing and in organizing and conducting expeditions to these great peaks. In addition to Kangchenjunga via its difficult north face in May 1998, she had summited three other 8000ers, including Everest in October, 1993.

A Nepalese Sherpa who was climbing with a French expedition, Dawa Dorje, was also killed by the avalanche that struck Ginette Harrison. The others who died on Nepalese mountains were two South Koreans, Han Do-Kyu and Hyun Myeong-Kun, on the north side of Kangchenjunga and Sange Sherpa with a South Korean team on the normal Northwest route for Makalu.

ELIZABETH HAWLEY

Trekking Peaks of Nepal, Ascents and Attempts. In an effort to climb all 18 trekking peaks in Nepal as catalogued by Bill O'Connor's book, *The Trekking Peaks of Nepal*, the British Army Nepal Expedition sent different teams to all the respective mountains with the objective of making "field observations" of the routes described in the book while climbing the routes. Changes were to be noted in updated descriptions that would be the basis for a new publication on the same topic. Fifteen out of the 18 peaks were summitted. Those that defeated attempts were Hiunchuli, Singu Chuli and Ramdung. Further details are lacking.

Kanjiroba, Ascent. It was reported that Britons Richard Bull, Neil Cooper, Andy Hawes, Mal Lewis, Andy Lind, Josie Poole, Ben Steele and Alison and Tom Wedgwood made the fifth ascent of Kanjiroba Main Summit (6883m). It was the first time in 20 years that the mountain had seen an ascent. The crux was the approach to the mountain. Taking the route pioneered in 1961 by John Tyson, the team proceeded up the Jagdula Gorge in a ten-day bushwhack that involved the building of four bridges, a number of rappels and Tyrolean traverses and construction of wooden ladders to navigate vertical rock walls. Base Camp was established at 4200 meters at the foot of the mountain. From an Advanced Base Camp at 5200 meters, Bull, Cooper, Hawes, Lewis and Steele, along with a climbing Sherpa and cook, Ringi, proceed to fix 200 meters of rope on a 45-degree snow slope to reach the southeast ridge at ca. 6000 meters. On September 26, they continued up the ridge in deep snow, led by Ringi, who broke trail for the team and fixed a 12-meter ice wall that would prove to be the hardest section of the climb. Following Ringi, Bull and Cooper reached the summit, a feat repeated on September 28 by Lind, Pemba Sherpa and Tom Wedgwood. A helicopter rescue was initiated to save Lind, who back at BC found that he had developed frostbite in one foot. The journey back to Hurikot followed a route to the west of the Jagdula that crossed two high passes, including the last col in the ridge that runs southeast from Milch Berg (Palta Thumba, 6126m), and traversed a series of high plateaus well above the gorge before following a long gully down to the main valley. (*High Mountain Sports* 212)

Kangtokla, First Official Ascent. Kangtokla (6294m) was one of the ten peaks opened to foreign expeditions in 1998. Miguel Angel Videl led a four-member Spanish team that made the first official ascent of the peak via the southeast ridge. The summit was reached on October 11. (*High Mountain Sports* 212)

Raksha Urai, Attempt. Hubert Fitzwallner led an Austro-German expedition that on October 20 reached a high point of just under 6000 meters on one of the summits of Rakshi Urai. The team climbed the east ridge to the east face in their attempt. (*High Mountain Sports* 212)

Himlung, Attempt. The members of the expedition were Götz Wiegand (leader), Frank Meutzner, Olaf Zill, Matthias Braun, Tilo Bähr and myself. We started our expedition in September. Before starting out to attempt Himlung, we met Miss Elizabeth Hawley in Kathmandu. We have heard about the fact that Himlung was quite hard to find. It seemed that other expedition teams would possibly be there, too. But the information we received was very poor and conflicting. The biggest problem for us was that everything we heard about Himlung could possibly refer to Nemjung, located close to Himlung. So we collected all the available information and started for Base Camp at the foot of Himlung, Gyachikang and Nemjung. This BC was used by a Japanese expedition in 1992.

Left to right: Himlung, Gyachikang and Nemjung I as seen from the summit of the 5800-meter peak climbed by the German Himlung expedition. The team attempted the ridge on Himlung that runs up from right to left. ANGELA HAMPEL

The weather was very unusual for the time: very cloudy and a lot of snow. We tried to find a good route to Camp I, which we set up on a saddle at 5300 meters on the west ridge. The next day, we climbed up to establish Camp II. At an altitude of 6000 meters we had to stop. It was hard to progress; deep new snow and thin ice crust prohibited us from going on. Götz and Matthias kept on going to find a place for CII. After setting up that camp at 6150 meters, Frank and Olaf went higher. They told us that it was very difficult to find the route through the glacier they had to cross. It was very dangerous, because there was an extremely high possibility of avalanches all the time. The route went along a ridge with snow cornices. Two cornices in particular, each 200 meters long, on the top of an 800-meter, 60-degree wall, made us turn back on October 10. It was too difficult to keep on going and the possibility that the cornices might crash down was very high. So we went back to climb another summit, a 5800-meter peak nearby.

ANGELA HAMPEL, *Germany*

Manaslu and Dhaulagiri, Ascents. Ed Viesturs and his Finnish partner, Veikka Gustafsson, surmounted Manaslu (8163m) and then Dhaulagiri I (8167m), the world's eighth- and seventh-highest mountains, in one month of climbing. They had no Sherpas, no fixed ropes and no bottled oxygen to assist them.

They arrived at the standard Manaslu Base Camp site at 4900 meters on April 4 and placed two more camps along the normal Northeast Face route in the following eight days. They then went down to rest at Base Camp before leaving it again on the 18th to establish one more high camp on the 21st at 7530 meters, just below the summit plateau out of the wind. The next day they went to the top. They were on Manaslu's summit on the 22nd despite very strong winds that "almost knocked us over a few times," according to Viesturs.

With the help of a helicopter, they arrived at Dhaulagiri I's Base Camp site on April 30 and on May 4 they were on its summit. They generally followed the standard climbing route along the northeast ridge but in getting to the ridge, they took a shortcut around an icefall and its crevasses and up a steep slope that avoided the usual longer route to the northeast col, where many expeditions place their first high camps. They pitched just two camps on the ridge on May 2-3 and climbed to the top on the 4th.

Viesturs has now summited ten of the world's 14 8000-meter mountains, including Everest five times and Cho Oyu twice; for Gustafsson this was his second ascent of Dhaulagiri I, but Manaslu was his seventh 8000er, including Everest twice.

ELIZABETH HAWLEY

DHAULAGIRI HIMAL

Dhaulagiri, South Face, New Route. From October 25-November 3, Slovenian Tomaž Humar soloed *The Mobitel Route* (VI 5.10d A0 M7+, ca. 4000m) on the south face of Dhaulagiri (8167m). A full account of his ascent appears earlier in this journal.

Nilgiri South, Attempt. It was reported that Tadej Golob led a five-member Slovenian expedition that attempted the first ascent of the southwest ridge on Nilgiri South (6839m). The team followed a line up the south face to connect with the crest of the ridge, reaching a high point of ca. 6600 meters on October 17 before strong winds and heavy snowfall forced an end to their efforts. (*High Mountain Sports* 212)

Annapurna I, North Face, New Route, and All 14 8000ers. This spring, Juanito Oyarzabal (or Oiarzabal, as it has sometimes been spelled), a 43-year-old Basque, climbed his 14th 8000er when he ascended Annapurna I (8091m), the tenth-highest mountain in the world. A man who has been scrupulous about his claims, Oyarzabal last year went back up to reach the highest point on Dhaulagiri I after realizing that he had gone to a false summit.

He and his team were forced to pioneer a new line up Annapurna I's north face from 5600 meters to the top because of frequent dangerous ice avalanching down the usual route to the right (west) of the line they climbed; the route they had to take was not completely safe from avalanches either, but it was much more so than others. "Annapurna is a very dangerous mountain—terrible," Oyarzabal reported.

Nonetheless he summited on April 29, when the mountain was still very dry, but it took him and his two Basque teammates eight hours to climb from their last camp at 7200 meters the very long distance to the top. His first 8000-meter success was on Cho Oyu in 1985; he had now summited 14 in 14 years on a total of 20 expeditions. He said he felt some relief at having done all 14, but no elation. He is not retiring: next year he wants to scale Everest without artificial oxygen. It seems to be extremely difficult for climbers to stop climbing.

This spring's other claim to have scaled all 14 of the 8000ers was made by Sergio Martini of Italy, who summited Everest from the north side on May 26 along with 12 others (and 11 from the south the same day). At the age of 49, he is the oldest person to claim all the 8000ers.

However, when he and his friend Fausto De Stefani were on Lhotse in the autumn of 1997, they reported that they had climbed to a point "very, very near" the summit but were unable to say how near it they had reached in very poor visibility, so their claim to Lhotse's summit is not accepted by many observers. Martini said now that he does not plan to stop climbing and perhaps he will return to the 8000ers, maybe including Lhotse.

ELIZABETH HAWLEY

Chhukung Ri, South Summit. Yoshio Morikubo led an expedition that climbed Chhukung Ri, reaching the South Summit (5550m) on August 16-17. Further details are lacking.

Ganchempo, South Face. On Ganchempo (or Gang Chhenpo, 6387m), in north central Nepal, a team of six Swiss led by Karl Kobler and Christoph Jezler succeeded in making a new route to the summit. One member, Markus Baumann, and a Nepalese "Sherpa" named Shyam Prasad Pun climbed the south face and were on the top on October 15, between the end of the monsoon season's snows and the beginning of Indian cyclone's new snowfall.

ELIZABETH HAWLEY

Everest in the Pre-Monsoon. This spring, 22 parties attempted to scale Everest from the north, 14 from the south and one from the east. A total of 117 people went to the summit of Everest from the three different sides: 48 from the north in Tibet via one of two standard routes which most climbers follow; 66 via the other standard route which begins on the southern side in Nepal; and three from the east, which, like the northern route, is in Tibet but is very seldom attempted. The total number of summitters for this season is just one person short of spring 1998's record number for any single season.

Forty-seven of this spring's successful climbers had been to the top in earlier years, so the season's net gain was a total of 70 new summitters. Altogether, 878 men and women have now reached the world's highest point, starting with Hillary and Tenzing, and they have been to the summit 1,177 times. A total of 136 people have now made more than one ascent including the second person to have summitted ten times, Apa Sherpa; on May 26, he equaled the record number of ascents first achieved in 1996 by the famous Ang Rita Sherpa, who now seems to have retired from high-altitude climbing.

About half of the 22 "parties" on the north side were not teams at all but only individuals or couples who were attempting the mountain independently of others above Advance Base Camp and who were assigned by their Kathmandu trekking agencies to the permits of teams who were glad to have some income from these independents' "memberships" but had no real responsibility for them. Eight of them never reached the top.

Some teams, especially those on the northern side where permits are considerably easier and less expensive to obtain, were ill-equipped to handle emergencies in terms of manpower, climbing equipment and supplies. When trouble arose, such as the disappearance or severe frostbite of members who could not descend alone, their groups were unable to cope. Other teams' leaders, climbing members, doctors and climbing Sherpas were then called upon to save people whom they did not know at all and for whom they had no responsibility except as one human being for another. A professional expedition leader and guide, New Zealander Russell Brice, who takes teams every spring to the north side, has found that year after year he must devote considerable time, expertise and plentiful supplies of oxygen and medical items to rescue people who do not belong to his teams.

Some of the new Everest records set this spring were as follows.

The oldest person to the top was Lev Sarkisov, who lives in Tbilisi and holds both Georgian and Armenian citizenship. He waited to make his summit bid until he would become the oldest on May 12 and thereby beat by exactly one day the previous record-holder, Ramon Blanco, a Spaniard resident in Venezuela, who on October 7, 1993 set an age record of 60 years and 160 days. Sarkisov became 60 years and 161 days old on his summit day.

The longest stay at the top was achieved by 33-year-old Babu Tshering (or Babu Chiri, as he now spells his name) Sherpa, who spent 21.5 hours on the very top or tucked into a tiny tent on a platform immediately below it. He declared in advance that his long stay was intended to establish "a new glory for Nepal and to encourage Nepalese and foreign climbers to conduct such courageous adventures." He used no artificial oxygen throughout his entire climb and, an exceedingly strong man, he now reached the summit in his eighth ascent (since October 1990) with two highly experienced Sherpa companions at 3:30 p.m. on May 6, after all other climbers had abandoned their attempts that day because of strong wind and fresh snowfall. His two Sherpa friends helped him to make a platform for his tent and prepare to remain there for his intended 20-hour stay, and after an hour they left him alone with his tent, mattress, cooking gear and a walkie-talkie.

Thomas and Mrs. Tina Sjogren, the Swedish leaders of the expedition who employed him to help gain the summit themselves, monitored his condition by talking with him hourly throughout the night from 9 p.m. onward (he had at first switched on to the wrong waveband). Babu spent an hour and a half chatting on his walkie-talkie with Sherpa friends, being interviewed by government-appointed liaison officers and packing up most of his belongings. He kept the valuable tent but left his mattress, somewhat to the annoyance of ecologically-minded summitters who came after him, but the mattress proved he got there. He was still in good health, and indeed went again to the top on May 26 with the Sjogrens for his ninth time atop Everest.

The first people to have summitted from all three sides were two members of an Indian expedition led by Mrs. Santosh Yadav, herself the first woman ever to have summitted Everest twice (see note on page 375). The first woman to go to the summit from both south and north sides was Miss Cathy O'Dowd of South Africa. She had summitted from the Nepalese side in May 1996 in the last ascent of a month that was notorious for its fatalities in a sudden storm about two weeks earlier. Now this May she has gone to the top from the north side on May 29, again on the last team to reach the summit, and found Babu Tshering's mattress still there, three weeks after he had abandoned it.

ELIZABETH HAWLEY

Mount Everest, Altitude Survey. In the spring of 1999, Boston's Museum of Science, the National Geographic Society and a number of very generous individual donors fielded a scientific expedition to Mount Everest, with five basic objectives.

1. To determine, as accurately as possible, the precise altitude of the summit of Mount Everest, using the latest Trimble 4800 Global Positioning Satellite (GPS) Receivers.

2. To coordinate every detail of this GPS work with both the United States' National Imagery and Mapping Agency (NIMA) and China's National Bureau of Surveying and Mapping, as a new altitude for Mount Everest is a matter of international interest.

3. To create a special geological collection (as planned by Dr. Kip Hodges of the Massachusetts Institute of Technology) as an important part of the Mount Everest Geologic Map Project, on which he and Dr. Michael Searle of Oxford University have already made significant progress.

4. To set up weather-monitoring equipment on bedrock at Everest's 7891-meter (25,889') South Col, Camp II and Base Camp for MIT's Media Laboratory, under the direction of Dr. Michael Hawley.

5. Jeff and Kellie Rhoads were to climb with our party and make as complete as possible a film of what was done and how. This was not in any way related to our budget, and all of the expenses and profits related to their work were a gamble taken by American Adventure Productions. This arrangement made it possible for us, at no cost, to get a video record of exactly what our team accomplished in the field.

In order to secure a very precise new altitude for Mount Everest's summit, as well as to have a good headquarters from which all of this work would be well coordinated, we set up Base Camp in early April at an altitude of 17,600 feet. Our team had reliable, constant communication by radiotelephone with the "outside world" as well as with our teams above on the mountain. David Mencin of Boulder, Colorado, was in charge of this coordination. Charles Corfield of Palo Alto, California, was science manager of the expedition.

On May 3, the leader of our party, Pete Athans, his assistant guide, Bill Crouse, and five experienced Sherpas reached our South Col camp with a plan to spend one full day there before moving up to the summit. These Sherpas were Chewang Nima, Phu Tashi, Dorje, Gyalgen and Nga Temba. May 4 was spent setting up a good camp and operating one of our Trimble 4800 GPS receivers at this critical location for at least 48 hours.

With excellent weather, they all reached the summit of Mount Everest at 10 a.m. on May 5. The conditions there were just about as perfect as we could have prayed for: -26°F, cloudless skies and a light breeze. The GPS Receiver was planted firmly in the summit snow at

10:13 a.m. and run continuously until 11:09 a.m. for a total of 56 minutes.

Pete and Bill took lots of pictures and carefully read the Kollsman altimeter, which was graciously loaned to us by Lou Bissoni. They also collected two tiny samples of ancient limestone from a small ledge just south of the top, stone that none of them had ever seen before. The same furious west-southwest winter gales that had revealed George Mallory's body on the other side of the peak had swept this lofty ledge clear, too, revealing very, very old limestone from the Ordovician period. This "new" ledge is certainly the highest bedrock anywhere in the world!

During their descent, Pete Athans replaced the GPS station bolt at Bishop Ledge (just below the summit) with a new, permanent one. Otherwise, the descent back to Base Camp was routine, and they carried with them the two precious GPS receivers.

I take pleasure in reporting the final results of our GPS data, now thoroughly coordinated with China, Nepal, India and the United States' NIMA. The newly-established altitude for Mount Everest is 29,035 feet (8850m).

BRADFORD WASHBURN

Medical Research at High Altitude. The E-3 expedition (Dr. Kenneth Kamler, expedition physician, and Dr. Christian Macedonia, director of medical research) was in the field from April 21-May 30. There were 15 expedition members, including five medical doctors. We used the standard approach to the south (Nepal) side of Everest, flying from Kathmandu to Lukla and then trekking to the standard expedition Base Camp area on the Khumbu Glacier. We returned via the same route. We were a medical research expedition and did not attempt to climb any peak.

The 1999 E-3 project's goals included high-altitude research, real-time biomonitoring, telemedicine and an education program involving "live transmission" from Mt. Everest to a number of schools. Research took place en route to, and at, Everest Base Camp (17,500'). Five members climbed through and above the Khumbu Icefall (19,000'+) in order to gather additional altitude data and to test the function of real-time biomonitoring equipment. We obtained permit space for Nuptse to do this, as the first two camps above Everest BC are the same as for Everest. The team treated numerous climbers and Sherpas at Everest Base Camp and also conducted free village medical clinics.

At various times en route, as well as during a climb through the Khumbu Icefall, team members wore compact, ca. four-pound biomonitoring devices. These instruments both recorded locally, and transmitted in real-time, vital signs including heart rate, core body temperature, skin temperature, activity level and GPS location. This data was displayed on computer screens showing the position of each climber "live" on a topographic map along with corresponding physiological information. Researchers at Base Camp and at Yale, 10,000 miles away, were able to monitor both the physical condition and precise location of the climbers. These devices functioned well and may serve as a useful adjunct to certain types of climbs in the future.

Newly available compact imaging duplex Doppler ultrasound equipment was used to gather data on how the blood flow rates in the carotid (neck) and brachial (arm) arteries change as a response to a hypoxic (low oxygen) environment. Comparing differences in circulatory flow rates, we were able to document significant change in blood flow patterns. The data appeared to show a significant shunting of the blood flow from one area of the body to another as an adaptation to a hypoxic environment. In some cases, the blood flow to the head more than doubled, while the blood flow to the arms and legs dropped to 25 percent of typical flow rates. The pounding headaches, poor appetite, muscle cramps, etc., that climbers experience may be explained, at least in part, by the significant redistribution of blood away from less vital organs and areas, such as the stomach, to the brain in an attempt to survive a low-oxygen environment. The project collected a large data set of imaging duplex Doppler ultrasound of blood flow at high altitude.

Drs. Kamler and Macedonia suggest that climbers going to high altitude consider the pneumococcus vaccination called Pneumovax. It is a one-time vaccination that is considered safe and effective at preventing the major subtypes of pneumonia caused by pneumococcus bacterium. Pneumovax is usually only given to the elderly and people with impaired immune systems. High altitude appears to produce similar risks in impairment of healing and in damage to the system that removes contaminants from our airways. Pneumovax has minimal risks to high-altitude climbers with potential life-saving properties.

SCOTT HAMILTON

Erkimkang, North Face, and Khatung Kang, Ascents. In mid-August I went to the Langtang region, north of Kathmandu, where I retraced the steps of Bill Tilman, who visited the area in the late 1940s. Like Tilman, I made a base at the yersa (temporary settlement) of Langshisa, exploring and making acclimatization hikes in the area. I made an ascent of "Buddha Peak" (Tilman's name, locally known as Erkimkang, ca. 6100m), in three days round-trip from base camp, via the north face. The climb involved some moderate mixed climbing but was mostly snow and ice. I descended to the west, down a glacier. Tilman approached this by crossing the river downstream of Langshisa near the Yersa of Numathang, but now there is a small bridge at Langshisa itself. This may or may not have been the peak's first ascent.

In September I went to Pokhara by bus, then flew to Jomsom. From there I trekked over the Thorung La, and to acclimate climbed Khatung Kang (6400m) from the east by a moderate snow/ice route.

CHARLIE FOWLER

Cho Polu, First Official Ascent. Our team was composed of Dieter Rüelker, Guenter Jung, Dr. Olaf Rieck and myself as leader. On October 13, we started from Kathmandu, reaching Lukla by airplane and continuing on via the normal trekking route to Namche Bazar in a few days of reasonably good weather. On October 18, just as we reached Dingboche, it started to snow heavily, forcing us to stop for two days before continuing via Chukhung to Island Peak (Imja Tse) Base Camp. On the last ten kilometers we broke trail through one meter of snow and dug out a path for the yaks with shovels (while lots of trekking groups waited behind us to enjoy the fruits of our work when it was done). On October 23 and 24, the yaks reached the porter shelter near Island BC, but were not able to continue further to Island Peak or even Cho Polu BC. We lost three more days carrying the loads by ourselves before establishing our BC on the moraine east of Island Peak on October 26 at about 5200 meters.

Two days later we started our first reconnaissance, but due to the vast amount of snow on the Lhotse Shar Glacier it took us until November 1 to reach the base of the mountain. We approached from the west and put in a line on the west face of the col ("Hardie's Col," 6183m) on November 1 after two days of climbing under continuous avalanche danger. Due

High camp at Hardie's Col (6183m), a snowy saddle on the ridge between Shartse and Cho Polu. The north face of Cho Polu is visible behind. It was climbed via a line right of center (Jung-Rieck-Rüelker-Walter) in 1999. MARKUS WALTER

to really bad snow conditions and unstable cornices, continuing via the north ridge to the summit would have been like playing Russian roulette. One day of reconnaissance on the ridge resulted in nothing other than cold fingers in the incredible winds. Stormy weather with heavy winds (but no snowfall) and not enough food for a longer summit attempt forced us to descend to Base Camp. We left two tents and some cooking and climbing equipment at Hardie's Col.

After three rest days in Base Camp, we reached our camp at Hardie's Col once more, this time with enough food for a longer stay during our summit attempt. The next day we descended down the east side of Hardie's Col, rappelling about 80 meters down onto a plateau of the Barun Glacier, at which point we crossed the glacier hollow through deep snow and reached the bergschrund on the north face of Cho Polu. We found excellent snow conditions on the steep wall above the bergschrund, and so we climbed 100 meters, fixed two ropes and returned to our High Camp, reaching it in darkness. The next morning, November 12, we started at 4 a.m., reached the bergschrund at 6 a.m. at dawn and climbed up our fixed ropes, taking them with us after reaching the highest point of the previous day's reconnaissance and continuing toward the summit. We climbed a direct line up the center of the north face, passing some seracs and small crevasses in the upper part of the wall. The whole face was about 600 meters high and up to 60 degrees. Because of -25°C temperatures and excellent ice conditions, we climbed unroped without belaying. Sixty meters below the summit cornice, we turned slightly to the right, gained a big crevasse and used the lower lip of this crevasse as a natural traverse line to reach the north ridge. A few steps on the broad ridge brought us to the summit of Cho Polu (6734m). Incredibly good weather with low winds and a fantastic view over hundreds of summits was waiting for us, and so we spent more than one hour on the very top, taking a 360-degree panoramic photograph and several hundred telephoto shots of the neighboring mountains. The ascent took us about four hours from the bergschrund, the descent via the same route two hours. We reached our camp at Hardie's Col late in the afternoon and over the next two days descended down to BC with all the equipment. Climbing on the sunny west face of Hardie's Col was still much more difficult and dangerous than on Cho Polu's north face because of the snow conditions.

Guenter Jung on the north face of Cho Polu. The summit above him is Kangchungtse (7640m), while to the left is Chomo Lönzö (7790m). MARKUS WALTER

Reaching BC on November 14, we completed our successful ascent of Cho Polu by all four team members. Before leaving BC on November 19, we celebrated Dieter Rüelker's 60th birthday on November 17 by making a short ascent of Island Peak in three hours from BC.

MARKUS WALTER, *Alpinclub Sachsen, Germany*

Cho Polu, First Ascent, Previously Unreported. Spanish mountaineer Nil Bohigas reports that he did very quick solo climbs to the summits of Cho Polu and of nearby Pethangtse in the autumn of 1984 and several days later also soloed Baruntse. However, he had no official permission for these ascents, and no one except a few of his friends knew about them until recently.

Bohigas says that he went up the north face to the northeast ridge of Cho Polo to the top on the same day, in late October or early November, on which he had just climbed Pethangtse (he does not remember the exact dates). He stayed at a bivouac at 6000 meters, left a cache of supplies there, went out at night and summitted Pethangtse (6710m) before sunrise in a very quick ascent and descent untroubled by any technical difficulties. He then moved south to Cho Polu. "I found the main difficulties on the north face's first section, especially on the descent. I reached the summit by the northeast ridge. I descended by the same route and I reached the glacier at night.... I did not take more than 16 hours in total. Three days later I soloed Baruntse."

He had already pioneered a new route on the difficult south face of Annapurna I with just one teammate, Enric Lucas (see 1985 *AAJ*, p. 285) and now "I felt perfectly acclimatized to the altitude." He also reports he found good snow conditions, which must have been significantly better than those the Germans encountered this autumn, and he does not mention any problems with the wind.

The Germans, without knowing the above exact details, found the claim by Bohigas to have summited Pethangtse and Cho Polu on the same day "unbelievable" because they were sure he would have had "just not enough time" to descend Pethangtse, cross an estimated five kilometers of plateau between these two mountains and scale the difficult north side of Cho Polu.

However, it is a truism that what one man cannot do another person can; skills, strengths and experience vary enormously. Also, one must consider the facts that the Germans had worse weather; they did not climb alpine style but pitched two fixed camps, which meant they carried heavy loads in their ascent, whereas Bohigas carried nothing; and they were a team of two men aged 59 years, one 35 and one, Walters, 26, the same age as Bohigas in 1984.

ELIZABETH HAWLEY

Tangkongma, Southeast/Northeast Ridge. It was reported that Jamie McGuinness (New Zealand) led an international commercial expedition that made perhaps the third official ascent of Tangkogma (6215m) via a possible new route. The mountain, which sits above the last approach stage to Kangchengjunga's Pangpema Base Camp, is easily approached, and other unauthorized ascents may thus have been made.

McGuinness, with one Sherpa and one Danish, one French and two American clients, climbed a snow gully from a high camp (ca. 5000m) before moving right onto the southeast ridge. They then traversed across a glacier on the right to connect with the northeast ridge, which they followed to the summit on October 29. The route was climbed without ropes; the next day, McGuinness, with three American clients and another Sherpa, repeated the route to the summit. (*High Mountain Sports* 212)

Jannu, North Face, Attempt. We (Fyodorov, Grekov, Mariev, Chabaline, Tukhvatulin, Slepnyov and Raljabov) arrived in Kathmandu September 2 with the goal of climbing the north face of Jannu. By September 11, the first team members arrived at Base Camp (4500m). The 13th marked the official opening of the event as we reconnaissanced the one-and-a-half hours' approach, cached gear at the base of the route and started to fix ropes through the ice-fall. Bad weather and heavy snowfall characterized the next month as we continued to work higher on the route. On October 11th, Chabaline, Tukhvatulin, Slepnyov and Radjabov fixed rope to 6700 meters, where they put a tent and spent a night. The next day, Tukhvatulin and Slepnyov fixed three more pitches. It snowed for the next three days. On October 16, when the team of Grekov, Fyodorov and Mariev went up to 6700 meters, they found the tent torn by snow and decided to go down. The general worsening of weather, permit deadlines and winter closing in forced the expedition to wind up.

Despite our failure to get to the summit, we consider the overall results to be good. We made a test of our climbing and team skills, made an active reconnaissance of the route up to 6800 meters, gathered information about route conditions in different weather, tested our equipment and worked out route tactics. We hope to return next spring and go on.

ILYAS TUKHVATULIN, *Russia*

TIBET

Lapche Kang, Attempt, Previously Unreported. The Kyoto Alpine League team, led by Kazunari Aihara and comprised of six members, made an attempt on the northeast ridge of Lapche Kang (7100m) in September-October, 1998, but abandoned the attempt 160 meters below the summit. We placed Base Camp (4500m) near Lango Village on September 12 and carried our supplies up by yak to ABC (5400m) on September 15. We set up Camp I (5750m) on September 21 and CII (6100m) on September 28 on the Duyannu Glacier. At first, we made an attempt via the ice fall on Duyannu Glacier, reaching about 6450 meters near the hanging glacier. We next tried the neighboring small ridge on the ice fall, placing CIII

(6700m) on the northeast ridge on October 14. We made the attempt for the summit from CIII on October 15-16. But we weren't blessed with fine weather and could not extend the route up further due to a shortage of fixed ropes. Snow conditions on the upper part of the summit ridge were very bad. By then we had little food and time. We had to abandon our climb on October 16.

MASAKI HAYASHI, *Kyoto Alpine League*

Kabang, Attempt, and Naimona'nyi, New Route. On September 10, Kinichi Yamamori (leader), Masayoshi Matsudate, Yoshihide Higami and Mitsuru Ito left Narita Airport and travelled to Lhasa via Beijing and Chengdu. On September 17, Ayumi Nozawai, Tomoyuki Furuya and I (Hiroshi Iwazaki), who had traveled overland from Pakistan after a Spantik expedition, joined the others at Zhangmu. On September 18, we crossed the Ma La (5234m) in jeeps and on the 19th came to the village of Gun. On the 21st, we established Base Camp at 4700 meters in a meadow on the north side of Kabang (6717m). The weather was not good because of the monsoon. On the 24th, we set up Camp I on the Nasu Glacier at 5180 meters and on October 2 made CII on the shoulder of the east ridge at 6050 meters. On October 4, we fixed 13 pitches to 6450 meters. The next day we reached 6550 meters, where we were confronted by a crevasse band that forced our retreat.

On October 10, Mitsuru Ito departed for Japan. We traveled to Saga, located on the north bank of the Yarlung Zangbo (Tsangpo), and then continued on via Zhongba and Paryang, looking over the mountains on the border with Nepal. On October 12, we established BC (4700m) on the banks of the Gurla Chu.

On the 15th, we made an Advanced Base Camp at 5450 meters. Matsudate and Higami attempted to ascend Guna La (6902m), which is located to the north of Naimona'nyi (Gurla Mondata, 7694m) across the Naimona'nyi Glacier, and Nozawai, Furuya and I went together for the purpose of exploring the north side of Naimona'nyi.

On October 17th, we bivied on the Naimona'nyi Glacier at 6095 meters. On the 18th, we climbed up the West Ridge route and all of us succeeded in reaching the summit together at 2:14 p.m. The same day, we bivied again at 6095 meters and returned to BC on the 19th.

On October 22, we started at first light (8 a.m.) for a new route on Naimona'nyi. Nozawai, Furuya and I traversed the rock-scrambling slope and went through an ablation valley to the Support Camp at 6000 meters on the Naimona'nyi Glacier. Then, Matsudate and Higami moved to the Support Camp as a countermeasure against accidents. There, we picked up deposits and carried up our heavy rucksacks. We shook hands with Matsudate and Higami and left. We entered a branch glacier from the southeast side of the Naimona'nyi's North Peak that we had explored while attempting Guna La. We went along the right side of the glacier for a while before crossing it and then continued on toward a col of the ridge between the main peak and north peak. The snow conditions were poor and the main difficulties were breaking trail in crusty snow. Nozawai and Furuya climbed up straight and I traversed right and ascended the contact line of rock and snow, and we reached the col. There, the whole of the north side of Naimona'nyi could be looked at. There was a serac which we had not been able to see before under the lower crevasse. Thus, we could not climb the north side directly. On this day, we stayed at 6380 meters just below a 6512-meter peak.

October 23 was a comfortable day. Although the serac was not so dangerous, we could not climb straight up and had to traverse to the right to avoid crevasses. We could not keep a rapid pace and gain altitude due to deep snow, and time passed. We went over two snow

The north face of Naimona'nyi as seen from Guna La, showing the route climbed by Furuya, Iwazaki and Nozawai. KINICHI YAMAMORI

bridges and at last climbed up to the upper great snow slope. After a short break, we started to climb the slope where, fortunately, the snow was in good condition, and we managed to make a rapid ascent of the slope. We continued to climb toward the upper part of the north ridge. The great white slope was long as we had expected, and our pace slowed down when we were over 7000 meters. Then came dark. We made a slow ascent without rest in high winds and blowing snow. We established a camp site at 7205 meters in blowing snow; one-third of our tent was in the air. We spent a long night holding down the tent against the storm.

On the 24th, we overslept because of fatigue, and our start was very late. We were forced to go roundabout to the east face because we didn't have rock pitons. The serac overhung the upper part of the face. Naimona'nyi threw a shadow upon the face. It was too late to climb the serac. Fortunately, we found a terrace on the face at 7410 meters that was wide enough to pitch a tent. We enjoyed the views of Tibet under fantastic moonlight.

The next morning, we found a weakness between a rock wall and an ice wall, but as we began climbing up, the slope became steep and our climbing pace slowed. The slope was over 75 degrees, thus we climbed with a rope for the last 50 meters. At last, we slipped out of the east face and climbed a gulley. Nozawai and Furuya climbed along the ridge and I traversed a snow face and climbed up. At 3:12 p.m., we reached the summit together, having completed a new route on the north side via the east face and the fourth ascent of the peak. Just after the ascent, we descended the Zaronmaromba Glacier on the west side and stayed at 6800 meters. On the 26th, we arrived at BC. After the climb, we drank in celebration of the ascent at Burang, and left for the pilgrimage to Mt. Kailash.

HIROSHI IWAZAKI, *Himalayan Association of Japan*

Nojin Kansa, Ascent. In the spring, Masakazu Okuda led a three-member Japanese expedition that made an ascent along the ridge between Togulon (ca. 6800m) and Nojin (Ningqing) Kansa (7206m), continuing to the summit of Nojin (Ningqing) Kansa via the west face. Exact details are uncertain; it is unclear whether this was a new route.

Lungma Ri Area, Various Activity, Previously Unreported. In July-August, 1997, we made a traverse of the Transhimalaya and climbed several 6000-meter peaks near Ombu Lake. Against our expectations, we found a mountain massif in this area with several peaks instead of only the one 7000-meter peak, Lungma Ri.

Čestmír Lukeš and Irene Oehninger, Switzerland

Pholha Khyung, Attempt. We departed Kathmandu on August 31 en route to Tibet's Transhimalaya. Our team was comprised of Britons Julian Freeman-Attwood, Lindsay Griffin and Phil Bartlett as climbers and Pat and Harry Reeves as trekkers. As the token American, my responsibilities included explaining this country's decision to give China permanent Most Favored Nation trading status as we drank Cokes and Pabst Blue Ribbon beers bought in the Tibetan hinterlands while listening to the locals talk about the relatives they had lost to the Han Chinese's efforts to domesticate Tibet. In one week of travel, we headed up through Nyalam and Tingri, hung a left at Lhatse, then took a right at a nondescript dirt track one and a half hours past Saga on the road to Mt. Kailash. One and a half more hours along this track through small collections of nomad houses brought us to Base Camp (4960m) in the middle of a beautiful basin on September 6. We were unable to find a lower altitude at which to place Base Camp; this would prove problematic for recovery from illness and general attempts at acclimatization. Other factors contributing to the nearly complete lack of climbing we would do were weather, lack of fitness and general disinclination on the part of most of the climbers. The highlights of the trip were the delightful locals. Nomads who tended their sheep and yak in these pristine mountain valleys during the summers, they would be our constant companions for the next month. Though they were quite familiar with the yeti that lived in a nearby valley and protected the region's holy mountain, they had never heard of Reinhold Messner and refused to believe he exists.

Our objectives as defined by our permits included an aesthetic 6530-meter peak the nomads called Pholha Khyung and the highest peak of the Gangdise Range, Loinbo Kangri (7095m). Loinbo Kangri, the only peak in the area to have received an ascent, had been attempted by a Himalayan Association of Japan expedition in 1994; the first ascent of the mountain was made in 1996 by a joint South Korea-China expedition. Julian and Lindsay had reconned the area the year before, following a route taken by Sven Hedin just after the turn of the century.

All the team minus Lindsay climbed up to ca. 6100 meters on a snow peak southeast of Phola Khyung on September 12. Pat, Harry, Phil and I climbed up the easy south flanks of Pt. 5916m (as measured by an unreliable wrist altimeter), a subsidiary summit of Peak ca. 6400m directly across from BC, on September 18. Pat and Harry departed BC on September 25. Lindsay continued to be kept low by illness; Phil and Julian decided they no longer wanted to try either of our permitted objectives. Instead, they climbed a ca. 6000-meter shoulder peak on the 28th, following a route that paralleled snow leopard tracks over the top, while I returned to BC to further recover from food poisoning and get psyched for a solo attempt on Pholha Khyung. On September 30, with Phil in support, I walked up to our high camp below

The southeast faces of Pholha Khyung (in front) and Loinbo Kangri. CHRISTAN BECKWITH

Pholha Khyung, then continued on up to recce the route for the next day. My high point of ca. 6200 meters on Pholha Khyung via a couloir on the southeast side would be the last effort of the trip, as the bad weather that had plagued our stay closed in for good that evening, signaling an end to the expedition.

Of note in the area is the southwest face of Pholha Khyung, which looked to yield a fine wall of golden granite perhaps as much as 800 meters high, and the striking ca. 6400-meter peak half a kilometer northeast of Pholha Khyung that would offer 800-meter mixed and/or rock routes. Himalayan wildlife, including lynx, ramchekor, wild sheep, wild asses, snow leopards and the oft-discussed but rarely seen yeti, along with the friendly and equally wild locals, would yield a wonderful adventure to those interested in exploratory climbing some distance from the usual haunts.

CHRISTIAN BECKWITH, *The Wayward Mountaineers*

Tangmonja, Attempt, and Machag, First Ascent. It was reported that Britons Derek Buckle, Gary Hill, Alyson Starling, John Town, John Whitely and Rik Wojtaszewski travelled to the Jomo Chu region of the western Nyangchen Tangla (Nyain-Qen-Tanglha) in July-August. From a Base Camp beneath the east face of Jomo Kangri (7048m), the team attempted the west ridge of the unclimbed Tangmonja (6328m). Advanced Base Camp (5525m) was established near the foot of the ridge. Poor weather prevented the team from climbing higher than 5850 meters, where the flat ridge quickly begins to steepen. Taking full advantage of a break in the weather, Buckle, Hill and Town made the first ascent of the prominent peak just to the southeast of Tangmonja via the 400-meter west face (AD-). The terrain involved excellent 45- to 50-degree granite and mixed ground; the ascent took nine hours from camp. They named the peak "Machag" (6025m) after the anvil-shaped summit block. (*High Mountain Sports* 210)

Peak 6250, Ascent, and Namlo Karpo, Attempt. New Zealanders Peter Cammell, John Cocks, Cam Falkner, Martin Hunter, John Nankervis and Adrian van Schie spent five weeks in the Kongpo region of eastern Tibet in the autumn. Accompanied by Tibetan mountaineer Ar Ke

Peaks of the Namlo Karpo massif in the Kongo region. JOHN NANKERVIS

Bu (liaison officer), Ang Tsering (Interpreter) and Ang Kami Sherpa (cook), they left Lhasa on October 7 and travelled by road, initially on the Tibet-Sichuan highway, to the picturesque village of Tsogo at the northern end of Draksum Latso (Pasum Tso). This was the soul lake and domain of King Gesar of Ling, a towering figure of Tibetan Buddhism. Base Camp was established in a forest at 3930 meters beyond a smaller steep-sided lake. This was a day's walk with porters up the Tsogo Valley and just below a glacier terminal. The short glacier was followed to a semi-circle of fierce icefalls. Access through these proved difficult. After a number of recces, a high camp was established above a smaller icefall at the northwestern end of the valley. However, unsettled weather, typical of that experienced in much of the eastern Himalaya in the 1999 post-monsoon season, prevented further progress. After investigating other side valleys, a camp was established in rather better weather on a col overlooking a beautiful meadow basin immediately west of BC at 5800 meters. For acclimatization purposes an unnamed peak of ca. 6250 meters was climbed via its southern ice arête by Cammell, Cocks, Falkner, Hunter and Nankervis on October 26. After returning to BC, a spirited attempt was then made on the principal objective of the expedition, the peak known as Namla Karpo (the White God of Heaven) by the villagers of Tsogo and mentioned by the famed English plant hunters Kingdon-Ward, Ludlow and Sherriff in the 1920s and 1930s. Good progress was made by Cammell, Falkner and Hunter to nearly 6000 meters, high on the western edge of the south face of the mountain, but a return to the daily snowfall and the expectation of difficulties on the cockscombed summit ridge discouraged further progress. Meanwhile, Cocks, Nankervis and van Schie made a further exploratory trip to the head of the valley. The expedition returned to Lhasa on November 7.

This highly glaciated area lies between the Po Yigrong and Gyamda watersheds. Distinct from both the eastern extension of the Himalaya culminating in Namcha Barwa, and the Nyenchen Tanglha visited recently by British teams led by Chris Bonington and others, it offers considerable potential for alpine-style ascents.

JOHN NANKERVIS, *New Zealand Alpine Club*

Mount Everest, Kanshung Face. Mrs. Santosh Yadav led an Indian expedition that largely repeated the line up Everest's east face pioneered by a small British-American-Canadian team (Anderson-Webster-Teare-Venables) in the spring of 1988. Kusang Dorjee Sherpa and Sange Sherpa, both Indian citizens, one a mountaineering instructor and the other a member of the Indo-Tibet Border Police, on May 28 ascended the east face out of Tibet, a feature rarely attempted and even more rarely climbed successfully (of only six previous attempts starting in 1981, three had succeeded). Mrs. Yadav and the other female on her climbing team, Miss Nari Dhami, reached the exit at the top of their face route onto the 7900-meter South Col and thereby became the first women to gain the Col from this side. They themselves were unable to proceed up from the Col, where they had placed their highest camp, to the top with Kusang Dorjee, Sange and a third team member, Amar Prakash, because they discovered that their oxygen masks were not functioning properly.

The Indians had a lucky escape from an avalanche of large ice blocks that struck their camp on the east face 450 meters below the Col not very long after they had begun their ascent from there on the 27th. Two of the four tents in the camp were completely buried and the other two were swept 200 meters down the mountainside; "if we had left camp a little later, eleven people would have died," Mrs. Yadav said.

After the three summitters returned to the Col late in the morning, all members then descended straight down, over and around the avalanche rubble, to the first camp they had pitched on the face, which was at 6450 meters, and arrived there after dark (at 8:30 p.m.) at the end of a very long day.

ELIZABETH HAWLEY

Mount Everest, Mallory and Irvine Research Expedition. The 1999 Mallory and Irvine Research Expedition was conducted to search for evidence of the 1924 British attempt on Mt. Everest and to recover information about the high point reached by George Leigh Mallory and Andrew Comyn Irvine during their ill-fated summit bid. Our predominantly American team consisted of climbers Conrad Anker, Dave Hahn, Graham Hoyland (UK), Jake Norton, Andy Politz, Tap Richards and Eric Simonson, expedition leader. In addition, we were joined by historians Jochen Hemmleb (Germany) and Larry Johnson, along with film crew members Liesl Clark, Peter Firstbrook (UK), Ned Johnston, Thom Pollard and Jyoti Rana (Nepal). Assisting us were 12 Sherpas led by Sirdar Dawa Nuru.

The team left Kathmandu on March 23, traveling overland to Rongbuk Base Camp (Tibet), which was established on March 30. For the next month, the entire team worked steadily on the North Ridge/Northeast Ridge route to establish the Advance Base Camp (6460m), Camp IV (7070m) and Camp V (7800m), eventually fixing this part of the route with 2500 meters of rope. During this period, the weather was quite good, and the upper mountain remained remarkably snow-free.

The first search team (Anker, Hahn, Norton, Politz, Richards) reached CV on April 30 and located the 1975 Chinese Camp VI the following day. That camp site was where Chinese climber Wang Hongbao started his famous "short walk" in 1975, during which he had report-edly come across an "English dead." After finding the Chinese campsite, they began searching to the west. Several hours later, Anker found the body of George Mallory at 8160 meters (see accompanying note by Anker below). The team spent three hours on site and buried Mallory's remains under stones before descending to CV. That night the weather worsened, with several feet of snow accumulating over the next two weeks. This effectively ended further searching.

The north face of Mt. Everest, showing Camp VI, the resting place of George Leigh Mallory (base of the cross) and the First (1), Second (2) and Third (3) steps. THOMAS POLLARD

On May 13, the team was back at CV for a summit attempt. Pinned down by high winds for three days, they were able to push to CVI on May 16, where Anker, Hahn, Norton and Richards remained to attempt the summit with Dawa Nuru and Ang Passang. Politz and Pollard, in support of the climbers, descended to CV, returning via the Mallory site on the way down to recheck the area with a metal detector for anything missed from the first search. On May 17, Anker and Hahn reached the summit in marginal weather, and returned to CVI. In the process, Anker attempted to free climb the Second Step. (His thoughtful analysis follows.) Norton, Richards, Dawa Nuru and Ang Passang abandoned their summit bid below the Second Step but recovered a 1924 oxygen cylinder on the North Ridge just below the First Step.

Interesting evidence of the 1924 climb was discovered by our team. In addition to the 1924 oxygen cylinder, we recovered various items of personal equipment from Mallory's remains, including an altimeter, goggles, a pocket knife and a complete inventory itemizing the provisions carried to CVI by the porters on June 7, 1924, for their summit bid. However, nothing recovered has definitively proven the high point of Mallory and Irvine's climb, and nothing about their route or summit bid is certain other than their ultimate demise on the mountain.

ERIC SIMONSON

Mount Everest, Discovery of the Body of George Mallory and Free Attempt of the Second Step. [On finding the body of George Mallory outside the search zone:] The probable location of the Chinese Camp VI, as defined by Jochen Hemmleb, was too high on the ill-defined ridge. There was no evidence of rock being moved, and it seemed unlikely anyone would pitch a camp that high. Traversing lower, I began scanning the basin and looked to the west.

George Leigh Mallory's hobnailed boot. THOMAS POLLARD

I had a great interest in the cliff bands (circumvented by Messner in August, 1980) that form the First and Second Step. At this point, I was well out of the search zone and began traversing back, which is when I saw the remains of George Mallory.

On June 8, 1924, Noel Odell sighted Mallory and Irvine topping one of the rock steps along the Northeast Ridge. Since that fateful afternoon, at which step they were last seen has been a matter of lengthy discussion. "I noticed far away on a snow slope leading up to what seemed to me to be the last step but one from the base of the final pyramid, a tiny object moving and approaching the rock step," recounted Odell. Was it the Second Step that Odell observed them climbing with relative ease?

Odell's observation places them on the Northeast Ridge, not the broad slopes below the First Step traversing in the Great (Norton) Couloir. If Mallory and Irvine were successful, their climbing route would include a 90-foot vertical barrier at an elevation of 28,300 feet: the Second Step, the most challenging bit of it all. The route ascends from the North Col, weaving through a series of slopes terraced with the occasional cliff until it intersects the Northeast Ridge, setting the stage for some of the finest high-altitude climbing. The real "business" begins at 27,760 feet with the First Step and continues on an exposed traverse for several rope lengths, culminating with the crest of the Second Step some 500 feet higher. Above and below this segment of the 1924 route, the terrain would be easily climbed, even 75 years ago with equipment of that era.

At the beginning of our expedition, I thought the Second Step to be possible for the 1924 climbers. Perhaps the arête or the rock in the vicinity would be peppered with incut holds, making the passage strenuous but feasible. On May 17, Dave Hahn, Jake Norton, Tap Richards, Danuru Sherpa, Ang Pasang Sherpa and I set out from high camp with the intention of filming my evaluation and attempt to free climb the Second Step.

Much has been speculated about a diagonal crack to the right of the dihedral. Could this be

The Second Step, with the ladder installed by the Chinese in 1975. Anker attempted to free the wide crack to the left of the ladder. FRED BARTH

the hidden passage that allowed Mallory and Irvine to climb the Second Step? Theorists speculated a grade (probably 5.6) without having ever been on it. With this in mind, I first probed about in an effort to climb it. The rock was rather loose, horribly unprotected and very strenuous in nature. I realized immediately that this was not the natural way, the line of least resistance. The dihedral climbed by the Chinese in 1960 is the logical line for the Second Step.

In the shady recesses of the Second Step, the opening moves begin at the base of the crack that defines this prow-like feature. Three large blocks lead the route slightly to the right, away from a wide flare to a chimney crack. The climbing is awkward—a series of high steps with insecure mantles. The last 20 feet of the shale cliff band end in a dihedral with a four-inch crack in the back. To the right of this, the 1975 Chinese expedition installed a ten-rung ladder which, along with the fixed rope, has been used ever since.

I removed my mittens, tied off my pack and spun my arms about in an attempt to warm my hands. With Dave's secure belay, I began with a series of fist jams, stemming with my right foot on good edges. The climbing was spectacular and demanding—rarely does one find a cliff of such a nature at altitude, steeped in such history.

The route moves to the right, intersecting the placement of the ladder. I placed a three-inch cam and fumbled about trying to find edges that weren't obscured by the ladder. Unfortunately, as one is prone to do at high altitude, I fizzled out. In desperation and weakness, I matched feet on the second to last rung of the Chinese ladder as I moved to the right.

How hard was it? Was it possible in 1924? I experienced the terrain in dry pre-monsoon Everest conditions similar to the type of ground Mallory and Irvine must have encountered. The climbing could best be described as "heads-up tricky terrain" on loose shale with the occasional patch of wind-hammered snow in between. The features slope the wrong direction; the cracks are shallow, brittle and poorly protectable. For a climber unfamiliar with exposure, as Irvine was, this terrain would be exhausting. The traversing forces one to move along a double fall line, which requires great concentration.

What would the rating be? As I climbed it, with the aid of the ladder, I would call it 5.10 A0—damn hard. To have basically "onsight" soloed this pitch with hobnail boots and no protection is beyond that of which I believe the early climbers were capable. No trace of their rappel setup was ever found on the block above the step, and for Mallory and Irvine to downclimb a tenuous fist crack would be even more demanding and unlikely.

My inability to make the moves reinforces my belief that Mallory and Irvine were not able to surmount this formidable obstacle.

CONRAD ANKER

Gyachung Kang, North Face, New Route, and Other Ascents. In the autumn, a Slovenian expedition led by Andrej Štremfelj made a number of first ascents in the Mahalangur Himal before climbing a new route on the north face of Gyachung Kang. A full account of the climbs appears in an article by Marko Prezelj earlier in this journal.

Cho Oyu, Tichy Route, Self-Supported Women's Ascent. We were a team of American women friends (Supy Bullard, leader, and Georgie Stanley, co-leader; Caroline Byrd, Kathryn Hess, Cara Liberatore, Liane Owen) with a goal to be the first American women's team to climb an 8000-meter peak without supplemental oxygen or Sherpa support. We left Kathmandu on April 1. Since we were "trucking" to Base Camp at 16,600 feet, we wanted to start acclimatizing on the approach. To this end, we spent two nights in Nyalam and two nights in Tingri. After spending three days at "Chinese" BC, we moved up to Advanced Base Camp at 18,600 feet and went to work on the mountain. The only glitch in our plans came early. A Norwegian team trying (later successfully) to climb Cho Oyu and Shishapangma in the same season had arrived early to Cho Oyu and their Sherpas had fixed the mountain. We thought it contrived to ignore these lines and fix our own set, so we used them, thereby compromising our goal of self-sufficiency.

We established Camp I at 21,000 feet, CII at 23,000 feet on April 20 and CIII at 24,500 feet. We climbed in two teams of three and on May 4, Supy, Kathryn and I reached the summit on a calm, clear day. On May 6, Cara, Caroline and Liane headed up but were turned back on their way to CIII by the first storm of the monsoon. We departed ABC on May 13. Thanks to the AAC and our friends and family for supporting our endeavor!

GEORGIE STANLEY, *unaffiliated*

Menlungtse, Attempt, and Milarepa, Ascent. We arrived at the upper meadows of the Menlung Valley beneath the north face of Menlungtse on September 3. We set up Base Camp (4900m) in the normal monsoon weather of clear mornings followed by rain in the afternoons and evenings. A few days later, Martin Zabaleta decided to return home. Mark Price, Andrew Brash, and I stayed on to attempt to climb both Menlungtse and several unclimbed and unnamed peaks just north of Menlungtse. Particularly interesting was point 6262 meters on the Chinese maps.

On September 14, we camped at 5420 meters on the compact west glacier of a small, unnamed peak northeast of our BC. On the morning of the 15th, after the normal snowfall during the night, I made what was probably the first ascent of this peak (ca. 5610m) by its

Point 6262m, a.k.a. Milarepa Peak. CARLOS BUHLER

short, exposed, granite west ridge. The climbing was not difficult, but several steep steps were tricky due to the newly fallen snow. I descended the east flank, a simple scree slope, and circled around the peak to the south. On September 23-24, all three of us hiked back up to the top of Pt. 5610m by the easy eastern scree slopes and spent the night a few meters under the summit for acclimatization. On September 26 and 28, following a line up an ice rib on the east end of the north face of Menlungtse, we fixed about 600 meters of 7- and 9mm line to a small, safe bivouac spot at the base of a 20-meter rock wall. Working as a threesome, we were able to carry up food and gear to the bivouac spot for a planned seven- to ten-day alpine-style ascent of the remaining 1600 meters of the peak. A nine-day storm ensued. So much snow fell that huge crown fractures were visible all along the top slopes of the north face of Menlungtse. On October 8, we made the decision to abandon the climb. Much less snow had accumulated on the two mountains north of Menlungtse, and we changed our objective to the unclimbed point 6262 meters.

On October 12 at 5 a.m., we three set off up the east face of point 6262m from a col (5550m) between it and another smaller peak. It was an ice face with a short mixed section at the bottom and another just under the summit. Not far up the face, Andrew decided to withdraw from the route. The face was about 50 degrees in overall steepness, and the ice climbing was moderate. Only the last two mixed pitches to the top were time consuming. At 3:30 p.m. we stood on the exposed, corniced summit, the junction of three steep ice ridges. The descent went quickly with two 60-meter ropes. Due to the threatening weather front approaching, we had rigged rappel anchors all the way up the route. By 7:30 p.m., we were back at the col. The following day, we descended to BC without urgency. On October 16, we left BC for the two-day return hike to Tsambouche Village.

We named point 6262m "Milarepa Peak" after the well-known Tibetan yogi and saint who died about 900 years ago in the Rongshar Valley. Milarepa's last days were spent in the sacred caves at the base of point 6262m, only a few hundred feet from the renowned Chuar Monastery.

CARLOS BUHLER

Chomo Lönzö, Attempt. The object of the expedition was the first ascent of Chomo Lönzö's Middle Peak via the southwest face and northwest ridge. We were Eduard Birnbacher (leader, Germany), Walter Hölzler and Stefan Wiebel from Germany and Manfred Feil from Italy. Because of problems with the trekking agency, liaison officer and yak owners, we failed to reach the south side of Chomo Lönzö (a six- to seven-day approach). At Kharta (the start of the trekking), we had to deposit half of the climbing equipment and food because of the exorbitant costs for the yaks. We did not have enough animals for the approach. All these circumstances left us no opportunity to climb the peak.

After five days' trekking we reached our new goal: the north face. Because of inadequate climbing equipment or food for the face and bad weather, the expedition failed to climb our new objective. After days on the mountain, I decided to abandon the expedition. My friends reached an altitude about 6100 meters on the north face.

EDUARD BIRNBACHER, *Deutscher Alpenverein*

Shishapangma, Southwest Face, Attempt and Tragedy. The idea behind this trip was to go over to the Himalaya with a group of friends and ski an 8000-meter peak. About half of the 14 8000ers have been skied by various lines, with the world-wide total being roughly ten to 20 individual descents off of the summits. Shishapangma has been skied via the regular route, but never by the steeper southwest side. The line that we were attempting, the Swiss/Polish Route, seemed to be a perfect candidate for a ski descent. It is a direct, continuously steep line with the hardest technical section being near the bottom. Our plan was to take our time getting up to a high advanced base camp, then do successively higher day skiing trips until we were acclimatized enough to climb and ski the route in a one-day push. If this didn't look like it was going to work out, plan B was to put a camp in somewhere on the route and do it as a two- to three-day outing.

Right from the start, this was an expensive trip and we were very fortunate that The North Face and MountainZone.com became major sponsors. We were also awarded a $6,000 grant through the Polartech Challenge, which helped defray many of the incidental costs along the way. As part of The North Face sponsorship, we agreed to make a film out of the outing through American Adventure Productions that was to be shown on NBC as part of a five-part series. This necessitated three more people on the trip: Kent Harvey, Michael Brown and David Bridges, who were not only excellent at their jobs but very experienced mountaineers and a great asset to the team.

Team members Andrew McLean (leader), Mark Holbrook, Alex Lowe, Kris Erickson, Hans Saari, Conrad Anker, David Bridges, Michael Brown and Kent Harvey arrived in Kathmandu on September 14 and spent four days there adjusting and doing last-minute provisioning before setting out to the north to cross into Tibet. After spending a night at the filthy border town of Kodari (where we picked up a few stomach bugs), we crossed into Tibet the next morning and were met by our CMA Liaison Officer and interpreter. The next stop was the outpost town of Nyalam, where we spent another day or so coordinating loads and yaks before finally setting out on the 15-mile approach to Base Camp at roughly 16,000 feet. As none of us had ever been there, we made the strategic error of letting the yak herders set the pace. The first day we did a placid three to five miles with about a 500-foot elevation gain. The next day, with all of our bivy gear loaded onto the yaks, they busted out ten miles and 4,000 feet of gain, which left some of us reeling with altitude sickness soon after arriving at BC. I hung in there for a few hours before recognizing the early signs of pulmonary edema and heading down with Alex and Michael in the middle of the night to spend four days recouping in Nyalam.

By the time I was able to return, the rest of the team had cleaned up BC, built a beautiful chorten and done a few short ski outings. With the snowline at above 18,000 feet, it required a major effort to do skiing day trips from BC. On one occasion, we were able to climb and ski a formation known as The Ice Tooth. A few days later, we split up and skied some of the stunning higher flanks surrounding Shishapanmga but only made it to about the 21,000-foot level before turning around due to poor weather.

Advanced Base Camp, which required a grueling effort to get to from BC, was a plush haven of soft, flat sand located right at the base of the south face. On October 4, after two to four trips apiece, we were finally established at the snowline, well acclimatized, completely provisioned and ready to start doing some skiing. On October 5, all of that changed. After spending our first night at ABC, we awoke the next morning to a clear, sunny day with a variety of nebulous plans. Alex, Conrad and David wanted to take a long loop over to check out a potential climb, then circle back to the base of the Swiss/Polish route. I was mainly interested in looking at our route, so I headed straight up toward it, with Mark, Hans and Kris about 20 minutes behind. After about an hour's climb straight up a gully, I reached a plateau and immediately spotted Alex, David and Conrad about half a mile off to my right. We were separated by a crevasse field and as I stood there wondering how to connect with them, we all noticed a small avalanche start far above. At first, it didn't seem to be a cause for alarm; it looked like it would probably stop on the first of three benches that it would come to. Instead, it did something far worse: it triggered a bigger slide, which in turn triggered an even bigger one. In a matter of seconds, the whole mountainside was in motion with Alex, David and Conrad directly below it. Conrad ran to the left while Alex and David ran downhill, perhaps to try and dive into a crevasse, still not realizing how large the slide was. From my view on a small knoll off to the side, my thoughts quickly turned from mild concern to blind panic as I realized they weren't going to make it.

The slide was huge. As it hit the apron above them, I saw the last of my friends before realizing that I was in the line of destruction. With five seconds to find a place to hide, I jumped into a small corner, covered my head and tried not to panic. The windblast flattened me, then filled every crevice with snow. When I dug myself out and climbed to the top of the knoll again, I was amazed to see a lone figure walking around on the debris pile. It was Conrad. "They're gone. Alex and David are gone."

We searched that day and again the next, but never found any trace of them. The debris pile was roughly 400 feet wide by 1,200 feet long and in places had filled in 30-foot crevasses.

A big part of this trip was the fact that we had all been good friends for years beforehand. With Alex and David gone, it completely took the wind out of our sails. The trip was over. Conrad was injured, our friends had died and the mountains seemed cold and inhospitable. We decided to head down.

ANDREW MCLEAN, *unaffiliated*

CHINA

East Kanthari, First Ascent. East Kanthari (6167m) lies on the Tibet-Qinghai (Changtang) Plateau in an area known as the Kokosiri that covers the borders between Tibet, Qinghai and Shinjyan. The Kokosiri is one of the most remote places in central Asia. Because of the numerous small streams that originate from glaciers to become the headwaters of the Yangtze River, it would take more than two weeks from the nearest village by jeep if you tried to reach here in summer. In mid-winter, the frozen ground and lakes make it possible to access the area relatively easily. The legendary explorer Sven Hedin commented on the Kanthari mountains 100 years ago, but no one had visited here for climbing, nor had anyone come in winter.

Our climbing trip was part of the 1998-'99 China-Japan joint Scientific Research Expedition to Kokosiri. Members were Shigeru Masuyama (leader), Kazuya Yamada, Noriyuki Muraguchi, Harik Muhamad, Shigeru Itoh, Yuji Kanazawa, Fumihiko Yamanushi, Daiki Hiroshima, Yuko Masuda, Noriyuki Otaishi and Huang Rong Fu. K. Yamada, our film leader, tried to reconnoiter the north face of the mountain in 1998, but his photos did not present a precise view of the peak. We also got two pictures taken by a 1991 Chinese scientific research party and another by a Kyushu University expedition. However, before leaving Japan, we could not tell from which direction these pictures were taken, nor could anyone confirm that they were really of Mt. East Kanthari.

On January 6, our five-day, 800-kilometer jeep caravan from Golmud (2800m) finally arrived at Base Camp (5200m) at the southern foot of East Kanthari. Though it was crazily cold, bitterly windy and dry, we were able to see Tibetan gazelle, antelope, wild ass, wild yak and wolf. After four days' recon of various possible routes, during which the temperature did not rise higher than -20°C, we decided the best route would be to establish an attack camp at the col of southeast ridge. From this camp, we would climb via the southeast ridge to the south peak and then on to the main peak via the south ridge.

On January 10 (-31°C), S. Masuyama, N. Muraguchi, F. Yamanushi, D. Hiroshima, K. Yamada and Y. Kanazawa carried all necessary equipment and food for six people to the attack camp at 5650 meters. As the temperatures were below -20°C, even at BC during daytime, we expected temperatures of -40°C at the top. In addition, strong winds were inevitably observed in the daytime. Because East Kanthari stands alone in the Kokosiri Plateau, daytime sunshine accelerates the airflow from 11 a.m. to 6 p.m. Serious difficulty would be raised by severe cold compounded by strong winds. We thus had to start early in the morning despite the severe cold.

On January 12, S. Masuyama, N. Muraguchi, F. Yamanushi, D. Hiroshima, K. Yamada and Y. Kanazawa moved from BC to Camp I, where we found a nice windless space for two tents. Muraguchi and Yamanushi, after reconnaissance to the foot of the south peak, reported, "Snow is stable, but wind is bitter!" The next day (-28°C at CI), the first attack team of S. Masuyama, N. Muraguchi, F. Yamanushi and D. Hiroshima departed at 6 a.m. (China has only one time zone; dawn here was around 9 a.m.) We wanted to reach the top before 11 a.m. when the strong winds began. An endless, wide snow ridge led us to the south peak. Drifting snow slowed our ascent. Masuyama and Yamanushi reached the south peak at 8 a.m.; Muraguchi and Hiroshima had gone ahead to film. The wind became stronger on the main ridge to the peak. Gusts knocked us off balance. Sensory feeling in our faces and in our fingers began to disappear. At the bottom of the last steep snow wall to the top, we noticed Muraguchi and Hiroshima descending. Hiroshima seemed too cold to respond promptly. He needed to descend to a safe zone. The other three continued to ascend the final wall. At 10 a.m., we arrived at the top, a wide snow peak, in -30°C temperatures with strong 20 m/second winds. We enjoyed the 360-degree view, including the Shin-Qing-Hong (6860m) in the east, and the twin-towered West Kanthari, which had been named "the beacon of Kokosiri" by Mr. Hedin, in the west.

We returned to CI at 1:30 p.m. Severe cold and strong winds gave Hiroshima frostbite on eight fingers. He was directed to go down to BC immediately with the support of Masuyama. (At BC, Masuyama sent e-mails asking friends in many countries for the best field treatment for Hiroshima's case. The responses helped save Hiroshima's fingers.)

On January 14, the second attack team of K. Yamada and Y. Kanazawa started from CI at 7 a.m., arriving at the south peak at 11 a.m. Further ascent was abandoned because of wind stronger than that of the day before. In the afternoon, CI was evacuated by K. Yamada and Y. Kanazawa, N. Muraguchi, F. Yamanushi and S. Itoh.

SHIGERU MASUYAMA, *Japanese Alpine Club*

Mushishan Group and Karangutagg Valley, First Ascents. It was reported that in August, 1998, a large group of Italian climbers and scientists travelled via Urumchi to Hotan on the southern fringes of the Taklimakan Desert. From there, they drove some 200 kilometers south to the small village of Houku, from which they were able to access the Mushishan Group, a group of glaciated peaks culminating in Mushishan (6638m), the high point on a long ridge of unclimbed summits. Renzo Corona and Franco Nicolini trekked to below the south flank of Mushishan, establishing a camp on August 19. Serac danger forced the pair to climb to a col on the ridge ("Col Lena," 6150m) via a vague rib on the southern snow slopes. On August 23, they followed the crest of the ridge west over Pt. 6450m ("Cima della Guide") to the high point of Mushishan.

In 1999, Corona and Nicolini returned to the region with an eight-member expedition to explore the Karangutagg Valley, a high valley they had reconned the year before. The peaks in this region offered technically straightforward snow climbs. Base Camp (3850m) was accessed via a three-day trek over a 3500-meter pass from the village of Kash Tash, itself a six-hour jeep drive from Hotan. In good weather, the team divided into two groups; Giacomo Corona, Nicolini and Omar Oprandi climbed Pt. 5850m while Renzo Corona, Mauro Fronza and Rocco Romagna made the first ascent of Pt. 5600m. On September 12, the group minus Romagna set out for the highest summit (6060m) of the area, reaching at it 5 p.m. (Fronza did not make the summit.) The team explored a pass into Tibet in 13 hours from BC, and Renzo Corona and Nicolini climbed a 5300-meter peak above BC that involved IV rock and 60-degree snow in its last 300 meters. On September 17, BC was struck and the team finished with a 1700-kilometer jeep drive across part of the Taklamakan Desert. (*High Mountain Sports* 210)

Gasherbrum II, Northeast Ridge, Attempt. In contrast to the relative ease of access from the west (Pakistan), the east side of the Gasherbrum mountains has been called, for geographical as well as political reasons, the "blank on the map" since the first expedition of Francis Edward Younghusband in 1887. And since the famous 1937 Eric Shipton expedition, highly acclaimed for its surveys of the unknown Aghil mountains and the eventual discovery of the Zug Shaksgam River, the area has been closed to foreigners. Not until the recent decade has the authorization to enter the upper Shaksgam river area (upstream from Durbin Jangal; downstream is relatively frequently trodden by expedition parties to the north face of K2) been issued to foreigners.

Since the successful 1993 first ascent of Mt. Chomo Lönzö (7816m), a satellite peak of Makalu, from the Chinese side, the Rikkyo University Alpine Club had nurtured a good relationship with the Chinese authorities. In 1998, it was granted the authorization to access the east face of the Gasherbrum region. Initially the main target of the expedition was the east ridge of GII, which was partially reconned by the 1989 Miyagi prefecture Federation of Mountaineering Expedition. As the recon progressed, however, the route was concluded to be too difficult mainly because of its distance to the summit via a line of knife-edge ridges liable to cause avalanches.

In 1998, a reconnaissance party reported the north ridge of GII was hopeless due to the heavy concentration of avalanches. Instead, they suggested the northeast ridge.

In 1999, the main party, led by Seisei Ajisaka and comprising seven members (including a medical doctor), five Sherpas and two Chinese staff (a liaison officer and an interpreter), started the mountaineering expedition to GII.

The Japanese members left Japan on June 1, organized the expedition party in Kashgar and started the 50-camel caravan with the assistance of 14 camel herders from Mazar Dara

Summit flags indicate the tops of (from left to right) GI, Gasherbrum East and GII. The line taken by the 1999 Rikkyo University expedition to the top of "Junction Peak" is shown. The glacier leading up to GII is the Upper Nakpo Glacier. SEISEI AJISAKA

on June 11. It took one week for them to cover the way to the Base Camp. On their way to Aghil Pass, they encountered an international party organized by Daniel Mazur. To their excitement, one of the eight members turned out to be Mr. Kurt Diemberger, who had a respectable climbing record in the Gasherbrum mountains. They exchanged friendship and were provided precious information on the climbing route to the exact northeast ridge of GII. Thanks to the information, the party adopted the East Nakpo Glacier route as the approach route to the Nakpo-Sagan col.

They passed the Aghil Pass (4780m) without any altitude trouble and covered the route on the broad river bed of the Shaksgam River. Although they did experience difficulty wading in the icy water, they at last reached Base Camp (4260m) at the confluence of the North Gasherbrum and the Urdok glaciers. Base Camp was placed on the Urdok Glacier side of the moraine on June 17.

They started climbing on June 18 and established Camp I (4500m) on the side moraine of the North Gasherbrum Glacier on June 20. They transported equipment and provisions to CI with the assistance of the camel herders. On June 22, they reached CII (4900m) which was located on the East Nakpo Glacier, just beneath the overwhelming great snow wall. After a struggle that included the fixing of 700 meters of rope on the 500-meter icy snow wall, they reached Nakpo-Sagan col and constructed CIII (5900m) on July 5. While advancing the route, they continued the transportation of supplies as well as acclimatization.

At 6400 meters on July 14, one of the three members fixing the route was hit by an slab avalanche and suffered a light bruise on his chest. As from the middle of July, with the change of the weather cycle pattern, heavy snowfall continued and avalanches were frequently observed. On July 24, two Sherpas who were transporting materials on the snow wall between CII to CIII were hit by an avalanche, barely escaping it. Two days after the avalanche (June 26), a second avalanche assaulted the route near CII and severely damaged the route by dislodging almost half of the fixed rope and isolating Camp III. On July 27, three members who had started to construct CIV found the uppermost fixed rope slashed away on the Sagan

Glacier side by an avalanche and were obliged to return to CIII. On July 28, Ajisaka ordered the retreat, and they started the descent, having reached a high point of 6780 meters. On August 2, they completed their climbing activity and gathered at BC.

After a week's stay at BC (on August 9), two of the camel herders arrived to report the inaccessibility by camel to BC due to the rising of the Shaksgam. (Two of their 35 camels had drowned in the flooded Shaksgam.) On August 10-11, the team transported equipment to the so-called American Base Camp with the assistance of nine camel herders. It was only on August 14 that they were at last able to start their return caravan. They reached the Mazar Dara on August 20.

TAKASHI MATSUDA, *Rikkyo University, Japan*

Lao Ding Shan and Mt. Desio, First Ascents, and Exploration of the Chinese Karakoram. It was an article by Kurt Diemberger in the 1995 volume of this journal that first inspired me to organize an expedition to the Chinese Karakoram. When I called the "Berg Fuehrer" himself to ask for information about the region, I couldn't believe my luck when Kurt wanted to join the expedition, which he promptly did. Around us gelled a team of Himalayan veterans including Dan Mazur, Greg Child, Chris Breemer, Andrew Brash, field technician Mark Dwyer and Nepalis Phurba Tamang, Kaji Tamang and Krishna XX. On April 9, we left for China with the considerable backing of Quokka.com, who would cover the expedition on a daily basis on their website.

After 3,500 miles of driving from Beijing to Mazar, six more days of walking with our caravan of 40 camels brought us to Base Camp on May 2, 1999. BC was situated in the Shaksgam Valley near the snout of the North Gasherbrum Glacier. This is an ideal base of operations for exploring this area as there is water and the spot is quite safe. However, camp must be placed on the north side of the glacier; otherwise, you stand a chance of being marooned when the Shaksgam River rises and floods the narrow gap between the glacier's snout and the opposite wall of the main valley. While the half-mile-wide Shaksgam River dries up almost completely every year (and wasn't there at all on our way in), the car-sized icebergs, torn from the North Gasherbrum Glacier and left strewn for miles along the riverbed, are a clear indication of the force the river can deliver when in flood.

From BC, we set out for our objectives, which were, in no particular order: to make a reconnaissance of the east face of Hidden Peak, to explore as far up the Shaksgam Valley as possible and to climb as many peaks as we were able. With the help of the camel drivers, we began by laying strategic food and gear depots in the Skyang Valley and on the south side of the North Gasherbrum Glacier.

The camel drivers are loath to go up the Shaksgam past the North Gasherbrum Glacier because of the danger of being trapped by a sudden flood. However, after cajoling them to help us, we headed en mass up the valley for approximately 35 kilometers to a point at which the Singhi Glacier flows across it and blocks further travel. We set up an Advanced Base Camp at the foot of the Shinghi's 80-meter ice towers. On the first day out from the Singhi camp, six members of the team, including Greg, Mark, Andrew, Phurba, Kaji and Dan, tried to climb a training peak. It is visible on the Russian maps of the area as the 5500-meter, ridge-shaped peak directly above the Shingi camp. The climb was mostly moderate scrambling; the team, exhausted and unacclimatized, turned around just under the summit. The weather was stunningly clear and the team was able to make extensive photographs of Teram Kangri, the Singhi Glacier and the Shaksgam valley. Greg christened the peak "Mount Beckwith." From

Dan Mazur above the Ramadan Glacier with "Lao Ding Shan" on the left. He and Andrew Brash made the first ascent of the peak two days after the photo was taken. ANDREW BRASH

this mountain, Andrew and Dan were able to get a clear view of their ascent line on the mountain they later named "Lao Ding Shan," after the Chinese staff's nickname for Kurt.

The following day we split into three parties: Kurt, Greg, Mark and the Tamang boys left to try to become the first since the Visser party in 1935 to see the Shaksgam beyond the Singhi Glacier barrier. Breemer and I set out on an ill-fated mission to make an end-run around the Singhi via a pass we were uncertain actually existed. Brash and Mazur, acting sensibly as usual, opted to attempt one of the many fine unclimbed peaks they'd seen from their practice climb, budgeting three days for the task.

After three days of searching, Kurt et al managed to find a passage through the towers. Kurt had tried this route 11 years before and there were tears in his eyes upon reaching yet another goal in a range so rich in his personal history. Ultimately, the team traveled as far as the next major barrier, the Kyagar Glacier, which also completely blocks the Shaksgam Valley. There they found that the lake formed by Kyagar Dam, which we'd seen in a satellite photo from the year before, was completely gone.

After threading our way up a dangerous gorge, Chris and I located our pass, which turned out to be very close to the source of the Zug Shaksgam River. We decided that the avalanche conditions were too dangerous to cross it, not to mention our uncertainty over whether or not we would have enough food to retrace our steps back over it should our companions, with whom we were out of contact, fail to find us a way back to ABC through the Shinghi. Krishna was thrilled, suggesting that the pass be named "Shoe Leather Pass" as it reminded him of one near his village so named for what those who try to cross it generally end up eating along the way.

Andrew and Dan bit off a bit more than they expected, fighting for six days through chest-deep snow to make the first ascent of Lao Ding Shan (6200m). While the climbing was not terribly difficult, this was a huge achievement given the totally remote location of this mountain.

Everyone headed back to BC at various times, repacked and set off for another round of exploring. Breemer and I headed up the Urdok Glacier to scope the east side of Hidden Peak. We picked up food from our earlier cache and after two days of walking and scrambling, we could finally see the east ridge. Given its size, location and appearance, it is the most impressive feature I have ever seen in the Himalaya. It rises roughly 10,000 feet and is incredibly steep. At one-third height, a horizontal section of wildly corniced gendarmes stretches for roughly a kilometer. It was this feature that stopped the only attempt on this face, by the Japanese in 1991, dead in its tracks. We left what is surely one of the "Last Great Problems" and headed further up the Urdok.

The goal was to try to be the first to reach the Indira Col from China. Unfortunately, snow conditions were terrible and stopped us as they had Younghusband and Desio decades before. Instead we opted for a small nunatak peak at the head of the Urdok. We climbed it the following day and named it Mt. Desio (5700m) for the pioneering explorer of the Duke of Spoleto's 1929 Karakoram Expedition. At the time, we assumed Desio was long dead.

Just before we returned to BC a second time, Kurt and his team headed up the North Gasherbrum Glacier to have a look at some nearby peaks and Dan and Andrew went up the Skyang Glacier to explore Skyang Kangri as a possible objective. Unfortunately, storms soon pushed both parties back to BC, where we were all reunited after more than two weeks apart. In typical Karakoram fashion, the weather never really improved and snow fell for the next nine days, during which we had the worst scare of the trip. Greg, who has previously climbed both Everest and K2 without oxygen, suddenly became seriously ill with what our doctor diagnosed (via sat phone) as either a stroke or HACE. Keeping Greg in the Gamov bag for an entire day improved his condition dramatically, though the episode got everyone thinking about wrapping things up. Fortunately, the camels arrived a few days later with the surprising news that the river was still just a trickle. This made for a nicely uneventful start to the long journey home.

As a footnote to the trip, I discovered in a discussion with Kurt that Professor Desio was in fact still alive at 102 and living in Rome. Via e-mail from BC, we arranged to go there and meet him after the trip. Still totally sharp in his second century, Desio reminded us of just how magic the Chinese Karakoram is. Three-quarters of a century had passed between our respective expeditions and unlike so many other mountains areas, nothing has changed there. The entire trip can be seen in exhaustive detail by looking for the First Ascent Expedition on www.quokka.com.

JOHN CLIMACO

GONGKA MOUNTAINS

Mt. Reddomain, First Ascent. Not a few virgin 6000-meter peaks still remain in Sichuan, China. One photograph, taken by a Japanese trekker in 1998, attracted our interest. Reddomain (6112m) rises fifteen kilometers north of Mt. Gongka Shan. The first introduction of Reddomain was in *National Geographic Magazine* in 1930. In the 70 years since, however, nobody had tried to climb this beautiful mountain. In May, we began to gather information on Reddomain and also commenced negotiating for climbing permission with the Chinese Mountaineering Association through Sichuan Adventure Travel. We got the permission in July and started preparing for our expedition.

Reddomain from Liuch Pass. ICHIRO ARAKAWA

We left for Chengdu on September 12. Our team was made up of 11 members, including eight undergraduate students of Gakushuin University: Yasushi Tanahashi, university leader; Masayuki Harada, subleader, Norisuke Ogawa, Yuji Tashiro, Maiko Uchino (f), Shotaro Yahagi, Yoshiaki Shimura, Hiroyuki Takahashi, Takuo Fukushima, Aya Yamane (f) and Ichiro Arakawa, adviser. Three of the 11 were mountaineering novices. On September 15, we travelled to Kangding, 400 kilometers west of Chengdu, by a chartered bus and to Raoyulin (3100m), the last village on our route, the following day. After two nights there, we departed into the Liuch Valley on September 18. For acclimation, we took four days to travel the distance of about 30 kilometers to Base Camp (4500m) in Mohsigoh Valley at the foot of Reddomain. In this way, we crossed the Liuch Pass (4910m) at the end of the west ridge of Reddomain.

We chose this west ridge as our route to the summit and started climbing on September 22. First we climbed up the scree-covered gully, where we were often frightened by rock fall, to get on the west ridge at 5150 meters, where we set up Camp I. We used fixed ropes all the way from CI to CII (5550m), including five pitches on a rock ridge and 16 pitches on snow, for the extra safety of the unskilled members. These ropes were carried down after the climb together with all other equipment.

Our first attempt was made by Harada and Tashiro on October 4. They approached the summit along the steep snow ridge. Just a few pitches from the summit, a cornice collapsed while Harada was belaying Tashiro. Unfortunately, Harada lost his rucksack and transceiver and they had to turn back halfway. The next day, Tanahashi, Ogawa and Tashiro attempted the summit again. After six hours of struggling on the snow ridge, they finally climbed up the steep snow wall and reached the top of Reddomain at noon of October 5.

Although not all the members were successful in reaching the summit, we really enjoyed our expedition and had unforgettable experiences during our trip in Sichuan. The Gongka range is a glorious place for climbing with many mountains to be explored.

YASUSHI TANAHASHI, *Gakushuin Alpine Club*

Gankarpunzum, Reconnaissance, and Liankang Kangri, First Ascent. When we attended the 40th Celebration of Chinese Mountaineering Association (CMA) in May, 1998, in Peking, we inquired about the possibility of receiving a mountaineering permit for a peak on the China-Bhutan border. We received a good reply. We set about planning the expedition to Gankarpunzum (7570m), the highest peak of Bhutan, for the next year, and sent a reconnaissance party to the mountain in mid-October, 1998. Prior to our attempt, successful ascents on the China-Bhutan border included both Khula Kangri (7538m) by a 1986 Kobe University party and Chomolari (7326m) by a joint China-Japan party in 1996.

The members of the reconnaissance were T. Itami, S. Nakamura and A. Yamamoto, and two news reporters for the newspaper Yomiuri. The approach to the mountain was made in a ten-hour ride from Lhasa by Landcruiser; we traveled alongside Yamudo Tso Lake and over the Monda La pass to arrive at Yojitsongtso (4500m), the last village. We gathered information from all the available sources in this village, after which we went on horseback into the old valley trail used by traders from Tibet to Bhutan. We set up Base Camp at Sumdo (4750m), the confluence of the glaciated valley of Namsang and Liankang Glacier. In the beginning, we entered the Namsang Glacier and made a camp on the left bank of the glacier. We advanced up the Namsang Glacier to see the upper side of the valley and the summit of Gankarpunzum. We found two possible routes to the summit, one on the northeast ridge via Liankang Kangri and the other directly up the east face of Gankarpunzum. Still more reconnoitering led to the south side of Khula Kangri Massif, which gave a general view of the possible routes on Gankarpunzum. (We also reconnoitered the Liankang Glacier, but found that there is no secure route to the upper part of the glacier.) We stayed in the hills for three days, and returned to Lhasa on November 12.

After returning home, we formed a mountaineering expedition to Gankarpunzum by selected JAC members. In February, the JAC received a notice from the CMA: the climbing permit for Gankarpunzum was postponed. The authorities in Bhutan had protested, stating that the peak lay on the Bhutan border and was thus forbidden. The notice confused the expedition committee, but we decided to send a younger members party to Liankang Kangri, which the CMA had proposed as a substitute.

Gankarpunzum, the highest unclimbed peak in the world. N. KOBAYASHI

We established Base Camp on April 21 at the same place as we had the year before. From Camp I, we made a route toward some seraced slopes, veered off the crevasse zone to CII, and pitched CIII below the 6921-meter pinnacle. On May 9, K. Suzuki and four men stood on the summit of Liankang Kangri (7534m), and the next day A. Yamamoto and four men climbed to the top as well. From the summit of Liankang Kangri, we could see the long knife-edged ridge stretching toward the summit of Gankarpunzum; it looked very serious, especially below the summit. Members of the expedition were T. Itami (leader), S. Nakamura, A. Yamamoto, K. Suzuki, H. Kadoya, H. Kobayashi, H. Takeuchi, K. Takahashi, Y. Kato, J. Takahashi and T. Sato.

TSUGUYASU ITAMI, *Japan*

Rock Peaks of the Siguniang Region. Japanese explorer Tamotsu Nakamura's photographs of the rock peaks near Mt. Siguniang in the Qionglai mountains make up an article that appears earlier in this journal.

MALAYSIAN BORNEO

SARAWAK

Batu Lawi, South Face. On March 5, Volker Shoeffl, Scott Morley, photographer Chris Noble, videographers Jim Surrette and Ken Sauls and I began the first leg of our ascent of Batu Lawi (6,703'), a remote spire in the Kelabit Highlands of Borneo. After a hair-raising flight (one engine failure) to the Highland community of Bario, then a short walk to the longhouse at Pa Ukat where we hired porters, the group began trekking toward the spire. We hiked for four days in an almost continuous downpour before reaching the base of the spire.

Our first attempt was on the east face, the largest and most striking side of the spire. Not much is known about this part of the world, and despite a scientific study claiming the spire to be of karst limestone, we found it to be Melingan Sandstone. Being porous, this rock absorbs a lot of the 300-plus inches of rain the Highlands receive each year and can thus be very weak. We had a limited amount of time, and after a few days of attempting to aid on hooks and knife blades up thin, water-weakened cracks (something none of us specialized in), we were forced to attempt the more moderate-looking south face.

The ca. 800-foot south face had its own difficulties. Large clumps of thick vegetation hung over many of the cracks like seracs, and their overhanging

The south face of Batu Lawi.
SAM LIGHTNER, JR.

undersides thwarted us on numerous crack lines. We eventually made it up via chimneys, hand cracks and occasional face climbing. At one point, two of us passed over a bamboo viper, one of the world's deadliest snakes. We reached the summit between storms and were given a clear view of the unspoiled rainforest.

Batu Lawi had been climbed twice before, once via the south ridge in 1986 by a British Army team and again by an Australian team in 1996. Our route went just west of the Australian line on the south face, then connects with it for the last pitch. The difficulty is hard to say as the standard rock ratings don't fit. The hardest rock pitch was 5.10a or b and with good protection, but the true crux was in dealing with the jungle, both on the trek and on the wall. Climbing over the overhanging clumps of moss as they pull away from the wall deserves its own rating system! One overhang near the top that had no gear was perhaps 20 feet long and would probably get the jungle rating of J4. The wetness of the mountain, its remote location and the difficulties of climbing in the jungle will no doubt steer other ascentionists away, but it shouldn't. Batu Lawi is one of the most beautiful mountains in the world, and getting to see the ever-shrinking rain forest in its pristine state truly makes this a worthy objective.

SAM LIGHTNER, JR.

SABAH

Mt. Kinabalu, Low's Gully, East Face, Attempt. Climbers Steve Long, Dave Turnbull, Paul Platt and Chris Parkin, with Paul "Chip" Rafferty, Charles Stead and Jon Rees in support, attempted the first big wall style climb in Malaysia from March 14–29 when they tried the east face of Low's Gully on Kinabalu (4101m). The east-facing wall is a 1000-meter wall in a remote setting, involving a complex abseil approach to the gully floor. The objective failed due to poor weather and blank granite, but the team pioneered a relatively safe approach route for future parties. We also made a recce of other potential climbing objectives.

The expedition was planned to coincide with the dry season. However, this year was unseasonably wet and we experienced an average of 12 hours of rain per day. Given the prevailing weather pattern, the only relatively safe options were the golden walls higher up the gully, which are overhanging for more than 2,000 feet but apparently devoid of cracklines in the lower sections, plus an area at the right-hand end of the wall that appeared to have three parallel cracks and is relatively protected from the waterfalls. This is the line we attempted.

Fixing an approach line into the base of Low's Gully took considerable effort, as we needed to conserve as much rope as possible. We took a total of 450 meters of static line and 180 meters of dynamic rope. A further 200 meters of static line would be appropriate for any attempt on the golden walls. The descent to the base of Low's Gully required ca. 300 meters of fixed line, essential for access and escape. Due to the rain, we decided that portaledges were not a safe option, and planned to fix 300 meters of rope to a ledge system and then sprint for the top. Unfortunately, the cracks proved to be dangerous and "blind." We only made about 80 meters of progress at about 5.8 and modern A3 before loose blocks and poor protection forced a retreat. Without bolt protection, this part of the wall is too dangerous.

The rock on Low's Gully is recent granite and seems to lack cracks. The exception to this is the Commando Cauldron area, which has potential for 400- to 500-meter routes. The walls opposite Lone Tree and stretching back toward Commando Cauldron are vertical to overhanging for 800-1000 meters. There is a long corner system which may be possible to reach from directly below, some 200 meters back up the gully from our abseil line where the gully makes an abrupt turn. However, binocular inspection did not reveal any cracks in the corner.

There is scope for a long buttress climb on Cirque Peak; this is clearly visible from the summit of Kinabalu and was photographed by Paul Pritchard in 1998 as a potential objective. This would require two days' bushwhacking through virgin jungle from Lone Tree, and the first 200 meters of steep slabs would probably require bolt protection. Above this would be excellent climbing on good cracks. This would be a feasible objective for a future expedition. The 250-meter Japanese route from 1969, *Tetsujin*, is on very poor rock, and still sports almost continuous fixed ropes and vast numbers of bolts.

There is considerable opportunity for climbs based at the four-man West Gurkha hut near the summit of Kinabalu, ranging from one to 15-plus pitches. Dewall Peak looks particularly promising for long ridge climbs.

STEVE LONG, *United Kingdom*

Mount Kinabalu, West Plateau, Victoria Peak, Southeast Face. Mount Kinabulu (4095m) in the Kinabalu National Park is the highest peak of Southeast Asia. Low's Gully, as the name suggests, is a deep gully that runs from the top of Kinabalu for more than 3000 meters down where the pluvial forest begins. It divides Kinabalu in two parts. The complete descent of the Low's Gully was accomplished by an Pat Gunson's joint Malaysian-British team in 1998.

The top of Mount Kinabalu is formed by the West and East plateaus, with spires that offer many climbs. The granite of this mountain is very young, and it is therefore advisable to come equipped with a good number of bolts. The walls of the spires on the big plateau are between 200-300 meters high. The most important peaks on the West Plateau are Victoria Peak (4094m) and Alexandra Peak (4003m); on the East Plateau, they are the Donkey's Ears (4052m), King Edward Peak (4081m) and Tunku Abdul Rahman Peak (3948m). The highest mountain of Kinabalu is Low's Peak (4095m).

Many Japanese parties have climbed in this area, as have British and Spanish teams. In 1998, on the east face of Victoria Peak, two Spanish parties opened new routes. Carles Albesa and Jordi Marti established *Figures 98* (A3 6c, seven pitches), and Xavier Vilella and Pep Soldevilla put up the nine-pitch route *L'Ullal d'en Godzilla* (A2 6b+). Meanwhile, on one of the Low's Gully walls, a Japanese team opened a route with almost 300 bolts.

Fabrizio Defrancesco, Giorgio Nicolodi and I left for Kota Kinabalu, the capital of Sabah, at the beginning of November. Once at Gurkha Hut, we decided on a new route on the southeast face of Victoria Peak. The rock is young and compact and cracks are very few. The rock on the first pitch was very solid, and it felt like climbing on Yosemite's walls. On the second pitch, the difficulties increased. We climbed the only crack offered to us. Then it abruptly ended in a very technical compact and crackless slab. We belayed on two bolts. We started climbing again on the crackless slab, but the weather changed suddenly, bringing rain, and we left the ropes on the wall and went back to Gurkha Hut.

We waited one more day, then decided to start climbing very early the next morning to precede the onset of the fog that usually comes up in the middle of the day. The rock was beautiful; some parts of the climb proceeded on rock so compact and crackless that we had difficulties progressing. There was one roof to surmount, which we passed with aid. We climbed on, this time along a new crack, until we reached a ledge. Fabrizio led the final slab, using two bolts. After passing the slab we got to the final ridge. From there to the top it was an easy walk. *La Perla di Labuan* (6c A1, 250m) is dedicated to our friend Valentino Scopoli.

MARIO MANICA, *Italy*

Corrections

In the 1995 *AAJ* (pp. 315-316) is a note that details the first ascent of Chiring (Karpo Gar) by a Japanese expedition under the leadership of Hiroshi Pujii. Cestmír Lukeš and Irene Oehninger (Switzerland) wrote that they climbed this peak in July, 1989, and left a snarg with a red sling near the summit. They gave the mountain a new name—Soglio Peak—because there are two names for the peak (Chiring Peak or Sarpo Laggo Peak 1) in the maps they consulted. They communicated this afterward to Mr. H. Adams Carter, but the correspondence never reached the current editor.

Regarding the note in the 1996 *AAJ*, pp. 213-215, Peter Carse writes, "On May 4 we climbed the southwest face of Pt. 5600m (just north of Quitoraju) via four pitches of 70-degree ice flutes. On May 12 we climbed the northwest face of Artesonraju, after an arduous approach up a hanging valley from the Quebrada Santa Cruz. Our route put us on the west ridge at about 5875 meters; it was composed almost entirely of good ice, except for one mixed section about 300 meters above the 'schrund. The lower third of the route was exposed to significant rock and ice fall during the afternoon hours."

In the 1997 *AAJ*, on p. 313, Redakh Brakk was reported as having received a first ascent by David Wilkinson and party. Mr. Wilkinson wrote to inform us that in fact, the mountain had previously been climbed as long ago as 1959 by members of the British Army Mountaineering Asociation Expedition, and named Engineers' Peak. The ascent routes differed in their upper parts; the first ascent in 1959 was made by the big couloir to the right of the ridge, while the second ascent (1996) was by the west-northwest ridge. The name Engineers' Peak has apparently been approved by the Pakistani authorities.

In the 1998 *AAJ*, pp. 325-327, we published an account of a variation of the 1981 Waseda University team's West Ridge route on K2 by the Tokai branch of the Japanese Alpine Club. In the 1999 *AAJ*, we published a correction to that note on page 429. We now publish the photo that appeared in the 1998 *AAJ* with the correct route drawn in.

In the 1999 *AAJ*, on p. 196, Tupilak East (2264m) is not in the Tasermiut Fjord area as reported, but actually in the Schweizerland area at N 66° 19' W 36° 32'.

On page 211, a note by Charlie Fowler regarding ascents in the Qionglai Range was inadvertently placed under Tibet. The Qionglai Range is in China.

On page 263, we published a report by Jeremy Frimer that mentioned an apparent first ascent of "Southeast Macaulay" in the St. Elias Range, Canada, in 1998. (The peak was incorrectly spelled Macauley.) The first ascent was actually by Kaj Bune and party in 1996, as reported in 1997 *AAJ*, page 199.

On pages 299-301, we published a note on the route *War and Poetry* (Bechtel-Bechtel-Lilygren-Mallamo-Piana-Skinner, 1998) by Steve Bechtel. Though fixed pitons, bolts, established bolt anchors and fixed copperheads

The north and west faces of K2 above 7000 meters as seen from Crown Peak, showing the line taken by the 1997 JAC-Tokai Branch. Osamu Tanabe

were found by the 1998 team on their ascent, the account did not mention that the 30-pitch *War and Poetry* shared pitches 5 through 27 with the previously established *Geneva Diedre* (Dalphin-Piola-Probst-Wiestliback, 1983). It is reported in *High Mountain Sports* magazine (issue 210) that Paul Piana believes the significant difference between the two routes lies in philosophy. *War and Poetry* is a free climb, while large parts of *Geneva Diedre* were climbed with aid. Piana believes that as a free route, *War and Poetry* is a superior climb.

The ascent of the southeast face of "Brakk Zang" via the route *Ganyips* by Pep Masip and Sílvia Vidal (see p. 398) and that of "Sotulpa Peak" via the route *Ramchekor* on the south face/pillar by Louise Thomas and Libby Peter (p. 393) appear to have occured on the same mountain.

Corrections to the on-going saga of the first ascents of Gya and Mukut Parvat East in India can be found in the Climbs and Expeditions: India section on pages 351 and 354.

We spelled Eric Bjørnstad's name incorrectly throughout the 1999 *AAJ*.

For these and any other mistakes we may have made, we offer our sincere apologies.

SEAN McCABE

Reviews

Edited by David Stevenson

Tibet's Secret Mountain: the Triumph of Sepu Kangri. Chris Bonington and Charles Clarke. London: Weidenfeld and Nicolson, 1999. 250 pages. £20.00.

This is an account of three expeditions led by Chris Bonington to a heretofore untrodden massif in Eastern Tibet in 1996, 1997 and 1998. On the first, Bonington and his friend, Charles Clarke, M.D., using a map purchased at the Lhasa airport and a single photograph from a Chinese mountaineering book, set out to find and explore the terrain around Sepu Kangri (7400m). The result is a fine tale in the Shipton-Tilman tradition, with touches of British amateurism evocative of the Newby's *Short Walk in the Hindu Kush.* For instance, they'd done no research on the weather and would discover that summer rains in Tibet are as bad as the monsoon in Nepal. On the drive from Lhasa, their guide forbade them to stay in towns, fearing the military or the police would find their travel permit flawed. "The reconnaissance had been one of the best trips I have ever undertaken," Bonington concludes. "We had done practically no climbing, we had attained no major summits, and yet I had enjoyed a quality of exploratory adventure that I had not experienced since the first trip I made to the Himalaya, to Annapurna II, in 1960."

On the second visit, Bonington decides on a strong infrastructure of climbers, expenditure, sponsorship and supporting communications technology. In addition to Clarke, he recruits stalwart, near-to-middle-age names of British climbing: John Porter, Jim Lowther, Jim Fotheringham. In addition to three Sherpas, there is filmmaker Jim Curran (also Bonington's biographer) plus a techie to run the communications paraphernalia. Beset with bad weather and avalanche-prone snow, the team fail fairly low on the mountain.

The following year, Bonington and Clarke are accompanied by four different climbers—less gray hair on sideburns and beards—and a three-man film team. Separately, Clarke and one of the climbers take a month-long different approach to base camp via terra incognita before the others arrive and explore the eastern side of the range. The weather is poor and the terrain treacherous for the climbing team and the expedition fails to get to the summit. Nobody but a desperate publisher would find anything triumphal here. In fact, the amount of prose dedicated to climbing (where we know triumph is to be found) is perhaps less than a third of the text. The most interesting parts of the book are the accounts of the two lightweight probes (in part because they have more contact with the land and the local people) and also Clarke's history of exploration of the region and his essay on Tibetan medical practices.

For me, *Tibet's Secret Mountain* is a fascinating record of the penetration of information technology into expeditionary life and the degree to which it reshapes the mountaineering experience. First, a little gear talk. The 1997 attempt on the mountain had a Saturn dish data terminal (30 kilos), and two British Telecom Mobiqs, each about the size of a laptop, linked to a satellite above the Indian Ocean. Bonington is pretty thrilled with his new altimeter that records rate of ascent and other data. The communications tent at base camp had three tables "so that several people could work at the same time." To kill time, Bonington plays *Warcraft,* a computer game to which he is addicted.

He writes that, "The other team members, and I too at first, had had reservations about our satellite link to the world, feeling that one of the charms of an expedition was getting away from worries of home and work. But 'because it was there' I noticed my companions were not slow to use the benefits of instant communications. John Porter was able to talk to his two children before they went off to school, Jim Lowther checked up on his estate, and Duncan was conducting by e-mail the final tortuous stages of selling a house. Were we losing some of the romance of mountaineering in our use of modern technology? I don't think so. There was room for the Shiptonesque as well as the satellite."

The second attempt on Sepu Kangri had greater technological scope. As Clarke writes: "Chris was keen that the expedition should have a strong communications background, ideally with the ability to transmit TV film direct from base camp." And so strong was his commitment that Bonington insisted that Clarke's two-man advance reconnaissance probe, traveling more than 200 kilometers and over at least six 5000-meter passes, carry satellite phones, digital cameras, walkie talkies, global positioning devices and computers and solar panels. This "made our baggage more cumbersome than originally planned, but it did add another dimension to travel through a remote region," Clarke writes. "Also, if difficult to put into any useful practice, communications could be valuable in case of accident or illness."

Clarke's somewhat tortuous language seems to barely suppress the thought that technology on this scale does not add, but subtracts a dimension from exploratory mountaineering. It undeniably leads to some pretty bizarre events, such as when Clarke visits the chief lama of a remote monastery that is being renovated. He asks the lama if he would like to talk on the phone to the superior of his order, who lives in Scotland.

"From an open first-floor window we aimed the satellite dish south and dialed the number. It seemed ludicrous to hear the Eskdalemuir monastery's answering phone playing its recorded message: 'This office opens at 9 a.m. Please try later.' " When the call goes through to the high lama, Clarke writes: "In this place where wood and yak dung were the source of power and the rooms lit with butter lamp, the solar panel and digital technology allowed one reincarnate lama to speak to another. The talk was mainly secular about supplies and the progress of building work."

In addition to the previous equipage, for the third venture Bonington has two wind generators and video transmission links to the ITN studios in London, powered by the two generators. The expedition's gear list contains three printers. Alas, there was rarely enough juice for them because the 20-kilo battery pack was dysfunctional. Meanwhile, lack of wind made these generators almost useless, only one of a score of disappointments caused by techno-overreaching or inadequate testing. Still, thanks to ITN's generators, there was usually enough juice for 20 e-mails daily, web site picture downloads, four computers and two satellite phones to run most of the day. Even Bonington's technophilia gets stressed at times. After he returns to Base Camp from an initial probe up to Camp I, he writes, "I had time to sort myself out and prepare for the climb ahead in a way that I had been unable to do before. There had been too many external pressures with ITN reports, answering e-mails, worries about my health and whether I was getting too old for it all."

The TV coverage meant that he appeared in staged video scenes as the climbers made their way up the mountain. At one point, when things are going well, he "dreamt of what it was going to be like reaching the summit and (I) even rehearsed my piece to the camera for the benefit of ITN." When it is clear that the team is more likely to succeed without him than with him, he opts to go down.

"I tried to do a piece to the camera for ITN explaining what we'd decided. The first time I tried I couldn't control my emotions and slumped down and cried." He later checks his emotions and explains his decision to the audience.

Bonington is too ingenuous in claiming technology is a convenience that can be used without compromises. The fact that he climbs while rehearsing scripts for the video camera induces a state of mind that must be different from merely slogging up a hill with one's thoughts, or with no thought at all. The climbers' obligations to feed the website is equally mind-altering. The quotidian stuff that Shipton would have scribbled in his diary now gets typed on laptops and packaged as up-to-the-minute "news." Climbing becomes intermingled with show biz values: a private experience, a personal challenge, is morphed into a public spectacle of dubious veracity (for instance, the makeover of Bonington's tearful moment of truth).

After the media binge, after the last of Bonington's "reports from Central Tibet" to the slack-jawed couch potatoes back home, there must come the realization that it was much ado about nothing. The diurnal events on this failed attempt on a modest-sized peak (where their high point was 6830 meters) are not likely to hold much interest for climbers, far less the general public, unless quite ordinary acts and thoughts of a celebrity like Bonington are the equivalent, or better than, real news.

Many generations of climbers have sought to impose exalted missions to their activities, such as scientific research or goals of national conquest. The narrative of *Tibet's Secret Mountain* tells the story of technological pioneers symbolically preparing the ground for utopian technological futures. Their picture of reality and their mental states are deeply influenced by the requirements of real-time communication. I do not argue that this is a bad choice. God knows, it may be a wonderful cure for the base camp blahs that readers of this journal are familiar with. But I do wish that Bonington showed more awareness of the Faustian bargain's irreversible consequences.

JOHN THACKRAY

Ascent. Allen Steck, Steve Roper, and David Harris, editors. Golden, CO: The American Alpine Club Press, 1999. Large format, numerous color and black-and-white photographs. 314 pages. $24.95.

S hortly after the New Year, the *New York Times* published a list of sports and the American sportspersons who excelled at them in 1999. As I recall, there were close to 100 activities, not all of them athletic, including more than a handful of which I had never heard. Rock climbing was not on the list, not even in the version known as sport climbing. The lack of regulated and publicized competition complete with spectators leading to "national" or "world" championships probably has a lot to do with this omission.

At the same time, climbing is almost alone in having a literature produced by the actual participants. Deep-water sailing can also lay a claim here, and perhaps it is the isolation and the accompanying lack of spectators that forces climbers and sailors to the equally isolated task of writing. If they don't do it, nobody else will or even can, and climbers intuitively know that the as-told-to gambit common in other sports just isn't going to come close to what they experienced. The surprising thing is not that some climbers write, but that some of them write very well.

So we have the doing, then the talking (writing) about the doing, and then the talking about the talking about the doing: action, narration, criticism. There must be something about the first that justifies the second, and, similarly, climbing is the only sport I know of where the quality of the narration has given rise to a discussion of the writing in itself. Of course, as intertwined (incestuous?) as this all is, to discover or perceive something about the narrator through his story is also to discover something about the climber and, perhaps, about climbing.

Which brings us to the 14th issue of *Ascent*. It reminds me of the thick stews that Chouinard used to cook up after collecting 50 cents each (half of our daily budget) from the exposed-ribbed and culinarily-challenged climbers hanging around camp. Only about a third of the articles are narratives of climbs in the traditional manner (meat). About half of the articles attempt in one way or another to get at climbing through writing about the peripheries of climbing (assorted vegetables in season). There are some fictional pieces and poetry (spices, I suppose). And then one finds several interesting articles directly addressing issues of climbing writing. One wonders, are there articles on golf writing, baseball writing, even ski writing?

Sampling the meat category, Stephen Venables goes off the beaten track in the Himalaya for a first ascent on Kasum Kanguru; Andy Selters wins the Palm d' Sweat Award while testing the proposition that as far as adventure goes, failure is just as good as success; and Greg Crouch gives a vivid account of going up, then down, then up, then down, then up, etc., for more than two months before finally bivouacking on the summit of Cerro Torre. Without such exploits and the engaging stories that connect the rest of us to them (if only in our imagination), the other varieties of climbing writing would provide less nourishing fare.

As it is, however, when David Pagel goes to have dinner with Anderl Heckmair, the Eigerwand looms in the background as we get a view different from the standard one recounted by Heinrich Harrer in *The White Spider*. Pagel brings Heckmair alive (like others, I had assumed he was dead by now, but he is not only alive, he twinkles), and Heckmair resuscitates the rivalries, the politics, the personality differences that surround climbers, then as now. (Why was Heckmair standing on a balcony with Hitler with his right hand behind his back? Read the article.) And when Amy Irvine goes into the Tetons alone in the wake of the disappearance of another woman in the Wind Rivers, we feel what we probably knew—not only that the wilderness is smaller, but also that other humans can now be counted as among the objective dangers, in Wyoming as well as in Pakistan. The more extreme joustings also lead John Thackray to consider anew why we do it, why some but not others actively seek sensation. But this time around he offers various psychological and neurobiological theories, not so much to explain our motivations as to provide needed ammunition against those, especially those in authoritarian or influential positions, who see climbing as not only senseless but also irresponsible.

If a main motivation of the editors is to publish pieces that somehow touch on and illuminate the more ineffable aspects of our sport, two pieces in particular must have been especially satisfying: John Embank's "Ironmongers of the Dreamtime" and Joe Kelsey's "Too Old for 5.12, Too Young for Obituaries." Both climbers are now in their 50s; both are grounded in a place, Ewbank in New South Wales, Kelsey in Joshua Tree; both know there is no direct line to where they want to go, so they look around a corner, wander across a face, double back to a slanting crack, hoping it will all connect. Ewbank observes, "Climbers are obsessed with an experience they wish to share, but which they do not wish to be altered or lessened." Ewbank has in mind physical altering—piton scars, bolts, that sort of thing—but, of course, even the telling will alter it, and even a good climb can be lessened by trying to make it seem like an even better climb. His article was originally a speech delivered a few years ago at the Escalade Festival, and it flows with a raconteur's ease from Australian climbing history to his own history to discussions of ethics and trends and finally to a kind of verbal arm-waving that indicates it's up there somewhere, whatever it is we're after.

For both Ewbank and Kelsey, silence, specifically the silence of rock, enters into the equation. Kelsey avers that he seeks "not the meaning of climbing but the experience of climbing. Given rock's silence, there's not much to say about the experience, other than that I'd like to hear the silence, be so at home that a cliff transfigures into Eden." Like, perhaps, when we were young, before we stumbled into self-consciousness and started trying to shape the narrative of our lives. Kelsey's piece continues a previous account of middle-aged Joshua Tree adventures, and in both cases we sense that while the JT trips are experiences in their own right, they also provide an excuse for Kelsey to write well about what he loves.

And there is much more in this issue, photos, drawings, paintings, a history of climbing gear from grappling hook to bat hook and beyond, and a history and survey of, of all things, climbing magazines. I found that not everything appealed to me, but I am willing to say that's just me. I think the book is best put on a coffee table, not for show, but to be dipped into from time to time. That way each of the pieces has some time to breath, like a good cabernet.

The front cover of *Ascent* shows two very small climbers ascending a relatively gentle but corniced ridge. One suspects that what seems to be the summit is not the summit (never mind that the photo credit says that it is). The back cover, however, provides for me the better metaphor for our sport. A climber, arms raised, legs akimbo, is caught leaping from one pinnacle to an adjacent one while below, a quaint village nestles against a fjord. It's up there, somewhere, whatever it is we are after.

JOE FITSCHEN

The Totem Pole—And a Whole New Adventure. Paul Pritchard. Seattle: Mountaineers Books, 1999. 16-page photo insert. 216 pages. $22.95.

*T*he *Totem Pole*, Paul Pritchard's first work since winning the Boardman Tasker award in 1997 for *Deep Play*, is a first-person account of a struggle with catastrophic injury and the possibility of permanent disability. Whereas I may not have been overly impressed with his last work, I found *The Totem Pole* to be one of the finest books ever written by a climber, a deeply moving account of the triumph of the human spirit in the face of a life-changing injury. Going from super hardman alpinist to a guy struggling to feed himself, Pritchard's hope and optimism throughout his painfully slow (and only partial) recovery is a truly inspirational story.

Celia Bull, Pritchard's girlfriend and climbing partner at the time, is responsible for his heroic rescue. She later wrote in her journal regarding the accident:

"He is there beneath me, hung by a thread of fate and nylon. He is suspended navel up. Limbs thrown out. He is limp and lifeless, faded. Here are the dying petals of a once exuberant flower. Just beyond, the sea is drinking thirstily at his blood. Horror is roaring in my ears. These tentacles of seaweed, they're unfurling, they're stroking softly at the sacrificial red, beckoning him to join them in their sempiternal kingdom." (p. 206)

Can you imagine the terror of seeing someone you love dying before your eyes? And what if you were in a strange country (Tasmania), miles from anyone, looking at a technical climbing rescue that would require at least a helicopter and a powerboat, not to mention advanced life support?

But this is not just yet another imitation of *Touching the Void*. This is a deeply unsettling book based upon Pritchard's later interpretations of tape recordings made at the beginnings of his recovery as soon as he had learned to speak again. Keep in mind he had his brain literally knocked halfway out of his head and then stuffed back in. Now, talking in a tape recorder as soon as one regains their power of speech is not an ordinary thing one might think of doing. But Pritchard is obviously no ordinary guy.

What we are left with is the perfect postmodern account of a man trying to literally rethink himself and understand what his thoughts once were. Then comes the haunting question of how to interpret it all. So what exactly is the "self"? Who is Paul Pritchard? Before the accident, we have a fanatically gifted climber and writer; during recovery, an individual fighting for his life and against despair, disappointment and depression; after the accident, a non-climber and brilliant writer.

In the end, Pritchard states, "I have seen things with new eyes since my accident, especially the relative importance of climbing. I once thought I would rather die than do without."

Have you ever wondered what you would do without? I know I have.

So why did Pritchard push himself so hard? Why do some climbers tempt fate over and over again, barely escape, then turn right around and hurl themselves back into the maelstrom?

Much has been made of totems in anthropology. They are the embodiments of spirits, gods and power. Cliffs, towers and mountains are the climber's totems of power. Friedrich Neitzsche wrote in *Will to Power*, "Thus a man climbs on dangerous paths in the highest mountains so as to mock his fears and trembling knees." This mocking, this "oppression" of our fears is a "tyranny of the soul" whereupon the prudent, the timid, the cautious part of all of our souls is demonized. Why? So that we may idolize and worship, in the highest form of vanity, our false courage as gods.

In Ovid's *Metamorphoses*, Hesiod's *Theogony* and Plato's "Symposium," there are retellings of an ancient Greek myth. The story is always the same: the Titans—half men, half gods—attempt to storm the heavens, located fittingly on Mount Olympus. Such hubris invited the wrath of all the gods. Pritchard's story is a cautionary one. We should be careful when we tread upon high places. We are not gods, and we tempt their patience.

DAVID HALE

A Life on the Edge: Memoirs of Everest and Beyond. Jim Whittaker. Seattle: Mountaineers Books. 24 color photos, 50 black-and-white photos. 272 pages. $24.95.

The superb description by Jon Krakauer of the tragedy on Mt. Everest has increased the audience for mountaineering literature from a limited group of cognoscenti to the general public who frequent airport book shops. Many of the books that have recently been written to attract this audience have included far too much material best left in personal diaries or in the offices of psychiatrists.

Happily, this autobiography by Jim Whittaker, the first American to reach the summit of Everest, is an exception. The addict of storm and tragedy who wishes to read about death-defying actions in perilous circumstances will find relatively little to satisfy in *A Life on the Edge*. Instead, the book provides a view of a life well led by a mountaineer who has always stretched his own boundaries, has used fame wisely, has always been willing to take risks to advance good causes and has never lost his reverence for nature.

Jim Whittaker achieved national fame when he reached the summit of Everest with Nawang Gombu in 1963. His fame is memorialized through his life-sized statue in the Mt. Rainier Visitor's Center. In an era when $65,000 will provide almost anyone with an excellent chance for the summit and reasonable odds of a round trip on expeditions directed by able Sherpas and professional guides, it is difficult to remember how challenging this summit was in 1963. Moreover, while the attention of the public has always been focused upon "Big Jim," the imagination of climbers was immediately captured by the first ascent of the West Ridge of Everest by Unsoeld and Hornbein and their heroic bivouac above 28,000 feet. It has consequently seemed puzzling to climbers that so much attention has been focused upon the first American to summit when other climbers produced the most gripping story and enduring achievement of this expedition. That being said, readers will finish this book with an appreciation of how large and extraordinary a life Whittaker has led. Similar to Sir Edmund Hillary, Whittaker has used his fame and the opportunities it has provided to him for many altruistic and admirable purposes.

The early chapters describe Whittaker's life before it was transformed by Everest. Of particular interest are his descriptions of his career as a Rainier guide and his role in directing the early growth of REI. This mountain "jock" proved to be an unusually able and interesting businessman, transforming REI from a one-employee organization to a large and thriving business. The chapters also describe the most harrowing of Whittaker's mountain experiences, the expedition that he and his brother Louis took to Denali with Pete Schoening and John Day. By ignoring all prudence in acclimatization, they established a speed record to the summit. This was followed by an accident in which the entire climbing party tumbled 500 feet down the slope below Denali Pass. Their evacuation required several days of massive rescue efforts in which two people died and an altitude record for evacuation by helicopter was established. The honesty of the writing in this section will appeal to all readers.

Whittaker then went to Everest, where his life was transformed by fame, which also ensured that his future actions would be subjected to skeptical scrutiny. Following the assassination of President John F. Kennedy, Whittaker was asked to guide the president's brother Bobby on the first ascent of Mt. Kennedy. This expedition resulted in a lifetime friendship with Bobby, his family and the Kennedy clan. Some of the most fascinating passages in the book describe the friendship and their shared idealism. Whittaker directed Bobby's primary campaign in Oregon and Washington. Bobby's assassination devastated Whittaker and the American body politic but did not destroy Whittaker's enduring optimism and confidence, which permeate every page in this book.

Together with his second wife, Diane, Whittaker then led two ambitious expeditions to K2, at that time unclimbed by Americans. On the first expedition, it soon became clear that the ambitious route was beyond the team's grasp. A combination of bad weather and difficulties with Balti porters destroyed their self-confidence before they really came to grips with the mountain. Whittaker returned to K2 in 1978, but the Pakistanis requested that he not begin the climb before the start of the monsoon.

The best of climbers' personalities often emerges in heroic circumstances; the worst almost inevitably becomes visible during weeks of weather-imposed inactivity. The text provides a compelling description of his personal frustration in leading a group of able, ambitious, but not entirely altruistic individuals during 70-odd days of monsoon storms. Happily, a last-minute break in weather after porters had been summoned to evacuate Base Camp made it possible for the expedition to succeed in the end.

While the retreat from the mountain had gripping moments, Whittaker emerged as a victor who brought all members of his two expeditions home safely. Shortly after returning from K2, Whittaker left REI to start his own business. While his K2 comrades were often difficult, his business partner proved to be wickedly treacherous. Whittaker's faith in the comparative stranger led to his personal bankruptcy.

Somehow, Whittaker's confidence and idealism survived the trauma. While rebuilding his financial security, he assembled a joint Soviet-Chinese-American expedition with the simple goal of putting representatives of each nation on the summit of Mt. Everest together. Whittaker clearly felt that success could inspire world leaders to eliminate the scourge of war. The text provides a fascinating description of the difficulties he encountered both before and during the expedition in making the dream a reality, relying upon climbers who came from very different cultures. In the end, leadership experience on K2 served Whittaker well and he achieved an amazing goal.

Whittaker is now in the midst of a voyage around the world with Diane and his second family, a voyage that seems likely to be equally rich in adventure.

Whittaker emerges from the pages of this book as a heroic, but also very human figure. The peaks and valleys in his life are much larger than those most of us will experience. His heroism lies not in his successes on Everest and K2, but in his perseverance, optimism and enduring love of nature despite betrayal, tragedy and other severe personal challenges.

Whittaker clearly wrote this book with the objective of educating as well as entertaining us. As usual, he has succeeded admirably.

LOU REICHARDT

Ghosts of Everest: The Search for Mallory & Irvine. Jochen Hemmleb, Larry A. Johnson, Eric R. Simonson, as told to William E. Nothdurft. Seattle: Mountaineers Books, 1999. 80 color photos. 208 pages. $29.95.

It was on George Leigh-Mallory's third expedition to Mt. Everest in 1924 that he and Andrew Irvine disappeared several hundred vertical feet from the summit. Over the years, this vaulted the two to legendary status, with speculation that they, and not Hillary and Tenzing nearly 30 years later, were the first to climb to the top of the world. One of the great unsolved mysteries of 20th century exploration, it would take until nearly the end of it before the most chillingly compelling evidence in this intriguing enigma would be discovered by the 1999 Mallory and Irvine Research Expedition.

Ghosts of Everest: The Search for Mallory & Irvine impressively tells the tale of this ambitious team effort led by veteran mountaineer Eric Simonson, and it is a must-read for aficionados of the subject and anyone else who would be riveted by a recounting of the courage of the 1924 expedition and the high drama of the 1999 team in searching for its two most famous members.

Seattle writer Bill Nothdurft, through expedition members Jochen Hemmleb, Larry Johnson and Eric Simonson, has crafted a powerful story, neatly combining the adventure of both expeditions until their two destinies converged with the discovery of Mallory's remains. The result provides a sharp contrast of the two eras and an invaluable appreciation of how success in the costliest human endeavors stands nobly on the shoulders of those who tried first.

Although Nothdurft's text effortlessly reads like good fiction, it is artfully woven with sepia-toned images from the pioneer Everesters and the more brightly spun Fuji and Kodachrome photography of the 1999 team. And utterly compelling are the images of the artifacts recovered from George Mallory's body. While not the Shroud of Turin, their collective impact comes close, and one has the sense in viewing them of the mythical Mallory made tangibly, warmly mortal. We see a broken, Everyman's wristwatch, the embroidered initials

"GLM" on a still-fresh linen handkerchief, battered Crooks goggles, the frayed frail rope once connecting him to Irvine, handwriting neatly chronicling the needs of the moment so many years ago.

Although the reverence for Mallory-in-death held by Simonson's team is always clear, there seemed something still naggingly vexing in *Ghosts'* portrayal of his remains. There is no question of the coldly historical relevance of these images, and the depiction of his final resting position is almost as effective as the magic of an oracle in helping to reconstruct the circumstances of his fatal fall. It is clear, too, that remnants of his body's graceful majesty still survive the ravages of the mountain. And yet, I wondered at the cumulative impact these images may have had on Mallory's surviving family members.

Ghosts' chapter eight is perhaps the most compelling with a wonderfully written account of the expedition's newly-discovered evidence, in an effort to circumstantially reconstruct the events of Mallory and Irvine's last hours. Both fact and intricate inference lead to plausible scenarios suggested by this combined authorship, though the end result of most of them seem to argue against summit success. But not completely, either, given the "tantalizing, if indirect clue" of team members failing to find a photograph of Mallory's wife Ruth on his body, suggesting that he may have delivered it to the summit as he was believed to have intended.

I was especially fascinated with *Ghosts'* conjecture that put Mallory and Irvine above the crux Second Step, and perhaps the Third, when they were last sighted by teammate Noel Odell "going strong for the top." This is crucial to an assessment of the likelihood of their summit success because of its bearing on their distance from the top and the time it would take to reach it and return. And it is a point of continuing controversy as well, given Odell's revision of his initial sighting that placed his two friends above the Second Step and not the First, as he later believed. Despite this, *Ghosts* proposes that, given their potential oxygen supply and climbing speed, even a charitable analysis of Mallory and Irvine's progress under favorable conditions presented such significant difficulties that it is improbable they reached their great goal.

There is the subtle sense in *Ghosts* of a whole stream of synchronistic occurrences leading to the solution of the mystery, as though the universe was gently orchestrating the actions of each team member. From Conrad Anker's "intuition of looking low" in his discover of Mallory's body to the fortuitous recovery of a key 1924 oxygen bottle as an emerging piece of the greater puzzle, this is a delicately interesting dimension to what is already a richly deserving read, refreshingly adding thoughtful perspective sometimes missing from the usual mountain fare. A symmetry emerges in *Ghosts* with the expedition's discovery, delivering yet another element of closure to the Mallory family circle.

In the end, the magnitude of the tragedy of George Mallory and Andrew Irvine still teaches, with *Ghosts* offering not only insight into the circumstances of their youthful passing, but of the players themselves in this Golden Age of high-altitude mountaineering and exploration. *Ghosts* paints a wonderfully compelling tribute to the determination of two expeditions separated in time, with Everest's First Knight, George Mallory, never far from Earth's highest center stage. The gift of this book reminds that any great endeavor begins first in the imagination, where the seed that may one day bring it fully to life is enriched and then empowered by a brightly spun dream. This most certainly was the force with Mallory and his wool-clad, hobnailed teammates, and Simonson's team, too, as they both struggled against great odds in reaching for the summit of their highest expectations.

PAUL PFAU

The Lost Explorer: Finding Mallory on Mt. Everest. Conrad Anker and David Roberts. New York: Simon and Schuster, 1999. 192 pages. $22.00.

In 1924, it took ten days for the news to reach London that George Mallory and Andrew Irvine had disappeared on Mt. Everest. In 1999, when members of the Mallory and Irvine Research Expedition finally located Mallory's remains on a rocky slope beneath the Northwest Ridge, people around the world (myself included) looked on with spellbound fascination as the dramatic events unfolded almost in real time on the World Wide Web. When news of the discovery first broke, regularly logging on to the expedition website became as much a part of my day-to-day routine as eating and sleeping. Daily postings describing the climbers' experiences and emotions, the details of what they had found, how they had found it and what light the discovery might shed on mountaineering's greatest mystery kept me glued to my screen like a teenage boy hacked into a Victoria's Secret changing room.

Then came the magazine articles. As the days after the discovery lengthened into weeks and months, the story seemed to be splashed across every glossy page that wasn't a cosmetic advertisement. The copy, largely more polished and fleshed-out forms of the same information that had already saturated the internet, was beginning to wear thin, but the fact that the articles were supplemented with macabre, arguably exploitative and utterly compelling photographs insured that they remained eminently salable.

Finally, inevitably, the parade of books: the "official expedition" story, scholarly dissertations by alpine historians and other pundits and then the personal accounts of various individuals both directly and peripherally connected with the discovery. Frankly, by the time Conrad Anker's *The Lost Explorer*, one of the last titles to appear on the shelves of my local bookstore, came to market, the whiff of commercialization had thickened into a full-fledged stink. Granted, Anker is the man who actually "found the body," but did we really need another 192 pages telling us about it? How could anybody justify yet another entire book devoted to such an over-told and oversold story?

It was with a weary, almost reluctant, skepticism that I opened this book and began to read. What I discovered was a surprisingly worthy tale and a refreshing perspective: the anti-Mallory point of view.

Without a doubt, the greatest stumbling block to objectively deciphering the evidence of the Mallory discovery is history itself. The courage of the ill-equipped yet resolute early Everest expeditions, the burning ambition of the tenacious Mallory to finally conquer "his" peak, the drama of Mallory and Irvine's final attempt and their mysterious disappearance into the clouds, are heroic and epic ingredients that have simmered in the pots of imagination and speculation for three quarters of a century—ample time to stew the collective consciousness. The fact is, the vast majority of us yearn for concrete evidence that Mallory and Irvine made the summit. Barring that, however, many seem willing to give them—by virtue of their colorful personalities, experience and grit—the benefit of the doubt. By virtue of his own experiences and personality, Conrad Anker cannot.

Few writers are as qualified to judge the mental and physical obstacles that George Mallory faced on that fateful day in 1924. Like Mallory, Anker is the cream of his generation. The consummate mountaineer, he has climbed the world over, demonstrating time and again his technical mastery on mountainous terrain. Perhaps more importantly, the book makes clear that he has also bridged the crevasse that separates mind and body, fine-tuning his mental screws to the point of achieving a dispassionate recognition of his own strengths and limitations. As one of the best in the game, widening the scope of this self-awareness to include others is a short leap for Anker. Such clarity permits him to perceive events without embell-ishment and render opinions unfettered by ego or popular perceptions. In short, Anker is able to detach himself from the heady romance of the Mallory-Irvine mystery and give an honest and well-supported assessment of the probability that the ill-fated pair reached the summit. His conclusion is that they almost certainly did not.

Rather than debating the significance of tantalizing but circumstantial evidence (numbers on oxygen bottles, cryptic notes and the like), Anker's opinions are based almost solely upon his own firsthand experiences during the expedition: his tainted attempt to free climb the for-midable technical crux of the Second Step, the surprisingly difficult and dangerous terrain he encountered between the Third Step and the summit, his own difficulties in shepherding a debilitated summit partner (whose experience and equipment far exceeded those of the rela-tively novice Irvine) and ultimately, the position and location of Mallory's remains. For Anker, it all adds up to a tragic anticlimax: an aborted summit bid (almost certainly below the Second Step), a disastrous slip on the descent, a long and fatal fall. Though the hackles may rise, his reasoning is so compelling that even the most rabid pro-Mallory advocates must pay heed. And his discovery of the body brings added credibility to his logic and instincts. It was, after all, Anker's mountain sense that led him to the spot where Mallory lay—well outside the expedition's designated search area.

This is not to say that Anker is unaffected by the Mallory-Irvine legend. His reverence and admiration for the early Everest climbers is evident both in his writing and in his determina-tion to thoroughly investigate the possibilities of that time period (i.e., free climbing the Second Step). In context, he is clearly awed by what these men attempted and by what they achieved. To this end, co-author David Roberts does his usual admirable job of distilling all the historical information into a thorough and well-crafted back-story. But in the end, there is no doubt that *The Lost Explorer* is Anker's book; amid the avalanche of media hype and over-exposure surrounding the Mallory discovery, it is his objective, unencumbered and honest per-spective that makes this title a unique and important addition to the literature of Everest.

DAVID PAGEL

Last Climb: The Legendary Everest Expeditions of George Mallory. David Breashears and Audrey Salkeld. Washington, D.C.: National Geographic Society, 1999. Numerous archival photos. 240 pages. $35.00.

How would the discovery of George Mallory's body have been reported and marketed if it had occurred before Everest went to the top of the charts in 1996? Probably the way it was when Wang Hongbao reported seeing "old English" near his 1975 camp where Conrad Anker found Mallory in May, 1999. The new context of the discovery has led to a lot more romantic speculation obfuscated through the fog of hero worship. Nothing discovered reveals more than we already knew: Mallory and Irvine died in an accident of unknown cause dur-ing an unsuccessful yet courageous and prudent attempt that reached an amazing height on Everest, even by modern standards.

Thanks to the maturity of these seasoned authors, *Last Climb* treats the discovery with an hon-esty of perspective that will stand the test of time and accords Mallory and Irvine the respect and dignity they deserve by recognizing them as real humans rather than sensationalizing and mythol-ogizing them. The result is a much more powerful tribute to their efforts than the simultaneously wishful and gratuitously brutal analyses of the more commercial exploitations of the discovery.

Salkeld and Breashears, while not on last year's expedition, both have a long-standing involvement with Everest in general and Mallory in particular. Salkeld is an eminent mountaineering historian and winner of last year's AAC literary award, while Breashears has on various occasions climbed and guided the mountain and filmed the IMAX Everest movie (not to mention highly acclaimed documentaries on Tibet). Rather than focusing on the current rediscovery and forensic analysis, Breashears and Salkeld emphasize the far more interesting and significant circumstances of the three British expeditions of the early 1920s. The adventure and camaraderie that marked these expeditions is apparent in the abundant selection of striking photographs supplemented by judiciously researched background material. The images alone, of early Himalayan mountaineering and the undisturbed Tibetan civilization through which these expeditions approached, make this book a great addition to the coffee table, while the text provides substantial insight into the attitudes held by Mallory and a variety of his contemporaries toward their dream of climbing the virgin Chomolungma.

The tone of the book is set in a dignified forward by Mallory's son, John. He puts the tragic cost of his father's boldness in perspective, which reminds us of the more recent deaths of Alison Hargreaves, Rob Hall and Alex Lowe and the consequences for their families.

Consideration of the mysterious final day is deliberate and reserved. I'm sure the authors would have liked no less than anyone else to be able to conceive of a way that Mallory and Irvine could have summitted without attributing to them a reckless "glory or death" attitude. Going on to the top when the consequence is certain death is no more praiseworthy on an unclimbed Everest than it is today, and the authors do not demean Mallory and Irvine by suggesting such a scenario. (Breashears is only too aware of the numerous ways a summit attempt could have ended early and turned tragic.) Regarding the famous step on the ridge, which Odell last saw the climbers ascend through a break in the clouds, Odell later pointed to what we now call the First Step on a Brad Washburn photo. Conrad Anker, whose own first-person account, *Lost Explorer*, demonstrates the same realistic and sensitive understanding of his fellow climbers that Breashears brings to *Last Climb*, recognized that the Chinese ladder provided significant psychological protection for his ascent of the Second Step, even if he hadn't stepped on it when it blocked a resting hold. (Breashears also understands that the off-width technique involved is a specialty of Anker's; while holding the highest regard for Mallory's ability, he also understands it was still not the equal of Conrad's "on a bad day.") Guided by Carl Sagan's dictum, "Extraordinary claims require extraordinary evidence," the authors resisted the increased sales potential of the summit fantasy, and instead produced an infinitely more worthy record of historic adventure turned tragic only by accident. (It is also worth noting that Breashears turned down offers for photos of the bodies of friends Hall and Fisher, the kind of situation others have been less reticent to exploit.)

In the conclusion of *Last Climb*, the authors quote Mallory's friend Howard Somervell who prophetically "saw their deaths as 'a clarion call to a materialistic age.' " Fortunately, their own book lives up to the better impulses that guided—and still guides—the true adventurers.

BOB PALAIS

Life and Death on Mt. Everest: Sherpas and Himalayan Mountaineering. Sherry B. Ortner. Princeton, NJ: Princeton University Press, 1999. 396 pages. $26.95.

*L*ife and Death on Mt. Everest by Sherry Ortner is a fascinating exploration of the complex and changing relationship between international mountaineers ("sahibs") and the Sherpas who have helped them make their climbs—and suffered the greatest number of climbing deaths in the Himalaya. The book traces the history of this relationship, showing how both Western and Sherpa attitudes toward climbing and each other have evolved over time.

Ortner points out that the sahibs began with a paternalistic, colonial attitude toward the Sherpas, whom they viewed as children to be taken care of and disciplined. Over time, as Western culture changed and mountaineering reflected egalitarian and countercultural influences, sahibs came to view Sherpas as friends and equals. This change is highlighted in the fact that starting in the 1970s, Sherpas stopped calling sahibs "sahibs" and began addressing them by their first names.

In the beginning of Himalayan mountaineering, climbing Sherpas came from the lower economic and social classes of Sherpa society—those who were disenfranchised, needed money and would carry loads, something that "big" people with status looked down on as demeaning work. Today, however, climbing Sherpas and those in the trekking industry have become the social and economic leaders of Khumbu, the Sherpa homeland near Everest.

Ortner focuses on changes in Sherpa culture and society during the period of Himalayan mountaineering and how the Sherpas have handled the advent of powerful outside influences. In a chapter titled "Monks," she presents an interesting parallel between the effects of the introduction of Western values by sahibs on the one hand and the introduction of monastic Buddhism by tulkus or incarnate lamas on the other hand. Before this period, Sherpas had relatively little to do with Westerners, and their religious life was dominated by village temples with married priests and the shamanistic healing practices of spirit mediums.

Ortner argues that the Sherpas and their culture have been much more resilient than many outside observers think. Rather than passively react to outside pressures, Sherpas have taken an active role in molding these influences to their own purposes. Ortner recounts a number of contemporary stories that contradict a widespread impression that the Sherpas have lost their old, selfless values and become materialistic money-grubbers.

A particularly interesting chapter goes into the complex attitudes that Sherpas have toward death, particularly deaths on Himalayan expeditions. Ortner shows that Western notions that Sherpas are fatalistic and accept death easily are simplistic and misleading. Climbing deaths in particular can have a profound impact. This I know firsthand. Annulu, a well-known Sherpa who put in the route to the South Col so that Tenzing Norgay and Edmund Hillary could make the first ascent of Everest, was killed in a climbing accident. When I visited his family afterward, people avoided talking about what had happened, and I could see how much his death had affected his wife and sons.

Ortner is a well-known anthropologist who knows the Sherpas well and received a prestigious MacArthur Award for her research on their religion and society. Accordingly, she has written the book from an anthropological perspective. She attempts to combine two approaches that have dominated recent scholarship in anthropology. One sees culture as primarily the creation of meaning, exemplified in the work of Clifford Geertz; the others sees it as the product of political and economic forces, as highlighted in Edward Said's critiques of Orientalism. Ortner also makes use of a distinction between "high" and "low" religion popular in anthropological circles. Her expertise lies in the extensive fieldwork she has done on "low" or village Buddhism. She is less knowledgeable about "high" or monastic Buddhism and its subtle systems of thought and meditative practice.

For her study of sahibs and their climbing culture and history, Ortner has drawn on extensive reading of mountaineering literature. She hasn't climbed herself and readily admits that she looks a bit askance on the sport and the risks it entails, both for sahibs and Sherpas:

"The mountaineering sahibs seemed in many ways more alien to me than the Sherpas. In the end I think I 'got it.' I have not entirely lost my critical sense about the senseless [this word appears with a slash through it in the book] risking of lives, and I could not imagine doing it myself." (pp. 8-9)

A strong feature of the book that commends it to climbers and many other readers is the range of perspectives it provides. In few other places will you find such a well-balanced and rich mix of points of view. Ortner does an excellent job of presenting sahib views of Sherpas, Sherpa views of sahibs and sahib and Sherpa views of themselves and the life and death they have shared on the highest mountain in the world.

EDWIN BERNBAUM

30 Years of Climbing Magazine. Climbing Magazine. Carbondale, CO: Primedia, 1999. 337 pages. $18.95.

The Best of Rock & Ice: An Anthology. Dougald MacDonald, Editor. Seattle: The Mountaineers, 1999. 200 pages, black-and-white photographs. $17.95.

Whether it's end-of-the-millennium angst or anniversary efforts to account for their existence, *Climbing* and *Rock & Ice* magazines have each released an anthology of what they consider the best writing of their respective 30- and 15-year histories. The notion of "best of" in climbing literature invokes many possible responses, from rabid reading to dismissal, appreciation for a forgotten gem to outrage at the absence of a favorite. Tallying tastes in this way tells more about the reader than the book, and when I first flipped through the pages, I skimmed through the essays that spoke to my preferences: clipping bolts on steep stone and a longing to be back on Yosemite's walls. In *30 Years of Climbing*, this meant Matt Samet's "How to Climb 5.14," a sardonic how-to of just that; Dave Pegg's "What's Your Problem," an indictment of the low standard of U.S. sportclimbing; John Long's "Wall Rats," his chronicle of Yosemite big wall climbers of the 1970s; and Tyler Stableford's "The Wild Bunch," a look at the Valley's search and rescue team. In *The Best of Rock & Ice*, my first look was to Will Gadd's "Verve," an interview with sport pioneer Christian Griffith; Cameron Burns' "Bad Boy," an ironic take on sport climbing's seamier side of one-upmanship and chipping; and Jeff Long's story, "Revenge," a fictional recount of innocence lost on the first pitches of the *Salathé*.

But these aren't the articles I necessarily turn to again and again, and this returning marks a difference between the anthologies and the magazines from which the stories emerge. As John Hart pointed out in his 1999 *Ascent* article "The Climbing Magazines: Read, Skim, or Ignore?," it's common practice to scan the current issues for topics of interest and then set them aside. For some readers it's "Hot Flashes" or "Cliff Notes," for others the photos in "High Exposure" or "The Gallery," equipment reviews or mountaineering epics. Many climbers keep a collection of issues on a shelf, but we have to be pretty bored or looking for a particular mini-guide to pull one from that stack and leaf through it. Not so with the books, which have a more singular formality, a coffee table quality with their glossy covers, a sense of seriousness in their lack of pictures and advertisements. "Best of" and "30 Years" sound lasting, enduring in a way that the flavor of the month, whether climber or route, never could.

So it's certain stories that stand out, stories that become history in their telling, narratives of climbing that engage a reader even if they have little in common with that reader's own climbing—like Martin Atkinson's "Over the Edge," in which he recounts his third ascent of the gritstone classic, *Master's Edge*. I've never climbed grit, and it's been years since I roped up on anything both hard and run-out, but I read and re-read this piece that opens the Rock & Ice anthology for its humor and voice. Most articles of the *R&I* collection follow suit, offering particular climbs and climbers in concert, telling in the first person a history made from a particularly personal narrative, sharing with other selections in the volume what editor Dougald MacDonald calls "unique characters and originality."

Climbing magazine's collection offers a different sort of truth, a survey of characters, often investigation rather than introspection, more journalism than personal essay. Greg Child's opening article sets the tone, and "The Big Easy: Everest the Weird Way" presents less of Child's own travail than a motley band of who's, how's, and why's. *30 Years of Climbing* features a daypack's worth of investigative articles, the backbone of journalism, whether the puzzle at hand is Alison Hargreaves' alpine career, the life of Heinrich Harrer, the 1996 Everest tragedy or Herzog's account of Annapurna. While *Climbing's* collection includes plenty of emphasis on the personal and the individual ascent, it finds its favored truth in research, in exploration, rather than (as is the case with the stories in the *Rock & Ice* anthology) truth made in exposition.

Which is not to say that these books are in the end all that different. The names remain the same, as Jim Bridwell, Greg Child, Jeff Long, John Long and Alison Osius appear in both venues; unfortunately, both also feature the typical polemic-epic from Marc (or Mark, now that he's back in the U.S.) Twight. In addition, all but four of *Climbing's* 38 articles are from the 1990s, most from the past four years. Similarly, only four of *Rock & Ice's* 25 are from the 1980s—though to be fair, the latter magazine only began in 1984 and was much shorter in its early years. In both cases, the "best" writing seems to be the most recent. In the alternative, the editors considered the datedness of earlier writing too much of a hard sell. Either way, the reader of these books sadly is left without a broader historical spectrum of writing about climbing.

Perhaps more important than their history is the present and future purpose these books serve—a critical purpose that perhaps can't be filled anywhere else, not in the magazines themselves or in the cragside conversations that might (or might not) be the origins of the adventures that the stories document and the magazines publish. These anthologies are neither beginnings nor endings but intersections, common places for readers, for climbers from rads to trads, from V9 no-name boulderers to big-time mountaineers to weekend warriors, all of whom, if they were to meet at the local coffee joint, might have little or nothing to say to one another. These two anthologies remind us that we are a "we," bound not even by ropes (for those who would emulate Bachar or Gill or Messner) but by a common passion for testing one's self against a little patch of nothing, be it in Chamonix or Central Park.

That sense of "we," of unity across the sub-specialties of our sport, is a sense of sameness that climbers, given current access problems ranging from closed cliffs to bans on wilderness fixed protection to skyrocketing peak and rescue fees, definitely need. There is strength in numbers, and when climbers recognize their plurality rather than their differences, they can more effectively act on access issues that, if unaddressed, will make climbing itself a thing only of history rather than the future. By joining tales of bouldering with mountain adventures, sportclimbing roadtrips alongside Tibetan treks, these two books hail the broadest bandwidth of climbers imaginable.

If you can buy only one of them, go with 30 *Years of Climbing* instead of *The Best of Rock & Ice*; for a buck extra, you get at least 100 more pages, a glossier cover photo and a hard binding. But better yet, read three issues of the mags at the climbing shop counter instead of purchasing them, and buy both books. They may lack the photos and up-to-date information of the magazines, but their stories are more lasting, their histories more telling than the hot send of the moment.

PETER CASTER

High Exposure: An Enduring Passion for Everest and Other Unforgiving Places. David Breashears. New York: Simon and Schuster, 1999. 16 color photos. 309 pages. $26.00.

It would be a great injustice for *High Exposure* to be regarded in any potential reader's mind as the work of just another climber trying to cash in on the big E while the market is hot. Breashears' claim on Everest (actually, he would have it the other way around) is both long-standing and intimate: four times to the summit in eight expeditions over 16 years (1981-97). Along the way, Breashears had a quiet role, either as firsthand observer, participant or leader, of every sensational Everest story of the last 15 years. But in *High Exposure*, Breashears just tells us what he's done. It's an impressive accounting.

Most of us know Breashears as the cameraman and director of the Everest IMAX film. (Or maybe we don't, as he's mostly behind the camera and the scenes.) And most people know that the IMAX team was on the mountain in the spring of 1996 at the same time as the teams decimated by storm. It's even common knowledge that the IMAX team members were generous in their assistance to climbers in trouble (though this, too, is a bit understated in the film). In *High Exposure*, though, we get the more thorough story. Why was Breashears' team going down when the others were going up? The reason: not mere dumb luck or some sort of mystical intuition, but because of an intuition earned by hard-won experience.

Breashears' opinions on the tragedies may come off as strong, but they never seem personal. In fact, he raises questions about people for whom he clearly has deep affection. Doubtless, some readers will disagree with his views, but they would do well to remember his opinions weren't formed while sitting on the couch. He's writing about a world he knows better than almost any reader—better, for that matter, than most on the mountain at the time.

It's hard for the average movieviewer to imagine the supreme effort that went into the making of the Everest IMAX film. The problem is that the film is so beautiful and the climbers so graceful that it's possible to walk away from it thinking that it was easily made. Here, Breashears tells us of the difficulties involved—not merely the brute physical effort of hauling the equipment, but the technical intricacies of operating the equipment at altitude as well as the aesthetic problems of the art maker. In a world that requires most climbers' full attention to simply put one foot in front of the other, Breashears ticks off a 15-item camera checklist that ends with "take a good picture with story value."

Breashears was also part of Tom Holzel's 1980 trip, the first expedition to search for Mallory. In addition, he was one of the first to "guide" Everest, leading Dick Bass to the summit in 1985. What struck me in this description was Breashears' obvious sense of respect for Bass—not a hint of leader/client arrogance or condescension. So, yes, Everest takes up a certain proportion of the book, a certain proportion of Breashears' life, but these excursions are the rewards of a long and, to me, more interesting mountain life.

The trip to Kwangde with Jeff Lowe is the climb Breashears rates as his finest mountaineering achievement. This is clearly the judgment first and foremost of a climber, not someone seeking the public eye. Likewise, the early rock climb upon which Breashears first made his reputation was *Kloberdanz*, a relatively obscure route in a relatively obscure place.

The recognition one receives from such climbs is limited to a relatively small group of climbers. It's quiet climbs like *Kloberdanz*, and especially *Perilous Journey*, that formed the character and made the man.

There are deaths depicted in this book, but there is no sense of Breashears taking advantage of this for the sake of his story. Instead, his attitude toward death is utterly respectful and heartbreakingly rendered, even when he happens to disagree with the decision-making processes that led to those deaths.

Death is not the only risk a climber takes; one also risks being alone. Breashears writes about his marriage—a marriage basically sacrificed on the altar of climbing and ambition—and seems to realize its dissolution was in essence his fault. Though that aspect of his life is not center stage as subject of the book, when he needs to talk to someone after the debacle on Everest, he realizes he's forfeited the right to call his wife, and that calling his mother would only worry her unnecessarily. If Breashears is harsh, he casts an equally harsh eye upon himself.

Like a lot of climbers, Breashears did not take to formal schooling but sought out an education in the mountains on his own terms. Numerous times we see Breashears the student absorbing his material: on an early Himalaya trip, he writes, "my eye was being educated to the light," or, regarding a mentor, "he was teaching me about removing myself from the story." Like all good students, Breashears sought out the best teachers, a pedigree line that includes Pat Ament, Tom Frost, Greg Lowe and Kurt Diemberger. In the acknowledgments that follow the book, he thanks many for the "collaborative effort" that went into *High Exposure*, especially Jeff Long, who helped structure the book. Breashears has learned from the best, and this learning is evident in the story of his life.

One can not, and should not, remove oneself from the story of one's own life. Yet there's a way of telling a story, and Breashears accomplishes it here, of writing a book about oneself that somehow doesn't come across as egocentric. Perhaps this sense of humility comes from repeated trips to the greatest of mountains, perhaps as a result of repeatedly witnessing the loss of friends and strangers. Perhaps it is only the rhetorical trick of good writing. However Breashears accomplishes it, the book works incredibly well. Don't give this one a miss if you're tired of Everest. Read it, in fact, because you're tired of the other Everest portrayals. This one, and its writer, stand apart.

DAVID STEVENSON

Summit: Vittorio Sella, Mountaineer and Photographer, The Years 1879-1909. Essays by Ansel Adams, David Brower, Greg Child, Paul Kalmes and Wendy Watson. Newark, NJ: Aperture, 1999. 125 duotone photographs. 129 pages. $50.00.

Vittorio Sella's eye, heart and mind danced in the mountains. Scion of a wealthy, cultivated and politically influential Italian family, Sella participated in many of the most important mountaineering expeditions of the late 19th and early 20th centuries. He developed his considerable skills as climber and photographer in the Alps, but his most extraordinary projects brought him farther afield. Sella took part in Douglas Freshfield's fabled 1899 circuit of the Kangchenjunga massif; the epic first ascent, with the Duke of Abruzzi, of Alaska's Mt. Saint Elias in 1897; first ascents in the Ruwenzori's Mountains of the Moon; and an audacious 1909 probe into the Karakoram that reached 24,500 feet on Chogolisa.

Sella's art bridges two eras. Behind him lay the main current of European Romanticism, a sensibility that celebrated the sublime majesty of nature. No photographer before or since has better expressed the Romantics' reverence for mountain grandeur than he. His mountains are nothing less than epic and stupendous, the abode of spirits and gods. But ahead of Sella lay Modernism, which, even as he trekked Karakoram glaciers, was being born in France. Modernists in photography would soon focus on the barest essentials of "the thing itself" (to use Edward Weston's term). Sella uncannily anticipated this trend with spare, clean compositions celebrating air, snow, rock—and form.

Nowhere is Sella's blend of romanticism and modernism better articulated than in the cover image of Siniolchun. As an expression of sheer "mountain-ness," the shot is incredibly perfect Modernism. Yet Sella also made the mountain seem like a goddess wrapped in bridal tule, romantic as she could possibly be. As David Brower says in the book's introduction, no mountain should be allowed to be that beautiful.

How is it that mountains can carry such symbolic intensity? How do they become the abode of dream and fantasy, of otherworldly kingdoms buried inside the human mind? There is no answer, of course. But curator Wendy Watson comes up with an intriguing notion in her essay. Playing with C.G. Jung's idea of the collective unconscious, she suggests that Sella tapped into an "optical unconscious" through a convergence of technical craft and inner spirituality.

One of the most exceptional landscape images this reviewer has ever seen shows Sella standing on the Baltoro Glacier. His camera stares simultaneously at the peaks above Urdukas and a cave plunging through unknowable depths within the ice. Sella has become a kind of Orpheus, traveling both in the conscious world and in the infinite underworld. That picture alone justified Sella's lifetime of visual exploration.

We are fortunate to partake of that odyssey in this astounding book, an essential volume for any lover of mountain imagery.

JAMES BALOG

Patagonia: Images of a Wild Land. David Neilson. Emerald, Australia: Snowgum Press, 1999. Color and black-and-white photos. 96 pages. $37.50.

Australian photographer David Neilson's *Patagonia: Images of a Wild Land* is a large-format book containing 43 color and 18 black-and-white plates. These images were culled from photos accumulated during three visits he made to Patagonia in the 1970s. Essays on the exploration, climbing and natural history of Patagonia, along with three memoirs from his journeys, accompany the photos.

Through narrative and photos, Neilson takes us to Tierra del Fuego (not properly in Patagonia), the Paine region, the Fitz Roy/Cerro Torre area, the Southern Patagonia Icecap and a remote valley adjacent to the Northern Patagonia Icecap. Neilson traces the exploration of these lands by Europeans, beginning with Magellan's epic voyage of discovery. Magellan is said to have bestowed the name "Patagonia" on the native peoples he encountered, though the origin of the word is unclear. As Neilson points out, these people were eventually exterminated. Though not exhaustive, Neilson also sketches out an overview of the climbing history of each area. He recounts in detail Maestri and Egger's climb on Cerro Torre, offering up the rarely voiced opinion that Maestri is telling the truth.

The scope of this book is one of its virtues. While most visitors to Patagonia limit themselves to the eastern sides of the Fitz Roy and Paine areas, Neilson has ventured into the heart of the matter, most notably on a voyage in 1977 and 1978 that began in Scotland on a sail-boat. Neilson and his comrades sailed to Tierra del Fuego for a climbing interlude, then continued up the coast of Chile to an obscure fiord from which three of them launched out across the Southern Patagonia Icecap to traverse east to the Fitz Roy area. The view from out on the icecap looking east toward the clustered and improbable western aspects of Cerro Torre, Fitz Roy, et al, is one of the great transcendent vistas on this planet.

Neilson's personal stories come from an already bygone era. In 1974, the year of Neilson's first visit, the ice-sheathed spires of Patagonia were still shrouded in an aura of almost mystic impregnability: Cerro Torre had maybe been climbed twice, the west face only first climbed that year. Any endeavor in these storm-swept mountains and icefields was regarded to be an adventure at the ends of the earth. Though Tierra del Fuego and the fiords of Chile may still not be popular destinations, time and familiarity have stolen some of the magic. The busy village of El Chalten that now sits at the road head below Fitz Roy (where 25 years ago there was only a ranger's cabin) notwithstanding, not all change is bad. Neilson's most potentially deadly episode was when he and his friends were arrested by the Argentine army in the bad old days of the military junta for an illegal border crossing out on the icecap.

A good bit of the mountain photography we see from Patagonia comes from climbers standing outside their tent or while on the go. A portion of the photos in this book fall into this category, and they have their own authenticity because of that. But Neilson was in Patagonia with a photographer's eye, and we are treated to photos that are crafted, taken with a photographer's patience and tenacity to find that perfect perspective and moment. Familiar vistas are revisited as well as far more esoteric images of remote fiords, valleys, mountain- and icescapes. Patagonia is not necessarily all harsh and edgy; a soft light can suffuse at times. Neilson has not ignored this, nor the wildlife.

Patagonia is things extreme, near earth's end, where outworldly landscapes are made manifest and primal forces remain unbridled. Some of this Patagonian essence can be experienced vicariously: Neilson's 25,000 words and 61 plates do a superb job of conveying it. However (and I suspect Neilson might agree with this), there is a dimension to Patagonia, more so than any other place I've been, that can only be experienced viscerally. There is nothing like standing out in the middle of the icecap as a big Patagonian storm powers up to full throttle. This you have to go feel for yourself.

MICHAEL BEARZI

Sherman Exposed: Slightly Censored Climbing Stories. John Sherman. Seattle: Mountaineers Books, 1999. 238 pages. $24.95.

Here we have John Sherman's collected articles—30 of them, almost all written during the 1990s and most having first appeared in *Climbing* magazine. The book is organized into four parts: the first is a mock self-interview titled "A Brief History of Vermin." The second part is called "Verm's World," collected articles from the column of the same name that ran in *Climbing* from 1995-'99. These are not organized chronologically but in general categories of "history, ethics, approaches to the sport, and general satire." Part three is organized by Place ("life has been one extended road trip for me"). And part four is "Characters." Sherman has added brief introductions and afterwords to most of the pieces, commenting on their origins, timeliness and the editorial battles fought on their behalf, all of which make for interesting reading and give readers a behind-the-scenes view of how articles find their way into print, as well as how climbing media shapes the experience of their readers.

In his preface, Sherman proclaims two self-imposed roles. First, by exposing "a new generation of climbers to the values of traditional climbing—sheep, inebriation and lowering after every fall—I hoped to give something back to the sport. Second, by providing lovably vulgar satire, I hoped to get climbers to take themselves less seriously." It would seem appropriate to use these criteria to judge how successful he's been. But the goals themselves pose the exact problems some readers will have with the whole. How many traditional climbers hold to the values of traditional climbing as Sherman sees them? Sheep and inebriation? Come on—it's a joke, folks, lighten up! In fact, that's the other goal: lightening up. It's just that some readers will never find vulgarity "lovable." About those would-be readers, I can only say that they're missing out on a lot of sharp observations about the state of the art, as well as brilliantly drawn portraits of places and people.

In Sherman we see the embodiment of both Royal Robbins and Warren Harding, a pair whose individual values are generally understood to be mutually exclusive. But Sherman somehow takes Harding's *semper farcimas* and combines it with Robins pure, ground-up ethic. I suppose one of the tricks to reading Sherman is to know when he's joking and when he's serious: the answer is usually both a and b.

One of the more rewarding pleasures of reading the pieces as a whole book is that you realize that Sherman very seldom writes about himself. When you read the whole, though you glimpse the "brief autobiographical" content, you realize the amazing range of his actual climbs. His commitment to bouldering has been well-documented in his twin labors of love, *Stone Crusade: A Historical Guide to Bouldering in America* and *Hueco Tanks: A Climbing and Bouldering Guide*, so it's no surprise he's done *The Thimble, Ripper Traverse*, and *Midnight Lightning*. But add *Astroman* and the first third (the easy third—he's clear about this) of the north face of the Eiger and throw in a season as a volunteer ranger on Denali, and it all adds up to the climbing life.

The portraits of places and people are the strongest pieces in the book. I took equal satisfaction in reading about places I know well, like Deadman's on the east side of the Sierra where I've bouldered dozens of times, or the gripping, committing, disintegrating, muddy towers of southern Utah's sandstone, where I've never climbed at all. In the case of Deadman's, I recognized the place perfectly, but felt I was seeing it anew through the eyes of someone who pays closer attention than I often do. In the case of the Fisher Towers, I was reading about a kind of climbing utterly foreign to me and utterly terrifying, and I had no doubt it was being accurately portrayed.

I doubt it's an accident that the portraits of people is titled "Characters," because his subjects possess it in aces. One key ingredient to character is that none of the characters ever seemed to particularly seek out the public eye. I think his two-part tribute to Robbie Slater, lost descending K2 in 1995, is as good as writing about friendship, partners and loss gets. Period.

I appreciated the previously unpublished pieces and their commentaries as much as the pieces already published. If anything, the writing that's being newly presented to the public is a little less censored, a little more personal, targeting Everest baggers, hold chippers and film makers, all of whom should understand that a little criticism goes with the territory.

If you're of the opinion that Sherman is a raving lunatic, he'd probably be the last to argue with you. In fact, you'd do well to remember that he's the one who very self-consciously gave you that impression in the first place. Don't let the hyperbolic style fool you—this is one very smart guy. And don't miss the one-paragraph history of climbing since about 1970 that ends with the sentence "Climbing is now decidedly mainstream, as proven by the media's insistence on calling it 'extreme.'"

At this late point in the review, I feel obligated to confess that I have a juvenile sense of humor and that I enjoy a glass (or more) of beer. I'm also male, of roughly the same generation as Sherman and am a traditional climber (a bad one, though). While I'm being confessional, I should add that I never saw a bolt I didn't clip; further, I admit with much regret that this year I may "climb" more days indoors than out. I suppose I'm saying that, when I'm reading, Sherman is preaching to the converted. I doubt that he will win many converts, but like all the devout, I believe that even if I don't need Sherman to remind me that "climbing" indoors isn't climbing, others do.

DAVID STEVENSON

Close Calls: Climbing Mishaps and Near-Death Experiences. John Long. Helena, MT: Falcon Publishing, 1999. 182 pages. $12.95.

John Long is a Yosemite hardman from the 1970s and the author or editor of some 17 books on rock climbing. In *Rock Jocks, Wall Rats, & Hang Dogs*, his account of his early career in and around the Valley, he recounts free-soloing 2,000 feet of 5.10 routes in a day at Joshua Tree—and nearly dying capping the day off with a 5.11. Evidently, he has grown more circumspect with age. His latest book, *Close Calls*, is devoted to safety.

In Close Calls, Mr. Long applies the droll style he has honed over the years to the accident-and-analysis format of *Accidents in North American Mountaineering*. He can get away with taking a comic approach to such a serious subject because, despite their carelessness and recklessness, the anti-heroes of these dramas all survived (miraculously, in many cases) to tell their tales. Collectively, they constitute a madcap Accidental Survivals in North American Mountaineering. Each story is followed by some pointed commentary, sensible advice and a cartoon by Tami Knight that vividly captures either the state of mindlessness of the perpetrator or the dire consequences of the deed. The locations range from Yosemite to local crags and rock gyms, the climbers from world-class to beginner. The names have been changed to protect the negligent, and the stories embellished with amusing details unabashedly supplied by the author.

The morals of most of these fables are timeless verities that every climber knows, but which many occasionally neglect: fasten your harness; rope up; set protection at regular intervals; bring water; don't climb drunk; don't test anchors with swan dives; watch out for rockfall; be careful with knives when dangling from ropes; be wary of gasoline stoves in nylon tents and romantic entanglements; don't climb with strange felons; don't drop your gear; don't rappel from rotten slings or off the end of the rope.

Other mistakes are more subtle, and yield more advanced lessons: don't belay directly beneath the climber; set anchors to withstand lateral pulls; anticipate both rope drag and stretch; plot the trajectories of both your own and others' likely pendulums; if you must climb drunk, don't puke on your rockshoes; keep in mind that real handholds may break and that gym holds may spin; the speed of long rappels increases as the rope runs out, lowering the tension on the braking device; and, given the extreme difficulty of have sex with harnesses on, the deed is best accomplished on hanging bivouacs by tying off one ankle apiece with a hangman's noose.

Many readers will find themselves sorting the various incidents into such categories as: stunts so wantonly reckless that there is absolutely no possibility of their engaging in anything remotely comparable; blunders which, although egregious, they could at least imagine themselves making in an unguarded moment; and, finally, stuff they've actually done. Others will find themselves recalling antics of their own that were easily as brainless as any in the book, but which, happily, have not been recorded for posterity.

In short, *Close Calls* is entertaining enough to keep the reader going and serious enough to be worth the investment. While no one is going to remember each incident, their cumulative impact should be adequate to make many a bit more careful, which amply justifies the project.

JOHN MCINERNEY

CORRECTION

In the 1999 *AAJ* (pp. 430-431), I reviewed the Everest IMAX film and mistakenly suggested that the "summit" footage was shot lower on the mountain. According to David Breashears, this is not true; the footage in question was indeed shot from the summit. After watching the film twice, I had incorrectly assumed from the unusually high camera angle (which eliminated background and placed the climbers on a mound of snow in a blue sky) that this shot must have been covered under the disclaimer that appears in the front of the film, "some shots were recreated." As Mr. Breashears explained to me, with only a mono-pod to stabilize the 65-pound camera, they were forced to secure it to the summit slope to achieve a viewable image. I particularly regret the implied comparison to Frederick Cook. I certainly did not mean to suggest that the film makers were perpetrating a hoax on their viewers. My abject apologies to David Breashears and his teammates for a mistake that could easily have been avoided.

I hope that this error does not detract from my attempt to convey my belief that the filmmakers of Everest made super-human efforts to complete its production. The result is the best IMAX film made to date.

MICHAEL GRABER

IN BRIEF

Despite our general policy of not reviewing how-to manuals and guidebooks, at least two titles stand out as exceptional: Mark F. Twight's *Extreme Alpinism: Climbing Light Fast, & High* is a manual for accomplished climbers who want to push to the next level. Twight is one of the few people who use the word "extreme" accurately. Excellent photos, many by Jim Martin, and first-rate anecdotes bolster a text that could be useful to most of us.

R.J. Secor's *The High Sierra: Peaks, Passes, and Trails* is now in its second edition. Secor has added 80 new routes and 60-plus new pages to the book that was already the definitive guide to the Range of Light; 570 peaks are described here. Both titles are from Mountaineers Books.

Ultimate High: My Everest Odyssey is the story of author Goran Kropp's bike trip from Sweden to Kathmandu and subsequent "solo" ascent of Everest. Reviewer Jeff apple Benowitz notes that anyone who enjoyed the death-mongering accounts of the 1996 Everest tragedies will like this one, and that the title should be changed to Ultimate Kropp to better fit the cover and text behind it. Discovery Books.

The Top of the World: Climbing Mount Everest is a beautifully illustrated book for children (ages 5 to 12; all ages for the artwork) about climbing by Steve Jenkins. Reviewers Marian and Neale Creamer were particularly impressed by the illustrations of cut paper and collage that create effective images of wind, snow plumes and valley clouds, as well as frostbite and breathing at altitude. Informative and beautiful. Houghton Mifflin Company.

In *North Cascades Crest: Notes and Images from America's Alps*, James Martin provides an overview of the geology, ecology, personalities and history of Washington's North Cascades mountain range using a mere 128 pages. Reviewer Lloyd Athearn admired the 75 sumptuous color photographs that bring the range to life, but found that the written text makes the book. Martin recalls six journeys to assorted corners of the range, from multi-day trips across the Northern Pickets and the Ptarmigan Traverse to day and weekend outings. Sasquatch Books.

Climbing High: A Woman's Account of Surviving the Everest Tragedy is Lene Gammelgaard's account of her successful climb as a member of Scott Fisher's 1996 team. Reviewer Jeanne Panek notes that "the stream-of-consciousness quality of her writing style matches the dream-like reverie of a mind at high elevation. Gammelgaard's style is not sensational. It is an intensely introspective, unpolished and analytical journal which focuses on events that touched her directly. She is unabashedly honest about her own self-doubts." Finally, Panek's opinions were mixed: "While I embrace including new styles in an otherwise male-dominated literature, her unfocused, self-absorbed journal narrative style felt shallow and left me wondering what her goal was in writing the book." Seal Press.

In *The High Lonesome: Epic Solo Climbing Stories*, editors John Long and Hai-Van K. Sponholz have given us a splendid selection of 21 previously published stories from soloists (several of whom have been killed in action) including household names: Beghin, Casarotto, Cesen, Child, Croft, Hargreaves, Messner, Twight. Reviewer Steve Roper says this compilation "speaks of the bravest of us all. Or the craziest of us all. This is a compelling and enjoyable book, one I recommend to all climbers except to impressionable ones." Falcon Press.

Lost on Everest: The Search for Mallory and Irvine is Peter Firstbrook's first-hand account of the 1999 Mallory and Irvine Research Expedition. The author, who produced the BBC film of the same name, devotes only two of ten chapters to the 1999 recovery mission, its findings and conclusions. These chapters are, in the opinion of reviewer Margaret Ann Sinex, without question the best portion of the volume. Contemporary Books.

David Robertson has reissued his biography, *George Mallory*, originally published in 1969. This is one of the primary sources of biographical materials for most of the new Mallory-Irvine tomes. In addition, Robertson has published *North of India*, portraits of six early Himalayan explorers. Both books are published by Orchid Press, Bangkok. David Robertson, a longtime AAC member and former co-editor of this journal, should not be confused with David Roberts, co-author of *The Lost Explorer* and numerous other titles familiar to our readers.

Also available in a new paperback edition is Tom Holzel and Audrey Salkeld's *First on Everest: The Mystery of Mallory & Irvine*, first published in 1986. This was the original ground-breaking work upon whose shoulders much of the "new" speculation stands. Mountaineers Books.

Evelio Echevarría has published a second edition of his history of climbing in Chile, *Chile Andinista: Su Historia*. Echevarría calls this labor of love his "final enlarged edition." Enhanced with numerous archival photographs and thoroughly documented with appendices and footnotes, this scholarly work will stand as the world-wide record. In Spanish.

Nanda Devi: Exploration and Ascent. Eric Shipton and H.W. Tilman. This book reprints the two classics *Nanda Devi* and *The Ascent of Nanda Devi*. In addition to combining the two-in-one volume, included here is a terrific new introductory memoir by Charles Houston, one of the co-leaders of the 1936 expedition. From Bâton Wicks.

Twenty-Five Letters from Norman Clyde, 1923-1964 is a limited edition (500 copies) book by Dennis Kruska, who has provided a short biography as well as thoughtful annotations of these previously unpublished letters. From The Castle Press, Pasadena, this is a most elegant production, made by and for people who love Norman Clyde, the Sierra and fine books.

Spirit of the Mountains collects "more than 200 photographs of the most sought-out mountains in the world." Published by Grivel, the French hardware makers, this is a beautiful collection, printed in paperback with a dust wrapper. It's a glossy magazine with high production values, no editorial content and next to no space devoted to advertising. Distributed in the U.S. by Stackpole Books.

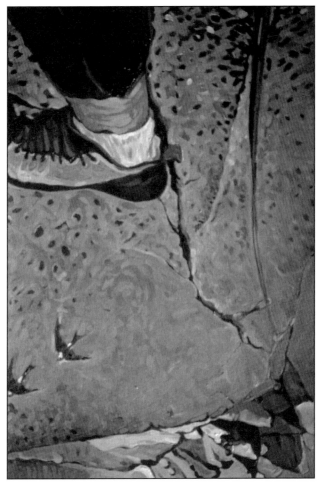

SEAN McCABE

Club Activities, 1999

Edited by Frederick O. Johnson

AAC, Sierra Nevada Section. Over the past two years, the Sierra Nevada Section has worked diligently to engage the National Park Service in meaningful dialogues regarding the use of resources within Yosemite National Park. In 1999, we began to reap some benefits from these efforts. Many of our activities were centered around continued work and education on Yosemite planning issues as well as celebrations of milestones from this work. We also took time to simply get together and climb or share our experiences.

In February, we gathered in Reno for a Section dinner at the Patagonia outlet. The program included Kath Pyke of the Central Rockies Section, Joe Kelsey, Tommy Herbert and T.M. Herbert. T.M. shared with us some classic photos and stories from the first ascent of El Capitan's Muir Wall, which he and Yvon Chouinard completed in 1965.

True classics themselves, Allen Steck and Steve Roper teamed up as editors of the long-awaited 14th issue of that premier collection of mountaineering writing and photography, *Ascent*. (For a review of the book, see page 399.)

Throughout 1999, planning issues in Yosemite continued on the forefront of member activities. Early in the year, it became evident that the El Portal road project undertaken by the Yosemite Park Service was going to have long-reaching, adverse effects on the seven-mile stretch it would follow along the wild and scenic Merced River. Thanks to Greg Adair's organization, The Friends of Yosemite Valley, and coordinated efforts with the Sierra Club and local citizen groups, the project was halted. The YPS then wrote the Merced River Management Plan to provide protection for this precious resource. Dozens of our members attended public hearings and wrote comments to the Park Service regarding this plan.

Some truly remarkable events also occurred this year in Yosemite. First, Camp 4 became officially eligible for the National Registry of Historic Places. This in large part was due to the enormous efforts of Dick Duane, who wrote the "Supplementary Application for Placement of Camp 4 on the National Historical Register" in 1998, and the negotiating efforts led by Tom Frost. In September, a Camp 4 celebration, hosted by Tom and Joyce Frost and the AAC, was held in the Valley to thank all who worked to make this possible and to celebrate this outstanding recognition of mountaineering history. Attended by 650 climbers from around the world and by park personnel, this was an grand testament to the new relationship the climbing community has forged with the NPS, as well as to how enduring the values and benefits of climbing remain over time. (For a full account of the celebration, see the note on pages 169-172 earlier in this journal.) It was a great honor for members of the Sierra Nevada Section to participate by donating hundreds of volunteer hours to the planning and execution of the event.

In May, in order to heighten community awareness of Yosemite planning issues, we hosted a climber's forum in the Bay Area. Mark Fincher, Gary Colliver and Amy Schneckenberger of the National Park Service provided presentations to help communicate ideas and plans for changes in Yosemite Valley. Similar events are planned so that climbers can remain engaged in the challenging planning process that Yosemite Park officials struggle with daily.

In its third year of operation, the Volunteer in Parks (VIP) program continues under George Gluck's direction to help build a cooperative relationship with the NPS in Yosemite. One of its many accomplishments in 1999 was the contribution of hundreds of hours to the construction of a new Tuolumne Backcountry Permit Office. With the old permit office, restrooms were half a mile away, bear canisters were picked up at a concession stand approximately a mile away, and permits were issued at the backcountry parking lot. The new office, constructed in an already developed area, eliminates much inconvenience to backpackers and reduces parking problems and the excessive use of cars. Other milestones included some 800 volunteer hours contributed by more than 80 of our members and their guests, who came from Germany, Spain, Italy, Poland, France, England and China.

Many Section members made the trek to Washington, D.C., for the Club's Annual Meeting in November. Dick Duane and Tom Frost were awarded the Gold Medal for their dedication in representing the Club with great integrity, humor, and compassion in negotiations and meetings with the National Park Service. This is not an annual award, but is reserved for occasions when individuals make a significant contribution to the AAC and the climbing community as a whole. While in Washington, Linda McMillan, newly elected AAC vice president, represented the Club's interests in visits to government officials in the departments of Interior and Agriculture as well as to officials in the National Parks and Conservation Association, Natural Resources Defense Council, the Wilderness Society and the Keeper of the Historic Registry.

LYNN BAMFORD, *Chair*

AAC, Central Rockies Section. Perhaps it's the proximity of the AAC offices or just that Coloradoans are being drawn to the great outdoors more than ever, but the Central Rockies Section continues to see phenomenal growth. Only four years after the division of the Rocky Mountain Section into two parts (North and Central), the Central Rockies Section has outgrown the previous total membership for the section. As we move into the 21st century, the CRS membership will break 1,400, and we may once again look into division to maximize the personal connection between the AAC and its membership.

The Central Rockies Section was involved in several events and projects in 1999 that we hope will show the climbing community that the AAC is an advocate voice and interested partner, able to attract new members while stimulating existing members to get involved. Naturally, it's a shame that we can't "just go climbing" anymore, that issues have arisen that require either response or the possible loss of our wilderness freedom. It is imperative that we help manage the land and freedom that we have taken for granted for so long.

Immediately north of the AAC offices in Golden are the basalt cliffs of Table Mountain, which offer sport and traditional climbs through most of the winter. The Section strengthened its alliance with the Access Fund in 1999 by donating $1,500 to the construction of the Golden Cliffs project, which provided a legal and formal access road, parking lot, trail system and restroom for the crag. The fund raising for this money was member-driven through support of the Annual Section Banquet, auction and sale items.

In April, the CRS wrote to the Jefferson County Planning Commission in Golden and attended public meetings to voice our concern regarding the proposed mining adjacent to Eldorado State Park. The open-pit mining proposal threatens the nature of the Park, which is an international destination for rock climbing. At the time of this writing, the proposal has been tabled.

In June, the Chairman met with leaders of two Russian climbing clubs in hopes of creating an exchange. Although the Russians are happy to receive guests, their economic conditions will prevent them from sending any of their climbers to this country for some time to come. If there are interested parties wishing to pursue an adventure in Russia, whether alpine ascents or rock climbing near the Black Sea, please feel free to inquire.

July saw Section members team up with the Colorado Fourteeners Initiative to provide labor toward trail restoration on Mount Harvard (14,420'). This organization, with an office in the American Mountaineering Center in Golden, is working to create a sustainable trail system on all 53 of Colorado's 14,000-foot peaks. In most cases our high peaks are being loved to death, and new trails are needed to get foot traffic onto rock and off the tundra.

For current events in our area, please visit our web site at http://crs.alpineclub. org. We have added a List Service for our e-mail members. On it, you may post inquiries, reports, gear wanted or for sale, or other news. It is exempt from solicitation and marketing and is solely for members' use and enjoyment. To subscribe, please visit our web site and follow the prompt on the Home Page.

GREG SIEVERS, *Chairman*

AAC, North Central Section. The North Central Section covers Minnesota, Iowa, Nebraska, South Dakota and North Dakota. In July, 1999, Scott Christensen took over the post of chairman, which had been vacant in 1997-'98. A first goal was to make a web site similar to those of the other sections. This was completed in October and now provides members and visitors a means to learn about specific North Central items as well as national AAC issues. The web site has sections on our parent organization, upcoming events and news of the region. It also has a message board for climbers to find one another and to post messages pertinent to the local crags. Contact our web site at www.ncs.alpineclub.org.

The chairman attended the AAC Annual Meeting in Washington, D.C., representing the Section at committee meetings and meeting with members who performed much of the Club's work in the Yosemite Camp 4 development. Also, members worked at the local clean-up day at Interstate Park on the north side of metropolitan Twin Cities. This is a very popular top-rope area for Minnesota and the Midwest. As in most areas of the country, more and more restrictions have been placed on climbing. Interstate is no exception; climbing permits are now required. The good-will from our support of the clean-up day goes a long way in keeping climbers climbing.

SCOTT CHRISTENSEN, *Chairman*

AAC, South Central Section. The South Central Section held an annual meeting in Dallas, Texas, on October 16. The newly elected officers for 2000 are Andy Jones, chair; Mike Doyle, co-chair; and Gail Billings, treasurer. Mike Lewis will assist the Section in an advisory capacity. The well-attended meeting was bolstered by public attendees who were there to see Kurt Diemberger. Kurt presented his K2 classic, "Mountain of Dreams and Destiny," and held the whole crowd in the palm of his hand throughout. The meeting was sponsored by (and could not have happened without) the generous help of Whole Earth Provision Company. Donors for the silent auction included The Sullivan Agency, Mountain Hideout, *Climbing* and *Rock & Ice* magazines, REI, Rollerblade, Camelback, Stone Works Climbing Gym, Metolius and Mike Hall (a retired climbing gear donation). The successful auction allowed the Section to make contributions to the Central Asian Institute and to the family of Alex Lowe.

The Section surveyed its membership, with 218 surveys mailed out and 40 returned. The survey was comprised of 12 questions related to the Annual Meeting, Section activities, communication and needs. The key responses were that there was interest in more activities, stepping up the political activism (e.g., the access arena), keeping the current meeting format, and gaining more information on the "goings-on in the climbing world."

With those interests in mind, it is important to know that several of our members have been heavily involved in the Sunset Report on Texas Parks and Wildlife. The Sunset Report on TPW is available at www.sunset.statetx.us and can be downloaded from the report section. This is an important document in that, after comments and final approval, it will be used in the 2001 Legislative Session to change the laws governing TPW. Access restrictions at Hueco Tanks State Park are still a topic of discussion between climbing organizations in Texas and TPW. TPW has issued a final management plan that still severely regulates access to the park for any activity, but especially climbing. Many members have been very active in meetings concerning the park management and have provided numerous written comments to the agency, requesting a better management approach. A request to TPW to open a climbing area in McKinney Falls State Park near Austin has, so far, been received favorably by the park manager and the new parks director. The area is a limestone outcrop that will support a few climbers at one time with bouldering activities. Other climbing areas are being developed in the state but are not yet ready for open access due to unresolved issues with the landowner.

The Section continued to support the trailbuilding effort at Enchanted Rock State Natural Area in Texas with monthly volunteer trailbuilding days held throughout the year. Participation has been good, and new areas of construction began this year, including the Blue Trail to the News Wall. To date, more than 200 tons of rock have been transported to the park and moved by wheelbarrow for building critical retaining walls, water breaks and trail sections. Funding for this effort was obtained through grants from the AAC Conservation Committee. Many thanks to all of the volunteers who have spent long hours on this project.

ANDY JONES, *Chair*

AAC, New York Section. As the millennium approached, the New York Section could look back on 25 years of continued growth and a strong tradition of volunteerism and financial support on behalf of Club causes. Now numbering more than 600 members—a 50 percent increase in just the last five years—the Section busies itself with a series of climbing and social events designed to bring together its varied and diversified membership.

Perhaps best known to the outside world is the Annual Section Dinner, a gala black-tie fundraiser which celebrated its 20th anniversary last year. Special guests Brad and Barbara Washburn, pioneer Alaskan climbers and extraordinary storytellers, kept the capacity audience of 160 members and guests, some from as far away as Oregon and Washington, in thrall as they told of their various adventures spanning back over 60 years. Another octogenarian, Gerry Bloch, recounted his recent 11-day ascent of El Capitan's formidable *Aquarian Wall*, thereby decisively breaking his own age record, one that will undoubtedly stand for a long time to come. Youth was served as well. Among the record 20 new members initiated into the Section that night were the first father-and-son pair, Irving Oppenheim and his son, Dan, a precocious 17-year-old who has an El Capitan solo as part of his climbing resume. The Dinner benefited *The American Alpine Journal* and the AAC Library Acquisition Fund.

Earlier in April, the Section had the honor and pleasure of welcoming Fosco Maraini, the Italian author, scholar, photographer and pioneer climber. At a Section-hosted dinner, Fosco told of his travels to Tibet both before and immediately after World War II as well as his climbs in the 1950s in the Hindu Kush and Karakoram. There he met and became good friends with former AAC President Nick Clinch, and Clinch journeyed from California to meet with Fosco once again. The dinner was part of a three-day, non-stop series of events that included a slide show and gallery opening in Manhattan. Fosco and his wife Meiko will be long remembered here for their grace and charm.

In May, the Club once again co-sponsored Alpinfilm, the New York International Mountain Film Festival, which celebrated its tenth anniversary. The Festival is a juried competition with cash prizes to winning filmmakers. The Rolex Award for the Best Film of the Festival went to AAC member and one-time New Yorker Ken Bailey for his powerful *Ode to Avalanche*, set to Beethoven's Ninth Symphony. Other winners were *Escoba de Dios* ("The Broom of God") and *War and Poetry*, a John Wilcox film starring Todd Skinner and friends in Greenland. The film premiered that night at the Festival. Before the screenings, Section members, filmmakers and guests mingled at a pre-theater reception and dinner at a nearby restaurant. Finally, on the following day, well-known author David Roberts presented a fascinating slide show on the Telem people of Mali, who may have been pre-history's first and finest climbers. June saw the Section convene once again at its historic haunts, the Ausable Club in Keene Valley, New York, for a weekend of climbing, hiking and canoeing in the heart of the Adirondack High Peaks. Earlier in January, members had climbed many of the same routes but with ice axes and crampons. These Adirondack Outings, both winter and summer, always attract capacity throngs and, in a pristine setting, are a welcome change of pace from the oft-crowded local routes.

Because the Gunks still remain the primary venue for local climbers, the Section helped the Mohonk Preserve fund a series of important initiatives at the local cliffs, including creating some badly needed new rappel stations and rebuilding some eroded access trails. These were funded in part by grants from the Club's Lyman Spitzer Fund.

Finally, tribute should be paid to Vaclav (Vic) Benes, our webmaster, for creating a lively, entertaining, and newsworthy Section web site, enhanced with superb pictorials and graphics. Among the new features introduced this year is an interactive slide show. So to keep abreast of what's going on in the Big Apple, do log on to http://nys.alpineclub.org.

PHILIP ERARD, *Chair*

AAC, New England Section. Chris Dame and friends began 1999 by attaining the summit of Chile's El Novado Juncal (6110m) for the first American ascent. In June, Dave and Debbie Duncanson topped out on Denali via the West Buttress.

Al Hospers and Yuki Fujita started their year at the Alpine Club of Canada's Cranmore, BC, facility, where they enjoyed many routes, among them *Kitty Hawk* and climbs on the Weeping Wall. They returned in the summer to climb Mount Athabasca.

Jim McCarthy, our special guest for our Fourth Annual Dinner, gave a 50-year reminiscence that ranged from the 'Gunk days of Wiessner, Kraus and Vulgarian yore to today's world of dynos and flashes. Our reception exhibit comprised the "Magical Snowcolors" of AAC Alaskan guide and water colorist John Svenson.

The Harvard Mountaineering Club selected Barry Rugo as guest speaker for their spring dinner. In April, various souls among us went West to climb at Red Rocks, Joshua Tree and Zion.

At our second Northcountry "Basecamp" at Jim Ansara's in North Conway, NH, we screened three of Ken Henderson's newly restored films of l930s ice and rock climbing, as we did again in the fall for a Connecticut "Camp I" group organized by Walt Hampton and Pauline Eng. In the fall, Ken Henderson retired from our midst to his daughter's realm in Hanover, NH.

Paul Dale trekked to the top of Pokalde (5800m) in the Nepal Himalaya. Bob Wadja returned from France, having visited Verdon Gorge, La Meije (3982m) in the Haute Dauphine, and later the summits of La Tour Ronde and Mont Blanc in Chamonix. Also in the Dauphine, Bill Atkinson and Nancy Savickas took a few days off to do Aiguille Dibona (3100m) from the Soreiller Hut, where we (almost) encountered Isabelle Bey on the same mission.

In 1999, Section membership increased from about 400 to 480, a gain of 20 percent, which we find gratifying but for which we are reluctant to claim any credit.

BILL ATKINSON, *Chair, and* NANCY SAVICKAS, *Vice-Chair*

Mountaineering Club of Alaska. In February, Mark Miraglia and Dolly Lefever climbed the Northeast Ridge of Mt. Tasman in New Zealand. Dolly's climb is thought to be the first ascent of this peak by someone with artificial hips. Meanwhile in Alaska, Cory Hinds and Richard Baranow made the first ascent of *Nigelina*, a 230-foot WI4+ ice climb in Eagle River (Chugach Mountains). Two weeks later, Carl Oswald, Richard Baranow and Wendy Sanem completed its previously unclimbed twin, *Luther's Delight* (WI4+, 230').

In April, a strong team including David Hart, Paul Barry, Jim McDonough, Shawn O'Donnell and Kirk Towner made multiple ascents in the Canadian St. Elias Range. The following peaks were climbed: Mt. Slaggard (15,557'), Mt. Macaulay (15,387'), Southeast Macaulay (14,501') and

Northwest Steele (13,845'). Richard Baranow, Wendy Sanem, Paul Templeton, Fred West and Tim Griffin summitted Mt. Marcus Baker (13,176') in the Chugach Mountains via the Northeast Ridge. Baranow, Sanem and West skied up the Matanuska Glacier, summitted, then skied out the Marcus Baker and Knik glaciers.

In May, David Hart, Dawn Groth, Cory Hinds, Elena Hinds, Wayne Todd, Kathy Still and Ben Still went ski touring on the upper Nabesna Glacier in the Alaskan Wrangell Mountains near Mt. Blackburn. Several 4,000-foot ski descents were made. Two strong teams summitted the Moose's Tooth via the *Ham and Eggs* route (WI4 5.7). Harry Hunt and Peter Haeussler summitted in May, and David Hart and Brad Gessner summitted in June (for further information on these climbs, see Climbs and Expeditions: Alaska).

In July, David Hart, Bryan Carey and Ron Rickman visited Bolivia's Cordillera Real and climbed Huayana Potosi, Pequeño Alpamayo, Ilusion, and Blanca. In October, David Hart and Kurt Bauer visited the Nepal Himalaya and climbed the South Ridge of Baruntse (23,400').

The club's training activities included general mountaineering, winter camping, snow and ice climbing, glacier travel and crevasse rescue, winter camping and knots.

Community involvement activities included the hiker/climber sign project and public-use cabin construction. The joint MCA/AAC Alaska Section Climber/Hiker Sign Project was originally started in 1998. Its purpose was to provide a positive message to hikers/climbers with regard to their activities on public lands and to show the general public that there is a group of responsible outdoor recreationalists who care about their impact on other user groups. Funding was provided by grants from the AAC and REI. This project was completed in spring of 1999 when signs were installed at various rock/ice climbing areas and popular trailheads.

The Alaska Division of Parks and Outdoor Recreation and MCA, in collaboration with the AAC, sponsored the construction of a public use cabin in the Chugach State Park. Architectural work was provided on a pro bono basis; the Club supplied a work force of skilled volunteers and materials were purchased with funds obtained from grants and donations. The cabin is conveniently located in a prime ice climbing area.

CORY HINDS, *Secretary*

The Mountaineers. The Mountaineers' Seattle climbing program, under the leadership of Ron Eng, continues to maintain a long-standing focus on alpine climbing in the Pacific Northwest. However, the program has continued to expand significantly. In addition to the Basic and Intermediate Climbing courses, which are its foundation and continue to draw high demand, the climbing program now offers the Waterfall Ice Climbing Course. This course, which includes winter trips to the waterfall ice climbing areas of Colorado, British Columbia and Alberta, is designed for the experienced alpinist and represents a significant expansion of the traditional curricular and geographic scopes.

The program also continues to offer a variety of climbing seminars designed to foster further development of the climbing course graduates' technical skills. Seminar offerings range from basic climbing skills (e.g., friction climbing and risk assessment) to "Advanced Climbing Experience" seminars (e.g., aid climbing and planning an expedition to Denali). In addition to numerous climbs of mountains in the Pacific Northwest, the program also sponsored trips to Yosemite Valley and Tuolumne Meadows, British Columbia and Alberta.

Program administration includes the increasing use of electronic technology. A growing number of climb leaders are taking advantage of the climb leader web page trip registration system to schedule trips. More and more information is being incorporated on the climbing program general web page. The climbing program web page URL is http://www.eskimo.com/-pc22/CC/cc.html.

Mountaineers Books published a number of books in 1999, among them *The Totem Pole*, by Paul Pritchard, Mark Twight's *Extreme Alpinism* and *A Life on the Edge: Memoirs of Everest and Beyond*, by Big Jim Whittaker. We also pulled off a minor publishing miracle in late September with the publication of *Ghosts of Everest: The Search for Mallory and Irvine*. On May 1, when we learned of the discovery of Mallory's body, we had no manuscript. On September 25, we printed 55,000 copies of a 200-page, full-color book. Typically it takes an author several years to complete a manuscript and at least nine months for us to edit, design and produce a book. In addition, Mountaineers Books has now completed two reprints for a current total of 85,000 copies in print (see reviews of the above titles beginning on page 397).

DONNA PRICE, *Trustee*

The Mazamas. The Climbing Committee, chaired by Gerald Itkin, scheduled 266 climbs, including 16 in winter. The Basic Climbing Committee, headed by Dave Sauerbrey, enrolled participants into groups of nine with about four instructors for each group. In addition to rock and snow training, the groups were required to make several day hikes into difficult terrain. Basic Climbing School suffered a serious setback, however, when the previous requirement for a mountain climb was canceled. The elimination of a "graduation" climb was forced by the efforts of the U.S. Forest Service to classify mountaineering clubs as guide services.

The Intermediate Climbing Program (ICP) was conducted by Richard Caldwell. This program develops and screens future climb leaders and provides instruction of higher levels of rock and snow climbing. The fatal avalanche in a Basic School climb in May, 1998, prompted a further tightening of safety procedures and a restructuring of the ICP in 1999. Intermediate students were routed through a series of instruction stations, each designated to teach a particular skill in rock and snow climbing sessions. Group coordinators were responsible for each station teacher as they covered the required curriculum.

The Advanced Rock Program enrolled 23 students under the lead of Don Erickson. The sessions were held at local rock gyms and local crags. A study group reviewed the course and made changes to improve safety and teaching techniques. Outdoor sessions were held at Horsethief Butte and Smith Rock. Field trips went to Yosemite, City of Rocks National Reserve in Idaho and Squamish in British Columbia.

The Advanced Snow and Ice Program had evolved into a program of vertical ice climbing. However, John Youngman led a study group in 1999 to redirect the training toward steep snow and crevasse terrain, the type of climbing that Club members actually do.

The Leadership Training Program further tightened requirements. Ten experienced leaders must evaluate the knowledge and leadership skill of each candidate. By October 1, the end of the 1998-1999 fiscal year, there were 16 leadership development candidates and five new provisional leaders. Now in its third year, a new Leadership Continuing Education Committee, chaired by David Wedge, was requiring further training, such as avalanche awareness and rescue, for established leaders.

Recipients of Mazama Climbing Awards were: Guardian Peaks (Hood, St. Helens, Adams): Anita Bieker, Richard Busing, Keith Childers, Christy Crandall, Steve Hallock, Skip Smith, Lee Wilson, Joan Zuber. Oregon Cascades (Jefferson, Three-Fingered Jack, Washington, Three Sisters): Elly Branch, Joan Zuber. Sixteen Major Peaks (all of the above plus Olympus, Baker, Shuksan, Glacier, Stuart, Shasta): Eric Hoem, Dean Odenthal. Fifteen-Point Leadership: Terry Cone.

The Outing Committee, chaired by Joe Boyce, sponsored several outings: backpacks in Guatemala and in Oregon's Wallowas and Steens Mountain and hiking trips to Maui, the Tetons, Peru, Ecuador, the Dolomites and Tuscany. The Trail Trips Committee, chaired by Richard Getgen, sponsored hikes with a total of 4,190 participant days. Street Rambles in Portland parks and streets continued as popular events on Tuesday and Thursday evenings. The Trail Tenders subcommittee continued a program of weekend trail improvement by volunteers wielding picks, shovels, axes and pruning shears to maintain trails at Mount Hood and the Columbia Gorge.

The Expedition Committee granted funds to three projects: climbing in Ecuador by John Youngman and Lloyd Athearn; exploration of the Cordon del Plata region of Argentina by Bill Brownlee and Tammee Stump; and an expedition to Mount Walsh in Canada's Yukon Territory by Jim Anderson and Mark Simmons. On the Executive Council, President Christine Mackert was re-elected. Joe Whittington was elected treasurer on October 1, and Susan Pyle Erickson, Josh Lockerby and Doug Wilson were elected council members.

Major William D. Hackett, U.S. Army Retired, died August 9, 1999, at age 81. Bill joined The Mazamas in 1933. An obituary can be found on page 436.

JACK GRAUER, *Historian*

California Mountaineering Club. The California Mountaineering Club is now ten years old. We have nearly 300 members, mostly from southern California but with a growing number from all regions of the state and many from other states. We climb mostly in the Sierra Nevada, but have scheduled climbs of Mount Rainier, other Cascade peaks, desert peaks, and the Mexican volcanoes.

In 1999, R. J. Secor led a Club outing to explore some of the more obscure approaches to Pico de Orizaba and Iztaccihuatl in Mexico. The Club had several ice climbing outings at June Lake and Lee Vining. It continues its monthly rock climbing outings at Joshua Tree and Tahquitz and held several well-attended training and practice sessions. The Club has a monthly newsletter. Interested mountaineers are invited to visit our web site at www.californiamountaineer.com.

JACK MILLER, *President*

Arizona Mountaineering Club. The Arizona Mountaineering Club (AMC) increased its membership in 1999 to more than 500 and added new programs for its members. The Club meets the fourth Monday of each month in Phoenix. Speakers at these meetings included nationally known climbers as well as Club members who added their own exciting adventures to the programs.

AMC involvement in access-related issues has kept members busy. We continue to help with trail building at Pinnacle Peak. Trails for both recreational use and climbing are being developed with the guidance of the City of Scottsdale Parks and Recreation Department. Parking and restroom facilities are in the planning stage. This climbing area, very popular in past years, has been closed since about 1995 because of development. With the peak about to become an official park and ownership of the land soon to be in the hands of Scottsdale, we look forward to climbing (perhaps) sometime late in 2001. The McDowell Mountains and the Little Granite Mountain area, bordering Scottsdale to the north and east, are also under intense threat from development. Thanks to voter approval, the City of Scottsdale is working on the purchase of right-of-access to these areas through taxes. We continue to be an active partner in The Access Fund through strong fiscal support and membership drives. Wayne Schroeter, access chairman, monitors and leads the activism on access-related issues.

Strong membership interest has led to the formation of a committee to explore offering alpine and mountaineering outings, the risks involved, and the criteria for approving leaders for such outings. Snow skills seminars were conducted on Humphreys Peak, where students learned ice axe arrest, crampon use, simulated glacier travel and simulated crevasse rescue systems. We also arranged for a professional company to provide ice climbing weekend seminars in Durango, Colorado.

The AMC's basic, anchors and lead rock climbing classes continue to be a great success. Each is held twice a year, and all are always sold out. A number of annual outings, such as Thanksgiving at Joshua Tree National Monument and spring in Lower Devils Canyon, bring large turnouts. The "Over The Rim" at the south rim of the Grand Canyon, when we rappel over the rim and clean up trash for the NPS, results in a fun weekend of cleanup, barbeque and climbing for members. Twice a year we do highway cleanup on U.S. 60 east of Superior for our Adopt-A-Mile conservation project.

After cleanup, the rest of the day is spent climbing in the Magma Mine area. There is at least one outing every weekend, more than enough to keep members climbing happily all over Arizona.

As an outgrowth of new activities, increased membership and more students in our rock climbing classes, the AMC board and the outing leaders are addressing risk-management issues, including the need for insurance and ongoing leader training. President Sue Goins attended the NOLS Wilderness Risk Management Conference in Sierra Vista, where much useful information on these matters was obtained for review and discussion within the AMC and with other organizations facing these same issues.

SUE GOINS, *President*

The Colorado Mountain Club. 1999 was a busy year for The Colorado Mountain Club. The Club graduated 258 students in its technical climbing schools and led three international expeditions of note. Basic Mountaineering Schools graduated 216 students, the Advanced Mountaineering 20, and the High Altitude Mountaineering School 22 with a graduation exercise of an ascent of Mount Rainier in Washington.

International climbing expeditions included ascents of Mount Kilimanjaro in Africa, Mount Elbrus in Russia and a volcano ascent in Ecuador. A total of 34 CMC climbers went on these trips with 32 reaching the actual summits. There were also trips to New Zealand, Peru and Alaska.

The CMC again had a successful year with thousands of volunteer-led trips to peaks, alpine attractions of the region and excellent local crags of Colorado and the surrounding states. Multiple conservation and education projects rounded out the year to help fulfill the CMC mission statement and provide for sustainable recreation in the future. Further information is available on the Club web page at www.cmc.org/cmc or by contacting the Colorado Mountain Club headquarters at the American Mountaineering Center, Golden, Colorado.

DARRAN BORNN

SEAN MCCABE

In Memoriam

Edited by David Harrah and Angus Thuermer, Jr.

MARJORY BRIDGE FARQUHAR
1903-1999

Marjory Farquhar, one of America's outstanding pioneer women climbers, died in San Francisco on January 22 after a short illness. Together with her late husband, Francis Farquhar, Marj was a great force in western American mountaineering and especially in the Sierra Club and the AAC. Besides bringing technical climbing to the Sierra Nevada and Yosemite Valley, the two of them were mentors to generations of California climbers. For decades, their home on Avalon Avenue in Berkeley was the AAC West. Climbers would introduce themselves with, "Remember me? I met you at the Farquhars'."

Marj was born on November 7 or 17, 1903, in San Francisco. (The original record was destroyed in the earthquake and fire and another record is difficult to read.) She went to school in the Bay Area and graduated from the University of California at Berkeley in 1925. She was a fine photographer and had her own photographic businesses from time to time.

She began her climbing with various ascents in the Sierra Nevada beginning in 1929. In 1931, when Francis Farquhar persuaded Robert Underhill to come to California to teach modern rock climbing techniques, she was a member of the small group of Sierra Club climbers who received that instruction and who began to pioneer new technical climbs in the Sierra Nevada and Yosemite Valley. In 1934, she made an early ascent of the Higher Cathedral Spire and was the first woman to do that climb, which remained for many years the test piece for all Yosemite climbers. She also made an early ascent of the East Face of Whitney, a climb she repeated several times.

She married Francis Farquhar in 1934. Besides rearing a family, she was active in the Sierra Club, and together with Francis she hosted a never-ending succession of dinners, receptions, AAC meetings and numerous other events. For 40 years their house was the ground zero for the conservation movement in California. She also served on the boards of the Sierra Club, the Save the Redwoods League and the AAC, among other organizations. If people were mountains, Marj Farquhar would be Lhotse, fourth highest mountain in the world, strong, impressive and rising far above most other mountains. Yet because she was married to Francis, an Everest of a man, her contribution to everything they accomplished is not fully appreciated by many people, even by some of their friends.

Marj was a woman of tremendous talent and unbelievable energy. She always was surrounded by her three children, Peter, Suzanne and Roger, their spouses and various grandchildren, as well as many other, more distant members of the family. In addition to everything else, she served as a mother hen to two generations of college students who lived at Avalon Avenue, not to mention various strays and waifs of the climbing world who would drift in from time to time. She was one of those remarkable persons who could love you, encourage you and shape you up, all simultaneously.

Marj also had a sharp sense of humor. One time, when someone commented to her how great Francis looked in a photograph taken on the top of Mt. Whitney, she replied, "He should. He rode a mule to the summit."

One could not be blessed with better friends than Francis and Marj. They may not have moved mountains, but they certainly moved mountaineers. Although they are both gone, their combined beneficial influence and example will continue to reverberate through American mountaineering for a long, long time.

NICHOLAS B. CLINCH

THOMAS HUGHES JUKES
1906-1999

Tom Jukes was born in Hastings, England, in 1906 and died on November 1, 1999, in Berkeley, CA, after a short illness. He was a classical environmentalist, a scientist of the first order and a long-time mountaineer and explorer of the Sierra Nevada. All who knew him were impressed with his devotion to accuracy in science, his unwillingness to suffer fools gladly, his sense of humor and his unequalled energy. At the age of 93, Tom was still working at the University of California.

Tom's first backpack trip in the Sierra took place in the summer of 1935, when he went from Kearsarge Pass to Bishops Pass along the John Muir Trail. From then until 1980, he spent part of every summer in the Sierra, where he climbed innumerable peaks, fished scores of its lakes and crossed most of the highest passes. On his last backpack trip in the Sierra, he went again through Kearsarge Pass and from there to Charlotte Lake, a favorite fishing spot.

That year, a knee replacement put an end to his backpacking, but beginning the next year he went with his wife, Marguerite, his children and grandchildren to Virginia Lake in the Northern Sierra each summer until just three years ago. There were only two summers when he did not visit the Sierra—the war years of 1943 and 1944.

Tom was a life member and an ardent supporter of the Sierra Club, founding its Atlantic Chapter in 1950. It was the first chapter to be formed outside of California and became one of the more successful. In the late 1960s, he became disillusioned with the direction the Sierra Club was taking. He believed that control was moving from genuine environmentalists such as Ansel Adams, Francis Farquhar, Dick Leonard and Raffi Bedayn to those who, for the most part, had little experience in the wilderness and no knowledge of the science that makes up the environment.

Tom's first skirmish with the new environmentalism occurred in 1962 with the publication of Rachel Carson's *Silent Spring*. The Sierra Club extolled the book, despite its lack of science and its failure to acknowledge that DDT had been responsible for saving innumerable lives and for its potential to continue to do so, particularly in the Third World. This was a crusade that he led until the end of his life.

In November, 1985, he again took up battle, this time against the banning of all Sierra Club climbing activities. The fight was unsuccessful. The new leadership could not be persuaded that climbing was an important aspect and a part of the appreciation of the wilderness. They did not much care that early climbers such as John Muir, Dick Leonard, David Brower, and Francis Farquhar were responsible for what the Sierra Club stood for and for the policies that made it what it had become by the 1960s.

I think it apt to quote a poem composed and sent to Tom by Ansel Adams in 1972 during one of Tom's duels with the Sierra Club.

We cannot trust the bastards
No matter what their stripe!

Wild or modest, sweet or sour
They never fail to gripe!!

My rhyme has failed,
My vision paled,
I won't be strafed or Holy Grailed!!! Or to the
GROUPTHINK Cross be nailed!
Enough—enough; you understand!
A few things left are truly GRAND!!
—AA
The Bearded Bard

Although Tom Jukes was dedicated to California and the Sierra, he spent many years on the East Coast during and after WWII. Many California mountaineers in the 1940s and '50s showed up on his doorstep for one reason or another, be it graduate study or passing through on the way to Europe. All of us will remember the warm welcome and hospitality that he and Marguerite offered, no matter the time of day or night.

ROBIN HANSEN

PAUL KIESOW PETZOLDT
1908-1999

Legendary mountaineer, educator and conservationist Paul Kiesow Petzoldt died in Maine on October 6.

From the moment of his birth on January 16, 1908, Paul's character was forged on an anvil of resourceful poverty with a view. He was the youngest of nine children on an Iowa homestead; lost his father, Charles, to diphtheria in 1911; accompanied his mother, Emma, on the family trek to the promise of farming in the Magic Valley in Idaho; and endured the consequent lack of financial security that dogged them.

Paul was pretty much self-supporting by 1923 when, at the age of 15, he rode the rails across the country and back. At 16, he found his true destiny during an ill-conceived yet successful ascent of the Grand Teton in Jackson's Hole, WY. His was only the fourth or fifth ascent of the peak. He loved to tell this story, and does so in his 1995 book, Teton Tales. His appetite for mountain adventure was irrevocably whetted by an experience that might have put most people off climbing for life. "If hypothermia'd been in the dictionary we'd've died of it," Petzoldt said.

When I met Paul in 1967 at the National Outdoor Leadership School, I was 21, which was about Paul's age when the Tetons became part of Grand Teton National Park in 1929 and he officially established his American School of Mountaineering. He'd already been guiding and exploring the Tetons for five years, honing his skills and creating climbing systems still in use today (voice signals, sliding middleman [a snow-climbing belay system], rhythmic breathing and other practical innovations.) He trained Glenn Exum, three years his junior, to guide and made him a partner in his little business, renaming it the Petzoldt-Exum Climbing School in 1932. He turned the concession over to Exum in 1955. It continues today under the Exum name.

In the years before WWII, Paul pioneered numerous, now classic routes in the Tetons, Wind River Range, Sawtooths and in Columbia's Sierra Nevada de Santa Marta. Many were made with clients, his brothers or his first wife, Bernice, in tow. Despite his proclamation that "there are no old bold climbers," Paul's solo first ascent of Mount Owen's Northeast Snowfields in 1934 still has climbers in awe of his boldness. His first ascent of the Grand Teton's North Face (1936, with Eldon "Curly" Petzoldt and Jack Durrance), and first winter ascent of the Grand (1935, with Curly and Fred Brown) are two other remarkable feats among many. In 1934, Paul and a partner made the (British) *Alpine Journal* by climbing the Matterhorn from Switzerland to Italy and back in the same day.

Paul always felt gratified to have been selected to fill a last-minute vacancy on the elite 1938 American K2 expedition. He reached a record altitude of the time—higher than 26,000 feet—without auxiliary oxygen as he and his team reconnoitered the route that would be used for the first ascent in 1954 by Italians.

Paul often was called upon for rescues in the early days, notably for the parachutist stranded in 1941 on the summit of Devils Tower, and the crash of the New Tribes Mission plane on Mount Moran in November, 1950. When the U.S. entered the war, he joined and helped train the Army's 10th Mountain Division ski and mountaineering troops.

Paul was a pragmatic genius, iconoclast and humanitarian, though few could venture to be as self-promoting as he. His controversial annual New Year's attempts on the Grand with students were both adventurous and great advertising for his fledgling school.

Accompanying Paul on his 50th, 60th, and 70th anniversary climbs of the Grand Teton taught me more about spirit than I knew existed. On his last successful ascent in 1984, he took a new-fangled camming device from my hand and placed it himself for the belay with obvious satisfaction. On the 1994 climb, his claims to have turned around out of his own good judgment (as quoted by Ray Ringholtz in her 1998 biography *On Belay*) are not exactly accurate. He was ready to go on as long as any of us dared. It was only his crew's desire not to become the people who killed Paul Petzoldt that put the kibosh on that climb at 11,000 feet, at the base of the fixed ropes just below the Lower Saddle.

Now I'm in my 50s, about the age Paul was in 1965 when he started the National Outdoor Leadership School in the Wind River Range of Wyoming. I'm dreaming of retirement and travel, but his dream was bold. In creating NOLS, Paul tapped a universal desire for adventure and communion with wild nature. Maybe because of his own youthful successes, he taught and then trusted us kids to do the most amazing things: climb mountains, ford rivers, plan long trips to unknown places and survive in style while leaving no trace. Because of Paul, NOLS graduates are stronger, braver, kinder and more conscious. His students and their students and offspring number tens of thousands now and Paul's philosophy of expedition behavior, planning and pacing ripples outward into the 21st century and beyond, where his legacy will endure.

Paul tried many things in his life, and some of his failures were subjects of his stories. Others were not. Gambling and golfing for money and wagons of bootleg whiskey, drinking, fighting and smoking were not beneath him. A student at the universities of Idaho, Wyoming and Utah, he never finished a degree, but gladly adopted the title "Doctor" when it was awarded him by Kansas State University in the early 1970s and later by Unity College, Maine. His capitalist ventures in sheep herding, alfalfa farming, used car sales, real estate and outdoor equipment were not his most successful. And he had some choice words about the folks who

Teton climbing pioneers Alex Lowe and Paul Petzoldt in Garnet Canyon, Grand Teton National Park, Wyoming, in 1994. Lowe and Petzoldt died within two days of each other in October, 1999.
NANCY WISE CARSON

ousted him from NOLS in 1976, his beloved school lost to him until Jim Ratz reconciled them for NOLS' 20th anniversary in 1985. It does often happen that the innovator has to step aside and let the next generation take charge, though I wish he could have stayed at NOLS' helm where he belonged and been spared the bitterness. But Paul was indomitable. He went on to create the Wilderness Education Association to train and certify outdoor leaders countrywide and was three years into the Paul Petzoldt Outdoor Leadership School to instruct Raymond, Maine, school kids at the time of his death.

Paul always warned us not to "pick a lemon in the garden of love," but now I see he considered himself one. Paul's first three marriages (to Bernice Patricia McGarrity, who wrote his first biography *On Top of the World* in 1953, Dorothy Dewhurst Reed and Joan Brodbeck) ended in divorce. His fourth wife, however, made lemonade. How grateful all Paul's "kids" are to Virginia Stroud Pyle (Ginnie) for treasuring and encouraging Paul during the last decades of his life and gamely accompanying him to the ends of the earth. And to Kelly Munson, who at the age of 21 became Paul's final protege and director of his ambitious Maine project. While he was dying of prostate cancer in a nursing home, Paul was lovingly attended by his beautiful old Ginnie, who came to feed and comfort him every meal, and beautiful young Kelly, who used the interims for Robert Service poetry and foot rubs. Add the visits from his friends, many of whom had celebrated his glorious 90th birthday with him in the Tetons in 1998, and one can certainly say he went out in style.

Paul was inducted into the Explorers' Club, was a recipient of the Eddie Bauer Award for conservation, and was posthumously elected as an honorary member of the AAC. He was honored as a senior guide by the American Mountain Guides Association shortly before his death. He wrote *The Wilderness Handbook* in 1974 and *Petzoldt's Teton Trails* in 1976. He received numerous conservation awards, was in *Who's Who in America 1967-1968*, was honored with the Banquet of the Golden Plate Award from the American Academy of Achievement and the Conservation Award from the Department of Interior, among other honors.

Even though Paul was no angel, I can imagine a future when a religion of the outdoors arises in recognition of the holiness of the earth's remaining wildness. Paul will surely be one of its saints. He devoted his life to exploring and treasuring the wild and getting people and wilderness together without harm to either and to the benefit of all.

NANCY WISE CARSON

HAROLD L. PINSCH
1917-1999

The mountain rescue community, and in particular Olympic Mountain Rescue (OMR), lost a strong advocate and well-respected friend with the passing of Harold on August 30. Harold was a really unique person; no one but he would become interested in mountaineering and sign up for formal training in such madness at the age of 45. In spite of being a bit long of tooth at the start, he quickly made up for lost time, compiling an excellent climbing record and providing a major contribution to the Northwest mountain rescue scene for a span of roughly 20 years.

It didn't take long for Harold to jump square into the climbing scene, and he was equally enamored with the separate joys provided by either rock or snow. While his home range, the Olympic Mountains of Washington, drew much of his attention, his adventuresome nature took him to places like the Sawtooth Range in Idaho, the Tetons and Wind River ranges of Wyoming, the Selkirks and the Purcells in Canada and Mt. Shasta in California. His first love was obviously the Sawtooth Range, as he returned to that majestic area time after time, accompanied by his wife and an ever-changing assortment of climbing associates. He accomplished a number of first ascents, mostly in the Olympics, and there are not-so-fond memories of brush crashes in the rain while trying to reach some of these places. His most notable ascents were undoubtedly his pioneering work in the Valhallas (a hard to reach sub-range in the Olympics) and the difficult *Ptarmigan Ridge* route on Mt. Rainier.

His love for climbing also extended to the teaching of others. He returned to his climbing "roots" at Olympic College, where he was an instructor in the Winter and Intermediate Climbing classes for several years and drilled into legions of budding climbers the fear of wearing wet blue jeans and hypothermia. He was a longstanding member of both the AAC and The Mountaineers. However, I believe that his finest hours were achieved in the mountain rescue forum.

My first recollection of Harold was "this old guy" sitting in the front row at one of our OMR meetings. In those years long past, everyone past 30 looked old, and at 45, Harold seemed ancient. However, it didn't take long for me to realize that this guy was going to be a force in the unit. At one time or another he probably held every office in OMR and was on the main team in regard to actually participating in rescues. I will never forget the call from Harold at 2 o'clock one morning as he, in quick order, sang reveille and then invited me on another middle-of-the-night mission.

However, his big contributions were the two terms he served as OMR Chairman and his work in both the Washington Mountain Rescue Association and the Mountain Rescue Association (MRA). Harold was quite a visionary and on his watch catalyzed the Unit into embarking on some really interesting actions. Included were: purchase of the Unit's first truck, joint practices with Olympic National Park, establishment of OMR as a United Way

Agency, OMR publication of *The Climber's Guide to the Olympic Mountains*, establishing a mountaineering equipment sales activity and, notably, his leadership in hosting one of the annual MRA meetings. In those days, OMR was a small, somewhat out-of-the-way operation, and successful hosting of this meeting was viewed as a pretty big deal. Harold was respected by all, and no one was pleased when he finally retired from OMR as he approached the age of 70.

I knew Harold as a valued climbing companion, a tough and resourceful rescue associate, but mostly as a good friend. His loyalty, keen intellect, sharp wit and fun-loving manner made him exciting to be around and I, and certainly others, am honored to have been his friend.

I would like to thank Lois, his enduring wife of 58 years, and two daughters, Pat Harrington and Joyce Magnusson, for their support in preparing this reflection.

Harold, rest in peace. We will miss you!

KEITH SPENCER

WILLIAM D. HACKETT
1918-1999

Bill Hackett died in Portland from complications following heart surgery.

Bill had a distinguished military career, a successful business career and a lifelong career of worldwide mountaineering, skiing, travel, and exploration. He combined his careers in interesting and fruitful ways. Growing up in Portland, OR, he began climbing at age 14. By age 22, when he entered the U.S. Army, he had made 50 ascents of Mt. Hood by 11 different routes, including three first ascents and two second ascents. In the Army in WWII, he served more than three years in the 10th Mountain Division, first as an instructor and then as a combat infantry unit commander in the Appenines and the Julian Alps. He was promoted to First Lieutenant of Infantry and awarded the Combat Infantry Badge, two Bronze Stars and the Silver Star for gallantry in action. After WWII, he remained in regular Army for 21 years. He served as an intelligence officer in Korea and in Vietnam. Following WWII, he served four years as a research and development field test officer for equipment and clothing. In that duty, he made many cold-weather ascents in Canada and Alaska, and his efforts helped in the improvement of various cold-weather gear (e.g., streamlining the arctic uniform from 23 to 14 pounds.)

Bill served as chief of training at the Mountain and Cold Weather Training Command at Fort Carson, CO, and as environmental training general staff officer at Fort Monroe, VA. He also served in Europe in a variety of posts. In 1963, with the rank of major, he took a disability retirement.

After leaving the Army, he returned to Portland and formed the Bill Hackett Company, a sporting goods manufacturers' representative organization. This proved to be a successful enterprise.

Bill made many ascents in the Cascades, Colorado, Canada, Mexico and the Alps. In five expeditions to Mt. McKinley, he ascended the South Peak four times and the North Peak twice, making first ascents of the West Buttress from Kahiltna Glacier and the Northwest Buttress via Peters Glacier. Two of these expeditions, with Bradford Washburn, accomplished survey work that fixed the elevation of the summit at 20,320 feet.

Bill Hackett was the first person to reach the summits of both McKinley and Logan. He was the first American to climb Aconcagua and the first American to climb Mt. Kenya. He was the first person to reach the summits of five continents. In 1960, he organized and led an American-German expedition to K2 that reached 25,000 feet. In 1985, at age 67, he joined a Canadian-American expedition to Antarctica to climb Mt. Vinson.

Miscellaneous travel included trips to both the North and South Poles, two journeys around the world and a voyage on a Russian icebreaker. Miscellaneous honors include the Army Commendation Medal for meritorious achievement in the field of expeditionary mountaineering.

The foregoing is only a brief summary of a rich life. A full-length biography is currently being written by June Hackett and Thorn Bacon. The title is *Climb to Glory* and publication is set for Fall, 2000.

DAVID HARRAH

HENRY W. KENDALL
1926-1999

Henry Kendall died during an underwater photography dive at Wakulla Springs, FL, on February 15. He suffered gastrointestinal bleeding as reported in some news stories, but other factors caused him to lose consciousness and subsequently die. The medical examiner ruled his death accidental.

Henry learned from his father a love of and respect for the outdoors growing up in the small town of Sharon, south of Boston. Sea-related activities took root early, and he began diving at 12. Bored by school work as a boy, Henry became a great scientist, a brilliant professor of physics and, as chairman of the Union of Concerned Scientists, an internationally respected public policy advocate. He was an avid diver, pilot, photographer and mountaineer who made ascents on four continents.

He trained at the U.S. Merchant Marine Academy, resigning from the Navy in 1946 to attend Amherst College. He earned a B.A. in mathematics from Amherst in 1950, followed by a Ph.D. in nuclear physics from M.I.T. in 1955. In the years just after WWII, he ran a summer diving and salvage business on Cape Cod. In the early 1950s he made numerous trips to the Florida Keys, taking underwater stills and movies, later co-authoring a technical book on the subject.

Henry did not even "see real mountains," as he put it, until he was 29, when he got a view of the Tetons on a cross-country drive to join a physics research project at Stanford University in the summer of 1956. Upon his arrival at Stanford, he "instantly" joined the Stanford Alpine Club. He hit it off with Club president John Harlin who, as Henry said, "took me under his wing and taught me how to climb." By the winter of 1956-57, they were climbing together in Yosemite Valley almost every weekend, doing most of the established routes and attempting some new ones, including the unclimbed Nose of El Capitan. Hobey DeStaebler, Henry's Stanford roommate and frequent climbing companion, said that the 21-year-old Harlin and 29-year-old Kendall had "a kind of sympathetic determination" so far as climbing was concerned. "It was the drive to excel."

In the SAC, Henry also met Leigh Ortenburger, Irene Ortenburger, Herb Hultgren and Tom Frost. All would become future climbing companions. Frost credited Henry with being his mentor at Stanford. Frost's first new route in Yosemite Valley, *The Roof* on Lower Cathedral Rock, was done with Henry, as was the first ascent of the North Face of Mt. Clark in the Yosemite high country (also with DeStaebler, and Herb Swedlund). Henry joined Harlin, Gary Hemming and DeStaebler in the 1957 Battle Range exploration, where the foursome made the first ascent of the North Ridge of Mt. Butters.

Left to right: Gary Hemming, John Harlin and Henry Kendall before setting out on their Battle Range exploration in British Columbia in 1957.
Photo by HOBEY DESTAEBLER, *courtesy of John Rawlings*

Leigh Ortenburger invited Henry to Peru in 1958 (the first of three Peruvian expeditions for Henry) on the basis of his Yosemite and Battle Range climbs. Henry's ascents in the Cordillera Blanca included a new route on Huascaran Sur and the second ascents by new routes on Huandoy Sur and Palcaraju.

"It wasn't in his nature to achieve something at some other person's expense," Richard Blankenbecler recalled. "He taught me that while climbing was no mere game, it ought to be fun. And while there's competition, it need not be outright competition. You climb with a partner and there's a fellowship there. That was at the essence of the activity."

Diving and mountaineering contributed to his professional successes, teaching him to complete projects safely. At Stanford, he took long rambles in the Yosemite high country with fellow SAC member James "BJ" Bjorken. Bjorken did the mathematical work that proved essential to the understanding and interpretation of Henry's discovery with Jerome Friedman and Richard Taylor of quarks, the most fundamental building blocks in nature.

Henry was in Europe doing physics research in the summer of 1962 and decided to contact Harlin and Hemming. Hemming was determined to make the first American ascent of the Walker Spur of the Grandes Jorasses and, upon hearing from Henry, invited him along. After their success, the relationship between the two men blossomed, and it was with deep sadness that Henry penned Hemming's obituary for the 1970 *AAJ*. Within a few years, some of Henry's closest mountain companions—Harlin, Dave Sowles, Dan Doody, Hugo Stadtmueller, Hemming—had died, and he stopped climbing soon after Hemming's death.

Then, in 1983, Frost wrote, "Join me and Jeff Lowe in the Himalaya. We're going to Kantega." In the Khumbu in 1985, Lowe and Kendall climbed a new route on Lobuje East. It involved front-pointing up steep ice, Henry's first go at the technique. Lowe decided that

Henry wasn't experienced enough in modern ice technique to go on a planned Kantega route, but Henry believed that he could have made the climb. At 59, he still wanted to go where no one had been before.

Climbing remained an important facet of Henry's productive, larger life. It was partially motivated by the photographic opportunities mountains provided. In the 1962 *Sierra Club Bulletin*, he wrote: "In one way... a camera is an essential piece of equipment because, beyond tenuous memory, photography is the only means by which the climber can relive and re-enjoy the qualities of an ascent."

Henry's commitment to service applied to the SAC and later the AAC, as well as to individuals. He was faculty advisor to the SAC for several years, contributed to the *Stanford Alpine Club Journal*, and joined the AAC in 1959. Appointed a councilor in 1966, he served as an AAC vice-president from 1968-'70.

Awarded the Nobel Prize for physics in 1990, Henry said, "I like to go where no human being has been before. I have done that in physics, done it a number of times with colleagues. We sometimes find things, and sometimes do not, but it is extraordinarily interesting.

"I like to go in the mountains to places where no one has been before. The world is an astonishingly beautiful place. It's beautiful at the deep level of physics, way down inside things. What we know of the universe that's visible to us is also of astonishing beauty, and I like to see that and explore it."

"A privilege and an inspiration" is how Frost characterized their shared experiences. "Henry always gave back more than he took."

JOHN RAWLINGS

CHARLES DAVIS HOLLISTER
1936-1999

Charley Hollister was an inexhaustibly cheerful and upbeat person with a Will Rogers-like wit, an adolescent's playfulness and an unassuming folksy manner that masked a keen and creative intellect, exceptional drive and purposefulness. Charley was by profession an earth scientist who loved the extremes—the tops of mountains and the bottoms of the oceans. He had a lifelong commitment to adventurous undertakings in research and education in marine geology and in expeditionary mountaineering. He died on August 23 of injuries sustained in a fall while scrambling during a family vacation in Wyoming. He was 63, still living life the way he drove his jeep as a teenager—pedal to the floor.

Charley's love of the out-of-doors grew from his boyhood adventures on his family's cattle ranch on the Santa Barbara, CA, coast. Charley was given free rein by the cowboys and ranch hands who ran the place. Consequently, by his early teens he was poaching deer on adjoining ranches, testing the limits of tractors, experimenting with dynamite and generally raising hell.

Charley's family enrolled him at Fountain Valley School in Colorado Springs. That's where I met him and first heard his Santa Barbara exploits. Even as a teenager, Charley was a good story teller.

Charley didn't stay at Fountain Valley. For a time it was uncertain whether he would finish high school at all. He did, of course, thanks to one of the older Santa Barbara ranch hands, who convinced him that conserving and building was preferable to wasting and breaking. After a stint in the Army, he entered Oregon State University. There, he fell under the spell of two people who altered his life's course.

The first was Jalien Green, whom he married in 1957. Jalien encouraged him to aim high, and he did. He never chose a subsidiary peak when there was a bigger one in the neighborhood. The second was Willi Unsoeld, who encouraged him to acquire technical mountaineering skills, take up climbing seriously and join the mountain rescue group. He received his B.S. degree from Oregon State in 1960.

Oregon State stimulated Charley's interests in oceanography. Lionel Walford, then head of fisheries in Washington, D.C., recognized Charley's natural talents and recommended him to Maurice Ewing, then director of Lamont Geological Observatory at Columbia University and a world leader in oceanography. Ewing decided to take a chance on Charley and offered him a fellowship. Charley never looked back. He did an outstanding Ph.D. thesis, and his career was launched.

In the winter of 1962, Boyd Everett and I were planning an expedition to Denali's then-unclimbed southeast spur. I suggested inviting Charley. He accepted, and somehow convinced Bruce Heezen, his thesis advisor, that a trip to Alaska would do him good.

The route we had selected involved the most difficult ice climbing any of us had done. The weather didn't make it easier. It stormed nearly half the days we were on Denali. On one occasion, the wind blew so hard it shredded one of our two Logan tents. Had Charley not brought an extra two-man mountain tent, the expedition might have failed.

Despite these adversities, Charley never lost his composure. His optimism buoyed us all. Whenever I felt down about our prospects for success, Charley would cheer me up. "Now Sam," he'd say with a twinkle in his eye, a grin on his face and a waggle of his index finder, "let's examine this situation...." Charley helped you believe in yourself.

Charley wasn't an athlete whose spectacular physical abilities enabled him to climb effortlessly. But he was always there and ready when needed. On one occasion he probably saved four lives when Hank Abraons slipped, pulling Chris Wren off a ridge.

By any measure, Charley had an exceptional career. At the time of his death he was a senior scientist in the Department of Geology and Geophysics and vice president of the Corporation of Woods Hole Oceanographic Institution in Woods Hole, MA. That Charley would become one of the pillars of the Oceanographic Institution was by no means a certainty, given the way his career at Woods Hole started.

By 1964, Charley was completing the research on the effects of deep ocean currents on sediment deposition, which formed the core of his Ph.D. thesis and the focus of his future life work. Anticipating that he would soon graduate, he accepted a post-doctoral position with K.O. Emery at the Woods Hole Oceanographic Institution, to begin in the fall of 1965.

But first, he had to finish his thesis. And he and Bruce Heezen devoted much of their time to writing *The Face of the Deep*, the first book to describe the fauna, flora and sediments of the floor of the oceans. Finally, Charley left for an expedition to Antarctica, somewhat exasperating Emery.

Charley's handling of this situation characterized his approach to life: do those things that excite your imagination and fulfill your spirit. The rest will follow. The Antarctic expedition was a great success, in no small measure due to Charley. He was the expedition's chief humorist. He participated in four first ascents (the Vinson Massif, and Mts. Shinn, Gardner and Ostenso) and did some geology.

Charley's doctoral dissertation and the papers that resulted from it initiated a new subfield of marine geology called sediment dynamics. He and collaborators identified the global effects on sediment texture and distribution of currents that run parallel to ocean ridges and

Charles Hollister.
Photo courtesy of SAMUEL C. SILVERSTEIN

continental margins as well as those that scour the deep ocean basins. He coined the term "contourite" to describe sediments transported by currents that parallel bathymetric contours and to distinguish them from previously described turbidites, sediments carried downhill by turbidity currents.

I recall in particular his proud and joyful smile when he told me of the cruise on which he and his colleagues obtained sediments that enabled them to identify the age of separation of the African and American continents, thereby establishing continuity between the Northern and Southern Atlantic Oceans.

"We have dated the big flush," he said.

Charley invented a device to sample ocean sediments that was almost seven times longer than existing instruments. The 100-foot-long "super straw" piston corer produced the single longest continuous record—65 million years—of ocean basin sedimentary history ever.

Charley's expertise in the dynamics of sediment transport made him among the first to recognize that large areas of the deep sea are swept by strong episodic currents known as "benthic storms." From 1979-1989, Charley was dean of the MIT-Woods Hole Oceanographic Institution's Ph.D. program. He was committed to creating opportunities for young people in oceanography.

Charley's leadership in graduate education has been recognized by the establishment at Woods Hole Oceanographic Institution of two permanent funds: a graduate student fellowship fund and the Endowed Fund for Support of Innovative Research, both in Charley's name.

In the 1980s, he made two trips to the Bhutan Himalaya, exploring the rarely visited Lunana Valley and making the first ascent of 20,000-foot Kang Tjito Ja with John Evans.

Charley became one of the Woods Hole Oceanographic Institution's most effective fund raisers. Together with his wife Jacqueline, he raised more than $50 million in unrestricted funds.

Charley published more than 90 papers on marine geology, graduate education in oceanography and nuclear waste disposal. He co-authored one book and edited six more. He was a Fellow of the Geological Society of America and of the American Association for the Advancement of Science; an advisor to UNESCO, U.S. government agencies, the National Academy of Sciences, several national and international scientific societies, and major corporations; a Keystone Center trustee; and a director (1971-'74), vice president (1967 and 1971-'73), and briefly president (1973) of the AAC. He was a co-recipient of the John Oliver La Gorce Medal of the National Geographic Society for exploration in Antarctica, a Henry Bryant Bigelow Distinguished Lecturer at Harvard University in 1984, the Doherty Lecturer of the U.S. House of Representatives in 1997 and the posthumous recipient of a Lifetime Science Achievement Award from the International Oceanography Society in 2000. He was a member of the Union of Concerned Scientists, Bohemian Club, Explorers Club, Rancheros

Vistadores and an honorary deputy sheriff of Santa Barbara County.

He is deeply missed by those who survive him, and by his many friends and colleagues with whom he joyously shared his adventurous and productive life.

SAMUEL C. SILVERSTEIN, M.D.

ALEX LOWE
1958-1999

"The best climber in the world is the one having the most fun!"
—Alex Lowe

By the time of his sudden, tragic death beneath an avalanche on Tibet's forbidding Mount Shishapangma, Alex Lowe had become a mountain character larger than life. Many called him the greatest contemporary climber on earth (a title he personally eschewed), but he was far more than just a phenomenal mountaineer. He was an intellectual, a family man, a prankster, a communicator and an open-hearted soul who could make friends with almost anyone, from the president of the National Geographic Society to a barefoot Balti porter.

Alex touched the lives of almost everyone he met, and this was clearly demonstrated in the wake of his passing. Two of America's biggest national network news programs devoted long minutes to news of the accident—more than is often earned by prominent ambassadors or senators—and virtually every major newspaper and outdoor magazine eulogized him. Thousands of people wrote condolences to his family. The mere fact that a person as talented, experienced and powerful as Alex could perish in the mountains was a wake-up call to everyone.

Ironically, Alex never set out to become famous; he just loved to climb. He was the second son of James and Dorothea Lowe and grew up in Missoula, MT, where James was a professor at the University of Montana and Dorothea taught fourth and fifth grades. "I was a nerdy kid," Alex once told me. "I was usually the last kid chosen for basketball or baseball games."

But Alex loved the outdoors, and his parents encouraged him. He became an Eagle Scout and started climbing seriously while still in high school, pioneering many classic routes in the Bitteroot Mountains. In 1982, Alex married Jennifer Daly, a fellow climber who is now a renowned artist and the mother of his three sons, Max, Sam and Isaac. This was a devoted partnership that brought Alex great comfort, but also dismay at the ever-extended periods of time that climbing—soon to become his career —took him away from home.

At times, Alex did try to become a workaday guy. He earned a degree in engineering mechanics from Montana State University and worked briefly doing seismic surveys in Wyoming. He also looked after quality control for Black Diamond Equipment. But always the mountains lured him away.

To readers of this journal, there is little point in trying to list Alex's many mountaineering achievements. They've filled numerous pages of the *AAJ*. He climbed Mount Everest twice, put up some of the hardest mixed climbs ever achieved, forged the lead up some of earth's most remote big walls and set speed records everywhere he went. He guided for Exum in the Tetons, smiled from the pages of *National Geographic* and lectured to audiences all over the world. No one could keep up, and often no one could follow. When it came to raw talent and energy, he was in a league of his own.

Alex did have his foibles. Notably, he was addicted to exercise. He might have been one of the first climbers to understand that fitness has something to do with alpine performance.

While working the oil rigs in Wyoming, he used to sneak away from his fellow roughnecks during lunch break and do pullups in the outhouse. In later years, he would wake at 3 a.m., climb a mountain near his home in Bozeman, MT, ski down and be home in time to wake up the kids for school. Then he'd make a few dozen phone calls and head to the health club, where he'd make muscle-bound weight lifters look like 98-pound weaklings. During one climb I shared with him on Baffin Island, he'd often spend the day hauling huge bags 1,000 feet up the wall, then return to base camp and do a pyramid of 400 pullups.

But Alex wasn't just an athlete. He was always thinking about how things in the world worked, and, in a storm-bound tent, it was humiliating to swap books with him. In exchange for your own tawdry novel (which he was not above reading), you'd likely get some textbook on quantum mechanics or a spiritual tome by the Dalai Lama.

Given his array of talents, Alex was one of the most remarkable people I have ever had the joy to meet. But simply spending time with him was exhausting. His favorite quote, for example, was from Pascal, something along the lines that life is motion, and when you stop moving, you die. And how he could move.

Alex was a friend who led by example. He always did more than his share of the climbing and camping chores. Just watching him almost always inspired his companions to try a little harder, to be a better person, a stronger climber. I owe two of my own proudest accomplishments (my photography of Antarctica's Queen Maud Land, and of our climb of Great Sail Peak on Baffin Island) to his intense energy and thoughtfulness to my own needs and weaknesses. With him around, how could I do anything but my best? But then again, as one climber once said, "to bring Alex along is cheating."

What really set Alex apart, however, was his growing abilities as a communicator. Much as he never considered himself a writer, his internet messages from Great Trango Tower rank among some of the best mountaineering prose ever written. Even after a long day on the ropes, he'd come back to the portaledge and sit down with a keyboard, wiring his thoughts to the world. He did a live interview with *National Public Radio* that inspired tens of thousands of traffic-jammed commuters.

But these skills were honed with his characteristic energy and hard work. The first time I heard Alex lecture, for example, I thought it was the worst slide show I'd ever seen. His pictures were blurry and his narrative rambling. How that changed over the years. He found his voice and was able to articulate how he viewed life and what was most important to him. While his friends and family are only now beginning to fathom the depth of his loss, at least we have some of his writings to hold close. The following was written July 6, 1999, from high up on the northwest face of Great Trango Tower:

What to say about the climbing. You know, for me, the climbing is insignificant in relation to the moments spent reclined on a ledge watching clouds transmogrify from one ethereal form to another even more evanescent shape. (What marvelous beasts would Max and Sam identify in the mists?) And while lost in cloud reverie an old tattered gorak drifts carelessly and silently upward, cocking his hoary head at me curiously as though asking why I struggle so hard for such measured upward gain. I'd love to borrow his wings for a magical waltz through these magnificent towers.

But—the climbing: The last three leads of the day fell to me. They involved incipient and unprotectable seams and face climbing where peaceful determination, trust and a huge smiling heart gets you up pitches you would never find rational justification to lead. I love the heady climbing best of all! Stepping out, believing I'll find a knifeblade seam somewhere in the next 50 feet and scratching out a stalwart belay at the end—ah, that's the good stuff!

I'll beg to take your leave now. Venus is rising over Uli Biaho and I yearn to snuggle deep in my bag here on my ledge in the starry sky and fall away into resplendent slumber.

Farewell, Alex. The world will miss you.

GORDON WILTSIE

YOSSI BRAIN
1967-1999

When trying to write of someone when they are gone, it becomes necessary to call up a mental image, so as to have something to work with. In my mind's eye, Yossarian Brain is standing, holding court in Mungo's Bar in La Paz, Bolivia, his audience—i.e., everyone—looking toward him. He stands well over six feet, his blonde hair long and of Viking style, his head thrown back as a booming laugh drowns out all others. He is wearing an old black leather jacket of heavy metal vintage, and his trousers are of incredibly impractical red leather. In both hands, he holds a beer, and the story he is telling is both unbelievable and true. I suspect Yossi once saw the phrase "larger than life," liked it and decided to make it his own. He was killed in an avalanche in September 1999, whilst climbing in Bolivia's Apolobamba range. Here is what I know of his story.

I first met Yossi at University College, London, where he was studying a subject that as far as anyone could tell involved no work of any kind. He was from Walsall, in England's West Midlands and he wanted to climb. He also wanted to drink and fight the government, so all-in-all university life suited him fine.

As far as climbing was concerned, his talents suited the mountains, where his stamina and sheer appetite for the outdoors stood him in good stead. On leaving college, part-time jobs and lengthy climbing trips sustained him for a while, and it was in this period that he first visited Bolivia. This lifestyle, though fun, did not give Yossi all that he needed, and by 1990 he had become focused on what was to become the third love of his life: journalism (in case you hadn't noticed, climbing and drinking were the other two).

For the next several years, he followed the classic path of an up-and-coming political journalist, and by 1992 he was working for the Coventry Evening News, a major provincial paper and one step away from the nationals. At this point, his life took something of a dramatic turn. He was climbing in the Alps during the summer with school friend Mike Clarke when they somehow conspired to fall all the way down the 1000-meter North Face of Les Courtes. Remarkably, they both survived almost unscathed, but for Yossi the experience left a powerful impression and led to a new outlook on life. Within a few months, he had quit his job and was off to Bolivia where, with remarkable self-assurance, he had decided to set up a guiding agency.

The next few years were a struggle as he strove to establish himself and become accepted by the Bolivians. During this period, he managed a huge amount of exploratory mountaineering and began work on what were to become his trekking and climbing guidebooks. By 1997, business was good; he was the acknowledged authority on mountaineering in Boliva and responsible for more exploration than anyone. His trekking guide had just been published, and the climbing guide was nearing completion. He had become the regional expert and correspondent for many journals, including Britain's *High* magazine and, of course, the *AAJ*.

At this time, he was operating the guiding business in partnership with girlfriend Ulli Scultz. Their break-up in the latter part of the year led to the closure of their Bolivian office, and Yossi becoming more focused on his writing and research. His *Climbing Guide to Bolivia*, published in 1998, was received with much praise, and, at the time of his death, he had virtually completed work on a guide to trekking in Equador. Yossi had also amassed a huge volume of historical information, and family and friends are at present working to collate and preserve this work.

In September, 1999, Yossi teamed up with three La Paz-based friends to try and grab a last new route of the season. Their objective was El Presidente (5700m) in the remote Apolobamba range. Yossi was climbing with Dana Witzel when they triggered the avalanche that caught them both. Their two friends were climbing nearby and saw the slope go. They were quickly on the scene, but both Yossi and Dana were already dead.

The Apolobamba Range is probably the least-visited Andean range in South America. Yossi was the acknowledged expert and had probably done more routes in the range than any other climber.

Yossi was a complex character, and it would be wrong to suggest he was perfect. He was thoroughly uncompromising and entirely intolerant of anything that got in the way of his passions. If you climbed, drank or wrote, he was your friend, and a good one. If you didn't, then you were at best a potential client. His relationships were generally short and tended to end abruptly. He made enemies as well as friends, both easily and in great numbers. He had crossed swords, literally at times, with many a Bolivian, but in the end the country gave him a medal. He left a legacy of work that will leave generations of visitors to Bolivia and Equador indebted to him. You loved him or hated him, but I suspect even his enemies will miss him.

ANDY MacNAE

DAVE BRIDGES
1970-1999

"The only death you die is the death you die every day by not living. Dream big and dare to fail."
—Norman Vaughan

A dventure as an addiction, as a passionate need, true compassion for life on the "front lines"—there was no other way. Dave Bridges just had to have it. Dave always used to say, "It's not the age, it's the mileage." At only 29, he had managed to accumulate more mileage and accomplish more than most people would dream of doing.

Dave had climbed throughout North and South America, Asia, Europe and Australia, moving from technical alpine testpieces in Chamonix to sport climbing in Thailand, alpine rock routes of the High Sierra to the world's highest summits. In 1994, he led the successful American K2 South Spur Expedition, personally reaching 8300 meters, 311 meters shy of the summit. A total of eight expeditions to the Himalaya and Karakoram yielded success on Annapurna IV, Island Peak, Ama Dablam, Baruntse, Kusum Kangaru and most recently, Makalu. Dave's passion for high places fueled a competitive edge that rewarded him with two consecutive United States National Paragliding Championships, in 1995 and 1996.

High-altitude filmmaking suddenly entered Dave's repertoire of talents on the trips to Baruntse and Makalu. His footage was impressive, but when given the opportunity to join The North Face American Shishapangma Ski Expedition, Dave just couldn't believe his luck. He politely asked what I thought of the invitation to work for American Adventure Productions as their high-altitude specialist. My first thought was that any footage Dave took would always be looking down on the climbers or skiers in a broken track—certainly an embarrassing angle to document lead climbers. I also imagined the pleasant surprise to fellow team members when they realized they had a second "secret weapon" with them (Alex Lowe being the first).

The postcard Dave sent from Kathmandu confirmed the solidarity of the group and his excitement to finally be "out there with the big boys." Without a doubt, Dave Bridges was on his way to the top of the stack, the heir to the alpine throne of his 11-year senior, Alex.

When the avalanche sheared a full monsoon season's snowpack down the southwest face of Shishapangma, the luck for Dave and Alex ran out. Thirty seconds after the initial, "Oh, shit! It's an avalanche!," the deed was done. Conrad Anker miraculously escaped burial, his injuries masked by adrenaline and the urgency to search for his friends. Not a trace. The devastated team reluctantly returned home with the empty, sick feeling of leaving the mountain without their friends.

What couldn't Dave do well? All disciplines of mountaineering, plus the rigorous demands of high-altitude super-alpinism and filmmaking, were as natural to Dave as world-class competition paragliding. His enthusiasm for this last adventure was as extreme as the undertaking. Dave was on top of his game. He was absolutely in his prime, an aerobic monster, mentally focused and passionately committed in all aspects of his life. His strength and stamina were second only to his humility and modest approach in his relations with others. He was a minimalist when it came to self-promotion, and he constantly joked about the abundance of opportunities to do so. Dave could and would laugh at himself, and none of us will ever forget his unique way of laughing. What a privilege it was for anyone to have spent time with Dave.

Friendship as an intimate relationship is not as relative to the amount of time shared as to the quality of the experience. Dave naturally connected with people. He literally shared quality time with hundreds each year. He guided rock climbs and alpine peaks, introduced many to the freedom of soaring flight through tandem paragliding and just could not get enough time skiing the soft snow of the high country. Dave was a great friend and teacher to all of us. His spirit knows only success, as he totally displayed in his hold-nothing-back lifestyle. Even death for Dave is life's next great adventure. He was ultimately mature in his self-esteem, confident in his actions to speak for themselves and sober in his awareness of life's fine line of existence when close to the "edge." He felt the pain of other close friends lost in the high mountains.

The very real connection of spiritual soaring with physical death lends comfort to Dave's rendezvous with Alex and the avalanche on Shishapangma. Close encounters with the soaring birds of the high mountains leave no question as to the appropriate metaphor in this case: Dave Bridges' passion for flying and high places is now one with the higher performance of winged carriers of the spiritual realm.

Dave Bridges settled in Aspen, yet he was a resident of the mountains everywhere. All his family and friends in so many places have gained a part of him simply through his authentic love and friendship. Dave was certainly very good at living in the moment, accepting the reality of his impermanence as he resisted the possibility of failure.

There are no guarantees in the lives that we lead. The entire worldwide mountain community is once again reminded of the risks that we assume. The distance and time away mean so much when a friend leaves on a one-way trip. While Dave may no longer out-run, out-fly, out-climb and out-power-mow us in tacos and margaritas, his spirit will live on in the countless people that he touched and inspired day in and day out. Those of us who got to share these experiences with him know that we lost our greatest partner—but more than that, we lost a great friend.

Namaste, Dave.

DICK JACKSON

NECROLOGY

Otto Titus Trott (1911-1999)
Anderson Bakewell (1912-1999)
Paul V. Livingston (1914-1999)
Harold W. Stevenson (1921-1999)
Ralph Johnson (1923-1999)
Akio Horiuchi (1933-1999)
Terry Alpine Murphy (1944-1999)
Keith Boskoff (1950-1999)
Myron William Smith (1963-1999)

Rock Climbing Classifications

YDS	UIAA	FR	AUS	SAX	CIS	SCA	BRA	UK	UK
5.2	II	1	10	II	III	3			D
5.3	III	2	11	III	III+	3+			D
5.4	IV- / IV	3	12		IV-	4			VD
5.5	IV+		13		IV	4+			VD
5.6	V-	4	14		IV+	5-		4a	S / HS
5.7	V / V+		15	VIIa		5		4b	VS
5.8	V+	5a	16	VIIb	V-	5+	4 / 4+	4c	HVS
5.9	VI-	5b	17	VIIc		6- / 5+	5 / 5+	5a	E1
5.10a	VI	5c	18				6a		
5.10b	VI+	6a		VIIIa	V	6		5b	E2
5.10c	VII-	6a+	19	VIIIb		6+	6b		
5.10d	VII	6b	20	VIIIc	V+	7-	6c	5c	E3
5.11a	VII+	6b+		IXa			7a		
5.11b		6c	21	IXb		7			
5.11c	VIII-	6c+	22		VI-	7+	7b		E4
5.11d	VIII	7a	23	IXc			7c	6a	
5.12a		7a+	24			8-	8a		E5
5.12b	VIII+	7b	25	Xa	VI	8	8b		
5.12c	IX-	7b+	26	Xb		8+	8c		
5.12d	IX	7c	27				9a	6b	E6
5.13a		7c+	28	Xc		9-	9b		
5.13b	IX+	8a	29				9c		
5.13c	X-	8a+	30	XIa		9	10a	6c	E7
5.13d	X	8b	31		VI+		10b		
5.14a	X+	8b+	32	XIb			10c	7a	E8
5.14b		8c	33			9+			
5.14c	XI-	8c+		XIc				7b	E9
5.14d	XI	9a							

YDS=Yosemite Decimal System; UIAA=Union Internationale des Associations D'Alpinisme; Fr=France; Aus=Australia; Sax=Saxony; CIS=Commonwealth of Independent States; Sca=Scandinavia; Bra=Brazil; UK=United Kingdom

Contributors' Guidelines

The *American Alpine Journal* records the significant climbing accomplishments of the world in an annual volume. We encourage climbers to submit brief (250-500 words), factual accounts of their climbs and expeditions. While we welcome submissions in a variety of forms, contributors are encouraged to follow certain guidelines when submitting materials. Accounts should be submitted by e-mail. Alternatively, submit accounts by regular post both as a hard copy and on disk; both Mac and PC disks are acceptable. When submitting an account on disk, please save it as a text file. Please include your club affiliation when submitting accounts.

Deadlines for all accounts are February 1 for the preceding calendar year of January 1 to December 31. For Patagonian climbs, the deadline is extended to February 15.

We encourage contributors to submit relevant photographs; we accept both black-and-white and color slides and prints. When submitting an image to show a route line, we ask that you submit the image along with a photo- or laser-copy and draw the lines in on the copy. Please do not draw directly on the photograph.

We prefer original slides and artwork in all instances. Duplicates should be reproduction quality. Please send all images via registered mail. *The American Alpine Journal* is not responsible for images lost or damaged in the mail. Topos and maps are also encouraged; camera-ready original copies are necessary for quality reproduction.

We do not pay for accounts or lead articles. Those accounts from which we publish a photograph will receive a complimentary copy of the *Journal*. Authors of lead articles and the photographer of the cover photo will receive a one-year complimentary membership to The American Alpine Club.

Please address all correspondences to:

The American Alpine Journal
710 Tenth Street, Suite 140
Golden, Colorado 80401
Tel.: (303) 384 0110
Fax: (303) 384 0111
E-mail:aaj@americanalpineclub.org
http://www.americanalpineclub.org

Index

Compiled by Jessica Kany

Z